THE U.S. CONSTITUTION

A Reader

THE U.S. CONSTITUTION

A Reader

EDITED BY THE HILLSDALE COLLEGE POLITICS FACULTY

HILLSDALE COLLEGE PRESS

Hillsdale, Michigan

HILLSDALE COLLEGE PRESS

The U.S. Constitution: A Reader
©2012 Hillsdale College Press, Hillsdale, Michigan 49242

Printed in the United States of America.

Cover design
Hesseltine & DeMason, Ann Arbor, Michigan

Library of Congress Control Number: 2011938176

ISBN 978-0-916308-36-0

Contents

Editorial Note

Spelling and punctuation in some of the documents in this book have been modernized. Ampersands have been converted. Footnotes have been omitted unless integral to the text. Misspelled names have been corrected and abbreviations eliminated in the lists of the signers of the Declaration of Independence, the Articles of Confederation, and the Constitution.

Foreword

The U.S Constitution: A Reader is made up of original source documents that bear upon the founding of the American republic, the making of its Constitution, and the struggle to preserve that document and govern under it to the current day.

The *Reader* is used in the Hillsdale College core course on the Constitution required of every student. About one-half of Hillsdale's curriculum is to be found in its core, which is organized to present the basic and necessary elements of a liberal arts education—an education oriented to the ultimate purposes in human life, the goods at which all activity is properly aimed.

The Hillsdale College Articles of Association state the reasons why the College takes this approach. The Articles promise a kind of learning that is "sound." This learning is said to "develop the minds" and "improve the hearts" of the students; in other words, it teaches the intellectual and the moral virtues. The ultimate effect of this kind of learning on the society is to perpetuate the "inestimable blessings" of "civil and religious liberty" and "intelligent piety."

Civil and religious liberty are political goods. The classic works that have always been taught here at Hillsdale College say that the nature of man is essentially political, that our gift of speech, a synonym for reason, makes us more social and moral than any beings on earth, and in the combination of these is our political nature. For this reason, politics has always been essential to the liberal arts curriculum.

The political goods of "civil and religious liberty" were first achieved here in the United States of America, the nation to which Hillsdale College has always been loyal. Its oldest building was dedicated on the Fourth of July in 1853, when the second president of the college, later one of the founders of the Republican Party, gave a speech on the relation of freedom and education. Its sons and daughters have fought in honorable numbers in all our nation's wars since the founding of the College. In the Civil War, some 400 young Hillsdale men fought for the Union, the highest percentage of any non-military school in the North. Since the founding of the College, it has played a part in the great movements to defend the Constitution from the many threats it has faced.

These actions, which form a noble part of the history of the College, do not stem from any agitation on the campus except that of teaching the Constitution as part of the core curriculum. To study the place of man in nature, and to study the meaning of the greatest of modern nations, is to place oneself in the middle of a series of great arguments carried on among exceptional people who often differ. This activity has always resulted in a thoughtful—and sometimes in a fierce—patriotism here at Hillsdale. When arguments arise about the meaning of our country, we can relate them to the great arguments that have already taken place in its history. We do not come to contemporary debates unarmed. This, said several of the Founders of our nation, is necessary to the training of statesmen and to the preservation of our republic in freedom and justice.

The *Reader* is divided into eleven sections, each with a brief introduction by a member of the Hillsdale College politics faculty.

Section I is organized according to the view that the Constitution is rooted in a certain basic understanding of man, his rights, and his relation to the other beings in nature—to the beasts below and to God above. This order of nature, we will find James Madison arguing in *Federalist* 51, gives rise to the structure of the Constitution itself, and to the "external and internal controls" on the government that are so obvious in the Constitution. If laws are required by the fact that men are not angels, Madison writes, controls on the government are required by the fact that angels do not govern men. In this Madison repeats in different words the appearance of God repeatedly in the Declaration, the association He has in that document to the branches of government, and the relation He has to man. The Declaration and the Constitution are in this sense partners in a unique enterprise.

Little surprise, the founding of America being without precedent, that it was not accomplished easily. Sections II through VI of the *Reader* present the reasoning, unfolding through a debate that lasted a generation, that gave the Constitution its form. The quality of this debate both for and against the Declaration, and both for and against the Constitution, is one reason that the Constitution has proved resilient and effective beyond any precedent. The *Reader* presents the key expressions of that reasoning and its results.

Sections VII through XI describe the two great challenges to the Declaration and the Constitution. These two challenges are very different in large respects, but they have something in common. The positive good school of slavery, which would have read the Declaration out of the American political tradition, and which would have made the Constitution the shield of human slavery in the federal territories and in the slave states, arises from a new view of nature, a historical view. Progressivism, which has in modern times remade the federal government both in purpose and in scope, also arises from a historical view. In its early account, "the laws of nature and of nature's God" are themselves constructs of a particular time and set of circumstances and not the abiding things they purport to be. In a later Progressive account, these eternal laws are indeed eternal, but because they are eternal the arrangements of the Constitution cannot be. In the nature of things, circumstances change radically. As they change, government must be able to adapt freely, without constraint. The protection of our property, argues Franklin Roosevelt, requires that we surrender that property to the government freely. The defense of our rights, he argues, requires that we empower the government far beyond the limits permitted by the Constitution.

The early progressivism differed from Jefferson as to whether there are laws that abide, located in nature and discovered by reason. The later progressivism differs from Madison as to whether the distinction between men and angels makes necessary limits on the law. Whether these differences amount to a similarity is a key question. Whether either form is compatible with the rights of man is another.

The last section especially brings us to the current day, to the debates swirling about us concerning the nature of American government and the nature of right. Both sides in the debate lay claim to the authority of the principles and the institutions of America. One cannot judge these claims intelligently, unless first he master the documents in this *Reader*, and elsewhere in our core curriculum. We look forward to undertaking this work with you.

LARRY P. ARNN
President
Hillsdale College

I
THE APPLE OF GOLD AND
THE FRAME OF SILVER

This first section of *The U.S. Constitution: A Reader* includes parts of two classic works of political philosophy by Aristotle, the first political scientist. They explain how politics arises from the nature of the human being, from the specific faculty that makes him able to reason, to talk, to choose according to moral criteria, and to live in connection with one another more profoundly than any other living beings on earth. We Americans, living in a liberal (in the old sense) regime, rightly believe that the purpose of government is to protect our private rights, our rights to our property, to our conscience, to our liberty to speak and worship as we please. We think the government must not exercise any authority over us except by our consent. This being so, we might forget the other side of American politics, or rather something at its foundation. The classics of Western civilization can help us understand why we Americans salute our flag, love our country and sacrifice for it, and pay our highest honors to those who give to it the "last full measure of devotion." The Founders built a different regime than the kind of regime known to ancient thinkers. But the Founders counseled that the reading of the classics was essential to understanding our nation, too. Their republicanism built, they believed, upon the best examples of the past.

Section I also includes letters by two statesmen on the meaning of the Declaration of Independence and its relation to the Constitution. There is no mention of the Constitution in the Declaration of Independence; it came later. There is no mention of the Declaration in the Constitution, either, and this fact has led to debate about the relationship between them. To examine that debate is one of the key purposes of any study of the Constitution, and this *Reader* contains many of the basic sources that bear on that question.

We think the fragment of text written by Abraham Lincoln included in Section I to be authoritative. Lincoln described the relation between the Declaration and the Constitution as the relationship between "an apple of gold" and "the picture," or frame, of silver. The Declaration is the golden apple, and the Constitution the silver frame around it that holds it in place and provides the structure. In the first we may find the purposes of the American republic. In the second we may find its method of operation.

3

The terms of the Declaration lead one to consider the most basic issues. Those who wrote the Declaration were committing an act of treason against the most powerful sovereign on earth. As they did this, they made the claim that they were acting according to certain laws, higher laws, "the laws of nature and of nature's God." To understand the foundation of the Constitution, Lincoln suggests that we must examine these laws. Alexander Hamilton said that the rights named in both the Declaration and the Constitution "are not to be rummaged for, among old parchments," but rather "they are written, as with a sun beam, in the whole volume of human nature, by the hand of divinity itself."

This *Reader* is full of dusty parchments, for which fact perhaps we should apologize. On the other hand, we know that Hamilton wrote that beautiful passage only because we have the dusty parchment in which it is preserved.

LARRY P. ARNN
President
Hillsdale College

THE DECLARATION
OF INDEPENDENCE

With the War for Independence over a year old and hope for a peaceful resolution nonexistent, the Continental Congress appointed a Committee of Five—including Thomas Jefferson, John Adams, and Benjamin Franklin— to draft a document "declar[ing] the causes which impel [the American colonies] to the separation." Thirty-three-year-old Jefferson composed the initial draft, completing it in seventeen days. The committee submitted its draft to Congress on June 28, 1776, and on July 2, Congress voted for independence. Two days later, after numerous edits, Congress approved the Declaration of Independence by unanimous vote.

JULY 4, 1776

THE UNANIMOUS DECLARATION OF THE
THIRTEEN UNITED STATES OF AMERICA

When in the Course of human events, it becomes necessary for one people to dissolve the political bands which have connected them with another, and to assume among the powers of the earth, the separate and equal station to which the Laws of Nature and of Nature's God entitle them, a decent respect to the opinions of mankind requires that they should declare the causes which 5 impel them to the separation.

We hold these truths to be self-evident, that all men are created equal, that they are endowed by their Creator with certain unalienable Rights, that among these are Life, Liberty and the pursuit of Happiness.—That to secure these rights, Governments are instituted among Men, deriving their just powers 10 from the consent of the governed,—That whenever any Form of Government becomes destructive of these ends, it is the Right of the People to alter or to abolish it, and to institute new Government, laying its foundation on such principles and organizing its powers in such form, as to them shall seem most likely to effect their Safety and Happiness. Prudence, indeed, will dictate that 15 Governments long established should not be changed for light and transient causes; and accordingly all experience hath shown, that mankind are more disposed to suffer, while evils are sufferable, than to right themselves by abolishing the forms to which they are accustomed. But when a long train of abuses and usurpations, pursuing invariably the same Object evinces a design to reduce them under absolute Despotism, it is their right, it is their duty, to throw off such Government, and to provide new Guards for their future security.—Such has been the patient sufferance of these Colonies; and such is now the necessity which constrains them to alter their former Systems of Government. The history of the present King of Great Britain is a history of repeated injuries and usurpations, all having in direct object the establishment of an absolute Tyranny over these States. To prove this, let Facts be submitted to a candid world.

He has refused his Assent to Laws, the most wholesome and necessary for the public good.

He has forbidden his Governors to pass Laws of immediate and pressing importance, unless suspended in their operation till his Assent should be obtained; and when so suspended, he has utterly neglected to attend to them.

He has refused to pass other Laws for the accommodation of large districts of people, unless those people would relinquish the right of Representation in the Legislature, a right inestimable to them and formidable to tyrants only.

He has called together legislative bodies at places unusual, uncomfortable, and distant from the depository of their public Records, for the sole purpose of fatiguing them into compliance with his measures.

He has dissolved Representative Houses repeatedly, for opposing with manly firmness his invasions on the rights of the people.

He has refused for a long time, after such dissolutions, to cause others to be elected; whereby the Legislative powers, incapable of Annihilation, have returned to the People at large for their exercise; the State remaining in the mean time exposed to all the dangers of invasion from without, and convulsions within.

He has endeavored to prevent the population of these States; for that purpose obstructing the Laws for Naturalization of Foreigners; refusing to pass others to encourage their migrations hither, and raising the conditions of new Appropriations of Lands.

He has obstructed the Administration of Justice, by refusing his Assent to Laws for establishing Judiciary powers.

He has made Judges dependent on his Will alone, for the tenure of their offices, and the amount and payment of their salaries.

He has erected a multitude of New Offices, and sent hither swarms of Officers to harrass our people, and eat out their substance.

He has kept among us, in times of peace, Standing Armies without the   5 Consent of our legislatures.

He has affected to render the Military independent of and superior to the Civil power.

He has combined with others to subject us to a jurisdiction foreign to our constitution, and unacknowledged by our laws; giving his Assent to their   10 Acts of pretended Legislation:

For Quartering large bodies of armed troops among us:

For protecting them, by a mock Trial, from punishment for any Murders which they should commit on the Inhabitants of these States:

For cutting off our Trade with all parts of the world: 15

For imposing Taxes on us without our Consent:

For depriving us in many cases, of the benefits of Trial by Jury:

For transporting us beyond Seas to be tried for pretended offenses:

For abolishing the free System of English Laws in a neighboring Province, establishing therein an Arbitrary government, and enlarging its Boundaries   20 so as to render it at once an example and fit instrument for introducing the same absolute rule into these Colonies:

For taking away our Charters, abolishing our most valuable Laws, and altering fundamentally the Forms of our Governments:

For suspending our own Legislatures, and declaring themselves invested with   25 power to legislate for us in all cases whatsoever.

He has abdicated Government here, by declaring us out of his Protection and waging War against us.

He has plundered our seas, ravaged our Coasts, burnt our towns, and destroyed the lives of our people.   30

He is at this time transporting large Armies of foreign Mercenaries to complete the works of death, desolation and tyranny, already begun with circumstances of Cruelty and perfidy scarcely paralleled in the most barbarous ages, and totally unworthy the Head of a civilized nation.

He has constrained our fellow Citizens taken Captive on the high Seas to bear Arms against their Country, to become the executioners of their friends and Brethren, or to fall themselves by their Hands.

He has excited domestic insurrections amongst us, and has endeavored to
5   bring on the inhabitants of our frontiers, the merciless Indian Savages, whose known rule of warfare, is an undistinguished destruction of all ages, sexes and conditions.

In every stage of these Oppressions We have Petitioned for Redress in the most humble terms: Our repeated Petitions have been answered only by
10   repeated injury. A Prince whose character is thus marked by every act which may define a Tyrant, is unfit to be the ruler of a free people.

Nor have We been wanting in attentions to our British brethren. We have warned them from time to time of attempts by their legislature to extend an unwarrantable jurisdiction over us. We have reminded them of the
15   circumstances of our emigration and settlement here. We have appealed to their native justice and magnanimity, and we have conjured them by the ties of our common kindred to disavow these usurpations, which, would inevitably interrupt our connections and correspondence. They too have been deaf to the voice of justice and of consanguinity. We must, therefore, acquiesce in
20   the necessity, which denounces our Separation, and hold them, as we hold the rest of mankind, Enemies in War, in Peace Friends.

We, therefore, the Representatives of the united States of America, in General Congress, Assembled, appealing to the Supreme Judge of the world for the rectitude of our intentions, do, in the Name, and by Authority of the good
25   People of these Colonies, solemnly publish and declare, That these United Colonies are, and of Right ought to be Free and Independent States; that they are Absolved from all Allegiance to the British Crown, and that all political connection between them and the State of Great Britain, is and ought to be totally dissolved; and that as Free and Independent States, they have full Power
30   to levy War, conclude Peace, contract Alliances, establish Commerce, and to do all other Acts and Things which Independent States may of right do. And for the support of this Declaration, with a firm reliance on the protection of divine Providence, we mutually pledge to each other our Lives, our Fortunes and our sacred Honor.

GEORGIA
Button Gwinnett, Lyman Hall, George Walton

NORTH CAROLINA
William Hooper, Joseph Hewes, John Penn

SOUTH CAROLINA
Edward Rutledge, Thomas Heyward, Jr., Thomas Lynch, Jr.,
Arthur Middleton

MARYLAND
Samuel Chase, William Paca, Thomas Stone,
Charles Carroll of Carrollton

VIRGINIA
George Wythe, Richard Henry Lee, Thomas Jefferson,
Benjamin Harrison, Thomas Nelson, Jr., Francis Lightfoot Lee,
Carter Braxton

PENNSYLVANIA
Robert Morris, Benjamin Rush, Benjamin Franklin, John Morton,
George Clymer, James Smith, George Taylor, James Wilson,
George Ross

DELAWARE
Caesar Rodney, George Read, Thomas McKean

NEW YORK
William Floyd, Philip Livingston, Francis Lewis, Lewis Morris

NEW JERSEY
Richard Stockton, John Witherspoon, Francis Hopkinson,
John Hart, Abraham Clark

NEW HAMPSHIRE
Josiah Bartlett, William Whipple, Matthew Thornton

MASSACHUSETTS
John Hancock, Samuel Adams, John Adams, Robert Treat Paine,
Elbridge Gerry

RHODE ISLAND
Stephen Hopkins, William Ellery

CONNECTICUT
Roger Sherman, Samuel Huntington, William Williams,
Oliver Wolcott

LETTER TO HENRY LEE
THOMAS JEFFERSON (1743–1826)

The elder Thomas Jefferson answered hundreds of letters, including, in this instance, a query about the Declaration of Independence, explaining that it drew upon a long political and philosophical tradition and reflected principles widely understood by Americans of the founding era.

MAY 8, 1825

DEAR SIR:

... That George Mason was the author of the bill of rights, and of the constitution founded on it, the evidence of the day established fully in my mind. Of the paper you mention, purporting to be instructions to the Virginia delegation in Congress, I have no recollection. If it were anything more than a project of some private hand, that is to say, had any such instructions 5 been ever given by the convention, they would appear in the journals, which we possess entire. But with respect to our rights, and the acts of the British government contravening those rights, there was but one opinion on this side of the water. All American whigs thought alike on these subjects. When forced, therefore, to resort to arms for redress, an appeal to the tribunal of 10 the world was deemed proper for our justification. This was the object of the Declaration of Independence. Not to find out new principles, or new arguments, never before thought of, not merely to say things which had never been said before; but to place before mankind the common sense of the subject, in terms so plain and firm as to command their assent, and to justify 15 ourselves in the independent stand we are compelled to take. Neither aiming at originality of principle or sentiment, nor yet copied from any particular and previous writing, it was intended to be an expression of the American mind, and to give to that expression the proper tone and spirit called for by the occasion. All its authority rests then on the harmonizing sentiments of 20

Thomas Jefferson, "To Henry Lee," May 8, 1825, in Paul Leicester Ford, ed., *The Works of Thomas Jefferson,* "Federal Edition," Vol. 10 (New York: G. P. Putnam's Sons, 1904–5), 342–43.

the day, whether expressed in conversation, in letters, printed essays, or in the elementary books of public right, as Aristotle, Cicero, Locke, Sidney, etc. The historical documents which you mention as in your possession, ought all to be found, and I am persuaded you will find, to be corroborative of the facts and principles advanced in that Declaration. Be pleased to accept assurances of my great esteem and respect.

NICOMACHEAN ETHICS
ARISTOTLE (384–322 B.C.)

Written in the tradition of Aristotle's teacher, Plato—and of Plato's teacher, Socrates—the Nicomachean Ethics *addresses the question, "What is the best life for man?" An extended reflection on virtue, happiness, and friendship, it helped to inform the moral and political thought of America's Founders. There are echoes of it, for instance, in President George Washington's First Inaugural Address, when he states "that there exists in the economy and course of nature, an indissoluble union between virtue and happiness."*

C. 350 B.C.

BOOK I

CHAPTER 1. Every art and every inquiry, and likewise every action and choice, seems to aim at some good, and hence it has been beautifully said that the good is that at which all things aim. But a certain difference is apparent among ends, since some are ways of being at work, while others are certain kinds of works produced, over and above the being-at-work. And in those 5 cases in which there are ends of any kind beyond the actions, the works produced are by nature better things than the activities. And since there are many actions and arts and kinds of knowledge, the ends also turn out to be many: of medical knowledge the end is health, of shipbuilding skill it is a boat, of strategic art it is victory, of household management it is wealth. But in as 10 many such pursuits as are under some one capacity—in the way that bridle making and all the other skills involved with implements pertaining to horses come under horsemanship, while this and every action pertaining to war come under strategic art, and in the same way other pursuits are under other capacities—in all of them the ends of all the master arts are more worthy of 15 choice than are the ends of the pursuits that come under them, since these latter are pursued for the sake of those arts. And it makes no difference whether

Aristotle, *Nicomachean Ethics*, trans. Joe Sachs (Newbury, MA: Focus Publishing/R. Pullins, 2002), 1–12. Reproduced with permission of Focus Publishing in the format Textbook via Copyright Clearance Center.

the ends of the actions are the ways of being at work themselves, or something else beyond these, as they are with the kinds of knowledge mentioned.

CHAPTER 2. If, then, there is some end of the things we do that we want on account of itself, and the rest on account of this one, and we do not choose
5   everything on account of something else (for in that way the choices would go beyond all bounds, so that desire would be empty and pointless), it is clear that this would be the good, and in fact the highest good. Then would not an awareness of it have great weight in one's life, so that, like archers who have a target, we would be more apt to hit on what is needed? But if this is so, one
10   ought to try to get a grasp, at least in outline, of what it is and to what kind of knowledge or capacity it belongs.

And it would seem to belong to the one that is most governing and most a master art, and politics appears to be of this sort, since it prescribes which kinds of knowledge ought to be in the cities, and what sorts each person ought to
15   learn and to what extent; also, we see that the most honored capacities, such as generalship, household economics, and rhetorical skill, are under this one. Since this capacity makes use of the rest of the kinds of knowledge, and also lays down the law about what one ought to do and from what one ought to refrain, the end of this capacity should include the ends of the other pursuits,
20   so that this end would be the human good. For even if the good is the same for one person and for a city, that of the city appears to be greater, at least, and more complete both to achieve and to preserve; for even if it is achieved for only one person that is something to be satisfied with, but for people or for cities it is something more beautiful and more divine. So our pursuit aims at
25   this, and is in a certain way political.

CHAPTER 3. One would speak adequately if one were to attain the clarity that goes along with the underlying material, for precision ought not to be sought in the same way in all kinds of discourse, any more than in things made by the various kinds of craftsmen. The things that are beautiful and just, about which
30   politics investigates, involve great disagreement and inconsistency, so that they are thought to belong only to convention and not to nature. And the things that are good also involve some inconsistency of this sort, because harm results from them for many people, for before now some people have been ruined by wealth, and others by courage. So one ought to be content, when speaking about
35   such things and reasoning from such things, to point out the truth roughly and in outline, and when speaking about things that are so for the most part, and reasoning from things of that short, to reach conclusions that are also of that sort. And it is necessary also to take each of the things that are said in the same way, for it belongs to an educated person to look for just so much precision in

Happiness is a personal opinion - People who have achieved happiness think differently than people who are trying to achieve happiness.

each kind of discourse as the nature of the thing one is concerned with admits; for to demand demonstrations from a rhetorician seems about like accepting probable conclusions from a mathematician.

All people are good at making distinctions about the things they are acquainted with, and each is a good judge of those things. Therefore, good judgment goes 5 along with the way each one is educated, and the one who has been educated about everything has it in an unqualified way. For this reason, it is not appropriate for a young person to be a student of politics, since the young are inexperienced in the actions of life, while these are the things about which politics speaks and from which it reasons. Also, since the young are apt to follow their impulses, 10 they would hear such discourses without purpose or benefit, since their end is not knowing but action. And it makes no difference whether one is young in age or immature in character, for the deficiency doesn't come from the time, but from living in accord with feeling and following every impulse. For knowledge comes to such people without profit, as it does to those who lack self-restraint; 15 but to those who keep their desires in proportion and act in that way, knowing about these things would be of great benefit.

About the one who is to hear this discourse, and how it ought to be received, and what task we have set before ourselves, let these things serve as a prelude.

CHAPTER 4. Now taking up the thread again, since every kind of knowing and 20 every choice reach toward some good, let us say what it is that we claim politics aims at, and what, of all the goods aimed at by action, is the highest. In name, this is pretty much agreed about by the majority of people, for most people, as well as those who are more refined, say it is happiness, and assume that living well and doing well are the same thing as being happy. But about happiness—what it 25 is—they are in dispute, and most people do not give the same account of it as the wise. Some people take it to be something visible and obvious, such as pleasure or wealth or honor, and different ones say different things, and even the same person often says different things; when sick one thinks it is health, but when poor, that it is wealth, and when they are conscious of ignorance in themselves, 30 people marvel at those who say it is something grand and above them. And some people believe that, besides these many good things, there is some other good, by itself, which is also responsible for the being good of all these other things.

Now to review all the opinions is perhaps rather pointless, and it would be sufficient to review the ones that come most to prominence or seem to have 35 some account to give. And let it not escape our notice that arguments from first principles differ from those that go up toward first principles. For Plato rightly raised this question, and used to inquire whether the road is from first principles or up to first principles, just as, on a race course, the run is either from the judges to the boundary or back again. One must begin from what is known, but this has two meanings, the things known to us and the things that are known simply. Perhaps then we, at any rate, ought to begin from the things that are known to us. This is why one who is going to listen adequately to discourse about things that are beautiful and just, and generally about things that pertain to political matters, needs to have been beautifully brought up by means of habits. For the primary thing is that something is so, and if this is sufficiently evident, there is no additional need for the reason why. And such a person either has or easily gets hold of the things that come first. If one neither has them nor has it in him to get hold of them, let him harken to Hesiod:

> Altogether best is he who himself has insight into all things,
> But good in his turn is he who trusts one who speaks well.
> But whoever neither himself discerns, nor, harkening to another,
> Lays to heart what he says, that one for his part is a useless man.

CHAPTER 5. For our part, let us speak from the point where we digressed. Most people and the crudest people seem, not without reason, to assume from people's lives that pleasure is the good and is happiness. For this reason they are content with a life devoted to enjoyment. For there are three ways of life especially that hold prominence: the one just now mentioned, and the political life, and third, the contemplative life. Now most people show themselves to be completely slavish by choosing a life that belongs to fatted cattle, but they happen to get listened to because most people who have power share the feeling of Sardanapalus. But refined and active people choose honor, for this is pretty much the goal of political life. Now this appears to be too superficial to be what is sought, for it seems to be in the ones who give honor rather than in the one who is honored, but we divine that the good is something of one's own and hard to take away. Also, people seem to pursue honor in order to be convinced that they themselves are good. At any rate they seek to be honored by the wise and by those who know them, and for virtue; it is clear, then, that at least according to these people, virtue is something greater, and one might perhaps assume that this, rather than honor, is the end of the political life.

But even this seems too incomplete, since it seems possible, while having virtue, even to be asleep or to be inactive throughout life, and on top of these things, to suffer evils and the greatest misfortunes. No one would consider one who lived in that way to be happy, except when defending a hypothesis. And this is enough about these things, since they are spoken of sufficiently in the current popular writings. And the third way of life is the contemplative one, about which we shall make an investigation in what follows. The life of money making is a type of compulsory activity, and it is clear that wealth is not the good being sought,

Wealth is the result of the pursuit of happiness, not the happiness itself.

since it is instrumental and for the sake of something else. For this reason one might suppose that the things spoken of before are more properly ends, since they provide contentment on account of themselves, though it appears that even they are not what is sought, even though many arguments connected with them are tossed around. So let these things be put aside. 5

CHAPTER 6. No doubt the better thing to do is to examine the universal good and go through the difficulties in the way it is spoken of, and yet such an inquiry becomes like trudging uphill because the men who introduced the forms were my friends. But no doubt it would be admitted to be better, indeed to be necessary when keeping the truth safe is at stake, even to abandon the things 10 that are one's own, both for other reasons and because we are philosophers; for while both [the truth and one's friends] are loved, it is a sacred thing to give the higher honor to the truth.

Now those who brought in this opinion did not make forms within which a primary and a derivative instance were spoken of (which is why they did not 15 construct a form of number), but the good is attributed to what something is and also to the sort of thing it is and to a relation it has, while the thinghood of something, which is something on its own, by nature has priority over a relation it has (for this is like an offshoot and incidental attribute of what is), so that there could not be any form common to these. Further, since *good* is 20 meant in just as many ways as *being* is (for in the sense of what something is, the good is spoken of as, for instance, the good or the intellect; in the sense of being of a certain sort, it is spoken of as the excellences; in the sense of being a certain amount, it is spoken of as the proper limit; in the sense of being related to something, it is spoken of as the useful; in the sense of being some time, it 25 is spoken of as an opportune moment; and in the sense of place, it is spoken of as a dwelling or other things of that sort), it is clear that there could not be any common good that is one and universal, for if there were it could not have been meant in all the ways of attributing being but only in one.

Further, since, of the things that come under one form, there is also one kind 30 of knowledge, there would also be some one kind of knowledge of all things that are good, but as it is there are many, even of the good things that come under one way of attributing being; for example, of the opportune moment, in war, the knowledge of it is the general's art, while in disease it is the physician's art, and of the proper limit in food, the knowledge is the physician's art, 35 while in exercises it is the art of the gymnastic trainer. And one might raise the question even of what in the world they mean by speaking of each whatever-itself, seeing as how there is one and the same meaning for both a human being and the human-being-itself, namely the meaning of human-ness. For insofar

> What is good is not always useful, and what is useful is not always good.

as something is a human being, there will be no difference, and if that is the way it is, there will be no difference either insofar as something is good. Surely it will not be any more good by being everlasting, inasmuch as a long-lasting thing is no more white than one that lasts only a day. The Pythagoreans seem
5 to speak in a more credible way about the good, when they place one-ness in the column of good things, and Speusippus seems to have followed them. But about these things let there be some other discussion.

But a certain debatable point in the things that have been said comes to light, on the grounds that the arguments were not meant to be about every sort of
10 good, but that the goods spoken of as coming under one form are those that are pursued, and with which people are satisfied, for their own sake, while the things that tend to produce these, or to preserve them in some way, or to prevent their opposites are spoken of as good by derivation from these and in a different way. It is clear, then, that good things would be meant in two ways, some on
15 account of themselves and others derived from these. Then separating the things that are good in themselves from the useful things, let us examine whether the former are meant in accordance with one form. But what sort of things should one set down as good in themselves? Are they not those things that one pursues even when they are isolated from everything else, such as having good sense,
20 or seeing, or certain pleasures and honors? For even if we pursue these things by reason of some other thing, one would still place them among things good in themselves. Or is there nothing else except the form that is good in itself? But then the form would be of no use. But if the things mentioned are among things good on account of themselves, the meaning of the good in all of these
25 would have to show itself as the same, just as the meaning of whiteness is the same in snow and in lead paint. But of honor and good sense and pleasure there are distinct and divergent meanings of that by which they are good. Therefore there is not any good that is shared and comes under one form.

But then in what way is good meant? For these things certainly do not seem
30 to have the same name by chance. But do they have the same name by being derived from one thing, or by all adding up together into one thing, or rather by analogy? For as sight is in relation to the body, intellect is in relation to the soul, and some other thing is in relation to something else. But perhaps these things ought to be let go for now, since to be precise about them would be more
35 at home in another kind of philosophic inquiry. And it is similar with the form, for even if there is some one good that is attributed in common, or is something separate itself by itself, it is clear that it is not a thing done or possessed by a human being, and something of that sort is being looked for now. But perhaps it might seem to someone that it would be better to be acquainted with it with

a view to those good things that can be possessed or done; for having this as a sort of pattern, we would also know the things that are good for us better, and if we know them, we will hit upon them.

Now while the argument has a certain plausibility, it seems to be discordant with the kinds of knowledge we have, for all of them leave aside an acquaintance 5 with the good itself in order to aim at some particular good and hunt for what they lack. And surely it is not reasonable that all those skilled in arts should be ignorant of, and not even look for, something of such great assistance. And it is impossible to say in what respect a weaver or a carpenter will be benefitted in relation to his art by knowing this good itself, or how one who has beheld the 10 form itself will be a better doctor or general. For it appears that the doctor does not consider health in that way, but the health of a human being, or perhaps rather that of this particular person, since he heals them each by each. So let these things have been spoken of just this much.

CHAPTER 7. And let us go back again to the good that is being sought, what- 15 ever it may be. For it seems to be a different thing in the medical art and the general's art, since it is a different thing in each different action and art, and similarly with the rest. What then is the good in each of them? Or is it that for the sake of which they do everything else? In the medical art this is health, in the general's art it is victory, in the housebuilder's art it is a house, and in a 20 different art it is something else, and in every action and choice it is the end, since everyone does everything else for the sake of this. And so, if there is some end for all actions, this would be the good that belongs to action, and if there is more than one such end, these would constitute that good. So the argument, in transforming itself, has reached the same place; and one must try to make 25 this still more clear.

Now since the ends seem to be more than one, while we choose some of them on account of something else, such as wealth, flutes, and instrumental things generally, it is clear that they are not all complete, but it is manifest that the highest good is something complete. So if there is some one thing alone that is 30 complete, this would be what is being sought, but if there are more than one of them, it would be the most complete of these. And we say that a thing that is pursued on account of itself is more complete than a thing pursued on account of something else, and that what is never chosen on account of anything else is more complete than things chosen both for themselves and on account of 35 something else, and hence that, in an unqualified sense, the complete is what is chosen always for itself and never on account of anything else. And happiness seems to be of this sort most of all, since we choose this always on account of itself and never on account of anything else, while we choose honor and pleasure

and intelligence and every virtue indeed on account of themselves (for even if nothing resulted from them we would choose each of them), but we choose them also for the sake of happiness, supposing that we will be happy by these means. But no one chooses happiness for the sake of these things, nor for the
5   sake of anything else at all.

And the same thing appears to follow from its self-sufficiency, for the complete good seems to be self-sufficient. And by the self-sufficient we mean not what suffices for oneself alone, living one's life as a hermit, but also with parents and children and a wife, and friends and fellow citizens generally, since a human
10 being is by nature meant for a city. But one must take some limit for these connections, since by stretching out to ancestors and descendants and friends of one's friends they go beyond all bounds; but this must be examined later. But we set down as self-sufficient that which, by itself, makes life choiceworthy and lacking in nothing, and such a thing we suppose happiness to be. What's
15 more, we suppose happiness to be the most choiceworthy of all things while not counting it as one of those things, since if it were counted among them it is clear that it would be more choiceworthy together with the tiniest amount of additional good, for the thing added becomes a preeminence of good, and of good things, the greater is always more worthy of choice. So happiness
20 appears to be something complete and self-sufficient, and is, therefore, the end of actions.

But perhaps to say that the highest good is happiness is obviously something undisputed, while it still begs to be said in a more clear and distinct way what happiness is. Now this might come about readily if one were to grasp the work
25 of a human being. For just as with a flute player or sculptor or any artisan, and generally with those to whom some work or action belongs, the good and the doing it well seem to be in the work, so too it would seem to be the case with a human being, if indeed there is some work that belongs to one. But is there some sort of work for a carpenter or a leather worker, while for a human being
30 there is none? Is a human being by nature idle? Or, just as for an eye or a hand or a foot or generally for each of the parts, there seems to be some sort of work, ought one also to set down some work beyond all these for the human being? But then what in the world would this be? For living seems to be something shared in even by plants, but something peculiarly human is being sought. Therefore,
35 one must divide off the life that consists in nutrition and growth. Following this would be some sort of life that consists in perceiving, but this seems to be shared in by a horse and a cow and by every animal. So what remains is some sort of life that puts into action that in us that has articulate speech; of this capacity, one aspect is what is able to be persuaded by reason, while the other

is what has reason and thinks things through. And since this is still meant in two ways, one must set it down as a life in a state of being-at-work, since this seems to be the more governing meaning.

And if the work of a human being is a being-at-work of the soul in accordance with reason, or not without reason, while we say that the work of a certain sort of person is the same in kind as that of a serious person of that sort, as in the case of a harpist and of a serious harpist, and this is simply because in all cases the superiority in excellence is attached to the work, since the work of a harpist is to play the harp and the work of a serious harpist is the play the harp well—if this is so and we set down that the work of a human being is a certain sort of life, while this life consists of a being-at-work of the soul and actions that go along with reason, and it belongs to a man of serious stature to do these things well and beautifully, while each thing is accomplished well as a result of the virtue appropriate to it—if this is so, the human good comes to be disclosed as a being-at-work of the soul in accordance with virtue, and if the virtues are more than one, in accordance with the best and most complete virtue. But also, this must be in a complete life, for one swallow does not make a Spring, nor one day, and in the same way one day or a short time does not make a person blessed and happy.

So let the good have been sketched in outline in this way, for presumably one needs to rough it in first and then inscribe the details later. And it would seem to be in the power of anyone to carry forward and articulate things that are in good shape in the outline, and that time is a good discoverer of such things, or makes the work easier; in fact the advances in the arts have come from this, since it is in anyone's power to add what is left out. But it behooves one to remember the things that were said before, and not to look for precision in the same way in all things, but in accordance with the underlying material in each case, and to the extent that it is appropriate to that course of inquiry. For both a carpenter and a geometrician look for a right angle, but in different ways, for the one seeks it to the extent that it is useful to the work, while the other seeks for what it is or what it is a property of, since he is someone who beholds the truth. So one ought to do the same in other things, so that side issues do not become greater than the work being done.

And one ought not to demand a reason in all things alike, either, but it is sufficient in some cases for it to be shown beautifully that something is so, in particular such things as concern first principles; that something is so comes first and is a first principle. And of first principles, some are beheld by way of examples, others by sense perception, others by becoming experienced in some habit, and others in other ways. So one must try to go after each of them by the means that belong to its nature, and be serious about distinguishing them rightly, since this has great weight in what follows. For the beginning seems to be more than half of the whole, and many of the things that are inquired after become illuminated along with it.

One may not know they are happy until after they have discovered the thing that makes them happy

THE POLITICS
ARISTOTLE

*Thomas Jefferson began studying Greek at the age of nine, and later in
life employed so many Greek phrases in his letters that John Adams, his
frequent correspondent, complained of them. The Founders' interest in clas-
sical languages was not academic, but political and philosophical. Among
the ancient books that they drew upon was Aristotle's Politics, a catalog of
constitutions and a guide to understanding regimes.*

C. 335–322 B.C.

BOOK I

CHAPTER 1. (1) Since we see that every city is some sort of partnership, and that
every partnership is constituted for the sake of some good (for everyone does
everything for the sake of what is held to be good), it is clear that all partnerships
aim at some good, and that the partnership that is most authoritative of all and
embraces all the others does so particularly, and aims at the most authoritative   5
good of all. This is what is called the city or the political partnership.

(2) Those who suppose that the same person is expert in political [rule], kingly
[rule], managing the household and being a master [of slaves] do not argue
rightly. For they consider that each of these differs in the multitude or few-
ness [of those ruled and not in kind—for example, [the ruler] of a few is a   10
master, of more a household manager, and of still more an expert in political
or kingly [rule]—the assumption being that there is no difference between a
large household and a small city; and as for the experts in political and kingly
[rule], they consider an expert in kingly [rule] one who has charge himself, and
in political [rule] one who, on the basis of the precepts of this sort of science,   15
rules and is ruled in turn. But these things are not true. (3) This will be clear to
those investigating in accordance with our normal sort of inquiry. For just as it
is necessary elsewhere to divide a compound into its uncompounded elements
(for these are the smallest parts of the whole), so too by investigating what the

Aristotle, *The Politics,* trans. Carnes Lord (Chicago: University of Chicago Press, 1984), 35–41.
Reproduced with permission of University of Chicago Press–Books in the format Textbook via
Copyright Clearance Center.

city is composed of we shall gain a better view concerning these [kinds of rulers] as well, both as to how they differ from one another and as to whether there is some expertise characteristic of an art that can be acquired in connection with each of those mentioned.

5   CHAPTER 2. (1) Now in these matters as elsewhere it is by looking at how things develop naturally from the beginning that one may best study them. (2) First, then, there must of necessity be a conjunction of persons who cannot exist without one another: on the one hand, male and female, for the sake of reproduction (which occurs not from intentional choice but—as is also the 10 case with the other animals and plants—from a natural striving to leave behind another that is like oneself); on the other, the naturally ruling and ruled, on account of preservation. For that which can foresee with the mind is the naturally ruling and naturally mastering element, while that which can do these things with the body is the naturally ruled and slave; hence the same thing is 15 advantageous for the master and slave. (3) Now the female is distinguished by nature from the slave. For nature makes nothing in an economizing spirit, as smiths make the Delphic knife, but one thing with a view to one thing; and each instrument would perform most finely if it served one task rather than many. (4) The barbarians, though, have the same arrangement for female and slave. 20 The reason for this is that they have no naturally ruling element; with them, the partnership [of man and woman] is that of female slave and male slave. This is why the poets say "it is fitting for Greeks to rule barbarians"—the assumption being that barbarian and slave are by nature the same thing.

(5) From these two partnerships, then, the household first arose, and Hesiod's 25 verse is rightly spoken: "first a house, and woman, and ox for plowing"—for poor persons have an ox instead of a servant. The household is the partnership constituted by nature for [the needs of] daily life; Charondas calls its members "peers of the mess," Epimenides of Crete "peers of the manger." The first partnership arising from [the union of] several households and for the sake of nondaily 30 needs is the village. (6) By nature the village seems to be above all an extension of the household. Its members some call "milk-peers"; they are "the children and the children's children." This is why cities were at first under kings, and nations are even now. For those who joined together were already under kings: every household was under the eldest as king, and so also were the extensions [of the 35 household constituting the village] as a result of kinship. (7) This is what Homer meant when he says that "each acts as law to his children and wives"; for [men] were scattered and used to dwell in this manner in ancient times. And it is for this reason that all assert that the gods are under a king—because they themselves are under kings now, or were in ancient times. For human beings assimilate not 40 only the looks of the gods to themselves, but their ways of life as well.

(8) The partnership arising from [the union of] several villages that is complete is the city. It reaches a level of full self-sufficiency, so to speak; and while coming into being for the sake of living, it exists for the sake of living well. Every city, therefore, exists by nature, if such also are the first partnerships. For the city is their end, and nature is an end: what each thing is—for example, a human being, 5 a horse, or a household—when its coming into being is complete is, we assert, the nature of that thing. (9) Again, that for the sake of which [a thing exists], or the end, is what is best; and self-sufficiency is an end and what is best.

From these things it is evident, then, that the city belongs among the things that exist by nature, and that man is by nature a political animal. He who is 10 without a city through nature rather than chance is either a mean sort or superior to man; he is "without clan, without law, without hearth," like the person reproved by Homer; (10) for the one who is such by nature has by this fact a desire for war, as if he were an isolated piece in a game of chess. That man is much more a political animal than any kind of bee or any herd animal is clear. 15 For, as we assert, nature does nothing in vain; and man alone among the animals has speech. (11) The voice indeed indicates the painful or pleasant, and hence is present in other animals as well; for their nature has come this far, that they have a perception of the painful and pleasant and indicate these things to each other. But speech serves to reveal the advantageous and the harmful, and 20 hence also the just and the unjust. (12) For it is peculiar to man as compared to the other animals that he alone has a perception of good and bad and just and unjust and other things [of this sort]; and partnership in these things is what makes a household and a city.

The city is thus prior by nature to the household and to each of us. (13) For 25 the whole must of necessity be prior to the part; for if the whole [body] is destroyed there will not be a foot or a hand, unless in the sense that the term is similar (as when one speaks of a hand made of stone), but the thing itself will be defective. Everything is defined by its task and its power, and if it is no longer the same in these respects it should not be spoken of in the same way, 30 but only as something similarly termed. (14) That the city is both by nature and prior to each individual, then, is clear. For if the individual when separated [from it] is not self-sufficient, he will be in a condition similar to that of the other parts in relation to the whole. One who is incapable of participating or who is in need of nothing through being self-sufficient is no part of a city, and 35 so is either a beast or a god.

(15) Accordingly, there is in everyone by nature an impulse toward this sort of partnership. And yet the one who first constituted [a city] is responsible for the greatest of goods. For just as man is the best of the animals when completed, when separated from law and adjudication he is the worst of all. (16) For 40

injustice is harshest when it is furnished with arms; and man is born naturally possessing arms for [the use of] prudence and virtue which are nevertheless very susceptible to being used for their opposites. This is why, without virtue, he is the most unholy and the most savage [of the animals], and the worst with regard to sex and food. [The virtue of] justice is a thing belonging to the city. For adjudication is an arrangement of the political partnership, and adjudication is judgment as to what is just.

CHAPTER 3. (1) Since it is evident out of what parts the city is constituted, it is necessary first to speak of household management; for every city is composed of households. The parts of household management correspond to the parts out of which the household itself is constituted. Now the complete household is made up of slaves and free persons. Since everything is to be sought for first in its smallest elements, and the first and smallest parts of the household are master, slave, husband, wife, father, and children, three things must be investigated to determine what each is and what sort of thing it ought to be. (2) These are expertise in mastery, in marital [rule] (there is no term for the union of man and woman), and thirdly in parental [rule] (this too has not been assigned a term of its own). (3) So much, then, for the three we spoke of. There is a certain part of it, however, which some hold to be [identical with] household management, and others its greatest part; how the matter really stands has to be studied. I am speaking of what is called business expertise.

Let us speak first about master and slave, so that we may see at the same time what relates to necessary needs and whether we cannot acquire something in the way of knowledge about these things that is better than current conceptions. (4) For some hold that mastery is a kind of science, and that managing the household, mastery, and expertise in political and kingly [rule] are the same, as we said at the beginning. Others hold that exercising mastery is against nature; for [as they believe] it is by law that one person is slave and another free, there being no difference by nature, and hence it is not just, since it rests on force.

CHAPTER 4. (1) Now possessions are a part of the household, and expertise in acquiring possessions a part of household management (for without the necessary things it is impossible either to live or to live well); and just as the specialized arts must of necessity have their proper instruments if their work is to be performed, so too must the expert household manager. (2) Now of instruments some are inanimate and others animate—the pilot's rudder, for example, is an inanimate one, but his lookout an animate one; for the subordinate is a kind of instrument for the arts. A possession too, then, is an instrument for life, and one's possessions are the multitude of such instruments; and the slave is a possession of the animate sort. Every subordinate, moreover, is an instrument that wields many instruments, (3) for if each of the instruments were able to perform its work on command or by anticipation, as they assert those of Daedalus did, or the tripods of Hephaestus (which the poet says "of their own accord came to the gods' gathering"), so that shuttles would weave themselves and picks play the lyre, master craftsmen would no longer have a need for subordinates, or masters   5 for slaves. (4) Now the instruments mentioned are productive instruments, but a possession is an instrument of action. For from the shuttle comes something apart from the use of it, while from clothing or a bed the use alone. Further, since production and action differ in kind and both require instruments, these must of necessity reflect the same difference. (5) Life is action, not production;   10 the slave is therefore a subordinate in matters concerning action.

A possession is spoken of in the same way as a part. A part is not only part of something else, but belongs wholly to something else; similarly with a possession. Accordingly, while the master is only master of the slave and does not belong to him, the slave is not only slave to the master but belongs wholly to him.   15

(6) What the nature of the slave is and what his capacity, then, is clear from these things. For one who does not belong to himself by nature but is another's, though a human being, is by nature a slave; a human being is another's who, though a human being, is a possession; and a possession is an instrument of action and separable [from its owner].   20

CHAPTER 5. (1) Whether anyone is of this sort by nature or not, and whether it is better and just for anyone to be a slave or not, but rather all slavery is against nature, must be investigated next. It is not difficult either to discern [the answer] by reasoning or to learn it from what actually happens. (2) Ruling and being ruled belong not only among things necessary but also among things advanta-   25 geous. And immediately from birth certain things diverge, some toward being ruled, others toward ruling. There are many kinds both of ruling and ruled [things], and the better rule is always that over ruled [things] that are better, for example over a human being rather than a beast; (3) for the work performed by the better is better, and wherever something rules and something is ruled   30 there is a certain work belonging to these together. For whatever is constituted out of a number of things—whether continuous or discrete—and becomes a single common thing always displays a ruling and a ruled element; (4) this is something that animate things derive from all of nature, for even in things that do not share in life there is a sort of rule, for example in a harmony. But these   35 matters perhaps belong to a more external sort of investigation. But an animal is the first thing constituted out of soul and body, of which the one is the ruling element by nature, the other the ruled. (5) It is in things whose condition is according to nature that one ought particularly to investigate what is by nature, not in things that are defective. Thus the human being to be studied is one whose state is best both in body and in soul—in him this is clear; for in the case of the depraved, or those in a depraved condition, the body is often held to rule the soul on account of their being in a condition that is bad and unnatural.

5   (6) It is then in an animal, as we were saying, that one can first discern both the sort of rule characteristic of a master and political rule. For the soul rules the body with the rule characteristic of a master, while intellect rules appetite with political and kingly rule; and this makes it evident that it is according to nature and advantageous for the body to be ruled by the soul, and the passionate part
10   [of the soul] by intellect and the part having reason, while it is harmful to both if the relation is equal or reversed. (7) The same holds with respect to man and the other animals: tame animals have a better nature than wild ones, and it is better for all of them to be ruled by man, since in this way their preservation is ensured. Further, the relation of male to female is by nature a relation of
15   superior to inferior and ruler to ruled. The same must of necessity hold in the case of human beings generally.

(8) Accordingly, those who are as different [from other men] as the soul from the body or man from beast—and they are in this state if their work is the use of the body, and if this is the best that can come from them—are slaves by nature.
20   For them it is better to be ruled in accordance with this sort of rule, if such is the case for the other things mentioned. (9) For he is a slave by nature who is capable of belonging to another—which is also why he belongs to another—and who participates in reason only to the extent of perceiving it, but does not have it. (The other animals, not perceiving reason, obey their passions.) Moreover,
25   the need for them differs only slightly: bodily assistance in the necessary things is forthcoming from both, from slaves and from tame animals alike.

(10) Nature indeed wishes to make the bodies of free persons and slaves different as well [as their souls]—those of the latter strong with a view to necessary needs, those of the former straight way of life (which is itself divided between
30   the needs of war and those of peace); yet the opposite often results, some having the bodies of free persons while others have the souls. It is evident, at any rate, that if they were to be born as different only in body as the images of the gods, everyone would assert that those not so favored merited being their slaves. (11) But if this is true in the case of the body, it is much more justifiable to make this
35   distinction in the case of the soul; yet it is not as easy to see the beauty of the soul as it is that of the body. That some persons are free and others slaves by nature, therefore, and that for these slavery is both advantageous and just, is evident.

ON THE COMMONWEALTH
MARCUS TULLIUS CICERO (c. 106–43 B.C.)

Marcus Tullius Cicero was the great defender of the Roman republic and a master of oratory. The author of several books on politics, philosophy, and rhetoric, he was the first to speak of natural law as a moral or political law, and was an important influence on the Founders.

C. 54–51 B.C.

…[33] True law is right reason, consonant with nature, spread through all people. It is constant and eternal; it summons to duty by its orders, it deters from crime by its prohibitions. Its orders and prohibitions to good people are never given in vain; but it does not move the wicked by these orders or prohibitions. It is wrong to pass laws obviating this law; it is not permitted to   5
abrogate any of it; it cannot be totally repealed. We cannot be released from this law by the senate or the people, and it needs no exegete or interpreter like Sextus Aelius. There will not be one law at Rome and another at Athens, one now and another later; but all nations at all times will be bound by this one eternal and unchangeable law, and the god will be the one common   10
master and general (so to speak) of all people. He is the author, expounder, and mover of this law; and the person who does not obey it will be in exile from himself. Insofar as he scorns his nature as a human being, by this very fact he will pay the greatest penalty, even if he escapes all the other things that are generally recognized as punishments.…   15

obviate - make unnecessary
abrogate - annul

Marcus Tullius Cicero, "On the Commonwealth," in James E.G. Zetzel, ed., *On the Commonwealth and On the Laws* (Cambridge: Cambridge University Press, 1999), 71–72.

SECOND TREATISE OF GOVERNMENT
JOHN LOCKE (1632–1704)

John Locke's Two Treatises of Government *presented a critique of the divine right of kings and outlined the principles of natural rights and government by consent. Written during the 1670s, they were not published until after the Glorious Revolution of 1688 and the passage of the English Bill of Rights in 1689. Locke was the political theorist quoted most frequently by Americans in the 1770s.*

1690

CHAPTER II. OF THE STATE OF NATURE.

4. To understand political power right, and derive it from its original, we must consider what state all men are naturally in, and that is, a state of perfect freedom to order their actions and dispose of their possessions, and persons, as they think fit, within the bounds of the law of nature; without asking leave, or depending upon the will of any other man. 5

A state also of equality, wherein all the power and jurisdiction is reciprocal, no one having more than another; there being nothing more evident, than that creatures of the same species and rank, promiscuously born to all the same advantages of nature, and the use of the same faculties, should also be equal one amongst another without subordination or subjection; unless the lord and 10 master of them all should, by any manifest declaration of his will, set one above another, and confer on him, by an evident and clear appointment, an undoubted right to dominion and sovereignty....

6. But though this be a state of liberty, yet it is not a state of licence: though man in that state have an uncontrollable liberty to dispose of his person or pos- 15 sessions, yet he has not liberty to destroy himself, or so much as any creature in his possession, but where some nobler use than its bare preservation calls

John Locke, "Book II," in *Two Treatises of Government* (London: C. and J. Rivington, 1824), 131–34, 159–61, 175, 179–81, 186–88, 203–6, 208–9, 215–16, 256–57, 261–65, 275–76.

for it. The state of nature has a law of nature to govern it, which obliges every one: and reason, which is that law, teaches all mankind, who will but consult it, that being all equal and independent, no one ought to harm another in his life, health, liberty, or possessions: for men being all the workmanship of one
5   omnipotent and infinitely wise Maker; all the servants of one sovereign master, sent into the world by his order, and about his business; they are his property, whose workmanship they are, made to last during his, not another's pleasure: and being furnished with like faculties, sharing all in one community of nature, there cannot be supposed any such subordination among us, that may authorize
10   us to destroy another, as if we were made for one another's uses, as the inferior ranks of creatures are for ours. Every one, as he is bound to preserve himself, and not to quit his station wilfully, so by the like reason, when his own preservation comes not in competition, ought he, as much as he can, to preserve the rest of mankind, and may not, unless it be to do justice to an offender, take away
15   or impair the life, or what tends to the preservation of life, the liberty, health, limb, or goods of another.

7. And that all men may be restrained from invading others' rights, and from doing hurt to one another, and the law of nature be observed, which willeth the peace and preservation of all mankind, the execution of the law of nature is, in
20   that state, put into every man's hands, whereby every one has a right to punish the transgressors of that law to such a degree as may hinder its violation: for the law of nature would, as all other laws that concern men in this world, be in vain, if there were nobody that in the state of nature had a power to execute that law, and thereby preserve the innocent and restrain offenders. And if any
25   one in the state of nature may punish another for any evil he has done, every one may do so: for in that state of perfect equality, where naturally there is no superiority or jurisdiction of one over another, what any may do in prosecution of that law, every one must needs have a right to do.

8. And thus, in the state of nature, "one man comes by a power over another;"
30   but yet no absolute or arbitrary power, to use a criminal, when he has got him in his hands, according to the passionate heats, or boundless extravagancy of his own will; but only to retribute to him, so far as calm reason and conscience dictate, what is proportionate to his transgression; which is so much as may serve for reparation and restraint: for these two are the only reasons, why one
35   man may lawfully do harm to another, which is that we call punishment. In transgressing the law of nature, the offender declares himself to live by another rule than that of reason and common equity, which is that measure God has set to the actions of men, for their mutual security; and so he becomes dangerous to mankind, the tie, which is to secure them from injury and violence, being

slighted and broken by him. Which being a trespass against the whole species, and the peace and safety of it, provided for by the law of nature; every man upon this score, by the right he hath to preserve mankind in general, may restrain, or, where it is necessary, destroy things noxious to them, and so may bring such evil on any one, who hath transgressed that law, as may make him repent the 5 doing of it, and thereby deter him, and by his example others, from doing the like mischief. And in this case, and upon this ground, "every man hath a right to punish the offender, and be executioner of the law of nature."…

CHAPTER VI. OF PATERNAL POWER.

54. Though I have said above…"That all men by nature are equal," I cannot be supposed to understand all sorts of equality: age or virtue may give men 10 a just precedency: excellency of parts and merit may place others above the common level: birth may subject some, and alliance or benefits others, to pay an observance to those whom nature, gratitude, or other respects, may have made it due: and yet all this consists with the equality, which all men are in, in respect of jurisdiction or dominion one over another; which was the equality 15 I there spoke of, as proper to the business in hand, being that equal right, that every man hath, to his natural freedom, without being subjected to the will or authority of any other man.…

CHAPTER VII. OF POLITICAL OR CIVIL SOCIETY.

87. Man being born, as has been proved, with a title to perfect freedom, and uncontrolled enjoyment of all the rights and privileges of the law of nature, 20 equally with any other man, or number of men in the world, hath by nature a power, not only to preserve his property, that is, his life, liberty, and estate, against the injuries and attempts of other men; but to judge of and punish the breaches of that law in others, as he is persuaded the offense deserves, even with death itself, in crimes where the heinousness of the fact, in his opinion, requires 25 it. But because no political society can be, nor subsist, without having in itself the power to preserve the property, and, in order thereunto, punish the offenses of all those of that society; there and there only is political society, where every one of the members hath quitted his natural power, resigned it up into the hands of the community in all cases that excludes him not from appealing for protection 30 to the law established by it. And thus all private judgment of every particular member being excluded, the community comes to be umpire by settled standing rules, indifferent, and the same to all parties; and by men having authority from the community, for the execution of those rules, decides all the differences that may happen between any members of that society concerning any matter of 35 right; and punishes those offenses which any member hath committed against

the society, with such penalties as the law has established, whereby it is easy to discern, who are, and who are not, in political society together. Those who are united into one body, and have a common established law and judicature to appeal to, with authority to decide controversies between then, and punish

5   offenders, are in civil society one with another: but those who have no such common appeal, I mean on earth, are still in the state of nature, each being, where there is no other, judge for himself, and executioner: which is, as I have before showed, the perfect state of nature.

88. And thus the commonwealth comes by a power to set down what punish-
10   ment shall belong to the several transgressions which they think worthy of it, committed amongst the members of that society, (which is the power of making laws) as well as it has the power to punish any injury done unto any of its members, by any one that is not of it, (which is the power of war and peace,) and all this for the preservation of the property of all the members of that
15   society, as far as is possible. But though every man who has entered into civil society, and is become a member of any commonwealth, has thereby quitted his power to punish offenses against the law of nature, in prosecution of his own private judgment; yet with the judgment of offenses, which he has given up to the legislative in all cases, where he can appeal to the magistrate, he has given a
20   right to the commonwealth to employ his force, for the execution of the judgments of the commonwealth, whenever he shall be called to it; which indeed are his own judgments, they being made by himself, or his representative. And herein we have the original of the legislative and executive power of civil society, which is to judge by standing laws, how far offenses are to be punished, when
25   committed within the commonwealth; and also to determine, by occasional judgments founded on the present circumstances of the fact, how far injuries from without are to be vindicated; and in both these to employ all the force of all the members, when there shall be need.

89. Whenever therefore any number of men are so united into one society, as
30   to quit every one his executive power of the law of nature, and to resign it to the public, there and there only is a political, or civil society. And this is done, wherever any number of men, in the state of nature, enter into society to make one people, one body politic, under one supreme government; or else when any one joins himself to, and incorporates with any government already made:
35   for hereby he authorizes the society, or, which is all one, the legislative thereof, to make laws for him, as the public good of the society shall require; to the execution whereof, his own assistance (as to his own degrees) is due. And this puts men out of a state of nature into that of a commonwealth, by setting up a judge on earth, with authority to determine all the controversies, and redress

the injuries that may happen to any member of the commonwealth: which judge is the legislative, or magistrate appointed by it. And wherever there are any number of men, however associated, that have no such decisive power to appeal to, there they are still in the state of nature....

CHAPTER VIII. OF THE BEGINNING OF POLITICAL SOCIETIES.

95. Men being, as has been said, by nature, all free, equal, and independent, no one can be put out of this estate, and subjected to the political power of another, without his own consent. The only way, whereby any one divests himself of his natural liberty, and puts on the bonds of civil society, is by agreeing with other men to join and unite into a community, for their comfortable, safe, and peaceable living one amongst another, in a secure enjoyment of their properties, and a greater security against any, that are not of it. This any number of men may do, because it injures not the freedom of the rest; they are left as they were in the liberty of the state of nature. When any number of men have so consented to make one community or government, they are thereby presently incorporated, and make one body politic, wherein the majority have a right to act and conclude the rest.

96. For when any number of men have, by the consent of every individual, made a community, they have thereby made that community one body, with a power to act as one body, which is only by the will and determination of the majority: for that which acts any community, being only the consent of the individuals of it, and it being necessary to that which is one body to move one way; it is necessary the body should move that way whither the greater force carries it, which is the consent of the majority: or else it is impossible it should act or continue one body, one community, which the consent of every individual that united into it, agreed that it should; and so every one is bound by that consent to be concluded by the majority. And therefore we see, that in assemblies, empowered to act by positive laws, where no number is set by that positive law which empowers them, the act of the majority passes for the act of the whole, and of course determines; as having, by the law of nature and reason, the power of the whole.

97. And thus every man, by consenting with others to make one body politic under one government, puts himself under an obligation, to every one of that society, to submit to the determination of the majority, and to be concluded by it; or else this original compact, whereby he with others incorporate into one society, would signify nothing, and be no compact, if he be left free, and under no other ties than he was in before in the state of nature. For what appearance would there be of any compact? What new engagement if he were

no farther tied by any decrees of the society, than he himself thought fit, and did actually consent to? This would be still as great a liberty, as he himself had before his compact, or any one else in the state of nature hath, who may submit himself, and consent to any acts of it if he thinks fit.

5   98. For if the consent of the majority shall not, in reason, be received as the act of the whole, and conclude every individual; nothing but the consent of every individual can make any thing to be the act of the whole but such a consent is next to impossible ever to be had, if we consider the infirmities of health, and avocations of business, which in a number, though much less than that of

10 a commonwealth, will necessarily keep many away from the public assembly. To which if we add the variety of opinions, and contrariety of interest, which unavoidably happen in all collections of men, the coming into society upon such terms would be only like Cato's coming into the theatre, only to go out again. Such a constitution as this would make the mighty leviathan of a shorter

15 duration, than the feeblest creatures, and not let it outlast the day it was born in: which cannot be supposed, till we can think, that rational creatures should desire and constitute societies only to be dissolved; for where the majority cannot conclude the rest, there they cannot act as one body, and consequently will be immediately dissolved again.

20 99. Whosoever therefore out of a state of nature unite into a community, must be understood to give up all the power, necessary to the ends for which they unite into society, to the majority of the community, unless they expressly agreed in any number greater than the majority. And this is done by barely agreeing to unite into one political society, which is all the compact that is, or needs be,

25 between the individuals, that enter into, or make up a commonwealth. And thus that, which begins and actually constitutes any political society, is nothing, but the consent of any number of freemen capable of a majority, to unite and incorporate into such a society. And this is that, and that only, which did, or could give beginning to any lawful government in the world....

CHAPTER IX. OF THE ENDS OF POLITICAL SOCIETY AND GOVERNMENT.

30 123. If man in the state of nature be so free, as has been said; if he be absolute lord of his own person and possessions, equal to the greatest, and subject to nobody, why will he part with his freedom? Why will he give up his empire, and subject himself to the dominion and control of any other power? To which it is obvious to answer, that though in the state of nature he hath such

35 a right, yet the enjoyment of it is very uncertain, and constantly exposed to the invasion of others; for all being kings as much as he, every man his equal, and the greater part no strict observers of equity and justice, the enjoyment of

the property he has in this state is very unsafe, very unsecure. This makes him willing to quit a condition, which, however free, is full of fears and continual dangers: and it is not without reason, that he seeks out, and is willing to join in society with others, who are already united, or have a mind to unite, for the mutual preservation of their lives, liberties, and estates, which I call by the   5
general name, property.

124. The great and chief end, therefore, of men's uniting into commonwealths, and putting themselves under government, is the preservation of their property. To which in the state of nature there are many things wanting.

First, There wants an established, settled, known law, received and allowed   10
by common consent to be the standard of right and wrong, and the common measure to decide all controversies between them: for though the law of nature be plain and intelligible to all rational creatures; yet men being biased by their interest, as well as ignorant for want of studying it, are not apt to allow of it as a law binding to them in the application of it to their particular cases.   15

125. Secondly, In the state of nature there wants a known and indifferent judge, with authority to determine all differences according to the established law: for every one in that state being both judge and executioner of the law of nature, men being partial to themselves, passion and revenge is very apt to carry them too far, and with too much heat, in their own cases; as well as negligence, and   20
unconcernedness, to make them too remiss in other men's.

126. Thirdly, In the state of nature there often wants power to back and support the sentence when right, and to give it due execution. They who by any injustice offend, will seldom fail, where they are able, by force to make good their injustice; such resistance many times makes the punishment dangerous,   25
and frequently destructive, to those who attempt it.

127. Thus mankind, notwithstanding all the privileges of the state of nature, being but in an ill condition, while they remain in it, are quickly driven into society. Hence it comes to pass that we seldom find any number of men live any time together in this state. The inconveniencies that they are therein exposed to,   30
by the irregular and uncertain exercise of the power every man has of punishing the transgressions of others, make them take sanctuary under the established laws of government, and therein seek the preservation of their property. It is this makes them so willingly give up every one his single power of punishing, to be exercised by such alone, as shall be appointed to it amongst them; and   35
by such rules as the community, or those authorized by them to that purpose, shall agree on. And in this we have the original right of both the legislative and executive power, as well as of the governments and societies themselves.

128. For in the state of nature, to omit the liberty he has of innocent delights, a man has two powers.

The first is to do whatsoever he thinks fit for the preservation of himself and others within the permission of the law of nature: by which law, common to
5 them all, he and all the rest of mankind are one community, make up one society, distinct from all other creatures. And, were it not for the corruption and viciousness of degenerate men, there would be no need of any other; no necessity that men should separate from this great and natural community, and by positive agreements combine into smaller and divided associations.

10 The other power a man has in the state of nature, is the power to punish the crimes committed against that law. Both these he gives up, when he joins in a private, if I may so call it, or particular politic society, and incorporates into any commonwealth, separate from the rest of mankind.

129. The first power, viz. "of doing whatsoever he thought fit for the preserva-
15 tion of himself," and the rest of mankind, he gives up to be regulated by laws made by the society, so far forth as the preservation of himself and the rest of that society shall require; which laws of the society in many things confine the liberty he had by the law of nature.

130. Secondly, The power of punishing he wholly gives up, and engages his natu-
20 ral force, (which he might before employ in the execution of the law of nature, by his own single authority, as he thought fit) to assist the executive power of the society, as the law thereof shall require: for being now in a new state, wherein he is to enjoy many conveniencies, from the labor, assistance, and society of others in the same community, as well as protection from its whole strength; he is to part
25 also, with as much of his natural liberty, in providing for himself, as the good, prosperity, and safety of the society shall require; which is not only necessary, but just, since the other members of the society do the like....

CHAPTER XI. OF THE EXTENT OF THE LEGISLATIVE POWER.

134. The great end of men's entering into society being the enjoyment of their properties in peace and safety, and the great instrument and means of that being
30 the laws established in that society; the first and fundamental positive law of all commonwealths is the establishing of the legislative power; as the first and fundamental natural law, which is to govern even the legislative itself, is the preservation of the society, and (as far as will consist with the public good) of every person in it. This legislative is not only the supreme power of the com-
35 monwealth, but sacred and unalterable in the hands where the community have once placed it; nor can any edict of any body else, in what form soever

conceived, or by what power soever backed, have the force and obligation of a law, which has not its sanction from that legislative which the public has chosen and appointed; for without this the law could not have that, which is absolutely necessary to its being a law, the consent of the society; over whom nobody can have a power to make laws, but by their own consent, and by authority received   5 from them. And therefore all the obedience, which by the most solemn ties any one can be obliged to pay, ultimately terminates in this supreme power, and is directed by those laws which it enacts; nor can any oaths to any foreign power whatsoever, or any domestic subordinate power, discharge any member of the society from his obedience to the legislative, acting pursuant to their trust; nor   10 oblige him to any obedience contrary to the laws so enacted, or farther than they do allow; it being ridiculous to imagine one can be tied ultimately to obey any power in the society, which is not supreme....

142. These are the bounds which the trust, that is put in them by the society and the law of God and nature, have set to the legislative power of every com-   15 monwealth, in all forms of government.

First, they are to govern by promulgated established laws, not to be varied in particular cases, but to have one rule for rich and poor, for the favorite at court, and the countryman at plow.

Secondly, These laws also ought to be designed for no other end ultimately, but   20 the good of the people.

Thirdly, they must not raise taxes on the property of the people, without the consent of the people, given by themselves or their deputies. And this properly concerns only such governments where the legislative is always in being, or at least where the people have not reserved any part of the legislative to deputies,   25 to be from time to time chosen by themselves.

Fourthly, The legislative neither must nor can transfer the power of making laws to any body else, or place it any where, but where the people have....

CHAPTER XIX. OF THE DISSOLUTION OF GOVERNMENT.

211. He that will with any clearness speak of the dissolution of government, ought in the first place to distinguish between the dissolution of the society and   30 the dissolution of the government. That which makes the community, and brings men out of the loose state of nature into one politic society, is the agreement which every one has with the rest to incorporate, and act as one body, and so be one distinct commonwealth. The usual, and almost only way whereby this union is dissolved, is the inroad of foreign force making a conquest upon them....   35

212. Besides this overturning from without, governments are dissolved from within....

222. The reason why men enter into society, is the preservation of their property; and the end why they choose and authorize a legislative, is, that there

5   may be laws made, and rules set, as guards and fences to the properties of all the members of the society: to limit the power, and moderate the dominion, of every part and member of the society: for since it can never be supposed to be the will of the society, that the legislative should have a power to destroy that which every one designs to secure by entering into society, and for which

10   the people submitted themselves to legislators of their own making; whenever the legislators endeavor to take away and destroy the property of the people, or to reduce them to slavery under arbitrary power, they put themselves into a state of war with the people, who are thereupon absolved from any farther obedience, and are left to the common refuge, which God hath provided for

15   all men, against force and violence. Whensoever therefore the legislative shall transgress this fundamental rule of society; and either by ambition, fear, folly or corruption, endeavor to grasp themselves, or put into the hands of any other, an absolute power over the lives, liberties, and estates of the people; by this breach of trust they forfeit the power the people had put into their hands for

20   quite contrary ends, and it devolves to the people, who have a right to resume their original liberty, and, by the establishment of a new legislative, (such as they shall think fit) provide for their own safety and security, which is the end for which they are in society. What I have said here, concerning the legislative in general, holds true also concerning the supreme executor, who having a

25   double trust put in him, both to have a part in the legislative, and the supreme execution of the law, acts against both, when he goes about to set up his own arbitrary will as the law of the society. He acts also contrary to his trust, when he either employs the force, treasure, and offices of the society, to corrupt the representatives, and gain them to his purposes; or openly pre-engages the elec-

30   tors, and prescribes to their choice, such, whom he has, by solicitations, threats, promises, or otherwise, won to his designs: and employs them to bring in such, who have promised beforehand, what to vote, and what to enact....

223. To this perhaps it will be said, that the people being ignorant, and always discontented, to lay the foundation of government in the unsteady opinion and

35   uncertain humor of the people, is to expose it to certain ruin; and no government will be able long to subsist, if the people may set up a new legislative, whenever they take offense at the old one. To this I answer, quite the contrary. People are not so easily got out of their old forms, as some are apt to suggest. They are hardly to be prevailed with to amend the acknowledged faults in the

frame they have been accustomed to. And if there be any original defects, or adventitious ones introduced by time, or corruption: it is not an easy thing to get them changed, even when all the world sees there is an opportunity for it. This slowness and aversion in the people to quit their old constitutions, has in the many revolutions which have been seen in this kingdom, in this and former ages, still kept us to, or, after some interval of fruitless attempts, still brought us back again to, our old legislative of king, lords, and commons: and whatever provocations have made the crown be taken from some of our princes' heads, they never carried the people so far as to place it in another line.

224. But it will be said, this hypothesis lays a ferment for frequent rebellion. To which I answer,

First, No more than any other hypothesis: for when the people are made miserable, and find themselves exposed to the ill-usage of arbitrary power, cry up their governors as much as you will, for sons of Jupiter; let them be sacred or divine, descended, or authorized from heaven; give them out for whom or what you please, the same will happen. The people generally ill-treated, and contrary to right, will be ready upon any occasion to ease themselves of a burden that sits heavy upon them. They will wish, and seek for the opportunity, which in the change, weakness, and accidents of human affairs, seldom delays long to offer itself. He must have lived but a little while in the world, who has not seen examples of this in his time; and he must have read very little, who cannot produce examples of it in all sorts of governments in the world.

225. Secondly, I answer, such revolutions happen not upon every little mismanagement in public affairs. Great mistakes in the ruling part, many wrong and inconvenient laws, and all the slips of human frailty, will be borne by the people without mutiny or murmur. But if a long train of abuses, prevarications and artifices, all tending the same way, make the design visible to the people, and they cannot but feel what they lie under, and see whither they are going; it is not to be wondered, that they should then rouse themselves, and endeavor to put the rule into such hands which may secure to them the ends for which government was at first erected; and without which, ancient names, and specious forms, are so far from being better, that they are much worse, than the state of nature, or pure anarchy; the inconveniences being all as great and as near, but the remedy farther off and more difficult.

226. Thirdly, I answer, That this doctrine of a power in the people of providing for their safety anew, by a new legislative, when their legislators have acted contrary to their trust, by invading their property, is the best fence against rebellion, and the probablest means to hinder it: for rebellion being an opposition,

not to persons, but authority, which is founded only in the constitutions and laws of the government; those, whoever they be, who by force break through, and by force justify their violation of them, are truly and properly rebels: for when men, by entering into society and civil government, have excluded force, and introduced laws for the preservation of property, peace, and unity amongst themselves; those who set up force again in opposition to the laws, do *rebellare*, that is, bring back again the state of war, and are properly rebels; which they who are in power, (by the pretence they have to authority, the temptation of force they have in their hands, and the flattery of those about them) being likeliest to do; the properest way to prevent the evil, is to show them the danger and injustice of it, who are under the greatest temptation to run into it....

240. Here, it is like, the common question will be made, "Who shall be judge, whether the prince or legislative act contrary to their trust?" This, perhaps, ill-affected and factious men may spread amongst the people, when the prince only makes use of his due prerogative. To this I reply, "The people shall be judge;" for who shall be judge whether his trustee or deputy acts well, and according to the trust reposed in him, but he who deputes him, and must by having deputed him, have still a power to discard him, when he fails in his trust? If this be reasonable in particular cases of private men, why should it be otherwise in that of the greatest moment, where the welfare of millions is concerned, and also where the evil, if not prevented, is greater, and the redress very difficult, dear, and dangerous?...

DISCOURSES CONCERNING GOVERNMENT
ALGERNON SIDNEY (1623–1683)

Involved in some of the same anti-monarchical causes as John Locke, Algernon Sidney was caught up in the conspiracy to oust King Charles II. He was beheaded on December 7, 1683, a martyr to the English Whig cause. Fifteen years after his death, his Discourses Concerning Government *was published. A hero to John Adams and widely read in the American colonies, Sidney famously inscribed the following in the Visitor's Book at the University of Copenhagen: "This hand, enemy to tyrants, by the sword seeks peace under liberty." This inscription later inspired the state motto of Massachusetts.*

1698

CHAPTER ONE

SECTION 17. *God having given the Government of the World to no one Man, nor declared how it should be divided, left it to the Will of Man.*

...But if the dominion of the whole world cannot belong to any one man, and every one have an equal title to that which should give it; or if it did belong to one, none did ever exercise it in governing the whole, or dividing it; or if   5
he did divide it, no man knows how, when, and to whom; so that they who lay claim to any parcels can give no testimony of that division, nor show any better title than other men derived from his first progenitor, to whom 'tis said to have been granted; and that we have neither a word, nor the promise of a word from God to decide the controversies arising thereupon, nor any prophet   10
giving testimony of his mission that takes upon him to do it, the whole fabric of our author's patriarchical dominion falls to the ground; and they who propose these doctrines, which (if they were received) would be a root of perpetual and irreconcilable hatred in every man against every man, can be accounted no less than ministers of the Devil, tho they want the abilities he has sometimes   15

Algernon Sidney, *Discourses Concerning Government,* Thomas G. West, ed. (Indianapolis, IN: Liberty Fund, 1996), 53, 56–57, 439–40, 442, 444. This material appears on the Online Library of Liberty [http://app.libraryof liberty.org] hosted by Liberty Fund, Inc.

infused into those who have been employed upon the like occasions. And we may justly conclude that God having never given the whole world to be governed by one man, not prescribed any rule for the division of it; nor declared where the right of dividing or subdividing that which every man has should
5   terminate; we may safely affirm that the whole is forever left to the will and discretion of man: We may enter into, form, and continue in greater or lesser societies, as best pleases ourselves: The right of paternity as to dominion is at an end, and no more remains, but the love, veneration, and obedience, which proceeding from a due sense of the benefits of birth and education, have their
10   root in gratitude, and are esteemed sacred and inviolable by all that are sober and virtuous. And as 'tis impossible to transfer these benefits by inheritance, so 'tis impossible to transfer the rights arising from them. No man can be my father but he that did beget me; and 'tis as absurd to say I owe that duty to one who is not my father, which I owe to my father, as to say, he did beget me, who
15   did not beget me; for the obligation that arises from benefits can only be to him that conferred them. 'Tis in vain to say the same is due to his heir; for that can take place only when he has but one, which in this case signifies nothing: For if I being the only son of my father, inherit his right, and have the same power over my children as he had over me; if I had one hundred brothers, they
20   must all inherit the same; and the law of England, which acknowledges one only heir, is not general, but municipal, and is so far from being general, as the precept of God and nature, that I doubt whether it was ever known or used in any nation of the world beyond our island. The words of the Apostle, *If we are children, we are therefore heirs and co-heirs with Christ*, are the voice of God and
25   nature; and as the universal law of God and nature is always the same, every one of us who have children have the same right over them, as Abraham, Isaac, and Jacob had over theirs; and that right which was not devolved to any one of them, but inherited by them all (I mean the right of father as father) not the peculiar promises, which were not according to the law of nature, but the
30   election of grace, is also inherited by every one of us, and ours, that is, by all mankind. But if that which could be inherited was inherited by all, and it be impossible that a right of dominion over all can be due to everyone, then all that is or can be inherited by everyone is that exemption from the dominion of another, which we call liberty, and is the gift of God and nature....

CHAPTER THREE

35   SECTION 21. *It cannot be for the good of the People that the Magistrate have a power above the Law: and he is not a Magistrate who has not his power by Law.*

...But nothing can be more absurd than to say, that one man has an absolute power above law to govern according to his will, *for the people's good, and the preservation of their liberty....*

...And as 'tis folly to suppose that princes will always be wise, just and good, when we know that few have been able alone to bear the weight of a govern-   5 ment, or to resist the temptations to ill, that accompany an unlimited power, it would be madness to presume they will for the future be free from infirmities and vices....

...If the public safety be provided, liberty and propriety secured, justice admin- istered, virtue encouraged, vice suppressed, and the true interest of the nation   10 advanced, the ends of government are accomplished; and the highest must be contented with such a proportion of glory and majesty as is consistent with the public; since the magistracy is not instituted, nor any person placed in it for the increase of his majesty, but for the preservation of the whole people, and the defence of the liberty, life and estate of every private man....   15

THE CONSTITUTION OF THE UNITED STATES OF AMERICA

Fifty-five delegates from twelve states (Rhode Island declined to partici-pate) traveled to Philadelphia to attend the Constitutional Convention, which began in May 1787. They quickly scrapped the existing Articles of Confederation, and after four months they concluded their business by adopting a new frame of government. On September 17, thirty-nine delegates signed the Constitution. It was nine months before the requisite nine states ratified the Constitution, putting it into effect. The thirteenth state, Rhode Island, did not ratify it until 1790. Subsequently it has been amended twenty-seven times.

SEPTEMBER 17, 1787

PREAMBLE

We the People of the United States, in Order to form a more perfect Union, establish Justice, insure domestic Tranquility, provide for the common defense, promote the general Welfare, and secure the Blessings of Liberty to ourselves and our Posterity, do ordain and establish this Constitution for the United States of America. 5

ARTICLE I

SECTION 1. All legislative Powers herein granted shall be vested in a Congress of the United States, which shall consist of a Senate and House of Representatives.

SECTION 2. The House of Representatives shall be composed of Members chosen every second Year by the People of the several States, and the Electors in each State shall have the Qualifications requisite for Electors of the most numerous 10 Branch of the State Legislature.

No person shall be a Representative who shall not have attained to the Age of twenty five Years, and been seven Years a Citizen of the United States, and who shall not, when elected, be an Inhabitant of that State in which he shall be chosen.

Representatives and direct Taxes shall be apportioned among the several States 15 which may be included within this Union, according to their respective Numbers,

47

which shall be determined by adding to the whole Number of free Persons, including those bound to Service for a Term of Years, and excluding Indians not taxed, three fifths of all other Persons. The actual Enumeration shall be made within three Years after the first Meeting of the Congress of the United
5   States, and within every subsequent Term of ten Years, in such Manner as they shall by Law direct. The Number of Representatives shall not exceed one for every thirty Thousand, but each State shall have at Least one Representative; and until such enumeration shall be made, the State of New Hampshire shall be entitled to choose three, Massachusetts eight, Rhode-Island and Providence
10   Plantations one, Connecticut five, New-York six, New Jersey four, Pennsylvania eight, Delaware one, Maryland six, Virginia ten, North Carolina five, South Carolina five, and Georgia three.

When vacancies happen in the Representation from any State, the Executive Authority thereof shall issue Writs of Election to fill such Vacancies.

15   The House of Representatives shall choose their Speaker and other Officers; and shall have the sole Power of Impeachment.

SECTION 3. The Senate of the United States shall be composed of two Senators from each State, chosen by the Legislature thereof, for six Years; and each Senator shall have one Vote.

20   Immediately after they shall be assembled in Consequence of the first Election, they shall be divided as equally as may be into three Classes. The Seats of the Senators of the first Class shall be vacated at the Expiration of the second Year, of the second Class at the Expiration of the fourth Year, and of the third Class at the Expiration of the sixth Year, so that one third may be chosen every second
25   Year; and if Vacancies happen by Resignation, or otherwise, during the Recess of the Legislature of any State, the Executive thereof may make temporary Appointments until the next Meeting of the Legislature, which shall then fill such Vacancies.

No Person shall be a Senator who shall not have attained to the Age of thirty
30   Years, and been nine Years a Citizen of the United States, and who shall not, when elected, be an Inhabitant of that State for which he shall be chosen.

The Vice President of the United States shall be President of the Senate, but shall have no Vote, unless they be equally divided.

The Senate shall choose their other Officers, and also a President pro tempore,
35   in the Absence of the Vice President, or when he shall exercise the Office of President of the United States.

The Senate shall have the sole Power to try all Impeachments. When sitting for that Purpose, they shall be on Oath or Affirmation. When the President of the United States is tried, the Chief Justice shall preside: And no Person shall be convicted without the Concurrence of two thirds of the Members present.

Judgment in Cases of Impeachment shall not extend further than to removal from Office, and disqualification to hold and enjoy any Office of honor, Trust or Profit under the United States: but the Party convicted shall nevertheless be liable and subject to Indictment, Trial, Judgment and Punishment, according to Law.

Section 4. The Times, Places and Manner of holding Elections for Senators and Representatives, shall be prescribed in each State by the Legislature thereof; but the Congress may at any time by Law make or alter such Regulations, except as to the Places of choosing Senators.

The Congress shall assemble at least once in every Year, and such Meeting shall be on the first Monday in December, unless they shall by Law appoint a different Day.

Section 5. Each House shall be the Judge of the Elections, Returns and Qualifications of its own Members, and a Majority of each shall constitute a Quorum to do Business; but a smaller Number may adjourn from day to day, and may be authorized to compel the Attendance of absent Members, in such Manner, and under such Penalties as each House may provide.

Each House may determine the Rules of its Proceedings, punish its Members for disorderly Behavior, and, with the Concurrence of two thirds, expel a Member.

Each House shall keep a Journal of its Proceedings, and from time to time publish the same, excepting such Parts as may in their Judgment require Secrecy; and the Yeas and Nays of the Members of either House on any question shall, at the Desire of one fifth of those Present, be entered on the Journal.

Neither House, during the Session of Congress, shall, without the Consent of the other, adjourn for more than three days, nor to any other Place than that in which the two Houses shall be sitting.

Section 6. The Senators and Representatives shall receive a Compensation for their Services, to be ascertained by Law, and paid out of the Treasury of the United States. They shall in all Cases, except Treason, Felony and Breach of the Peace, be privileged from Arrest during their Attendance at the Session of their respective Houses, and in going to and returning from the same; and for any Speech or Debate in either House, they shall not be questioned in any other Place.

No Senator or Representative shall, during the Time for which he was elected, be appointed to any civil Office under the Authority of the United States, which shall have been created, or the Emoluments whereof shall have been encreased during such time; and no Person holding any Office under the United States,
5   shall be a Member of either House during his Continuance in Office.

Section 7. All Bills for raising Revenue shall originate in the House of Representatives; but the Senate may propose or concur with Amendments as on other Bills.

Every Bill which shall have passed the House of Representatives and the Senate,
10 shall, before it become a Law, be presented to the President of the United States; If he approve he shall sign it, but if not he shall return it, with his Objections to that House in which it shall have originated, who shall enter the Objections at large on their Journal, and proceed to reconsider it. If after such Reconsideration two thirds of that House shall agree to pass the Bill, it shall be
15 sent, together with the Objections, to the other House, by which it shall likewise be reconsidered, and if approved by two thirds of that House, it shall become a Law. But in all such Cases the Votes of both Houses shall be determined by yeas and Nays, and the Names of the Persons voting for and against the Bill shall be entered on the Journal of each House respectively. If any Bill shall not
20 be returned by the President within ten days (Sundays excepted) after it shall have been presented to him, the Same shall be a Law, in like Manner as if he had signed it, unless the Congress by their Adjournment prevent its Return in which Case it shall not be a Law.

Every Order, Resolution, or Vote to which the Concurrence of the Senate
25 and House of Representatives may be necessary (except on a question of Adjournment) shall be presented to the President of the United States; and before the Same shall take Effect, shall be approved by him, or being disapproved by him, shall be repassed by two thirds of the Senate and House of Representatives, according to the Rules and Limitations prescribed in the
30 Case of a Bill.

Section 8. The Congress shall have Power To lay and collect Taxes, Duties, Imposts and Excises, to pay the Debts and provide for the common Defense and general Welfare of the United States; but all Duties, Imposts and Excises shall be uniform throughout the United States;

35 To borrow Money on the credit of the United States;

To regulate Commerce with foreign Nations, and among the several States, and with the Indian Tribes;

To establish an uniform Rule of Naturalization, and uniform Laws on the subject of Bankruptcies throughout the United States;

To coin Money, regulate the Value thereof, and of foreign Coin, and fix the Standard of Weights and Measures;

To provide for the Punishment of counterfeiting the Securities and current 5 Coin of the United States;

To establish Post Offices and post Roads;

To promote the Progress of Science and useful Arts, by securing for limited Times to Authors and Inventors the exclusive Right to their respective Writings and Discoveries; 10

To constitute Tribunals inferior to the supreme Court;

To define and punish Piracies and Felonies committed on the high Seas, and Offenses against the Law of Nations;

To declare War, grant Letters of Marque and Reprisal, and make Rules concerning Captures on Land and Water; 15

To raise and support Armies, but no Appropriation of Money to that Use shall be for a longer Term than two Years;

To provide and maintain a Navy;

To make Rules for the Government and Regulation of the land and naval Forces;

To provide for calling forth the Militia to execute the Laws of the Union, suppress 20 Insurrections and repel Invasions;

To provide for organizing, arming, and disciplining, the Militia, and for governing such Part of them as may be employed in the Service of the United States, reserving to the States respectively, the Appointment of the Officers, and the Authority of training the Militia according to the discipline prescribed 25 by Congress;

To exercise exclusive Legislation in all Cases whatsoever, over such District (not exceeding ten Miles square) as may, by Cession of particular States, and the Acceptance of Congress, become the Seat of the Government of the United States, and to exercise like Authority over all Places purchased by the Consent 30 of the Legislature of the State in which the Same shall be, for the Erection of Forts, Magazines, Arsenals, dock-Yards, and other needful Buildings;—And

To make all Laws which shall be necessary and proper for carrying into Execution the foregoing Powers, and all other Powers vested by this Constitution in the Government of the United States, or in any Department or Officer thereof. 35

SECTION 9. The Migration or Importation of such Persons as any of the States now existing shall think proper to admit, shall not be prohibited by the Congress prior to the Year one thousand eight hundred and eight, but a Tax or duty may be imposed on such Importation, not exceeding ten dollars for each Person.

5   The Privilege of the Writ of Habeas Corpus shall not be suspended, unless when in Cases of Rebellion or Invasion the public Safety may require it.

No Bill of Attainder or ex post facto Law shall be passed.

No Capitation, or other direct, Tax shall be laid, unless in Proportion to the Census or Enumeration herein before directed to be taken.

10   No Tax or Duty shall be laid on Articles exported from any State.

No Preference shall be given by any Regulation of Commerce or Revenue to the Ports of one State over those of another: nor shall Vessels bound to, or from, one State, be obliged to enter, clear, or pay Duties in another.

No Money shall be drawn from the Treasury, but in Consequence of Appropri-
15   ations made by Law; and a regular Statement and Account of the Receipts and Expenditures of all public Money shall be published from time to time.

No Title of Nobility shall be granted by the United States: And no Person holding any Office of Profit or Trust under them, shall, without the Consent of the Congress, accept of any present, Emolument, Office, or Title, of any
20   kind whatever, from any King, Prince, or foreign State.

SECTION 10. No State shall enter into any Treaty, Alliance, or Confederation; grant Letters of Marque and Reprisal; coin Money; emit Bills of Credit; make any Thing but gold and silver Coin a Tender in Payment of Debts; pass any Bill of Attainder, ex post facto Law, or Law impairing the Obligation of Contracts,
25   or grant any Title of Nobility.

No State shall, without the Consent of the Congress, lay any Imposts or Duties on Imports or Exports, except what may be absolutely necessary for executing its inspection Laws: and the net Produce of all Duties and Imposts, laid by any State on Imports or Exports, shall be for the Use of the Treasury of the United
30   States; and all such Laws shall be subject to the Revision and Control of the Congress.

No State shall, without the Consent of Congress, lay any duty of Tonnage, keep Troops, or Ships of War in time of Peace, enter into any Agreement or Compact with another State, or with a foreign Power, or engage in War, unless actually
35   invaded, or in such imminent Danger as will not admit of delay.

Article II

Section 1. The executive Power shall be vested in a President of the United States of America. He shall hold his Office during the Term of four Years, and, together with the Vice-President chosen for the same Term, be elected as follows:

Each State shall appoint, in such Manner as the Legislature thereof may direct, a Number of Electors, equal to the whole Number of Senators and   5
Representatives to which the State may be entitled in the Congress: but no Senator or Representative, or Person holding an Office of Trust or Profit under the United States, shall be appointed an Elector.

The Electors shall meet in their respective States, and vote by Ballot for two Persons, of whom one at least shall not be an Inhabitant of the same State   10
with themselves. And they shall make a List of all the Persons voted for, and of the Number of Votes for each; which List they shall sign and certify, and transmit sealed to the Seat of the Government of the United States, directed to the President of the Senate. The President of the Senate shall, in the Presence of the Senate and House of Representatives, open all the Certificates, and the   15
Votes shall then be counted. The Person having the greatest Number of Votes shall be the President, if such Number be a Majority of the whole Number of Electors appointed; and if there be more than one who have such Majority, and have an equal Number of Votes, then the House of Representatives shall immediately choose by Ballot one of them for President; and if no Person have   20
a Majority, then from the five highest on the List the said House shall in like Manner choose the President. But in choosing the President, the Votes shall be taken by States, the Representation from each State having one Vote; a quorum for this Purpose shall consist of a Member or Members from two thirds of the States, and a Majority of all the States shall be necessary to a Choice. In every   25
Case, after the Choice of the President, the Person having the greatest Number of Votes of the Electors shall be the Vice President. But if there should remain two or more who have equal Votes, the Senate shall choose from them by Ballot the Vice President.

The Congress may determine the Time of choosing the Electors, and the Day   30
on which they shall give their Votes; which Day shall be the same throughout the United States.

No Person except a natural born Citizen, or a Citizen of the United States, at the time of the Adoption of this Constitution, shall be eligible to the Office of President; neither shall any Person be eligible to that Office who shall not   35
have attained to the Age of thirty-five Years, and been fourteen Years a Resident within the United States.

In Case of the Removal of the President from Office, or of his Death, Resignation, or Inability to discharge the Powers and Duties of the said Office, the Same shall devolve on the Vice President, and the Congress may by Law provide for the Case of Removal, Death, Resignation or Inability, both of the
5   President and Vice President, declaring what Officer shall then act as President, and such Officer shall act accordingly, until the Disability be removed, or a President shall be elected.

The President shall, at stated Times, receive for his Services, a Compensation, which shall neither be increased nor diminished during the Period for which
10 he shall have been elected, and he shall not receive within that Period any other Emolument from the United States, or any of them.

Before he enter on the Execution of his Office, he shall take the following Oath or Affirmation:—"I do solemnly swear (or affirm) that I will faithfully execute the Office of President of the United States, and will to the best of my Ability,
15 preserve, protect and defend the Constitution of the United States."

SECTION 2. The President shall be Commander in Chief of the Army and Navy of the United States, and of the Militia of the several States, when called into the actual Service of the United States; he may require the Opinion, in writing, of the principal Officer in each of the executive Departments, upon any subject
20 relating to the Duties of their respective Offices, and he shall have Power to grant Reprieves and Pardons for Offenses against the United States, except in Cases of Impeachment.

He shall have Power, by and with the Advice and Consent of the Senate, to make Treaties, provided two thirds of the Senators present concur; and he shall
25 nominate, and by and with the Advice and Consent of the Senate, shall appoint Ambassadors, other public Ministers and Consuls, Judges of the supreme Court, and all other Officers of the United States, whose Appointments are not herein otherwise provided for, and which shall be established by Law: but the Congress may by Law vest the Appointment of such inferior Officers, as they
30 think proper, in the President alone, in the Courts of Law, or in the Heads of Departments.

The President shall have Power to fill up all Vacancies that may happen during the Recess of the Senate, by granting Commissions which shall expire at the End of their next Session.

35 SECTION 3. He shall from time to time give to the Congress Information of the State of the Union, and recommend to their Consideration such Measures as he shall judge necessary and expedient; he may, on extraordinary Occasions,

convene both Houses, or either of them, and in Case of Disagreement between them, with Respect to the Time of Adjournment, he may adjourn them to such Time as he shall think proper; he shall receive Ambassadors and other public Ministers; he shall take Care that the Laws be faithfully executed, and shall Commission all the Officers of the United States.   5

Section 4. The President, Vice President and all civil Officers of the United States, shall be removed from Office on Impeachment for, and Conviction of, Treason, Bribery, or other high Crimes and Misdemeanors.

Article III

Section 1. The judicial Power of the United States, shall be vested in one supreme Court, and in such inferior Courts as the Congress may from time to   10 time ordain and establish. The Judges, both of the supreme and inferior Courts, shall hold their Offices during good Behavior, and shall, at stated Times, receive for their Services a Compensation, which shall not be diminished during their Continuance in Office.

Section 2. The judicial Power shall extend to all Cases, in Law and Equity, arising   15 under this Constitution, the Laws of the United States, and Treaties made, or which shall be made, under their Authority;—to all Cases affecting Ambassadors, other public Ministers and Consuls;—to all Cases of admiralty and maritime Jurisdiction; —to Controversies to which the United States shall be a Party;—to Controversies between two or more States;—between a State and Citizens of   20 another State;—between Citizens of different States;—between Citizens of the same State claiming Lands under Grants of different States, and between a State, or the Citizens thereof, and foreign States, Citizens or Subjects.

In all Cases affecting Ambassadors, other public Ministers and Consuls, and those in which a State shall be Party, the supreme Court shall have original   25 Jurisdiction. In all the other Cases before mentioned, the supreme Court shall have appellate Jurisdiction, both as to Law and Fact, with such Exceptions, and under such Regulations as the Congress shall make.

The Trial of all Crimes, except in Cases of Impeachment, shall be by Jury; and such Trial shall be held in the State where the said Crimes shall have been   30 committed; but when not committed within any State, the Trial shall be at such Place or Places as the Congress may by Law have directed.

Section 3. Treason against the United States, shall consist only in levying War against them, or in adhering to their Enemies, giving them Aid and Comfort. No Person shall be convicted of Treason unless on the Testimony of two Witnesses   35 to the same overt Act, or on Confession in open Court.

The Congress shall have Power to declare the Punishment of Treason, but no Attainder of Treason shall work Corruption of Blood, or Forfeiture except during the Life of the Person attainted.

ARTICLE IV

SECTION 1. Full Faith and Credit shall be given in each State to the public Acts, Records, and judicial Proceedings of every other State. And the Congress may by general Laws prescribe the Manner in which such Acts, Records and Proceedings shall be proved, and the Effect thereof.

SECTION 2. The Citizens of each State shall be entitled to all Privileges and Immunities of Citizens in the several States.

A Person charged in any State with Treason, Felony, or other Crime, who shall flee from Justice, and be found in another State, shall on Demand of the executive Authority of the State from which he fled, be delivered up, to be removed to the State having Jurisdiction of the Crime.

No Person held to Service or Labor in one State, under the Laws thereof, escaping into another, shall, in Consequence of any Law or Regulation therein, be discharged from such Service or Labor, but shall be delivered up on Claim of the Party to whom such Service or Labor may be due.

SECTION 3. New States may be admitted by the Congress into this Union; but no new State shall be formed or erected within the Jurisdiction of any other State; nor any State be formed by the Junction of two or more States, or parts of States, without the Consent of the Legislatures of the States concerned as well as of the Congress.

The Congress shall have Power to dispose of and make all needful Rules and Regulations respecting the Territory or other Property belonging to the United States; and nothing in this Constitution shall be so construed as to Prejudice any Claims of the United States, or of any particular State.

SECTION 4. The United States shall guarantee to every State in this Union a Republican Form of Government, and shall protect each of them against Invasion; and on Application of the Legislature, or of the Executive (when the Legislature cannot be convened) against domestic Violence.

ARTICLE V

The Congress, whenever two thirds of both Houses shall deem it necessary, shall propose Amendments to this Constitution, or, on the Application of the Legislatures of two thirds of the several States, shall call a Convention for proposing Amendments, which, in either Case, shall be valid to all Intents and Purposes, as Part of this Constitution, when ratified by the Legislatures of three fourths of the several States, or by Conventions in three fourths thereof, as the one or the other Mode of Ratification may be proposed by the Congress; Provided that no Amendment which may be made prior to the Year One thousand eight hundred and eight shall in any Manner affect the first and fourth Clauses in the Ninth Section of the first Article; and that no State, without its Consent, shall be deprived of its equal Suffrage in the Senate.

Article VI

All Debts contracted and Engagements entered into, before the Adoption of this Constitution, shall be as valid against the United States under this Constitution, as under the Confederation.

This Constitution, and the Laws of the United States which shall be made in Pursuance thereof; and all Treaties made, or which shall be made, under the Authority of the United States, shall be the supreme Law of the Land; and the Judges in every State shall be bound thereby, any Thing in the Constitution or Laws of any State to the Contrary notwithstanding.

The Senators and Representatives before mentioned, and the Members of the several State Legislatures, and all executive and judicial Officers, both of the United States and of the several States, shall be bound by Oath or Affirmation, to support this Constitution; but no religious Test shall ever be required as a Qualification to any Office or public Trust under the United States.

Article VII

The Ratification of the Conventions of nine States, shall be sufficient for the Establishment of this Constitution between the States so ratifying the Same.

Done in Convention by the Unanimous Consent of the States present the Seventeenth Day of September in the Year of our Lord one thousand seven hundred and Eighty seven and of the Independence of the United States of America the Twelfth In witness whereof We have hereunto subscribed our Names.

George Washington—
President and deputy from Virginia

Delaware
George Read, Gunning Bedford, Jr., John Dickinson, Richard Bassett, Jacob Broom

Maryland
James McHenry, Daniel of St. Thomas Jenifer, Daniel Carroll

VIRGINIA
John Blair, James Madison, Jr.

NORTH CAROLINA
William Blount, Richard Dobbs Spaight, Hugh Williamson

SOUTH CAROLINA
John Rutledge, Charles Cotesworth Pinckney, Charles Pinckney,
Pierce Butler

GEORGIA
William Few, Abraham Baldwin

NEW HAMPSHIRE
John Langdon, Nicholas Gilman

MASSACHUSETTS
Nathaniel Gorham, Rufus King

CONNECTICUT
William Samuel Johnson, Roger Sherman

NEW YORK
Alexander Hamilton

NEW JERSEY
William Livingston, David Brearley, William Paterson,
Jonathan Dayton

PENNSYLVANIA
Benjamin Franklin, Thomas Mifflin, Robert Morris,
George Clymer, Thomas FitzSimmons, Jared Ingersoll,
James Wilson, Gouverneur Morris

Attest William Jackson Secretary

AMENDMENTS TO THE
CONSTITUTION OF THE UNITED STATES OF AMERICA

AMENDMENT I
Ratified December 15, 1791

Congress shall make no law respecting an establishment of religion, or prohibiting the free exercise thereof; or abridging the freedom of speech, or of the press; or the right of the people peaceably to assemble, and to petition the Government for a redress of grievances.

Amendment II
Ratified December 15, 1791

A well regulated Militia, being necessary to the security of a free State, the right of the people to keep and bear Arms, shall not be infringed.

Amendment III
Ratified December 15, 1791

No Soldier shall, in time of peace be quartered in any house, without the consent of the Owner, nor in time of war, but in a manner to be prescribed by law.

Amendment IV
Ratified December 15, 1791

The right of the people to be secure in their persons, houses, papers, and effects,   5
against unreasonable searches and seizures, shall not be violated, and no Warrants shall issue, but upon probable cause, supported by Oath or affirmation,
and particularly describing the place to be searched, and the persons or things
to be seized.

Amendment V
Ratified December 15, 1791

No person shall be held to answer for a capital, or otherwise infamous crime,
unless on a presentment or indictment of a Grand Jury, except in cases arising   10
in the land or naval forces, or in the Militia, when in actual service in time of
War or public danger; nor shall any person be subject for the same offense to
be twice put in jeopardy of life or limb; nor shall be compelled in any criminal
case to be a witness against himself, nor be deprived of life, liberty, or property,
without due process of law; nor shall private property be taken for public use,   15
without just compensation.

Amendment VI
Ratified December 15, 1791

In all criminal prosecutions, the accused shall enjoy the right to a speedy and
public trial, by an impartial jury of the State and district wherein the crime shall
have been committed, which district shall have been previously ascertained by
law, and to be informed of the nature and cause of the accusation; to be con-   20
fronted with the witnesses against him; to have compulsory process for obtaining
witnesses in his favor, and to have the Assistance of Counsel for his defence.

Amendment VII
Ratified December 15, 1791

In Suits at common law, where the value in controversy shall exceed twenty
dollars, the right of trial by jury shall be preserved, and no fact tried by a jury,

shall be otherwise re-examined in any Court of the United States, than according to the rules of the common law.

AMENDMENT VIII
Ratified December 15, 1791
Excessive bail shall not be required, nor excessive fines imposed, nor cruel and unusual punishments inflicted.

AMENDMENT IX
Ratified December 15, 1791
5 The enumeration in the Constitution, of certain rights, shall not be construed to deny or disparage others retained by the people.

AMENDMENT X
Ratified December 15, 1791
The powers not delegated to the United States by the Constitution, nor prohibited by it to the States, are reserved to the States respectively, or to the people.

AMENDMENT XI
Ratified February 7, 1795
The Judicial power of the United States shall not be construed to extend to any
10 suit in law or equity, commenced or prosecuted against one of the United States by Citizens of another State, or by Citizens or Subjects of any Foreign State.

AMENDMENT XII
Ratified June 15, 1804
The Electors shall meet in their respective states and vote by ballot for President and Vice-President, one of whom, at least, shall not be an inhabitant of the same state with themselves; they shall name in their ballots the person voted
15 for as President, and in distinct ballots the person voted for as Vice-President, and they shall make distinct lists of all persons voted for as President, and of all persons voted for as Vice-President, and of the number of votes for each, which lists they shall sign and certify, and transmit sealed to the seat of the government of the United States, directed to the President of the Senate;—the President of
20 the Senate shall, in the presence of the Senate and House of Representatives, open all the certificates and the votes shall then be counted;—The person having the greatest number of votes for President, shall be the President, if such number be a majority of the whole number of Electors appointed; and if no person have such majority, then from the persons having the highest num-
25 bers not exceeding three on the list of those voted for as President, the House of Representatives shall choose immediately, by ballot, the President. But in

choosing the President, the votes shall be taken by states, the representation
from each state having one vote; a quorum for this purpose shall consist of a
member or members from two-thirds of the states, and a majority of all the
states shall be necessary to a choice. And if the House of Representatives shall
not choose a President whenever the right of choice shall devolve upon them,   5
before the fourth day of March next following, then the Vice-President shall act
as President, as in the case of the death or other constitutional disability of the
President.—The person having the greatest number of votes as Vice-President,
shall be the Vice-President, if such number be a majority of the whole number of
Electors appointed, and if no person have a majority, then from the two highest   10
numbers on the list, the Senate shall choose the Vice-President; a quorum for
the purpose shall consist of two-thirds of the whole number of Senators, and
a majority of the whole number shall be necessary to a choice. But no person
constitutionally ineligible to the office of President shall be eligible to that of
Vice-President of the United States.   15

Amendment XIII
Ratified December 6, 1865

Section 1. Neither slavery nor involuntary servitude, except as a punishment
for crime whereof the party shall have been duly convicted, shall exist within
the United States, or any place subject to their jurisdiction.

Section 2. Congress shall have power to enforce this article by appropriate
legislation.   20

Amendment XIV
Ratified July 9, 1868

Section 1. All persons born or naturalized in the United States, and subject
to the jurisdiction thereof, are citizens of the United States and of the State
wherein they reside. No State shall make or enforce any law which shall abridge
the privileges or immunities of citizens of the United States; nor shall any State
deprive any person of life, liberty, or property, without due process of law; nor   25
deny to any person within its jurisdiction the equal protection of the laws.

Section 2. Representatives shall be apportioned among the several States
according to their respective numbers, counting the whole number of persons
in each State, excluding Indians not taxed. But when the right to vote at any
election for the choice of electors for President and Vice-President of the United   30
States, Representatives in Congress, the Executive and Judicial officers of a State,
or the members of the Legislature thereof, is denied to any of the male inhabitants
of such State, being twenty-one years of age, and citizens of the United States,
or in any way abridged, except for participation in rebellion, or other crime,

the basis of representation therein shall be reduced in the proportion which the number of such male citizens shall bear to the whole number of male citizens twenty-one years of age in such State.

SECTION 3. No person shall be a Senator or Representative in Congress, or elector
5　of President and Vice-President, or hold any office, civil or military, under the United States, or under any State, who, having previously taken an oath, as a member of Congress, or as an officer of the United States, or as a member of any State legislature, or as an executive or judicial officer of any State, to support the Constitution of the United States, shall have engaged in insurrection or
10　rebellion against the same, or given aid or comfort to the enemies thereof. But Congress may by a vote of two-thirds of each House, remove such disability.

SECTION 4. The validity of the public debt of the United States, authorized by law, including debts incurred for payment of pensions and bounties for services in suppressing insurrection or rebellion, shall not be questioned. But neither the
15　United States nor any State shall assume or pay any debt or obligation incurred in aid of insurrection or rebellion against the United States, or any claim for the loss or emancipation of any slave; but all such debts, obligations and claims shall be held illegal and void.

SECTION 5. The Congress shall have power to enforce, by appropriate legislation,
20　the provisions of this article.

AMENDMENT XV
Ratified February 3, 1870

SECTION 1. The right of citizens of the United States to vote shall not be denied or abridged by the United States or by any State on account of race, color, or previous condition of servitude.

SECTION 2. The Congress shall have power to enforce this article by appropriate
25　legislation.

AMENDMENT XVI
Ratified February 3, 1913

The Congress shall have power to lay and collect taxes on incomes, from whatever source derived, without apportionment among the several States, and without
30　regard to any census or enumeration.

AMENDMENT XVII
Ratified April 8, 1913

The Senate of the United States shall be composed of two Senators from each State, elected by the people thereof, for six years; and each Senator shall have one vote. The electors in each State shall have the qualifications requisite for electors of the most numerous branch of the State legislatures.

When vacancies happen in the representation of any State in the Senate, the executive authority of such State shall issue writs of election to fill such vacancies: *Provided,* That the legislature of any State may empower the executive thereof to make temporary appointments until the people fill the vacancies by election as the legislature may direct.

This amendment shall not be so construed as to affect the election or term of any Senator chosen before it becomes valid as part of the Constitution.

Amendment XVIII
Ratified January 16, 1919

Section 1. After one year from the ratification of this article the manufacture, sale, or transportation of intoxicating liquors within, the importation thereof into, or the exportation thereof from the United States and all territory subject to the jurisdiction thereof for beverage purposes is hereby prohibited.

Section 2. The Congress and the several States shall have concurrent power to enforce this article by appropriate legislation.

Section 3. This article shall be inoperative unless it shall have been ratified as an amendment to the Constitution by the legislatures of the several States, as provided in the Constitution, within seven years from the date of the submission hereof to the States by the Congress.

Amendment XIX
Ratified August 18, 1920

The right of citizens of the United States to vote shall not be denied or abridged by the United States or by any State on account of sex.

Congress shall have power to enforce this article by appropriate legislation.

Amendment XX
Ratified January 23, 1933

Section 1. The terms of the President and the Vice President shall end at noon on the 20th day of January, and the terms of Senators and Representatives at noon on the 3rd day of January, of the years in which such terms would have ended if this article had not been ratified; and the terms of their successors shall then begin.

Section 2. The Congress shall assemble at least once in every year, and such meeting shall begin at noon on the 3rd day of January, unless they shall by law appoint a different day.

SECTION 3. If, at the time fixed for the beginning of the term of the President, the President elect shall have died, the Vice President elect shall become President. If a President shall not have been chosen before the time fixed for the beginning of his term, or if the President elect shall have failed to qualify, then the Vice President elect shall act as President until a President shall have qualified; and the Congress may by law provide for the case wherein neither a President elect nor a Vice President shall have qualified, declaring who shall then act as President, or the manner in which one who is to act shall be selected, and such person shall act accordingly until a President or Vice President shall have qualified.

SECTION 4. The Congress may by law provide for the case of the death of any of the persons from whom the House of Representatives may choose a President whenever the right of choice shall have devolved upon them, and for the case of the death of any of the persons from whom the Senate may choose a Vice President whenever the right of choice shall have devolved upon them.

SECTION 5. Sections 1 and 2 shall take effect on the 15th day of October following the ratification of this article.

SECTION 6. This article shall be inoperative unless it shall have been ratified as an amendment to the Constitution by the legislatures of three-fourths of the several States within seven years from the date of its submission.

AMENDMENT XXI
Ratified December 5, 1933

SECTION 1. The eighteenth article of amendment to the Constitution of the United States is hereby repealed.

SECTION 2. The transportation or importation into any State, Territory, or possession of the United States for delivery or use therein of intoxicating liquors, in violation of the laws thereof, is hereby prohibited.

SECTION 3. This article shall be inoperative unless it shall have been ratified as an amendment to the Constitution by conventions in the several States, as provided in the Constitution, within seven years from the date of the submission hereof to the States by the Congress.

AMENDMENT XXII
Ratified February 27, 1951

SECTION 1. No person shall be elected to the office of the President more than twice, and no person who has held the office of President, or acted as President, for more than two years of a term to which some other person was elected President shall be elected to the office of President more than once. But this Article shall not apply to any person holding the office of President when this

Article was proposed by the Congress, and shall not prevent any person who may be holding the office of President, or acting as President, during the term within which this Article becomes operative from holding the office of President or acting as President during the remainder of such term.

SECTION 2. This article shall be inoperative unless it shall have been ratified as an amendment to the Constitution by the legislatures of three-fourths of the several States within seven years from the date of its submission to the States by the Congress.

AMENDMENT XXIII
Ratified March 29, 1961

SECTION 1. The District constituting the seat of Government of the United States shall appoint in such manner as the Congress may direct:

A number of electors of President and Vice President equal to the whole number of Senators and Representatives in Congress to which the District would be entitled if it were a State, but in no event more than the least populous State; they shall be in addition to those appointed by the States, but they shall be considered, for the purposes of the election of President and Vice President, to be electors appointed by a State; and they shall meet in the District and perform such duties as provided by the twelfth article of amendment.

SECTION 2. The Congress shall have power to enforce this article by appropriate legislation.

AMENDMENT XXIV
Ratified January 23, 1964

SECTION 1. The right of citizens of the United States to vote in any primary or other election for President or Vice President, for electors for President or Vice President, or for Senator or Representative in Congress, shall not be denied or abridged by the United States or any State by reason of failure to pay any poll tax or other tax.

SECTION 2. The Congress shall have power to enforce this article by appropriate legislation.

AMENDMENT XXV
Ratified February 10, 1967

SECTION 1. In case of the removal of the President from office or of his death or resignation, the Vice President shall become President.

SECTION 2. Whenever there is a vacancy in the office of the Vice President, the President shall nominate a Vice President who shall take office upon confirmation by a majority vote of both Houses of Congress.

SECTION 3. Whenever the President transmits to the President pro tempore of the Senate and the Speaker of the House of Representatives his written declaration that he is unable to discharge the powers and duties of his office, and until he transmits to them a written declaration to the contrary, such powers and duties
5   shall be discharged by the Vice President as Acting President.

SECTION 4. Whenever the Vice President and a majority of either the principal officers of the executive departments or of such other body as Congress may by law provide, transmit to the President pro tempore of the Senate and the Speaker of the House of Representatives their written declaration that the President is
10   unable to discharge the powers and duties of his office, the Vice President shall immediately assume the powers and duties of the office as Acting President.

Thereafter, when the President transmits to the President pro tempore of the Senate and the Speaker of the House of Representatives his written declaration that no inability exists, he shall resume the powers and duties of his office unless
15   the Vice President and a majority of either the principal officers of the executive department or of such other body as Congress may by law provide, transmit within four days to the President pro tempore of the Senate and the Speaker of the House of Representatives their written declaration that the President is unable to discharge the powers and duties of his office. Thereupon Congress
20   shall decide the issue, assembling within forty-eight hours for that purpose if not in session. If the Congress, within twenty-one days after receipt of the latter written declaration, or, if Congress is not in session, within twenty-one days after Congress is required to assemble, determines by two-thirds vote of both Houses that the President is unable to discharge the powers and duties of his office,
25   the Vice President shall continue to discharge the same as Acting President; otherwise, the President shall resume the powers and duties of his office.

AMENDMENT XXVI
Ratified July 1, 1971

SECTION 1. The right of citizens of the United States, who are eighteen years of age or older, to vote shall not be denied or abridged by the United States or by any State on account of age.

30   SECTION 2. The Congress shall have power to enforce this article by appropriate legislation.

AMENDMENT XXVII
Ratified May 7, 1992

No law varying the compensation for the services of the Senators and Representatives shall take effect, until an election of Representatives shall have intervened.

FRAGMENT ON THE CONSTITUTION AND THE UNION
ABRAHAM LINCOLN (1809–1865)

This never appeared in Abraham Lincoln's public speeches, but it is possible that he composed it while writing his First Inaugural Address. It draws upon the King James translation of Proverbs 25:11—"A word fitly spoken is like apples of gold in pictures of silver"—to describe the relationship between the principles of the Declaration and the purpose of the Constitution.

JANUARY 1861

All this is not the result of accident. It has a philosophical cause. Without the *Constitution* and the *Union*, we could not have attained the result; but even these, are not the primary cause of our great prosperity. There is something back of these, entwining itself more closely about the human heart. That something, is the principle of "Liberty to all"—the principle that clears the *path* for all—gives *hope* to all—and, by consequence, *enterprise*, and *industry* to all.   5

The *expression* of that principle, in our Declaration of Independence, was most happy, and fortunate. *Without* this, as well as *with* it, we could have declared our independence of Great Britain; but *without* it, we could not,   10 I think, have secured our free government, and consequent prosperity. No oppressed, people will *fight*, and *endure*, as our fathers did, without the promise of something better, than a mere change of masters.

The assertion of that *principle*, at *that time*, was *the* word, *"fitly spoken"* which has proved an "apple of gold" to us. The *Union*, and the *Constitution*, are the   15 *picture* of *silver*, subsequently framed around it. The picture was made, not to *conceal*, or *destroy* the apple; but to *adorn*, and *preserve* it. The *picture* was made *for* the apple—*not* the apple for the picture.

Abraham Lincoln, "Fragment on the Constitution and the Union," January 1861, in Roy P. Basler, ed., *The Collected Works of Abraham Lincoln*, Vol. 4 (New Brunswick, NJ: Rutgers University Press, 1953), 168–69. Reprinted with the permission of the Abraham Lincoln Association, Springfield, IL.

So let us act, that neither *picture*, or *apple* shall ever be blurred, or bruised or broken.

That we may so act, we must study, and understand the points of danger.

II
NATURAL RIGHTS AND
THE AMERICAN REVOLUTION

The readings in this section illustrate four basic principles of the American Revolution. These principles, America's Founders held, are true always and everywhere. These principles guided the statesmen and citizens of the colonies as they protested and resisted the changes in policy enacted by the British government following the end of the French and Indian War in 1763, as they fought from Lexington and Concord in 1775 to victory at Yorktown in 1781, and as they concluded the Treaty of Paris in 1783, in which Britain recognized the independence of the United States of America.

I. EVERY HUMAN BEING IS EQUALLY A CREATURE OF GOD ENDOWED WITH A NATURAL RIGHT TO LIFE, LIBERTY, AND PROPERTY.

The Founders believed that every human being—regardless of race, gender, birth, national origin, or religion—is a creature of God and, as such, endowed with a right to life, liberty, and property. Human beings are unequal in many respects, but they are equal in their possession of natural rights. This means, as Thomas Paine argues, that no man is naturally king and another naturally subject. Similarly, James Otis, Thomas Jefferson, Gad Hitchcock, and Alexander Hamilton argue in this section that while every man is subject to God, the only true monarch in the universe, no man is naturally or divinely ruler of or subject to another man.

II. THE PURPOSE OF GOVERNMENT IS LIMITED TO SECURING NATURAL RIGHTS.

Natural rights exist prior to any government. Thus government is not the source of rights. Rather, governments are created to secure natural rights. Limited government derives from this principle. According to the selections in this section, we learn this principle by reflecting on the divine and natural order. As Otis and Paine explain at length, understanding of this principle has been a long time coming. The history of mankind is primarily the history of governments founded on usurpation, force, or fraud of one kind or another. Most governments throughout recorded history have been tyrannies. Many have usurped legal authority through force. Others have been the result of fraud, usually by a monarch surrounded by willing flatterers who employ deception, persuading the weak that the king rules by divine right. All of these governments are illegitimate. Moreover, those who govern—whether one, a few, or many—are not free to determine the purpose of government, but are required to serve the common good. Justice is the true end or purpose of government.

III. The authority of government derives from the consent of the governed.

Following from the principle of equality, every man is (or ought to be) subject to and obligated only to God, and not obligated to obey or be subject to the authority of any government except that to which he has consented or with which he continues to associate voluntarily. (The Founders used the word "consent" interchangeably with the words "compact" and "contract," each of which also imply voluntary association.) Through consent, men create government to secure the rights they cannot secure by themselves, delegating certain powers to government. These powers are circumscribed by the original contract. No government can violate legitimately "the laws of nature and of nature's God" or deviate from the social contract by transferring, altering, or expanding the powers granted it without recourse to the constituent authority—we the people.

IV. Whenever any government routinely and continually goes beyond the consent of the governed, free men must resist its tyrannical usurpations, even at the risk of their lives and fortunes, as required by sacred honor.

As the state motto of New Hampshire has it, every man has an obligation to live free or die. When government usurps powers that it was never granted, it becomes illegitimate and the people, if they acquiesce, become slaves. Men have a duty to defend their natural rights against whatever authority would enslave them. The selections in this section document the long train of abuses perpetrated by King George III in concert with the pretended acts of legislation by Parliament against the American colonies. These violations of "the laws of nature and of nature's God"—including especially the power to tax without representation, and manifold other arbitrary expansions, corruptions, and violations of legitimate executive and legislative powers—required the people of the American colonies to unite against the British tyranny and establish a free government.

Mickey Craig
William and Berniece Grewcock
Professor of Politics
Hillsdale College

Rights of the British Colonies Asserted and Proved
James Otis (1725–1783)

James Otis rose to prominence in 1761, after he gave a courtroom speech opposing the Writs of Assistance—blanket warrants issued by the British for searching suspect property. He edited that speech into this essay three years later, after the passage of the Sugar Act. Its arguments contain the seed of the American Revolution—an appeal to natural rights applied against particular abuses of political power. Struck by lightning in 1783, Otis did not live beyond the Revolution. But John Adams remarked that he had never known a man "whose service for any ten years of his life were so important and essential to the cause of his country as those of Mr. Otis from 1760 to 1770."

1764

Let no Man think I am about to commence advocate for *despotism*, because I affirm that government is founded on the necessity of our natures; and that an original supreme Sovereign, absolute, and uncontrollable, *earthly* power *must* exist in and preside over every society; from whose final decisions there can be no appeal but directly to Heaven. It is therefore *originally* and *ultimately* in the people. I say this supreme absolute power is *originally* and *ultimately* in the people; and they never did in fact *freely*, nor can they *rightfully* make an absolute, unlimited renunciation of this divine right. It is ever in the nature of the thing given in *trust*, and on a condition, the performance of which no mortal can dispence with; namely, that the person or persons on whom the sovereignty is conferred by the people, shall *incessantly* consult *their* good. Tyranny of all kinds is to be abhorred, whether it be in the hands of one, or of the few, or of the many.—And though "in the last age a generation of men sprung up that would flatter Princes with an opinion that *they* have a *divine right* to absolute power;" Yet "slavery is so vile and miserable an estate of man, and so directly opposite to 5

10

15

James Otis, "The Rights of the British Colonies Asserted and Proved," 1764, in Jack P. Greene, ed., *Colonies to Nation 1763–1789: A Documentary History of the American Revolution* (New York: W. W. Norton & Company, 1975), 28–33. Reprinted from James Otis, *The Rights of the British Colonies*, 1764.

the generous temper and courage of our nation, that it is hard to be conceived that an *Englishman*, much less a *gentleman*, should plead for it"....

But let the *origin* of government be placed where it may, the *end* of it is manifestly the good of *the whole*. *Salus populi suprema lex esto*, is of the law of nature, and
5   part of that grand charter given the human race (though too many of them are afraid to assert it) by the only monarch in the universe, who has a clear and indisputable right to *absolute* power; because he is the *only* one who is *omniscient* as well as *omnipotent*....

The *British* constitution in theory and in the present administration of it, in
10   general comes nearest the idea of perfection, of any that has been reduced to practice; and if the principles of it are adhered to, it will, according to the infallible prediction of *Harrington*, always keep the *Britons* uppermost in *Europe,* 'till their *only* rival nation shall either embrace that perfect model of a commonwealth given us by that author, or come as near it as *Great-Britain* is. Then indeed, and
15   not 'till then, will that rival and our nation either be eternal confederates, or contend in greater earnest than they have ever yet done, till one of them shall sink under the power of the other, and rise no more....

Every British Subject born on the continent of America, or in any other of the British dominions, is by the law of God and nature, by the common law, and
20   by act of parliament, (exclusive of all charters from the crown) entitled to all the natural, essential, inherent and inseparable rights of our fellow subjects in Great-Britain. Among those rights are the following, which it is humbly conceived no man or body of men, not excepting the parliament, justly, equitably and consistently with their own rights and the constitution, can take away.

25   1st. *That the supreme and subordinate powers of legislation should be free and sacred in the hands where the community have once rightfully placed them.*

2dly. The supreme national legislative cannot be altered justly till the commonwealth is dissolved, nor a subordinate legislative taken away without forfeiture or other good cause. Nor then can the subjects in the subordinate government be reduced to a
30   state of slavery, and subject to the despotic rule of others. A state has no right to make slaves of the conquered. Even when the subordinate right of legislature is forfeited, and so declared, this cannot effect the natural persons either of those who were invested with it, or the inhabitants, so far as to deprive them of the rights of subjects and of men.—The colonists will have an equitable right, not-
35   withstanding any such forfeiture of charter, to be represented in parliament, or to have some new subordinate legislature among themselves. It would be best if they had both. Deprived, however, of their common rights as subjects, they cannot lawfully be, while they remain such....

3dly. *No legislative, supreme or subordinate, has a right to make itself arbitrary.*

It would be a most manifest contradiction, for a free legislative, like that of Great-Britain, to make itself arbitrary.

4thly. *The supreme legislative cannot justly assume a power of ruling by extempore arbitrary decrees, but is bound to dispense justice by known settled rules, and by duly authorized independent judges.*

5thly. *The supreme power cannot take from any man any part of his property, without his consent in person or by representation.*

6thly. *The legislative cannot transfer the power of making laws to any other hands.*

These are their bounds, which by God and nature are fixed, hitherto have they a right to come, and no further.

1. *To govern by stated laws.*
2. *Those laws should have no other end ultimately, but the good of the people.*
3. *Taxes are not to be laid on the people, but by their consent in person, or by deputation.*
4. *Their whole power is not transferable.*

These are the first principles of law and justice, and the great barriers of a free state, and of the British constitution in particular. I ask, I want no more—Now let it be shown how it is reconcileable with these principles, or to many other fundamental maxims of the British constitution, as well as the natural and civil rights, which by the laws of their country, all British subjects are entitled to, as their best inheritance and birth-right, that all the northern colonies, who are without one representative in the house of commons, should be taxed by the British parliament.

That the colonists, black and white, born here, are free born British subjects, and entitled to all the essential civil rights of such, is a truth not only manifest from the provincial charters, from the principles of the common law, and acts of parliament; but from the British constitution which was re-established at the revolution, with a professed design to secure the liberties of all the subjects to all generations....

... [T]he liberties of the subject are spoken of as their best birth-rights—No one ever dreamed, surely, that these liberties were confined to the realm. At that rate, no British subjects in the dominions could, without a manifest contradiction, be declared entitled to all the privileges of subjects born within the realm, to all intents and purposes, which are rightly given foreigners, by parliament, after residing seven years. These expressions of parliament, as well as of the charters, must be vain and empty sounds, unless we are allowed the essential rights of our fellow-subjects in Great-Britain.

5   Now can there be any liberty, where property is taken away without consent? Can it with any color of truth, justice or equity, be affirmed, that the northern colonies are represented in parliament? Has this whole continent, of near three thousand miles in length, and in which, and his other American dominions, his Majesty has, or very soon will have, some millions of as good, loyal and
10   useful subjects, white and black, as any in the three kingdoms, the election of one member of the house of commons?

Is there the least difference, as to the consent of the Colonists, whether taxes and impositions are laid on their trade, and other property, by the crown alone, or by the parliament? As it is agreed on all hands, the crown alone cannot impose
15   them, we should be justifiable in refusing to pay them, but must and ought to yield obedience to an act of parliament, though erroneous, till repealed.

I can see no reason to doubt, but that the imposition of taxes, whether on trade, or on land, or houses, or ships, on real or personal, fixed or floating property, in the colonies, is absolutely irreconcilable with the rights of the Colonists, as
20   British subjects, and as men. I say men, for in a state of nature, no man can take my property from me, without my consent: If he does, he deprives me of my liberty, and makes me a slave. If such a proceeding is a breach of the law of nature, no law of society can make it just.—The very act of taxing, exercised over those who are not represented, appears to me to be depriving them of
25   one of their most essential rights, as freemen; and if continued, seems to be in effect an entire disfranchisement of every civil right. For what one civil right is worth a rush, after a man's property is subject to be taken from him at pleasure, without his consent? If a man is not his *own assessor* in person, or by deputy, his liberty is gone, or lays entirely at the mercy of others.

30   I think I have heard it said, that when the Dutch are asked why they enslave their colonies, their answer is, that the liberty of Dutchmen is confined to Holland; and that it was never intended for Provincials in America, or any where else. A sentiment this, very worthy of modern Dutchmen; but if their brave and worthy ancestors had entertained such narrow ideas of liberty, seven
35   poor and distressed provinces would never have asserted their rights against the whole Spanish monarchy, of which the present is but a shadow. It is to be hoped, none of our fellow subjects of Britain, great or small, have borrowed this Dutch maxim of plantation politics; if they have, they had better return it from

whence it came; indeed they had. Modern Dutch or French maxims of state, never will suit with a British constitution. It is a maxim, that the King can do no wrong; and every good subject is bound to believe his King is not inclined to do any. We are blessed with a prince who has given abundant demonstrations, that in all his actions, he studies the good of his people, and the true glory of his crown, which are inseparable. It would therefore be the highest degree of impudence and disloyalty to imagine that the King, at the head of his parliament, could have any, but the most pure and perfect intentions of justice, goodness and truth, that human nature is capable of. All this I say and believe of the King and parliament, in all their acts; even in that which so nearly affects the interest of the colonists; and that a most perfect and ready obedience is to be yielded to it, while it remains in force. I will go further, and really admit, that the intention of the ministry was not only to promote the public good, by this act, but that Mr. Chancellor of the Exchequer had therein a particular view to the "ease, the quiet, and the good will of the Colonies," he having made this declaration more than once. Yet, I hold that it is possible he may have erred in his kind intentions towards the Colonies, and taken away our fish, and given us a stone. With regard to the parliament, as infallibility belongs not to mortals, it is possible *they* may have been misinformed and deceived. The power of parliament is uncontrollable, but by themselves, and we must obey. They only can repeal their own acts. There would be an end of all government, if one or a number of subjects or subordinate provinces should take upon them so far to judge of the justice of an act of parliament, as to refuse obedience to it. If there was nothing else to restrain such a step, prudence ought to do it, for forcibly resisting the parliament and the King's laws, is high treason. Therefore, let the parliament lay what burdens they please on us, we must, it is our duty to submit and patiently bear them, till they will be pleased to relieve us. And it is to be presumed, the wisdom and justice of that august assembly, always will afford us relief by repealing such acts, as through mistake, or other human infirmities, have been suffered to pass, if they can be convinced that their proceedings are not constitutional, or not for the common good....

Every subject has a right to give his sentiments to the public, of the utility or inutility of any act whatsoever, even after it is passed, as well as while it is pending.—The equity and justice of a bill may be questioned, with perfect submission to the legislature. Reasons may be given, why an act ought to be repealed, and yet obedience must be yielded to it till that repeal takes place. If the reasons that can be given against an act, are such as plainly demonstrate that it is against *natural* equity, the executive courts will adjudge such acts void. It may be questioned by some, though I make no doubt of it, whether they are

not obliged by their oaths to adjudge such acts void. If there is not a right of
private judgment to be exercised, so far at least as to petition for repeal, or to
determine the expediency of risking a trial at law, the parliament might make
itself arbitrary, which it is conceived it cannot by the constitution.—I think
5   every man has a right to examine as freely into the origin, spring and foundation of every power and measure in a commonwealth, as into a piece of curious
machinery, or a remarkable phenomenon in nature; and that it ought to give
no more offense to say, the parliament have erred, or are mistaken, in a matter
of fact, or of right, than to say it of a private man, if it is true of both. If the
10 assertion can be proved with regard to either, it is a kindness done them to shew
them the truth. With regard to the public, it is the duty of every good citizen
to point out what he thinks erroneous in the commonwealth....

To say the parliament is absolute and arbitrary, is a contradiction. The parliament cannot make two and two, five: Omnipotency cannot do it. The supreme
15 power in a state, is *jus dicere* only:—*jus dare*, strictly speaking, belongs alone to
God. Parliaments are in all cases to *declare* what is for the good of the whole; but
it is not the *declaration* of parliament that makes it so: There must be in every
instance, a higher authority, *viz.* God. Should an act of Parliament be against any
of *his* natural laws, which are *immutably* true, *their* declaration would be contrary
20 to eternal truth, equity and justice, and consequently void: and so it would be
adjudged by the parliament itself, when convinced of their mistake. Upon this
great principle, parliaments repeal such act, as soon as they find they have been
mistaken, in having declared them to be for the public good, when in fact they
were not so. When such mistake is evident and palpable, as in the instances
25 in the appendix, the judges of the executive courts have declared the act "of a
whole parliament void." See here the grandeur of the British constitution! See
the wisdom of our ancestors! The supreme *legislative*, and the supreme *executive*,
are a perpetual check and balance to each other. If the supreme executive errs, it
is informed by the supreme legislative in Parliament: if the supreme legislative
30 errs, it is informed by the supreme executive in the King's courts of law. Here,
the King appears, as represented by his judges, in the highest luster and majesty,
as supreme executor of the commonwealth; and he never shines brighter, but
on his throne, at the head of the supreme legislative. This is government! This,
is a constitution! to preserve which, either from foreign or domestic foes, has
35 cost oceans of blood and treasure in every age; and the blood and the treasure
have upon the whole been well spent....

The sum of my argument is, That civil government is of God: that the administrators of it were originally the whole people: that they might have devolved
it on whom they pleased: that this devolution is fiduciary, for the good of the

whole: that by the British constitution, this devolution is on the King, lords and commons, the supreme, sacred and uncontrollable legislative power, not only in the realm, but through the dominions: that by the abdication, the original compact was broken to pieces: that by the revolution, it was renewed, and more firmly established, and the rights and liberties of the subject in all parts of the   5 dominions, more fully explained and confirmed: that in consequence of this establishment and the acts of succession and union, His Majesty George III is rightful king and sovereign, and with his parliament, the supreme legislative of Great-Britain, France and Ireland, and the dominions thereunto belonging: that this constitution is the most free one, and by far the best, now existing on   10 earth: that by this constitution, every man in the dominions is a free man: that no parts of his Majesty's dominions can be taxed without their consent: that every part has a right to be represented in the supreme or some subordinate legislature: that the refusal of this, would seem to be a contradiction in practice to the theory of the constitution: that the colonies are subordinate dominions,   15 and are now in such a state, as to make it best for the good of the whole, that they should not only be continued in the enjoyment of subordinate legislation, but be also represented in some proportion to their number and estates in the grand legislation of the nation: that this would firmly unite all parts of the British empire, in the greatest peace and prosperity; and render it invulnerable   20 and perpetual.

A Summary View of the Rights
of British America
Thomas Jefferson

Thomas Jefferson began his public career in 1769 in the Virginia House of Burgesses, the colonial legislature. British implementation of the Coercive Acts of 1774 (also known as the Intolerable Acts)—passed in response to the Boston Tea Party—prompted the "Summary View," Jefferson's first publication. Written for Virginians who were choosing delegates to the First Continental Congress, it laid the groundwork for later appeals by a "free people, claiming their rights as derived from the laws of nature."

JULY 1774

Resolved, that it be an instruction to the said deputies when assembled in General Congress with the deputies from the other states of British America to propose to the said Congress that an humble and dutiful address be presented to his majesty begging leave to lay before him as chief magistrate of the British empire the united complaints of his majesty's subjects in America; complaints 5 which are excited by many unwarrantable encroachments and usurpations, attempted to be made by the legislature of one part of the empire, upon those rights which god and the laws have given equally and independently to all. To represent to his majesty that these his states have often individually made humble application to his imperial throne, to obtain through its intervention 10 some redress of their injured rights; to none of which was ever even an answer condescended. Humbly to hope that this their joint address, penned in the language of truth, and divested of those expressions of servility which would persuade his majesty that we are asking favors and not rights, shall obtain from his majesty a more respectful acceptance. And this his majesty will think we 15 have reason to expect when he reflects that he is no more than the chief officer of the people, appointed by the laws, and circumscribed with definite powers, to assist in working the great machine of government erected for their use, and

Thomas Jefferson, "Draft of Instructions to the Virginia Delegates in the Continental Congress," July 1774, in Julian P. Boyd, ed., *The Papers of Thomas Jefferson*, Vol. 1 (Princeton, NJ: Princeton University Press, 1950–1992), 121–23, 125–35.

consequently subject to their superintendence. And in order that these our rights, as well as the invasions of them, may be laid more fully before his majesty, to take a view of them from the origin and first settlement of these countries.

To remind him that our ancestors, before their emigration to America, were
5 the free inhabitants of the British dominions in Europe, and possessed a right, which nature has given to all men, of departing from the country in which chance, not choice has placed them, of going in quest of new habitations, and of there establishing new societies, under such laws and regulations as to them shall seem most likely to promote public happiness. That their Saxon ancestors
10 had under this universal law, in like manner, left their native wilds and woods in the North of Europe, had possessed themselves of the island of Britain then less charged with inhabitants, and had established there that system of laws which has so long been the glory and protection of that country. Nor was ever any claim of superiority or dependance asserted over them by that mother country
15 from which they had migrated: and were such a claim made it is believed his majesty's subjects in Great Britain have too firm a feeling of the rights derived to them from their ancestors to bow down the sovereignty of their state before such visionary pretensions. And it is thought that no circumstance has occurred to distinguish materially the British from the Saxon emigration. America was
20 conquered, and her settlements made and firmly established, at the expense of individuals, and not of the British public. Their own blood was spilt in acquiring lands for their settlement, their own fortunes expended in mak- ing that settlement effectual. For themselves they fought, for themselves they conquered, and for themselves alone they have right to hold. No shilling was
25 ever issued from the public treasures of his majesty, or his ancestors, for their assistance, till of very late times, after the colonies had become established on a firm and permanent footing. That then indeed, having become valuable to Great Britain for her commercial purposes, his parliament was pleased to lend them assistance against an enemy who would fain have drawn to herself the
30 benefits of their commerce to the great aggrandisement of herself and danger of Great Britain. Such assistance, and in such circumstances, they had often before given to Portugal and other allied states, with whom they carry on a commercial intercourse. Yet these states never supposed that, by calling in her aid, they thereby submitted themselves to her sovereignty. Had such terms been
35 proposed, they would have rejected them with disdain, and trusted for better to the moderation of their enemies, or to a vigorous exertion of their own force. We do not however mean to underrate those aids, which to us were doubtless valuable, on whatever principles granted: but we would shew that they cannot give a title to that authority which the British parliament would arrogate over

us; and that they may amply be repaid, by our giving to the inhabitants of Great Britain such exclusive privileges in trade as may be advantageous to them, and at the same time not too restrictive to ourselves. That settlements having been thus effected in the wilds of America, the emigrants thought proper to adopt that system of laws under which they had hitherto lived in the mother country, and to continue their union with her by submitting themselves to the same common sovereign, who was thereby made the central link connecting the several parts of the empire thus newly multiplied.

But that not long were they permitted, however far they thought themselves removed from the hand of oppression, to hold undisturbed the rights thus acquired at the hazard of their lives and loss of their fortunes. A family of princes was then on the British throne, whose treasonable crimes against their people brought on them afterwards the exertion of those sacred and sovereign rights of punishment, reserved in the hands of the people for cases of extreme necessity, and judged by the constitution unsafe to be delegated to any other judicature. While every day brought forth some new and unjustifiable exertion of power over their subjects on that side the water, it was not to be expected that those here, much less able at that time to oppose the designs of despotism, should be exempted from injury. Accordingly that country which had been acquired by the lives, the labors and the fortunes of individual adventurers, was by these princes at several times parted out and distributed among the favorites and followers of their fortunes; and by an assumed right of the crown alone were erected into distinct and independent governments....

That the exercise of a free trade with all parts of the world, possessed by the American colonists as of natural right, and which no law of their own had taken away or abridged, was next the object of unjust encroachment.... The true ground on which we declare these acts void is that the British parliament has no right to exercise authority over us....

That thus have we hastened through the reigns which preceded his majesty's, during which the violation of our rights were less alarming, because repeated at more distant intervals, than that rapid and bold succession of injuries which is likely to distinguish the present from all other periods of [the] American story. Scarcely have our minds been able to emerge from the astonishment into which one stroke of parliamentary thunder has involved us, before another more heavy and more alarming is fallen on us. Single acts of tyranny may be ascribed to the accidental opinion of a day; but a series of oppressions, begun at a distinguished period, and pursued unalterably through every change of ministers, too plainly prove a deliberate, systematical plan of reducing us to slavery.

That the act passed in the fourth year of his majesty's reign entitled "an act for granting certain duties in the British colonies and plantations in America, etc.";
one other act passed in the fifth year of his reign entitled "an act for granting and applying certain stamp duties in the British colonies and plantations in America, etc."; one other act passed in the sixth year of his reign entitled "an act
5   for the better securing the dependency of His Majesty's dominions in America upon the crown and parliament of Great Britain"; and one other act, passed in the seventh year of his reign, entitled "an act for granting duties on paper, tea, etc.," form that connected chain of parliamentary usurpation which has
10   already been the subject of frequent applications to his majesty and the houses of Lords and Commons of Great Britain; and, no answers having yet been condescended to any of these, we shall not trouble his majesty with a repetition of the matters they contained.

But that one other act passed in the same seventh year of his reign, having been
15   a peculiar attempt, must ever require peculiar mention. It is entitled "an act for suspending the legislature of New York." One free and independent legislature hereby takes upon itself to suspend the powers of another, free and independent as itself, thus exhibiting a phaenomenon, unknown in nature, the creator and creature of it's own power. Not only the principles of common sense, but the
20   common feelings of human nature must be surrendered up, before his majesty's subjects here can be persuaded to believe that they hold their political existence at the will of a British parliament. Shall these governments be dissolved, their property annihilated, and their people reduced to a state of nature, at the imperious breath of a body of men whom they never saw, in whom they never
25   confided, and over whom they have no powers of punishment or removal, let their crimes against the American public be ever so great?...

That by "an act to discontinue in such manner and for such time as are therein mentioned the landing and discharging, lading or shipping of Goods wares and merchandise at the town and within the harbor of Boston in the province
30   of Massachusett's bay in North America" which was passed at the last session of British parliament, a large and populous town, whose trade was their sole subsistence, was deprived of that trade, and involved in utter ruin. Let us for a while suppose the question of right suspended, in order to examine this act on principles of justice. An act of parliament had been passed imposing duties
35   on teas to be paid in America, against which act the Americans had protested as inauthoritative. The East India company, who till that time had never sent a pound of tea to America on their own account, step forth on that occasion the asserters of parliamentary right, and send hither many ship loads of that obnoxious commodity. The masters of their several vessels however, on their

arrival in America, wisely attended to admonition, and returned with their cargoes. In the province of New England alone the remonstrances of the people were disregarded, and a compliance, after being many days waited for, was flatly refused. Whether in this the master of the vessel was governed by his obstinacy or his instructions, let those who know, say. There are extraordinary   5 situations which require extraordinary interposition. An exasperated people, who feel that they possess power, are not easily restrained within limits strictly regular. A number of them assembled in the town of Boston, threw the tea into the ocean and dispersed without doing any other act of violence. If in this they did wrong, they were known, and were amenable to the laws of the land,   10 against which it could not be objected that they had ever in any instance been obstructed or diverted from their regular course in favor of popular offend- ers. They should therefore not have been distrusted on this occasion. But that ill-fated colony had formerly been bold in their enmities against the house of Stuart, and were now devoted to ruin by that unseen hand which governs the   15 momentous affairs of this great empire. On the partial representations of a few worthless ministerial dependants, whose constant office it has been to keep that government embroiled, and who by their treacheries hope to obtain the dignity of the British knighthood, without calling for a party accused, without asking a proof, without attempting a distinction between the guilty and the innocent, the   20 whole of that ancient and wealthy town is in a moment reduced from opulence to beggary. Men who had spent their lives in extending the British commerce, who had invested in that place the wealth their honest endeavors had merited, found themselves and their families thrown at once on the world for subsistence by it's charities. Not the hundredth part of the inhabitants of that town had   25 been concerned in the act complained of; many of them were in Great Britain and in other parts beyond sea; yet all were involved in one indiscriminate ruin, by a new executive power unheard of till then, that of a British parliament. A property of the value of many millions of money was sacrificed to revenge, not repay, the loss of a few thousands. This is administering justice with a heavy   30 hand indeed! And when is this tempest to be arrested in its course? Two wharfs are to be opened again when his majesty shall think proper: the residue which lined the extensive shores of the bay of Boston are forever interdicted the exercise of commerce. This little exception seems to have been thrown in for no other purpose than that of setting a precedent for investing his majesty with legisla-   35 tive powers. If the pulse of his people shall beat calmly under this experiment, another and another will be tried till the measure of despotism be filled up. It would be an insult on common sense to pretend that this exception was made in order to restore its commerce to that great town. The trade which cannot be received at two wharfs alone, must of necessity be transferred to some other   40 place; to which it will soon be followed by that of the two wharfs. Considered in this light it would be an insolent and cruel mockery at the annihilation of the town of Boston.

By the act for the suppression of riots and tumults in the town of Boston,
5   passed also in the last session of parliament, a murder committed there is, if the governor pleases, to be tried in the court of King's bench in the island of Great Britain, by a jury of Middlesex. The witnesses too, on receipt of such a sum as the Governor shall think it reasonable for them to expend, are to enter into recognisance to appear at the trial. This is in other words taxing them to
10 the amount of their recognisance; and that amount may be whatever a Governor pleases. For who does his majesty think can be prevailed on to cross the Atlantick for the sole purpose of bearing evidence to a fact? His expenses are to be borne indeed as they shall be estimated by a Governor; but who are to feed the wife and children whom he leaves behind, and who have had no other
15 subsistence but his daily labor? Those epidemical disorders too, so terrible in a foreign climate, is the cure of them to be estimated among the articles of expense, and their danger to be warded off by the almighty power of a parliament? And the wretched criminal, if he happen to have offended on the American side, stripped of his privilege of trial by peers, of his vicinage, removed from the place
20 where alone full evidence could be obtained, without money, without counsel, without friends, without exculpatory proof, is tried before judges predetermined to condemn. The cowards who would suffer a countryman to be torn from the bowels of their society in order to be thus offered a sacrifice to parliamentary tyranny, would merit that everlasting infamy now fixed on the authors of the
25 act! A clause for a similar purpose had been introduced into an act passed in the twelfth. year of his majesty's reign entitled "an act for the better securing and preserving his majesty's dock-yards, magazines, ships, ammunition and stores," against which as meriting the same censures the several colonies have already protested.

30 That these are the acts of power assumed by a body of men foreign to our constitutions, and unacknowleged by our laws; against which we do, on behalf of the inhabitants of British America, enter this our solemn and determined protest. And we do earnestly intreat his majesty, as yet the only mediatory power between the several states of the British empire, to recommend to his parliament of Great
35 Britain the total revocation of these acts, which however nugatory they be, may yet prove the cause of further discontents and jealousies among us.

That we next proceed to consider the conduct of his majesty, as holding the executive powers of the laws of these states, and mark out his deviations from the line of duty. By the constitution of Great Britain as well as of the several

American states, his majesty possesses the power of refusing to pass into a law any bill which has already passed the other two branches of legislature. His majesty however and his ancestors, conscious of the impropriety of opposing their single opinion to the united wisdom of two houses of parliament, while their proceedings were unbiased by interested principles, for several ages past 5 have modestly declined the exercise of this power in that part of his empire called Great Britain. But by change of circumstances, other principles than those of justice simply have obtained an influence on their determinations. The addition of new states to the British empire has produced an addition of new, and sometimes opposite interests. It is now therefore the great office of his majesty 10 to resume the exercise of his negative power, and to prevent the passage of laws by any one legislature of the empire which might bear injuriously on the rights and interests of another. Yet this will not excuse the wanton exercise of this power which we have seen his majesty practice on the laws of the American legislatures. For the most trifling reasons, and sometimes for no conceivable reason at all, his 15 majesty has rejected laws of the most salutary tendency. The abolition of domestic slavery is the great object of desire in those colonies where it was unhappily introduced in their infant state. But previous to the infranchisement of the slaves we have, it is necessary to exclude all further importations from Africa. Yet our repeated attempts to effect this by prohibitions, and by imposing duties which 20 might amount to a prohibition, have been hitherto defeated by his majesty's negative: thus preferring the immediate advantages of a few British corsairs to the lasting interests of the American states, and to the rights of human nature deeply wounded by this infamous practice. Nay the single interposition of an interested individual against a law was scarcely ever known to fail of success, 25 tho' in the opposite scale were placed the interests of a whole country. That this is so shameful an abuse of a power trusted with his majesty for other purposes, as if not reformed would call for some legal restrictions.

With equal inattention to the necessities of his people here, has his majesty permitted our laws to lie neglected in England for years, neither confirming 30 them by his assent, nor annulling them by his negative: so that such of them as have no suspending clause, we hold on the most precarious of all tenures, his majesty's will, and such of them as suspend themselves till his majesty's assent be obtained we have feared might be called into existence at some future and distant period, when time and change of circumstances shall have rendered them 35 destructive to his people here. And to render this grievance still more oppressive, his majesty by his instructions has laid his governors under such restrictions that they can pass no law of any moment unless it have such suspending clause: so that, however immediate may be the call for legislative interposition, the law cannot be executed till it has twice crossed the Atlantic, by which time the evil may have spent its whole force....

One of the articles of impeachment against Tresilian and the other judges of Westminster Hall in the reign of Richard the second, for which they suffered
5   death as traitors to their country, was that they had advised the king that he might dissolve his parliament at any time: and succeeding kings have adopted the opinion of these unjust judges. Since the establishment however of the British constitution at the glorious Revolution on it's free and ancient principles, neither his majesty nor his ancestors have exercised such a power of dissolution
10 in the island of Great Britain; and when his majesty was petitioned by the united voice of his people there to dissolve the present parliament, who had become obnoxious to them, his ministers were heard to declare in open parliament that his majesty possessed no such power by the constitution. But how different their language and his practice here! To declare as their duty required the known
15 rights of their country, to oppose the usurpation of every foreign judicature, to disregard the imperious mandates of a minister or governor, have been the avowed causes of dissolving houses of representatives in America. But if such powers be really vested in his majesty, can he suppose they are there placed to awe the members from such purposes as these? When the representative body
20 have lost the confidence of their constituents, when they have notoriously made sale of their most valuable rights, when they have assumed to themselves powers which the people never put into their hands, then indeed their continuing in office becomes dangerous to the state, and calls for an exercise of the power of dissolution. Such being the causes for which the representative body should
25 and should not be dissolved, will it not appear strange to an unbiased observer that that of Great Britain was not dissolved, while those of the colonies have repeatedly incurred that sentence?

But your majesty or your Governors have carried this power beyond every limit known or provided for by the laws. After dissolving one house of representa-
30 tives, they have refused to call another, so that for a great length of time the legislature provided by the laws has been out of existence. From the nature of things, every society must at all times possess within itself the sovereign powers of legislation. The feelings of human nature revolt against the supposition of a state so situated as that it may not in any emergency provide against dangers
35 which perhaps threaten immediate ruin. While those bodies are in existence to whom the people have delegated the powers of legislation, they alone possess and may exercise those powers. But when they are dissolved by the lopping off one or more of their branches, the power reverts to the people, who may use it to unlimited extent, either assembling together in person, sending deputies,

or in any other way they may think proper. We forbear to trace consequences
further; the dangers are conspicuous with which this practice is replete.

That we shall at this time also take notice of an error in the nature of our land-
holdings, which crept in at a very early period of our settlement. The introduction of the Feudal tenures into the kingdom of England, though ancient, is well   5
enough understood to set this matter in a proper light. In the earlier ages of
the Saxon settlement feudal holdings were certainly altogether unknown, and
very few, if any, had been introduced at the time of the Norman conquest. Our
Saxon ancestors held their lands, as they did their personal property, in absolute
dominion, disencumbered with any superior, answering nearly to the nature of   10
those possessions which the Feudalists term Allodial: William the Norman first
introduced that system generally. The lands which had belonged to those who
fell in the battle of Hastings, and in the subsequent insurrections of his reign,
formed a considerable proportion of the lands of the whole kingdom. These he
granted out, subject to feudal duties, as did he also those of a great number of   15
his new subjects, who by persuasions or threats were induced to surrender them
for that purpose. But still much was left in the hands of his Saxon subjects, held
of no superior, and not subject to feudal conditions. These therefore by express
laws, enacted to render uniform the system of military defence, were made liable
to the same military duties as if they had been feuds: and the Norman lawyers   20
soon found means to saddle them also with all the other feudal burthens. But
still they had not been surrendered to the king, they were not derived from his
grant, and therefore they were not holden of him. A general principle indeed
was introduced that "all lands in England were held either mediately or immediately of the crown": but this was borrowed from those holdings which were   25
truly feudal, and only applied to others for the purposes of illustration. Feudal
holdings were therefore but exceptions out of the Saxon laws of possession, under
which all lands were held in absolute right. These therefore still form the basis
or groundwork of the Common law, to prevail wheresoever the exceptions have
not taken place. America was not conquered by William the Norman, nor its   30
lands surrendered to him or any of his successors. Possessions there are undoubtedly of the Allodial nature. Our ancestors however, who migrated hither, were
laborers, not lawyers. The fictitious principle that all lands belong originally to
the king, they were early persuaded to believe real, and accordingly took grants
of their own lands from the crown. And while the crown continued to grant   35
for small sums and on reasonable rents, there was no inducement to arrest the
error and lay it open to public view. But his majesty has lately taken on him to
advance the terms of purchase and of holding to the double of what they were,
by which means the acquisition of lands being rendered difficult, the popula-

tion of our country is likely to be checked. It is time therefore for us to lay this matter before his majesty, and to declare that he has no right to grant lands of himself. From the nature and purpose of civil institutions, all the lands within the limits which any particular society has circumscribed around itself, are
5 assumed by that society, and subject to their allotment only. This may be done by themselves assembled collectively, or by their legislature to whom they may have delegated sovereign authority: and, if they are allotted in neither of these ways, each individual of the society may appropriate to himself such lands as he finds vacant, and occupancy will give him title.

10 That, in order to inforce the arbitrary measures before complained of, his majesty has from time to time sent among us large bodies of armed forces, not made up of the people here, nor raised by the authority of our laws. Did his majesty possess such a right as this, it might swallow up all our other rights whenever he should think proper. But his majesty has no right to land a single armed
15 man on our shores; and those whom he sends here are liable to our laws for the suppression and punishment of Riots, Routs, and unlawful assemblies, or are hostile bodies invading us in defiance of law. When in the course of the late war it became expedient that a body of Hanoverian troops should be brought over for the defence of Great Britain, his majesty's grandfather, our late sovereign,
20 did not pretend to introduce them under any authority he possessed. Such a measure would have given just alarm to his subjects in Great Britain, whose liberties would not be safe if armed men of another country, and of another spirit, might be brought into the realm at any time without the consent of their legislature. He therefore applied to parliament who passed an act for that
25 purpose, limiting the number to be brought in and the time they were to continue. In like manner is his majesty restrained in every part of the empire. He possesses indeed the executive power of the laws in every state; but they are the laws of the particular state which he is to administer within that state, and not those of any one within the limits of another. Every state must judge for itself
30 the number of armed men which they may safely trust among them, of whom they are to consist, and under what restrictions they are to be laid. To render these proceedings still more criminal against our laws, instead of subjecting the military to the civil power, his majesty has expressly made the civil subordinate to the military. But can his majesty thus put down all law under his feet? Can
35 he erect a power superior to that which erected himself? He has done it indeed by force; but let him remember that force cannot give right.

That these are our grievances which we have thus laid before his majesty with that freedom of language and sentiment which becomes a free people, claiming their rights as derived from the laws of nature, and not as the gift of their chief magistrate. Let those flatter, who fear: it is not an American art. To give praise where it is not due, might be well from the venal, but would ill beseem those who are asserting the rights of human nature. They know, and will therefore say, that kings are the servants, not the proprietors of the people. Open your breast Sire, to liberal and expanded thought. Let not the name of George the third be a blot in the page of history. You are surrounded by British counsellors, but remember that they are parties. You have no ministers for American affairs, because you have none taken from among us, nor amenable to the laws on which they are to give you advice. It behooves you therefore to think and to act for yourself and your people. The great principles of right and wrong are legible to every reader: to pursue them requires not the aid of many counsellors. The whole art of government consists in the art of being honest. Only aim to do your duty, and mankind will give you credit where you fail. No longer persevere in sacrificing the rights of one part of the empire to the inordinate desires of another: but deal out to all equal and impartial right. Let no act be passed by any one legislature which may infringe on the rights and liberties of another. This is the important post in which fortune has placed you, holding the balance of a great, if a well poised empire. This, Sire, is the advice of your great American council, on the observance of which may perhaps depend your felicity and future fame, and the preservation of that harmony which alone can continue both to Great Britain and America the reciprocal advantages of their connection. It is neither our wish nor our interest to separate from her. We are willing on our part to sacrifice every thing which reason can ask to the restoration of that tranquility for which all must wish. On their part let them be ready to establish union on a generous plan. Let them name their terms, but let them be just. Accept of every commercial preference it is in our power to give for such things as we can raise for their use, or they make for ours. But let them not think to exclude us from going to other markets, to dispose of those commodities which they cannot use, nor to supply those wants which they cannot supply. Still less let it be proposed that our properties within our own territories shall be taxed or regulated by any power on earth but our own. The god who gave us life, gave us liberty at the same time: the hand of force may destroy, but cannot disjoin them. This, Sire, is our last, our determined resolution: and that you will be pleased to interpose with that efficacy which your earnest endeavors may insure to procure redress of these our great grievances, to quiet the minds of your subjects in British America against any apprehensions of future encroachment, to establish fraternal love and harmony through the whole empire, and that that may continue to the latest ages of time, is the fervent prayer of all British America.

AN ELECTION SERMON
GAD HITCHCOCK (1718–1803)

Pastors and ministers were among the highest educated citizens in the American colonies, and often addressed politics from the pulpit. This sermon by Gad Hitchcock was delivered on election day in 1774, in the presence of General Thomas Gage, the British military governor of the Province of Massachusetts Bay. It decries British monarchical rule and celebrates the idea of the consent of the governed, appealing to reason as well as revelation.

1774

…In a mixed government, such as the British, public virtue and religion, in the several branches, though they may not be exactly of a mind in every measure, will be the security of order and tranquility—Corruption and venality, the certain source of confusion and misery to the state.

This form of government, in the opinion of subjects and strangers, is happily   5
calculated for the preservation of the Rights and Liberties of mankind.—Much, however, depends on union; and the concern of every part to pursue the great ends of government.…

In such a government, rulers have their distinct powers assigned them by the people, who are the only source of civil authority on earth, with the view of   10
having them exercised for the public advantage; and in proportion as this worthy end of their investiture is kept in sight, and prosecuted, the bands of society are strengthened, and its interests promoted.…

Rulers are under the most sacred ties to consult the good of society. 'Tis the only grand design of their appointment. For the promotion of this valuable   15
end, they are ordained of God, and clothed with authority by men.

Gad Hitchcock, "An Election Sermon," 1774, in Charles S. Hyneman and Donald S. Lutz, eds., *American Political Writing during the Founding Era, 1760–1805*, Vol. 1 (Indianapolis, IN: Liberty Fund, 1983), 287–89. This material appears on the Online Library of Liberty [http://app.libraryof liberty.org] hosted by Liberty Fund, Inc.

In a state of nature men are equal, exactly on a par in regard to authority: each one is a law to himself, having the law of God, the sole rule of conduct, written on his heart.

No individual has any authority, or right to attempt to exercise any, over the
5 rest of the human species, however he may be supposed to surpass them in wisdom and sagacity. The idea of superior wisdom giving a right to rule, can answer the purpose of power but to one; for on this plan the Wisest of all is Lord of all. Mental endowments, though excellent qualifications for rule, when men have entered into combination and erected government, and previous to
10 government, bring the possessors under moral obligation, by advice, persuasion and argument, to do good proportionate to the degrees of them; yet do not give any antecedent right to the exercise of authority. Civil authority is the production of combined society—not born with, but delegated to certain individuals for the advancement of the common benefit.

15 And as its origin is from the people, who have not only a right, but are bound in duty, for the preservation of the property and liberty of the whole society, to lodge it in such hands as they judge best qualified to answer its intention; so when it is misapplied to other purposes, and the public, as it always will, receives damage from the abuse, they have the same original right, grounded
20 on the same fundamental reasons, and are equally bound in duty to resume it, and transfer it to others.—These are principles which will not be denied by any good and loyal subject of his present Majesty King George, either in Great-Britain or America—The royal right to the throne absolutely depends on the truth of them,—and the revolution, an event seasonable and happy
25 both to the mother country and these colonies, evidently supports them, and is supported by them....

THE FARMER REFUTED
ALEXANDER HAMILTON (1755–1804)

When loyalist writings began to appear in New York newspapers in 1775, nineteen-year-old Alexander Hamilton responded with an essay defending the colonists' right of revolution. Still a student at King's College, he followed up with this second pamphlet, expanding his argument on the purpose of legitimate government.

FEBRUARY 23, 1775

I shall, for the present, pass over to that part of your pamphlet, in which you endeavor to establish the supremacy of the British Parliament over America. After a proper eclaircissement of this point, I shall draw such inferences, as will sap the foundation of every thing you have offered.

The first thing that presents itself is a wish, that "*I* had, explicitly, declared to   5
the public my ideas of the *natural rights* of mankind. Man, in a state of nature (you say) may be considered, as perfectly free from all restraints of *law* and *government,* and, then, the weak must submit to the strong."

I shall, henceforth, begin to make some allowance for that enmity, you have discovered to the *natural rights* of mankind. For, though ignorance of them in   10
this enlightened age cannot be admitted, as a sufficient excuse for you; yet, it ought, in some measure, to extenuate your guilt. If you will follow my advice, there still may be hopes of your reformation. Apply yourself, without delay, to the study of the law of nature. I would recommend to your perusal, Grotius, Puffendorf, Locke, Montesquieu, and Burlemaqui. I might mention other   15
excellent writers on this subject; but if you attend, diligently, to these, you will not require any others.

There is so strong a similitude between your political principles and those maintained by Mr. Hobb[e]s, that, in judging from them, a person might very easily *mistake* you for a disciple of his. His opinion was, exactly, coincident   20
with yours, relative to man in a state of nature. He held, as you do, that he was,

Alexander Hamilton, "The Farmer Refuted," February 23, 1775, in Harold Coffin Syrett, ed., *The Papers of Alexander Hamilton, 1768–1778*, Vol. 1 (New York: Columbia University Press, 1961–1987), 86–89, 121–22, 135–36. Reproduced with permission of Columbia University Press in the format Textbook via Copyright Clearance Center.

then, perfectly free from all restraint of *law* and *government*. Moral obligation, according to him, is derived from the introduction of civil society; and there is no virtue, but what is purely artificial, the mere contrivance of politicians, for the maintenance of social intercourse. But the reason he run into this absurd
5   and impious doctrine, was, that he disbelieved the existence of an intelligent superintending principle, who is the governor, and will be the final judge of the universe.

As you, sometimes, swear *by him that made you,* I conclude, your sentiment does not correspond with his, in that which is the basis of the doctrine, you
10 both agree in; and this makes it impossible to imagine whence this congruity between you arises. To grant, that there is a supreme intelligence, who rules the world, and has established laws to regulate the actions of his creatures; and, still, to assert, that man, in a state of nature, may be considered as perfectly free from all restraints of *law* and *government,* appear to a common understanding,
15 altogether irreconcileable.

Good and wise men, in all ages, have embraced a very dissimilar theory. They have supposed, that the deity, from the relations, we stand in, to himself and to each other, has constituted an eternal and immutable law, which is, indispensibly, obligatory upon all mankind, prior to any human institution whatever.

20 This is what is called the law of nature, "which, being coeval with mankind, and dictated by God himself, is, of course, superior in obligation to any other. It is binding over all the globe, in all countries, and at all times. No human laws are of any validity, if contrary to this; and such of them as are valid, derive all their authority, mediately, or immediately, from this original." Blackstone.

25 Upon this law, depend the natural rights of mankind, the supreme being gave existence to man, together with the means of preserving and beatifying that existence. He endowed him with rational faculties, by the help of which, to discern and pursue such things, as were consistent with his duty and interest, and invested him with an inviolable right to personal liberty, and personal safety.

30 Hence, in a state of nature, no man had any *moral* power to deprive another of his life, limbs, property or liberty; nor the least authority to command, or exact obedience from him; except that which arose from the ties of consanguinity.

Hence also, the origin of all civil government, justly established, must be a voluntary compact, between the rulers and the ruled; and must be liable to such
35 limitations, as are necessary for the security of the *absolute rights* of the latter; for what original title can any man or set of men have, to govern others, except their own consent? To usurp dominion over a people, in their own despite, or

to grasp at a more extensive power than they are willing to entrust, is to violate that law of nature, which gives every man a right to his personal liberty; and can, therefore, confer no obligation to obedience.

"The principal aim of society is to protect individuals, in the enjoyment of those absolute rights, which were vested in them by the immutable laws of nature;   5
but which could not be preserved, in peace, without that mutual assistance, and intercourse, which is gained by the institution of friendly and social communities. Hence it follows, that the first and primary end of human laws, is to maintain and regulate these *absolute rights* of individuals." Blackstone.

If we examine the pretensions of parliament, by this criterion, which is evidently,   10
a good one, we shall, presently detect their injustice. First, they are subversive of our natural liberty, because an authority is assumed over us, which we by no means assent to. And secondly, they divest us of that moral security, for our lives and properties, which we are entitled to, and which it is the primary end of society to bestow. For such security can never exist, while we have no part   15
in making the laws, that are to bind us; and while it may be the interest of our uncontrolled legislators to oppress us as much as possible.

To deny these principles will be not less absurd, than to deny the plainest axioms: I shall not, therefore, attempt any further illustration of them....

Thus Sir, I have taken a pretty general survey of the American Charters; and   20
proved to the satisfaction of every unbiased person, that they are entirely, discordant with that sovereignty of parliament, for which you are an advocate. The disingenuity of your extracts (to give it no harsher name) merits the severest censure; and will no doubt serve to discredit all your former, as well as future labors, in your favorite cause of despotism.   25

It is true, that New-York has no Charter. But, if it could support its claim to liberty in no other way, it might, with justice, plead the common principles of colonization: for, it would be unreasonable, to seclude one colony, from the enjoyment of the most important privileges of the rest. There is no need, however, of this plea: The sacred rights of mankind are not to be rummaged   30
for, among old parchments, or musty records. They are written, as with a sun beam, in the whole *volume* of human nature, by the hand of the divinity itself; and can never be erased or obscured by mortal power.

The nations of Turkey, Russia, France, Spain, and all other despotic kingdoms, in the world, have an inherent right, when ever they please, to shake off the yoke   35
of servitude, (though sanctified by the immemorial usage of their ancestors;) and to model their government, upon the principles of civil liberty....

Had the rest of America passively looked on, while a sister colony was subjugated, the same fate would gradually have overtaken all. The safety of the whole depends upon the mutual protection of every part. If the sword of oppression be permitted to lop off one limb without opposition, reiterated strokes will
5   soon dismember the whole body. Hence it was the duty and interest of all the colonies to succour and support the one which was suffering. It is sometimes sagaciously urged, that we ought to commisserate the distresses of the people of Massachusetts; but not intermeddle in their affairs, so far, as perhaps to bring ourselves into like circumstances with them. This might be good reasoning, if
10   our neutrality would not be more dangerous, than our participation: But I am unable to conceive how the colonies in general would have any security against oppression, if they were once to content themselves, with barely *pitying* each other, while parliament was prosecuting and enforcing its demands. Unless they continually protect and assist each other, they must all inevitably fall a
15   prey to their enemies.

Extraordinary emergencies, require extraordinary expedients. The best mode of opposition was that in which there might be an union of councils. This was necessary to ascertain the boundaries of our rights; and to give weight and dignity to our measures, both in Britain and America. A Congress was accordingly
20   proposed, and universally agreed to.

You, Sir, triumph in the supposed *illegality* of this body; but, granting your supposition were true, it would be a matter of no real importance. When the first principles of civil society are violated, and the rights of a whole people are invaded, the common forms of municipal law are not to be regarded. Men
25   may then betake themselves to the law of nature; and, if they but conform their actions, to that standard, all cavils against them, betray either ignorance or dishonesty. There are some events in society, to which human laws cannot extend; but when applied to them lose all their force and efficacy. In short, when human laws contradict or discountenance the means, which are necessary
30   to preserve the essential rights of any society, they defeat the proper end of all laws, and so become null and void....

COMMON SENSE
THOMAS PAINE (1737–1809)

Published anonymously in January 1776, by an Englishman who had come to Philadelphia two years before, Common Sense became the most published work of the founding era. Printed over half a million times in a nation of three million people, it made a passionate case for liberty and against monarchy. Unpopular in later life for his attacks on Christianity, Thomas Paine will always be remembered for this pamphlet—a pamphlet often said to have launched the American Revolution.

JANUARY 10, 1776

ON THE ORIGIN AND DESIGN OF GOVERNMENT IN GENERAL, WITH CONCISE REMARKS ON THE ENGLISH CONSTITUTION

Some writers have so confounded society with government, as to leave little or no distinction between them; whereas they are not only different, but have different origins. Society is produced by our wants and government by our wickedness; the former promotes our happiness *positively* by uniting our affections, the latter *negatively* by restraining our vices. The one encourages intercourse, the other 5 creates distinctions. The first is a patron, the last a punisher.

Society in every state is a blessing, but government, even in its best state, is but a necessary evil; in its worst state an intolerable one; for when we suffer, or are exposed to the same miseries *by a government,* which we might expect in a country *without government,* our calamity is heightened by reflecting that 10 we furnish the means by which we suffer. Government, like dress, is the badge of lost innocence; the palaces of kings are built upon the ruins of the bowers of paradise. For were the impulses of conscience clear, uniform and irresistibly obeyed, man would need no other law-giver; but that not being the case, he finds it necessary to surrender up a part of his property to furnish means for the 15

Thomas Paine, "Common Sense," in William M. Van der Weyde, ed., *The Life and Works of Thomas Paine*, "Patriot's Edition," Vol. 2 (New Rochelle, NY: Thomas Paine National Historical Association, 1925), 97–110, 114–22. Thomas Paine National Historical Association, New Rochelle, NY. www.thomaspaine.org.

protection of the rest; and this he is induced to do by the same prudence which in every other case advises him, out of two evils to choose the least. Wherefore, security being the true design and end of government, it unanswerably follows that whatever form thereof appears most likely to ensure it to us, with the least
5   expense and greatest benefit, is preferable to all others.

In order to gain a clear and just idea of the design and end of government, let us suppose a small number of persons settled in some sequestered part of the earth, unconnected with the rest; they will then represent the first peopling of any country, or of the world. In this state of natural liberty, society will be their
10   first thought. A thousand motives will excite them thereto; the strength of one man is so unequal to his wants, and his mind so unfitted for perpetual solitude, that he is soon obliged to seek assistance and relief of another, who in his turn requires the same. Four or five united would be able to raise a tolerable dwelling in the midst of a wilderness, but one man might labor out the common period
15   of life without accomplishing any thing; when he had felled his timber he could not remove it, nor erect it after it was removed; hunger in the mean time would urge him to quit his work, and every different want would call him a different way. Disease, nay even misfortune, would be death; for though neither might be mortal, yet either would disable him from living, and reduce him to a state
20   in which he might rather be said to perish than to die.

Thus necessity, like a gravitating power, would soon form our newly arrived emigrants into society, the reciprocal blessings of which would supercede, and render the obligations of law and government unnecessary while they remained perfectly just to each other; but as nothing but Heaven is impregnable to vice, it
25   will unavoidably happen that in proportion as they surmount the first difficulties of emigration, which bound them together in a common cause, they will begin to relax in their duty and attachment to each other; and this remissness will point out the necessity of establishing some form of government to supply the defect of moral virtue.

30   Some convenient tree will afford them a State House, under the branches of which the whole colony may assemble to deliberate on public matters. It is more than probable that their first laws will have the title only of regulations and be enforced by no other penalty than public disesteem. In this first parliament every man by natural right will have a seat.

35   But as the colony increases, the public concerns will increase likewise, and the distance at which the members may be separated, will render it too inconvenient for all of them to meet on every occasion as at first, when their number was small, their habitations near, and the public concerns few and

trifling. This will point out the convenience of their consenting to leave the legislative part to be managed by a select number chosen from the whole body, who are supposed to have the same concerns at stake which those have who appointed them, and who will act in the same manner as the whole body would act were they present. If the colony continue increasing, it will become   5 necessary to augment the number of representatives, and that the interest of every part of the colony may be attended to, it will be found best to divide the whole into convenient parts, each part sending its proper number: and that the *elected* might never form to themselves an interest separate from the *electors,* prudence will point out the propriety of having elections often: 10 because as the *elected* might by that means return and mix again with the general body of the *electors* in a few months, their fidelity to the public will be secured by the prudent reflection of not making a rod for themselves. And as this frequent interchange will establish a common interest with every part of the community, they will mutually and naturally support each other, and on   15 this, (not on the unmeaning name of king,) depends the *strength of government, and the happiness of the governed.*

Here then is the origin and rise of government; namely, a mode rendered necessary by the inability of moral virtue to govern the world; here too is the design and end of government, viz. freedom and security. And however our eyes   20 may be dazzled with show, or our ears deceived by sound; however prejudice may warp our wills, or interest darken our understanding, the simple voice of nature and reason will say, 'tis right.

I draw my idea of the form of government from a principle in nature which no art can overturn, viz. that the more simple any thing is, the less liable it is to be   25 disordered; and the easier repaired when disordered; and with this maxim in view I offer a few remarks on the so much boasted Constitution of England. That it was noble for the dark and slavish times in which it was erected, is granted. When the world was overrun with tyranny the least remove therefrom was a glorious rescue. But that it is imperfect, subject to convulsions, and incapable   30 of producing what it seems to promise, is easily demonstrated.

Absolute governments, (though the disgrace of human nature) have this advantage with them, they are simple; if the people suffer, they know the head from which their suffering springs; know likewise the remedy; and are not bewildered by a variety of causes and cures. But the Constitution of England is   35 so exceedingly complex, that the nation may suffer for years together without being able to discover in which part the fault lies; some will say in one and some in another, and every political physician will advise a different medicine.

I know it is difficult to get over local or long standing prejudices, yet if we will suffer ourselves to examine the component parts of the English Constitution, we shall find them to be the base remains of two ancient tyrannies, compounded with some new Republican materials.

5   *First.*—The remains of monarchical tyranny in the person of the king.

Secondly.—The remains of aristocratical tyranny in the persons of the peers.

Thirdly.—The new Republican materials, in the persons of the Commons, on whose virtue depends the freedom of England.

The two first, by being hereditary, are independent of the people; wherefore in a
10 *constitutional sense* they contribute nothing towards the freedom of the State.

To say that the Constitution of England is an *union* of three powers, reciprocally *checking* each other, is farcical; either the words have no meaning, or they are flat contradictions.

To say that the Commons is a check upon the king, presupposes two things.

15 *First.*—That the king is not to be trusted without being looked after; or in other words, that a thirst for absolute power is the natural disease of monarchy.

Secondly.—That the Commons, by being appointed for that purpose, are either wiser or more worthy of confidence than the crown.

But as the same constitution which gives the Commons a power to check the
20 king by withholding the supplies, gives afterwards the king a power to check the Commons, by empowering him to reject their other bills; it again supposes that the king is wiser than those whom it has already supposed to be wiser than him. A mere absurdity!

There is something exceedingly ridiculous in the composition of monarchy; it
25 first excludes a man from the means of information, yet empowers him to act in cases where the highest judgment is required. The state of a king shuts him from the world, yet the business of a king requires him to know it thoroughly; wherefore the different parts, by unnaturally opposing and destroying each other, prove the whole character to be absurd and useless.

30 Some writers have explained the English Constitution thus: the king, say they, is one, the people another; the peers are a house in behalf of the king, the Commons in behalf of the people; but this hath all the distinctions of a house divided against itself; and though the expressions be pleasantly arranged, yet when examined they appear idle and ambiguous; and it will always happen,
35 that the nicest construction that words are capable of, when applied to the

description of something which either cannot exist, or is too incomprehensible to be within the compass of description, will be words of sound only, and though they may amuse the ear, they cannot inform the mind: for this explanation includes a previous question, viz. *how came the king by a power which the people are afraid to trust, and always obliged to check?* Such a power could not be the gift of a wise people, neither can any power, *which needs checking,* be from God; yet the provision which the Constitution makes supposes such a power to exist.

But the provision is unequal to the task; the means either cannot or will not accomplish the end, and the whole affair is a *Felo de se*; for, as the greater weight will always carry up the less, and as all the wheels of a machine are put in motion by one, it only remains to know which power in the constitution has the most weight, for that will govern: and though the others, or a part of them, may clog, or, as the phrase is, check the rapidity of its motion, yet so long as they cannot stop it, their endeavors will be ineffectual: the first moving power will at last have its way, and what it wants in speed is supplied by time.

That the crown is this overbearing part in the English Constitution needs not be mentioned, and that it derives its whole consequence merely from being the giver of places and pensions is self-evident; wherefore, though we have been wise enough to shut and lock a door against absolute Monarchy, we at the same time have been foolish enough to put the crown in possession of the key.

The prejudice of Englishmen, in favor of their own government, by king, lords and Commons, arises as much or more from national pride than reason. Individuals are undoubtedly safer in England than in some other countries: but the will of the king is as much the law of the land in Britain as in France, with this difference, that instead of proceeding directly from his mouth, it is handed to the people under the formidable shape of an act of Parliament. For the fate of Charles the First hath only made kings more subtle—not more just.

Wherefore, laying aside all national pride and prejudice in favor of modes and forms, the plain truth is that *it is wholly owing to the constitution of the people, and not to the constitution of the government* that the crown is not as oppressive in England as in Turkey.

An inquiry into the *constitutional errors* in the English form of government, is at this time highly necessary; for as we are never in a proper condition of doing justice to others, while we continue under the influence of some leading partiality, so neither are we capable of doing it to ourselves while we remain fettered by any obstinate prejudice. And as a man who is attached to a prostitute is unfitted to choose or judge of a wife, so any prepossession in favor of a rotten constitution of government will disable us from discerning a good one.

OF MONARCHY AND HEREDITARY SUCCESSION

Mankind being originally equals in the order of creation, the equality could only be destroyed by some subsequent circumstance: the distinctions of rich and poor may in a great measure be accounted for, and that without having recourse to the harsh ill-sounding names of oppression and avarice. Oppression
5 is often the *consequence,* but seldom or never the *means* of riches; and though avarice will preserve a man from being necessitously poor, it generally makes him too timorous to be wealthy.

But there is another and greater distinction for which no truly natural or religious reason can be assigned, and that is the distinction of men into kings
10 and subjects. Male and female are the distinctions of nature, good and bad the distinctions of heaven; but how a race of men came into the world so exalted above the rest, and distinguished like some new species, is worth inquiring into, and whether they are the means of happiness or of misery to mankind.

In the early ages of the world, according to the scripture chronology there
15 were no kings; the consequence of which was, there were no wars; it is the pride of kings which throws mankind into confusion. Holland, without a king hath enjoyed more peace for this last century than any of the monarchical governments in Europe. Antiquity favors the same remark; for the quiet and rural lives of the first Patriarchs have a happy something in them, which vanishes
20 when we come to the history of Jewish royalty.

Government by kings was first introduced into the world by the heathens, from whom the children of Israel copied the custom. It was the most prosperous invention the devil ever set on foot for the promotion of idolatry. The heathens paid divine honors to their deceased kings, and the Christian world has
25 improved on the plan by doing the same to their living ones. How impious is the title of sacred majesty applied to a worm, who in the midst of his splendor is crumbling into dust!

As the exalting one man so greatly above the rest cannot be justified on the equal rights of nature, so neither can it be defended on the authority of scripture;
30 for the will of the Almighty as declared by Gideon, and the prophet Samuel, expressly disapproves of government by kings. All anti-monarchical parts of scripture, have been very smoothly glossed over in monarchical governments, but they undoubtedly merit the attention of countries which have their governments yet to form. *Render unto Caesar the things which are Caesar's,* is the scripture
35 doctrine of courts, yet it is no support of monarchical government, for the Jews at that time were without a king, and in a state of vassalage to the Romans.

Near three thousand years passed away, from the Mosaic account of the creation, till the Jews under a national delusion requested a king. Till then their form of government (except in extraordinary cases where the Almighty interposed) was a kind of Republic, administered by a judge and the elders of the tribes. Kings they had none, and it was held sinful to acknowledge any being under that title 5 but the Lord of Hosts. And when a man seriously reflects on the idolatrous homage which is paid to the persons of kings, he need not wonder that the Almighty, ever jealous of his honor, should disapprove a form of government which so impiously invades the prerogative of heaven....

These portions of scripture are direct and positive. They admit of no equiv- 10 ocal construction. That the Almighty hath here entered his protest against monarchical government is true, or the scripture is false. And a man hath good reason to believe that there is as much of kingcraft as priestcraft in withholding the scripture from the public in popish countries. For monarchy in every instance, is the popery of government. 15

To the evil of monarchy we have added that of hereditary succession; and as the first is a degradation and lessening of ourselves, so the second, claimed as a matter of right, is an insult and imposition on posterity. For all men being originally equals, no one by birth could have a right to set up his own family in perpetual preference to all others for ever, and though himself might deserve 20 some decent degree of honors of his cotemporaries, yet his descendants might be far too unworthy to inherit them. One of the strongest natural proofs of the folly of hereditary right in kings, is that nature disapproves it, otherwise she would not so frequently turn it into ridicule, by giving mankind an *ass for a lion*.

Secondly, as no man at first could possess any other public honors than were 25 bestowed upon him, so the givers of those honors could have no power to give away the right of posterity, and though they might say, "We choose you for our head," they could not without manifest injustice to their children say "that your children and your children's children shall reign over ours forever." Because such an unwise, unjust, unnatural compact might (perhaps) in the next succession 30 put them under the government of a rogue or a fool. Most wise men in their private sentiments have ever treated hereditary right with contempt; yet it is one of those evils which when once established is not easily removed: many submit from fear, others from superstition, and the more powerful part shares with the king the plunder of the rest. 35

This is supposing the present race of kings in the world to have had an honorable origin: whereas it is more than probable, that, could we take off the dark covering of antiquity and trace them to their first rise, we should find the

first of them nothing better than the principal ruffian of some restless gang; whose savage manners or pre-eminence in subtlety obtained him the title of chief among plunderers: and who by increasing in power and extending his depredations, overawed the quiet and defenceless to purchase their safety by
5   frequent contributions. Yet his electors could have no idea of giving hereditary right to his descendants, because such a perpetual exclusion of themselves was incompatible with the free and unrestrained principles they professed to live by. Wherefore, hereditary succession in the early ages of monarchy could not take place as a matter of claim, but as something casual or complemental; but as few
10   or no records were extant in those days, and traditionary history stuff'd with fables, it was very easy, after the lapse of a few generations, to trump up some superstitious tale conveniently timed . . . to cram hereditary right down the throats of the vulgar. Perhaps the disorders which threatened, or seemed to threaten, on the decease of a leader and the choice of a new one (for elections among ruffians
15   could not be very orderly) induced many at first to favor hereditary pretensions; by which means it happened, as it hath happened since, that what at first was submitted to as a convenience was afterwards claimed as a right.

England since the conquest hath known some few good monarchs, but groaned beneath a much larger number of bad ones; yet no man in his senses can say
20   that their claim under William the Conqueror is a very honorable one. A French bastard landing with an armed banditti and establishing himself king of England against the consent of the natives, is in plain terms a very paltry rascally original. It certainly hath no divinity in it. However it is needless to spend much time in exposing the folly of hereditary right; if there are any so weak as to believe
25   it, let them promiscuously worship the ass and the lion, and welcome. I shall neither copy their humility, nor disturb their devotion.

Yet I should be glad to ask how they suppose kings came at first? The question admits but of three answers, viz. either by lot, by election, or by usurpation. If the first king was taken by lot, it establishes a precedent for the next, which excludes
30   hereditary succession. Saul was by lot, yet the succession was not hereditary, neither does it appear from that transaction that there was any intention it ever should. If the first king of any country was by election, that likewise establishes a precedent for the next; for to say, that the right of all future generations is taken away, by the act of the first electors, in their choice not only of a king
35   but of a family of kings for ever, hath no parallel in or out of scripture but the doctrine of original sin, which supposes the free will of all men lost in Adam; and from such comparison, and it will admit of no other, hereditary succession can derive no glory. For as in Adam all sinned, and as in the first electors all men obeyed; as in the one all mankind were subjected to Satan, and in the other

to sovereignty; as our innocence was lost in the first, and our authority in the last; and as both disable us from reassuming some former state and privilege, it unanswerably follows that original sin and hereditary succession are parallels. Dishonorable rank! Inglorious connection! Yet the most subtle sophist cannot produce a juster simile.   5

As to usurpation, no man will be so hardy as to defend it; and that William the Conqueror was an usurper is a fact not to be contradicted. The plain truth is, that the antiquity of English monarchy will not bear looking into.

But it is not so much the absurdity as the evil of hereditary succession which concerns mankind. Did it insure a race of good and wise men it would have the   10
seal of divine authority, but as it opens a door to the *foolish,* the *wicked,* and the *improper,* it has in it the nature of oppression. Men who look upon themselves born to reign, and others to obey, soon grow insolent. Selected from the rest of mankind, their minds are early poisoned by importance; and the world they act in differs so materially from the world at large, that they have but little opportunity   15
of knowing its true interests, and when they succeed to the government are frequently the most ignorant and unfit of any throughout the dominions.

Another evil which attends hereditary succession is, that the throne is subject to be possessed by a minor at any age; all which time the regency acting under the cover of a king have every opportunity and inducement to betray their   20
trust. The same national misfortune happens when a king worn out with age and infirmity enters the last stage of human weakness. In both these cases the public becomes a prey to every miscreant who can tamper successfully with the follies either of age or infancy.

The most plausible plea which hath ever been offered in favor of hereditary   25
succession is, that it preserves a nation from civil wars; and were this true, it would be weighty; whereas it is the most barefaced falsity ever imposed upon mankind. The whole history of England disowns the fact. Thirty kings and two minors have reigned in that distracted kingdom since the conquest, in which time there has been (including the revolution) no less than eight civil wars and   30
nineteen rebellions. Wherefore instead of making for peace, it makes against it, and destroys the very foundation it seems to stand upon....

In short, monarchy and succession have laid (not this or that kingdom only) but the world in blood and ashes. 'Tis a form of government which the word of God bears testimony against, and blood will attend it.   35

If we inquire into the business of a king, we shall find that in some countries they may have none; and after sauntering away their lives without pleasure to themselves or advantage to the nation, withdraw from the scene, and leave their successors to tread the same idle round. In absolute monarchies, the whole weight of business civil and military lies on the king; the children of Israel in their request for a king urged this plea, "that he may judge us, and go out before us and fight our battles." But in countries where he is neither a judge nor a general, as in England, a man would be puzzled to know what *is* his business.

The nearer any government approaches to a Republic, the less business there is for a king. It is somewhat difficult to find a proper name for the government of England. Sir William Meredith calls it a Republic; but in its present state it is unworthy of the name, because the corrupt influence of the crown, by having all the places in its disposal, hath so effectually swallowed up the power, and eaten out the virtue of the House of Commons (the republican part in the Constitution) that the government of England is nearly as monarchical as that of France or Spain. Men fall out with names without understanding them. For 'tis the republican and not the monarchical part of the Constitution of England which Englishmen glory in, viz. the liberty of choosing an House of Commons from out of their own body—and it is easy to see that when republican virtues fail, slavery ensues. Why is the Constitution of England sickly, but because monarchy hath poisoned the Republic; the crown has engrossed the Commons.

In England a king hath little more to do than to make war and give away places; which, in plain terms, is to impoverish the nation and set it together by the ears. A pretty business indeed for a man to be allowed eight hundred thousand sterling a year for, and worshipped into the bargain! Of more worth is one honest man to society, and in the sight of God, than all the crowned ruffians that ever lived. . . .

Letter to Roger Weightman
Thomas Jefferson

Written just days before his death on July 4, 1826, this letter to the mayor of Washington, D.C., encapsulates the great cause of Thomas Jefferson's life.

June 24, 1826

Respected Sir:

The kind invitation I receive from you, on the part of the citizens of the city of Washington, to be present with them at their celebration on the fiftieth anniversary of American Independence, as one of the surviving signers of an instrument pregnant with our own, and the fate of the world, is most flattering to myself, and heightened by the honorable accompaniment proposed for   5
the comfort of such a journey. It adds sensibly to the sufferings of sickness, to be deprived by it of a personal participation in the rejoicings of that day. But acquiescence is a duty, under circumstances not placed among those we are permitted to control. I should, indeed, with peculiar delight, have met and exchanged there congratulations personally with the small band, the remnant of that host of worthies, who joined with us on that day, in the bold   10
and doubtful election we were to make for our country, between submission or the sword; and to have enjoyed with them the consolatory fact, that our fellow citizens, after half a century of experience and prosperity, continue to approve the choice we made. May it be to the world, what I believe it will be, (to some parts sooner, to others later, but finally to all,) the signal of arousing   15
men to burst the chains under which monkish ignorance and superstition had persuaded them to bind themselves, and to assume the blessings and security of self-government. That form which we have substituted, restores the free right to the unbounded exercise of reason and freedom of opinion. All eyes are opened, or opening, to the rights of man. The general spread of the light of science has   20
already laid open to every view the palpable truth, that the mass of mankind

---

Thomas Jefferson, "To Roger C. Weightman," June 24, 1826, in Paul Leicester Ford, ed., *The Works of Thomas Jefferson*, "Federal Edition," Vol. 10 (New York: G. P. Putnam's Sons, 1904–5), 390–92.

has not been born with saddles on their backs, nor a favored few booted and spurred, ready to ride them legitimately, by the grace of God. These are grounds of hope for others. For ourselves, let the annual return of this day forever refresh our recollections of these rights, and an undiminished devotion to them.

5   I will ask permission here to express the pleasure with which I should have met my ancient neighbors of the city of Washington and of its vicinities, with whom I passed so many years of a pleasing social intercourse; an intercourse which so much relieved the anxieties of the public cares, and left impressions so deeply engraved in my affections, as never to be forgotten. With my regret
10   that ill health forbids me the gratification of an acceptance, be pleased to receive for yourself, and those for whom you write, the assurance of my highest respect and friendly attachments.

III
THE FOUNDERS ON RELIGION, MORALITY, AND PROPERTY

"Almighty God hath created the mind free." Thus Thomas Jefferson begins the "Virginia Statute for Religious Freedom." The freedom of the human mind means that all individuals can choose between good and evil. The Founders believed that although human beings are capable of doing great good, they equally are capable of tremendous evil. In the words of Jefferson in the landmark Statute of 1786, all people, including rulers, are "but fallible and uninspired men." The theological conviction of early Americans was that all human beings are fallen; politically, this meant that all are fallible.

The political, religious, and moral framework of the founding started with the affirmation of a common, enduring, and immutable human nature. Human beings are admixtures of roiling passions and calming reason. Regardless of time, place, and social or economic status, all share the same propensity to pride and to evil. Despite these strong tendencies, man is not condemned to a mere animal existence. With careful cultivation of his soul, attention to "the laws of nature and of nature's God," and the uplifting assistance of family, church, and local community, human beings are able to tame their passions and act worthy of the "blessings of liberty."

As flawed but rational beings, humans should strive to let reason—a gift from God—rule their lives, the Founders urged, for with that rule comes the possibility of self-government. The implication for politics of this moral and religious conclusion is profound: Every person and every regime, or form of government, is imperfect and incapable of being perfected by mortal means.

The Founders concluded that we know the existence of human nature, natural law, and the mind's freedom not because we are members of any particular church or denomination, but because we are able as human beings to follow reason's path to these first principles. Reason's dictates are not opposed to those of revelation; on the contrary, the vital truths of human existence are affirmed by both reason and revelation.

Reason and revelation both counsel religious liberty. This principle, upheld by all of the American Founders, is among the most revolutionary tenets advanced in the history of ideas. Whereas throughout most of human history religious minorities had lived with the fear of political persecution, and religious toleration if established was put in place as a revocable policy, in America the *right* to religious liberty was established as a matter of principle. President George Washington expressed this new principle in a letter he sent in 1790 to the Hebrew Congregation of Newport, Rhode Island, included in this section.

Rights are the most precious possessions anyone may own. Our greatest property right, or claim to ownership, is found in our religious freedom, James Madison states in his 1792 article "On Property." Religion's role in social and political life is so important, Madison wrote in his "Memorial and Remonstrance Against Religious Assessments," that the religious liberties of all Americans— and all peoples everywhere—must be guarded with special vigilance.

Together, Madison and Jefferson were a powerful force for religious liberty. Working from the mid- to late-1770s until the adoption of the Virginia Statute of 1786, Madison and Jefferson waged an all-out assault on Virginia's establishment of the Anglican Church in what was the most pitched battle for religious liberty in American history. Their untiring work sought to establish the principle that no government in America could legitimately establish an official religion and compel taxpayers to support it to the exclusion of others.

If this conclusion about the sanctity of religious liberty calls to mind one of the most famous metaphors in American political and constitutional thought—"a wall of separation between church and state"—it is not because of the weight Jefferson himself placed upon the metaphor. Rather, the phrase, used by Jefferson in a letter in 1802, was freighted with enormous political and constitutional significance by the Supreme Court, which in the 1947 case *Everson* v. *Board of Education* transformed it into constitutional law.

For many Americans since then who have listened mainly to the Supreme Court for lessons about religious liberty, the wall separating church and state demands a strict separation of religion and politics. The Court's misreading of Jefferson's metaphor has contributed to a popular misunderstanding of politics, law, morality, and religion. This misreading is best corrected by allowing the Founders to speak for themselves, for their insistence upon religious liberty meant not the erection of a wall separating religion and politics, but the establishment of a principle that would let religion flourish.

David J. Bobb
Lecturer in Politics
Director, Allan P. Kirby, Jr. Center for
Constitutional Studies and Citizenship
Hillsdale College

VIRGINIA DECLARATION OF RIGHTS
GEORGE MASON (1725–1792)

The Virginia Declaration of Rights, a preamble to the Virginia Constitution drafted by George Mason, is—along with the Declaration of Independence that followed a month later—the clearest statement of the social contract theory of government found in major early American documents.

JUNE 12, 1776

A DECLARATION OF RIGHTS MADE BY THE REPRESENTATIVES OF THE GOOD PEOPLE OF VIRGINIA, ASSEMBLED IN FULL AND FREE CONVENTION; WHICH RIGHTS DO PERTAIN TO THEM AND THEIR POSTERITY, AS THE BASIS AND FOUNDATION OF GOVERNMENT.

SECTION 1. That all men are by nature equally free and independent, and have certain inherent rights, of which, when they enter into a state of society, they cannot, by any compact, deprive or divest their posterity; namely, the enjoyment of life and liberty, with the means of acquiring and possessing property, and pursuing and obtaining happiness and safety.   5

SECTION 2. That all power is vested in, and consequently derived from, the People; that magistrates are their trustees and servants, and at all times amenable to them.

SECTION 3. That Government is, or ought to be, instituted for the common benefit, protection, and security of the people, nation, or community;—of all the   10 various modes and forms of Government that is best which is capable of producing the greatest degree of happiness and safety, and is most effectually secured against the danger of mal-administration;—and that, whenever any Government shall be found inadequate or contrary to these purposes, a majority of the community hath an indubitable, unalienable, and indefeasible right, to reform, alter, or abolish it,   15 in such manner as shall be judged most conducive to the public weal.

George Mason, "Final Draft of the Virginia Declaration of Rights," from *The Papers of George Mason, 1727–1792*, edited by Robert A. Rutland and published in three volumes for the Omohundro Institute of Early American History and Culture. Copyright © 1970 by the University of North Carolina Press. Used by permission of the publisher. www.uncpress.unc.edu.

SECTION 4. That no man, or set of men, are entitled to exclusive or separate emoluments and privileges from the community, but in consideration of public services; which, not being descendible, neither ought the offices of Magistrate, Legislator, or Judge, to be hereditary.

5   SECTION 5. That the Legislative and Executive powers of the State should be separate and distinct from the Judicative; and, that the members of the two first may be restrained from oppression, by feeling and participating the burdens of the people, they should, at fixed periods, be reduced to a private station, return into that body from which they were originally taken, and the
10 vacancies be supplied by frequent, certain, and regular elections, in which all, or any part of the former members, to be again eligible, or ineligible, as the law shall direct.

SECTION 6. That elections of members to serve as Representatives of the people, in Assembly, ought to be free; and that all men, having sufficient evidence of
15 permanent common interest with, and attachment to, the community, have the right of suffrage, and cannot be taxed or deprived of their property for public uses without their own consent or that of their Representative so elected, nor bound by any law to which they have not, in like manner, assented, for the public good.

20 SECTION 7. That all power of suspending laws, or the execution of laws, by any authority, without consent of the Representatives of the people, is injurious to their rights, and ought not to be exercised.

SECTION 8. That in all capital or criminal prosecutions a man hath a right to demand the cause and nature of his accusation, to be confronted with the
25 accusers and witnesses, to call for evidence in his favor, and to a speedy trial by an impartial jury of his vicinage, without whose unanimous consent he cannot be found guilty, nor can he be compelled to give evidence against himself; that no man be deprived of his liberty except by the law of the land, or the judgment of his peers.

30 SECTION 9. That excessive bail ought not to be required, nor excessive fines imposed, nor cruel and unusual punishments inflicted.

SECTION 10. That general warrants, whereby any officer or messenger may be commanded to search suspected places without evidence of a fact committed, or to seize any person or persons not named, or whose offense is not particularly
35 described and supported by evidence, are grievous and oppressive, and ought not to be granted.

SECTION 11. That in controversies respecting property, and in suits between man and man, the ancient trial by Jury is preferable to any other, and ought to be held sacred.

SECTION 12. That the freedom of the Press is one of the greatest bulwarks of liberty, and can never be restrained but by despotic Governments.   5

SECTION 13. That a well-regulated Militia, composed of the body of the people, trained to arms, is the proper, natural, and safe defense of a free State; that Standing Armies, in time of peace, should be avoided as dangerous to liberty; and that, in all cases, the military should be under strict subordination to, and governed by, the civil power.   10

SECTION 14. That the people have a right to uniform Government; and, therefore, that no Government separate from, or independent of, the Government of *Virginia*, ought to be erected or established within the limits thereof.

SECTION 15. That no free Government, or the blessing of liberty, can be preserved to any people but by a firm adherence to justice, moderation, temperance,   15 frugality, and virtue, and by frequent recurrence to fundamental principles.

SECTION 16. That Religion, or the duty which we owe to our *Creator,* and the manner of discharging it, can be directed only by reason and conviction, not by force or violence; and, therefore, all men are equally entitled to the free exercise of religion, according to the dictates of conscience; and that it is the mutual duty   20 of all to practice Christian forbearance, love, and charity, towards each other.

FAST DAY PROCLAMATION OF THE CONTINENTAL CONGRESS

The petition of this Fast Day Proclamation was echoed repeatedly by Congresses in early American history.

DECEMBER 11, 1776

Whereas, the war in which the United States are engaged with Great Britain, has not only been prolonged, but is likely to be carried to the greatest extremity; and whereas, it becomes all public bodies, as well as private persons, to reverence the Providence of God, and look up to him as the supreme disposer of all events, and the arbiter of the fate of nations; therefore,   5

Resolved, That it be recommended to all the United States, as soon as possible, to appoint a day of solemn fasting and humiliation; to implore of Almighty God the forgiveness of the many sins prevailing among all ranks, and to beg the countenance and assistance of his Providence in the prosecution of the present just and necessary war.   10

The Congress do also, in the most earnest manner, recommend to all the members of the United States, and particularly the officers civil and military under them, the exercise of repentance and reformation; and further, require of them the strict observation of the articles of war, and particularly, that part of the said articles, which forbids profane swearing, and all immorality, of   15 which all such officers are desired to take notice.

It is left to each state to issue out proclamations fixing the days that appear most proper within their several bounds....

"Fast Day Proclamation of the Continental Congress," December 11, 1776, in Worthington C. Ford, Gaillard Hunt et al., eds., *The Journals of the Continental Congress, 1774–1789*, Vol. 6 (Washington, D.C.: Government Printing Office, 1904–37), 1022.

THE NORTHWEST ORDINANCE

Adopted by the Congress of the Confederation in 1787, the Northwest Ordinance set forth a model for the expansion of the American republic. Providing a governing structure for the territory that would later become Ohio, Indiana, Illinois, Michigan, and Wisconsin, it prohibited slavery, protected religious liberty, and encouraged education. Following the adoption of the Constitution, the new Congress passed the Northwest Ordinance again in 1789.

JULY 13,1787

An Ordinance for the government of the territory of the United States northwest of the river Ohio

SECTION 1. *Be it ordained by the United States in Congress assembled,* That the said territory, for the purpose of temporary government, be one district, subject, however, to be divided into two districts, as future circumstances may, in the opinion of Congress, make it expedient.

SECTION 2. *Be it ordained by the authority aforesaid,* That the estates both of resident and non-resident proprietors in the said territory, dying intestate, shall descend to, and be distributed among, their children and the descendants of a deceased child in equal parts, the descendants of a deceased child or grandchild to take the share of their deceased parent in equal parts among them; and where there shall be no children or descendants, then in equal parts to the next of kin, in equal degree; and among collaterals, the children of a deceased brother or sister of the intestate shall have, in equal parts among them, their deceased parent's share; and there shall, in no case, be a distinction between kindred of the whole and half blood; saving in all cases to the widow of the intestate, her third part of the real estate for life, and one-third part of the personal estate; and this law relative to descents and dower, shall remain in full force until altered by the legislature of the district. And until the governor and judges shall adopt laws as hereinafter mentioned, estates in the said territory may be devised or bequeathed by wills in writing, signed and sealed by him or her in whom the estate may

121

be, (being of full age,) and attested by three witnesses; and real estates may be conveyed by lease and release, or bargain and sale, signed, sealed, and delivered by the person, being of full age, in whom the estate may be, and attested by two witnesses, provided such wills be duly proved, and such conveyances be
5   acknowledged, or the execution thereof duly proved, and be recorded within one year after proper magistrates, courts, and registers, shall be appointed for that purpose; and personal property may be transferred by delivery, saving, however, to the French and Canadian inhabitants, and other settlers of the Kaskaskies, Saint Vincents, and the neighboring villages, who have heretofore
10   professed themselves citizens of Virginia, their laws and customs now in force among them, relative to the descent and conveyance of property.

SECTION 3. *Be it ordained by the authority aforesaid,* That there shall be appointed, from time to time, by Congress, a governor, whose commission shall continue in force for the term of three years, unless sooner revoked by Congress; he shall
15   reside in the district, and have a freehold estate therein, in one thousand acres of land, while in the exercise of his office.

SECTION 4. There shall be appointed from time to time, by Congress, a secretary, whose commission shall continue in force for four years, unless sooner revoked; he shall reside in the district, and have a freehold estate therein, in five hundred
20   acres of land, while in the exercise of his office. It shall be his duty to keep and preserve the acts and laws passed by the legislature, and the public records of the district, and the proceedings of the governor in his executive department, and transmit authentic copies of such acts and proceedings every six months to the Secretary of Congress. There shall also be appointed a court, to consist of
25   three judges, any two of whom to form a court, who shall have a common-law jurisdiction and reside in the district, and have each therein a freehold estate, in five hundred acres of land, while in the exercise of their offices; and their commissions shall continue in force during good behavior.

SECTION 5. The governor and judges, or a majority of them, shall adopt and
30   publish in the district such laws of the original States, criminal and civil, as may be necessary, and best suited to the circumstances of the district, and report them to Congress from time to time, which laws shall be in force in the district until the organization of the general assembly therein, unless disapproved of by Congress; but afterwards the legislature shall have authority to alter them
35   as they shall think fit.

SECTION 6. The governor, for the time being, shall be commander-in-chief of the militia, appoint and commission all officers in the same below the rank of general officers; all general officers shall be appointed and commissioned by Congress.

SECTION 7. Previous to the organization of the general assembly the governor shall appoint such magistrates, and other civil officers, in each county or township, as he shall find necessary for the preservation of the peace and good order in the same. After the general assembly shall be organized the powers and duties of magistrates and other civil officers shall be regulated and defined   5
by the said assembly; but all magistrates and other civil officers, not herein otherwise directed, shall, during the continuance of this temporary government, be appointed by the governor.

SECTION 8. For the prevention of crimes and injuries, the laws to be adopted or made shall have force in all parts of the district, and for the execution of process,   10
criminal and civil, the governor shall make proper divisions thereof; and he shall proceed, from time to time, as circumstances may require, to lay out the parts of the district in which the Indian titles shall have been extinguished, into counties and townships, subject, however, to such alterations as may thereafter be made by the legislature.   15

SECTION 9. So soon as there shall be five thousand free male inhabitants, of full age, in the district, upon giving proof thereof to the governor, they shall receive authority, with time and place, to elect representatives from their counties or townships, to represent them in the general assembly: *Provided,* That for every five hundred free male inhabitants there shall be one representative, and so   20
on, progressively, with the number of free male inhabitants, shall the right of representation increase, until the number of representatives shall amount to twenty-five; after which the number and proportion of representatives shall be regulated by the legislature: *Provided,* That no person be eligible or qualified to act as a representative, unless he shall have been a citizen of one of the United   25
States three years, and be a resident in the district, or unless he shall have resided in the district three years; and, in either case, shall likewise hold in his own right, in fee-simple, two hundred acres of land within the same: *Provided also,* That a freehold in fifty acres of land in the district, having been a citizen of one of the States, and being resident in the district, or the like freehold and   30
two years' residence in the district, shall be necessary to qualify a man as an elector of a representative.

SECTION 10. The representatives thus elected shall serve for the term of two years; and in case of the death of a representative, or removal from office, the governor shall issue a writ to the county or township, for which he was a member,   35
to elect another in his stead, to serve for the residue of the term.

SECTION 11. The general assembly or legislature shall consist of the governor, legislative council, and a house of representatives. The legislative council shall

consist of five members, to continue in office five years, unless sooner removed by Congress; any three of whom to be a quorum; and the members of the council shall be nominated and appointed in the following manner, to wit: As soon as representatives shall be elected the governor shall appoint a time and
5   place for them to meet together, and when met they shall nominate ten persons, resident in the district, and each possessed of a freehold in five hundred acres of land, and return their names to Congress, five of whom Congress shall appoint and commission to serve as aforesaid; and whenever a vacancy shall happen in the council, by death or removal from office, the house of representatives shall
10 nominate two persons, qualified as aforesaid, for each vacancy, and return their names to Congress, one of whom Congress shall appoint and commission for the residue of the term; and every five years, four months at least before the expiration of the time of service of the members of the council, the said house shall nominate ten persons, qualified as aforesaid, and return their names to
15 Congress, five of whom Congress shall appoint and commission to serve as members of the council five years, unless sooner removed. And the governor, legislative council, and house of representatives shall have authority to make laws in all cases for the good government of the district, not repugnant to the principles and articles in this ordinance established and declared. And all bills,
20 having passed by a majority in the house, and by a majority in the council, shall be referred to the governor for his assent; but no bill, or legislative act whatever, shall be of any force without his assent. The governor shall have power to convene, prorogue, and dissolve the general assembly when, in his opinion, it shall be expedient.

25 SECTION 12. The governor, judges, legislative council, secretary, and such other officers as Congress shall appoint in the district, shall take an oath or affirmation of fidelity, and of office; the governor before the President of Congress, and all other officers before the governor. As soon as a legislature shall be formed in the district, the council and house assembled, in one room, shall have authority, by
30 joint ballot, to elect a delegate to Congress, who shall have a seat in Congress with a right of debating, but not of voting, during this temporary government.

SECTION 13. And for extending the fundamental principles of civil and religious liberty, which form the basis whereon these republics, their laws and constitutions, are erected; to fix and establish those principles as the basis
35 of all laws, constitutions, and governments, which forever hereafter shall be formed in the said territory; to provide, also, for the establishment of States, and permanent government therein, and for their admission to a share in the Federal councils on an equal footing with the original States, at as early periods as may be consistent with the general interest:

SECTION 14. It is hereby ordained and declared, by the authority aforesaid, that the following articles shall be considered as articles of compact, between the original States and the people and States in the said territory, and forever remain unalterable, unless by common consent, to wit:

ARTICLE I

No person, demeaning himself in a peaceable and orderly manner, shall ever   5
be molested on account of his mode of worship, or religious sentiments, in the said territories.

ARTICLE II

The inhabitants of the said territory shall always be entitled to the benefits of the writs of *habeas corpus,* and of the trial by jury; of a proportionate representation of the people in the legislature, and of judicial proceedings according to the course of the common law. All persons shall be bailable, unless for capital   10
offenses, where the proof shall be evident, or the presumption great. All fines shall be moderate; and no cruel or unusual punishment shall be inflicted. No man shall be deprived of his liberty or property, but by the judgment of his peers, or the law of the land, and should the public exigencies make it necessary, for the common preservation, to take any person's property, or to demand his   15
particular services, full compensation shall be paid for the same. And, in the just preservation of rights and property, it is understood and declared, that no law ought ever to be made or have force in the said territory, that shall, in any manner whatever, interfere with or affect private contracts, or engagements, *bona fide,* and without fraud previously formed.   20

ARTICLE III

Religion, morality, and knowledge being necessary to good government and the happiness of mankind, schools and the means of education shall forever be encouraged. The utmost good faith shall always be observed towards the Indians; their lands and property shall never be taken from them without their consent; and in their property, rights, and liberty they never shall be invaded or disturbed   25
unless in just and lawful wars authorized by Congress; but laws founded in justice and humanity shall, from time to time, be made, for preventing wrongs being done to them, and for preserving peace and friendship with them.

ARTICLE IV

The said territory, and the States which may be formed therein, shall forever remain a part of this confederacy of the United States of America, subject   30
to the Articles of Confederation, and to such alterations therein as shall be constitutionally made; and to all the acts and ordinances of the United States

in Congress assembled, conformable thereto. The inhabitants and settlers in the said territory shall be subject to pay a part of the Federal debts, contracted, or to be contracted, and a proportional part of the expenses of government to be apportioned on them by Congress, according to the same common rule
5   and measure by which apportionments thereof shall be made on the other States; and the taxes for paying their proportion shall be laid and levied by the authority and direction of the legislatures of the district, or districts, or new States, as in the original States, within the time agreed upon by the United States in Congress assembled. The legislatures of those districts, or new States,
10   shall never interfere with the primary disposal of the soil by the United States in Congress assembled, nor with any regulations Congress may find necessary for securing the title in such soil to the *bona fide* purchasers. No tax shall be imposed on lands the property of the United States; and in no case shall non-resident proprietors be taxed higher than residents. The navigable waters leading
15   into the Mississippi and Saint Lawrence, and the carrying places between the same, shall be common highways, and forever free, as well to the inhabitants of the said territory as to the citizens of the United States, and those of any other States that may be admitted into the confederacy, without any tax, impost, or duty therefore.

ARTICLE V

20   There shall be formed in the said territory, not less than three nor more than five States; and the boundaries of the States, as soon as Virginia shall alter her act of cession and consent to the same, shall become fixed and established as follows, to wit: The western State, in the said territory, shall be bounded by the Mississippi, the Ohio, and the Wabash Rivers; a direct line drawn from
25   the Wabash and Post Vincents, due north, to the territorial line between the United States and Canada; and by the said territorial line to the Lake of the Woods and Mississippi. The middle State shall be bounded by the said direct line, the Wabash from Post Vincents to the Ohio, by the Ohio, by a direct line drawn due north from the mouth of the Great Miami to the said territorial
30   line, and by the said territorial line. The eastern State shall be bounded by the last-mentioned direct line, the Ohio, Pennsylvania, and the said territorial line: *Provided, however,* And it is further understood and declared, that the boundaries of these three States shall be subject so far to be altered, that, if Congress shall hereafter find it expedient, they shall have authority to form one or two States
35   in that part of the said territory which lies north of an east and west line drawn through the southerly bend or extreme of Lake Michigan. And whenever any of the said States shall have sixty thousand free inhabitants therein, such State shall be admitted by its delegates, into the Congress of the United States, on

an equal footing with the original States, in all respects whatever; and shall be at liberty to form a permanent constitution and State government: *Provided,* The constitution and government, so to be formed, shall be republican, and in conformity to the principles contained in these articles, and, so far as it can be consistent with the general interest of the confederacy, such admission shall   5 be allowed at an earlier period, and when there may be a less number of free inhabitants in the State than sixty thousand.

ARTICLE VI

There shall be neither slavery nor involuntary servitude in the said territory, otherwise than in the punishment of crimes, whereof the party shall have been duly convicted: *Provided always,* That any person escaping into the same, from   10 whom labor or service is lawfully claimed in any one of the original States, such fugitive may be lawfully reclaimed, and conveyed to the person claiming his or her labor or service as aforesaid.

Be it ordained by the authority aforesaid, That the resolutions of the twenty-third of April, 1784, relative to the subject of this ordinance, be, and the same are   15 hereby, repealed, and declared null and void.

Done by the United States, in Congress assembled, the thirteenth day of July, in the year of our Lord 1787, and of their sovereignty and independence the twelfth.

Memorial and Remonstrance against Religious Assessments
James Madison (1751–1836)

James Madison circulated the Memorial and Remonstrance anonymously in 1785 as part of the effort to pass the Virginia Statute for Religious Freedom. It appeals to Christian citizens by emphasizing that Christianity's own teachings preclude politically coerced support for particular sects, and to all citizens based on reason.

JUNE 20, 1785

To the Honorable the General Assembly of the Commonwealth of Virginia: A Memorial and Remonstrance

We the subscribers, citizens of the said Commonwealth, having taken into serious consideration, a Bill printed by order of the last Session of General Assembly, entitled "A Bill establishing a provision for Teachers of the Christian Religion," and conceiving that the same if finally armed with the sanctions of a law, will be a dangerous abuse of power, are bound as faithful members of a   5
free State to remonstrate against it, and to declare the reasons by which we are determined. We remonstrate against the said Bill,

1. Because we hold it for a fundamental and undeniable truth, "that Religion or the duty which we owe to our Creator and the manner of discharging it, can be directed only by reason and conviction, not by force or violence." The   10
Religion then of every man must be left to the conviction and conscience of every man; and it is the right of every man to exercise it as these may dictate. This right is in its nature an unalienable right. It is unalienable, because the opinions of men, depending only on the evidence contemplated by their own minds cannot follow the dictates of other men: It is unalienable also, because   15
what is here a right towards men, is a duty towards the Creator. It is the duty of every man to render to the Creator such homage and such only as he believes

James Madison, "To the Honorable the General Assembly of the Commonwealth of Virginia A Memorial and Remonstrance," June 20, 1785, in William T. Hutchinson et al., eds., *The Papers of James Madison*, Vol. 8 (Chicago: University of Chicago Press, 1962–present), 298–304. Reproduced with permission of University of Chicago Press–Books in the format Textbook via Copyright Clearance Center.

to be acceptable to him. This duty is precedent, both in order of time and in degree of obligation, to the claims of Civil Society. Before any man can be considered as a member of Civil Society, he must be considered as a subject of the Governor of the Universe: And if a member of Civil Society, who enters
5   into any subordinate Association, must always do it with a reservation of his duty to the General Authority; much more must every man who becomes a member of any particular Civil Society, do it with a saving of his allegiance to the Universal Sovereign. We maintain therefore that in matters of Religion, no mans right is abridged by the institution of Civil Society and that Religion
10   is wholly exempt from its cognizance. True it is, that no other rule exists, by which any question which may divide a Society, can be ultimately determined, but the will of the majority; but it is also true that the majority may trespass on the rights of the minority.

2. Because if Religion be exempt from the authority of the Society at large,
15   still less can it be subject to that of the Legislative Body. The latter are but the creatures and vicegerents of the former. Their jurisdiction is both derivative and limited: it is limited with regard to the coordinate departments, more necessarily is it limited with regard to the constituents. The preservation of a free Government requires not merely, that the metes and bounds which separate
20   each department of power be invariably maintained; but more especially that neither of them be suffered to overleap the great Barrier which defends the rights of the people. The Rulers who are guilty of such an encroachment, exceed the commission from which they derive their authority, and are Tyrants. The People who submit to it are governed by laws made neither by themselves nor by an
25   authority derived from them, and are slaves.

3. Because it is proper to take alarm at the first experiment on our liberties. We hold this prudent jealousy to be the first duty of Citizens, and one of the noblest characteristics of the late Revolution. The free men of America did not wait till usurped power had strengthened itself by exercise, and entangled the
30   question in precedents. They saw all the consequences in the principle, and they avoided the consequences by denying the principle. We revere this lesson too much soon to forget it. Who does not see that the same authority which can establish Christianity, in exclusion of all other Religions, may establish with the same ease any particular sect of Christians, in exclusion of all other Sects?
35   that the same authority which can force a citizen to contribute three pence only of his property for the support of any one establishment, may force him to conform to any other establishment in all cases whatsoever?

4. Because the Bill violates that equality which ought to be the basis of every law, and which is more indispensible, in proportion as the validity or expediency

of any law is more liable to be impeached. If "all men are by nature equally free and independent," all men are to be considered as entering into Society on equal conditions; as relinquishing no more, and therefore retaining no less, one than another, of their natural rights. Above all are they to be considered as retaining an "*equal* title to the free exercise of Religion according to the dictates of   5 Conscience." Whilst we assert for ourselves a freedom to embrace, to profess and to observe the Religion which we believe to be of divine origin, we cannot deny an equal freedom to those whose minds have not yet yielded to the evidence which has convinced us. If this freedom be abused, it is an offense against God, not against man: To God, therefore, not to man, must an account of it be rendered.   10 As the Bill violates equality by subjecting some to peculiar burdens, so it violates the same principle, by granting to others peculiar exemptions. Are the Quakers and Menonists the only sects who think a compulsive support of their Religions unnecessary and unwarrantable? Can their piety alone be entrusted with the care of public worship? Ought their Religions to be endowed above all others with   15 extraordinary privileges by which proselytes may be enticed from all others? We think too favorably of the justice and good sense of these denominations to believe that they either covet pre-eminences over their fellow citizens or that they will be seduced by them from the common opposition to the measure.

5. Because the Bill implies either that the Civil Magistrate is a competent Judge of   20 Religious Truth; or that he may employ Religion as an engine of Civil policy. The first is an arrogant pretension falsified by the contradictory opinions of Rulers in all ages, and throughout the world: the second an unhallowed perversion of the means of salvation.

6. Because the establishment proposed by the Bill is not requisite for the support   25 of the Christian Religion. To say that it is, is a contradiction to the Christian Religion itself, for every page of it disavows a dependence on the powers of this world: it is a contradiction to fact; for it is known that this Religion both existed and flourished, not only without the support of human laws, but in spite of every opposition from them, and not only during the period of miraculous   30 aid, but long after it had been left to its own evidence and the ordinary care of Providence. Nay, it is a contradiction in terms; for a Religion not invented by human policy, must have pre-existed and been supported, before it was established by human policy. It is moreover to weaken in those who profess this Religion a pious confidence in its innate excellence and the patronage of   35 its Author; and to foster in those who still reject it, a suspicion that its friends are too conscious of its fallacies to trust it to its own merits.

7. Because experience witnesseth that ecclesiastical establishments, instead of maintaining the purity and efficacy of Religion, have had a contrary operation.

During almost fifteen centuries has the legal establishment of Christianity been on trial. What have been its fruits? More or less in all places, pride and indolence in the Clergy, ignorance and servility in the laity, in both, superstition, bigotry and persecution. Inquire of the Teachers of Christianity for the ages in which
5   it appeared in its greatest lustre; those of every sect, point to the ages prior to its incorporation with Civil policy. Propose a restoration of this primitive State in which its Teachers depended on the voluntary rewards of their flocks, many of them predict its downfall. On which Side ought their testimony to have greatest weight, when for or when against their interest?

10   8. Because the establishment in question is not necessary for the support of Civil Government. If it be urged as necessary for the support of Civil Government only as it is a means of supporting Religion, and it be not necessary for the latter purpose, it cannot be necessary for the former. If Religion be not within the cognizance of Civil Government how can its legal establishment be necessary
15   to Civil Government? What influence in fact have ecclesiastical establishments had on Civil Society? In some instances they have been seen to erect a spiritual tyranny on the ruins of the Civil authority; in many instances they have been seen upholding the thrones of political tyranny: in no instance have they been seen the guardians of the liberties of the people. Rulers who wished to subvert
20   the public liberty, may have found an established Clergy convenient auxiliaries. A just Government instituted to secure and perpetuate it needs them not. Such a Government will be best supported by protecting every Citizen in the enjoyment of his Religion with the same equal hand which protects his person and his property; by neither invading the equal rights of any Sect, nor suffering
25   any Sect to invade those of another.

9. Because the proposed establishment is a departure from that generous policy, which, offering an Asylum to the persecuted and oppressed of every Nation and Religion, promised a luster to our country, and an accession to the number of its citizens. What a melancholy mark is the Bill of sudden degeneracy? Instead of
30   holding forth an Asylum to the persecuted, it is itself a signal of persecution. It degrades from the equal rank of Citizens all those whose opinions in Religion do not bend to those of the Legislative authority. Distant as it may be in its present form from the Inquisition, it differs from it only in degree. The one is the first step, the other the last in the career of intolerance. The magnanimous sufferer
35   under this cruel scourge in foreign Regions, must view the Bill as a Beacon on our Coast, warning him to seek some other haven, where liberty and philanthrophy in their due extent, may offer a more certain repose from his Troubles.

10. Because it will have a like tendency to banish our Citizens. The allurements presented by other situations are every day thinning their number. To superadd

a fresh motive to emigration by revoking the liberty which they now enjoy, would be the same species of folly which has dishonored and depopulated flourishing kingdoms.

11. Because it will destroy that moderation and harmony which the forbearance of our laws to intermeddle with Religion has produced among its several sects. Torrents of blood have been spilt in the old world, by vain attempts of the secular arm, to extinguish Religious discord, by proscribing all difference in Religious opinion. Time has at length revealed the true remedy. Every relaxation of narrow and rigorous policy, wherever it has been tried, has been found to assuage the disease. The American Theater has exhibited proofs that equal and complete liberty, if it does not wholly eradicate it, sufficiently destroys its malignant influence on the health and prosperity of the State. If with the salutary effects of this system under our own eyes, we begin to contract the bounds of Religious freedom, we know no name that will too severely reproach our folly. At least let warning be taken at the first fruits of the threatened innovation. The very appearance of the Bill has transformed "that Christian forbearance, love and charity," which of late mutually prevailed, into animosities and jealousies, which may not soon be appeased. What mischiefs may not be dreaded, should this enemy to the public quiet be armed with the force of a law?

12. Because the policy of the Bill is adverse to the diffusion of the light of Christianity. The first wish of those who enjoy this precious gift ought to be that it may be imparted to the whole race of mankind. Compare the number of those who have as yet received it with the number still remaining under the dominion of false Religions; and how small is the former! Does the policy of the Bill tend to lessen the disproportion? No; it at once discourages those who are strangers to the light of revelation from coming into the Region of it; and countenances by example the nations who continue in darkness, in shutting out those who might convey it to them. Instead of Levelling as far as possible, every obstacle to the victorious progress of Truth, the Bill with an ignoble and unchristian timidity would circumscribe it with a wall of defense against the encroachments of error.

13. Because attempts to enforce by legal sanctions, acts obnoxious to so great a proportion of Citizens, tend to enervate the laws in general, and to slacken the bands of Society. If it be difficult to execute any law which is not generally deemed necessary or salutary, what must be the case, where it is deemed invalid and dangerous? And what may be the effect of so striking an example of impotency in the Government, on its general authority?

14. Because a measure of such singular magnitude and delicacy ought not to be imposed, without the clearest evidence that it is called for by a majority of

citizens, and no satisfactory method is yet proposed by which the voice of the majority in this case may be determined, or its influence secured. "The people of the respective counties are indeed requested to signify their opinion respecting the adoption of the Bill to the next Session of Assembly." But the representation

5 must be made equal, before the voice either of the Representatives or of the Counties will be that of the people. Our hope is that neither of the former will, after due consideration, espouse the dangerous principle of the Bill. Should the event disappoint us, it will still leave us in full confidence, that a fair appeal to the latter will reverse the sentence against our liberties.

10 15. Because finally, "the equal right of every citizen to the free exercise of his Religion according to the dictates of conscience" is held by the same tenure with all our other rights. If we recur to its origin, it is equally the gift of nature; if we weigh its importance, it cannot be less dear to us; if we consult the "Declaration of those rights which pertain to the good people of Virginia, as the basis and

15 foundation of Government," it is enumerated with equal solemnity, or rather studied emphasis. Either then, we must say, that the Will of the Legislature is the only measure of their authority; and that in the plenitude of this authority, they may sweep away all our fundamental rights; or, that they are bound to leave this particular right untouched and sacred: Either we must say, that they may

20 control the freedom of the press, may abolish the Trial by Jury, may swallow up the Executive and Judiciary Powers of the State; nay that they may despoil us of our very right of suffrage, and erect themselves into an independent and hereditary Assembly or, we must say, that they have no authority to enact into law the Bill under consideration. We the Subscribers say, that the General

25 Assembly of this Commonwealth have no such authority: And that no effort may be omitted on our part against so dangerous an usurpation, we oppose to it, this remonstrance; earnestly praying, as we are in duty bound, that the Supreme Lawgiver of the Universe, by illuminating those to whom it is addressed, may on the one hand, turn their Councils from every act which would affront his

30 holy prerogative, or violate the trust committed to them: and on the other, guide them into every measure which may be worthy of his blessing, may redound to their own praise, and may establish more firmly the liberties, the prosperity and the happiness of the Commonwealth.

VIRGINIA STATUTE FOR
RELIGIOUS FREEDOM
THOMAS JEFFERSON

Thomas Jefferson asked to be remembered on his tombstone as author of the Declaration of Independence, father of the University of Virginia, and author of this law. Long delayed because of the contentiousness of the subject and the powerful interests arrayed against it, the Virginia Statute was drafted in 1777, introduced as a bill in the 1779 legislative session, and adopted in 1786. Eventually the laws of all thirteen originial states would prohibit an established church and guarantee religious liberty to all.

JANUARY 16, 1786

I. *Well aware that the opinions and belief of men depend not on their own will but follow involuntarily the evidence proposed to their minds; that* Almighty God hath created the mind free; *and manifested his supreme will that free it shall remain by making it altogether insusceptible of restraint;* that all attempts to influence it by temporal punishments, or burdens, or by civil incapacitations, tend only to beget 5 habits of hypocrisy and meanness, and are a departure from the plan of the holy author of our religion, who being lord both of body and mind, yet chose not to propagate it by coercions on either, as was in his Almighty power to do *but to extend it by its influence on reason alone*; that the impious presumption of legislators and rulers, civil as well as ecclesiastical, who, being themselves but fallible and 10 uninspired men, have assumed dominion over the faith of others, setting up their own opinions and modes of thinking as the only true and infallible, and as such endeavoring to impose them on others, hath established and maintained false religions over the greatest part of the world and through all time: That to compel a man to furnish contributions of money for the propagation of opinions which 15 he disbelieves *and abhors*, is sinful and tyrannical; that even the forcing him to support this or that teacher of his own religious persuasion, is depriving him of the comfortable liberty of giving his contributions to the particular pastor whose morals he would make his pattern, and whose powers he feels most persuasive to

Thomas Jefferson, "A Bill for Establishing Religious Freedom," in Julian P. Boyd, ed., *The Papers of Thomas Jefferson*, Vol. 2 (Princeton, NJ: Princeton University Press, 1950–1992), 545–47.

righteousness and is withdrawing from the ministry those temporary rewards, which proceeding from an approbation of their personal conduct, are an additional incitement to earnest and unremitting labors for the instruction of mankind; that our civil rights have no dependence on our religious opinions, any more than

5   our opinions in physics or geometry; that therefore the proscribing any citizen as unworthy the public confidence by laying upon him an incapacity of being called to offices of trust and emolument, unless he profess or renounce this or that religious opinion, is depriving him injuriously of those privileges and advantages to which, in common with his fellow citizens, he has a natural right; that it tends

10   also to corrupt the principles of that religion it is meant to encourage, by bribing, with a monopoly of worldly honors and emoluments, those who will externally profess and conform to it; that though indeed these are criminal who do not withstand such temptation, yet neither are those innocent who lay the bait in their way *that the opinions of men are not the object of civil government, nor under*

15   *its jurisdiction*; that to suffer the civil magistrate to intrude his powers into the field of opinion and to restrain the profession or propagation of principles on supposition of their ill tendency is a dangerous fallacy, which at once destroys all religious liberty, because he being of course judge of that tendency will make his opinions the rule of judgement, and approve or condemn the sentiments of

20   others only as they shall square with or differ from his own; that it is time enough for the rightful purposes of civil government for its officers to interfere when principles break out into overt acts against peace and good order; and finally, that truth is great and will prevail if left to herself; that she is the proper and sufficient antagonist to error, and has nothing to fear from the conflict unless by human

25   interposition disarmed of her natural weapons, free argument and debate; errors ceasing to be dangerous when it is permitted freely to contradict them.

II. *We the General Assembly of Virginia do enact,* that no man shall be compelled to frequent or support any religious worship, place, or ministry whatsoever, nor shall be enforced, restrained, molested, or burdened in his body or goods, nor

30   shall otherwise suffer, on account of his religious opinions or belief; but that all men shall be free to profess, and by argument to maintain, their opinions in matters of religion, and that the same shall in no wise diminish, enlarge, or affect their civil capacities.

And though we well know that this Assembly, elected by the people for the

35   ordinary purposes of legislation only, have no power to restrain the acts of succeeding Assemblies, constituted with powers equal to our own, and that therefore to declare this act to be irrevocable would be of no effect in law; yet we are free to declare, and do declare, that the rights hereby asserted are of the natural rights of mankind, and that if any act shall be hereafter passed to repeal the present

40   or to narrow its operation, such act will be an infringement of natural right.

LETTER TO THE
HEBREW CONGREGATION
GEORGE WASHINGTON (1732–1799)

The Constitution of 1787 said little directly about religion, with the notable exception of a ban on religious tests as a requirement for federal office. When George Washington was elected president, the Bill of Rights had not yet been adopted. Despite this, in his response to a congratulatory note sent to him by a group of Jewish Americans, President Washington characterized religious liberty not as a gift of government or a matter of toleration, but as a natural right possessed by every human being.

AUGUST 18, 1790

GENTLEMEN:

While I receive, with much satisfaction, your Address replete with expressions of esteem; I rejoice in the opportunity of assuring you, that I shall always retain grateful remembrance of the cordial welcome I experienced in my visit to New-port, from all classes of Citizens.

The reflection on the days of difficulty and danger which are past is rendered the   5
more sweet, from a consciousness that they are succeeded by days of uncommon prosperity and security. If we have wisdom to make the best use of the advantages with which we are now favored, we cannot fail, under the just administration of a good Government, to become a great and happy people.

The Citizens of the United States of America have a right to applaud themselves   10
for having given to mankind examples of an enlarged and liberal policy: a policy worthy of imitation. All possess alike liberty of conscience and immunities of citizenship. It is now no more that toleration is spoken of, as if it was by the indulgence of one class of people, that another enjoyed the exercise of their inherent natural rights. For happily the Government of the United States, which   15
gives to bigotry no sanction, to persecution no assistance requires only that they

George Washington, "To the Hebrew Congregation in Newport, Rhode Island," August 18, 1790, in W. W. Abbot et al., eds., *The Papers of George Washington, 1748–1799,* "Presidential Series," Vol. 6 (Charlottesville, VA: University of Virginia Press, 1976–present), 284–85.

who live under its protection should demean themselves as good citizens, in giving it on all occasions their effectual support.

It would be inconsistent with the frankness of my character not to avow that I am pleased with your favorable opinion of my Administration and fervent wishes for my felicity. May the Children of the Stock of Abraham, who dwell in this land, continue to merit and enjoy the good will of the other Inhabitants; while every one shall sit in safety under his own vine and figtree, and there shall be none to make him afraid. May the father of all mercies scatter light and not darkness in our paths, and make us all in our several vocations useful here, and in his own due time and way everlastingly happy.

GEORGE WASHINGTON

FAREWELL ADDRESS
GEORGE WASHINGTON

George Washington had first prepared a farewell address to be delivered in 1792, upon the conclusion of his first term as president. Having been convinced to stand for a second term, he was unanimously re-elected. When he finally issued this address in 1796, it was his last public work. After nearly forty-five years of service, he retired to Mount Vernon.

SEPTEMBER 19, 1796

FRIENDS, AND FELLOW CITIZENS:

The period for a new election of a Citizen, to Administer the Executive government of the United States, being not far distant, and the time actually arrived, when your thoughts must be employed in designating the person, who is to be clothed with that important trust, it appears to me proper, especially as it may conduce to a more distinct expression of the public voice, that I should   5
now apprise you of the resolution I have formed, to decline being considered among the number of those, out of whom a choice is to be made.

I beg you, at the same time, to do me the justice to be assured, that this resolution has not been taken, without a strict regard to all the considerations appertaining to the relation, which binds a dutiful citizen to his country, and   10
that, in withdrawing the tender of service which silence in my situation might imply, I am influenced by no diminution of zeal for your future interest, no deficiency of grateful respect for your past kindness; but am supported by a full conviction that the step is compatible with both.

The acceptance of, and continuance hitherto in, the office to which your Suf-   15
frages have twice called me, have been a uniform sacrifice of inclination to the opinion of duty, and to a deference for what appeared to be your desire.

George Washington, "Farewell Address," September 19, 1796, in W. B. Allen, ed., *George Washington: A Collection* (Indianapolis, IN: Liberty Fund, 1988), 512–17. This material appears on the Online Library of Liberty [http://app.libraryof liberty.org] hosted by Liberty Fund, Inc.

I constantly hoped, that it would have been much earlier in my power, consistently with motives, which I was not at liberty to disregard, to return to that retirement, from which I had been reluctantly drawn. The strength of my inclination to do this, previous to the last Election, had even led to the
5   preparation of an address to declare it to you; but mature reflection on the then perplexed and critical posture of our Affairs with foreign Nations, and the unanimous advice of persons entitled to my confidence, impelled me to abandon the idea.

I rejoice, that the state of your concerns, external as well as internal, no longer
10 renders the pursuit of inclination incompatible with the sentiment of duty, or propriety; and am persuaded whatever partiality may be retained for my services, that in the present circumstances of our country, you will not disapprove my determination to retire.

The impressions, with which I first undertook the arduous trust, were ex-
15 plained on the proper occasion. In the discharge of this trust, I will only say, that I have, with good intentions, contributed towards the Organization and Administration of the government, the best exertions of which a very fallible judgment was capable. Not unconscious, in the outset, of the inferiority of my qualifications, experience in my own eyes, perhaps still more in the eyes
20 of others, has strengthened the motives to diffidence of myself; and every day the increasing weight of years admonishes me more and more, that the shade of retirement is as necessary to me as it will be welcome. Satisfied that if any circumstances have given peculiar value to my services, they were temporary, I have the consolation to believe, that while choice and prudence invite me to
25 quit the political scene, patriotism does not forbid it.

In looking forward to the moment, which is intended to terminate the career of my public life, my feelings do not permit me to suspend the deep acknowledgment of that debt of gratitude which I owe to my beloved country, for the many honors it has conferred upon me; still more for the steadfast con-
30 fidence with which it has supported me; and for the opportunities I have thence enjoyed of manifesting my inviolable attachment, by services faithful and persevering, though in usefulness unequal to my zeal. If benefits have resulted to our country from these services, let it always be remembered to your praise, and as an instructive example in our annals, that, under circumstances
35 in which the Passions agitated in every direction were liable to mislead, amidst appearances sometimes dubious, vicissitudes of fortune often discouraging, in situations in which not unfrequently want of Success has countenanced the spirit of criticism, the constancy of your support was the essential prop of the efforts, and a guarantee of the plans by which they were effected. Profoundly

penetrated with this idea, I shall carry it with me to my grave, as a strong incitement to unceasing vows that Heaven may continue to you the choicest
tokens of its beneficence; that your Union and brotherly affection may be
perpetual; that the free constitution, which is the work of your hands, may
be sacredly maintained; that its Administration in every department may be   5
stamped with wisdom and Virtue; that, in fine, the happiness of the people of
these States, under the auspices of liberty, may be made complete, by so careful
a preservation and so prudent a use of this blessing as will acquire to them the
glory of recommending it to the applause, the affection, and adoption of every
nation which is yet a stranger to it.   10

Here, perhaps, I ought to stop. But a solicitude for your welfare, which cannot end but with my life, and the apprehension of danger, natural to that
solicitude, urge me on an occasion like the present, to offer to your solemn
contemplation, and to recommend to your frequent review, some sentiments;
which are the result of much reflection, of no inconsiderable observation, and   15
which appear to me all important to the permanency of your felicity as a
People. These will be offered to you with the more freedom, as you can only
see in them the disinterested warnings of a parting friend, who can possibly
have no personal motive to bias his counsel. Nor can I forget, as an encouragement to it, your indulgent reception of my sentiments on a former and not   20
dissimilar occasion.

Interwoven as is the love of liberty with every ligament of your hearts, no recommendation of mine is necessary to fortify or confirm the attachment.

The Unity of Government which constitutes you one people is also now dear
to you. It is justly so; for it is a main Pillar in the Edifice of your real indepen-   25
dence, the support of your tranquility at home; your peace abroad; of your
safety; of your prosperity; of that very Liberty which you so highly prize. But
as it is easy to foresee, that from different causes and from different quarters,
much pains will be taken, many artifices employed, to weaken in your minds
the conviction of this truth; as this is the point in your political fortress against   30
which the batteries of internal and external enemies will be most constantly
and actively (though often covertly and insidiously) directed, it is of infinite
moment, that you should properly estimate the immense value of your national Union to your collective and individual happiness; that you should cherish
a cordial, habitual, and immoveable attachment to it; accustoming yourselves   35
to think and speak of it as of the Palladium of your political safety and prosperity; watching for its preservation with jealous anxiety; discountenancing
whatever may suggest even a suspicion that it can in any event be abandoned,
and indignantly frowning upon the first dawning of every attempt to alienate

any portion of our Country from the rest, or to enfeeble the sacred ties which now link together the various parts.

For this you have every inducement of sympathy and interest. Citizens by birth or choice, of a common country, that country has a right to concentrate
5   your affections. The name of American, which belongs to You, in your national capacity, must always exalt the just pride of Patriotism, more than any appellation derived from local discriminations. With slight shades of difference, you have the same Religion, Manners, Habits and political Principles. You have in a common cause fought and triumphed together. The independence and
10   liberty you possess are the work of joint councils, and joint efforts; of common dangers, sufferings and successes.

But these considerations, however powerfully they address themselves to your sensibility are greatly outweighed by those which apply more immediately to your Interest. Here every portion of our country finds the most commanding
15   motives for carefully guarding and preserving the Union of the whole.

The *North,* in an unrestrained intercourse with the *South,* protected by the equal Laws of a common government, finds in the productions of the latter, great additional resources of Maritime and commercial enterprise and precious materials of manufacturing industry. The *South* in the same Intercourse,
20   benefitting by the Agency of the *North,* sees its agriculture grow and its commerce expand. Turning partly into its own channels the seamen of the *North,* it finds its particular navigation envigorated; and while it contributes, in different ways, to nourish and increase the general mass of the National navigation, it looks forward to the protection of a Maritime strength, to which itself is
25   unequally adapted. The *East,* in a like intercourse with the *West,* already finds, and in the progressive improvement of interior communications, by land and water, will more and more find, a valuable vent for the commodities which it brings from abroad, or manufactures at home. The *West* derives from the *East* supplies requisite to its growth and comfort, and what is perhaps of still greater
30   consequence, it must of necessity owe the *secure* enjoyment of indispensable *outlets* for its own productions to the weight, influence, and the future Maritime strength of the Atlantic side of the Union, directed by an indissoluble community of interest as *one Nation.* Any other tenure by which the *West* can hold this essential advantage, whether derived from its own separate strength,
35   or from an apostate and unnatural connection with any foreign Power, must be intrinsically precarious.

While then every part of our country thus feels an immediate and particular Interest in Union, all the parts combined cannot fail to find in the united mass

of means and efforts greater strength, greater resource, proportionably greater security from external danger, a less frequent interruption of their Peace
by foreign Nations; and, what is of inestimable value! they must derive from
Union an exemption from those broils and Wars between themselves, which
so frequently afflict neighboring countries, not tied together by the same gov-   5
ernment; which their own rivalships alone would be sufficient to produce, but
which opposite foreign alliances, attachments, and intrigues would stimulate
and embitter. Hence likewise they will avoid the necessity of those overgrown
Military establishments, which under any form of Government are inauspi-
cious to liberty, and which are to be regarded as particularly hostile to Repub-   10
lican Liberty: In this sense it is, that your Union ought to be considered as a
main prop of your liberty, and that the love of the one ought to endear to you
the preservation of the other.

These considerations speak a persuasive language to every reflecting and virtuous mind, and exhibit the continuance of the Union as a primary object of   15
Patriotic desire. Is there a doubt whether a common government can embrace
so large a sphere? Let experience solve it. To listen to mere speculation in such
a case were criminal. We are authorized to hope that a proper organization of
the whole, with the auxiliary agency of governments for the respective Subdivisions, will afford a happy issue to the experiment. 'Tis well worth a fair and   20
full experiment. With such powerful and obvious motives to Union, affecting
all parts of our country, while experience shall not have demonstrated its impracticability, there will always be reason, to distrust the patriotism of those,
who in any quarter may endeavor to weaken its bands.

In contemplating the causes which may disturb our Union, it occurs as matter   25
of serious concern, that any ground should have been furnished for character-
izing parties by *Geographical* discriminations: *Northern* and *Southern—Atlantic* and W*estern;* whence designing men may endeavor to excite a belief that
there is a real difference of local interests and views. One of the expedients of
Party to acquire influence, within particular districts, is to misrepresent the   30
opinions and aims of other Districts. You cannot shield yourselves too much
against the jealousies and heart burnings which spring from these misrepresentations. They tend to render Alien to each other those who ought to be
bound together by fraternal affection. The inhabitants of our Western country
have lately had a useful lesson on this head. They have seen, in the Negotia-   35
tion by the Executive; and in the unanimous ratification by the Senate, of
the Treaty with Spain, and in the universal satisfaction at that event throughout the United States, a decisive proof how unfounded were the suspicions
propagated among them of a policy in the General Government and in the

Atlantic States unfriendly to their interests [in] regard to the Mississippi. They have been witnesses to the formation of two Treaties, that with Great Britain and that with Spain, which secure to them every thing they could desire, in respect to our Foreign relations, towards confirming their prosperity. Will it
5 not be their wisdom to rely for the preservation of these advantages on the Union by which they were procured? Will they not henceforth be deaf to those advisers, if such there are, who would sever them from their Brethren and connect them with Aliens?

To the efficacy and permanency of your Union, a Government for the whole
10 is indispensable. No alliances however strict between the parts can be an adequate substitute. They must inevitably experience the infractions and interruptions which all Alliances in all times have experienced. Sensible of this momentous truth, you have improved upon your first essay, by the adoption of a Constitution of Government, better calculated than your former for an
15 intimate Union, and for the efficacious management of your common concerns. This government, the offspring of our own choice uninfluenced and unawed, adopted upon full investigation and mature deliberation, completely free in its principles, in the distribution of its powers, uniting security with energy, and containing within itself a provision for its own amendment, has a
20 just claim to your confidence and your support. Respect for its authority, compliance with its Laws, acquiescence in its measures, are duties enjoined by the fundamental maxims of true Liberty. The basis of our political systems is the right of the people to make and to alter their Constitutions of Government. But the Constitution which at any time exists, 'til changed by an explicit and
25 authentic act of the whole People, is sacredly obligatory upon all. The very idea of the power and the right of the People to establish Government presupposes the duty of every Individual to obey the established Government.

All obstructions to the execution of the Laws, all combinations and Associations, under whatever plausible character, with the real design to direct, con-
30 trol, counteract, or awe the regular deliberation and action of the Constituted authorities, are destructive of this fundamental principle and of fatal tendency. They serve to organize faction, to give it an artificial and extraordinary force; to put in the place of the delegated will of the nation, the will of a party; often a small but artful and enterprising minority of the Community; and,
35 according to the alternate triumphs of different parties, to make the public administration the Mirror of the ill-concerted and incongruous projects of faction, rather than the organ of consistent and wholesome plans digested by common councils and modified by mutual interests. However combinations or Associations of the above description may now and then answer popu-

lar ends, they are likely, in the course of time and things, to become potent engines, by which cunning, ambitious and unprincipled men will be enabled to subvert the Power of the People, and to usurp for themselves the reins of Government; destroying afterwards the very engines which have lifted them to unjust dominion.   5

Towards the preservation of your Government and the permanency of your present happy state, it is requisite, not only that you steadily discountenance irregular oppositions to its acknowledged authority, but also that you resist with care the spirit of innovation upon its principles however specious the pretexts. One method of assault may be to effect, in the forms of the Con-   10 stitution, alterations which will impair the energy of the system, and thus to undermine what cannot be directly overthrown. In all the changes to which you may be invited, remember that time and habit are at least as necessary to fix the true character of Governments, as of other human institutions; that experience is the surest standard, by which to test the real tendency of the   15 existing Constitution of a country; that facility in changes upon the credit of mere hypotheses and opinion exposes to perpetual change, from the endless variety of hypotheses and opinion, and remember, especially, that for the efficient management of your common interests, in a country so extensive as ours, a Government of as much vigor as is consistent with the perfect secu-   20 rity of Liberty is indispensable. Liberty itself will find in such a Government, with powers properly distributed and adjusted, its surest Guardian. It is indeed little else than a name, where the Government is too feeble to withstand the enterprises of faction, to confine each member of the Society within the limits prescribed by the Laws, and to maintain all in the secure and tranquil enjoy-   25 ment of the rights of person and property.

I have already intimated to you the danger of Parties in the State, with particular reference to the founding of them on Geographical discriminations. Let me now take a more comprehensive view, and warn you in the most solemn manner against the baneful effects of the Spirit of Party, generally.   30

This spirit, unfortunately, is inseparable from our nature, having its root in the strongest passions of the human Mind. It exists under different shapes in all Governments, more or less stifled, controlled, or repressed; but, in those of the popular form, it is seen in its greatest rankness and is truly their worst enemy.   35

The alternate domination of one faction over another, sharpened by the spirit of revenge natural to party dissention, which in different ages and countries has perpetrated the most horrid enormities, is itself a frightful despotism. But

this leads at length to a more formal and permanent despotism. The disorders and miseries, which result, gradually incline the minds of men to seek security and repose in the absolute power of an Individual; and sooner or later the chief of some prevailing faction more able or more fortunate than his competitors,
5   turns this disposition to the purposes of his own elevation, on the ruins of Public Liberty.

Without looking forward to an extremity of this kind (which nevertheless ought not to be entirely out of sight) the common and continual mischiefs of the spirit of Party are sufficient to make it the interest and the duty of a wise
10   People to discourage and restrain it.

It serves always to distract the Public Councils and enfeeble the Public administration. It agitates the Community with ill-founded jealousies and false alarms, kindles the animosity of one part against another, foments occasionally riot and insurrection. It opens the door to foreign influence and corruption, which find
15   a facilitated access to the government itself through the channels of party passions. Thus the policy and the will of one country, are subjected to the policy and will of another.

There is an opinion that parties in free countries are useful checks upon the Administration of the government and serve to keep alive the spirit of Liberty.
20   This within certain limits is probably true, and in Governments of a Monarchical cast Patriotism may look with indulgence, if not with favor, upon the spirit of party. But in those of the popular character, in Governments purely elective, it is a spirit not to be encouraged. From their natural tendency, it is certain there will always be enough of that spirit for every salutary purpose.
25   And there being constant danger of excess, the effort ought to be, by force of public opinion to mitigate and assuage it. A fire not to be quenched; it demands a uniform vigilance to prevent its bursting into a flame, lest instead of warming, it should consume.

It is important, likewise, that the habits of thinking in a free Country should
30   inspire caution in those entrusted with its administration, to confine themselves within their respective Constitutional spheres; avoiding in the exercise of the powers of one department to encroach upon another. The spirit of encroachment tends to consolidate the powers of all the departments in one, and thus to create whatever the form of government, a real despotism. A just
35   estimate of that love of power, and proneness to abuse it, which predominates in the human heart is sufficient to satisfy us of the truth of this position. The necessity of reciprocal checks in the exercise of political power; by dividing and distributing it into different depositories, and constituting each the Guard-

ian of the Public Weal against invasions by the others, has been evinced by
experiments ancient and modern, some of them in our country and under our
own eyes. To preserve them must be as necessary as to institute them. If in the
opinion of the People, the distribution or modification of the Constitutional
powers be in any particular wrong, let it be corrected by an amendment in the   5
way which the Constitution designates. But let there be no change by usurpation; for though this, in one instance, may be the instrument of good, it is the
customary weapon by which free governments are destroyed. The precedent
must always greatly overbalance in permanent evil any partial or transient benefit which the use can at any time yield.   10

Of all the dispositions and habits which lead to political prosperity, Religion
and morality are indispensable supports. In vain would that man claim the
tribute of Patriotism, who should labor to subvert these great Pillars of human
happiness, these firmest props of the duties of Men and citizens. The mere
Politician, equally with the pious man ought to respect and to cherish them.   15
A volume could not trace all their connections with private and public felicity.
Let it simply be asked where is the security for property, for reputation, for life,
if the sense of religious obligation *desert* the oaths, which are the instruments
of investigation in Courts of Justice? And let us with caution indulge the supposition, that morality can be maintained without religion. Whatever may be   20
conceded to the influence of refined education on minds of peculiar structure,
reason and experience both forbid us to expect that National morality can
prevail in exclusion of religious principle.

'Tis substantially true, that virtue or morality is a necessary spring of popular
government. The rule indeed extends with more or less force to every species of   25
free Government. Who that is a sincere friend to it, can look with indifference
upon attempts to shake the foundation of the fabric.

Promote then as an object of primary importance, Institutions for the general diffusion of knowledge. In proportion as the structure of a government gives force
to public opinion, it is essential that public opinion should be enlightened.   30

As a very important source of strength and security, cherish public credit. One
method of preserving it is to use it as sparingly as possible: avoiding occasions
of expense by cultivating peace, but remembering also that timely disbursements to prepare for danger frequently prevent much greater disbursements
to repel it; avoiding likewise the accumulation of debt, not only by shunning   35
occasions of expense, but by vigorous exertions in time of Peace to discharge
the Debts which unavoidable wars may have occasioned, not ungenerously
throwing upon posterity the burden which we ourselves ought to bear. The

execution of these maxims belongs to your Representatives, but it is necessary that public opinion should cooperate. To facilitate to them the performance of their duty, it is essential that you should practically bear in mind, that towards the payment of debts there must be Revenue; that to have Revenue there must
5   be taxes; that no taxes can be devised which are not more or less inconvenient and unpleasant; that the intrinsic embarrassment inseparable from the selection of the proper objects (which is always a choice of difficulties) ought to be a decisive motive for a candid construction of the Conduct of the Government in making it, and for a spirit of acquiescence in the measures for obtaining
10 Revenue which the public exigencies may at any time dictate.

Observe good faith and justice towards all Nations. Cultivate peace and harmony with all. Religion and morality enjoin this conduct; and can it be that good policy does not equally enjoin it? It will be worthy of a free, enlightened, and, at no distant period, a great Nation, to give to mankind the magnani-
15 mous and too novel example of a People always guided by an exalted justice and benevolence. Who can doubt that in the course of time and things the fruits of such a plan would richly repay any temporary advantages which might be lost by a steady adherence to it? Can it be, that Providence has not connected the permanent felicity of a nation with its virtue? The experiment,
20 at least, is recommended by every sentiment which ennobles human Nature. Alas! is it rendered impossible by its vices?

In the execution of such a plan nothing is more essential than that permanent, inveterate antipathies against particular Nations and passionate attachments for others should be excluded; and that in place of them just and ami-
25 cable feelings towards all should be cultivated. The Nation, which indulges towards another an habitual hatred, or an habitual fondness, is in some degree a slave. It is a slave to its animosity or to its affection, either of which is sufficient to lead it astray from its duty and its interest. Antipathy in one Nation against another, disposes each more readily to offer insult and injury,
30 to lay hold of slight causes of umbrage, and to be haughty and intractable, when accidental or trifling occasions of dispute occur. Hence frequent collisions, obstinate, envenomed, and bloody contests. The Nation, prompted by ill will and resentment sometimes impels to War the Government, contrary to the best calculations of policy. The Government sometimes participates
35 in the national propensity, and adopts through passion what reason would reject; at other times, it makes the animosity of the Nation subservient to projects of hostility instigated by pride, ambition and other sinister and pernicious motives. The peace often, sometimes perhaps the Liberty, of Nations has been the victim.

So, likewise, a passionate attachment of one Nation for another produces a variety of evils. Sympathy for the favorite nation, facilitating the illusion of an imaginary common interest, in cases where no real common interest exists, and infusing into one the enmities of the other, betrays the former into a participation in the quarrels and Wars of the latter, without adequate inducement or justification: It leads also to concessions to the favorite Nation of privileges denied to others, which is apt doubly to injure the Nation making the concession; by unnecessarily parting with what ought to have been retained, and by exciting jealousy, ill will, and a disposition to retaliate, in the parties from whom equal privileges are withheld: And it gives to ambitious, corrupted, or deluded citizens (who devote themselves to the favorite Nation) facility to betray, or sacrifice the interests of their own country, without odium sometimes even with popularity; gilding with the appearances of a virtuous sense of obligation a commendable deference for public opinion, or a laudable zeal for public good, the base or foolish compliances of ambition[,] corruption, or infatuation.

As avenues to foreign influence in innumerable ways, such attachments are particularly alarming to the truly enlightened and independent Patriot. How many opportunities do they afford to tamper with domestic factions, to practice the arts of seduction, to mislead public opinion, to influence or awe the public Councils! Such an attachment of a small or weak, towards a great and powerful Nation, dooms the former to be the satellite of the latter.

Against the insidious wiles of foreign influence (I conjure you to believe me, fellow citizens), the jealousy of a free people ought to be *constantly* awake; since history and experience prove that foreign influence is one of the most baneful foes of Republican Government. But that jealousy to be useful must be impartial; else it becomes the instrument of the very influence to be avoided, instead of a defense against it. Excessive partiality for one foreign nation and excessive dislike of another, cause those whom they actuate to see danger only on one side, and serve to veil and even second the arts of influence on the other. Real Patriots, who may resist the intrigues of the favorite, are liable to become suspected and odious; while its tools and dupes usurp the applause and confidence of the people, to surrender their interests.

The Great rule of conduct for us, in regard to foreign Nations is in extending our commercial relations, to have with them as little *political* connections as possible. So far as we have already formed engagements let them be fulfilled, with perfect good faith. Here let us stop.

Europe has a set of primary interests, which to us have none, or a very remote relation. Hence she must be engaged in frequent controversies, the causes of which are essentially foreign to our concerns. Hence therefore it must be unwise in us to implicate ourselves, by artificial ties, in the ordinary vicissitudes of her politics, or the ordinary combinations and collisions of her friendships, or enmities:

5   Our detached and distant situation invites and enables us to pursue a different course. If we remain one People, under an efficient government, the period is not far off, when we may defy material injury from external annoyance; when we may take such an attitude as will cause the neutrality we may at any time resolve upon to be scrupulously respected; when belligerent nations, under the
10   impossibility of making acquisitions upon us, will not lightly hazard the giving us provocation; when we may choose peace or war, as our interest guided by justice shall Counsel.

Why forego the advantages of so peculiar a situation? Why quit our own to stand upon foreign ground? Why, by interweaving our destiny with that of
15   any part of Europe, entangle our peace and prosperity in the toils of European Ambition, Rivalship, Interest, Humor or Caprice?

'Tis our true policy to steer clear of permanent Alliances, with any portion of the foreign world. So far, I mean, as we are now at liberty to do it, for let me not be understood as capable of patronizing infidelity to existing engagements
20   (I hold the maxim no less applicable to public than to private affairs, that honesty is always the best policy). I repeat it therefore, let those engagements be observed in their genuine sense. But in my opinion, it is unnecessary and would be unwise to extend them.

Taking care always to keep ourselves, by suitable establishments, on a respect-
25   ably defensive posture, we may safely trust to temporary alliances for extraordinary emergencies.

Harmony, liberal intercourse with all Nations, are recommended by policy, humanity and interest. But even our commercial policy should hold an equal and impartial hand: neither seeking nor granting exclusive favors or preferences;
30   consulting the natural course of things; diffusing and diversifying by gentle means the streams of Commerce, but forcing nothing; establishing with Powers so disposed; in order to give to trade a stable course, to define the rights of our Merchants, and to enable the Government to support them; conventional rules of intercourse, the best that present circumstances and mutual opinion
35   will permit, but temporary, and liable to be from time to time abandoned or varied, as experience and circumstances shall dictate; constantly keeping in view, that 'tis folly in one Nation to look for disinterested favors from another; that it must pay with a portion of its Independence for whatever it may accept under

that character; that by such acceptance, it may place itself in the condition of having given equivalents for nominal favors and yet, of being reproached with ingratitude for not giving more. There can be no greater error than to expect, or calculate upon real favors from Nation to Nation. 'Tis an illusion which experience must cure, which a just pride ought to discard.   5

In offering to you, my Countrymen, these counsels of an old and affectionate friend, I dare not hope they will make the strong and lasting impression, I could wish; that they will control the usual current of the passions, or prevent our Nation from running the course which has hitherto marked the Destiny of Nations. But if I may even flatter myself that they may be productive of 10 some partial benefit, some occasional good; that they may now and then recur to moderate the fury of party spirit, to warn against the mischiefs of foreign intrigue, to guard against the Impostures of pretended patriotism; this hope will be a full recompense for the solicitude for your welfare, by which they have been dictated.   15

How far in the discharge of my Official duties, I have been guided by the principles which have been delineated, the public Records and other evidences of my conduct must Witness to You and to the world. To myself, the assurance of my own conscience is, that I have at least believed myself to be guided by them.

In relation to the still subsisting War in Europe, my Proclamation of the 22d of 20 April, 1793 is the index to my Plan. Sanctioned by your approving voice and by that of Your Representatives in both Houses of Congress, the spirit of that measure has continually governed me; uninfluenced by any attempts to deter or divert me from it.

After deliberate examination with the aid of the best lights I could obtain I was 25 well satisfied that our Country, under all the circumstances of the case, had a right to take, and was bound in duty and interest, to take a Neutral position. Having taken it, I determined, as far as should depend upon me, to maintain it, with moderation, perseverance, and firmness.

The considerations, which respect the right to hold this conduct, it is not 30 necessary on this occasion to detail. I will only observe, that according to my understanding of the matter, that right, so far from being denied by any of the Belligerent powers has been virtually admitted by all.

The duty of holding a Neutral conduct may be inferred, without any thing more, from the obligation which justice and humanity impose on every 35 Nation, in cases in which it is free to act, to maintain inviolate the relations of Peace and amity towards other Nations.

The inducements of interest for observing that conduct will best be referred to your own reflections and experience. With me, a predominant motive has been to endeavor to gain time to our country to settle and mature its yet recent institutions, and to progress without interruption, to that degree of strength and consistency, which is necessary to give it, humanly speaking, the command of its own fortunes.

Though in reviewing the incidents of my Administration, I am unconscious of intentional error, I am nevertheless too sensible of my defects not to think it probable that I may have committed many errors. Whatever they may be I fervently beseech the Almighty to avert or mitigate the evils to which they may tend. I shall also carry with me the hope that my Country will never cease to view them with indulgence; and that after forty-five years of my life dedicated to its Service, with an upright zeal, the faults of incompetent abilities will be consigned to oblivion, as myself must soon be to the Mansions of rest.

Relying on its kindness in this as in other things, and actuated by that fervent love towards it, which is so natural to a man who views in it the native soil of himself and his progenitors for several Generations, I anticipate with pleasing expectation that retreat, in which I promise myself to realize, without alloy, the sweet enjoyment of partaking, in the midst of my fellow Citizens, the benign influence of good Laws under a free Government, the ever favorite object of my heart, and the happy reward, as I trust, of our mutual cares, labors and dangers.

LETTER TO THE
DANBURY BAPTIST ASSOCIATION
THOMAS JEFFERSON

The Danbury Baptist Association, aware of Thomas Jefferson's earlier role in overturning the Anglican establishment in Virginia, expressed hope that as president he might help liberate them from the religious constraints in Connecticut. Jefferson's response, in which he employs the famous "wall of separation between church and state" metaphor, is not a demand for the separation of religion and politics; rather, it addresses the principle of federalism. As president, Jefferson is unable to interfere in this state issue. Likewise, Congress is prohibited from doing so by the First Amendment's religion clauses. The citizens of Connecticut must remedy their situation by amending their state constitution and statutes—as eventually they did.

JANUARY 1, 1802

GENTLEMEN:

The affectionate sentiments of esteem and approbation which you are so good as to express towards me, on behalf of the Danbury Baptist Association, give me the highest satisfaction. My duties dictate a faithful and zealous pursuit of the interests of my constituents, and in proportion as they are persuaded of my fidelity to those duties, the discharge of them becomes more and more pleasing. 5
Believing with you that religion is a matter which lies solely between man and his God, that he owes account to none other for his faith or his worship, that the legislative powers of government reach actions only, and not opinions, I contemplate with sovereign reverence that act of the whole American people which declared that their legislature should "make no law respecting an estab- 10
lishment of religion, or prohibiting the free exercise thereof," thus building a wall of separation between Church and State. Adhering to this expression of the supreme will of the nation in behalf of the rights of conscience, I shall see

Thomas Jefferson, "Replies to Public Addresses," January 1, 1802, in A. A. Lipscomb and A. E. Bergh, eds., *The Writings of Thomas Jefferson*, Vol. 16 (Washington, D.C.: Thomas Jefferson Memorial Association, 1907), 281–82.

with sincere satisfaction the progress of those sentiments which tend to restore to man all his natural rights, convinced he has no natural right in opposition to his social duties.

I reciprocate your kind prayers for the protection and blessing of the common Father and Creator of man, and tender you for yourselves and your religious association, assurances of my high respect and esteem.

ON PROPERTY
JAMES MADISON

James Madison, known as the "Father of the Constitution," was elected from Virginia to the U.S. House of Representatives in 1788, and served four terms. This essay, which then-Congressman Madison wrote for a New York newspaper, connects the idea of property rights as commonly understood to man's natural rights, culminating in the right of conscience.

MARCH 29, 1792

This term in its particular application means "that dominion which one man claims and exercises over the external things of the world, in exclusion of every other individual."

In its larger and juster meaning, it embraces every thing to which a man may attach a value and have a right; and *which leaves to every one else the like advantage.*   5

In the former sense, a man's land, or merchandise, or money is called his property.

In the latter sense, a man has a property in his opinions and the free communication of them.   10

He has a property of peculiar value in his religious opinions, and in the profession and practice dictated by them.

He has a property very dear to him in the safety and liberty of his person.

He has an equal property in the free use of his faculties and free choice of the objects on which to employ them.   15

In a word, as a man is said to have a right to his property, he may be equally said to have a property in his rights.

James Madison, "Property," March 27, 1792, in William T. Hutchinson et al., eds., *The Papers of James Madison*, Vol. 14 (Chicago: University of Chicago Press, 1962–present), 266–68. Reproduced with permission of University of Chicago Press–Books in the format Textbook via Copyright Clearance Center.

Where an excess of power prevails, property of no sort is duly respected. No man is safe in his opinions, his person, his faculties, or his possessions.

Where there is an excess of liberty, the effect is the same, though from an opposite cause.

5   Government is instituted to protect property of every sort; as well that which lies in the various rights of individuals, as that which the term particularly expresses. This being the end of government, that alone is a *just* government, which *impartially* secures to every man, whatever is his *own*.

According to this standard of merit, the praise of affording a just securing
10   to property, should be sparingly bestowed on a government which, however scrupulously guarding the possessions of individuals, does not protect them in the enjoyment and communication of their opinions, in which they have an equal, and in the estimation of some, a more valuable property.

More sparingly should this praise be allowed to a government, where a man's
15   religious rights are violated by penalties, or fettered by tests, or taxed by a hierarchy. Conscience is the most sacred of all property; other property depending in part on positive law, the exercise of that, being a natural and unalienable right. To guard a man's house as his castle, to pay public and enforce private debts with the most exact faith, can give no title to invade a
20   man's conscience which is more sacred than his castle, or to withhold from it that debt of protection, for which the public faith is pledged, by the very nature and original conditions of the social pact.

That is not a just government, nor is property secure under it, where the property which a man has in his personal safety and personal liberty, is violated by
25   arbitrary seizures of one class of citizens for the service of the rest. A magistrate issuing his warrants to a press gang, would be in his proper functions in Turkey or Indostan, under appellations proverbial of the most complete despotism.

That is not a just government, nor is property secure under it, where arbitrary restrictions, exemptions, and monopolies deny to part of its citizens that free
30   use of their faculties, and free choice of their occupations, which not only constitute their property in the general sense of the word; but are the means of acquiring property strictly so called. What must be the spirit of legislation where a manufacturer of linen cloth is forbidden to bury his own child in a linen shroud, in order to favor his neighbour who manufactures woolen cloth;
35   where the manufacturer and wearer of woolen cloth are again forbidden the economical use of buttons of that material, in favor of the manufacturer of buttons of other materials!

A just security to property is not afforded by that government, under which unequal taxes oppress one species of property and reward another species: where arbitrary taxes invade the domestic sanctuaries of the rich, and excessive taxes grind the faces of the poor; where the keenness and competitions of want are deemed an insufficient spur to labor, and taxes are again applied, by an unfeeling   5 policy, as another spur; in violation of that sacred property, which Heaven, in decreeing man to earn his bread by the sweat of his brow, kindly reserved to him, in the small repose that could be spared from the supply of his necessities.

If there be a government then which prides itself in maintaining the inviolability of property; which provides that none shall be taken *directly* even for public   10 use without indemnification to the owner, and yet *directly* violates the property which individuals have in their opinions, their religion, their persons, and their faculties; nay more, which *indirectly* violates their property, in their actual possessions, in the labor that acquires their daily subsistence, and in the hallowed remnant of time which ought to relieve their fatigues and soothe their cares, the   15 influence will have been anticipated, that such a government is not a pattern for the United States.

If the United States mean to obtain or deserve the full praise due to wise and just governments, they will equally respect the rights of property, and the property in rights: they will rival the government that most sacredly guards the former; and   20 by repelling its example in violating the latter, will make themselves a pattern to that and all other governments.

IV
GOVERNMENT UNDER THE ARTICLES OF CONFEDERATION: THE PROBLEM OF LEGISLATIVE/MAJORITY TYRANNY

Having fought and won a revolution against unchecked political power, the American Founders were determined not to install a government of their own that would degenerate into tyranny. As they quickly discovered, however, the real scourge of the young confederation was not centralization, but the confederate form of government itself.

Historically, confederations had been effective in rallying disparate and small powers against larger common foes. The 1781 "Articles of Confederation and Perpetual Union" sought to unite the thirteen states against any external threat, especially Great Britain. Having seen the excesses of British rule, the colonists sought a form of government that would chasten rather than empower the central government. Designed to ward off foreign invasion, facilitate free trade among the states, and bring order to their interactions, the confederal constitution, Americans soon discovered, invited as many problems as it solved.

As attested by the great triumvirate of Founders featured in this section— George Washington, Thomas Jefferson, and James Madison—the Articles of Confederation created an enfeebled regime from the outset. In their common opinion, the American government under the Articles lacked the energy sufficient for good government. Congressional action on any serious question, for example, required the assent of nine of the thirteen states, which was almost impossible to achieve.

For General Washington, writing in his "Circular Letter to the States" of June 1783, the "theater" in which the "citizens of America" are given a stage "seems to be peculiarly designated by Providence for the display of human greatness and felicity." Geographical security, natural abundance, and above all, the age in which the nation was born—one in which natural rights were understood— all made possible an astonishing success. There was no guarantee of continued success, but the responsibility shared by all was great, "for with our fate will the destiny of unborn Millions be involved."

Three years later, in a 1786 letter to John Jay, who was to become the nation's first Supreme Court Chief Justice, Washington revisited many of his earlier arguments for the insufficiency of the Articles. "We have probably had too good an opinion of human nature in forming our confederation," he ruminated. "We must take human nature as we find it. Perfection falls not to the share of mortals."

By late March 1787, when Washington wrote Madison the letter included here, the Constitutional Convention was slated to start in May. Washington expresses his unstinting support of the Convention's aims, writing that it should "probe the defects of the Constitution to the bottom, and provide radical cures." And by "radical," with the Latin root *radix*, or "root," he meant nothing less than a complete extirpation of the old mode of government.

In the only book Jefferson published, *Notes on the State of Virginia*, the ever-loyal Virginian offers a friendly critique of the first Constitution of his state, much of which could with equal force be lodged against the Articles of Confederation. The Virginia Constitution, he wrote, was "formed when we were new and unexperienced in the science of government." From the ancient Greeks, for instance, the Founders learned that democracy in its pure form was to be avoided. When the people rule directly, a dictatorship of popular passions almost always ensues. Much preferred, the Founders concluded, echoing Aristotle, was a mixed regime in which neither rich nor poor had a monopoly on power, and in which no one sector of society would rule without checks.

The "Father of the Constitution," James Madison, earned his title, one might say, in no small measure because he, more than anyone at the Constitutional Convention, insisted that the Articles should not merely be amended but rather replaced by a new constitution. In April 1787, just before the Convention delegates gathered in Philadelphia, he composed what amounted to his own notes for a preliminary agenda for the Convention, titled "Vices of the Political System of the United States." Organized according to eleven major points, "Vices" begins with a reiteration of the major defects of the Articles. States ignore the Articles and usurp federal authorities. With so many parties to treaties, treaties often are violated. States trespass on the rights of other states, unity is impossible in commercial matters, and protections against internal violence are lacking. Furthermore, the violation of laws is not accompanied by punishment, and the Articles are authorized only by the legislature, not by the people as a whole. Laws are multiplying too rapidly, and even more problematic is that they are mutable.

The "multiplicity" and "mutability" of laws undermines the principle of majority rule by allowing it to degenerate into majority tyranny. Madison argues that although popular virtue has its place in restraining government, the longevity and success of a regime depends most upon a well-crafted system of governance, complete with separation of powers and checks and balances. Factions are inevitable because human beings are flawed, but factions can be controlled if none is able to become too powerful.

DAVID J. BOBB
Lecturer in Politics
Director, Allan P. Kirby, Jr. Center for
Constitutional Studies and Citizenship
Hillsdale College

THE ARTICLES OF CONFEDERATION

Pennsylvanian John Dickinson—who declined to sign the Declaration of Independence because he believed that the states should be organized politically before declaring independence—wrote the first draft of the Articles of Confederation in 1777. Signed into effect that year and ratified in 1781, the Articles provided the structure of government for the states until the Constitution was ratified in 1788. During that period the Articles' deficiencies became increasingly obvious, and by the time of the Constitutional Convention, few Founders, including Dickinson, defended its continuation.

MARCH 1, 1781

TO ALL TO WHOM THESE PRESENTS SHALL COME, WE THE UNDERSIGNED DELEGATES OF THE STATES AFFIXED TO OUR NAMES, SEND GREETING:

Whereas the Delegates of the United States of America in Congress assembled did on the fifteenth day of November in the Year of our Lord One Thousand Seven Hundred and Seventy-Seven, and in the Second Year of the Independence of America agree to certain articles of Confederation and perpetual Union between the States of New Hampshire, Massachusetts Bay, Rhode Island and Providence Plantations, Connecticut, New York, New Jersey, Pennsylvania, Delaware, Maryland, Virginia, North Carolina, South Carolina, and Georgia in the words following, viz.

Articles of Confederation and perpetual Union between the states of New Hampshire, Massachusetts Bay, Rhode Island and Providence Plantations, Connecticut, New York, New Jersey, Pennsylvania, Delaware, Maryland, Virginia, North Carolina, South Carolina, and Georgia.

ARTICLE I

The stile of this confederacy shall be "The United States of America."

ARTICLE II

Each State retains its sovereignty, freedom and independence, and every power, jurisdiction and right, which is not by this confederation expressly delegated to the United States, in Congress assembled.

Article III

The said States hereby severally enter into a firm league of friendship with each other, for their common defense, the security of their liberties, and their mutual and general welfare, binding themselves to assist each other, against all force offered to, or attacks made upon them, or any of them, on account of religion,
5   sovereignty, trade, or any other pretense whatever.

Article IV

The better to secure and perpetuate mutual friendship and intercourse among the people of the different States in this Union, the free inhabitants of each of these States, paupers, vagabonds and fugitives from justice excepted, shall be entitled to all privileges and immunities of free citizens in the several States;
10   and the people of each State shall have free ingress and regress to and from any other State and shall enjoy therein all the privileges of trade and commerce, subject to the same duties, impositions and restrictions as the inhabitants thereof respectively, provided that such restriction shall not extend so far as to prevent the removal of property imported into any State, to any other State of
15   which the owner is an inhabitant; provided also that no imposition, duties or restriction shall be laid by any State, on the property of the United States, or either of them.

If any person guilty of, or charged with treason, felony, or other high misdemeanor in any State, shall flee from justice, and be found in any of the
20   United States, he shall, upon demand of the Governor or Executive power, of the State from which he fled, be delivered up and removed to the State having jurisdiction of his offense.

Full faith and credit shall be given in each of these States to the records, acts and judicial proceedings of the courts and magistrates of every other State.

Article V

25   For the more convenient management of the general interests of the United States, delegates shall be annually appointed in such manner as the legislature of each State shall direct, to meet in Congress on the first Monday in November, in every year, with a power reserved to each State to recall its delegates, or any of them, at any time within the year, and to send others in their stead, for the
30   remainder of the year.

No State shall be represented in Congress by less than two, nor by more than seven members; and no person shall be capable of being a delegate for more than three years in any term of six years; nor shall any person, being a delegate, be capable of holding any office under the United States, for which he, or another
35   for his benefit receives any salary, fees or emolument of any kind.

Each State shall maintain its own delegates in a meeting of the States, and while they act as members of the committee of the States.

In determining questions in the United States, in Congress assembled, each State shall have one vote.

Freedom of speech and debate in Congress shall not be impeached or questioned in any court, or place out of Congress, and the members of Congress shall be protected in their persons from arrests and imprisonments, during the time of their going to and from, and attendance on Congress, except for treason, felony, or breach of the peace.

Article VI

No State without the consent of the United States in Congress assembled, shall send any embassy to, or receive any embassy from, or enter into any conference, agreement, alliance or treaty with any king, prince or state; nor shall any person holding any office of profit or trust under the United States, or any of them, accept of any present, emolument, office or title of any kind whatever from any king, prince or foreign state; nor shall the United States in Congress assembled, or any of them, grant any title of nobility.

No two or more States shall enter into any treaty, confederation or alliance whatever between them, without the consent of the United States in Congress assembled, specifying accurately the purposes for which the same is to be entered into, and how long it shall continue.

No State shall lay any imposts or duties, which may interfere with any stipulations in treaties, entered into by the United States in Congress assembled, with any king, prince or state, in pursuance of any treaties already proposed by Congress, to the courts of France and Spain.

No vessels of war shall be kept up in time of peace by any State, except such number only, as shall be deemed necessary by the United States in Congress assembled, for the defense of such State, or its trade; nor shall any body of forces be kept up by any State, in time of peace, except such number only, as in the judgment of the United States, in Congress assembled, shall be deemed requisite to garrison the forts necessary for the defense of such State; but every State shall always keep up a well regulated and disciplined militia, sufficiently armed and accoutred, and shall provide and constantly have ready for use, in public stores, a due number of field pieces and tents, and a proper quantity of arms, ammunition and camp equipage.

No State shall engage in any war without the consent of the United States in Congress assembled, unless such State be actually invaded by enemies, or shall

have received certain advice of a resolution being formed by some nation of Indians to invade such State, and the danger is so imminent as not to admit of a delay, till the United States in Congress assembled can be consulted: nor shall any State grant commissions to any ships or vessels of war, nor letters of
5   marque or reprisal, except it be after a declaration of war by the United States in Congress assembled, and then only against the kingdom or state and the subjects thereof, against which war has been so declared, and under such regulations as shall be established by the United States in Congress assembled, unless such State be infested by pirates, in which case vessels of war may be fitted out for
10   that occasion, and kept so long as the danger shall continue or until the United States in Congress assembled shall determine otherwise.

ARTICLE VII

When land-forces are raised by any State for the common defense, all officers of or under the rank of colonel, shall be appointed by the Legislature of each State respectively, by whom such forces shall be raised, or in such manner as
15   such State shall direct, and all vacancies shall be filled up by the State which first made the appointment.

ARTICLE VIII

All charges of war, and all other expenses that shall be incurred for the common defense or general welfare, and allowed by the United States in Congress assembled, shall be defrayed out of a common treasury, which shall be supplied
20   by the several States, in proportion to the value of all land within each State, granted to or surveyed for any person, as such land and the buildings and improvements thereon shall be estimated according to such mode as the United States in Congress assembled, shall from time to time direct and appoint.

The taxes for paying that proportion shall be laid and levied by the authority
25   and direction of the Legislatures of the several States within the time agreed upon by the United States in Congress assembled.

ARTICLE IX

The United States in Congress assembled, shall have the sole and exclusive right and power of determining on peace and war, except in the cases mentioned in the sixth article—of sending and receiving ambassadors—entering into treaties
30   and alliances, provided that no treaty of commerce shall be made whereby the legislative power of the respective States shall be restrained from imposing such imposts and duties on foreigners, as their own people are subjected to, or from prohibiting the exportation or importation of any species of goods or commodities, whatsoever—of establishing rules for deciding in all cases,
35   what captures on land or water shall be legal, and in what manner prizes taken

by land or naval forces in the service of the United States shall be divided or appropriated—of granting letters of marque and reprisal in times of peace—appointing courts for the trial of piracies and felonies committed on the high seas and establishing courts for receiving and determining finally appeals in all cases of captures, provided that no member of Congress shall be appointed a   5 judge of any of the said courts.

The United States in Congress assembled shall also be the last resort on appeal in all disputes and differences now subsisting or that hereafter may arise between two or more States concerning boundary, jurisdiction or any other cause whatever; which authority shall always be exercised in the manner following.   10 Whenever the legislative or executive authority or lawful agent of any State in controversy with another shall present a petition to Congress, stating the matter in question and praying for a hearing, notice thereof shall be given by order of Congress to the legislative or executive authority of the other State in controversy, and a day assigned for the appearance of the parties by their lawful agents, who   15 shall then be directed to appoint by joint consent, commissioners or judges to constitute a court for hearing and determining the matter in question: but if they cannot agree, Congress shall name three persons out of each of the United States, and from the list of such persons each party shall alternately strike out one, the petitioners beginning, until the number shall be reduced to thirteen; and from   20 that number not less than seven, nor more than nine names as Congress shall direct, shall in the presence of Congress be drawn out by lot, and the persons whose names shall be so drawn or any five of them, shall be commissioners or judges, to hear and finally determine the controversy, so always as a major part of the judges who shall hear the cause shall agree in the determination: and   25 if either party shall neglect to attend at the day appointed, without showing reasons, which Congress shall judge sufficient, or being present shall refuse to strike, the Congress shall proceed to nominate three persons out of each State, and the Secretary of Congress shall strike in behalf of such party absent or refusing; and the judgment and sentence of the court to be appointed, in the   30 manner before prescribed, shall be final and conclusive; and if any of the parties shall refuse to submit to the authority of such court, or to appear or defend their claim or cause, the court shall nevertheless proceed to pronounce sentence, or judgment, which shall in like manner be final and decisive, the judgment or sentence and other proceedings being in either case transmitted to Congress,   35 and lodged among the acts of Congress for the security of the parties concerned: provided that every commissioner, before he sits in judgment, shall take an oath to be administered by one of the judges of the supreme or superior court of the State where the cause shall be tried, "well and truly to hear and determine the matter in question, according to the best of his judgment, without favor, affection or hope of reward:" provided also that no State shall be deprived of territory for the benefit of the United States.

All controversies concerning the private right of soil claimed under different
5   grants of two or more States, whose jurisdictions as they may respect such lands, and the States which passed such grants are adjusted, the said grants or either of them being at the same time claimed to have originated antecedent to such settlement of jurisdiction, shall on the petition of either party to the Congress of the United States, be finally determined as near as may be in the
10   same manner as is before prescribed for deciding disputes respecting territorial jurisdiction between different States.

The United States in Congress assembled shall also have the sole and exclusive right and power of regulating the alloy and value of coin struck by their own authority, or by that of the respective States.—fixing the standard of weights and measures
15   throughout the United States.—regulating the trade and managing all affairs with the Indians, not members of any of the States, provided that the legislative right of any State within its own limits be not infringed or violated—establishing and regulating post-offices from one State to another, throughout all the United States, and exacting such postage on the papers passing thro' the same as may be requisite
20   to defray the expenses of the said office—appointing all officers of the land forces, in the service of the United States, excepting regimental officers—appointing all the officers of the naval forces, and commissioning all officers whatever in the service of the United States—making rules for the government and regulation of the said land and naval forces, and directing their operations.

25   The United States in Congress assembled shall have authority to appoint a committee, to sit in the recess of Congress, to be denominated "a Committee of the States", and to consist of one delegate from each State; and to appoint such other committees and civil officers as may be necessary for managing the general affairs of the United States under their direction—to appoint one of
30   their number to preside, provided that no person be allowed to serve in the office of president more than one year in any term of three years; to ascertain the necessary sums of money to be raised for the service of the United States, and to appropriate and apply the same for defraying the public expenses—to borrow money, or emit bills on the credit of the United States, transmitting every half
35   year to the respective States an account of the sums of money so borrowed or emitted,—to build and equip a navy—to agree upon the number of land forces, and to make requisitions from each State for its quota, in proportion to the number of white inhabitants in such State; which requisition shall be binding, and thereupon the Legislature of each State shall appoint the regimental officers,

raise the men and clothe, arm and equip them in a soldier-like manner, at the
expense of the United States; and the officers and men so clothed, armed and
equipped shall march to the place appointed, and within the time agreed on by
the United States in Congress assembled: but if the United States in Congress
assembled shall, on consideration of circumstances judge proper that any State   5
should not raise men, or should raise a smaller number than its quota, and that
any other State should raise a greater number of men than the quota thereof,
such extra number shall be raised, officered, clothed, armed and equipped in
the same manner as the quota of such State, unless the legislature of such State
shall judge that such extra number cannot be safely spared out of the same, in   10
which case they shall raise, officer, cloth, arm and equip as many of such extra
number as they judge can be safely spared. And the officers and men so clothed,
armed and equipped, shall march to the place appointed, and within the time
agreed on by the United States in Congress assembled.

The United States in Congress assembled shall never engage in a war, nor grant   15
letters of marque and reprisal in time of peace, nor enter into any treaties or
alliances, nor coin money, nor regulate the value thereof, nor ascertain the
sums and expenses necessary for the defense and welfare of the United States,
or any of them, nor emit bills, nor borrow money on the credit of the United
States, nor appropriate money, nor agree upon the number of vessels of war,   20
to be built or purchased, or the number of land or sea forces to be raised, nor
appoint a commander in chief of the army or navy, unless nine States assent to
the same; nor shall a question on any other point, except for adjourning from
day to day be determined, unless by the votes of a majority of the United States
in Congress assembled.   25

The Congress of the United States shall have power to adjourn to any time
within the year, and to any place within the United States, so that no period of
adjournment be for a longer duration than the space of six months, and shall
publish the journal of their proceedings monthly, except such parts thereof
relating to treaties, alliances or military operations, as in their judgment require   30
secrecy; and the yeas and nays of the delegates of each State on any question
shall be entered on the journal, when it is desired by any delegate; and the
delegates of a State, or any of them, at his or their request shall be furnished
with a transcript of the said journal, except such parts as are above excepted, to
lay before the legislatures of the several States.   35

Article X
The committee of the States, or any nine of them, shall be authorized to execute,
in the recess of Congress, such of the powers of Congress as the United States in
Congress assembled, by the consent of nine States, shall from time to time think

expedient to vest them with; provided that no power be delegated to the said committee, for the exercise of which, by the articles of confederation, the voice of nine states in the Congress of the United States assembled is requisite.

ARTICLE XI

Canada acceding to this confederation, and joining in the measures of the United
5   States, shall be admitted into, and entitled to all the advantages of this Union: but no other colony shall be admitted into the same, unless such admission be agreed to by nine States.

ARTICLE XII

All bills of credit emitted, monies borrowed and debts contracted by, or under the
10   authority of Congress, before the assembling of the United States, in pursuance of the present confederation, shall be deemed and considered as a charge against the United States, for payment and satisfaction whereof the said United States, and the public faith are hereby solemnly pledged.

ARTICLE XIII

Every State shall abide by the determinations of the United States in Congress
15   assembled, on all questions which by this confederation, are submitted to them. And the articles of this confederation shall be inviolably observed by every State, and the Union shall be perpetual; nor shall any alteration at any time hereafter be made in any of them; unless such alteration be agreed to in a Congress of the United States, and be afterwards confirmed by the Legislatures of every State.

20   And whereas it hath pleased the Great Governor of the world to incline the hearts of the Legislatures we respectively represent in Congress, to approve of, and to authorize us to ratify the said articles of confederation and perpetual Union. Know Ye that we, the undersigned delegates, by virtue of the power and authority to us given for that purpose, do by these presents, in the name and
25   in behalf of our respective constituents, fully and entirely ratify and confirm each and every of the said articles of confederation and perpetual Union, and all and singular the matters and things therein contained: and we do further solemnly plight and engage the faith of our respective constituents, that they shall abide by the determinations of the United States in Congress assembled,
30   on all questions, which by the said confederation are submitted to them. And that the Articles thereof shall be inviolably observed by the States we respectively represent, and that the Union shall be perpetual.

In witness whereof we have hereunto set our hands in Congress. Done at Philadelphia in the State of Pennsylvania the ninth day of July, in the year of
35   our Lord, one thousand seven hundred and seventy-eight, and in the third year of the independence of America.

On the part and behalf of the State of New Hampshire:
Josiah Bartlett, John Wentworth, Jr.

On the part and behalf of the State of Massachusetts Bay:
John Hancock, Samuel Adams, Elbridge Gerry, Francis Dana
James Lovell, Samuel Holten

*On the part and behalf of the State of Rhode Island and Providence
Plantations:*
Willam Ellery, Henry Marchant, John Collins

On the part and behalf of the State of Connecticut:
Roger Sherman, Samuel Huntington, Oliver Wolcott, Titus Hosmer,
Andrew Adams

On the part and behalf of the State of New York:
James Duane, Francis Lewis, William Duer, Gouverneur Morris

On the part and behalf of the State of New Jersey:
John Witherspoon, Nathaniel Scudder

On the part and behalf of the State of Pennsylvania:
Robert Morris, Daniel Roberdeau, Jonathan Bayard Smith,
William Clingan, Joseph Reed

On the part and behalf of the State of Delaware:
Thomas McKean, John Dickinson, Nicholas Van Dyke

On the part and behalf of the State of Maryland:
John Hanson, Daniel Carroll

On the part and behalf of the State of Virginia:
Richard Henry Lee, John Banister, Thomas Adams, John Harvie,
Francis Lightfoot Lee

On the part and behalf of the State of North Carolina:
John Penn, Cornelius Harnett, John Williams

On the part and behalf of the State of South Carolina:
Henry Laurens, William Henry Drayton, John Matthews,
Richard Hutson, Thomas Heyward, Jr.

On the part and behalf of the State of Georgia:
John Walton, Edward Telfair, Edward Langworthy

CIRCULAR LETTER TO THE STATES
GEORGE WASHINGTON

As Commander-in-Chief of the Continental Army, overseen by a national legislature that struggled to fund the War for Independence, General George Washington was as familiar as anyone with the defects of the Articles of Confederation. In this, his last circular letter to the states, which he sent to the thirteen governors, Washington emphasizes the need for unity in the maintenance of the nation's independence.

JUNE 8, 1783

SIR:

The great object for which I had the honor to hold an appointment in the Service of my Country, being accomplished, I am now preparing to resign it into the hands of Congress, and to return to that domestic retirement, which, it is well known, I left with the greatest reluctance, a Retirement, for which I have never ceased to sigh through a long and painful absence, and in which (remote from   5
the noise and trouble of the World) I meditate to pass the remainder of life in a state of undisturbed repose; But before I carry this resolution into effect, I think it a duty incumbent on me, to make this my last official communication, to congratulate you on the glorious events which Heaven has been pleased to produce in our favor, to offer my sentiments respecting some important sub-   10
jects, which appear to me, to be intimately connected with the tranquility of the United States, to take my leave of your Excellency as a public Character, and to give my final blessing to that Country, in whose service I have spent the prime of my life, for whose sake I have consumed so many anxious days and watchful nights, and whose happiness being extremely dear to me, will always   15
constitute no inconsiderable part of my own.

Impressed with the liveliest sensibility on this pleasing occasion, I will claim the indulgence of dilating the more copiously on the subjects of our mutual

George Washington, "Circular to the States," June 8, 1783, in W. W. Abbot et al., eds., *The Papers of George Washington, 1748–1799*, Vol. 26 (Charlottesville, VA: University of Virginia Press, 1976–present), 483–96.

felicitation. When we consider the magnitude of the prize we contended for, the doubtful nature of the contest, and the favorable manner in which it has terminated, we shall find the greatest possible reason for gratitude and rejoicing; this is a theme that will afford infinite delight to every benevolent and liberal 5 mind, whether the event in contemplation, be considered as the source of present enjoyment or the parent of future happiness; and we shall have equal occasion to felicitate ourselves on the lot which Providence has assigned us, whether we view it in a natural, a political or moral point of light.

The Citizens of America, placed in the most enviable condition, as the sole Lords 10 and Proprietors of a vast Tract of Continent, comprehending all the various soils and climates of the World, and abounding with all the necessaries and conveniencies of life, are now by the late satisfactory pacification, acknowledged to be possessed of absolute freedom and Independency; They are, from this period, to be considered as the Actors on a most conspicuous Theater, which 15 seems to be peculiarly designated by Providence for the display of human greatness and felicity; Here, they are not only surrounded with every thing which can contribute to the completion of private and domestic enjoyment, but Heaven has crowned all its other blessings, by giving a fairer opportunity for political happiness, than any other Nation has ever been favored with. 20 Nothing can illustrate these observations more forcibly, than a recollection of the happy conjuncture of times and circumstances, under which our Republic assumed its rank among the Nations; The foundation of our Empire was not laid in the gloomy age of Ignorance and Superstition, but at an Epocha when the rights of mankind were better understood and more clearly defined, than 25 at any former period; the researches of the human mind, after social happiness, have been carried to a great extent, the Treasures of knowledge, acquired by the labors of Philosophers, Sages and Legislatures, through a long succession of years, are laid open for our use, and their collected wisdom may be happily applied in the Establishment of our forms of Government; the free cultivation 30 of Letters, the unbounded extension of Commerce, the progressive refinement of Manners, the growing liberality of sentiment, and above all, the pure and benign light of Revelation, have had a meliorating influence on mankind and increased the blessings of Society. At this auspicious period, the United States came into existence as a Nation, and if their Citizens should not be completely 35 free and happy, the fault will be entirely their own.

Such is our situation, and such are our prospects: but notwithstanding the cup of blessing is thus reached out to us, notwithstanding happiness is ours, if we have a disposition to seize the occasion and make it our own; yet, it appears to me there is an option still left to the United States of America, that it is in their choice, and depends upon their conduct, whether they will be respectable and prosperous, or contemptible and miserable as a Nation; This is the time of their political probation, this is the moment when the eyes of the whole World are turned upon them, this is the moment to establish or ruin their national Character forever, this is the favorable moment to give such a tone to our Federal Government, as will enable it to answer the ends of its institution, or this may be the ill-fated moment for relaxing the powers of the Union, annihilating the cement of the Confederation, and exposing us to become the sport of European politics, which may play one State against another to prevent their growing importance, and to serve their own interested purposes. For, according to the system of Policy the States shall adopt at this moment, they will stand or fall, and by their confirmation or lapse, it is yet to be decided, whether the Revolution must ultimately be considered as a blessing or a curse: a blessing or a curse, not to the present age alone, for with our fate will the destiny of unborn Millions be involved.

With this conviction of the importance of the present Crisis, silence in me would be a crime; I will therefore speak to your Excellency, the language of freedom and of sincerity, without disguise; I am aware, however, that those who differ from me in political sentiment, may perhaps remark, I am stepping out of the proper line of my duty, and they may possibly ascribe to arrogance or ostentation, what I know is alone the result of the purest intention, but the rectitude of my own heart, which disdains such unworthy motives, the part I have hitherto acted in life, the determination I have formed, of not taking any share in public business hereafter, the ardent desire I feel, and shall continue to manifest, of quietly enjoying in private life, after all the toils of War, the benefits of a wise and liberal Government, will, I flatter myself, sooner or later convince my Countrymen, that I could have no sinister views in delivering with so little reserve, the opinions contained in this Address.

There are four things, which I humbly conceive, are essential to the well being, I may even venture to say, to the existence of the United States as an Independent Power:

1st. An indissoluble Union of the States under one Federal Head.

2dly. A Sacred regard to Public Justice.

3dly. The adoption of a proper Peace Establishment, and

4thly. The prevalence of that pacific and friendly Disposition, among the People of the United States, which will induce them to forget their local prejudices and policies, to make those mutual concessions which are requisite to the general prosperity, and in some instances, to sacrifice their individual advantages to the interest of the Community.

These are the Pillars on which the glorious Fabric of our Independency and National Character must be supported; Liberty is the Basis, and whoever would dare to sap the foundation, or overturn the Structure, under whatever specious pretexts he may attempt it, will merit the bitterest execration, and the severest
5   punishment which can be inflicted by his injured Country.

On the three first Articles I will make a few observations, leaving the last to the good sense and serious consideration of those immediately concerned.

Under the first head, although it may not be necessary or proper for me in this place to enter into a particular disquisition of the principles of the Union, and
10   to take up the great question which has been frequently agitated, whether it be expedient and requisite for the States to delegate a larger proportion of Power to Congress, or not, Yet it will be a part of my duty, and that of every true Patriot, to assert without reserve, and to insist upon the following positions, That unless the States will suffer Congress to exercise those prerogatives, they are
15   undoubtedly invested with by the Constitution, every thing must very rapidly tend to Anarchy and confusion, That it is indispensable to the happiness of the individual States, that there should be lodged somewhere, a Supreme Power to regulate and govern the general concerns of the Confederated Republic, without which the Union cannot be of long duration. That there must be a faithful
20   and pointed compliance on the part of every State, with the late proposals and demands of Congress, or the most fatal consequences will ensue, That whatever measures have a tendency to dissolve the Union, or contribute to violate or lessen the Sovereign Authority, ought to be considered as hostile to the Liberty and Independency of America, and the Authors of them treated accordingly,
25   and lastly, that unless we can be enabled by the concurrence of the States, to participate of the fruits of the Revolution, and enjoy the essential benefits of Civil Society, under a form of Government so free and uncorrupted, so happily guarded against the danger of oppression, as has been devised and adopted by the Articles of Confederation, it will be a subject of regret, that so much
30   blood and treasure have been lavished for no purpose, that so many sufferings have been encountered without a compensation, and that so many sacrifices have been made in vain. Many other considerations might here be adduced to prove, that without an entire conformity to the Spirit of the Union, we cannot exist as an Independent Power; it will be sufficient for my purpose to mention
35   but one or two which seem to me of the greatest importance. It is only in our united Character as an Empire, that our Independence is acknowledged, that our power can be regarded, or our Credit supported among Foreign Nations. The Treaties of the European Powers with the United States of America, will have no validity on a dissolution of the Union. We shall be left nearly in a

state of Nature, or we may find by our own unhappy experience, that there is a natural and necessary progression, from the extreme of anarchy to the extreme of Tyranny; and that arbitrary power is most easily established on the ruins of Liberty abused to licentiousness.

As to the second Article, which respects the performance of Public Justice, Congress have, in their late Address to the United States, almost exhausted the subject, they have explained their Ideas so fully, and have enforced the obligations the States are under, to render complete justice to all the Public Creditors, with so much dignity and energy, that in my opinion, no real friend to the honor and Independency of America, can hesitate a single moment respecting the propriety of complying with the just and honorable measures proposed; if their Arguments do not produce conviction, I know of nothing that will have greater influence; especially when we recollect that the System referred to, being the result of the collected Wisdom of the Continent, must be esteemed, if not perfect, certainly the least objectionable of any that could be devised; and that if it shall not be carried into immediate execution, a National Bankruptcy, with all its deplorable consequences will take place, before any different Plan can possibly be proposed and adopted, So pressing are the present circumstances! And such is the alternative now offered to the States!

The ability of the Country to discharge the debts which have been incurred in its defense, is not to be doubted, an inclination, I flatter myself, will not be wanting, the path of our duty is plain before us, honesty will be found on every experiment, to be the best and only true policy, let us then as a Nation be just, let us fulfill the public Contracts, which Congress had undoubtedly a right to make for the purpose of carrying on the War, with the same good faith we suppose ourselves bound to perform our private engagements; in the mean time, let an attention to the cheerful performance of their proper business, as Individuals, and as members of Society, be earnestly inculcated on the Citizens of America, that will they strengthen the hands of Government, and be happy under its protection: every one will reap the fruit of his labors, every one will enjoy his own acquisitions without molestation and without danger.

In this state of absolute freedom and perfect security, who will grudge to yield a very little of his property to support the common interest of Society, and insure the protection of Government? Who does not remember, the frequent declarations, at the commencement of the War, that we should be completely satisfied, if at the expense of one half, we could defend the remainder of our possessions? Where is the Man to be found, who wishes to remain indebted, for the defense of his own person and property, to the exertions, the bravery, and the blood of others, without making one generous effort to repay the debt of

honor and of gratitude? In what part of the Continent shall we find any Man, or body of Men, who would not blush to stand up and propose measures, purposely calculated to rob the Soldier of his Stipend, and the Public Creditor of his due? and were it possible that such a flagrant instance of Injustice could ever
5   happen, would it not excite the general indignation, and tend to bring down, upon the Authors of such measures, the aggravated vengeance of Heaven? If after all, a spirit of disunion or a temper of obstinacy and perverseness, should manifest itself in any of the States, if such an ungracious disposition should attempt to frustrate all the happy effects that might be expected to flow from
10   the Union, if there should be a refusal to comply with the requisitions for Funds to discharge the annual interest of the public debts, and if that refusal should revive again all those jealousies and produce all those evils, which are now happily removed, Congress, who have in all their Transaction shown a great degree of magnanimity and justice, will stand justified in the sight of God
15   and Man, and the State alone which puts itself in opposition to the aggregate Wisdom of the Continent, and follows such mistaken and pernicious Councils, will be responsible for all the consequences.

For my own part, conscious of having acted while a Servant of the Public, in the manner I conceived best suited to promote the real interests of my Country;
20   having in consequence of my fixed belief in some measure pledged myself to the Army, that their Country would finally do them complete and ample Justice; and not wishing to conceal any instance of my official conduct from the eyes of the World, I have thought proper to transmit to your Excellency the enclosed collection of Papers, relative to the half pay and commutation granted
25   by Congress to the Officers of the Army; From these communications, my decided sentiment will be clearly comprehended, together with the conclusive reasons which induced me, at an early period, to recommend the adoption of the measure, in the most earnest and serious manner. As the proceedings of Congress, the Army, and myself are open to all, and contain in my opinion,
30   sufficient information to remove the prejudices and errors which may have been entertained by any; I think it unnecessary to say any thing more, than just to observe, that the Resolutions of Congress, now alluded to, are undoubtedly as absolutely binding upon the United States, as the most solemn Acts of Confederation or Legislation. As to the Idea, which I am informed has in
35   some instances prevailed, that the half pay and commutation are to be regarded merely in the odious light of a Pension, it ought to be exploded forever; that Provision, should be viewed as it really was, a reasonable compensation offered by Congress, at a time when they had nothing else to give, to the Officers of the Army, for services then to be performed. It was the only means to prevent

a total dereliction of the Service, It was a part of their hire, I may be allowed to say, it was the price of their blood and of your Independency, it is therefore more than a common debt, it is a debt of honor, it can never be considered as a Pension or gratuity, nor be cancelled until it is fairly discharged.

With regard to a distinction between Officers and Soldiers, it is sufficient that the uniform experience of every Nation of the World, combined with our own, proves the utility and propriety of the discrimination. Rewards in proportion to the aids the public derives from them, are unquestionably due to all its Servants; In some Lines, the Soldiers have perhaps generally had as ample a compensation for their Services, by the large Bounties which have been paid to them, as their Officers will receive in the proposed Commutation, in others, if besides the donation of Lands, the payment of Arrearages of Clothing and Wages (in which Articles all the component parts of the Army must be put upon the same footing) we take into the estimate, the Bounties many of the Soldiers have received and the gratuity of one Year's full pay, which is promised to all, possibly their situation (every circumstance being duly considered) will not be deemed less eligible than that of the Officers. Should a farther reward, however, be judged equitable, I will venture to assert, no one will enjoy greater satisfaction than myself, on seeing an exemption from Taxes for a limited time, (which has been petitioned for in some instances) or any other adequate immunity or compensation, granted to the brave defenders of their Country's Cause; but neither the adoption or rejection of this proposition will in any manner affect, much less militate against, the Act of Congress, by which they have offered five years full pay, in lieu of the half pay for life, which had been before promised to the Officers of the Army.

Before I conclude the subject of public justice, I cannot omit to mention the obligations this Country is under, to that meritorious Class of veteran Non-commissioned Officers and Privates, who have been discharged for inability, in consequence of the Resolution of Congress of the twenty-third of April 1782, on an annual pension for life, their peculiar sufferings, their singular merits and claims to that provision need only be known, to interest all the feelings of humanity in their behalf: nothing but a punctual payment of their annual allowance can rescue them from the most complicated misery, and nothing could be a more melancholy and distressing sight, than to behold those who have shed their blood or lost their limbs in the service of their Country, without a shelter, without a friend, and without the means of obtaining any of the necessaries or comforts of Life; compelled to beg their daily bread from door to door! suffer me to recommend those of this description, belonging to your State, to the warmest patronage of your Excellency and your Legislature.

It is necessary to say but a few words on the third topic which was proposed, and which regards particularly the defense of the Republic, As there can be little doubt but Congress will recommend a proper Peace Establishment for the United States, in which a due attention will be paid to the importance of
5 placing the Militia of the Union upon a regular and respectable footing; If this should be the case, I would beg leave to urge the great advantage of it in the strongest terms. The Militia of this Country must be considered as the Palladium of our security, and the first effectual resort in case of hostility; It is essential, therefore, that the same system should pervade the whole; that the formation
10 and discipline of the Militia of the Continent should be absolutely uniform, and that the same species of Arms, Accoutrements and Military Apparatus, should be introduced in every part of the United States; No one, who has not learned it from experience, can conceive the difficulty, expense, and confusion which result from a contrary system, or the vague Arrangements which have
15 hitherto prevailed.

If in treating of political points, a greater latitude than usual has been taken in the course of this Address, the importance of the Crisis, and the magnitude of the objects in discussion, must be my apology: It is, however, neither my wish or expectation, that the preceding observations should claim any regard, except
20 so far as they shall appear to be dictated by a good intention, consonant to the immutable rules of Justice; calculated to produce a liberal system of policy, and founded on whatever experience may have been acquired by a long and close attention to public business. Here I might speak with the more confidence from my actual observations, and, if it would not swell this Letter (already too prolix)
25 beyond the bounds I had prescribed myself: I could demonstrate to every mind open to conviction, that in less time and with much less expense than has been incurred, the War might have been brought to the same happy conclusion, if the resources of the Continent could have been properly drawn forth, that the distresses and disappointments which have very often occurred, have in
30 too many instances, resulted more from a want of energy, in the Continental Government, than a deficiency of means in the particular States. That the inefficiency of measures, arising from the want of an adequate authority in the Supreme Power, from a partial compliance with the Requisitions of Congress in some of the States, and from a failure of punctuality in others, while it tended
35 to damp the zeal of those which were more willing to exert themselves; served also to accumulate the expenses of the War, and to frustrate the best concerted Plans, and that the discouragement occasioned by the complicated difficulties and embarrassments, in which our affairs were, by this means involved, would have long ago produced the dissolution of any Army, less patient, less virtuous

and less persevering, than that which I have had the honor to command. But while I mention these things, which are notorious facts, as the defects of our Federal Constitution, particularly in the prosecution of a War, I beg it may be understood, that as I have ever taken a pleasure in gratefully acknowledging the assistance and support I have derived from every Class of Citizens, so shall   5
I always be happy to do justice to the unparalleled exertion of the individual States, on many interesting occasions.

I have thus freely disclosed what I wished to make known, before I surrendered up my Public trust to those who committed it to me, the task is now accomplished, I now bid adieu to your Excellency as the Chief Magistrate of your State, at the   10
same time I bid a last farewell to the cares of Office, and all the employments of public life.

It remains then to be my final and only request, that your Excellency will communicate these sentiments to your Legislature at their next meeting, and that they may be considered as the Legacy of One, who has ardently wished,   15
on all occasions, to be useful to his Country, and who, even in the shade of Retirement, will not fail to implore the divine benediction upon it.

I now make it my earnest prayer, that God would have you, and the State over which you preside, in his holy protection, that he would incline the hearts of the Citizens to cultivate a spirit of subordination and obedience to Government, to   20
entertain a brotherly affection and love for one another, for their fellow Citizens of the United States at large, and particularly for their brethren who have served in the Field, and finally, that he would most graciously be pleased to dispose us all, to do Justice, to love mercy, and to demean ourselves with that Charity, humility and pacific temper of mind, which were the Characteristics of the   25
Divine Author of our blessed Religion, and without an humble imitation of whose example in these things, we can never hope to be a happy Nation.

LETTER TO JOHN JAY
GEORGE WASHINGTON

George Washington writes here as a private citizen to John Jay, who as Secretary of Foreign Affairs under the Articles of Confederation witnessed firsthand the Articles' shortcomings, as each state pursued a different foreign policy.

AUGUST 15, 1786

DEAR SIR:

I have to thank you very sincerely for your interesting letter of the twenty-seventh of June, as well as for the other communications you had the goodness to make at the same time.

I am sorry to be assured, of what indeed I had little doubt before, that we have been guilty of violating the treaty in some instances. What a misfortune it is the   5
British should have so well grounded a pretext for their palpable infractions? —and what a disgraceful part, out of the choice of difficulties before us, are we to act?

Your sentiments, that our affairs are drawing rapidly to a crisis, accord with my own. What the event will be is also beyond the reach of my foresight. We   10
have errors to correct. We have probably had too good an opinion of human nature in forming our confederation. Experience has taught us, that men will not adopt and carry into execution, measures the best calculated for their own good without the intervention of a coercive power. I do not conceive we can exist long as a nation, without having lodged somewhere a power which will pervade   15
the whole Union in as energetic a manner, as the authority of the different state governments extends over the several States. To be fearful of vesting Congress, constituted as that body is, with ample authorities for national purposes, appears to me the very climax of popular absurdity and madness. Could Congress exert them for the detriment of the public without injuring themselves in an equal   20

George Washington, "To John Jay," August 15, 1786, in W. W. Abbot et al., eds., *The Papers of George Washington,* "Confederation Series," Vol. 4 (Charlottesville, VA: University of Virginia Press, 1976–present), 212–13.

or greater proportion? Are not their interests inseparably connected with those of their constituents? By the rotation of appointment must they not mingle frequently with the mass of citizens? Is it not rather to be apprehended, if they were possessed of the power before described, that the individual members would
5 be induced to use them, on many occasions, very timidly and inefficaciously for fear of losing their popularity and future election? We must take human nature as we find it. Perfection falls not to the share of mortals. Many are of opinion that Congress have too frequently made use of the suppliant humble tone of requisition, in applications to the States, when they had a right to assume their
10 imperial dignity and command obedience. Be that as it may, requisitions are a perfect nihility, where thirteen sovereign, independent, disunited States are in the habit of discussing and refusing compliance with them at their option. Requisitions are actually little better than a jest and a byword throughout the Land. If you tell the Legislatures they have violated the treaty of peace and
15 invaded the prerogatives of the confederacy they will laugh in your face. What then is to be done? Things cannot go on in the same train forever. It is much to be feared, as you observe, that the better kind of people being disgusted with the circumstances will have their minds prepared for any revolution whatever. We are apt to run from one extreme into another. To anticipate and prevent
20 disastrous contingencies would be the part of wisdom and patriotism.

What astonishing changes a few years are capable of producing! I am told that even respectable characters speak of a monarchical form of government without horror. From thinking proceeds speaking, thence to acting is often but a single step. But how irrevocable and tremendous! What a triumph for the advocates of
25 despotism to find that we are incapable of governing ourselves, and that systems founded on the basis of equal liberty are merely ideal and fallacious! Would to God that wise measures may be taken in time to avert the consequences we have but too much reason to apprehend.

Retired as I am from the world, I frankly acknowledge I cannot feel myself an
30 unconcerned spectator. Yet having happily assisted in bringing the ship into port and having been fairly discharged; it is not my business to embark again on a sea of troubles. Nor could it be expected that my sentiments and opinions would have much weight on the minds of my Countrymen—they have been neglected, though given as a last legacy in the most solemn manner. I had then
35 perhaps some claims to public attention. I consider myself as having none at present. With sentiments of sincere esteem and friendship I am, my dear Sir, Your Most Obedient and Affectionate Humble Servant.

George Washington

LETTER TO JAMES MADISON
GEORGE WASHINGTON

George Washington writes here to James Madison two months before the Constitutional Convention was set to start in Philadelphia. A year earlier, only twelve men from five states attended a gathering held in Annapolis, Maryland, to amend the Articles of Confederation. Both men feared the consequences should the this convention similarly fail.

MARCH 31, 1787

MY DEAR SIR:

At the same time that I acknowledge the receipt of your obliging favor of the 21st. Ult. from New York, I promise to avail myself of your indulgence of writing only when it is convenient to me. If this should not occasion a relaxation on your part, I shall become very much your debtor—and possibly like others in similar circumstances (when the debt is burdensome) may feel a disposition 5 to apply the spunge—or, what is nearly a-kin to it—pay you off in depreciated paper, which being a legal tender, or what is tantamount, being *that* or *nothing*, you cannot refuse. You will receive the nominal value, and that you know quiets the conscience, and makes all things easy—with the debtors.

I am glad to find that Congress have recommended to the States to appear in the 10 Convention proposed to be holden in Philadelphia in May. I think the reasons in favor, have the preponderancy of those against the measure. It is idle in my opinion to suppose that the Sovereign can be insensible of the inadequacy of the powers under which it acts—and that seeing, it should not recommend a revision of the Federal system, when it is considered by many as the *only* 15 Constitutional mode by which the defects can be remedied. Had Congress proceeded to a delineation of the Powers, it might have sounded an Alarm; but as the case is, I do not conceive that it will have that effect.

George Washington, "To James Madison," March 31, 1787, in W. W. Abbot et al., eds., *The Papers of George Washington,* "Confederation Series," Vol. 5 (Charlottesville, VA: University of Virginia Press, 1976–present), 114–17.

From the acknowledged abilities of the Secretary for Foreign Affairs, I could have had no doubt of his having ably investigated the infractions of the Treaty on both sides.—Much is it to be regretted however, that there should have been any on ours. We seem to have forgotten, or never to have learnt, the policy of placing one's enemy in the wrong. Had we observed good faith on our part, we might have told our tale to the world with a good grace; but complaints illy become those who are found to be the first aggressors.

I am fully of opinion that those who lean to a Monarchical government have either not consulted the public mind, or that they live in a region where the levelling principles in which they were bred, being entirely eradicated, is much more productive of Monarchical ideas than are to be found in the Southern States, where from the habitual distinctions which have always existed among the people, one would have expected the first generation, and the most rapid growth of them. I also am clear, that even admitting the utility; nay necessity of the form—yet that the period is not arrived for adopting the change without shaking the Peace of this Country to its foundation.

That a thorough reform of the present system is indispensable, none who have capacities to judge will deny—and with hand and heart I hope the business will be essayed in a full Convention—After which, if more powers, and more decision is not found in the existing form—If it still wants energy and that secrecy and dispatch (either from the non-attendance, or the local views of its members) which is characteristic of good Government—And if it shall be found (the contrary of which however I have always been more afraid of, than of the abuse of them) that Congress will upon all proper occasions exercise the powers with a firm and steady hand, instead of frittering them back to the Individual States where the members in place of viewing themselves in their national character, are too apt to be looking. I say after this essay is made if the system proves inefficient, conviction of the necessity of a change will be disseminated among all classes of the People—Then, and not till then, in my opinion can it be attempted without involving all the evils of civil discord.

I confess however that my opinion of public virtue is so far changed that I have my doubts whether any system without the means of coercion in the Sovereign, will enforce obedience to the Ordinances of a General Government; without which, every thing else fails. Laws or Ordinances unobserved, or partially attended to, had better never have been made; because the first is a mere nihil—and the second is productive of much jealousy and discontent. But the kind of coercion you may ask?—This indeed will require thought; though the non-compliance of the States with the late requisition, is an evidence of the necessity.

It is somewhat singular that a State (New York) which used to be foremost in all federal measures, should now turn her face against them in almost every instance.

I fear the State of Massachusetts have exceeded the bounds of good policy in its disfranchisements—punishment is certainly due to the disturbers of a government, but the operations of this act is too extensive. It embraces too much—and probably   5
may give birth to new, instead of destroying the old leven.

Some Acts passed at the last Session of our Assembly respecting the trade of this Country, has given great, and general discontent to the Merchants of it. An application from the whole body of those at Norfolk has been made, I am told, to convene the Assembly.   10

I had written thus far, and was on the point of telling you how much I am your obliged Servant, when your favor of the eighteenth calls upon me for additional acknowledgments.

I thank you for the Indian Vocabulary which I dare say will be very acceptable in a general comparison. Having taken a copy, I return you the original with thanks.   15

It gives me great pleasure to hear that there is a probability of a full representation of the States in Convention; but if the delegates come to it under fetters, the salutary ends proposed will in my opinion be greatly embarrassed and retarded, if not altogether defeated. I am anxious to know how this matter really is, as my wish is, that the Convention may adopt no temporizing expedient, but   20
probe the defects of the Constitution to the bottom, and provide radical cures, whether they are agreed to or not—a conduct like this, will stamp wisdom and dignity on the proceedings, and be looked to as a luminary, which sooner or later will shed its influence.

I should feel pleasure, I confess in hearing that Vermont is received into the   25
Union upon terms agreeable to all parties—I took the liberty years ago to tell some of the first characters in the State of New York, that sooner or later it would come to that. That the longer it was delayed the terms on their part, would, probably be more difficult—and that the general interest was suffering by the suspense in which the business was held; as the asylum which it afforded, was   30
a constant drain from the Army in place of an aid which it offered to afford, and lastly, considering the proximity of it to Canada if they were not with us, they might become a sore thorn in our sides, which I verily believe would have been the case if the War had continued. The Western Settlements without good and wise management of them, may be equally troublesome. With sentiments   35
of the sincerest friendship I am—Dear Sir Your Affectionate Servant,

George Washington

Notes on the State of Virginia
Query XIII: Constitution
Thomas Jefferson

Virginia, the most populous state, adopted its state constitution in 1776, a month before the Declaration of Independence passed Congress. Thomas Jefferson, Virginia's governor from 1779 to 1781, addressed the problems that plagued the state's first attempt at self-government in his 1784 book, Notes on the State of Virginia.

1784

The Constitution of the State and its Several Charters

…This constitution was formed when we were new and unexperienced in the science of government. It was the first, too, which was formed in the whole United States. No wonder then that time and trial have discovered very capital defects in it.

1. The majority of the men in the State, who pay and fight for its support, 5 are unrepresented in the legislature, the roll of freeholders entitled to vote not including generally the half of those on the roll of the militia, or of the tax-gatherers.

2. Among those who share the representation, the shares are very unequal. Thus the county of Warwick, with only one hundred fighting men, has an 10 equal representation with the county of Loudon, which has 1,746. So that every man in Warwick has as much influence in the government as seventeen men in Loudon. But lest it should be thought that an equal interspersion of small among large counties, through the whole State, may prevent any danger of injury to particular parts of it, we will divide it into districts, and show the 15 proportions of land, of fighting men, and of representation in each.

Thomas Jefferson, *Notes on the State of Virginia,* "Query XIII: Constitution," in A. A. Lipscomb and A. E. Bergh, eds., *The Writings of Thomas Jefferson*, Vol. 2 (Washington, D.C.: Thomas Jefferson Memorial Association, 1907), 160–67, 172–78.

	Square Miles	Fighting Men	Delegates	Senators
Between the sea-coast and falls of the rivers	11,205	19,012	71	12
Between the falls of the rivers and the Blue Ridge of mountains	18,759	18,828	46	8
Between the Blue Ridge and the Alleghany	11,911	7,673	16	2
Between the Alleghany and Ohio	79,650	4,458	16	2
Total	121,525	49,971	149	24

An inspection of this table will supply the place of commentaries on it. It will appear at once that nineteen thousand men, living below the falls of the rivers, possess half the senate, and want four members only of possessing a majority of the house of delegates; a want more than supplied by the vicinity

5   of their situation to the seat of government, and of course the greater degree of convenience and punctuality with which their members may and will attend in the legislature. These nineteen thousand, therefore, living in one part of the country, give law to upwards of thirty thousand living in another, and appoint all their chief officers, executive and judiciary. From the difference of their

10   situation and circumstances, their interests will often be very different.

3. The senate is, by its constitution, too homogeneous with the house of delegates. Being chosen by the same electors, at the same time, and out of the same subjects, the choice falls of course on men of the same description. The purpose of establishing different houses of legislation is to introduce the

15   influence of different interests or different principles. Thus in Great Britain it is said their constitution relies on the house of commons for honesty, and the lords for wisdom; which would be a rational reliance, if honesty were to be bought with money, and if wisdom were hereditary. In some of the American States, the delegates and senators are so chosen, as that the first represent the persons,

20   and the second, the property of the State. But with us, wealth and wisdom have equal chance for admission into both houses. We do not, therefore, derive from the separation of our legislature into two houses, those benefits which a proper complication of principles are capable of producing, and those which alone can compensate the evils which may be produced by their dissensions.

25   4. All the powers of government, legislative, executive, and judiciary, result to the legislative body. The concentrating these in the same hands is precisely the

definition of despotic government. It will be no alleviation that these powers
will be exercised by a plurality of hands, and not by a single one. One hundred
seventy-three despots would surely be as oppressive as one. Let those who doubt
it turn their eyes on the republic of Venice. As little will it avail us that they are
chosen by ourselves. An *elective despotism* was not the government we fought for,   5
but one which should not only be founded upon free principles, but in which the
powers of government should be so divided and balanced among several bodies
of magistracy, as that no one could transcend their legal limits, without being
effectually checked and restrained by the others. For this reason that convention
which passed the ordinance of government, laid its foundation on this basis,   10
that the legislative, executive, and judiciary departments should be separate and
distinct, so that no person should exercise the powers of more than one of them
at the same time. But no barrier was provided between these several powers. The
judiciary and executive members were left dependent on the legislative, for their
subsistence in office, and some of them for their continuance in it. If, therefore,   15
the legislature assumes executive and judiciary powers, no opposition is likely
to be made; nor, if made, can it be effectual; because in that case they may put
their proceedings into the form of an act of assembly, which will render them
obligatory on the other branches. They have, accordingly, in many instances,
decided rights which should have been left to judiciary controversy; and the   20
direction of the executive, during the whole time of their session, is becoming
habitual and familiar. And this is done with no ill intention. The views of the
present members are perfectly upright. Whey they are led out of their regular
province, it is by art in others, and inadvertence in themselves. And this will
probably be the case for some time to come. But it will not be a very long time.   25
Mankind soon learn to make interested uses of every right and power which
they possess, or may assume. The public money and public liberty, intended to
have been deposited with three branches of magistracy, but found inadvertently
to be in the hands of one only, will soon be discovered to be sources of wealth
and dominion to those who hold them; distinguished, too, by this tempting   30
circumstance, that they are the instrument, as well as the object of acquisition.
With money we will get men, said Caesar, and with men we will get money.
Nor should our assembly be deluded by the integrity of their own purposes, and
conclude that these unlimited powers will never be abused, because themselves
are not disposed to abuse them. They should look forward to a time, and that   35
not a distant one, when a corruption in this, as in the country from which we
derive our origin, will have seized the heads of government, and be spread by
them through the body of the people; when they will purchase the voices of
the people, and make them pay the price. Human nature is the same on every
side of the Atlantic, and will be alike influenced by the same causes. The time   40

to guard against corruption and tyranny, is before they shall have gotten hold of us. It is better to keep the wolf out of the fold, than to trust to drawing his teeth and claws after he shall have entered. To render these considerations the more cogent, we must observe in addition:

5   5. That the ordinary legislature may alter the constitution itself. On the discontinuance of assemblies, it became necessary to substitute in their place some other body, competent to the ordinary business of government, and to the calling forth the powers of the State for the maintenance of our opposition to Great Britain. Conventions were therefore introduced, consisting of two

10   delegates from each county, meeting together and forming one house, on the plan of the former house of burgesses, to whose places they succeeded. These were at first chosen anew for every particular session. But in March 1775, they recommended to the people to choose a convention, which should continue in office a year. This was done, accordingly, in April 1775, and in the July following

15   that convention passed an ordinance for the election of delegates in the month of April annually. It is well known, that in July 1775, a separation from Great Britain and establishment of republican government, had never yet entered into any person's mind. A convention, therefore, chosen under that ordinance, cannot be said to have been chosen for purposes which certainly did not exist in the minds

20   of those who passed it. Under this ordinance, at the annual election in April 1776, a convention for the year was chosen. Independence, and the establishment of a new form of government, were not even yet the objects of the people at large. One extract from the pamphlet called *Common Sense* had appeared in the Virginia papers in February, and copies of the pamphlet itself had got in a few hands. But

25   the idea had not been opened to the mass of the people in April, much less can it be said that they had made up their minds in its favor.

So that the electors of April 1776, no more than the legislators of July 1775, not thinking of independence and a permanent republic, could not mean to vest in these delegates powers of establishing them, or any authorities other than those

30   of the ordinary legislature. So far as a temporary organization of government was necessary to render our opposition energetic, so far their organization was valid. But they received in their creation no powers but what were given to every legislature before and since. They could not, therefore, pass an act transcendent to the powers of other legislatures. If the present assembly pass an act, and declare

35   it shall be irrevocable by subsequent assemblies, the declaration is merely void, and the act repealable, as other acts are. So far, and no farther authorized, they organized the government by the ordinance entitled a constitution or form of government. It pretends to no higher authority than the other ordinances of the same session; it does not say that it shall be perpetual; that it shall be unalterable

by other legislatures; that it shall be transcendent above the powers of those who they knew would have equal power with themselves. Not only the silence of the instrument is a proof they thought it would be alterable, but their own practice also; for this very convention, meeting as a house of delegates in general assembly with the Senate in the autumn of that year, passed acts of assembly in 5 contradiction to their ordinance of government; and every assembly from that time to this has done the same. I am safe, therefore, in the position that the constitution itself is alterable by the ordinary legislature....

6. That the assembly exercises a power of determining the quorum of their own body which may legislate for us. After the establishment of the new form they 10 adhered to the *Lex majoris partis,* founded in common law as well as common right. It is the natural law of every assembly of men, whose numbers are not fixed by any other law. They continued for some time to require the presence of a majority of their whole number, to pass an act. But the British parliament fixes its own quorum; our former assemblies fixed their own quorum; and one 15 precedent in favor of power is stronger than an hundred against it. The house of delegates, therefore, have lately voted that, during the present dangerous invasion, forty members shall be a house to proceed to business. They have been moved to this by the fear of not being able to collect a house. But this danger could not authorize them to call that a house which was none; and if they may 20 fix it at one number, they may at another, till it loses its fundamental character of being a representative body. As this vote expires with the present invasion, it is probable the former rule will be permitted to revive; because at present no ill is meant. The power, however, of fixing their own quorum has been avowed, and a precedent set. From forty it may be reduced to four, and from four to 25 one; from a house to a committee, from a committee to a chairman or speaker, and thus an oligarchy or monarchy be substituted under forms supposed to be regular. "*Omnia mala exempla ex bonis orta sunt; sed ubi imperium ad ignaros aut minus bonos pervenit, novum illud exemplum ab dignis et edoneis abindignos et non ideoneos fertur.*"* When, therefore, it is considered, that there is no 30 legal obstacle to the assumption by the assembly of all the powers legislative, executive, and judiciary, and that these may come to the hands of the smallest rag of delegation, surely the people will say, and their representatives, while yet they have honest representatives, will advise them to say, that they will not acknowledge as laws any acts not considered and assented to by the major part 35 of their delegates.

---

*"All bad examples are derived from good ones; but when power comes to the ignorant or the less good, the new example is transferred from the worthy and fit to the unworthy and unfit."

In enumerating the defects of the Constitution, it would be wrong to count among them what is only the error of particular persons. In December 1776, our circumstances being much distressed, it was proposed in the house of delegates to create a *dictator*, invested with every power legislative, executive
5   and judiciary, civil and military, of life and of death, over our persons and over our properties; and in June 1781, again under calamity, the same proposition was repeated, and wanted a few votes only of being passed. One who entered into this contest from a pure love of liberty, and a sense of injured rights, who determined to make every sacrifice, and to meet every danger, for the re-
10   establishment of those rights on a firm basis, who did not mean to expend his blood and substance for the wretched purpose of changing this master for that, but to place the powers of governing him in a plurality of hands of his own choice, so that the corrupt will of no one man might in future oppress him, must stand confounded and dismayed when he is told, that a considerable
15   portion of that plurality had mediated the surrender of them into a single hand, and, in lieu of a limited monarchy, to deliver him over to a despotic one! How must we find his efforts and sacrifices abused and baffled, if he may still, by a single vote, be laid prostrate at the feet of one man! In God's name, from whence have they derived this power? Is it from our ancient laws? None such can be
20   produced. Is it from any principle in our new Constitution expressed or implied? Every lineament expressed or implied, is in full opposition to it. Its fundamental principle is, that the State shall be governed as a commonwealth. It provides a republican organization, proscribes under the name of *prerogative* the exercise of all powers undefined by the laws; places on this basis the whole system of
25   our laws; and by consolidating them together, chooses that they shall be left to stand or fall together, never providing for any circumstances, nor admitting that such could arise, wherein either should be suspended; no, not for a moment. Our ancient laws expressly declare, that those who are but delegates themselves shall not delegate to others powers which require judgment and integrity in
30   their exercise. Or was this proposition moved on a supposed right in the movers, of abandoning their posts in a moment of distress? The same laws forbid the abandonment of that post, even on ordinary occasions; and much more a transfer of their powers into other hands and other forms, without consulting the people. They never admit the idea that these, like sheep or cattle, may be
35   given from hand to hand without an appeal to their own will. Was it from the necessity of the case? Necessities which dissolve a government, do not convey its authority to an oligarchy or a monarchy. They throw back, into the hands of the people, the powers they had delegated, and leave them as individuals to shift for themselves. A leader may offer, but not impose himself, nor be imposed
40   on them. Much less can their necks be submitted to his sword, their breath to

be held at his will or caprice. The necessity which should operate these tremendous effects should at least be palpable and irresistible. Yet in both instances, where it was feared, or pretended with us, it was belied by the event. It was belied, too, by the preceding experience of our sister States, several of whom had grappled through greater difficulties without abandoning their forms of government. When the proposition was first made, Massachusetts had found even the government of committees sufficient to carry them through an invasion. But we at the time of that proposition, were under no invasion. When the second was made, there had been added to this example those of Rhode Island, New York, New Jersey, and Pennsylvania, in all of which the republican form had been found equal to the task of carrying them through the severest trials. In this State alone did there exist so little virtue, that fear was to be fixed in the hearts of the people, and to become the motive of their exertions, and the principle of their government? The very thought alone was treason against the people; was treason against mankind in general; as riveting for ever the chains which bow down their necks, by giving to their oppressors a proof, which they would have trumpeted through the universe, of the imbecility of republican government, in times of pressing danger, to shield them from harm. Those who assume the right of giving away the reins of government in any case, must be sure that the herd, whom they hand on to the rods and hatchet of the dictator, will lay their necks on the block when he shall nod to them. But if our assemblies supposed such a recognition in the people, I hope they mistook their character. I am of opinion, that the government, instead of being braced and invigorated for greater exertions under their difficulties, would have been thrown back upon the bungling machinery of county committees for administration, till a convention could have been called, and its wheels again set into regular motion. What a cruel moment was this for creating such an embarrassment, for putting to the proof the attachment of our countrymen to republican government! Those who meant well, of the advocates for this measure, (and most of them meant well, for I know them personally, had been their fellow-laborer in the common cause, and had often proved the purity of their principles) had been seduced in their judgment by the example of an ancient republic, whose constitution and circumstances were fundamentally different. They had sought this precedent in the history of Rome, where alone it was to be found, and where at length, too, it had proved fatal. They had taken it from a republic rent by the most bitter factions and tumults, where the government was of a heavy-handed unfeeling aristocracy, over a people ferocious, and rendered desperate by poverty and wretchedness; tumults which could not be allayed under the most trying circumstances, but by the omnipotent hand of a single despot. Their constitution, therefore, allowed a temporary tyrant to be erected, under

the name of a dictator; and that temporary tyrant, after a few examples, became perpetual. They misapplied this precedent to a people mild in their dispositions, patient under their trial, united for the public liberty, and affectionate to their leaders. But if from the constitution of the Roman government there resulted
5   to their senate a power of submitting all their rights to the will of one man; does it follow that the assembly of Virginia have the same authority? What clause in our constitution has substituted that of Rome, by way of residuary provision, for all cases not otherwise provided for? Or, if they may step *ad libitum* into any other form of government for precedents to rule us by, for
10   what oppression may not a precedent be found in this world of the *bellum omnium in omnia*? Searching for the foundations of this proposition, I can find none which may pretend a color of right or reason, but the defect before developed, that there being no barrier between the legislative, executive, and judiciary departments, the legislature may seize the whole; that having seized
15   it, and possessing a right to fix their own quorum, they may reduce that quorum to one, whom they may call a chairman, speaker, dictator, or by any other name they please. Our situation is indeed perilous, and I hope my countrymen will be sensible of it, and will apply, at a proper season, the proper remedy; which is a convention to fix the constitution, to amend its defects, to bind up the
20   several branches of government by certain laws, which, when they transgress, their acts shall become nullities; to render unnecessary an appeal to the people, or in other words a rebellion, on every infraction of their rights, on the peril that their acquiescence shall be construed into an intention to surrender those rights.

Vices of the Political System of the United States
James Madison

In this essay, James Madison outlines the main issues that the Constitutional Convention should address. His early arrival in Philadelphia allowed him to incorporate his ideas into a recommended plan for the Convention—what came to be called the Virginia Plan—representing no mere revision of the Articles of Association, but the adoption of an entirely new Constitution.

APRIL 1787

1. FAILURE OF THE STATES TO COMPLY WITH THE CONSTITUTIONAL REQUISITIONS.

This evil has been so fully experienced both during the war and since the peace, results so naturally from the number and independent authority of the States and has been so uniformly exemplified in every similar Confederacy, that it may be considered as not less radically and permanently inherent in, than it is fatal to the object of, the present System. 5

2. ENCROACHMENTS BY THE STATES ON THE FEDERAL AUTHORITY.

Examples of this are numerous and repetitions may be foreseen in almost every case where any favorite object of a State shall present a temptation. Among these examples are the wars and Treaties of Georgia with the Indians—The unlicensed compacts between Virginia and Maryland, and between Pennsylvania and New Jersey—the troops raised and to be kept up by Massachusetts. 10

3. VIOLATIONS OF THE LAW OF NATIONS AND OF TREATIES.

From the number of Legislatures, the sphere of life from which most of their members are taken, and the circumstances under which their legislative business is carried on, irregularities of this kind must frequently happen. Accordingly not

James Madison, "Vices of the Political System of the United States," April 1787, in William T. Hutchison et al., eds., *The Papers of James Madison,* Vol. 9 (Chicago: University of Chicago Press, 1962–present), 348–57. Reproduced with permission of University of Chicago Press–Books in the format Textbook via Copyright Clearance Center.

a year has passed without instances of them in some one or other of the States. The Treaty of peace—the treaty with France—the treaty with Holland have each been violated. The causes of these irregularities must necessarily produce frequent violations of the law of nations in other respects.

5   As yet foreign powers have not been rigorous in animadverting on us. This moderation however cannot be mistaken for a permanent partiality to our faults, or a permanent security against those disputes with other nations, which being among the greatest of public calamities, it ought to be least in the power of any part of the Community to bring on the whole.

4. TRESPASSES OF THE STATES ON THE RIGHTS OF EACH OTHER.

10   These are alarming symptoms, and may be daily apprehended as we are admonished by daily experience. See the law of Virginia restricting foreign vessels to certain ports—of Maryland in favor of vessels belonging to her own citizens—of New York in favor of the same.

Paper money, installments of debts, occlusion of Courts, making property a
15   legal tender, may likewise be deemed aggressions on the rights of other States. As the Citizens of every State aggregately taken stand more or less in the relation of Creditors or debtors, to the Citizens of every other States, Acts of the debtor State in favor of debtors, affect the Creditor State, in the same manner, as they do its own citizens who are relatively creditors towards other citizens. This remark
20   may be extended to foreign nations. If the exclusive regulation of the value and alloy of coin was properly delegated to the federal authority, the policy of it equally requires a control on the States in the cases above mentioned. It must have been meant 1. to preserve uniformity in the circulating medium throughout the nation. 2. to prevent those frauds on the citizens of other States, and the
25   subjects of foreign powers, which might disturb the tranquility at home, or involve the Union in foreign contests.

The practice of many States in restricting the commercial intercourse with other States, and putting their productions and manufactures on the same footing with those of foreign nations, though not contrary to the federal articles, is certainly
30   adverse to the spirit of the Union, and tends to beget retaliating regulations, not less expensive and vexatious in themselves, than they are destructive of the general harmony.

5. WANT OF CONCERT IN MATTERS WHERE COMMON INTEREST REQUIRES IT.

This defect is strongly illustrated in the state of our commercial affairs. How much has the national dignity, interest, and revenue suffered from this cause?
35   Instances of inferior moment are the want of uniformity in the laws concerning

naturalization and literary property; of provision for national seminaries, for grants of incorporation for national purposes, for canals and other works of general utility, which may at present be defeated by the perverseness of particular States whose concurrence is necessary.

6. WANT OF GUARANTY TO THE STATES OF THEIR CONSTITUTIONS AND LAWS AGAINST INTERNAL VIOLENCE.

The confederation is silent on this point and therefore by the second article   5
the hands of the federal authority are tied. According to Republican Theory, Right and power being both vested in the majority, are held to be synonymous. According to fact and experience a minority may in an appeal to force, be an overmatch for the majority. 1. If the minority happen to include all such as possess the skill and habits of military life, and such as possess the great pecuniary   10
resources, one third only may conquer the remaining two thirds. 2. One third of those who participate in the choice of the rulers, may be rendered a majority by the accession of those whose poverty excludes them from a right of suffrage, and who for obvious reasons will be more likely to join the standard of sedition than that of the established Government. 3. Where slavery exists the republican   15
Theory becomes still more fallacious.

7. WANT OF SANCTION TO THE LAWS, AND OF COERCION IN THE GOVERNMENT OF THE CONFEDERACY.

A sanction is essential to the idea of law, as coercion is to that of Government. The federal system being destitute of both, wants the great vital principles of a Political Constitution. Under the form of such a Constitution, it is in fact nothing more than a treaty of amity of commerce and of alliance, between so   20
many independent and Sovereign States. From what cause could so fatal an omission have happened in the articles of Confederation? from a mistaken confidence that the justice, the good faith, the honor, the sound policy, of the several legislative assemblies would render superfluous any appeal to the ordinary motives by which the laws secure the obedience of individuals: a confidence   25
which does honor to the enthusiastic virtue of the compilers, as much as the inexperience of the crisis apologizes for their errors. The time which has since elapsed has had the double effect, of increasing the light and tempering the warmth, with which the arduous work may be revised. It is no longer doubted that a unanimous and punctual obedience of thirteen independent bodies, to the   30
acts of the federal Government, ought not be calculated on. Even during the war, when external danger supplied in some degree the defect of legal and coercive sanctions, how imperfectly did the States fulfill their obligations to the Union? In time of peace, we see already what is to be expected. How indeed could it

be otherwise? In the first place, Every general act of the Union must necessarily bear unequally hard on some particular member or members of it. Secondly the partiality of the members to their own interests and rights, a partiality which will be fostered by the Courtiers of popularity, will naturally exaggerate the
5   inequality where it exists, and even suspect it where it has no existence. Thirdly a distrust of the voluntary compliance of each other may prevent the compliance of any, although it should be the latent disposition of all. Here are causes and pretexts which will never fail to render federal measures abortive. If the laws of the States, were merely recommendatory to their citizens, or if they were to be
10   rejudged by County authorities, what security, what probability would exist, that they would be carried into execution? Is the security or probability greater in favor of the acts of Congress which depending for their execution on the will of the state legislatures, which are though nominally authoritative, in fact recommendatory only.

8. WANT OF RATIFICATION BY THE PEOPLE OF THE ARTICLES OF CONFEDERATION.

15   In some of the States the Confederation is recognized by, and forms a part of the constitution. In others however it has received no other sanction than that of the Legislative authority. From this defect two evils result: 1. Whenever a law of a State happens to be repugnant to an act of Congress, particularly when the latter is of posterior date to the former, it will be at least questionable whether
20   the latter must not prevail; and as the question must be decided by the Tribunals of the State, they will be most likely to lean on the side of the State. 2. As far as the Union of the States is to be regarded as a league of sovereign powers, and not as a political Constitution by virtue of which they are become one sovereign power, so far it seems to follow from the doctrine of compacts, that a breach of
25   any of the articles of the confederation by any of the parties to it, absolves the other parties from their respective obligations, and gives them a right if they choose to exert it, of dissolving the Union altogether.

9. MULTIPLICITY OF LAWS IN THE SEVERAL STATES.

In developing the evils which vitiate the political system of the United States, it is proper to include those which are found within the States individually, as
30   well as those which directly affect the States collectively, since the former class have an indirect influence on the general malady and must not be overlooked in forming a complete remedy. Among the evils then of our situation may well be ranked the multiplicity of laws from which no State is exempt. As far as laws are necessary, to mark with precision the duties of those who are to obey them,
35   and to take from those who are to administer them a discretion, which might be abused, their number is the price of liberty. As far as the laws exceed this limit,

they are a nuisance: a nuisance of the most pestilent kind. Try the Codes of the several States by this test, and what a luxuriancy of legislation do they present. The short period of independency has filled as many pages as the century which preceded it. Every year, almost every session, adds a new volume. This may be the effect in part, but it can only be in part, of the situation in which the revolution has placed us. A review of the several codes will show that every necessary and useful part of the least voluminous of them might be compressed into one tenth of the compass, and at the same time be rendered tenfold as perspicuous.

10. MUTABILITY OF THE LAWS OF THE STATES.

This evil is intimately connected with the former yet deserves a distinct notice as it emphatically denotes a vicious legislation. We daily see laws repealed or superseded, before any trial can have been made of their merits; and even before a knowledge of them can have reached the remoter districts within which they were to operate. In the regulations of trade this instability becomes a snare, not only to our citizens but to foreigners also.

11. INJUSTICE OF THE LAWS OF STATES.

If the multiplicity and mutability of laws prove a want of wisdom, their injustice betrays a defect still more alarming: more alarming not merely because it is a greater evil in itself, but because it brings more into question the fundamental principle of republican Government, that the majority who rule in such Governments, are the safest Guardians both of public Good and of private rights. To what causes is this evil to be ascribed?

These causes lie: 1. In the Representative bodies. 2. In the people themselves.

1. Representative appointments are sought from three motives: 1. ambition, 2. personal interest, 3. public good. Unhappily the two first are proved by experience to be most prevalent. Hence the candidates who feel them, particularly, the second, are most industrious, and most successful in pursuing their object: and forming often a majority in the legislative Councils, with interested views, contrary to the interest, and views, of their Constituents, join in a perfidious sacrifice of the latter to the former. A succeeding election it might be supposed, would displace the offenders, and repair the mischief. But how easily are base and selfish measures, masked by pretexts of public good and apparent expediency? How frequently will a repetition of the same arts and industry which succeeded in the first instance, again prevail on the unwary to misplace their confidence?

How frequently too will the honest but unenlightened representative be the dupe of a favorite leader, veiling his selfish views under the professions of public good, and varnishing his sophistical arguments with the glowing colors of popular eloquence?

2. A still more fatal if not more frequent cause lies among the people themselves. All civilized societies are divided into different interests and factions, as they happen to be creditors or debtors—Rich or poor—husbandmen, merchants or manufacturers—members of different religious sects—followers of different political leaders—inhabitants of different districts—owners of different kinds of property, etc., etc. In republican Government the majority however composed, ultimately give the law. Whenever therefore an apparent interest or common passion unites a majority what is to restrain them from unjust violations of the rights and interests of the minority, or of individuals? Three motives only: 1. a prudent regard to their own good as involved in the general and permanent good of the Community. This consideration although of decisive weight in itself, is found by experience to be too often unheeded. It is too often forgotten, by nations as well as by individuals that honesty is the best policy. Secondly respect for character. However strong this motive may be in individuals, it is considered as very insufficient to restrain them from injustice. In a multitude its efficacy is diminished in proportion to the number which is to share the praise or the blame. Besides, as it has reference to public opinion, which within a particular Society, is the opinion of the majority, the standard is fixed by those whose conduct is to be measured by it. The public opinion without the Society, will be little respected by the people at large of any Country. Individuals of extended views, and of national pride, may bring the public proceedings to this standard, but the example will never be followed by the multitude. Is it to be imagined that an ordinary citizen or even an assemblyman of Rhode Island in estimating the policy of paper money, ever considered or cared in what light the measure would be viewed in France or Holland; or even in Massachusetts or Connecticut? It was a sufficient temptation to both that it was for their interest: it was a sufficient sanction to the latter that it was popular in the State; to the former that it was so in the neighbourhood. Thirdly will Religion, the only remaining motive be a sufficient restraint? It is not pretended to be such on men individually considered. Will its effect be greater on them considered in an aggregate view? quite the reverse. The conduct of every popular assembly acting on oath, the strongest of religious Ties, proves that individuals join without remorse in acts, against which their consciences would revolt if proposed to them under the like sanction, separately in their closets. When indeed Religion is kindled into enthusiasm, its force like that of other passions, is increased by the sympathy of a multitude. But enthusiasm is only a temporary state of religion, and while it lasts will hardly be seen with pleasure at the helm of Government.

Besides as religion in its coolest state, is not infallible, it may become a motive to oppression as well as a restraint from injustice. Place three individuals in a situation wherein the interest of each depends on the voice of the others, and give to two of them an interest opposed to the rights of the third? Will the latter be secure? The prudence of every man would shun the danger. The rules and forms   5 of justice suppose and guard against it. Will two thousand in a like situation be less likely to encroach on the rights of one thousand? The contrary is witnessed by the notorious factions and oppressions which take place in corporate towns limited as the opportunities are, and in little republics when uncontrolled by apprehensions of external danger. If an enlargement of the sphere is found to   10 lessen the insecurity of private rights, it is not because the impulse of a common interest or passion is less predominant in this case with the majority; but because a common interest or passion is less apt to be felt and the requisite combinations less easy to be formed by a great than by a small number. The Society becomes broken into a greater variety of interests, of pursuits, of passions, which check   15 each other, whilst those who may feel a common sentiment have less opportunity of communication and concert. It may be inferred that the inconveniences of popular States contrary to the prevailing Theory, are in proportion not to the extent, but to the narrowness of their limits.

The great desideratum in Government is such a modification of the Sovereignty   20 as will render it sufficiently neutral between the different interests and factions, to control one part of the society from invading the rights of another, and at the same time sufficiently controlled itself, from setting up an interest adverse to that of the whole society. In absolute Monarchies, the prince is sufficiently neutral towards his subjects, but frequently sacrifices their happiness to his   25 ambition or his avarice. In small Republics, the sovereign will is sufficiently controlled from such a Sacrifice of the entire Society, but is not sufficiently neutral towards the parts composing it. As a limited Monarchy tempers the evils of an absolute one; so an extensive Republic meliorates the administration of a small Republic.   30

An auxiliary desideratum for the melioration of the Republican form is such a process of elections as will most certainly extract from the mass of the Society the purest and noblest characters which it contains; such as will at once feel most strongly the proper motives to pursue the end of their appointment, and be most capable to devise the proper means of attaining it. . . .   35

V
Rethinking the Nature of Union and the Structure of Government

The Constitution establishes a structure of government without offering a defense of the principles that undergird it. For that we must look first to the Declaration of Independence, and also to *The Federalist.* In the words of Publius—the pen name chosen by Alexander Hamilton, James Madison, and John Jay to unify their argument and to invoke the memory of Publius Valerius Publicola, the savior of the early Roman republic—it would be up to the American people "to decide the important question, whether societies of men are really capable or not of establishing good government from reflection and choice, or whether they are forever destined to depend for their political constitutions on accident and force." Put another way, if republican government could not work here, how could it work anywhere? Reflecting and choosing will not matter if the finished product is not right. Americans must not only choose, but choose *well*.

With this in mind, Publius—in a series of essays that originally appeared in New York newspapers beginning on October 27, 1787—mounts a vigorous defense of the new Constitution. In doing so, he proceeds from what is necessary to good government, to an analysis of the new Constitution itself.

The first half of *The Federalist* (1 through 36) is composed of three parts. Following the introductory first paper, papers 2 through 14 are concerned with the Union. *Federalist* 9 and 10 contend that a large republic is not only possible—by means of representation—but absolutely necessary to overcome the problem of majority faction. The "multiplicity of interests" found in a large republic makes it much less likely that an unjust majority will form and oppress a minority, thereby providing a "republican remedy" for this peculiarly republican disease. Papers 15 through 22 consider the insufficiency of the Articles of Confederation as a means to secure the Union. Under the Articles, as *Federalist* 15 notes, there were in effect two supreme powers in the United States—the states and the national government—which resulted only in ineffective, weak, and ultimately unjust government. To overcome this and other failures of the Articles, papers 23 through 36 make the case for an energetic national government. As Publius observes in *Federalist* 23, if we will the ends of government, we must also will the means to achieve those ends.

In the second half of *The Federalist* (37 to 85), Publius turns from necessity to a more high-minded concern: the merits of the proposed Constitution.

Correspondingly, certainty about the necessity of government is replaced by a "spirit of moderation" in relation to its particular form. A perfect Constitution is not to be expected from fallible human beings.

Nor should adherence to the law trump the demands of justice. After establishing the Constitution's republican *bona fides*—in response to the general Anti-Federalist charge of "consolidation"—Publius defends the action of the Convention, despite its lack of legal authority. Reason itself dictates that the means—a mandate that extended only to a revision of the Articles—should be sacrificed for the sake of the end: good government.

If the real point at issue is whether the Constitution is good or not, then separation of powers (47 to 51) constitutes the heart of its defense. A principal objection is that the three branches are not strictly separated, and therefore a consolidation of powers, or tyranny, will eventually result. But it turns out that some overlap of powers is not only consistent with, but *required* for, free government. Most importantly, mere "parchment barriers" offer no defense against the "impetuous vortex" that is the legislature. Strict separation leads only to legislative tyranny, as happened so often under the Articles of Confederation. Paradoxically, in a popular government, the people must be most vigilant against their own branch. Nor would direct appeals to the people to decide separation of powers questions be of help: These would favor the same legislature and, even worse, deprive the Constitution of much-needed veneration.

Having demonstrated the insufficiency of "exterior provisions" (parchment barriers and direct appeal), Publius turns to his solution, to the "interior structure" of the Constitution. In doing so, he teaches us that self-interest and duty are not mutually exclusive. In fact, in this system of divided and arranged powers, a defense of one's own self-interest becomes a defense of the Constitution itself. (Think of the presidential veto, for example.) That such prudential safeguards are necessary is not an entirely flattering reflection on human nature, and yet, if men were angels, "no government would be necessary."

The prevention of tyranny, especially the legislative kind, is not the whole story. A proper separation allows each branch to perform its assigned task better: the legislative branch will be more deliberative, the executive more energetic, and the judicial more judicious. In sum, the internal structure of government will protect Americans' natural rights more effectively than any formal bill of rights ever could. The "Constitution is itself" a bill of rights and will lead to good government.

Timothy W. Caspar
Lecturer in Politics
Associate Vice President
for External Affairs
Hillsdale College

Letter Transmitting the Constitution
George Washington

As they affixed their names to the new Constitution, the Framers understood that their work had just begun. Four months of debate and compromise paled in comparison to the challenge of convincing the states to ratify. Unanimity was not necessary for the Constitution to go into effect—only nine of thirteen states were needed—but they knew that without the approval of the largest of the states, including New York, Virginia, and Pennsylvania, their work would be for naught. Congress sent this letter to each state to begin the ratification process.

SEPTEMBER 17, 1787

SIR:

We have now the honor to submit to the consideration of the United States in Congress assembled, that Constitution which has appeared to us the most advisable.

The friends of our country have long seen and desired, that the power of making war, peace and treaties, that of levying money and regulating commerce, and the correspondent executive and judicial authorities should be fully and effectually vested in the general government of the Union: but the impropriety of delegating such extensive trust to one body of men is evident—Hence results the necessity of a different organization.

It is obviously impracticable in the federal government of these States, to secure all rights of independent sovereignty to each, and yet provide for the interest and safety of all—Individuals entering into society, must give up a share of liberty to preserve the rest. The magnitude of the sacrifice must depend as well on situation and circumstance, as on the object to be obtained. It is at all times difficult to draw with precision the line between those rights which must be

George Washington, "Letter Transmitting the Proposed Constitution from the Federal Convention to the Confederation Congress," September 17, 1787, in George Anastaplo, *The Constitution of 1787: A Commentary* (Baltimore, MD: Johns Hopkins University Press, 1989), 283–84.

surrendered, and those which may be reserved; and on the present occasion this difficulty was increased by a difference among the several States as to their situation, extent, habits, and particular interests.

In all our deliberations on this subject we kept steadily in our view, that which
5   appears to us the greatest interest of every true American, the consolidation of our Union, in which is involved our prosperity, felicity, safety, perhaps our national existence. This important consideration, seriously and deeply impressed on our minds, led each State in the Convention to be less rigid on points of inferior magnitude, than might have been otherwise expected; and thus the
10   Constitution, which we now present, is the result of a spirit of amity, and of that mutual deference and concession which the peculiarity of our political situation rendered indispensable.

That it will meet the full and entire approbation of every State is not perhaps to be expected; but each will doubtless consider, that had her interests been
15   alone consulted, the consequences might have been particularly disagreeable or injurious to others; that it is liable to as few exceptions as could reasonably have been expected, we hope and believe; that it may promote the lasting welfare of that country so dear to us all, and secure her freedom and happiness, is our most ardent wish.

20   With great respect, We have the honor to be, Sir, Your Excellency's most Obedient and humble Servants,

George Washington, President

By unanimous Order of the Convention

Federalist 1
Alexander Hamilton

By the time the members of the New York ratifying convention gathered in June 1788, ratification had succeeded in eight states—only one shy of the nine required. The pro-ratification Federalist Party in New York was weak, outnumbered at the convention by more than two to one. Alexander Hamilton, sensing the danger posed by attacks on the Constitution that had been published in newspapers across the state, suggested to James Madison and John Jay that the three of them write a series of essays defending and explaining the Constitution. Published under the pen name "Publius" in three New York City newspapers beginning in October 1787, The Federalist was called by Thomas Jefferson "the best commentary on the principles of government which was ever written."

OCTOBER 27, 1787

General Introduction

After an unequivocal experience of the inefficiency of the subsisting federal government, you are called upon to deliberate on a new Constitution for the United States of America. The subject speaks its own importance; comprehending in its consequences nothing less than the existence of the UNION, the safety and welfare of the parts of which it is composed, the fate of an empire in many respects the most interesting in the world. It has been frequently remarked that it seems to have been reserved to the people of this country, by their conduct and example, to decide the important question, whether societies of men are really capable or not of establishing good government from reflection and choice, or whether they are forever destined to depend for their political constitutions on accident and force. If there be any truth in the remark, the crisis at which we are arrived may with propriety be regarded as the era in which that decision is to be made; and a wrong election of the part we shall act may, in this view, deserve to be considered as the general misfortune of mankind.

5

10

Alexander Hamilton, "No. 1: General Introduction," in Clinton Rossiter, ed., *The Federalist Papers* (New York: Mentor, 1999), 27–31.

This idea will add the inducements of philanthropy to those of patriotism, to heighten the solicitude which all considerate and good men must feel for the event. Happy will it be if our choice should be directed by a judicious estimate of our true interests, unperplexed and unbiased by considerations not
5   connected with the public good. But this is a thing more ardently to be wished than seriously to be expected. The plan offered to our deliberations affects too many particular interests, innovates upon too many local institutions, not to involve in its discussion a variety of objects foreign to its merits, and of views, passions, and prejudices little favorable to the discovery of truth.

10   Among the most formidable of the obstacles which the new Constitution will have to encounter may readily be distinguished the obvious interest of a certain class of men in every State to resist all changes which may hazard a diminution of the power, emolument, and consequence of the offices they hold under the State establishments; and the perverted ambition of another class of men, who
15   will either hope to aggrandize themselves by the confusions of their country, or will flatter themselves with fairer prospects of elevation from the subdivision of the empire into several partial confederacies than from its union under one government.

It is not, however, my design to dwell upon observations of this nature. I
20   am well aware that it would be disingenuous to resolve indiscriminately the opposition of any set of men (merely because their situations might subject them to suspicion) into interested or ambitious views. Candor will oblige us to admit that even such men may be actuated by upright intentions; and it cannot be doubted that much of the opposition which has made its appearance,
25   or may hereafter make its appearance, will spring from sources, blameless at least if not respectable—the honest errors of minds led astray by preconceived jealousies and fears. So numerous indeed and so powerful are the causes which serve to give a false bias to the judgment, that we, upon many occasions, see wise and good men on the wrong as well as on the right side of questions of
30   the first magnitude to society. This circumstance, if duly attended to, would furnish a lesson of moderation to those who are ever so thoroughly persuaded of their being in the right in any controversy. And a further reason for caution, in this respect, might be drawn from the reflection that we are not always sure that those who advocate the truth are influenced by purer principles than their
35   antagonists. Ambition, avarice, personal animosity, party opposition, and many other motives not more laudable than these, are apt to operate as well upon those who support as those who oppose the right side of a question. Were there not even these inducements to moderation, nothing could be more ill-judged than that intolerant spirit which has at all times characterized political parties.

For in politics, as in religion, it is equally absurd to aim at making proselytes by fire and sword. Heresies in either can rarely be cured by persecution.

And yet, however just these sentiments will be allowed to be, we have already sufficient indications that it will happen in this as in all former cases of great national discussion. A torrent of angry and malignant passions will be let loose. To judge from the conduct of the opposite parties, we shall be led to conclude that they will mutually hope to evince the justness of their opinions, and to increase the number of their converts by the loudness of their declamations and by the bitterness of their invectives. An enlightened zeal for the energy and efficiency of government will be stigmatized as the offspring of a temper fond of despotic power and hostile to the principles of liberty. An over-scrupulous jealousy of danger to the rights of the people, which is more commonly the fault of the head than of the heart, will be represented as mere pretense and artifice, the stale bait for popularity at the expense of public good. It will be forgotten, on the one hand, that jealousy is the usual concomitant of violent love, and that the noble enthusiasm of liberty is too apt to be infected with a spirit of narrow and illiberal distrust. On the other hand, it will be equally forgotten that the vigor of government is essential to the security of liberty; that, in the contemplation of a sound and well-informed judgment, their interests can never be separated; and that a dangerous ambition more often lurks behind the specious mask of zeal for the rights of the people than under the forbidden appearance of zeal for the firmness and efficiency of government. History will teach us that the former has been found a much more certain road to the introduction of despotism than the latter, and that of those men who have overturned the liberties of republics, the greatest number have begun their career by paying an obsequious court to the people, commencing demagogues and ending tyrants.

In the course of the preceding observations, I have had an eye, my fellow-citizens, to putting you upon your guard against all attempts, from whatever quarter, to influence your decision in a matter of the utmost moment to your welfare by any impressions other than those which may result from the evidence of truth. You will, no doubt, at the same time, have collected from the general scope of them that they proceed from a source not unfriendly to the new Constitution. Yes, my countrymen, I own to you that after having given it an attentive consideration, I am clearly of opinion it is your interest to adopt it. I am convinced that this is the safest course for your liberty, your dignity, and your happiness. I affect not reserves which I do not feel. I will not amuse you with an appearance of deliberation when I have decided. I frankly acknowledge to you my convictions, and I will freely lay before you the reasons on which they are founded. The consciousness of good intentions disdains ambiguity. I shall not, however, multiply professions on this head. My motives must remain in the depository of my own breast. My arguments will be open to all and may be judged of by all. They shall at least be offered in a spirit which will not disgrace the cause of truth.

5   I propose, in a series of papers, to discuss the following interesting particulars:

—*The utility of the* UNION *to your political prosperity*—*The insufficiency of the present Confederation to preserve that Union*—*The necessity of a government at least equally energetic with the one proposed, to the attainment of this object*—*The conformity of the proposed Constitution to the true principles of republican government*—*Its*

10   *analogy to your own State constitution*—and lastly, *The additional security which its adoption will afford to the preservation of that species of government, to liberty, and to property.*

In the progress of this discussion I shall endeavor to give a satisfactory answer to all the objections which shall have made their appearance, that may seem to

15   have any claim to your attention.

It may perhaps be thought superfluous to offer arguments to prove the utility of the UNION, a point, no doubt, deeply engraved on the hearts of the great body of the people in every State, and one which, it may be imagined, has no adversaries. But the fact is that we already hear it whispered in the private circles

20   of those who oppose the new Constitution, that the thirteen States are of too great extent for any general system, and that we must of necessity resort to separate confederacies of distinct portions of the whole. This doctrine will, in all probability, be gradually propagated, till it has votaries enough to countenance an open avowal of it. For nothing can be more evident to those who are able

25   to take an enlarged view of the subject than the alternative of an adoption of the new Constitution or a dismemberment of the Union. It will therefore be of use to begin by examining the advantages of that Union, the certain evils, and the probable dangers, to which every State will be exposed from its dissolution. This shall accordingly constitute the subject of my next address.

FEDERALIST 9
ALEXANDER HAMILTON

*If too powerful, the central government would be tyrannical. If not strong
enough, the Union would not hold together. In pointing out these problems,
Publius argues that a solution has been found through a "great improvement" in the "science of politics."*

NOVEMBER 21, 1787

THE UNION AS A SAFEGUARD AGAINST
DOMESTIC FACTION AND INSURRECTION

A firm Union will be of the utmost moment to the peace and liberty of the States
as a barrier against domestic faction and insurrection. It is impossible to read the
history of the petty republics of Greece and Italy without feeling sensations of
horror and disgust at the distractions with which they were continually agitated,
and at the rapid succession of revolutions by which they were kept in a state of   5
perpetual vibration between the extremes of tyranny and anarchy. If they exhibit
occasional calms, these only serve as short-lived contrasts to the furious storms
that are to succeed. If now and then intervals of felicity open themselves to view,
we behold them with a mixture of regret, arising from the reflection that the
pleasing scenes before us are soon to be overwhelmed by the tempestuous waves of   10
sedition and party rage. If momentary rays of glory break forth from the gloom,
while they dazzle us with a transient and fleeting brilliancy, they at the same time
admonish us to lament that the vices of government should pervert the direction
and tarnish the luster of those bright talents and exalted endowments for which
the favored soils that produced them have been so justly celebrated.   15

From the disorders that disfigure the annals of those republics the advocates
of despotism have drawn arguments, not only against the forms of republican
government, but against the very principles of civil liberty. They have decried
all free government as inconsistent with the order of society, and have indulged

---

Alexander Hamilton, "No. 9: The Union as a Safeguard Against Domestic Faction and Insurrection,"
in Clinton Rossiter, ed., *The Federalist Papers* (New York: Mentor, 1999), 66–71.

themselves in malicious exultation over its friends and partisans. Happily for mankind, stupendous fabrics reared on the basis of liberty, which have flourished for ages, have, in a few glorious instances, refuted their gloomy sophisms. And, I trust, America will be the broad and solid foundation of other edifices, not less

5   magnificent, which will be equally permanent monuments of their errors.

But it is not to be denied that the portraits they have sketched of republican government were too just copies of the originals from which they were taken. If it had been found impracticable to have devised models of a more perfect structure, the enlightened friends to liberty would have been obliged to abandon

10   the cause of that species of government as indefensible. The science of politics, however, like most other sciences, has received great improvement. The efficacy of various principles is now well understood, which were either not known at all, or imperfectly known to the ancients. The regular distribution of power into distinct departments; the introduction of legislative balances and checks;

15   the institution of courts composed of judges holding their offices during good behavior; the representation of the people in the legislature by deputies of their own election: these are wholly new discoveries, or have made their principal progress towards perfection in modern times. They are means, and powerful means, by which the excellencies of republican government may be retained

20   and its imperfections lessened or avoided. To this catalog of circumstances that tend to the amelioration of popular systems of civil government, I shall venture, however novel it may appear to some, to add one more, on a principle which has been made the foundation of an objection to the new Constitution; I mean the ENLARGEMENT of the ORBIT within which such systems are to revolve, either

25   in respect to the dimensions of a single State, or to the consolidation of several smaller States into one great Confederacy. The latter is that which immediately concerns the object under consideration. It will, however, be of use to examine the principle in its application to a single State, which shall be attended to in another place.

30   The utility of a Confederacy, as well to suppress faction and to guard the internal tranquility of States as to increase their external force and security, is in reality not a new idea. It has been practised upon in different countries and ages, and has received the sanction of the most applauded writers on the subjects of politics. The opponents of the PLAN proposed have, with great assiduity, cited

35   and circulated the observations of Montesquieu on the necessity of a contracted territory for a republican government. But they seem not to have been apprised of the sentiments of that great man expressed in another part of his work, nor to have adverted to the consequences of the principle to which they subscribe with such ready acquiescence.

When Montesquieu recommends a small extent for republics, the standards he had in view were of dimensions far short of the limits of almost every one of these States. Neither Virginia, Massachusetts, Pennsylvania, New York, North Carolina, nor Georgia can by any means be compared with the models from which he reasoned and to which the terms of his description apply. If we therefore take his ideas on this point as the criterion of truth, we shall be driven to the alternative either of taking refuge at once in the arms of monarchy, or of splitting ourselves into an infinity of little, jealous, clashing, tumultuous commonwealths, the wretched nurseries of unceasing discord and the miserable objects of universal pity or contempt. Some of the writers who have come forward on the other side of the question seem to have been aware of the dilemma; and have even been bold enough to hint at the division of the larger States as a desirable thing. Such an infatuated policy, such a desperate expedient, might, by the multiplication of petty offices, answer the views of men who possess not qualifications to extend their influence beyond the narrow circles of personal intrigue, but it could never promote the greatness or happiness of the people of America.

Referring the examination of the principle itself to another place, as has been already mentioned, it will be sufficient to remark here that, in the sense of the author who has been most emphatically quoted upon the occasion, it would only dictate a reduction of the SIZE of the more considerable MEMBERS of the Union, but would not militate against their being all comprehended in one confederate government. And this is the true question, in the discussion of which we are at present interested.

So far are the suggestions of Montesquieu from standing in opposition to a general Union of the States that he explicitly treats of a CONFEDERATE REPUBLIC as the expedient for extending the sphere of popular government and reconciling the advantages of monarchy with those of republicanism.

"It is very probable" (says he) "that mankind would have been obliged at length to live constantly under the government of a SINGLE PERSON, had they not contrived a kind of constitution that has all the internal advantages of a republican, together with the external force of a monarchical, government. I mean a CONFEDERATE REPUBLIC.

"This form of government is a convention by which several smaller *states* agree to become members of a larger *one*, which they intend to form. It is a kind of assemblage of societies that constitute a new one, capable of increasing, by means of new associations, till they arrive to such a degree of power as to be able to provide for the security of the united body.

"A republic of this kind, able to withstand an external force, may support itself without any internal corruptions. The form of this society prevents all manner of inconveniences.

"If a single member should attempt to usurp the supreme authority, he could
5   not be supposed to have an equal authority and credit in all the confederate states. Were he to have too great influence over one, this would alarm the rest. Were he to subdue a part, that which would still remain free might oppose him with forces independent of those which he had usurped, and overpower him before he could be settled in his usurpation.

10   "Should a popular insurrection happen in one of the confederate states, the others are able to quell it. Should abuses creep into one part, they are reformed by those that remain sound. The state may be destroyed on one side, and not on the other; the confederacy may be dissolved, and the confederates preserve their sovereignty.

15   "As this government is composed of small republics, it enjoys the internal happiness of each; and with respect to its external situation, it is possessed, by means of the association, of all the advantages of large monarchies."

I have thought it proper to quote at length these interesting passages, because they contain a luminous abridgment of the principal arguments in favor of the
20   Union, and must effectually remove the false impressions which a misapplication of other parts of the work was calculated to produce. They have, at the same time, an intimate connection with the more immediate design of this paper, which is to illustrate the tendency of the Union to repress domestic faction and insurrection.

25   A distinction, more subtle than accurate, has been raised between a *confederacy* and a *consolidation* of the States. The essential characteristic of the first is said to be the restriction of its authority to the members in their collective capacities, without reaching to the individuals of whom they are composed. It is contended that the national council ought to have no concern with any object of internal
30   administration. An exact equality of suffrage between the members has also been insisted upon as a leading feature of a confederate government. These positions are, in the main, arbitrary; they are supported neither by principle nor precedent. It has indeed happened that governments of this kind have generally operated in the manner which the distinction, taken notice of, supposes to be inherent
35   in their nature; but there have been in most of them extensive exceptions to the practice, which serve to prove, as far as example will go, that there is no absolute rule on the subject. And it will be clearly shown, in the course of this

investigation, that as far as the principle contended for has prevailed, it has been the cause of incurable disorder and imbecility in the government.

The definition of a *confederate republic* seems simply to be "an assemblage of societies," or an association of two or more states into one state. The extent, modifications, and objects of the federal authority are mere matters of discretion. 5 So long as the separate organization of the members be not abolished; so long as it exists, by a constitutional necessity, for local purposes; though it should be in perfect subordination to the general authority of the union, it would still be, in fact and in theory, an association of states, or a confederacy. The proposed Constitution, so far from implying an abolition of the State governments, makes 10 them constituent parts of the national sovereignty, by allowing them a direct representation in the Senate, and leaves in their possession certain exclusive and very important portions of sovereign power. This fully corresponds, in every rational import of the terms, with the idea of a federal government.

In the Lycian confederacy, which consisted of twenty-three CITIES, or republics, 15 the largest were entitled to *three* votes in the COMMON COUNCIL, those of the middle class to *two*, and the smallest to *one*. The COMMON COUNCIL had the appointment of all the judges and magistrates of the respective CITIES. This was certainly the most delicate species of interference in their internal administration; for if there be any thing that seems exclusively appropriated 20 to the local jurisdictions, it is the appointment of their own officers. Yet Montesquieu, speaking of this association, says: "Were I to give a model of an excellent Confederate Republic, it would be that of Lycia." Thus we perceive that the distinctions insisted upon were not within the contemplation of this enlightened civilian; and we shall be led to conclude that they are the novel 25 refinements of an erroneous theory.

ESSAY 1
BRUTUS

Supporters of the Constitution dubbed their opponents "Anti-Federalists." Opponents resented the label, but it stuck. The Anti-Federalist author Brutus—most likely New York lawyer Robert Yates—penned this essay, the first of sixteen, a month after the Constitution was completed. Having attended the first month of the Constitutional Convention, Yates had left, disgusted with what he perceived as a plan that would give far too much power to the central government.

OCTOBER 18, 1787

TO THE CITIZENS OF THE STATE OF NEW-YORK:

When the public is called to investigate and decide upon a question in which not only the present members of the community are deeply interested, but upon which the happiness and misery of generations yet unborn is in great measure suspended, the benevolent mind cannot help feeling itself peculiarly interested in the result.... 5

Perhaps this country never saw so critical a period in their political concerns. We have felt the feebleness of the ties by which these United States are held together, and the want of sufficient energy in our present confederation, to manage, in some instances, our general concerns. Various expedients have been proposed to remedy these evils, but none have succeeded. At length a Convention of the 10 states has been assembled, they have formed a constitution which will now, probably, be submitted to the people to ratify or reject, who are the fountain of all power, to whom alone it of right belongs to make or unmake constitutions, or forms of government, at their pleasure. The most important question that was ever proposed to your decision, or to the decision of any people under heaven, is 15 before you, and you are to decide upon it by men of your own election, chosen specially for this purpose. If the constitution, offered to your acceptance, be

Anonymous, "Essays of Brutus, I," October 18, 1787, in Herbert J. Storing, ed., *The Complete Anti-Federalist*, Vol. 2 (Chicago: University of Chicago Press, 1981), 363–72.

a wise one, calculated to preserve the invaluable blessings of liberty, to secure the inestimable rights of mankind, and promote human happiness, then, if you accept it, you will lay a lasting foundation of happiness for millions yet unborn; generations to come will rise up and call you blessed. You may rejoice
5 in the prospects of this vast extended continent becoming filled with freemen, who will assert the dignity of human nature. You may solace yourselves with the idea, that society, in this favored land, will fast advance to the highest point of perfection; the human mind will expand in knowledge and virtue, and the golden age be, in some measure, realised. But if, on the other hand, this form
10 of government contains principles that will lead to the subversion of liberty—if it tends to establish a despotism, or, what is worse, a tyrannic aristocracy; then, if you adopt it, this only remaining asylum for liberty will be shut up, and posterity will execrate your memory.

Momentous then is the question you have to determine, and you are called
15 upon by every motive which should influence a noble and virtuous mind, to examine it well, and to make up a wise judgment. It is insisted, indeed, that this constitution must be received, be it ever so imperfect. If it has its defects, it is said, they can be best amended when they are experienced. But remember, when the people once part with power, they can seldom or never resume it again but
20 by force. Many instances can be produced in which the people have voluntarily increased the powers of their rulers; but few, if any, in which rulers have willingly abridged their authority. This is a sufficient reason to induce you to be careful, in the first instance, how you deposit the powers of government.

With these few introductory remarks, I shall proceed to a consideration of this
25 constitution:

The first question that presents itself on the subject is, whether a confederated government be the best for the United States or not? Or in other words, whether the thirteen United States should be reduced to one great republic, governed by one legislature, and under the direction of one executive and judicial; or whether
30 they should continue thirteen confederated republics, under the direction and control of a supreme federal head for certain defined national purposes only?

This enquiry is important, because, although the government reported by the convention does not go to a perfect and entire consolidation, yet it approaches so near to it, that it must, if executed, certainly and infallibly terminate in it.

35 This government is to possess absolute and uncontrollable power, legislative, executive and judicial, with respect to every object to which it extends, for by the last clause of section 8th, article 1st, it is declared "that the Congress shall have power to make all laws which shall be necessary and proper for carrying

into execution the foregoing powers, and all other powers vested by this
constitution, in the government of the United States; or in any department
or office thereof." And by the 6th article, it is declared "that this constitution,
and the laws of the United States, which shall be made in pursuance thereof,
and the treaties made, or which shall be made, under the authority of the   5
United States, shall be the supreme law of the land; and the judges in every
state shall be bound thereby, any thing in the constitution, or law of any state
to the contrary notwithstanding." It appears from these articles that there is
no need of any intervention of the state governments, between the Congress
and the people, to execute any one power vested in the general government,   10
and that the constitution and laws of every state are nullified and declared
void, so far as they are or shall be inconsistent with this constitution, or the
laws made in pursuance of it, or with treaties made under the authority of the
United States.—The government then, so far as it extends, is a complete one,
and not a confederation. It is as much one complete government as that of   15
New-York or Massachusetts, has as absolute and perfect powers to make and
execute all laws, to appoint officers, institute courts, declare offenses, and annex
penalties, with respect to every object to which it extends, as any other in the
world. So far therefore as its powers reach, all ideas of confederation are given
up and lost. It is true this government is limited to certain objects, or to speak   20
more properly, some small degree of power is still left to the states, but a little
attention to the powers vested in the general government, will convince every
candid man, that if it is capable of being executed, all that is reserved for the
individual states must very soon be annihilated, except so far as they are barely
necessary to the organization of the general government. The powers of the   25
general legislature extend to every case that is of the least importance—there is
nothing valuable to human nature, nothing dear to freemen, but what is within
its power. It has authority to make laws which will affect the lives, the liberty,
and property of every man in the United States; nor can the constitution or
laws of any state, in any way prevent or impede the full and complete execution   30
of every power given. The legislative power is competent to lay taxes, duties,
imposts, and excises;—there is no limitation to this power, unless it be said
that the clause which directs the use to which those taxes, and duties shall be
applied, may be said to be a limitation: but this is no restriction of the power
at all, for by this clause they are to be applied to pay the debts and provide   35
for the common defense and general welfare of the United States; but the
legislature have authority to contract debts at their discretion; they are the sole
judges of what is necessary to provide for the common defense, and they only
are to determine what is for the general welfare; this power therefore is neither
more nor less, than a power to lay and collect taxes, imposts, and excises, at   40

their pleasure; not only [is] the power to lay taxes unlimited, as to the amount they may require, but it is perfect and absolute to raise them in any mode they please. No state legislature, or any power in the state governments, have any more to do in carrying this into effect, than the authority of one state has 5 to do with that of another. In the business therefore of laying and collecting taxes, the idea of confederation is totally lost, and that of one entire republic is embraced....

It might be here shown, that the power in the federal legislative, to raise and support armies at pleasure, as well in peace as in war, and their control over the 10 militia, tend, not only to a consolidation of the government, but the destruction of liberty.—I shall not, however, dwell upon these, as a few observations upon the judicial power of this government, in addition to the preceding, will fully evince the truth of the position.

The judicial power of the United States is to be vested in a supreme court, and 15 in such inferior courts as Congress may from time to time ordain and establish. The powers of these courts are very extensive; their jurisdiction comprehends all civil causes, except such as arise between citizens of the same state; and it extends to all cases in law and equity arising under the constitution. One inferior court must be established, I presume, in each state, at least, with the necessary executive 20 officers appendant thereto. It is easy to see, that in the common course of things, these courts will eclipse the dignity, and take away from the respectability, of the state courts. These courts will be, in themselves, totally independent of the states, deriving their authority from the United States, and receiving from them fixed salaries; and in the course of human events it is to be expected, that they 25 will swallow up all the powers of the courts in the respective states.

How far the clause in the 8th section of the 1st article may operate to do away all idea of confederated states, and to effect an entire consolidation of the whole into one general government, it is impossible to say. The powers given by this article are very general and comprehensive, and it may receive a construction 30 to justify the passing almost any law. A power to make all laws, which shall be *necessary and proper*, for carrying into execution, all powers vested by the constitution in the government of the United States, or any department or officer thereof, is a power very comprehensive and indefinite, and may, for ought I know, be exercised in a such manner as entirely to abolish the state 35 legislatures. Suppose the legislature of a state should pass a law to raise money to support their government and pay the state debt, may the Congress repeal this law, because it may prevent the collection of a tax which they may think proper and necessary to lay, to provide for the general welfare of the United

States? For all laws made, in pursuance of this constitution, are the supreme law of the land, and the judges in every state shall be bound thereby, any thing in the constitution or laws of the different states to the contrary notwithstanding.—By such a law, the government of a particular state might be overturned at one stroke, and thereby be deprived of every means of its support. 5

It is not meant, by stating this case, to insinuate that the constitution would warrant a law of this kind; or unnecessarily to alarm the fears of the people, by suggesting, that the federal legislature would be more likely to pass the limits assigned them by the constitution, than that of an individual state, further than they are less responsible to the people. But what is meant is, that the legislature 10 of the United States are vested with the great and uncontrollable powers, of laying and collecting taxes, duties, imposts, and excises; of regulating trade, raising and supporting armies, organizing, arming, and disciplining the militia, instituting courts, and other general powers. And are by this clause invested with the power of making all laws, *proper and necessary*, for carrying all these into 15 execution; and they may so exercise this power as entirely to annihilate all the state governments, and reduce this country to one single government. And if they may do it, it is pretty certain they will; for it will be found that the power retained by individual states, small as it is, will be a clog upon the wheels of the government of the United States; the latter therefore will be naturally inclined 20 to remove it out of the way. Besides, it is a truth confirmed by the unerring experience of ages, that every man, and every body of men, invested with power, are ever disposed to increase it, and to acquire a superiority over every thing that stands in their way. This disposition, which is implanted in human nature, will operate in the federal legislature to lessen and ultimately to subvert 25 the state authority, and having such advantages, will most certainly succeed, if the federal government succeeds at all. It must be very evident then, that what this constitution wants of being a complete consolidation of the several parts of the union into one complete government, possessed of perfect legislative, judicial, and executive powers, to all intents and purposes, it will necessarily 30 acquire in its exercise and operation.

Let us now proceed to enquire, as I at first proposed, whether it be best the thirteen United States should be reduced to one great republic, or not? It is here taken for granted, that all agree in this, that whatever government we adopt, it ought to be a free one; that it should be so framed as to secure the liberty of 35 the citizens of America, and such an one as to admit of a full, fair, and equal representation of the people. The question then will be, whether a government thus constituted, and founded on such principles, is practicable, and can be exercised over the whole United States, reduced into one state?

If respect is to be paid to the opinion of the greatest and wisest men who have ever thought or wrote on the science of government, we shall be constrained to conclude, that a free republic cannot succeed over a country of such immense extent, containing such a number of inhabitants, and these increasing in
5   such rapid progression as that of the whole United States. Among the many illustrious authorities which might be produced to this point, I shall content myself with quoting only two. The one is the Baron de Montesquieu, *Spirit of Laws*, chap. xvi. vol. I [book VIII]. "It is natural to a republic to have only a small territory, otherwise it cannot long subsist. In a large republic there are
10   men of large fortunes, and consequently of less moderation; there are trusts too great to be placed in any single subject; he has interest of his own; he soon begins to think that he may be happy, great and glorious, by oppressing his fellow citizens; and that he may raise himself to grandeur on the ruins of his country. In a large republic, the public good is sacrificed to a thousand views;
15   it is subordinate to exceptions, and depends on accidents. In a small one, the interest of the public is easier perceived, better understood, and more within the reach of every citizen; abuses are of less extent, and of course are less protected." Of the same opinion is the marquis Beccarari.

History furnishes no example of a free republic, any thing like the extent of
20   the United States. The Grecian republics were of small extent; so also was that of the Romans. Both of these, it is true, in process of time, extended their conquests over large territories of country; and the consequence was, that their governments were changed from that of free governments to those of the most tyrannical that ever existed in the world.

25   Not only the opinion of the greatest men, and the experience of mankind, are against the idea of an extensive republic, but a variety of reasons may be drawn from the reason and nature of things, against it. In every government, the will of the sovereign is the law. In despotic governments, the supreme authority being lodged in one, his will is law, and can be as easily expressed to a large
30   extensive territory as to a small one. In a pure democracy the people are the sovereign, and their will is declared by themselves; for this purpose they must all come together to deliberate, and decide. This kind of government cannot be exercised, therefore, over a country of any considerable extent; it must be confined to a single city, or at least limited to such bounds as that the people
35   can conveniently assemble, be able to debate, understand the subject submitted to them, and declare their opinion concerning it.

In a free republic, although all laws are derived from the consent of the people, yet the people do not declare their consent by themselves in person, but by representatives, chosen by them, who are supposed to know the minds of their constituents, and to be possessed of integrity to declare this mind.

In every free government, the people must give their assent to the laws by which they are governed. This is the true criterion between a free government and an arbitrary one. The former are ruled by the will of the whole, expressed in any manner they may agree upon; the latter by the will of one, or a few. If the people are to give their assent to the laws, by persons chosen and appointed by them, the manner of the choice and the number chosen, must be such, as to possess, be disposed, and consequently qualified to declare the sentiments of the people; for if they do not know, or are not disposed to speak the sentiments of the people, the people do not govern, but the sovereignty is in a few. Now, in a large extended country, it is impossible to have a representation, possessing the sentiments, and of integrity, to declare the minds of the people, without having it so numerous and unwieldly, as to be subject in great measure to the inconveniency of a democratic government.

The territory of the United States is of vast extent; it now contains near three millions of souls, and is capable of containing much more than ten times that number. Is it practicable for a country, so large and so numerous as they will soon become, to elect a representation, that will speak their sentiments, without their becoming so numerous as to be incapable of transacting public business? It certainly is not.

In a republic, the manners, sentiments, and interests of the people should be similar. If this be not the case, there will be a constant clashing of opinions; and the representatives of one part will be continually striving against those of the other. This will retard the operations of government, and prevent such conclusions as will promote the public good. If we apply this remark to the condition of the United States, we shall be convinced that it forbids that we should be one government. The United States includes a variety of climates. The productions of the different parts of the union are very variant, and their interests, of consequence, diverse. Their manners and habits differ as much as their climates and productions; and their sentiments are by no means coincident. The laws and customs of the several states are, in many respects, very diverse, and in some opposite; each would be in favor of its own interests and customs, and, of consequence, a legislature, formed of representatives from the respective parts, would not only be too numerous to act with any care or decision, but would be composed of such heterogenous and discordant principles, as would constantly be contending with each other.

The laws cannot be executed in a republic, of an extent equal to that of the United States, with promptitude.

The magistrates in every government must be supported in the execution of the laws, either by an armed force, maintained at the public expense for that
5   purpose; or by the people turning out to aid the magistrate upon his command, in case of resistance.

In despotic governments, as well as in all the monarchies of Europe, standing armies are kept up to execute the commands of the prince or the magistrate, and are employed for this purpose when occasion requires: But they have always
10   proved the destruction of liberty, and [are] abhorrent to the spirit of a free republic. In England, where they depend upon the parliament for their annual support, they have always been complained of as oppressive and unconstitutional, and are seldom employed in executing of the laws; never except on extraordinary occasions, and then under the direction of a civil magistrate.

15   A free republic will never keep a standing army to execute its laws. It must depend upon the support of its citizens. But when a government is to receive its support from the aid of the citizens, it must be so constructed as to have the confidence, respect, and affection of the people. Men who, upon the call of the magistrate, offer themselves to execute the laws, are influenced to do it
20   either by affection to the government, or from fear; where a standing army is at hand to punish offenders, every man is actuated by the latter principle, and therefore, when the magistrate calls, will obey: but, where this is not the case, the government must rest for its support upon the confidence and respect which the people have for their government and laws. The body of the people being
25   attached, the government will always be sufficient to support and execute its laws, and to operate upon the fears of any faction which may be opposed to it, not only to prevent an opposition to the execution of the laws themselves, but also to compel the most of them to aid the magistrate; but the people will not be likely to have such confidence in their rulers, in a republic so extensive
30   as the United States, as necessary for these purposes. The confidence which the people have in their rulers, in a free republic, arises from their knowing them, from their being responsible to them for their conduct, and from the power they have of displacing them when they misbehave: but in a republic of the extent of this continent, the people in general would be acquainted with very
35   few of their rulers: the people at large would know little of their proceedings, and it would be extremely difficult to change them. The people in Georgia and New-Hampshire would not know one another's mind, and therefore could not act in concert to enable them to affect a general change of representatives. The

different parts of so extensive a country could not possibly be made acquainted with the conduct of their representatives, nor be informed of the reasons upon which measures were founded. The consequence will be, they will have no confidence in their legislature, suspect them of ambitious views, be jealous of every measure they adopt, and will not support the laws they pass. Hence the government will be nerveless and inefficient, and no way will be left to render it otherwise, but by establishing an armed force to execute the laws at the point of the bayonet—a government of all others the most to be dreaded.

In a republic of such vast extent as the United States, the legislature cannot attend to the various concerns and wants of its different parts. It cannot be sufficiently numerous to be acquainted with the local condition and wants of the different districts, and if it could, it is impossible it should have sufficient time to attend to and provide for all the variety of cases of this nature, that would be continually arising.

In so extensive a republic, the great officers of government would soon become above the control of the people, and abuse their power to the purpose of aggrandizing themselves, and oppressing them. The trust committed to the executive offices, in a country of the extent of the United States, must be various and of magnitude. The command of all the troops and navy of the republic, the appointment of officers, the power of pardoning offenses, the collecting of all the public revenues, and the power of expending them, with a number of other powers, must be lodged and exercised in every state, in the hands of a few. When these are attended with great honor and emolument, as they always will be in large states, so as greatly to interest men to pursue them, and to be proper objects for ambitious and designing men, such men will be ever restless in their pursuit after them. They will use the power, when they have acquired it, to the purposes of gratifying their own interest and ambition, and it is scarcely possible, in a very large republic, to call them to account for their misconduct, or to prevent their abuse of power.

These are some of the reasons by which it appears, that a free republic cannot long subsist over a country of the great extent of these states. If then this new constitution is calculated to consolidate the thirteen states into one, as it evidently is, it ought not to be adopted.

Though I am of opinion, that it is a sufficient objection to this government, to reject it, that it creates the whole union into one government, under the form of a republic, yet if this objection was obviated, there are exceptions to it, which are so material and fundamental, that they ought to determine every man, who is a friend to the liberty and happiness of mankind, not to adopt it.

I beg the candid and dispassionate attention of my countrymen while I state these objections—they are such as have obtruded themselves upon my mind upon a careful attention to the matter, and such as I sincerely believe are well founded. There are many objections, of small moment, of which I shall take no notice—perfection is not to be expected in any thing that is the production of man—and if I did not in my conscience believe that this scheme was defective in the fundamental principles—in the foundation upon which a free and equal government must rest—I would hold my peace.

Federalist 10
James Madison

Whereas democracy entails direct rule of the people, in a republic the people rule indirectly, through their representatives. A republic can therefore encompass a greater population and geographical area. This difference is decisive in the American experiment, Publius argues, for an expansive republic is able to control the inherent danger of majority faction.

NOVEMBER 22, 1787

The Union as a Safeguard Against
Domestic Faction and Insurrection

Among the numerous advantages promised by a well-constructed Union, none deserves to be more accurately developed than its tendency to break and control the violence of faction. The friend of popular governments never finds himself so much alarmed for their character and fate as when he contemplates their propensity to this dangerous vice. He will not fail, therefore, to set a due value 5 on any plan which, without violating the principles to which he is attached, provides a proper cure for it. The instability, injustice, and confusion introduced into the public councils have, in truth, been the mortal diseases under which popular governments have everywhere perished, as they continue to be the favorite and fruitful topics from which the adversaries to liberty derive their 10 most specious declamations. The valuable improvements made by the American constitutions on the popular models, both ancient and modern, cannot certainly be too much admired; but it would be an unwarrantable partiality to contend that they have as effectually obviated the danger on this side, as was wished and expected. Complaints are everywhere heard from our most considerate and 15 virtuous citizens, equally the friends of public and private faith and of public and personal liberty, that our governments are too unstable, that the public good is disregarded in the conflicts of rival parties, and that measures are too often decided, not according to the rules of justice and the rights of the minor party,

James Madison, "No. 10: The Same Subject Continued," in Clinton Rossiter, ed., *The Federalist Papers* (New York: Mentor, 1999), 71–79.

231

but by the superior force of an interested and overbearing majority. However anxiously we may wish that these complaints had no foundation, the evidence of known facts will not permit us to deny that they are in some degree true. It will be found, indeed, on a candid review of our situation, that some of the
5   distresses under which we labor have been erroneously charged on the operation of our governments; but it will be found, at the same time, that other causes will not alone account for many of our heaviest misfortunes; and, particularly, for that prevailing and increasing distrust of public engagements and alarm for private rights which are echoed from one end of the continent to the other.
10   These must be chiefly, if not wholly, effects of the unsteadiness and injustice with which a factious spirit has tainted our public administration.

By a faction I understand a number of citizens, whether amounting to a majority or minority of the whole, who are united and actuated by some common impulse of passion, or of interest, adverse to the rights of other citizens, or to
15   the permanent and aggregate interests of the community.

There are two methods of curing the mischiefs of faction: the one, by removing its causes; the other, by controlling its effects.

There are again two methods of removing the causes of faction: the one, by destroying the liberty which is essential to its existence; the other, by giving to
20   every citizen the same opinions, the same passions, and the same interests.

It could never be more truly said than of the first remedy that it was worse than the disease. Liberty is to faction what air is to fire, an aliment without which it instantly expires. But it could not be a less folly to abolish liberty, which is essential to political life, because it nourishes faction than it would be to wish
25   the annihilation of air, which is essential to animal life, because it imparts to fire its destructive agency.

The second expedient is as impracticable as the first would be unwise. As long as the reason of man continues fallible, and he is at liberty to exercise it, different opinions will be formed. As long as the connection subsists between
30   his reason and his self-love, his opinions and his passions will have a reciprocal influence on each other; and the former will be objects to which the latter will attach themselves. The diversity in the faculties of men, from which the rights of property originate, is not less an insuperable obstacle to a uniformity of interests. The protection of these faculties is the first object of government.
35   From the protection of different and unequal faculties of acquiring property, the possession of different degrees and kinds of property immediately results; and from the influence of these on the sentiments and views of the respective proprietors ensues a division of the society into different interests and parties.

The latent causes of faction are thus sown in the nature of man; and we see them everywhere brought into different degrees of activity, according to the different circumstances of civil society. A zeal for different opinions concerning religion, concerning government, and many other points, as well as speculation as of practice; an attachment to different leaders ambitiously contending for pre-eminence and power; or to persons of other descriptions whose fortunes have been interesting to the human passions, have, in turn, divided mankind into parties, inflamed them with mutual animosity, and rendered them much more disposed to vex and oppress each other than to cooperate for their common good. So strong is this propensity of mankind to fall into mutual animosities that where no substantial occasion presents itself the most frivolous and fanciful distinctions have been sufficient to kindle their unfriendly passions and excite their most violent conflicts. But the most common and durable source of factions has been the various and unequal distribution of property. Those who hold and those who are without property have ever formed distinct interests in society. Those who are creditors, and those who are debtors, fall under a like discrimination. A landed interest, a manufacturing interest, a mercantile interest, a moneyed interest, with many lesser interests, grow up of necessity in civilized nations, and divide them into different classes, actuated by different sentiments and views. The regulation of these various and interfering interests forms the principal task of modern legislation and involves the spirit of party and faction in the necessary and ordinary operations of government.

No man is allowed to be a judge in his own cause because his interest would certainly bias his judgment, and, not improbably, corrupt his integrity. With equal, nay with greater reason, a body of men are unfit to be both judges and parties at the same time; yet what are many of the most important acts of legislation but so many judicial determinations, not indeed concerning the rights of single persons, but concerning the rights of large bodies of citizens? And what are the different classes of legislators but advocates and parties to the causes which they determine? Is a law proposed concerning private debts? It is a question to which the creditors are parties on one side and the debtors on the other. Justice ought to hold the balance between them. Yet the parties are, and must be, themselves the judges; and the most numerous party, or in other words, the most powerful faction must be expected to prevail. Shall domestic manufactures be encouraged, and in what degree, by restrictions on foreign manufactures? are questions which would be differently decided by the landed and the manufacturing classes, and probably by neither with a sole regard to justice and the public good. The apportionment of taxes on the various descriptions of property is an act which seems to require the most exact impartiality; yet there is, perhaps, no legislative act in which greater opportunity and temptation are given to a predominant party to trample on the rules of justice. Every shilling with which they overburden the inferior number is a shilling saved to their own pockets.

5   It is in vain to say that enlightened statesmen will be able to adjust these clashing interests and render them all subservient to the public good. Enlightened statesmen will not always be at the helm. Nor, in many cases, can such an adjustment be made at all without taking into view indirect and remote considerations, which will rarely prevail over the immediate interest which one
10   party may find in disregarding the rights of another or the good of the whole.

The inference to which we are brought is that the *causes* of faction cannot be removed and that relief is only to be sought in the means of controlling its *effects*.

If a faction consists of less than a majority, relief is supplied by the republican
15   principle, which enables the majority to defeat its sinister views by regular vote. It may clog the administration, it may convulse the society; but it will be unable to execute and mask its violence under the forms of the Constitution. When a majority is included in a faction, the form of popular government, on the other hand, enables it to sacrifice to its ruling passion or interest both
20   the public good and the rights of other citizens. To secure the public good and private rights against the danger of such a faction, and at the same time to preserve the spirit and the form of popular government, is then the great object to which our inquiries are directed. Let me add that it is the great desideratum by which alone this form of government can be rescued from the opprobrium
25   under which it has so long labored and be recommended to the esteem and adoption of mankind.

By what means is this object attainable? Evidently by one of two only. Either the existence of the same passion or interest in a majority at the same time must be prevented, or the majority, having such coexistent passion or interest, must be
30   rendered, by their number and local situation, unable to concert and carry into effect schemes of oppression. If the impulse and the opportunity be suffered to coincide, we well know that neither moral nor religious motives can be relied on as an adequate control. They are not found to be such on the injustice and violence of individuals, and lose their efficacy in proportion to the number
35   combined together, that is, in proportion as their efficacy becomes needful.

From this view of the subject it may be concluded that a pure democracy, by which I mean a society consisting of a small number of citizens, who assemble and administer the government in person, can admit of no cure for the mischiefs of faction. A common passion or interest will, in almost every case, be felt by a majority of the whole; a communication and concert result from the form of government itself; and there is nothing to check the inducements to sacrifice the weaker party or an obnoxious individual. Hence it is that such democracies have ever been spectacles of turbulence and contention; have ever been found incompatible with personal security or the rights of property; and have in general been as short in their lives as they have been violent in their deaths. Theoretic politicians, who have patronized this species of government, have erroneously supposed that by reducing mankind to a perfect equality in their political rights, they would at the same time be perfectly equalized and assimilated in their possessions, their opinions, and their passions.

A republic, by which I mean a government in which the scheme of representation takes place, opens a different prospect and promises the cure for which we are seeking. Let us examine the points in which it varies from pure democracy, and we shall comprehend both the nature of the cure and the efficacy which it must derive from the Union.

The two great points of difference between a democracy and a republic are: first, the delegation of the government, in the latter, to a small number of citizens elected by the rest; secondly, the greater number of citizens and greater sphere of country over which the latter may be extended.

The effect of the first difference is, on the one hand, to refine and enlarge the public views by passing them through the medium of a chosen body of citizens, whose wisdom may best discern the true interest of their country and whose patriotism and love of justice will be least likely to sacrifice it to temporary or partial considerations. Under such a regulation it may well happen that the public voice, pronounced by the representatives of the people, will be more consonant to the public good than if pronounced by the people themselves, convened for the purpose. On the other hand, the effect may be inverted. Men of factious tempers, of local prejudices, or of sinister designs, may, by intrigue, by corruption, or by other means, first obtain the suffrages, and then betray the interests of the people. The question resulting is, whether small or extensive republics are most favorable to the election of proper guardians of the public weal; and it is clearly decided in favor of the latter by two obvious considerations.

In the first place it is to be remarked that however small the republic may be the representatives must be raised to a certain number in order to guard against the cabals of a few; and that however large it may be they must be limited to a certain number in order to guard against the confusion of a multitude. Hence,

the number of representatives in the two cases not being in proportion to that of the two constituents, and being proportionally greatest in the small republic, it follows that if the proportion of fit characters be not less in the large than in the small republic, the former will present a greater option, and consequently
5   a greater probability of a fit choice.

In the next place, as each representative will be chosen by a greater number of citizens in the large than in the small republic, it will be more difficult for unworthy candidates to practise with success the vicious arts by which elections are too often carried; and the suffrages of the people being more free, will be
10   more likely to center on men who possess the most attractive merit and the most diffusive and established characters.

It must be confessed that in this, as in most other cases, there is a mean, on both sides of which inconveniences will be found to lie. By enlarging too much the number of electors, you render the representative too little acquainted with
15   all their local circumstances and lesser interests; as by reducing it too much, you render him unduly attached to these, and too little fit to comprehend and pursue great and national objects. The federal Constitution forms a happy combination in this respect; the great and aggregate interests being referred to the national, the local and particular to the State legislatures.

20   The other point of difference is the greater number of citizens and extent of territory which may be brought within the compass of republican than of democratic government; and it is this circumstance principally which renders factious combinations less to be dreaded in the former than in the latter. The smaller the society, the fewer probably will be the distinct parties and interests
25   composing it; the fewer the distinct parties and interests, the more frequently will a majority be found of the same party; and the smaller the number of individuals composing a majority, and the smaller the compass within which they are placed, the more easily will they concert and execute their plans of oppression. Extend the sphere and you take in a greater variety of parties and
30   interests; you make it less probable that a majority of the whole will have a common motive to invade the rights of other citizens; or if such a common motive exists, it will be more difficult for all who feel it to discover their own strength and to act in unison with each other. Besides other impediments, it may be remarked that, where there is a consciousness of unjust or dishonorable
35   purposes, communication is always checked by distrust in proportion to the number whose concurrence is necessary.

Hence, it clearly appears that the same advantage which a republic has over a democracy in controlling the effects of faction is enjoyed by a large over a small republic—is enjoyed by the Union over the States composing it. Does this advantage consist in the substitution of representatives whose enlightened views and virtuous sentiments render them superior to local prejudices and to schemes of injustice? It will not be denied that the representation of the Union will be most likely to possess these requisite endowments. Does it consist in the   5 greater security afforded by a greater variety of parties, against the event of any one party being able to outnumber and oppress the rest? In an equal degree, does the increased variety of parties comprised within the Union increase this security? Does it, in fine, consist in the greater obstacles opposed to the concert and accomplishment of the secret wishes of an unjust and interested majority?   10 Here again the extent of the Union gives it the most palpable advantage.

The influence of factious leaders may kindle a flame within their particular States but will be unable to spread a general conflagration through the other States. A religious sect may degenerate into a political faction in a part of the Confederacy; but the variety of sects dispersed over the entire face of it must   15 secure the national councils against any danger from that source. A rage for paper money, for an abolition of debts, for an equal division of property, or for any other improper or wicked project, will be less apt to pervade the whole body of the Union than a particular member of it, in the same proportion as such a malady is more likely to taint a particular county or district than an   20 entire State.

In the extent and proper structure of the Union, therefore, we behold a republican remedy for the diseases most incident to republican government. And according to the degree of pleasure and pride we feel in being republicans ought to be our zeal in cherishing the spirit and supporting the character of   25 federalists.

FEDERALIST 15
ALEXANDER HAMILTON

Echoing earlier critiques of the Articles of Confederation, Publius disputes the notion that the national government must be weak in order for liberty to be secured.

DECEMBER 1, 1787

THE INSUFFICIENCY OF THE PRESENT
CONFEDERATION TO PRESERVE THE UNION

In the course of the preceding papers I have endeavored, my fellow-citizens, to place before you in a clear and convincing light the importance of Union to your political safety and happiness. I have unfolded to you a complication of dangers to which you would be exposed, should you permit that sacred knot which binds the people of America together to be severed or dissolved by ambition or by avarice, by jealousy or by misrepresentation. In the sequel of the inquiry through which I propose to accompany you, the truths intended to be inculcated will receive further confirmation from facts and arguments hitherto unnoticed. If the road over which you will still have to pass should in some places appear to you tedious or irksome, you will recollect that you are in quest of information on a subject the most momentous which can engage the attention of a free people, that the field through which you have to travel is in itself spacious, and that the difficulties of the journey have been unnecessarily increased by the mazes with which sophistry has beset the way. It will be my aim to remove the obstacles from your progress in as compendious a manner as it can be done, without sacrificing utility to dispatch.

In pursuance of the plan which I have laid down for the discussion of the subject, the point next in order to be examined is the "insufficiency of the present Confederation to the preservation of the Union." It may perhaps be asked what need there is of reasoning or proof to illustrate a position which is not either controverted or doubted, to which the understandings and feelings of all classes

Alexander Hamilton, "No. 15: The Insufficiency of the Present Confederation to Preserve the Union," in Clinton Rossiter, ed., *The Federalist Papers* (New York: Mentor, 1999), 100–108.

of men assent, and which in substance is admitted by the opponents as well as by the friends of the new Constitution. It must in truth be acknowledged that, however these may differ in other respects, they in general appear to harmonize in this sentiment at least: that there are material imperfections in our
5 national system and that something is necessary to be done to rescue us from impending anarchy. The facts that support this opinion are no longer objects of speculation. They have forced themselves upon the sensibility of the people at large, and have at length extorted from those, whose mistaken policy has had the principal share in precipitating the extremity at which we are arrived, a
10 reluctant confession of the reality of those defects in the scheme of our federal government which have been long pointed out and regretted by the intelligent friends of the Union.

We may indeed with propriety be said to have reached almost the last stage of national humiliation. There is scarcely anything that can wound the pride or
15 degrade the character of an independent nation which we do not experience. Are there engagements to the performance of which we are held by every tie respectable among men? These are the subjects of constant and unblushing violation. Do we owe debts to foreigners and to our own citizens contracted in a time of imminent peril for the preservation of our political existence? These
20 remain without any proper or satisfactory provision for their discharge. Have we valuable territories and important posts in the possession of a foreign power which, by express stipulations, ought long since to have been surrendered? These are still retained to the prejudice of our interests, not less than of our rights. Are we in a condition to resent or to repel the aggression? We have neither troops,
25 nor treasury, nor government. Are we even in a condition to remonstrate with dignity? The just imputations on our own faith in respect to the same treaty ought first to be removed. Are we entitled by nature and compact to a free participation in the navigation of the Mississippi? Spain excludes us from it. Is public credit an indispensable resource in time of public danger? We seem to have
30 abandoned its cause as desperate and irretrievable. Is commerce of importance to national wealth? Ours is at the lowest point of declension. Is respectability in the eyes of foreign powers a safeguard against foreign encroachments? The imbecility of our government even forbids them to treat with us. Our ambassadors abroad are the mere pageants of mimic sovereignty. Is a violent and unnatural decrease
35 in the value of land a symptom of national distress? The price of improved land in most parts of the country is much lower than can be accounted for by the quantity of waste land at market, and can only be fully explained by that want of private and public confidence, which are so alarmingly prevalent among all ranks and which have a direct tendency to depreciate property of every kind. Is

private credit the friend and patron of industry? That most useful kind which relates to borrowing and lending is reduced within the narrowest limits, and this still more from an opinion of insecurity than from a scarcity of money. To shorten an enumeration of particulars which can afford neither pleasure nor instruction, it may in general be demanded, what indication is there of national 5 disorder, poverty, and insignificance that could befall a community so peculiarly blessed with natural advantages as we are, which does not form a part of the dark catalog of our public misfortunes?

This is the melancholy situation to which we have been brought by those very maxims and counsels which would now deter us from adopting the proposed 10 Constitution; and which, not content with having conducted us to the brink of a precipice, seem resolved to plunge us into the abyss that awaits us below. Here, my countrymen, impelled by every motive that ought to influence an enlightened people, let us make a firm stand for our safety, our tranquility, our dignity, our reputation. Let us at last break the fatal charm which has too long 15 seduced us from the paths of felicity and prosperity.

It is true, as has been before observed, that facts too stubborn to be resisted have produced a species of general assent to the abstract proposition that there exist material defects in our national system; but the usefulness of the concession on the part of the old adversaries of federal measures is destroyed by a strenuous 20 opposition to a remedy upon the only principles that can give it a chance of success. While they admit that the government of the United States is destitute of energy, they contend against conferring upon it those powers which are requisite to supply that energy. They seem still to aim at things repugnant and irreconcilable; at an augmentation of federal authority without a diminution of State authority; 25 at sovereignty in the Union and complete independence in the members. They still, in fine, seem to cherish with blind devotion the political monster of an *imperium in imperio*. This renders a full display of the principal defects of the Confederation necessary in order to show that the evils we experience do not proceed from minute or partial imperfections, but from fundamental errors in 30 the structure of the building, which cannot be amended otherwise than by an alteration in the first principles and main pillars of the fabric.

The great and radical vice in the construction of the existing Confederation is in the principle of LEGISLATION for STATES or GOVERNMENTS, in their CORPORATE or COLLECTIVE CAPACITIES, and as contradistinguished from the INDIVIDUALS of 35 which they consist. Though this principle does not run through all the powers delegated to the Union, yet it pervades and governs those on which the efficacy of the rest depends. Except as to the rule of apportionment, the United States have an indefinite discretion to make requisitions for men and money; but they have

no authority to raise either by regulations extending to the individual citizens of America. The consequence of this is that though in theory their resolutions concerning those objects are laws constitutionally binding on the members of the Union, yet in practice they are mere recommendations which the States
5   observe or disregard at their option.

It is a singular instance of the capriciousness of the human mind that after all the admonitions we have had from experience on this head, there should still be found men who object to the new Constitution for deviating from a principle which has been found the bane of the old and which is in itself evidently
10   incompatible with the idea of GOVERNMENT; a principle, in short, which, if it is to be executed at all, must substitute the violent and sanguinary agency of the sword to the mild influence of the magistracy.

There is nothing absurd or impracticable in the idea of a league or alliance between independent nations for certain defined purposes precisely stated in a
15   treaty regulating all the details of time, place, circumstance, and quantity, leaving nothing to future discretion, and depending for its execution on the good faith of the parties. Compacts of this kind exist among all civilized nations, subject to the usual vicissitudes of peace and war, of observance and nonobservance, as the interests or passions of the contracting powers dictate. In the early part of
20   the present century there was an epidemical rage in Europe for this species of compacts, from which the politicians of the times fondly hoped for benefits which were never realized. With a view to establishing the equilibrium of power and the peace of that part of the world, all the resources of negotiations were exhausted, and triple and quadruple alliances were formed; but they were scarcely formed
25   before they were broken, giving an instructive but afflicting lesson to mankind how little dependence is to be placed on treaties which have no other sanction than the obligations of good faith, and which oppose general considerations of peace and justice to the impulse of any immediate interest or passion.

If the particular States in this country are disposed to stand in a similar relation to
30   each other, and to drop the project of a general DISCRETIONARY SUPERINTENDENCE, the scheme would indeed be pernicious and would entail upon us all the mischiefs which have been enumerated under the first head; but it would have the merit of being, at least, consistent and practicable. Abandoning all views towards a confederate government, this would bring us to a simple alliance offensive and
35   defensive; and would place us in a situation to be alternate friends and enemies of each other, as our mutual jealousies and rivalships, nourished by the intrigues of foreign nations, should prescribe to us.

But if we are unwilling to be placed in this perilous situation; if we still will adhere to the design of a national government, or, which is the same thing, of a superintending power under the direction of a common council, we must resolve to incorporate into our plan those ingredients which may be considered as forming the characteristic difference between a league and a government; we must extend the authority of the Union to the persons of the citizens—the only proper objects of government.   5

Government implies the power of making laws. It is essential to the idea of a law that it be attended with a sanction; or, in other words, a penalty or punishment for disobedience. If there be no penalty annexed to disobedience, the resolutions or commands which pretend to be laws will, in fact, amount to nothing more than advice or recommendation. This penalty, whatever it may be, can only   10 be inflicted in two ways: by the agency of the courts and ministers of justice, or by military force; by the COERCION of the magistracy, or by the COERCION of arms. The first kind can evidently apply only to men; the last kind must of necessity be employed against bodies politic, or communities, or States. It is evident that there is no process of a court by which the observance of the laws   15 can in the last resort be enforced. Sentences may be denounced against them for violations of their duty; but these sentences can only be carried into execution by the sword. In an association where the general authority is confined to the collective bodies of the communities that compose it, every breach of the laws must involve a state of war; and military execution must become the only   20 instrument of civil obedience. Such a state of things can certainly not deserve the name of government, nor would any prudent man choose to commit his happiness to it.

There was a time when we were told that breaches by the States of the regulations of the federal authority were not to be expected; that a sense of common interest   25 would preside over the conduct of the respective members, and would beget a full compliance with all the constitutional requisitions of the Union. This language, at the present day, would appear as wild as a great part of what we now hear from the same quarter will be thought, when we shall have received further lessons from that best oracle of wisdom, experience. It at all times betrayed an ignorance   30 of the true springs by which human conduct is actuated, and belied the original inducements to the establishment of civil power. Why has government been instituted at all? Because the passions of men will not conform to the dictates of reason and justice without constraint. Has it been found that bodies of men act with more rectitude or greater disinterestedness than individuals? The contrary   35 of this has been inferred by all accurate observers of the conduct of mankind; and the inference is founded upon obvious reasons. Regard to reputation has a less active influence when the infamy of a bad action is to be divided among a number than when it is to fall singly upon one. A spirit of faction, which is apt to mingle its poison in the deliberations of all bodies of men, will often hurry the persons of whom they are composed into improprieties and excesses for which they would blush in a private capacity.

In addition to all this, there is in the nature of sovereign power an impatience of
5   control that disposes those who are invested with the exercise of it to look with an evil eye upon all external attempts to restrain or direct its operations. From this spirit it happens that in every political association which is formed upon the principle of uniting in a common interest a number of lesser sovereignties, there will be found a kind of eccentric tendency in the subordinate or inferior orbs
10   by the operation of which there will be a perpetual effort in each to fly off from the common center. This tendency is not difficult to be accounted for. It has its origin in the love of power. Power controlled or abridged is almost always the rival and enemy of that power by which it is controlled or abridged. This simple proposition will teach us how little reason there is to expect that the persons
15   entrusted with the administration of the affairs of the particular members of a confederacy will at all times be ready with perfect good humor and an unbiased regard to the public weal to execute the resolutions or decrees of the general authority. The reverse of this results from the constitution of man.

If, therefore, the measures of the Confederacy cannot be executed without the
20   intervention of the particular administrations, there will be little prospect of their being executed at all. The rulers of the respective members, whether they have a constitutional right to do it or not, will undertake to judge of the propriety of the measures themselves. They will consider the conformity of the thing proposed or required to their immediate interests or aims; the momentary conveniences
25   or inconveniences that would attend its adoption. All this will be done; and in a spirit of interested and suspicious scrutiny, without that knowledge of national circumstances and reasons of state, which is essential to a right judgment, and with that strong predilection in favor of local objects, which can hardly fail to mislead the decision. The same process must be repeated in every member of
30   which the body is constituted; and the execution of the plans, framed by the councils of the whole, will always fluctuate on the discretion of the ill-informed and prejudiced opinion of every part. Those who have been conversant in the proceedings of popular assemblies; who have seen how difficult it often is, where there is no exterior pressure of circumstances, to bring them to harmonious
35   resolutions on important points, will readily conceive how impossible it must be to induce a number of such assemblies, deliberating at a distance from each other, at different times and under different impressions, long to cooperate in the same views and pursuits.

In our case the concurrence of thirteen distinct sovereign wills is requisite under the Confederation to the complete execution of every important measure that proceeds from the Union. It has happened as was to have been foreseen. The measures of the Union have not been executed; and the delinquencies of the States have step by step matured themselves to an extreme, which has, at length, arrested all the wheels of the national government and brought them to an awful stand. Congress at this time scarcely possess the means of keeping up the forms of administration, till the States can have time to agree upon a more substantial substitute for the present shadow of a federal government. Things did not come to this desperate extremity at once. The causes which have been specified produced at first only unequal and disproportionate degrees of compliance with the requisitions of the Union. The greater deficiencies of some States furnished the pretext of example and the temptation of interest to the complying, or to the least delinquent States. Why should we do more in proportion than those who are embarked with us in the same political voyage? Why should we consent to bear more than our proper share of the common burden? These were suggestions which human selfishness could not withstand, and which even speculative men, who looked forward to remote consequences, could not without hesitation combat. Each State yielding to the persuasive voice of immediate interest or convenience has successively withdrawn its support, till the frail and tottering edifice seems ready to fall upon our heads and to crush us beneath its ruins.

Federalist 23
Alexander Hamilton

Publius argues that the Constitution creates a government limited in the objects it can pursue, but largely free to choose the best means to achieve those ends.

December 18, 1787

The Necessity of a Government as Energetic as the One Proposed to the Preservation of the Union

The necessity of a Constitution, at least equally energetic with the one proposed, to the preservation of the Union is the point at the examination of which we are now arrived.

This inquiry will naturally divide itself into three branches—the objects to be provided for by a federal government, the quantity of power necessary to the 5 accomplishment of those objects, the persons upon whom that power ought to operate. Its distribution and organization will more properly claim our attention under the succeeding head.

The principal purposes to be answered by union are these—the common defense of the members; the preservation of the public peace, as well against internal 10 convulsions as external attacks; the regulation of commerce with other nations and between the States; the superintendence of our intercourse, political and commercial, with foreign countries.

The authorities essential to the common defense are these: to raise armies; to build and equip fleets; to prescribe rules for the government of both; to direct 15 their operations; to provide for their support. These powers ought to exist without limitation, *because it is impossible to foresee or define the extent and variety of national exigencies, and the correspondent extent and variety of the means which may be necessary to satisfy them.* The circumstances that endanger the safety of nations are infinite, and for this reason no constitutional shackles can wisely be 20 imposed on the power to which the care of it is committed. This power ought

---

Alexander Hamilton, "No. 23: The Necessity of a Government as Energetic as the One Proposed to the Preservation of the Union," in Clinton Rossiter, ed., *The Federalist Papers* (New York: Mentor, 1999), 148–53.

to be coextensive with all the possible combinations of such circumstances; and ought to be under the direction of the same councils which are appointed to preside over the common defense.

This is one of those truths which to a correct and unprejudiced mind carries its
5   own evidence along with it, and may be obscured, but cannot be made plainer by argument or reasoning. It rests upon axioms as simple as they are universal; the *means* ought to be proportioned to the *end*; the persons from whose agency the attainment of any *end* is expected ought to possess the *means* by which it is to be attained.

10   Whether there ought to be a federal government entrusted with the care of the common defense is a question in the first instance open for discussion; but the moment it is decided in the affirmative, it will follow that that government ought to be clothed with all the powers requisite to complete execution of its trust. And unless it can be shown that the circumstances which may affect the public
15   safety are reducible within certain determinate limits; unless the contrary of this position can be fairly and rationally disputed, it must be admitted as a necessary consequence that there can be no limitation of that authority which is to provide for the defense and protection of the community in any matter essential to its efficacy—that is, in any matter essential to the *formation*, *direction*, or *support* of
20   the NATIONAL FORCES.

Defective as the present Confederation has been proved to be, this principle appears to have been fully recognized by the framers of it; though they have not made proper or adequate provision for its exercise. Congress have an unlimited discretion to make requisitions of men and money; to govern the army and navy;
25   to direct their operations. As their requisitions are made constitutionally binding upon the States, who are in fact under the most solemn obligations to furnish the supplies required of them, the intention evidently was that the United States should command whatever resources were by them judged requisite to the "common defense and general welfare." It was presumed that a sense of their true interests,
30   and a regard to the dictates of good faith, would be found sufficient pledges for the punctual performance of the duty of the members to the federal head.

The experiment has, however, demonstrated that this expectation was ill-founded and illusory; and the observations made under the last head will, I imagine, have sufficed to convince the impartial and discerning that there is an absolute necessity
35   for an entire change in the first principles of the system; that if we are in earnest about giving the Union energy and duration we must abandon the vain project of legislating upon the States in their collective capacities; we must extend the laws of the federal government to the individual citizens of America; we must discard the fallacious scheme of quotas and requisitions as equally impracticable

and unjust. The result from all this is that the Union ought to be invested with full power to levy troops; to build and equip fleets; and to raise the revenues which will be required for the formation and support of an army and navy in the customary and ordinary modes practiced in other governments.

If the circumstances of our country are such as to demand a compound instead of a simple, a confederate instead of a sole, government, the essential point which will remain to be adjusted will be to discriminate the OBJECTS, as far as it can be done, which shall appertain to the different provinces or departments of power; allowing to each the most ample authority for fulfilling the objects committed to its charge. Shall the Union be constituted the guardian of the common safety? Are fleets and armies and revenues necessary to this purpose? The government of the Union must be empowered to pass all laws, and to make all regulations which have relation to them. The same must be the case in respect to commerce, and to every other matter to which its jurisdiction is permitted to extend. Is the administration of justice between the citizens of the same State the proper department of the local governments? These must possess all the authorities which are connected with this object, and with every other that may be allotted to their particular cognizance and direction. Not to confer in each case a degree of power commensurate to the end would be to violate the most obvious rules of prudence and propriety, and improvidently to trust the great interests of the nation to hands which are disabled from managing them with vigor and success.

Who so likely to make suitable provisions for the public defense as that body to which the guardianship of the public safety is confided; which, as the center of information, will best understand the extent and urgency of the dangers that threaten; as the representative of the WHOLE, will feel itself most deeply interested in the preservation of every part; which, from the responsibility implied in the duty assigned to it, will be most sensibly impressed with the necessity of proper exertions; and which, by the extension of its authority throughout the States, can alone establish uniformity and concert in the plans and measures by which the common safety is to be secured? Is there not a manifest inconsistency in devolving upon the federal government the care of the general defense and leaving in the State governments the *effective* powers by which it is to be provided for? Is not a want of cooperation the infallible consequence of such a system? And will not weakness, disorder, an undue distribution of the burdens and calamities of war, an unnecessary and intolerable increase of expense, be its natural and inevitable concomitants? Have we not had unequivocal experience of its effects in the course of the revolution which we have just achieved?

Every view we may take of the subject, as candid inquirers after truth, will serve to convince us that it is both unwise and dangerous to deny the federal government

5

10

15

20

25

30

35

an unconfined authority in respect to all those objects which are entrusted to its management. It will indeed deserve the most vigilant and careful attention of the people to see that it be modeled in such a manner as to admit of its being safely vested with the requisite powers. If any plan which has been, or may be, offered
5 to our consideration should not, upon a dispassionate inspection, be found to answer this description, it ought to be rejected. A government, the constitution of which renders it unfit to be trusted with all the powers which a free people *ought to delegate to any government*, would be an unsafe and improper depositary of the NATIONAL INTERESTS. Wherever THESE can with propriety be confided,
10 the co-incident powers may safely accompany them. This is the true result of all just reasoning upon the subject. And the adversaries of the plan promulgated by the convention would have given a better impression of their candor if they had confined themselves to showing that the internal structure of the proposed government was such as to render it unworthy of the confidence of the people. They
15 ought not to have wandered into inflammatory declamations and unmeaning cavils about the extent of the powers. The POWERS are not too extensive for the OBJECTS of federal administration, or, in other words, for the management of our NATIONAL INTERESTS; nor can any satisfactory argument be framed to show that they are chargeable with such an excess. If it be true, as has been insinuated by some of the
20 writers on the other side, that the difficulty arises from the nature of the thing, and that the extent of the country will not permit us to form a government in which such ample powers can safely be reposed, it would prove that we ought to contract our views, and resort to the expedient of separate confederacies, which will move within more practicable spheres. For the absurdity must continually stare us in
25 the face of confiding to a government the direction of the most essential national interests, without daring to trust it to the authorities which are indispensible to their proper and efficient management. Let us not attempt to reconcile contradictions, but firmly embrace a rational alternative.

I trust, however, that the impracticability of one general system cannot be shown. I
30 am greatly mistaken if anything of weight has yet been advanced of this tendency; and I flatter myself that the observations which have been made in the course of these papers have served to place the reverse of that position in as clear a light as any matter still in the womb of time and experience is susceptible of. This, at all events, must be evident, that the very difficulty itself, drawn from the extent of
35 the country, is the strongest argument in favor of an energetic government; for any other can certainly never preserve the Union of so large an empire. If we embrace the tenets of those who oppose the adoption of the proposed Constitution as the standard of our political creed we cannot fail to verify the gloomy doctrines which predict the impracticability of a national system pervading the entire limits
40 of the present Confederacy.

Federalist 39
James Madison

Responding to the Anti-Federalist charge that the Constitution will con-
solidate power at the national level, Publius sets up a five-prong test to
demonstrate that the Constitution will establish neither a wholly national
government nor one in which all the power resides with the states. A com-
bination, he argues, creates the best chance for liberty.

JANUARY 16, 1788

THE CONFORMITY OF THE PLAN TO REPUBLICAN PRINCIPLES

The last paper having concluded the observations which were meant to introduce a candid survey of the plan of government reported by the convention, we now proceed to the execution of that part of our undertaking.

The first question that offers itself is whether the general form and aspect of the government be strictly republican. It is evident that no other form would be   5 reconcilable with the genius of the people of America; with the fundamental principles of the Revolution; or with that honorable determination which animates every votary of freedom to rest all our political experiments on the capacity of mankind for self-government. If the plan of the convention, therefore, be found to depart from the republican character, its advocates must abandon   10 it as no longer defensible.

What, then, are the distinctive characters of the republican form? Were an answer to this question to be sought, not by recurring to principles but in the application of the term by political writers to the constitutions of different States, no satisfactory one would ever be found. Holland, in which no particle of the   15 supreme authority is derived from the people, has passed almost universally under the denomination of a republic. The same title has been bestowed on Venice, where absolute power over the great body of the people is exercised in the most absolute manner by a small body of hereditary nobles. Poland,

James Madison, "No. 39: The Conformity of the Plan to Republican Principles," in Clinton Rossiter, ed., *The Federalist Papers* (New York: Mentor, 1999), 236–43.

which is a mixture of aristocracy and of monarchy in their worst forms, has been dignified with the same appellation. The government of England, which has one republican branch only, combined with an hereditary aristocracy and monarchy, has with equal impropriety been frequently placed on the list of
5   republics. These examples, which are nearly as dissimilar to each other as to a genuine republic, show the extreme inaccuracy with which the term has been used in political disquisitions.

If we resort for a criterion to the different principles on which different forms of government are established, we may define a republic to be, or at least may
10   bestow that name on, a government which derives all its powers directly or indirectly from the great body of the people, and is administered by persons holding their offices during pleasure for a limited period, or during good behavior. It is *essential* to such a government that it be derived from the great body of the society, not from an inconsiderable proportion or a favored class
15   of it; otherwise a handful of tyrannical nobles, exercising their oppressions by a delegation of their powers, might aspire to the rank of republicans and claim for their government the honorable title of republic. It is *sufficient* for such a government that the persons administering it be appointed, either directly or indirectly, by the people; and that they hold their appointments by either of
20   the tenures just specified; otherwise every government in the United States, as well as every other popular government that has been or can be well organized or well executed, would be degraded from the republican character. According to the constitution of every State in the Union, some or other of the officers of government are appointed indirectly only by the people. According to most
25   of them, the chief magistrate himself is so appointed. And according to one, this mode of appointment is extended to one of the coordinate branches of the legislature. According to all the constitutions, also, the tenure of the highest offices is extended to a definite period, and in many instances, both within the legislative and executive departments, to a period of years. According to the
30   provisions of most of the constitutions, again, as well as according to the most respectable and received opinions on the subject, the members of the judiciary department are to retain their offices by the firm tenure of good behavior.

On comparing the Constitution planned by the convention with the standard here fixed, we perceived at once that it is, in the most rigid sense, conformable
35   to it. The House of Representatives, like that of one branch at least of all the State legislatures, is elected immediately by the great body of the people. The Senate, like the present Congress and the Senate of Maryland, derives its appointment indirectly from the people. The President is indirectly derived from the choice of the people, according to the example in most of the States.

Even the judges, with all other officers of the Union, will, as in the several States, be the choice, though a remote choice, of the people themselves. The duration of the appointments is equally conformable to the republican standard and to the model of State constitutions. The House of Representatives is periodically elective, as in all the States; and for the period of two years, as in the State of   5
South Carolina. The Senate is elective for the period of six years, which is but one year more than the period of the Senate of Maryland, and but two more than that of the Senates of New York and Virginia. The President is to continue in office for the period of four years; as in New York and Delaware the chief magistrate is elected for three years, and in South Carolina for two years. In the   10
other States the election is annual. In several of the States, however, no explicit provision is made for the impeachment of the chief magistrate. And in Delaware and Virginia he is not impeachable till out of office. The President of the United States is impeachable at any time during his continuance in office. The tenure by which the judges are to hold their places is, as it unquestionably ought to   15
be, that of good behavior. The tenure of the ministerial offices generally will be a subject of legal regulation, conformably to the reason of the case and the example of the State constitutions.

Could any further proof be required of the republican complexion of this system, the most decisive one might be found in its absolute prohibition of titles of   20
nobility, both under the federal and the State governments; and in its express guaranty of the republican form to each of the latter.

"But it was not sufficient," say the adversaries of the proposed Constitution, "for the convention to adhere to the republican form. They ought with equal care to have preserved the *federal* form, which regards the Union as a *Confederacy*   25
of sovereign states; instead of which they have framed a *national* government, which regards the Union as a *consolidation* of the States." And it is asked by what authority this bold and radical innovation was undertaken? The handle which has been made of this objection requires that it should be examined with some precision.   30

Without inquiring into the accuracy of the distinction on which the objection is founded, it will be necessary to a just estimate of its force, first, to ascertain the real character of the government in question; secondly, to inquire how far the convention were authorized to propose such a government; and thirdly, how far the duty they owed to their country could supply any defect of regular   35
authority.

First.—In order to ascertain the real character of the government, it may be considered in relation to the foundation on which it is to be established; to the sources from which its ordinary powers are to be drawn; to the operation of those powers; to the extent of them; and to the authority by which future changes in the government are to be introduced.

On examining the first relation, it appears, on one hand, that the Constitution
5   is to be founded on the assent and ratification of the people of America, given by deputies elected for the special purpose; but, on the other, that this assent and ratification is to be given by the people, not as individuals composing one entire nation, but as composing the distinct and independent States to which they respectively belong. It is to be the assent and ratification of the several
10   States, derived from the supreme authority in each State—the authority of the people themselves. The act, therefore, establishing the Constitution will not be a *national* but a *federal* act.

That it will be a federal and not a national act, as these terms are understood by the objectors—the act of the people, as forming so many independent States, not
15   as forming one aggregate nation—is obvious from this single consideration: that it is to result neither from the decision of a *majority* of the people of the Union, nor from that of a *majority* of the States. It must result from the *unanimous* assent of the several States that are parties to it, differing no otherwise from their ordinary assent than in its being expressed, not by the legislative authority, but
20   by that of the people themselves. Were the people regarded in this transaction as forming one nation, the will of the majority of the whole people of the United States would bind the minority, in the same manner as the majority in each State must bind the minority; and the will of the majority must be determined either by a comparison of the individual votes, or by considering the will of the
25   majority of the States as evidence of the will of a majority of the people of the United States. Neither of these rules has been adopted. Each State, in ratifying the Constitution, is considered as a sovereign body independent of all others, and only to be bound by its own voluntary act. In this relation, then, the new Constitution will, if established, be a *federal* and not a *national* constitution.

30   The next relation is to the sources from which the ordinary powers of government are to be derived. The House of Representatives will derive its powers from the people of America; and the people will be represented in the same proportion and on the same principle as they are in the legislature of a particular State. So far the government is *national*, not *federal*. The Senate, on the other hand, will
35   derive its powers from the States as political and coequal societies; and these will be represented on the principle of equality in the Senate, as they now are in the existing Congress. So far the government is *federal*, not *national*. The executive power will be derived from a very compound source. The immediate election of the President is to be made by the States in their political characters. The

votes allotted to them are in a compound ratio, which considers them partly as distinct and coequal societies, partly as unequal members of the same society. The eventual election, again, is to be made by that branch of the legislature which consists of the national representatives; but in this particular act they are to be thrown into the form of individual delegations from so many distinct and coequal bodies politic. From this aspect of the government it appears to be of a mixed character, presenting at least as many *federal* as *national* features.

The difference between a federal and national government, as it relates to the *operation of the government*, is by the adversaries of the plan of the convention supposed to consist in this, that in the former the powers operate on the political bodies composing the Confederacy in their political capacities; in the latter, on the individual citizens composing the nation in their individual capacities. On trying the Constitution by this criterion, it falls under the *national* not the *federal* character; though perhaps not so completely as has been understood. In several cases, and particularly in the trial of controversies to which States may be parties, they must be viewed and proceeded against in their collective and political capacities only. But the operation of the government on the people in their individual capacities, in its ordinary and most essential proceedings, will, in the sense of its opponents, on the whole, designate it, in this relation, a *national* government.

But if the government be national with regard to the *operation* of its powers, it changes its aspect again when we contemplate it in relation to the extent of its powers. The idea of a national government involves in it not only an authority over the individual citizens, but an indefinite supremacy over all persons and things, so far as they are objects of lawful government. Among a people consolidated into one nation, this supremacy is completely vested in the national legislature. Among communities united for particular purposes, it is vested partly in the general and partly in the municipal legislatures. In the former case, all local authorities are subordinate to the supreme; and may be controlled, directed, or abolished by it at pleasure. In the latter, the local or municipal authorities form distinct and independent portions of the supremacy, no more subject, within their respective spheres, to the general authority than the general authority is subject to them, within its own sphere. In this relation, then, the proposed government cannot be deemed a *national* one; since its jurisdiction extends to certain enumerated objects only, and leaves to the several States a residuary and inviolable sovereignty over all other objects. It is true that in controversies relating to the boundary between the two jurisdictions, the tribunal which is ultimately to decide is to be established under the general government. But this does not change the principle of the case. The decision

is to be impartially made, according to the rules of the Constitution; and all the usual and most effectual precautions are taken to secure this impartiality. Some such tribunal is clearly essential to prevent an appeal to the sword and a dissolution of the compact; and that it ought to be established under the
5   general rather than under the local governments, or, to speak more properly, that it could be safely established under the first alone, is a position not likely to be combated.

If we try the Constitution by its last relation to the authority by which amendments are to be made, we find it neither wholly *national* nor wholly
10   *federal*. Were it wholly national, the supreme and ultimate authority would reside in the *majority* of the people of the Union; and this authority would be competent at all times, like that of a majority of every national society to alter or abolish its established government. Were it wholly federal, on the other hand, the concurrence of each State in the Union would be essential to every
15   alteration that would be binding on all. The mode provided by the plan of the convention is not founded on either of these principles. In requiring more than a majority, and particularly in computing the proportion by *States*, not by *citizens*, it departs from the national and advances towards the *federal* character; in rendering the concurrence of less than the whole number of States sufficient,
20   it loses again the *federal* and partakes of the *national* character.

The proposed Constitution, therefore, even when tested by the rules laid down by its antagonists, is, in strictness, neither a national nor a federal Constitution, but a composition of both. In its foundation it is federal, not national; in the sources from which the ordinary powers of the government are drawn, it is partly
25   federal and partly national; in the operation of these powers, it is national, not federal; in the extent of them, again, it is federal, not national; and, finally in the authoritative mode of introducing amendments, it is neither wholly federal nor wholly national.

Federalist 40
James Madison

*In creating the Constitution, the Constitutional Convention overstepped
its mandate, which was to amend the Articles of Confederation. Publius
cannot dispute this. Instead, he appeals to the principles of the Declaration
of Independence to support the Convention's work.*

January 18, 1788

The Powers of the Convention to Form a Mixed Government
Examined and Sustained

The *second* point to be examined is whether the convention were authorized to
frame and propose this mixed Constitution.

The powers of the convention ought, in strictness, to be determined by an
inspection of the commissions given to the members by their respective
constituents. As all of these, however, had reference either to the recommendation   5
from the meeting at Annapolis, in September, 1786, or to that from Congress,
in February, 1787, it will be sufficient to recur to these particular acts.

The act from Annapolis recommends the "appointment of commissioners to
take into consideration the situation of the United States; to devise *such further
provisions* as shall appear to them necessary to render the Constitution of the   10
federal government *adequate to the exigencies of the Union*; and to report such
an act for that purpose to the United States in Congress assembled, as when
agreed to by them, and afterwards confirmed by the legislature of every State,
will effectually provide for the same."

The recommendatory act of Congress is in the words following: "Whereas there   15
is provision in the articles of Confederation and perpetual Union for making
alterations therein, by the assent of a Congress of the United States and of the
legislatures of the several States; and whereas experience hath evinced that there

---

James Madison, "No. 40: The Powers of the Convention to Form a Mixed Government Examined and
Sustained," in Clinton Rossiter, ed., *The Federalist Papers* (New York: Mentor, 1999), 243–51.

are defects in the present Confederation; as a means to remedy which, several of the States, and *particularly the State of New York*, by express instructions to their delegates in Congress, have suggested a convention for the purposes expressed in the following resolution; and such convention appearing to be the most probable mean of establishing in these States *a firm national government*:

"*Resolved*—That in the opinion of Congress it is expedient that on the second Monday in May next a convention of delegates, who shall have been appointed by the several States, be held at Philadelphia for the sole and express purpose *of revising the articles of Confederation* and reporting to Congress and the several legislatures such *alterations and provisions therein* as shall, when agreed to in Congress and confirmed by the States, render the federal Constitution *adequate to the exigencies of government and the preservation of the Union*."

From these two acts, it appears, 1st, that the object of the convention was to establish in these States a *firm national government*; 2nd, that this government was to be such as would be *adequate to the exigencies of government* and *the preservation of the Union*; 3rd, that these purposes were to be affected by *alterations and provisions in the Articles of Confederation*, as it is expressed in the act of Congress, or by *such further provisions as should appear necessary*, as it stands in the recommendatory act from Annapolis; 4th, that the alterations and provisions were to be reported to Congress and to the States in order to be agreed to by the former and confirmed by the latter.

From a comparison and fair construction of these several modes of expression is to be deduced the authority under which the convention acted. They were to frame a *national government*, adequate to the *exigencies of government* and *of the Union*; and to reduce the articles of Confederation into such form as to accomplish these purposes.

There are two rules of construction, dictated by plain reason as well as founded on legal axioms. The one is that every part of the expression ought, if possible, to be allowed some meaning, and be made to conspire to some common end. The other is that where the several parts cannot be made to coincide, the less important should give way to the more important part; the means should be sacrificed to the end, rather than the end to the means.

Suppose, then, that the expressions defining the authority of the convention were irreconcilably at variance with each other; that a *national* and *adequate government* could not possibly, in the judgment of the convention, be affected by *alterations* and *provisions* in the *Articles of Confederation*; which part of the definition ought to have been embraced and which rejected? Which was the more important, which the less important part? Which the end; which the means?

Let the most scrupulous expositors of delegated powers, let the most inveterate objectors against those exercised by the convention answer these questions. Let them declare whether it was of most importance to the happiness of the people of America, that the Articles of Confederation should be disregarded, and an adequate government be provided, and the Union preserved; or that   5 an adequate government should be omitted, and the Articles of Confederation preserved. Let them declare whether the preservation of these articles was the end for securing which a reform of the government was to be introduced as the means; or whether the establishment of a government adequate to the national happiness was the end at which these articles themselves originally aimed, and   10 to which they ought, as insufficient means, to have been sacrificed.

But is it necessary to suppose that these expressions are absolutely irreconcilable to each other; that no *alterations* or *provisions* in the *Articles of the Confederation* could possibly mold them into a national and adequate government; into such a government as has been proposed by the convention?   15

No stress, it is presumed, will, in this case, be laid on the *title*, a change of that could never be deemed an exercise of ungranted power. *Alterations* in the body of the instrument are expressly authorized. *New provisions* therein are also expressly authorized. Here then is a power to change the title; to insert new articles; to alter old ones. Must it of necessity be admitted that this power is   20 infringed, so long as a part of the old articles remain? Those who maintain the affirmative ought at least to mark the boundary between authorized and usurped innovations; between that degree of change which lies within the compass of *alterations and further provisions* and that which amounts to a *transmutation* of the government. Will it be said that the alterations ought not to have touched   25 the substances of the Confederation? The States would never have appointed a convention with so much solemnity, nor described its objects with so much latitude, if some *substantial* reform had not been in contemplation. Will it be said that the *fundamental principles* of the Confederation were not within the purview of the convention, and ought not to have been varied? I ask, What are   30 these principles? Do they require that in the establishment of the Constitution the States should be regarded as distinct and independent sovereigns? They are so regarded by the Constitution proposed. Do they require that the members of the government should derive their appointment from the legislatures, not from the people of the States? One branch of the new government is to be   35 appointed by these legislatures; and under the Confederation the delegates to Congress *may all* be appointed immediately by the people, and in two States are actually so appointed. Do they require that the powers of the government should act on the States and not immediately on individuals? In some instances,

as has been shown, the powers of the new government will act on the States
in their collective characters. In some instances, also, those of the existing
government act immediately on individuals. In cases of capture; of piracy; of
the post office; of coins, weights, and measures; of trade with the Indians; of
5   claims under grants of land by different States; and, above all, in the case of
trials by courts-martial in the army and navy, by which death may be inflicted
without the intervention of a jury, or even of a civil magistrate—in all these
cases the powers of the Confederation operate immediately on the persons
and interests of individual citizens. Do these fundamental principles require,
10   particularly, that no tax should be levied without the intermediate agency of
the States? The Confederation itself authorizes a direct tax, to a certain extent,
on the post office. The power of coinage has been so construed by Congress
as to levy a tribute immediately from that source also. But pretermitting these
instances, was it not an acknowledged object of the convention and the universal
15   expectation of the people that the regulation of trade should be submitted to
the general government in such a form as would render it an immediate source
of general revenue? Had not Congress repeatedly recommended this measure as
not inconsistent with the fundamental principles of the Confederation? Had not
every State but one, had not New York herself, so far complied with the plan of
20   Congress as to recognize the *principle* of the innovation? Do these principles, in
fine, require that the powers of the general government should be limited, and
that, beyond this limit, the States should be left in possession of their sovereignty
and independence? We have seen that in the new government, as in the old, the
general powers are limited; and that the States, in all unenumerated cases, are
25   left in the enjoyment of their sovereign and independent jurisdiction.

The truth is that the great principles of the Constitution proposed by the
convention may be considered less as absolutely new than as the expansion of
principles which are found in the Articles of Confederation. The misfortune
under the latter system has been that these principles are so feeble and confined
30   as to justify all the charges of inefficiency which have been urged against it, and
to require a degree of enlargement which gives to the new system the aspect of
an entire transformation of the old.

In one particular it is admitted that the convention have departed from the tenor
of their commission. Instead of reporting a plan requiring the confirmation *of*
35   *all the States*, they have reported a plan which is to be confirmed and may be
carried into effect by *nine States only*. It is worthy of remark that this objection,
though the most plausible, has been the least urged in the publications which
have swarmed against the convention. The forbearance can only have proceeded
from an irresistible conviction of the absurdity of subjecting the fate of twelve

States to the perverseness or corruption of a thirteenth; from the example of inflexible opposition given by a *majority* of one sixtieth of the people of America to a measure approved and called for by the voice of twelve States, comprising fifty-nine sixtieths of the people—an example still fresh in the memory and indignation of every citizen who has felt for the wounded honor and prosperity 5 of his country. As this objection, therefore, has been in a manner waived by those who have criticized the powers of the convention, I dismiss it without further observation.

The *third* point to be inquired into is how far considerations of duty arising out of the case itself could have supplied any defect of regular authority. 10

In the preceding inquiries the powers of the convention have been analyzed and tried with the same rigor, and by the same rules, as if they had been real and final powers for the establishment of a Constitution for the United States. We have seen in what manner they have borne the trial even on that supposition. It is time now to recollect that the powers were merely advisory and recommendatory; 15 that they were so meant by the States and so understood by the convention; and that the latter have accordingly planned and proposed a Constitution which is to be of no more consequence than the paper on which it is written, unless it be stamped with the approbation of those to whom it is addressed. This reflection places the subject in a point of view altogether different, and will enable us to 20 judge with propriety of the course taken by the convention.

Let us view the ground on which the convention stood. It may be collected from their proceedings that they were deeply and unanimously impressed with the crisis, which had led their country almost with one voice to make so singular and solemn an experiment for correcting the errors of a system by which this crisis 25 had been produced; that they were no less deeply and unanimously convinced that such a reform as they have proposed was absolutely necessary to affect the purposes of their appointment. It could not be unknown to them that the hopes and expectations of the great body of citizens, throughout this great empire, were turned with the keenest anxiety to the event of their deliberations. They 30 had every reason to believe that the contrary sentiments agitated the minds and bosoms of every external and internal foe to the liberty and prosperity of the United States. They had seen in the origin and progress of the experiment the alacrity with which the *proposition*, made by a single State (Virginia) towards a partial amendment of the Confederation, had been attended to and promoted. 35 They had seen the *liberty assumed* by a *very few* deputies from a *very few* States, convened at Annapolis, of recommending a great and critical object, wholly foreign to their commission, not only justified by the public opinion, but actually carried into effect by twelve out of the thirteen States. They had seen, in a variety

of instances, assumptions by Congress, not only of recommendatory, but of operative, powers, warranted, in the public estimation, by occasions and objects infinitely less urgent than those by which their conduct was to be governed. They must have reflected that in all great changes of established governments
5   forms ought to give way to substance; that a rigid adherence in such cases to the former would render nominal and nugatory the transcendent and precious right of the people to "*abolish or alter their governments* as to them shall seem most likely to affect their safety and happiness,"* since it is impossible for the people spontaneously and universally to move in concert towards their object;
10   and it is therefore essential that such changes be instituted by some *informal and unauthorized propositions,* made by some patriotic and respectable citizen or number of citizens. They must have recollected that it was by this irregular and assumed privilege of proposing to the people plans for their safety and happiness that the States were first united against the danger with which they
15   were threatened by their ancient government; that committees and congresses were formed for concentrating their efforts and defending their rights; and that *conventions* were *elected* in *the several States* for establishing the constitutions under which they are now governed; nor could it have been forgotten that no little ill-timed scruples, no zeal for adhering to ordinary forms, were anywhere
20   seen, except in those who wished to indulge, under these masks, their secret enmity to the substance contended for. They must have borne in mind that as the plan to be framed and proposed was to be submitted to *the people themselves,* the disapprobation of this supreme authority would destroy it forever; its approbation blot out antecedent errors and irregularities. It might even have
25   occurred to them that where a disposition to cavil prevailed, their neglect to execute the degree of power vested in them, and still more their recommendation of any measure whatever not warranted by their commission, would not less excite animadversion than a recommendation at once of a measure fully commensurate to the national exigencies.

30   Had the convention, under all these impressions and in the midst of all these considerations, instead of exercising a manly confidence in their country, by whose confidence they had been so peculiarly distinguished, and of pointing out a system capable, in their judgment, of securing its happiness, taken the cold and sullen resolution of disappointing its ardent hopes, of sacrificing substance to
35   forms, of committing the dearest interests of their country to the uncertainties of delay and the hazard of events, let me ask the man who can raise his mind to one elevated conception, who can awaken in his bosom one patriotic emotion, what judgment ought to have been pronounced by the impartial world, by the

---

*Declaration of Independence—PUBLIUS.

friends of mankind, by every virtuous citizen, on the conduct and character of this assembly? Or if there be a man whose propensity to condemn is susceptible of no control, let me then ask what sentence he has in reserve for the twelve States who *usurped the power* of sending deputies to the convention, a body, utterly unknown to their constitutions; for Congress, who recommended the 5 appointment of this body, equally unknown to the Confederation; and for the State of New York, in particular, which first urged and then complied with this unauthorized interposition?

But that the objectors may be disarmed of every pretext it shall be granted for a moment that the convention were neither authorized by their commission, nor 10 justified by circumstances in proposing a Constitution for their country: does it follow that the Constitution ought, for that reason alone, to be rejected? If, according to the noble precept, it be lawful to accept good advice even from an enemy, shall we set the ignoble example of refusing such advice even when it is offered by our friends? The prudent inquiry, in all cases, ought surely to be not 15 so much *from whom* the advice comes, as whether the advice be *good*.

The sum of what has been here advanced and proved is that the charge against the convention of exceeding their powers, except in one instance little urged by the objectors, has no foundation to support it; that if they had exceeded their powers, they were not only warranted, but required as the confidential servants 20 of their country, by the circumstances in which they were placed to exercise the liberty which they assumed; and that finally, if they had violated both their powers and their obligations in proposing a Constitution, this ought nevertheless to be embraced, if it be calculated to accomplish the views and happiness of the people of America. How far this character is due to the Constitution is the 25 subject under investigation.

LETTERS I AND II
FEDERAL FARMER

Alexander Hamilton acknowledged the Federal Farmer—believed to be either New Yorker Melancton Smith or Virginian Richard Henry Lee—as "the most plausible" Anti-Federalist. Here the Federal Farmer argues that the federalism of the Constitution is a mirage, for it sets up a structure in which all power will flow to the center.

OCTOBER 8, 1787

LETTER I

DEAR SIR:

...The present moment discovers a new face in our affairs. Our object has been all along, to reform our federal system, and to strengthen our governments—to establish peace, order and justice in the community—but a new object now presents. The plan of government now proposed is evidently calculated totally to change, in time, our condition as a people. Instead of being thirteen republics, 5 under a federal head, it is clearly designed to make us one consolidated government. Of this, I think, I shall fully convince you, in my following letters on this subject. This consolidation of the states has been the object of several men in this country for some time past. Whether such a change can ever be affected in any manner; whether it can be affected without convulsions and 10 civil wars; whether such a change will not totally destroy the liberties of this country—time only can determine....

In the first place, I shall premise, that the plan proposed is a plan of accommodation—and that it is in this way only, and by giving up a part of our opinions, that we can ever expect to obtain a government founded in freedom 15 and compact. This circumstance candid men will always keep in view, in the discussion of this subject.

Anonymous, "Letters from the Federal Farmer I, II," in Herbert J. Storing, ed., *The Complete Anti-Federalist*, Vol. 2 (Chicago: University of Chicago Press, 1981), 223, 226, 228–30.

The plan proposed appears to be partly federal, but principally however, calculated ultimately to make the states one consolidated government.

The first interesting question, therefore suggested, is, how far the states can be consolidated into one entire government on free principles. In considering this question extensive objects are to be taken into view, and important changes in the forms of government to be carefully attended to in all their consequences. The happiness of the people at large must be the great object with every honest statesman, and he will direct every movement to this point. If we are so situated as a people, as not to be able to enjoy equal happiness and advantages under one government, the consolidation of the states cannot be admitted.

There are three different forms of free government under which the United States may exist as one nation; and now is, perhaps, the time to determine to which we will direct our views. 1. Distinct republics connected under a federal head. In this case the respective state governments must be the principal guardians of the peoples' rights, and exclusively regulate their internal police; in them must rest the balance of government. The congress of the states, or federal head, must consist of delegates amenable to, and removeable by the respective states: This congress must have general directing powers; powers to require men and monies of the states; to make treaties, peace and war; to direct the operations of armies, etc. Under this federal modification of government, the powers of congress would be rather advisory or recommendatory than coercive. 2. We may do away the several state governments, and form or consolidate all the states into one entire government, with one executive, one judiciary, and one legislature, consisting of senators and representatives collected from all parts of the union: In this case there would be a complete consolidation of the states. 3. We may consolidate the states as to certain national objects, and leave them severally distinct independent republics, as to internal police generally. Let the general government consist of an executive, a judiciary, and balanced legislature, and its powers extend exclusively to all foreign concerns, causes arising on the seas to commerce, imports, armies, navies, Indian affairs, peace and war, and to a few internal concerns of the community; to the coin, post-offices, weights and measures, a general plan for the militia, to naturalization, *and, perhaps to bankruptcies*, leaving the internal police of the community, in other respects, exclusively to the state governments; as the administration of justice in all causes arising internally, the laying and collecting of internal taxes, and the forming of the militia according to a general plan prescribed. In this case there would be a complete consolidation, *quoad* certain objects only.

Touching the first, or federal plan, I do not think much can be said in its favor: The sovereignty of the nation, without coercive and efficient powers to collect the strength of it, cannot always be depended on to answer the purposes of government; and in a congress of representatives of sovereign states, there must necessarily be an unreasonable mixture of powers in the   5
same hands.

As to the second, or complete consolidating plan, it deserves to be carefully considered at this time, by every American: If it be impracticable, it is a fatal error to model our governments, directing our views ultimately to it.

The third plan, or partial consolidation, is, in my opinion, the only one   10
that can secure the freedom and happiness of this people. I once had some general ideas that the second plan was practicable, but from long attention, and the proceedings of the convention, I am fully satisfied, that this third plan is the only one we can with safety and propriety proceed upon. Making this the standard to point out, with candor and fairness, the parts of the new   15
constitution which appear to be improper, is my object. The convention appears to have proposed the partial consolidation evidently with a view to collect all powers ultimately, in the United States into one entire government; and from its views in this respect, and from the tenacity of the small states to have an equal vote in the senate, probably originated the greatest defects   20
in the proposed plan.

Independent of the opinions of many great authors, that a free elective government cannot be extended over large territories, a few reflections must evince, that one government and general legislation alone, never can extend equal benefits to all parts of the United States: Different laws, customs, and   25
opinions exist in the different states, which by a uniform system of laws would be unreasonably invaded. The United States contain about a million of square miles, and in half a century will, probably, contain ten millions of people; and from the center to the extremes is about 800 miles.

Before we do away the state governments, or adopt measures that will tend   30
to abolish them, and to consolidate the states into one entire government, several principles should be considered and facts ascertained:—These, and my examination into the essential parts of the proposed plan, I shall pursue in my next.

LETTER II

OCTOBER 9, 1787

DEAR SIR:

The essential parts of a free and good government are a full and equal
representation of the people in the legislature, and the jury trial of the vicinage
in the administration of justice—a full and equal representation, is that which
possesses the same interests, feelings, opinions, and views the people themselves
5   would were they all assembled—a fair representation, therefore, should be so
regulated, that every order of men in the community, according to the common
course of elections, can have a share in it—in order to allow professional men,
merchants, traders, farmers, mechanics, etc. to bring a just proportion of their
best informed men respectively into the legislature, the representation must
10   be considerably numerous—We have about 200 state senators in the United
States, and a less number than that of federal representatives cannot, clearly, be
a full representation of this people, in the affairs of internal taxation and police,
were there but one legislature for the whole union. The representation cannot
be equal, or the situation of the people proper for one government only—if the
15   extreme parts of the society cannot be represented as fully as the central—It is
apparently impracticable that this should be the case in this extensive country—it
would be impossible to collect a representation of the parts of the country five,
six, and seven hundred miles from the seat of government. . . .

Federalist 47
James Madison

Anti-Federalists argued that the Constitution violated the maxim of the French political philosopher Montesquieu that the three branches of government should be "separate and distinct" in order to guard against tyranny. Using Montesquieu's own examples and the examples of American state constitutions, Publius refutes the idea that partial overlap of the branches is dangerous to liberty.

January 30, 1788

The Particular Structure of the New Government and the Distribution of Power Among its Different Parts

Having reviewed the general form of the proposed government and the general mass of power allotted to it, I proceed to examine the particular structure of this government, and the distribution of this mass of power among its constituent parts.

One of the principal objections inculcated by the more respectable adversaries 5 to the Constitution is its supposed violation of the political maxim that the legislative, executive, and judiciary departments ought to be separate and distinct. In the structure of the federal government no regard, it is said, seems to have been paid to this essential precaution in favor of liberty. The several departments of power are distributed and blended in such a manner as at once 10 to destroy all symmetry and beauty of form, and to expose some of the essential parts of the edifice to the danger of being crushed by the disproportionate weight of other parts.

No political truth is certainly of greater intrinsic value, or is stamped with the authority of more enlightened patrons of liberty than that on which the objection 15 is founded. The accumulation of all powers, legislative, executive, and judiciary,

James Madison, "No. 47: The Particular Structure of the New Government and the Distribution of Power Among Its Different Parts," in Clinton Rossiter, ed., *The Federalist Papers* (New York: Mentor, 1999), 297–304.

in the same hands, whether of one, a few, or many, and whether hereditary, self-appointed, or elective, may justly be pronounced the very definition of tyranny. Were the federal Constitution, therefore, really chargeable with this accumulation of power, or with a mixture of powers, having a dangerous
5   tendency to such an accumulation, no further arguments would be necessary to inspire a universal reprobation of the system. I persuade myself, however, that it will be made apparent to everyone that the charge cannot be supported, and that the maxim on which it relies has been totally misconceived and misapplied. In order to form correct ideas on this important subject it will be proper to
10 investigate the sense in which the preservation of liberty requires that the three great departments of power should be separate and distinct.

The oracle who is always consulted and cited on this subject is the celebrated Montesquieu. If he be not the author of this invaluable precept in the science of politics, he has the merit at least of displaying and recommending it most
15 effectually to the attention of mankind. Let us endeavor, in the first place, to ascertain his meaning on this point.

The British Constitution was to Montesquieu what Homer has been to the didactic writers on epic poetry. As the latter have considered the work of the immortal bard as the perfect model from which the principles and rules of the epic art were to
20 be drawn, and by which all similar works were to be judged, so this great political critic appears to have viewed the Constitution of England as the standard, or to use his own expression, as the mirror of political liberty; and to have delivered, in the form of elementary truths, the several characteristic principles of that particular system. That we may be sure, then, not to mistake his meaning in this case, let us
25 recur to the source from which the maxim was drawn.

On the slightest view of the British Constitution, we must perceive that the legislative, executive, and judiciary departments are by no means totally separate and distinct from each other. The executive magistrate forms an integral part of the legislative authority. He alone has the prerogative of making treaties with
30 foreign sovereigns which, when made, have, under certain limitations, the force of legislative acts. All the members of the judiciary department are appointed by him, can be removed by him on the address of the two Houses of Parliament, and form, when he pleases to consult them, one of his constitutional councils. One branch of the legislative department forms also a great constitutional council
35 to the executive chief, as, on another hand, it is the sole depositary of judicial power in cases of impeachment, and is invested with the supreme appellate jurisdiction in all other cases. The judges, again, are so far connected with the legislative department as often to attend and participate in its deliberations, though not admitted to a legislative vote.

From these facts, by which Montesquieu was guided, it may clearly be inferred that in saying "There can be no liberty where the legislative and executive powers are united in the same person, or body of magistrates," or, "if the power of judging be not separated from the legislative and executive powers," he did not mean that these departments ought to have no *partial agency* in, or no *control* over, the acts 5 of each other. His meaning, as his own words import, and still more conclusively as illustrated by the example in his eye, can amount to no more than this, that where the *whole* power of one department is exercised by the same hands which possess the *whole* power of another department, the fundamental principles of a free constitution are subverted. This would have been the case in the constitution 10 examined by him, if the king, who is the sole executive magistrate, had possessed also the complete legislative power, or the supreme administration of justice; or if the entire legislative body had possessed the supreme judiciary, or the supreme executive authority. This, however, is not among the vices of that constitution. The magistrate in whom the whole executive power resides cannot of himself 15 make a law, though he can put a negative on every law; nor administer justice in person, though he has the appointment of those who do administer it. The judges can exercise no executive prerogative, though they are shoots from the executive stock; nor any legislative function, though they may be advised by the legislative councils. The entire legislature can perform no judiciary act, though 20 by the joint act of two of its branches the judges may be removed from their offices, and though one of its branches is possessed of the judicial power in the last resort. The entire legislature, again, can exercise no executive prerogative, though one of its branches constitutes the supreme executive magistracy, and another, on the impeachment of a third, can try and condemn all the subordinate 25 officers in the executive department.

The reasons on which Montesquieu grounds his maxim are a further demonstration of his meaning. "When the legislative and executive powers are united in the same person or body," says he, "there can be no liberty, because apprehensions may arise lest *the same* monarch or senate should *enact* tyrannical laws to *execute* 30 them in a tyrannical manner." Again: "Were the power of judging joined with the legislative, the life and liberty of the subject would be exposed to arbitrary control, for *the judge* would then be *the legislator*. Were it joined to the executive power, *the judge* might behave with all the violence of *an oppressor*." Some of these reasons are more fully explained in other passages; but briefly stated as 35 they are here they sufficiently establish the meaning which we have put on this celebrated maxim of this celebrated author.

If we look into the constitutions of the several States we find that, notwithstanding the emphatical and, in some instances, the unqualified terms in which this

axiom has been laid down, there is not a single instance in which the several departments of power have been kept absolutely separate and distinct. New Hampshire, whose constitution was the last formed, seems to have been fully aware of the impossibility and inexpediency of avoiding any mixture whatever
5   of these departments, and has qualified the doctrine by declaring "that the legislative, executive, and judiciary powers ought to be kept as separate from, and independent of, each other *as the nature of a free government will admit; or as is consistent with that chain of connection that binds the whole fabric of the constitution in one indissoluble bond of unity and amity.*" Her constitution accordingly mixes
10   these departments in several respects. The Senate, which is a branch of the legislative department, is also a judicial tribunal for the trial of impeachments. The President, who is the head of the executive department, is the presiding member also of the Senate; and, besides an equal vote in all cases, has a casting vote in case of a tie. The executive head is himself eventually elective every year
15   by the legislative department and his council is every year chosen by and from the members of the same department. Several of the officers of state are also appointed by the legislature. And the members of the judiciary department are appointed by the executive department.

The constitution of Massachusetts has observed a sufficient though less pointed
20   caution in expressing this fundamental article of liberty. It declares "that the legislative department shall never exercise the executive and judicial powers, or either of them; the executive shall never exercise the legislative and judicial powers, or either of them; the judicial shall never exercise the legislative and executive powers, or either of them." This declaration corresponds precisely with
25   the doctrine of Montesquieu, as it has been explained, and is not in a single point violated by the plan of the convention. It goes no farther than to prohibit any one of the entire departments from exercising the powers of another department. In the very Constitution to which it is prefixed, a partial mixture of powers has been admitted. The executive magistrate has a qualified negative on the legislative body,
30   and the Senate, which is a part of the legislature, is a court of impeachment for members both of the executive and judiciary departments. The members of the judiciary department, again, are appointable by the executive department, and removable by the same authority on the address of the two legislative branches. Lastly, a number of the officers of government are annually appointed by the
35   legislative department. As the appointment to offices, particularly executive offices, is in its nature an executive function, the compilers of the Constitution have, in this last point at least, violated the rule established by themselves.

I pass over the constitutions of Rhode Island and Connecticut, because they were formed prior to the Revolution and even before the principle under examination
40   had become an object of political attention.

The constitution of New York contains no declaration on this subject, but appears very clearly to have been framed with an eye to the danger of improperly blending the different departments. It gives, nevertheless, to the executive magistrate, a partial control over the legislative department; and, what is more, gives a like control to the judiciary department; and even blends the executive and judiciary departments in the exercise of this control. In its council of appointment members of the legislative are associated with the executive authority, in the appointment of officers, both executive and judiciary. And its court for the trial of impeachments and correction of errors is to consist of one branch of the legislature and the principal members of the judiciary department.

The constitution of New Jersey has blended the different powers of government more than any of the preceding. The governor, who is the executive magistrate, is appointed by the legislature; is chancellor and ordinary, or surrogate of the State; is a member of the Supreme Court of Appeals, and president, with a casting vote, of one of the legislative branches. The same legislative branch acts again as executive council to the governor, and with him constitutes the Court of Appeals. The members of the judiciary department are appointed by the legislative department, and removable by one branch of it, on the impeachment of the other.

According to the constitution of Pennsylvania, the president, who is the head of the executive department, is annually elected by a vote in which the legislative department predominates. In conjunction with an executive council, he appoints the members of the judiciary department and forms a court of impeachment for trial of all officers, judiciary as well as executive. The judges of the Supreme Court and justices of the peace seem also to be removable by the legislature; and the executive power of pardoning, in certain cases, to be referred to the same department. The members of the executive council are made EX OFFICIO justices of peace throughout the State.

In Delaware, the chief executive magistrate is annually elected by the legislative department. The speakers of the two legislative branches are vice-presidents in the executive department. The executive chief, with six others appointed, three by each of the legislative branches, constitutes the Supreme Court of Appeals; he is joined with the legislative department in the appointment of the other judges. Throughout the States it appears that the members of the legislature may at the same time be justices of the peace; in this State, the members of one branch of it are EX OFFICIO justices of the peace; as are also the members of the executive council. The principal officers of the executive department are appointed by the legislative; and one branch of the latter forms a court of impeachments. All officers may be removed on address of the legislature.

Maryland has adopted the maxim in the most unqualified terms; declaring that the legislative, executive, and judicial powers of government ought to be forever separate and distinct from each other. Her constitution, notwithstanding, makes the executive magistrate appointable by the legislative department; and 5 the members of the judiciary by the executive department.

The language of Virginia is still more pointed on this subject. Her constitution declares "that the legislative, executive, and judiciary departments shall be separate and distinct; so that neither exercises the powers properly belonging to the other; nor shall any person exercise the powers of more than one of them 10 at the same time, except that the justices of county courts shall be eligible to either House of Assembly." Yet we find not only this express exception with respect to the members of the inferior courts, but that the chief magistrate, with his executive council, are appointable by the legislature; that two members of the latter are triennially displaced at the pleasure of the legislature; and that 15 all the principal offices, both executive and judiciary, are filled by the same department. The executive prerogative of pardon, also, is in one case vested in the legislative department.

The constitution of North Carolina, which declares "that the legislative, executive, and supreme judicial powers of government ought to be forever separate and 20 distinct from each other," refers, at the same time, to the legislative department, the appointment not only of the executive chief but all the principal officers within both that and the judiciary department.

In South Carolina, the constitution makes the executive magistracy eligible by the legislative department. It gives to the latter, also, the appointment of the 25 members of the judiciary department, including even justices of the peace and sheriffs; and the appointment of officers in the executive department, down to captains in the army and navy of the State.

In the constitution of Georgia where it is declared "that the legislative, executive, and judiciary departments shall be separate and distinct, so that neither 30 exercise the powers properly belonging to the other," we find that the executive department is to be filled by appointments of the legislature; and the executive prerogative of pardon to be finally exercised by the same authority. Even justices of the peace are to be appointed by the legislature.

In citing these cases, in which the legislative, executive, and judiciary departments 35 have not been kept totally separate and distinct, I wish not to be regarded as an advocate for the particular organizations of the several State governments. I am fully aware that among the many excellent principles which they exemplify they carry strong marks of the haste, and still stronger of the inexperience, under which they were framed. It is but too obvious that in some instances the fundamental principle under consideration has been violated by too great a mixture, and even an actual consolidation of the different powers; and that in no instance has a competent provision been made for maintaining in practice the separation delineated on paper. What I have wished to evince is that the   5 charge brought against the proposed Constitution of violating the sacred maxim of free government is warranted neither by the real meaning annexed to that maxim by its author, nor by the sense in which it has hitherto been understood in America. This interesting subject will be resumed in the ensuing paper.

Federalist 48
James Madison

Taking the argument of the previous paper one step further, Publius argues that overlapping branches are essential to the maintenance of separation of powers. Unless each branch possesses "practical security" against the other two, departmental boundaries will be mere "parchment barriers" and the legislative branch will likely absorb all power to itself.

February 1, 1788

These Departments Should Not Be So Far Separated as to Have No Constitutional Control Over Each Other

It was shown in the last paper that the political apothegm there examined does not require that the legislative, executive, and judiciary departments should be wholly unconnected with each other. I shall undertake, in the next place, to show that unless these departments be so far connected and blended as to give to each a constitutional control over the others, the degree of separation which 5 the maxim requires, as essential to a free government, can never in practice be duly maintained.

It is agreed on all sides that the powers properly belonging to one of the departments ought not to be directly and completely administered by either of the other departments. It is equally evident that none of them ought to 10 possess, directly or indirectly, an overruling influence over the others in the administration of their respective powers. It will not be denied that power is of an encroaching nature and that it ought to be effectually restrained from passing the limits assigned to it. After discriminating, therefore, in theory, the several classes of power, as they may in their nature be legislative, executive, or 15 judiciary, the next and most difficult task is to provide some practical security for each, against the invasion of the others. What this security ought to be is the great problem to be solved.

James Madison, "No. 48: These Departments Should Not Be So Far Separated as to Have No Constitutional Control Over Each Other," in Clinton Rossiter, ed., *The Federalist Papers* (New York: Mentor, 1999), 305–10.

Will it be sufficient to mark, with precision, the boundaries of these departments in the constitution of the government, and to trust to these parchment barriers against the encroaching spirit of power? This is the security which appears to have been principally relied on by the compilers of most of the American
5   constitutions. But experience assures us that the efficacy of the provision has been greatly overrated; and that some more adequate defense is indispensably necessary for the more feeble against the more powerful members of the government. The legislative department is everywhere extending the sphere of its activity and drawing all power into its impetuous vortex.

10   The founders of our republics have so much merit for the wisdom which they have displayed that no task can be less pleasing than that of pointing out the errors into which they have fallen. A respect for truth, however, obliges us to remark that they seem never for a moment to have turned their eyes from the danger, to liberty, from the overgrown and all-grasping prerogative of an
15   hereditary magistrate, supported and fortified by an hereditary branch of the legislative authority. They seem never to have recollected the danger from legislative usurpations, which, by assembling all power in the same hands, must lead to the same tyranny as is threatened by executive usurpations.

In a government where numerous and extensive prerogatives are placed in
20   the hands of an hereditary monarch, the executive department is very justly regarded as the source of danger, and watched with all the jealousy which a zeal for liberty ought to inspire. In a democracy, where a multitude of people exercise in person the legislative functions and are continually exposed, by their incapacity for regular deliberation and concerted measures, to the ambitious
25   intrigues of their executive magistrates, tyranny may well be apprehended, on some favorable emergency, to start up in the same quarter. But in a representative republic where the executive magistracy is carefully limited, both in the extent and the duration of its power; and where the legislative power is exercised by an assembly, which is inspired by a supposed influence over the people with an
30   intrepid confidence in its own strength; which is sufficiently numerous to feel all the passions which actuate a multitude, yet not so numerous as to be incapable of pursuing the objects of its passions by means which reason prescribes; it is against the enterprising ambition of this department that the people ought to indulge all their jealousy and exhaust all their precautions.

35   The legislative department derives a superiority in our governments from other circumstances. Its constitutional powers being at once more extensive, and less susceptible of precise limits, it can, with the greater facility, mask, under complicated and indirect measures, the encroachments which it makes on the coordinate departments. It is not unfrequently a question of real nicety in

legislative bodies whether the operation of a particular measure will, or will not, extend beyond the legislative sphere. On the other side, the executive power being restrained within a narrower compass and being more simple in its nature, and the judiciary being described by landmarks still less uncertain, projects of usurpation by either of these departments would immediately betray and defeat themselves. Nor is this all: as the legislative department alone has access to the pockets of the people, and has in some constitutions full discretion, and in all a prevailing influence, over the pecuniary rewards of those who fill the other departments, a dependence is thus created in the latter, which gives still greater facility to encroachments of the former.

I have appealed to our own experience for the truth of what I advance on this subject. Were it necessary to verify this experience by particular proofs, they might be multiplied without end. I might collect vouchers in abundance from the records and archives of every State in the Union. But as a more concise and at the same time equally satisfactory evidence, I will refer to the example of two States, attested by two unexceptionable authorities.

The first example is that of Virginia, a State which, as we have seen, has expressly declared in its constitution that the three great departments ought not to be intermixed. The authority in support of it is Mr. Jefferson, who, besides his other advantages for remarking the operation of the government, was himself the chief magistrate of it. In order to convey fully the ideas with which his experience had impressed him on this subject, it will be necessary to quote a passage of some length from his very interesting *Notes on the State of Virginia...* "All the powers of government, legislative, executive, and judiciary, result to the legislative body. The concentrating these in the same hands is precisely the definition of despotic government. It will be no alleviation that these powers will be exercised by a plurality of hands, and not by a single one. One hundred and seventy-three despots would surely be as oppressive as one. Let those who doubt it turn their eyes on the republic of Venice. As little will it avail us that they are chosen by ourselves. An *elective despotism* was not the government we fought for; but one which should not only be founded on free principles, but in which the powers of government should be so divided and balanced among several bodies of magistracy as that no one could transcend their legal limits without being effectually checked and restrained by the others. For this reason that convention which passed the ordinance of government laid its foundation on this basis, that the legislative, executive, and judiciary departments should be separate and distinct, so that no person should exercise the powers of more than one of them at the same time. *But no barrier was provided between these several powers*. The judiciary and the executive members were left dependent

on the legislative for their subsistence in office, and some of them for their continuance in it. If, therefore, the legislature assumes executive and judiciary powers, no opposition is likely to be made; nor, if made, can be effectual; because in that case they may put their proceedings into the form of acts of
5   Assembly, which will render them obligatory on the other branches. They have accordingly, *in many* instances, *decided rights* which should have been left to *judiciary controversy*, and *the direction of the executive, during the whole time of their session, is becoming habitual and familiar.*"

The other State which I shall take for an example is Pennsylvania; and the other
10   authority, the Council of Censors, which assembled in the years 1783 and 1784. A part of the duty of this body, as marked out by the Constitution, was "to inquire whether the Constitution had been preserved inviolate in every part; and whether the legislative and executive branches of government had performed their duty as guardians of the people, or assumed to themselves, or exercised,
15   other or greater powers than they are entitled to by the Constitution." In the execution of this trust, the council were necessarily led to a comparison of both the legislative and executive proceedings with the constitutional powers of these departments; and from the facts enumerated, and to the truth of most of which both sides in the council subscribed, it appears that the Constitution had been
20   flagrantly violated by the legislature in a variety of important instances.

A great number of laws had been passed violating, without any apparent necessity, the rule requiring that all bills of a public nature shall be previously printed for the consideration of the people; although this is one of the precautions chiefly relied on by the Constitution against improper acts of the legislature.

25   The constitutional trial by jury had been violated and powers assumed which had not been delegated by the Constitution.

Executive powers had been usurped.

The salaries of the judges, which the Constitution expressly requires to be fixed, had been occasionally varied; and cases belonging to the judiciary department
30   frequently drawn within legislative cognizance and determination.

Those who wish to see the several particulars falling under each of these heads may consult the journals of the council which are in print. Some of them, it will be found, may be imputable to peculiar circumstances connected with the war; but the greater part of them may be considered as the spontaneous shoots
35   of an ill-constituted government.

It appears, also, that the executive department had not been innocent of frequent breaches of the Constitution. There are three observations, however, which

ought to be made on this head: *first*, a great proportion of the instances were either immediately produced by the necessities of the war, or recommended by Congress or the commander-in-chief; *second*, in most of the other instances they conformed either to the declared or the known sentiments of the legislative department; *third*, the executive department of Pennsylvania is distinguished   5
from that of the other States by the number of members composing it. In this respect, it has as much affinity to a legislative assembly as to an executive council. And being at once exempt from the restraint of an individual responsibility for the acts of the body, and deriving confidence from mutual example and joint influence, unauthorized measures would, of course, be more freely hazarded,   10
than where the executive department is administered by a single hand, or by a few hands.

The conclusion which I am warranted in drawing from these observations is that a mere demarcation on parchment of the constitutional limits of the several departments is not a sufficient guard against those encroachments which lead to a   15
tyrannical concentration of all the powers of government in the same hands.

FEDERALIST 49
JAMES MADISON

Thomas Jefferson proposed a direct appeal to the people as a method of solving constitutional disputes among the branches. Publius argues that in addition to being dangerous, such a system would inherently favor the legislative branch. What is more, such appeals would give the impression that the Constitution is defective, thus depriving it of veneration.

FEBRUARY 2, 1788

METHOD OF GUARDING AGAINST THE ENCROACHMENTS OF
ANY ONE DEPARTMENT OF GOVERNMENT BY
APPEALING TO THE PEOPLE THROUGH A CONVENTION

The author of the *Notes on the State of Virginia*, quoted in the last paper, has subjoined to that valuable work the draught of a constitution, which had been prepared in order to be laid before a convention expected to be called in 1783, by the legislature, for the establishment of a constitution for that commonwealth. The plan, like everything from the same pen, marks a turn of thinking, original, comprehensive, and accurate; and is the more worthy of attention as it equally displays a fervent attachment to republican government and an enlightened view of the dangerous propensities against which it ought to be guarded. One of the precautions which he proposes, and on which he appears ultimately to rely as a palladium to the weaker departments of power against the invasions of the stronger, is perhaps altogether his own, and as it immediately relates to the subject of our present inquiry, ought not to be overlooked. 5

His proposition is "that whenever any two of the three branches of government shall concur in opinion, each by the voices of two thirds of their whole number, that a convention is necessary for altering the Constitution, or *correcting breaches of it*, a convention shall be called for the purpose." 15

James Madison, "No. 49: Method of Guarding Against the Encroachments of Any One Department of Government by Appealing to the People Through a Convention," in Clinton Rossiter, ed., *The Federalist Papers* (New York: Mentor, 1999), 310–14.

As the people are the only legitimate fountain of power, and it is from them that the constitutional charter, under which the several branches of government hold their power, is derived, it seems strictly consonant to the republican theory to recur to the same original authority, not only whenever it may be necessary to
5 enlarge, diminish, or new-model the powers of government, but also whenever any one of the departments may commit encroachments on the chartered authorities of the others. The several departments being perfectly coordinate by the terms of their common commission, neither of them, it is evident, can pretend to an exclusive or superior right of settling the boundaries between
10 their respective powers; and how are the encroachments of the stronger to be prevented, or the wrongs of the weaker to be redressed, without an appeal to the people themselves, who, as the grantors of the commission, can alone declare its true meaning, and enforce its observance?

There is certainly great force in this reasoning, and it must be allowed to prove
15 that a constitutional road to the decision of the people ought to be marked out and kept open, for certain great and extraordinary occasions. But there appear to be insuperable objections against the proposed recurrence to the people, as a provision in all cases for keeping the several departments of power within their constitutional limits.

20 In the first place, the provision does not reach the case of a combination of two of the departments against the third. If the legislative authority, which possesses so many means of operating on the motives of the other departments, should be able to gain to its interest either of the others, or even one third of its members, the remaining department could derive no advantage from this
25 remedial provision. I do not dwell, however, on this objection, because it may be thought to lie rather against the modification of the principle, than against the principle itself.

In the next place, it may be considered as an objection inherent in the principle that as every appeal to the people would carry an implication of some defect
30 in the government, frequent appeals would, in great measure, deprive the government of that veneration which time bestows on everything, and without which perhaps the wisest and freest governments would not possess the requisite stability. If it be true that all governments rest on opinion, it is no less true that the strength of opinion in each individual, and its practical influence on his
35 conduct, depend much on the number which he supposes to have entertained the same opinion. The reason of man, like man himself, is timid and cautious when left alone, and acquires firmness and confidence in proportion to the number with which it is associated. When the examples which fortify opinion are *ancient* as well as *numerous*, they are known to have a double effect. In a

nation of philosophers, this consideration ought to be disregarded. A reverence for the laws would be sufficiently inculcated by the voice of an enlightened reason. But a nation of philosophers is as little to be expected as the philosophical race of kings wished for by Plato. And in every other nation, the most rational government will not find it a superfluous advantage to have the prejudices of the community on its side.

The danger of disturbing the public tranquility by interesting too strongly the public passions is a still more serious objection against a frequent reference of constitutional questions to the decision of the whole society. Notwithstanding the success which has attended the revisions of our established forms of government and which does so much honor to the virtue and intelligence of the people of America, it must be confessed that the experiments are of too ticklish a nature to be unnecessarily multiplied. We are to recollect that all the existing constitutions were formed in the midst of a danger which repressed the passions most unfriendly to order and concord; of an enthusiastic confidence of the people in their patriotic leaders, which stifled the ordinary diversity of opinions on great national questions; of a universal ardor for new and opposite forms, produced by a universal resentment and indignation against the ancient government; and whilst no spirit of party connected with the changes to be made, or the abuses to be reformed, could mingle its leaven in the operation. The future situations in which we must expect to be usually placed do not present any equivalent security against the danger which is apprehended.

But the greatest objection of all is that the decisions which would probably result from such appeals would not answer the purpose of maintaining the constitutional equilibrium of the government. We have seen that the tendency of republican governments is to an aggrandizement of the legislative at the expense of the other departments. The appeals to the people, therefore, would usually be made by the executive and judiciary departments. But whether made by one side or the other, would each side enjoy equal advantages on the trial? Let us view their different situations. The members of the executive and judiciary departments are few in number, and can be personally known to a small part only of the people. The latter, by the mode of their appointment, as well as by the nature and permanency of it, are too far removed from the people to share much in their prepossessions. The former are generally the objects of jealousy and their administration is always liable to be discolored and rendered unpopular. The members of the legislative department, on the other hand, are numerous. They are distributed and dwell among the people at large. Their connections of blood, of friendship, and of acquaintance embrace a great proportion of the most influential part of the society. The nature of their public trust implies a personal influence among the people, and that they are more immediately the confidential guardians of the rights and liberties of the people. With these advantages it can hardly be supposed that the adverse party would have an equal chance for a favorable issue.

5   But the legislative party would not only be able to plead their cause most successfully with the people. They would probably be constituted themselves the judges. The same influence which had gained them an election into the legislature would gain them a seat in the convention. If this should not be the case with all, it would probably be the case with many, and pretty certainly
10 with those leading characters, on whom everything depends in such bodies. The convention, in short, would be composed chiefly of men who had been, who actually were, or who expected to be, members of the department whose conduct was arraigned. They would consequently be parties to the very question to be decided by them.

15 It might, however, sometimes happen, that appeals would be made under circumstances less adverse to the executive and judiciary departments. The usurpations of the legislature might be so flagrant and so sudden, as to admit of no specious coloring. A strong party among themselves might take side with the other branches. The executive power might be in the hands of a peculiar
20 favorite of the people. In such a posture of things, the public decision might be less swayed by prepossessions in favor of the legislative party. But still it could never be expected to turn on the true merits of the question. It would inevitably be connected with the spirit of preexisting parties, or of parties springing out of the question itself. It would be connected with persons of distinguished
25 character and extensive influence in the community. It would be pronounced by the very men who had been agents in, or opponents of, the measures to which the decision would relate. The *passions*, therefore, not the *reason*, of the public would sit in judgment. But it is the reason, alone, of the public, that ought to control and regulate the government. The passions ought to be controlled and
30 regulated by the government.

We found in the last paper that mere declarations in the written Constitution are not sufficient to restrain the several departments within their legal rights. It appears in this that occasional appeals to the people would be neither a proper nor an effectual provision for that purpose. How far the provisions of a different
35 nature contained in the plan above quoted might be adequate I do not examine. Some of them are unquestionably founded on sound political principles, and all of them are framed with singular ingenuity and precision.

Federalist 51
James Madison

Publius argues that the Constitution will maintain separation of powers by means of its "interior structure." The "great security" against tyranny is to give the members of each department the "necessary constitutional means" combined with the requisite "personal motives" to resist encroachments on their power. The fact "that such devices should be necessary to control the abuses of government" is a "reflection on human nature."

February 6, 1788

The Structure of the Government Must Furnish the Proper Checks and Balances Between the Different Departments

To what expedient, then, shall we finally resort, for maintaining in practice the necessary partition of power among the several departments as laid down in the Constitution? The only answer that can be given is that as all these exterior provisions are found to be inadequate the defect must be supplied, by so contriving the interior structure of the government as that its several constituent 5 parts may, by their mutual relations, be the means of keeping each other in their proper places. Without presuming to undertake a full development of this important idea I will hazard a few general observations which may perhaps place it in a clearer light, and enable us to form a more correct judgment of the principles and structure of the government planned by the convention. 10

In order to lay a due foundation for that separate and distinct exercise of the different powers of government, which to a certain extent is admitted on all hands to be essential to the preservation of liberty, it is evident that each department should have a will of its own; and consequently should be so constituted that the members of each should have as little agency as possible in 15 the appointment of the members of the others. Were this principle rigorously adhered to, it would require that all the appointments for the supreme executive,

---

James Madison, "No. 51: The Structure of the Government Must Furnish the Proper Checks and Balances Between the Different Departments," in Clinton Rossiter, ed., *The Federalist Papers* (New York: Mentor, 1999), 317–22.

legislative, and judiciary magistracies should be drawn from the same fountain of authority, the people, through channels having no communication whatever with one another. Perhaps such a plan of constructing the several departments would be less difficult in practice than it may in contemplation appear. Some
5 difficulties, however, and some additional expense would attend the execution of it. Some deviations, therefore, from the principle must be admitted. In the constitution of the judiciary department in particular, it might be inexpedient to insist rigorously on the principle: first, because peculiar qualifications being essential in the members, the primary consideration ought to be to select that
10 mode of choice which best secures these qualifications; second, because the permanent tenure by which the appointments are held in that department must soon destroy all sense of dependence on the authority conferring them.

It is equally evident that the members of each department should be as little dependent as possible on those of the others for the emoluments annexed to
15 their offices. Were the executive magistrate, or the judges, not independent of the legislature in this particular, their independence in every other would be merely nominal.

But the great security against a gradual concentration of the several powers in the same department consists in giving to those who administer each
20 department the necessary constitutional means and personal motives to resist encroachments of the others. The provision for defense must in this, as in all other cases, be made commensurate to the danger of attack. Ambition must be made to counteract ambition. The interest of the man must be connected with the constitutional rights of the place. It may be a reflection on human nature
25 that such devices should be necessary to control the abuses of government. But what is government itself but the greatest of all reflections on human nature? If men were angels, no government would be necessary. If angels were to govern men, neither external nor internal controls on government would be necessary. In framing a government which is to be administered by men over men, the
30 great difficulty lies in this: you must first enable the government to control the governed; and in the next place oblige it to control itself. A dependence on the people is, no doubt, the primary control on the government; but experience has taught mankind the necessity of auxiliary precautions.

This policy of supplying, by opposite and rival interests, the defect of better
35 motives, might be traced through the whole system of human affairs, private as well as public. We see it particularly displayed in all the subordinate distributions of power, where the constant aim is to divide and arrange the several offices in such a manner as that each may be a check on the other—that the private interest of every individual may be a sentinel over the public rights. These inventions

of prudence cannot be less requisite in the distribution of the supreme powers of the State.

But it is not possible to give to each department an equal power of self-defense. In republican government, the legislative authority necessarily predominates. The remedy for this inconveniency is to divide the legislature into different branches; and to render them, by different modes of election and different principles of action, as little connected with each other as the nature of their common functions and their common dependence on the society will admit. It may even be necessary to guard against dangerous encroachments by still further precautions. As the weight of the legislative authority requires that it should be thus divided, the weakness of the executive may require, on the other hand, that it should be fortified. An absolute negative on the legislature appears, at first view, to be the natural defense with which the executive magistrate should be armed. But perhaps it would be neither altogether safe nor alone sufficient. On ordinary occasions it might not be exerted with the requisite firmness, and on extraordinary occasions it might be perfidiously abused. May not this defect of an absolute negative be supplied by some qualified connection between this weaker department and the weaker branch of the stronger department, by which the latter may be led to support the constitutional rights of the former, without being too much detached from the rights of its own department?

If the principles on which these observations are founded be just, as I persuade myself they are, and they be applied as a criterion to the several State constitutions, and to the federal Constitution, it will be found that if the latter does not perfectly correspond with them, the former are infinitely less able to bear such a test.

There are, moreover, two considerations particularly applicable to the federal system of America, which place that system in a very interesting point of view.

First. In a single republic, all the power surrendered by the people is submitted to the administration of a single government; and the usurpations are guarded against by a division of the government into distinct and separate departments. In the compound republic of America, the power surrendered by the people is first divided between two distinct governments, and then the portion allotted to each subdivided among distinct and separate departments. Hence a double security arises to the rights of the people. The different governments will control each other, at the same time that each will be controlled by itself.

Second. It is of great importance in a republic not only to guard the society against the oppression of its rulers, but to guard one part of the society against

the injustice of the other part. Different interests necessarily exist in different classes of citizens. If a majority be united by a common interest, the rights of the minority will be insecure. There are but two methods of providing against this evil: the one by creating a will in the community independent
5   of the majority—that is, of the society itself; the other, by comprehending in the society so many separate descriptions of citizens as will render an unjust combination of a majority of the whole very improbable, if not impracticable. The first method prevails in all governments possessing an hereditary or self-appointed authority. This, at best, is but a precarious security; because a power
10   independent of the society may as well espouse the unjust views of the major as the rightful interests of the minor party, and may possibly be turned against both parties. The second method will be exemplified in the federal republic of the United States. Whilst all authority in it will be derived from and dependent on the society, the society itself will be broken into so many parts, interests, and
15   classes of citizens, that the rights of individuals, or of the minority, will be in little danger from interested combinations of the majority. In a free government the security for civil rights must be the same as that for religious rights. It consists in the one case in the multiplicity of interests, and in the other in the multiplicity of sects. The degree of security in both cases will depend on the number of
20   interests and sects; and this may be presumed to depend on the extent of country and number of people comprehended under the same government. This view of the subject must particularly recommend a proper federal system to all the sincere and considerate friends of republican government, since it shows that in exact proportion as the territory of the Union may be formed into more
25   circumscribed Confederacies, or States, oppressive combinations of a majority will be facilitated; the best security, under the republican forms, for the rights of every class of citizen will be diminished; and consequently the stability and independence of some member of the government, the only other security, must be proportionately increased. Justice is the end of government. It is the end of
30   civil society. It ever has been and ever will be pursued until it be obtained, or until liberty be lost in the pursuit. In a society under the forms of which the stronger faction can readily unite and oppress the weaker, anarchy may as truly be said to reign as in a state of nature, where the weaker individual is not secured against the violence of the stronger; and as, in the latter state, even the stronger
35   individuals are prompted, by the uncertainty of their condition, to submit to a government which may protect the weak as well as themselves; so, in the former state, will the more powerful factions or parties be gradually induced, by a like motive, to wish for a government which will protect all parties, the weaker as well as the more powerful. It can be little doubted that if the State of Rhode
40   Island was separated from the Confederacy and left to itself, the insecurity of

rights under the popular form of government within such narrow limits would
be displayed by such reiterated oppressions of factious majorities that some
power altogether independent of the people would soon be called for by the
voice of the very factions whose misrule had proved the necessity of it. In the
extended republic of the United States, and among the great variety of interests,   5
parties, and sects which it embraces, a coalition of a majority of the whole
society could seldom take place on any other principles than those of justice
and the general good; whilst there being thus less danger to a minor from the
will of a major party, there must be less pretext, also, to provide for the security
of the former, by introducing into the government a will not dependent on the   10
latter, or, in other words, a will independent of the society itself. It is no less
certain than it is important, notwithstanding the contrary opinions which have
been entertained, that the larger the society, provided it lie within a practicable
sphere, the more duly capable it will be of self-government. And happily for the
republican cause, the practicable sphere may be carried to a very great extent by   15
a judicious modification and mixture of the *federal principle*.

FEDERALIST 84
ALEXANDER HAMILTON

Although New York had ratified the Constitution by the time this essay was published, the debate it addresses lived on. The original Constitution did not include what came to be known as the Bill of Rights. Many Anti-Federalists ended up supporting the Constitution because of the concession made in some states that the first Congress would adopt a Bill of Rights. Publius here makes no such concession, arguing that a listing of rights would be potentially dangerous. In the end, Publius lost this battle, and even James Madison, despite his earlier opposition, ended up championing the Bill of Rights.

AUGUST 9, 1788

CERTAIN GENERAL AND MISCELLANEOUS OBJECTIONS TO THE CONSTITUTION CONSIDERED AND ANSWERED

In the course of the foregoing review of the Constitution, I have taken notice of, and endeavored to answer most of the objections which have appeared against it. There however remain a few which either did not fall naturally under any particular head or were forgotten in their proper places. These shall now be discussed; but as the subject has been drawn into great length, I shall so 5 far consult brevity as to comprise all my observations on these miscellaneous points in a single paper.

The most considerable of the remaining objections is that the plan of the convention contains no bill of rights. Among other answers given to this, it has been upon different occasions remarked that the constitutions of several of 10 the States are in a similar predicament. I add that New York is of this number. And yet the opposers of the new system, in this State, who profess an unlimited admiration for its constitution, are among the most intemperate partisans of a bill of rights. To justify their zeal in this matter they allege two things: one is

Alexander Hamilton, "No. 84: Certain General and Miscellaneous Objections to the Constitution Considered and Answered," in Clinton Rossiter, ed., *The Federalist Papers* (New York: Mentor, 1999), 509–20.

that, though the constitution of New York has no bill of rights prefixed to it, yet it contains, in the body of it, various provisions in favor of particular privileges and rights which, in substance, amount to the same thing; the other is that the Constitution adopts, in their full extent, the common and statute law of Great
5   Britain, by which many other rights not expressed in it are equally secured.

To the first I answer that the Constitution proposed by the convention contains, as well as the constitution of this State, a number of such provisions.

Independent of those which relate to the structure of the government, we find the following: Article 1, section 3, clause 7—"Judgment in cases of impeachment
10   shall not extend further than to removal from office and disqualification to hold and enjoy any office of honor, trust, or profit under the United States; but the party convicted shall nevertheless be liable and subject to indictment, trial, judgment, and punishment according to law." Section 9, of the same article, clause 2—"The privilege of the writ of *habeas corpus* shall not be suspended,
15   unless when in cases of rebellion or invasion the public safety may require it." Clause 3—"No bill of attainder or *ex post facto* law shall be passed." Clause 7—"No title of nobility shall be granted by the United States; and no person holding any office of profit or trust under them shall, without the consent of the Congress, accept of any present, emolument, office, or title of any kind
20   whatever, from any king, prince, or foreign state." Article 3, section 2, clause 3—"The trial of all crimes, except in cases of impeachment, shall be by jury; and such trial shall be held in the State where the said crimes shall have been committed; but when not committed within any State, the trial shall be at such place or places as the Congress may by law have directed." Section 3, of the same
25   article—"Treason against the United States shall consist only in levying war against them, or in adhering to their enemies, giving them aid and comfort. No person shall be convicted of treason, unless on the testimony of two witnesses to the same overt act, or on confession in open court." And clause 3, of the same section—"The Congress shall have power to declare the punishment of treason;
30   but no attainder of treason shall work corruption of blood, or forfeiture, except during the life of the person attainted."

It may well be a question whether these are not, upon the whole, of equal importance with any which are to be found in the constitution of this State. The establishment of the writ of *habeas corpus*, the prohibition of *ex post facto*
35   laws, and of TITLES OF NOBILITY, *to which we have no corresponding provision in our Constitution*, are perhaps greater securities to liberty and republicanism than any it contains. The creation of crimes after the commission of the fact, or, in other words, the subjecting of men to punishment for things which, when they were done, were breaches of no law, and the practice of arbitrary imprisonments,

have been, in all ages, the favorite and most formidable instruments of tyranny. The observations of the judicious Blackstone, in reference to the latter, are well worthy of recital: "To bereave a man of life [says he] or by violence to confiscate his estate, without accusation or trial, would be so gross and notorious an act of despotism as must at once convey the alarm of tyranny throughout the whole   5
nation; but confinement of the person, by secretly hurrying him to jail, where his sufferings are unknown or forgotten, is a less public, a less striking, and therefore a *more dangerous engine* of arbitrary government." And as a remedy for this fatal evil he is everywhere peculiarly emphatical in his encomiums on the *habeas corpus* act, which in one place he calls "the BULWARK of the British   10
Constitution."

Nothing need be said to illustrate the importance of the prohibition of titles of nobility. This may truly be denominated the cornerstone of republican government; for so long as they are excluded there can never be serious danger that the government will be any other than that of the people.   15

To the second, that is, to the pretended establishment of the common and statute law by the Constitution, I answer that they are expressly made subject "to such alterations and provisions as the legislature shall from time to time make concerning the same." They are therefore at any moment liable to repeal by the ordinary legislative power, and of course have no constitutional sanction. The   20
only use of the declaration was to recognize the ancient law and to remove doubts which might have been occasioned by the Revolution. This consequently can be considered as no part of a declaration of rights, which under our constitutions must be intended as limitations of the power of the government itself.

It has been several times truly remarked that bills of rights are, in their origin,   25
stipulations between kings and their subjects, abridgements of prerogative in favor of privilege, reservations of rights not surrendered to the prince. Such was MAGNA CHARTA, obtained by the barons, sword in hand, from King John. Such were the subsequent confirmations of that charter by subsequent princes. Such was the *Petition of Right* assented to by Charles the First in the beginning of   30
his reign. Such, also, was the Declaration of Right presented by the Lords and Commons to the Prince of Orange in 1688, and afterwards thrown into the form of an act of Parliament called the Bill of Rights. It is evident, therefore, that, according to their primitive signification, they have no application to constitutions, professedly founded upon the power of the people and executed   35
by their immediate representatives and servants. Here, in strictness, the people surrender nothing; and as they retain everything they have no need of particular reservations, "WE, THE PEOPLE of the United States, to secure the blessings of liberty to ourselves and our posterity, do *ordain* and *establish* this Constitution

for the United States of America." Here is a better recognition of popular rights than volumes of those aphorisms which make the principal figure in several of our State bills of rights and which would sound much better in a treatise of ethics than in a constitution of government.

5 But a minute detail of particular rights is certainly far less applicable to a Constitution like that under consideration, which is merely intended to regulate the general political interests of the nation, than to a constitution which has the regulation of every species of personal and private concerns. If, therefore, the loud clamors against the plan of the convention, on this score, are well founded,
10 no epithets of reprobation will be too strong for the constitution of this State. But the truth is that both of them contain all which, in relation to their objects, is reasonably to be desired.

I go further and affirm that bills of rights, in the sense and to the extent in which they are contended for, are not only unnecessary in the proposed Constitution
15 but would even be dangerous. They would contain various exceptions to powers which are not granted; and, on this very account, would afford a colorable pretext to claim more than were granted. For why declare that things shall not be done which there is no power to do? Why, for instance; should it be said that the liberty of the press shall not be restrained, when no power is given by
20 which restrictions may be imposed? I will not contend that such a provision would confer a regulating power; but it is evident that it would furnish, to men disposed to usurp, a plausible pretense for claiming that power. They might urge with a semblance of reason that the Constitution ought not to be charged with the absurdity of providing against the abuse of an authority which was not
25 given, and that the provision against restraining the liberty of the press afforded a clear implication that a power to prescribe proper regulations concerning it was intended to be vested in the national government. This may serve as a specimen of the numerous handles which would be given to the doctrine of constructive powers, by the indulgence of an injudicious zeal for bills of rights.

30 On the subject of the liberty of the press, as much as has been said, I cannot forbear adding a remark or two: in the first place, I observe, that there is not a syllable concerning it in the constitution of this State; in the next, I contend that whatever has been said about it in that of any other State amounts to nothing. What signifies a declaration that "the liberty of the press shall be
35 inviolably preserved"? What is the liberty of the press? Who can give it any definition which would not leave the utmost latitude for evasion? I hold it to be impracticable; and from this I infer that its security, whatever fine declarations may be inserted in any constitution respecting it, must altogether depend on public opinion, and on the general spirit of the people and of the government.

And here, after all, as is intimated upon another occasion, must we seek for the only solid basis of all our rights.

There remains but one other view of this matter to conclude the point. The truth is, after all the declamations we have heard, that the Constitution is itself, in every rational sense, and to every useful purpose, a BILL OF RIGHTS. The several bills of rights in Great Britain form its Constitution, and conversely the constitution of each State is its bill of rights. And the proposed Constitution, if adopted, will be the bill of rights of the Union. Is it one object of a bill of rights to declare and specify the political privileges of the citizens in the structure and administration of the government? This is done in the most ample and precise manner in the plan of the convention; comprehending various precautions for the public security which are not to be found in any of the State constitutions. Is another object of a bill of rights to define certain immunities and modes of proceeding, which are relative to personal and private concerns? This we have seen has also been attended to in a variety of cases in the same plan. Adverting therefore to the substantial meaning of a bill of rights, it is absurd to allege that it is not to be found in the work of the convention. It may be said that it does not go far enough though it will not be easy to make this appear; but it can with no propriety be contended that there is no such thing. It certainly must be immaterial what mode is observed as to the order of declaring the rights of the citizens if they are to be found in any part of the instrument which establishes the government. And hence it must be apparent that much of what has been said on this subject rests merely on verbal and nominal distinctions, entirely foreign from the substance of the thing.

Another objection which has been made, and which, from the frequency of its repetition, it is to be presumed is relied on, is of this nature: "It is improper [say the objectors] to confer such large powers as are proposed upon the national government, because the seat of that government must of necessity be too remote from many of the States to admit of a proper knowledge on the part of the constituent of the conduct of the representative body." This argument, if it proves anything, proves that there ought to be no general government whatever. For the powers which, it seems to be agreed on all hands, ought to be vested in the Union, cannot be safely entrusted to a body which is not under every requisite control. But there are satisfactory reasons to show that the objection is in reality not well founded. There is in most of the arguments which relate to distance a palpable illusion of the imagination. What are the sources of information by which the people in Montgomery County must regulate their judgment of the conduct of their representatives in the State legislature? Of personal observation they can have no benefit. This is confined to the citizens on the spot. They must therefore depend on the information of intelligent men, in whom they confide; and how must these men obtain their information? Evidently from the complexion of public measures, from the public prints, from correspondences with their representatives, and with other persons who reside at the place of their

5   deliberations. This does not apply to Montgomery County only, but to all the counties at any considerable distance from the seat of government.

It is equally evident that the same sources of information would be open to the people in relation to the conduct of their representatives in the general government, and the impediments to a prompt communication which distance

10   may be supposed to create will be overbalanced by the effects of the vigilance of the State governments. The executive and legislative bodies of each State will be so many sentinels over the persons employed in every department of the national administration; and as it will be in their power to adopt and pursue a regular and effectual system of intelligence, they can never be at a loss to know the

15   behavior of those who represent their constituents in the national councils, and can readily communicate the same knowledge to the people. Their disposition to apprise the community of whatever may prejudice its interests from another quarter may be relied upon, if it were only from the rivalship of power. And we may conclude with the fullest assurance that the people, through that channel,

20   will be better informed of the conduct of their national representatives than they can be by any means they now possess, of that of their State representatives.

It ought also to be remembered that the citizens who inhabit the country at and near the seat of government will, in all questions that affect the general liberty and prosperity, have the same interest with those who are at a distance,

25   and that they will stand ready to sound the alarm when necessary, and to point out the actors in any pernicious project. The public papers will be expeditious messengers of intelligence to the most remote inhabitants of the Union.

Among the many extraordinary objections which have appeared against the proposed Constitution, the most extraordinary and the least colorable one is

30   derived from the want of some provision respecting the debts due *to* the United States. This has been represented as a tacit relinquishment of those debts, and as a wicked contrivance to screen public defaulters. The newspapers have teemed with the most inflammatory railings on this head; and yet there is nothing clearer than that the suggestion is entirely void of foundation, and is the offspring of

35   extreme ignorance or extreme dishonesty. In addition to the remarks I have made upon the subject in another place, I shall only observe that as it is a plain dictate of common sense, so it is also an established doctrine of political law, that *"States neither lose any of their rights, nor are discharged from any of their obligations, by a change in the form of their civil government."*

The last objection of any consequence, which I at present recollect, turns upon the article of expense. If it were even true that the adoption of the proposed government would occasion a considerable increase of expense, it would be an objection that ought to have no weight against the plan.

The great bulk of the citizens of America are with reason convinced that Union   5
is the basis of their political happiness. Men of sense of all parties now with few exceptions agree that it cannot be preserved under the present system, nor without radical alterations; that new and extensive powers ought to be granted to the national head, and that these require a different organization of the federal government—a single body being an unsafe depositary of such ample   10
authorities. In conceding all this, the question of expense must be given up; for it is impossible, with any degree of safety, to narrow the foundation upon which the system is to stand. The two branches of the legislature are, in the first instance, to consist of only sixty-five persons, which is the same number of which Congress, under the existing Confederation, may be composed. It is true that   15
this number is intended to be increased; but this is to keep pace with the increase of the population and resources of the country. It is evident that a less number would, even in the first instance, have been unsafe, and that a continuance of the present number would, in a more advanced stage of population, be a very inadequate representation of the people.   20

Whence is the dreaded augmentation of expense to spring? One source pointed out is the multiplication of offices under the new government. Let us examine this a little.

It is evident that the principal departments of the administration under the present government are the same which will be required under the new. There   25
are now a Secretary of War, a Secretary for Foreign Affairs, a Secretary for Domestic Affairs, a Board of Treasury, consisting of three persons, a treasurer, assistants, clerks, etc. These offices are indispensable under any system and will suffice under the new as well as under the old. As to ambassadors and other ministers and agents in foreign countries, the proposed Constitution can make   30
no other difference than to render their characters, where they reside, more respectable, and their services more useful. As to persons to be employed in the collection of the revenues, it is unquestionably true that these will form a very considerable addition to the number of federal officers; but it will not follow that this will occasion an increase of public expense. It will be in most   35
cases nothing more than an exchange of State officers for national officers. In the collection of all duties, for instance, the persons employed will be wholly of the latter description. The States individually will stand in no need of any for this purpose. What difference can it make in point of expense to pay officers of

the customs appointed by the State or those appointed by the United States? There is no good reason to suppose that either the number or the salaries of the latter will be greater than those of the former.

Where then are we to seek for those additional articles of expense which are
5   to swell the account to the enormous size that has been represented to us? The chief item which occurs to me respects the support of the judges of the United States. I do not add the President, because there is now a president of Congress, whose expenses may not be far, if anything, short of those which will be incurred on account of the President of the United States. The support of
10   the judges will clearly be an extra expense, but to what extent will depend on the particular plan which may be adopted in practice in regard to this matter. But it can upon no reasonable plan amount to a sum which will be an object of material consequence.

Let us now see what there is to counterbalance any extra expense that may attend
15   the establishment of the proposed government. The first thing that presents itself is that a great part of the business which now keeps Congress sitting through the year will be transacted by the President. Even the management of foreign negotiations will naturally devolve upon him, according to general principles concerted with the Senate, and subject to their final concurrence.
20   Hence it is evident that a portion of the year will suffice for the session of both the Senate and the House of Representatives; we may suppose about a fourth for the latter and a third, or perhaps a half, for the former. The extra business of treaties and appointments may give this extra occupation to the Senate. From this circumstance we may infer that, until the House of Representatives shall be
25   increased greatly beyond its present number, there will be a considerable saving of expense from the difference between the constant session of the present and the temporary session of the future Congress.

But there is another circumstance of great importance in the view of economy. The business of the United States has hitherto occupied the State legislatures,
30   as well as Congress. The latter has made requisitions which the former have had to provide for. Hence it has happened that the sessions of the State legislatures have been protracted greatly beyond what was necessary for the execution of the mere local business of the States. More than half their time has been frequently employed in matters which related to the United States. Now the
35   members who compose the legislatures of the several States amount to two thousand and upwards, which number has hitherto performed what under the new system will be done in the first instance by sixty-five persons, and probably at no future period by above a fourth or fifth of that number. The Congress under the proposed government will do all the business of the United States

themselves, without the intervention of the State legislatures, who thenceforth will have only to attend to the affairs of their particular States, and will not have to sit in any proportion as long as they have heretofore done. This difference in the time of the sessions of the State legislatures will be all clear gain, and will alone form an article of saving, which may be regarded as an equivalent   5 for any additional objects of expense that may be occasioned by the adoption of the new system.

The result from these observations is that the sources of additional expense from the establishment of the proposed Constitution are much fewer than may have been imagined; that they are counterbalanced by considerable objects of saving;   10 and that while it is questionable on which side the scale will preponderate, it is certain that a government less expensive would be incompetent to the purposes of the Union.

VI
THE THREE BRANCHES
OF GOVERNMENT

Publius moves in *The Federalist*'s second half to explain the separation of powers and the three branches of government: Congress, including the House (52 to 58) and the Senate (62 to 66), the presidency (67 to 77), and the judiciary (78–83). In response to the Anti-Federalist demand for a more responsive government, Publius teaches us a lesson about the true meaning of "responsibility." Good government is not defined by its responsiveness to popular demands, but is responsible to the true, long-term interests of the people. In other words, it protects their natural rights. In his attempt to heal the American body politic, Publius here offers a strong dose of political moderation. A government that is responsive to every popular whim suffers from the fatal weakness of wanting to enforce those whims.

The separation of powers doctrine makes clear we can never expect good results if the government consists only in a legislative branch. Indeed, the Constitution's powers are arranged in such a way as to lean most of all against the legislature. Publius took seriously the threat to liberty posed by the "impetuous vortex."

Republican government is impossible without a legislature. Consider that the virtue of the House, according to *Federalist* 52, is its "immediate dependence on" and "intimate sympathy with the people," fostered especially through the mechanism of frequent elections. Combined with minimal qualifications for office, this close proximity of the people to their elected representatives ensures that the various interests of a large and diverse people are well-represented.

Yet Publius does not favor change for its own sake: If republican government is to succeed, some members must be distinguished by their talents and service to the people, and through constant re-election become "masters of the public business," as Publius writes in *Federalist* 53. Two-year terms may be necessary, but good government requires talented and experienced members who can apply their accumulated knowledge to the pressing issues of the day.

Frequent elections are a virtue for the House, but they will prove to be a vice for the Senate, which aims at stability. A senator's longer term of service (six years), combined with their small number (two per state), will lead to a body that is more stable, cool, and deliberate. Publius makes the case for the Senate indirectly. In *Federalist* 62 and 63, he explains six "inconveniences" that any government lacking a Senate must endure—the most important being the lack of a sense of responsibility. The frequent elections that produce a certain kind of responsibility in the House destroy responsibility in the Senate.

A numerous and changeable body is inherently incapable of taking the kind of long-term view that the "collective and permanent welfare" of the country demands. Senators, by contrast, will take "personal responsibility" for measures whose benefit will only be fully realized over a series of years. The Senate is institutionally equipped to counter the inherently myopic view of the House.

In addition—and here is another hard lesson for partisans of republican government—the Senate will be able to stand up to the people themselves, whenever they may suffer from "temporary errors and delusions" brought on by passions run amok. Rather, "the cool and deliberate sense of the community" should always prevail and will prevail, as long as there is some "temperate and respectable body of citizens" that can keep the people from acting against their own best interests until reason returns.

The virtues of the legislature—deliberation above all—become vices in the case of presidency. Instead, the president's primary virtue is energy. Perhaps the most important ingredient of energy is unity, which allows the president to act with "decision, activity, secrecy, and dispatch." As Publius observes in *Federalist* 70, "feeble" execution is "bad" execution, and a "government ill executed" is nothing other than "a bad government."

As with the Senate, the president's longer, four-year term will cause him to feel a personal responsibility for his actions. Not only will this lead to a more stable system of administration, it will, in the words of *Federalist* 71, supply the president with the "personal firmness" he needs to stand up to the "almost irresistible" legislative branch—especially by means of his veto power—and to defend against whatever "temporary delusion" may arise in the people.

The judiciary is the capstone of the Constitution. It appears at first glance to be the least republican branch, and the most dangerous to republican liberties. Yet Publius in *Federalist* 78 retorts that without the power of the sword or the purse, it is the "least dangerous" branch. It will possess "neither force nor will but merely judgment."

What the judiciary can do—what it will have the "independent spirit" to do, thanks to life tenure with good behavior—is check the legislature by declaring "all acts contrary to the manifest tenor of the Constitution void." This does not mean, Publius hastens to add, that the judiciary will be superior to Congress, but rather that the Constitution will be superior to both—a view confirmed by Supreme Court Chief Justice John Marshall in *Marbury* v. *Madison*.

The benefits of an independent judiciary do not end here. It will also have the ability to "guard the Constitution and the rights of individuals" against the "people themselves," should they be misled by artful politicians or overcome by a momentary and unjust desire to trample on minority rights. In sum, without the addition of this indispensable and "important feature of good government," the constitution would have been inexcusably "defective."

Publius leaves us with yet another profound lesson in political moderation. A well-formed Constitution aims not at efficient or responsive government, but at good government, and in so doing it teaches the people who live under it that there are limits to what the majority may rightfully do.

TIMOTHY W. CASPAR
Lecturer in Politics
Associate Vice President
for External Affairs
Hillsdale College

FEDERALIST 52
JAMES MADISON

The House of Representatives is designed, Publius explains, to be closest to the people.

FEBRUARY 8, 1788

THE HOUSE OF REPRESENTATIVES

From the more general inquiries pursued in the four last papers, I pass on to a more particular examination of the several parts of the government. I shall begin with the House of Representatives.

The first view to be taken of this part of the government relates to the qualifications of the electors and the elected. Those of the former are to be the same with those of the electors of the most numerous branch of the State legislatures. The definition of the right of suffrage is very justly regarded as a fundamental article of republican government. It was incumbent on the convention, therefore, to define and establish this right in the Constitution. To have left it open for the occasional regulation of the Congress would have been improper for the reason just mentioned. To have submitted it to the legislative discretion of the States would have been improper for the same reason; and for the additional reason that it would have rendered too dependent on the State governments that branch of the federal government which ought to be dependent on the people alone. To have reduced the different qualifications in the different States to one uniform rule would probably have been as dissatisfactory to some of the States as it would have been difficult to the convention. The provision made by the convention appears, therefore, to be the best that lay within their option. It must be satisfactory to every State, because it is comfortable to the standard already established, or which may be established, by the State itself. It will be safe to the United States because, being fixed by the State constitutions, it is not alterable by the State governments, and it cannot be feared that the people of the States will alter this part of their constitutions in such a manner as to abridge the rights secured to them by the federal Constitution.

James Madison, "No. 52: The House of Representatives," in Clinton Rossiter, ed., *The Federalist Papers* (New York: Mentor, 1999), 322–27.

The qualifications of the elected, being less carefully and properly defined by the State constitutions, and being at the same time more susceptible of uniformity, have been very properly considered and regulated by the convention. A representative of the United States must be of the age of twenty-five years; must have been
5   seven years a citizen of the United States; must, at the time of his election, be an inhabitant of the State he is to represent; and, during the time of his service, must be in no office under the United States. Under these reasonable limitations, the door of this part of the federal government is open to merit of every description, whether native or adoptive, whether young or old, and without regard to poverty
10   or wealth, or to any particular profession of religious faith.

The term for which the representatives are to be elected falls under a second view which may be taken of this branch. In order to decide on the propriety of this article, two questions must be considered: first, whether biennial elections will, in this case, be safe; secondly, whether they be necessary or useful.

15   *First.* As it is essential to liberty that the government in general should have a common interest with the people, so it is particularly essential that the branch of it under consideration should have an immediate dependence on, and an intimate sympathy with, the people. Frequent elections are unquestionably the only policy by which this dependence and sympathy can be effectually secured.
20   But what particular degree of frequency may be absolutely necessary for the purpose does not appear to be susceptible of any precise calculation, and must depend on a variety of circumstances with which it may be connected. Let us consult experience, the guide that ought always to be followed whenever it can be found.

25   The scheme of representation as a substitute for a meeting of the citizens in person being at most but very imperfectly known to ancient polity, it is in more modern times only that we are to expect instructive examples. And even here, in order to avoid a research too vague and diffusive, it will be proper to confine ourselves to the few examples which are best known, and which bear the
30   greatest analogy to our particular case. The first to which this character ought to be applied is the House of Commons in Great Britain. The history of this branch of the English Constitution, anterior to the date of Magna Charta, is too obscure to yield instruction. The very existence of it has been made a question among political antiquaries. The earliest records of subsequent date prove that
35   parliaments were to *sit* only every year; not that they were to be *elected* every year. And even these annual sessions were left so much at the discretion of the monarch, that, under various pretexts, very long and dangerous intermissions were often contrived by royal ambition. To remedy this grievance, it was provided by a statute in the reign of Charles II that the intermissions should not be

protracted beyond a period of three years. On the accession of William III, when a revolution took place in the government, the subject was still more seriously resumed, and it was declared to be among the fundamental rights of the people that parliaments ought to be held *frequently*. By another statute, which passed a few years later in the same reign, the term "frequently," which had alluded   5 to the triennial period settled in the time of Charles II, is reduced to a precise meaning, it being expressly enacted that a new parliament shall be called within three years after the termination of the former. The last change, from three to seven years, is well known to have been introduced pretty early in the present century, under an alarm for the Hanoverian succession. From these facts it   10 appears that the greatest frequency of elections which has been deemed necessary in that kingdom for binding the representatives to their constituents does not exceed a triennial return of them. And if we may argue from the degree of liberty retained even under septennial elections, and all the other vicious ingredients in the parliamentary Constitution, we cannot doubt that a reduction of the period   15 from seven to three years, with the other necessary reforms, would so far extend the influence of the people over their representatives as to satisfy us that biennial elections, under the federal system, cannot possibly be dangerous to the requisite dependence of the House of Representatives on their constituents.

Elections in Ireland, till of late, were regulated entirely by the discretion of the   20 crown, and were seldom repeated, except on the accession of a new prince, or some other contingent event. The Parliament which commenced with George II was continued throughout his whole reign, a period of about thirty-five years. The only dependence of the representatives on the people consisted in the right of the latter to supply occasional vacancies by the election of new members, and   25 in the chance of some event which might produce a general new election. The ability also of the Irish parliament to maintain the rights of their constituents, so far as the disposition might exist, was extremely shackled by the control of the crown over the subjects of their deliberation. Of late, these shackles, if I mistake not, have been broken; and octennial parliaments have besides been   30 established. What effect may be produced by this partial reform must be left to further experience. The example of Ireland, from this view of it, can throw but little light on the subject. As far as we can draw any conclusion from it, it must be that if the people of that country have been able under all these dis- advantages to retain any liberty whatever, the advantage of biennial elections   35 would secure to them every degree of liberty, which might depend on a due connection between their representatives and themselves.

Let us bring our inquiries nearer home. The example of these States, when British colonies, claims particular attention, at the same time that it is so well known as

to require little to be said on it. The principle of representation, in one branch of the legislature at least, was established in all of them. But the periods of election were different. They varied from one to seven years. Have we any reason to infer, from the spirit and conduct of the representatives of the people, prior to
5   the Revolution, that biennial elections would have been dangerous to the public liberties? The spirit which everywhere displayed itself at the commencement of the struggle, and which vanquished the obstacles to independence, is the best of proofs that a sufficient portion of liberty had been everywhere enjoyed to inspire both a sense of its worth and a zeal for its proper enlargement. This
10   remark holds good as well with regard to the then colonies whose elections were least frequent, as to those whose elections were most frequent. Virginia was the colony which stood first in resisting the parliamentary usurpations of Great Britain; it was the first also in espousing, by public act, the resolution of independence. In Virginia, nevertheless, if I have not been misinformed, elec-
15   tions under the former government were septennial. This particular example is brought into view, not as a proof of any peculiar merit, for the priority in those instances was probably accidental; and still less of any advantage in *septennial* elections, for when compared with a greater frequency they are inadmissible; but merely as a proof, and I conceive it to be a very substantial proof, that the
20   liberties of the people can be in no danger from *biennial* elections.

The conclusion resulting from these examples will be not a little strengthened by recollecting three circumstances. The first is, that the federal legislature will possess a part only of that supreme legislative authority which is vested completely in the British Parliament; and which, with a few exceptions, was
25   exercised by the colonial assemblies and the Irish legislature. It is a received and well-founded maxim that where no other circumstances affect the case, the greater the power is, the shorter ought to be its duration; and, conversely, the smaller the power, the more safely may its duration be protracted. In the second place it has, on another occasion, been shown that the federal legislature
30   will not only be restrained by its dependence on the people, as other legislative bodies are, but that it will be, moreover, watched and controlled by the several collateral legislatures, which other legislative bodies are not. And in the third place, no comparison can be made between the means that will be possessed by the more permanent branches of the federal government for seducing, if they
35   should be disposed to seduce, the House of Representatives from their duty to the people, and the means of influence over the popular branch possessed by the other branches of the government above cited. With less power, therefore, to abuse, the federal representatives can be less tempted on one side, and will be doubly watched on the other.

FEDERALIST 53
JAMES MADISON

Publius often returns to the problem posed by majority tyranny. Here he expresses his preference for biennial over annual elections.

THE SAME SUBJECT CONTINUED: THE HOUSE OF REPRESENTATIVES

I shall here, perhaps, be reminded of a current observation "that where annual elections end, tyranny begins." If it be true, as has often been remarked, that sayings which become proverbial are generally founded in reason, it is not less true that when once established they are often applied to cases to which the reason of them does not extend. I need not look for a proof beyond the case before us. 5
What is the reason on which this proverbial observation is founded? No man will subject himself to the ridicule of pretending that any natural connection subsists between the sun or the seasons, and the period within which human virtue can bear the temptations of power. Happily for mankind, liberty is not, in this respect, confined to any single point of time, but lies within extremes, 10
which afford sufficient latitude for all the variations which may be required by the various situations and circumstances of civil society. The election of magistrates might be, if it were found expedient, as in some instances it actually has been, daily, weekly, or monthly, as well as annual; and if circumstances may require a deviation from the rule on one side, why not also on the other side? Turn- 15
ing our attention to the periods established among ourselves, for the election of the most numerous branches of the State legislatures, we find them by no means coinciding any more in this instance than in the elections of other civil magistrates. In Connecticut and Rhode Island, the periods are half-yearly. In the other States, South Carolina excepted, they are annual. In South Carolina they 20
are biennial—as is proposed in the federal government. Here is a difference, as four to one, between the longest and shortest periods; and yet it would be not easy to show, that Connecticut or Rhode Island is better governed, or enjoys a

James Madison, "No. 53: The Same Subject Continued," in Clinton Rossiter, ed., *The Federalist Papers* (New York: Mentor, 1999), 327–33.

greater share of rational liberty, than South Carolina; or that either the one or
the other of these States is distinguished in these respects, and by these causes,
from the States whose elections are different from both.

In searching for the grounds of this doctrine, I can discover but one, and that is
5   wholly inapplicable to our case. The important distinction so well understood
in America between a Constitution established by the people and unalterable
by the government, and a law established by the government and alterable by
the government, seems to have been little understood and less observed in any
other country. Wherever the supreme power of legislation has resided, has been
10 supposed to reside also a full power to change the form of the government.
Even in Great Britain, where the principles of political and civil liberty have
been most discussed, and where we hear most of the rights of the Constitution, it is maintained that the authority of the Parliament is transcendent and
uncontrollable as well with regard to the Constitution as the ordinary objects
15 of legislative provision. They have accordingly, in several instances, actually
changed, by legislative acts, some of the most fundamental articles of the
government. They have in particular, on several occasions, changed the period
of election; and, on the last occasion, not only introduced septennial in place
of triennial elections, but by the same act, continued themselves in place four
20 years beyond the term for which they were elected by the people. An attention
to these dangerous practices has produced a very natural alarm in the votaries
of free government, of which frequency of elections is the cornerstone; and has
led them to seek for some security to liberty, against the danger to which it is
exposed. Where no Constitution, paramount to the government, either existed
25 or could be obtained, no constitutional security, similar to that established in
the United States, was to be attempted. Some other security, therefore, was to be
sought for; and what better security would the case admit than that of selecting
and appealing to some simple and familiar portion of time as a standard for
measuring the danger of innovations, for fixing the national sentiment, and for
30 uniting the patriotic exertions? The most simple and familiar portion of time
applicable to the subject was that of a year; and hence the doctrine has been
inculcated by a laudable zeal to erect some barrier against the gradual innovations of an unlimited government, that the advance towards tyranny was to be
calculated by the distance of departure from the fixed point of annual elections.
35 But what necessity can there be of applying this expedient to a government
limited, as the federal government will be, by the authority of a paramount
Constitution? Or who will pretend that the liberties of the people of America
will not be more secure under biennial elections, unalterably fixed by such a
Constitution, than those of any other nation would be, where elections were

annual, or even more frequent, but subject to alterations by the ordinary power
of the government?

The second question stated is whether biennial elections be necessary or useful.
The propriety of answering this question in the affirmative will appear from
several very obvious considerations.

No man can be a competent legislator who does not add to an upright intention and a sound judgment a certain degree of knowledge of the subjects on
which he is to legislate. A part of this knowledge may be acquired by means of
information which lie within the compass of men in private as well as public
stations. Another part can only be attained, or at least thoroughly attained, by   10
actual experience in the station which requires the use of it. The period of service ought, therefore, in all such cases, to bear some proportion to the extent of
practical knowledge requisite to the due performance of the service. The period
of legislative service established in most of the States for the more numerous
branch is, as we have seen, one year. The question then may be put into this   15
simple form: does the period of two years bear no greater proportion to the
knowledge requisite for federal legislation than one year does to the knowledge
requisite for State legislation? The very statement of the question, in this form,
suggests the answer that ought to be given to it.

In a single State, the requisite knowledge relates to the existing laws which are   20
uniform throughout the State and with which all the citizens are more or less
conversant; and to the general affairs of the State, which lie within a small compass, are not very diversified, and occupy much of the attention and conversation
of every class of people. The great theater of the United States presents a very
different scene. The laws are so far from being uniform that they vary in every   25
State; whilst the public affairs of the Union are spread throughout a very extensive
region and are extremely diversified by the local affairs connected with them,
and can with difficulty be correctly learned in any other place than in the central
councils, to which a knowledge of them will be brought by the representatives
of every part of the empire. Yet some knowledge of the affairs, and even of the   30
laws, of all the States, ought to be possessed by the members from each of the
States. How can foreign trade be properly regulated by uniform laws without
some acquaintance with the commerce, the ports, the usages, and the regulations
of the different States? How can the trade between the different States be duly
regulated without some knowledge of their relative situations in these and other   35
points? How can taxes be judiciously imposed and effectually collected if they
be not accommodated to the different laws and local circumstances relating to
these objects in the different States? How can uniform regulations for the militia

be duly provided without a similar knowledge of some internal circumstances by which the States are distinguished from each other? These are the principal objects of federal legislation and suggest most forcibly the extensive information which the representatives ought to acquire. The other inferior objects will
5   require a proportional degree of information with regard to them.

It is true that all these difficulties will, by degrees, be very much diminished. The most laborious task will be the proper inauguration of the government and the primeval formation of a federal code. Improvements on the first draught will every year become both easier and fewer. Past transactions of the government
10   will be a ready and accurate source of information to new members. The affairs of the Union will become more and more objects of curiosity and conversation among the citizens at large. And the increased intercourse among those of different States will contribute not a little to diffuse a mutual knowledge of their affairs, as this again will contribute to a general assimilation of their manners
15   and laws. But with all these abatements, the business of federal legislation must continue so far to exceed, both in novelty and difficulty, the legislative business of a single State, as to justify the longer period of service assigned to those who are to transact it.

A branch of knowledge which belongs to the acquirements of a federal representa-
20   tive and which has not been mentioned is that of foreign affairs. In regulating our own commerce, he ought to be not only acquainted with the treaties between the United States and other nations, but also with the commercial policy and laws of other nations. He ought not to be altogether ignorant of the law of nations; for that, as far as it is a proper object of municipal legislation, is sub-
25   mitted to the federal government. And although the House of Representatives is not immediately to participate in foreign negotiations and arrangements, yet from the necessary connection between the several branches of public affairs, those particular branches will frequently deserve attention in the ordinary course of legislation and will sometimes demand particular legislative sanction and
30   cooperation. Some portion of this knowledge may, no doubt, be acquired in a man's closet; but some of it also can only be derived from the public sources of information; and all of it will be acquired to best effect by a practical attention to the subject during the period of actual service in the legislature.

There are other considerations, of less importance perhaps, but which are not
35   unworthy of notice. The distance which many of the representatives will be obliged to travel and the arrangements rendered necessary by that circumstance might be much more serious objections with fit men to this service, if limited to a single year, than if extended to two years. No argument can be drawn on

this subject from the case of the delegates to the existing Congress. They are elected annually, it is true; but their re-election is considered by the legislative assemblies almost as a matter of course. The election of the representatives by the people would not be governed by the same principle.

A few of the members, as happens in all such assemblies, will possess superior   5
talents; will, by frequent re-elections, become members of long standing; will be thoroughly masters of the public business, and perhaps not unwilling to avail themselves of those advantages. The greater the proportion of new members and the less the information of the bulk of the members, the more apt will they be to fall into the snares that may be laid for them. This remark   10
is no less applicable to the relation which will subsist between the House of Representatives and the Senate.

It is an inconvenience mingled with the advantages of our frequent elections, even in single States, where they are large, and hold but one legislative session in a year, that spurious elections cannot be investigated and annulled in time   15
for the decision to have its due effect. If a return can be obtained, no matter by what unlawful means, the irregular member, who takes his seat of course, is sure of holding it a sufficient time to answer his purposes. Hence, a very pernicious encouragement is given to the use of unlawful means for obtaining irregular returns. Were elections for the federal legislature to be annual this   20
practice might become a very serious abuse, particularly in the more distant States. Each house is, as it necessarily must be, the judge of the elections, qualifications, and returns of its members; and whatever improvements may be suggested by experience for simplifying and accelerating the process in disputed cases, so great a portion of a year would unavoidably elapse before an   25
illegitimate member could be dispossessed of his seat that the prospect of such an event would be little check to unfair and illicit means of obtaining a seat.

All these considerations taken together warrant us in affirming that biennial elections will be as useful to the affairs of the public as we have seen that they will be safe to the liberties of the people.   30

Federalist 55
James Madison

Under the Constitution's original formula, the House would have sixty-five members. This number was too small according to Anti-Federalists. Publius employs a number of arguments to demonstrate that the ratio of elected representatives to constitutents is prudent.

FEBRUARY 13, 1788

The Total Number of the House of Representatives

The number of which the House of Representatives is to consist forms another and a very interesting point of view under which this branch of the federal legislature may be contemplated. Scarce any article, indeed, in the whole Constitution seems to be rendered more worthy of attention by the weight of character and the apparent force of argument with which it has been   5
assailed. The charges exhibited against it are, first, that so small a number of representatives will be an unsafe depositary of the public interests; second, that they will not possess a proper knowledge of the local circumstances of their numerous constituents; third, that they will be taken from that class of citizens which will sympathize least with the feelings of the mass of the people and be   10
most likely to aim at a permanent elevation of the few on the depression of the many; fourth, that defective as the number will be in the first instance, it will be more and more disproportionate, by the increase of the people and the obstacles which will prevent a correspondent increase of the representatives.

In general it may be remarked on this subject that no political problem is less   15
susceptible of a precise solution than that which relates to the number most convenient for a representative legislature; nor is there any point on which the policy of the several States is more at variance, whether we compare their legislative assemblies directly with each other, or consider the proportions which

James Madison, "No. 55: The Total Number of the House of Representatives," in Clinton Rossiter, ed., *The Federalist Papers* (New York: Mentor, 1999), 338–43.

they respectively bear to the number of their constituents. Passing over the difference between the smallest and largest States, as Delaware, whose most numerous branch consists of twenty-one representatives, and Massachusetts, where it amounts to between three and four hundred, a very considerable dif-
5 ference is observable among States nearly equal in population. The number of representatives in Pennsylvania is not more than one fifth of that in the State last mentioned. New York, whose population is to that of South Carolina as six to five, has little more than one third of the number of representatives. As great a disparity prevails between the States of Georgia and Delaware or Rhode
10 Island. In Pennsylvania, the representatives do not bear a greater proportion to their constituents than of one for every four or five thousand. In Rhode Island, they bear a proportion of at least one for every thousand. And according to the constitution of Georgia, the proportion may be carried to one to every ten electors; and must unavoidably far exceed the proportion in any of
15 the other States.

Another general remark to be made is that the ratio between the representatives and the people ought not to be the same where the latter are very numerous as where they are very few. Were the representatives in Virginia to be regulated by the standard in Rhode Island, they would, at this time, amount to between
20 four and five hundred; and twenty or thirty years hence, to a thousand. On the other hand, the ratio of Pennsylvania, if applied to the State of Delaware, would reduce the representative assembly of the latter to seven or eight members. Nothing can be more fallacious than to found our political calculations on arithmetical principles. Sixty or seventy men may be more properly trusted
25 with a given degree of power than six or seven. But it does not follow that six or seven hundred would be proportionably a better depositary. And if we carry on the supposition to six or seven thousand, the whole reasoning ought to be reversed. The truth is that in all cases a certain number at least seems to be necessary to secure the benefits of free consultation and discussion, and to
30 guard against too easy a combination for improper purposes; as, on the other hand, the number ought at most to be kept within a certain limit, in order to avoid the confusion and intemperance of a multitude. In all very numerous assemblies, of whatever characters composed, passion never fails to wrest the scepter from reason. Had every Athenian citizen been a Socrates, every Athenian
35 assembly would still have been a mob.

It is necessary also to recollect here the observations which were applied to the case of biennial elections. For the same reason that the limited powers of the Congress, and the control of the State legislatures, justify less frequent elections than the public safely might otherwise require, the members of the

Congress need be less numerous than if they possessed the whole power of legislation, and were under no other than the ordinary restraints of other legislative bodies.

With these general ideas in our minds, let us weigh the objections which have been stated against the number of members proposed for the House of Representatives. It is said, in the first place, that so small a number cannot be safely trusted with so much power.

The number of which this branch of the legislature is to consist, at the outset of the government, will be sixty-five. Within three years a census is to be taken, when the number may be augmented to one for every thirty thousand inhabitants; and within every successive period of ten years the census is to be renewed, and augmentations may continue to be made under the above limitation. It will not be thought an extravagant conjecture that the first census will, at the rate of one for every thirty thousand, raise the number of representatives to at least one hundred. Estimating the Negroes in the proportion of three fifths, it can scarcely be doubted that the population of the United States will by that time, if it does not already, amount to three millions. At the expiration of twenty-five years, according to the computed rate of increase, the number of representatives will amount to two hundred; and of fifty years, to four hundred. This is a number which, I presume, will put an end to all fears arising from the smallness of the body. I take for granted here what I shall, in answering the fourth objection, hereafter show, that the number of representatives will be augmented from time to time in the manner provided by the Constitution. On a contrary supposition, I should admit the objection to have very great weight indeed.

The true question to be decided, then, is whether the smallness of the number, as a temporary regulation, be dangerous to the public liberty? Whether sixty-five members for a few years, and a hundred or two hundred for a few more, be a safe depositary for a limited and well-guarded power of legislating for the United States? I must own that I could not give a negative answer to this question, without first obliterating every impression which I have received with regard to the present genius of the people of America, the spirit which actuates the State legislatures, and the principles which are incorporated with the political character of every class of citizens. I am unable to conceive that the people of America, in their present temper, or under any circumstances which can speedily happen, will choose, and every second year repeat the choice of, sixty-five or a hundred men who would be disposed to form and pursue a scheme of tyranny or treachery. I am unable to conceive that the State legislatures, which must feel so many motives to watch and which possess so many means of counteracting the federal legislature, would fail either to detect or to defeat a conspiracy of the latter against the liberties of their common constituents. I am equally unable to conceive that there are at this time, or can be in any short time, in the United States, any sixty-five or a hundred men capable

5   of recommending themselves to the choice of the people at large, who would either desire or dare, within the short space of two years, to betray the solemn trust committed to them. What change of circumstances time, and a fuller population of our country may produce requires a prophetic spirit to declare, which makes no part of my pretensions. But judging from the circumstances

10   now before us, and from the probable state of them within a moderate period of time, I must pronounce that the liberties of America cannot be unsafe in the number of hands proposed by the federal Constitution.

From what quarter can the danger proceed? Are we afraid of foreign gold? If foreign gold could so easily corrupt our federal rulers and enable them to

15   ensnare and betray their constituents, how has it happened that we are at this time a free and independent nation? The Congress which conducted us through the Revolution was a less numerous body than their successors will be; they were not chosen by, nor responsible to, their fellow-citizens at large; though appointed from year to year, and recallable at pleasure, they were

20   generally continued for three years, and, prior to the ratification of the federal articles, for a still longer term. They held their consultations always under the veil of secrecy; they had the sole transaction of our affairs with foreign nations; through the whole course of the war they had the fate of their country more in their hands than it is to be hoped will ever be the case with our future

25   representatives; and from the greatness of the prize at stake, and the eagerness of the party which lost it, it may well be supposed that the use of other means than force would not have been scrupled. Yet we know by happy experience that the public trust was not betrayed; nor has the purity of our public councils in this particular ever suffered, even from the whispers of calumny.

30   Is the danger apprehended from the other branches of the federal government? But where are the means to be found by the President, or the Senate, or both? Their emoluments of office, it is to be presumed, will not, and without a previous corruption of the House of Representatives cannot, more than suffice for very different purposes; their private fortunes, as they must all be American

35   citizens, cannot possibly be sources of danger. The only means, then, which they can possess, will be in the dispensation of appointments. Is it here that suspicion rests her charge? Sometimes we are told that this fund of corruption is to be exhausted by the President in subduing the virtue of the Senate. Now, the fidelity of the other House is to be the victim. The improbability of such a

mercenary and perfidious combination of the several members of government, standing on as different foundations as republican principles will well admit, and at the same time accountable to the society over which they are placed, ought alone to quiet this apprehension. But, fortunately, the Constitution has provided a still further safeguard. The members of the Congress are rendered ineligible to any civil offices that may be created, or of which the emoluments may be increased, during the term of their election. No offices therefore can be dealt out to the existing members but such as may become vacant by ordinary casualties: and to suppose that these would be sufficient to purchase the guardians of the people, selected by the people themselves, is to renounce every rule by which events ought to be calculated, and to substitute an indiscriminate and unbounded jealousy, with which all reasoning must be vain. The sincere friends of liberty who give themselves up to the extravagancies of this passion are not aware of the injury they do their own cause. As there is a degree of depravity in mankind which requires a certain degree of circumspection and distrust, so there are other qualities in human nature which justify a certain portion of esteem and confidence. Republican government presupposes the existence of these qualities in a higher degree than any other form. Were the pictures which have been drawn by the political jealousy of some among us faithful likenesses of the human character, the inference would be that there is not sufficient virtue among men for self-government; and that nothing less than the chains of despotism can restrain them from destroying and devouring one another.

FEDERALIST 57
JAMES MADISON

Publius explains the necessity of virtue in elected representatives and of a spirit of manly vigilance in the American people.

FEBRUARY 19, 1788

THE ALLEGED TENDENCY OF THE NEW PLAN TO ELEVATE
THE FEW AT THE EXPENSE OF THE MANY
CONSIDERED IN CONNECTION WITH REPRESENTATION

The *third* charge against the House of Representatives is that it will be taken from that class of citizens which will have least sympathy with the mass of the people, and be most likely to aim at an ambitious sacrifice of the many to the aggrandizement of the few.

Of all the objections which have been framed against the federal Constitution, this is perhaps the most extraordinary. Whilst the objection itself is leveled against a pretended oligarchy, the principle of it strikes at the very root of republican government.

The aim of every political constitution is, or ought to be, first to obtain for rulers men who possess most wisdom to discern, and most virtue to pursue, the common good of the society, and in the next place, to take the most effectual precautions for keeping them virtuous whilst they continue to hold their public trust. The elective mode of obtaining rulers is the characteristic policy of republican government. The means relied on in this form of government for preventing their degeneracy are numerous and various. The most effectual one is such a limitation of the term of appointments as will maintain a proper responsibility to the people.

Let me now ask what circumstance there is in the constitution of the House of Representatives that violates the principles of republican government, or favors

---

James Madison, "No. 57: The Alleged Tendency of the New Plan to Elevate the Few at the Expense of the Many Considered in Connection with Representation," in Clinton Rossiter, ed., *The Federalist Papers* (New York: Mentor, 1999), 348–53.

the elevation of the few on the ruins of the many? Let me ask whether every circumstance is not, on the contrary, strictly conformable to these principles, and scrupulously impartial to the rights and pretensions of every class and description of citizens?

5   Who are to be the electors of the federal representatives? Not the rich, more than the poor; not the learned, more than the ignorant; not the haughty heirs of distinguished names, more than the humble sons of obscure and unpropitious fortune. The electors are to be the great body of the people of the United States. They are to be the same who exercise the right in every State of electing the
10 corresponding branch of the legislature of the State.

Who are to be the objects of popular choice? Every citizen whose merit may recommend him to the esteem and confidence of his country. No qualification of wealth, of birth, of religious faith, or of civil profession is permitted to fetter the judgment or disappoint the inclination of the people.

15 If we consider the situation of the men on whom the free suffrages of their fellow-citizens may confer the representative trust, we shall find it involving every security which can be devised or desired for their fidelity to their constituents.

In the first place, as they will have been distinguished by the preference of their fellow-citizens, we are to presume that in general they will be somewhat
20 distinguished also by those qualities which entitle them to it, and which promise a sincere and scrupulous regard to the nature of their engagements.

In the second place, they will enter into the public service under circumstances which cannot fail to produce a temporary affection at least to their constituents. There is in every breast a sensibility to marks of honor, of favor, of esteem,
25 and of confidence, which, apart from all considerations of interests, is some pledge for grateful and benevolent returns. Ingratitude is a common topic of declamation against human nature; and it must be confessed that instances of it are but too frequent and flagrant, both in public and in private life. But the universal and extreme indignation which it inspires is itself a proof of the energy
30 and prevalence of the contrary sentiment.

In the third place, those ties which bind the representative to his constituents are strengthened by motives of a more selfish nature. His pride and vanity attach him to a form of government which favors his pretensions and gives him a share in its honors and distinctions. Whatever hopes or projects might be entertained
35 by a few aspiring characters, it must generally happen that a great proportion of the men deriving their advancement from their influence with the people would have more to hope from a preservation of the favor than from innovations in the government subversive of the authority of the people.

All these securities, however, would be found very insufficient without the restraint of frequent elections. Hence, in the fourth place the House of Representatives is so constituted as to support in the members an habitual recollection of their dependence on the people. Before the sentiments impressed on their minds by the mode of their elevation can be effaced by the exercise of power, they will be compelled to anticipate the moment when their power is to cease, when their exercise of it is to be reviewed, and when they must descend to the level from which they were raised; there forever to remain unless a faithful discharge of their trust shall have established their title to a renewal of it.

I will add, as a fifth circumstance in the situation of the House of Representatives, restraining them from oppressive measures, that they can make no law which will not have its full operation on themselves and their friends, as well as on the great mass of the society. This has always been deemed one of the strongest bonds by which human policy can connect the rulers and the people together. It creates between them that communion of interests and sympathy of sentiments of which few governments have furnished examples; but without which every government degenerates into tyranny. If it be asked, what is to restrain the House of Representatives from making legal discriminations in favor of themselves and a particular class of the society? I answer: the genius of the whole system; the nature of just and constitutional laws; and, above all, the vigilant and manly spirit which actuates the people of America—a spirit which nourishes freedom, and in return is nourished by it.

If this spirit shall ever be so far debased as to tolerate a law not obligatory on the legislature, as well as on the people, the people will be prepared to tolerate anything but liberty.

Such will be the relation between the House of Representatives and their constituents. Duty, gratitude, interest, ambition itself, are the cords by which they will be bound to fidelity and sympathy with the great mass of the people. It is possible that these may all be insufficient to control the caprice and wickedness of man. But are they not all that government will admit, and that human prudence can devise? Are they not the genuine and the characteristic means by which republican government provides for the liberty and happiness of the people? Are they not the identical means on which every State government in the Union relies for the attainment of these important ends? What, then, are we to understand by the objection which this paper has combated? What are we to say to the men who profess the most flaming zeal for republican government, yet boldly impeach the principle of it; who pretend to be champions for the right and the capacity of the people to choose their own rulers, yet maintain that they will prefer those only who will immediately and infallibly betray the trust committed to them?

Were the objection to be read by one who had not seen the mode prescribed by the Constitution for the choice of representatives, he could suppose nothing less than that some unreasonable qualification of property was annexed to the right of suffrage; or that the right of eligibility was limited to persons of particular families or fortunes; or at least that the mode prescribed by the State constitutions was, in some respect or other, very grossly departed from. We have seen how far such a supposition would err, as to the two first points. Nor would it, in fact, be less erroneous as to the last. The only difference discoverable between the two cases is that each representative of the United States will be elected by five or six thousand citizens; whilst in the individual States, the election of a representative is left to about as many hundreds. Will it be pretended that this difference is sufficient to justify an attachment to the State governments and an abhorrence to the federal government? If this be the point on which the objection turns, it deserves to be examined.

Is it supported by *reason*? This cannot be said, without maintaining that five or six thousand citizens are less capable of choosing a fit representative, or more liable to be corrupted by an unfit one, than five or six hundred. Reason, on the contrary, assures us that as in so great a number a fit representative would be most likely to be found, so the choice would be less likely to be diverted from him by the intrigues of the ambitious or the ambitious or the bribes of the rich.

Is the *consequence* from this doctrine admissible? If we say that five or six hundred citizens are as many as can jointly exercise their right of suffrage, must we not deprive the people of the immediate choice of their public servants in every instance where the administration of the government does not require as many of them as will amount to one for that number of citizens?

Is the doctrine warranted by *facts*? It was shown in the last paper that the real representation in the British House of Commons very little exceeds the proportion of one for every thirty thousand inhabitants. Besides a variety of powerful causes not existing here, and which favor in that country the pretensions of rank and wealth, no person is eligible as a representative of a county unless he possess real estate of the clear value of six hundred pounds sterling per year; nor of a city or borough, unless he possess a like estate of half that annual value. To this qualification on the part of the county representatives is added another on the part of the county electors, which restrains the right of suffrage to persons having a freehold estate of the annual value of more than twenty pounds sterling, according to the present rate of money. Notwithstanding these unfavorable circumstances, and notwithstanding some very unequal laws in the British code, it cannot be said that the representatives of the nation have elevated the few on the ruins of the many.

But we need not resort to foreign experience on this subject. Our own is explicit and decisive. The districts in New Hampshire in which the senators are chosen immediately by the people are nearly as large as will be necessary for her representatives in the Congress. Those of Massachusetts are larger than will be necessary for that purpose; and those of New York still more so. In the last State the members of Assembly for the cities and counties of New York and Albany are elected by very nearly as many voters as will be entitled to a representative in the Congress, calculating on the number of sixty-five representatives only. It makes no difference that in these senatorial districts and counties a number of representatives are voted for by each elector at the same time. If the same electors at the same time are capable of choosing four or five representatives, they cannot be incapable of choosing one. Pennsylvania is an additional example. Some of her counties, which elect her State representatives, are almost as large as her districts will be by which her federal representatives will be elected. The city of Philadelphia is supposed to contain between fifty and sixty thousand souls. It will therefore form nearly two districts for the choice of federal representatives. It forms, however, but one county, in which every elector votes for each of its representatives in the State legislature. And what may appear to be still more directly to our purpose, the whole city actually elects a *single member* for the executive council. This is the case in all the other counties of the State.

Are not these facts the most satisfactory proofs of the fallacy which has been employed against the branch of the federal government under consideration? Has it appeared on trial that the senators of New Hampshire, Massachusetts, and New York, or the executive council of Pennsylvania, or the members of the Assembly in the two last States, have betrayed any peculiar disposition to sacrifice the many to the few, or are in any respect less worthy of their places than the representatives and magistrates appointed in other States by very small divisions of the people?

But there are cases of a stronger complexion than any which I have yet quoted. One branch of the legislature of Connecticut is so constituted that each member of it is elected by the whole State. So is the governor of that State, of Massachusetts, and of this State, and the president of New Hampshire. I leave every man to decide whether the result of any one of these experiments can be said to countenance a suspicion that a diffusive mode of choosing representatives of the people tends to elevate traitors and to undermine the public liberty.

Federalist 62
James Madison

The Senate, with its equal representation of each state and members selected by state legislatures, was at once a concession to small states and a bulwark of federalism. Due to its structure, it would also lend the legislative branch stability and wisdom.

FEBRUARY 27, 1788

The Senate

Having examined the constitution of the House of Representatives, and answered such of the objections against it as seemed to merit notice, I enter next on the examination of the Senate. The heads into which this member of the government may be considered are: I. The qualification of senators; II. The appointment of them by the State legislatures; III. The equality of representation in the Senate; IV. The number of senators, and the term for which they are to be elected; V. The powers vested in the Senate.

I. The qualifications proposed for senators, as distinguished from those of representatives, consist in a more advanced age and a longer period of citizenship. A senator must be thirty years of age at least; as a representative must be twenty-five. And the former must have been a citizen nine years; as seven years are required for the latter. The propriety of these distinctions is explained by the nature of the senatorial trust, which, requiring greater extent of information and stability of character, requires at the same time that the senator should have reached a period of life most likely to supply these advantages; and which, participating immediately in transactions with foreign nations, ought to be exercised by none who are not thoroughly weaned from the prepossessions and habits incident to foreign birth and education. The term of nine years appears to be a prudent mediocrity between a total exclusion of adopted citizens,

James Madison, "No. 62: The Senate," in Clinton Rossiter, ed., *The Federalist Papers* (New York: Mentor, 1999), 374–80.

whose merits and talents may claim a share in the public confidence, and an indiscriminate and hasty admission of them, which might create a channel for foreign influence on the national councils.

II. It is equally unnecessary to dilate on the appointment of senators by the
5   State legislatures. Among the various modes which might have been devised for constituting this branch of the government, that which has been proposed by the convention is probably the most congenial with the public opinion. It is recommended by the double advantage of favoring a select appointment, and of giving to the State governments such an agency in the formation of the
10 federal government as must secure the authority of the former, and may form a convenient link between the two systems.

III. The equality of representation in the Senate is another point which, being evidently the result of compromise between the opposite pretensions of the large and the small States, does not call for much discussion. If indeed it be
15 right that among a people thoroughly incorporated into one nation every district ought to have a *proportional* share in the government and that among independent and sovereign States, bound together by a simple league, the parties, however unequal in size, ought to have an *equal* share in the common councils, it does not appear to be without some reason that in a compound
20 republic, partaking both of the national and federal character, the government ought to be founded on a mixture of the principles of proportional and equal representation. But it is superfluous to try, by the standard of theory, a part of the Constitution which is allowed on all hands to be the result, not of theory, but "of a spirit of amity, and that mutual deference and concession which
25 the peculiarity of our political situation rendered indispensable." A common government, with powers equal to its objects, is called for by the voice, and still more loudly by the political situation, of America. A government founded on principles more consonant to the wishes of the larger States is not likely to be obtained from the smaller States. The only option, then, for the former lies
30 between the proposed government and a government still more objectionable. Under this alternative, the advice of prudence must be to embrace the lesser evil; and instead of indulging a fruitless anticipation of the possible mischiefs which may ensue, to contemplate rather the advantageous consequences which may qualify the sacrifice.

35 In this spirit it may be remarked that the equal vote allowed to each State is at once a constitutional recognition of the portion of sovereignty remaining in the individual States and an instrument for preserving that residuary sovereignty. So far the equality ought to be no less acceptable to the large than to the small states; since they are not less solicitous to guard, by every

possible expedient, against an improper consolidation of the States into one simple republic.

Another advantage accruing from this ingredient in the constitution of the Senate is the additional impediment it must prove against improper acts of legislation. No law or resolution can now be passed without the concurrence, first, of a majority of the people, and then of a majority of the States. It must be acknowledged that this complicated check on legislation may in some instances be injurious as well as beneficial; and that the peculiar defense which it involves in favor of the smaller States would be more rational if any interests common to them and distinct from those of the other States would otherwise be exposed to peculiar danger. But as the larger States will always be able, by their power over the supplies, to defeat unreasonable exertions of this prerogative of the lesser States, and as the facility and excess of lawmaking seem to be the diseases to which our governments are most liable, it is not impossible that this part of the Constitution may be more convenient in practice than it appears to many in contemplation.

IV. The number of senators and the duration of their appointment come next to be considered. In order to form an accurate judgment on both these points it will be proper to inquire into the purposes which are to be answered by a senate; and in order to ascertain these it will be necessary to review the inconveniences which a republic must suffer from the want of such an institution.

First. It is a misfortune incident to republican government, though in a less degree than to other governments, that those who administer it may forget their obligations to their constituents and prove unfaithful to their important trust. In this point of view a senate, as a second branch of the legislative assembly distinct from and dividing the power with a first, must be in all cases a salutary check on the government. It doubles the security to the people by requiring the concurrence of two distinct bodies in schemes of usurpation or perfidy, where the ambition or corruption of one would otherwise be sufficient. This is a precaution founded on such clear principles, and now so well understood in the United States, that it would be more than superfluous to enlarge on it. I will barely remark that as the improbability of sinister combinations will be in proportion to the dissimilarity in the genius of the two bodies, it must be politic to distinguish them from each other by every circumstance which will consist with a due harmony in all proper measures and with the genuine principles of republican government.

Second. The necessity of a senate is not less indicated by the propensity of all single and numerous assemblies to yield to the impulse of sudden and violent

passions, and to be seduced by factious leaders into intemperate and pernicious resolutions. Examples on this subject might be cited without number; and from proceedings within the United States, as well as from the history of other nations. But a position that will not be contradicted need not be proved.
5   All that need be remarked is that a body which is to correct this infirmity ought itself to be free from it, and consequently ought to be less numerous. It ought, moreover, to possess great firmness, and consequently ought to hold its authority by a tenure of considerable duration.

Third. Another defect to be supplied by a senate lies in a want of due
10 acquaintance with the objects and principles of legislation. It is not possible that an assembly of men called for the most part from pursuits of a private nature continued in appointment for a short time and led by no permanent motive to devote the intervals of public occupation to a study of the laws, the affairs, and the comprehensive interests of their country, should, if left
15 wholly to themselves, escape a variety of important errors in the exercise of their legislative trust. It may be affirmed, on the best grounds, that no small share of the present embarrassments of America is to be charged on the blunders of our governments; and that these have proceeded from the heads rather than the hearts of most of the authors of them. What indeed are
20 all the repealing, explaining, and amending laws, which fill and disgrace our voluminous codes, but so many monuments of deficient wisdom; so many impeachments exhibited by each succeeding against each preceding session; so many admonitions to the people of the value of those aids which may be expected from a well-constituted senate?

25 A good government implies two things: first, fidelity to the object of government, which is the happiness of the people; secondly, a knowledge of the means by which that object can be best attained. Some governments are deficient in both these qualities; most governments are deficient in the first. I scruple not to assert that in American governments too little attention has
30 been paid to the last. The federal Constitution avoids this error; and what merits particular notice, it provides for the last in a mode which increases the security for the first.

Fourth. The mutability in the public councils arising from a rapid succession of new members, however qualified they may be, points out, in the strongest
35 manner, the necessity of some stable institution in the government. Every new election in the States is found to change one half of the representatives. From this change of men must proceed a change of opinions; and from a change of opinions, a change of measures. But a continual change even of

good measures is inconsistent with every rule of prudence and every prospect of success. The remark is verified in private life, and becomes more just, as well as more important, in national transactions.

To trace the mischievous effects of a mutable government would fill a volume. I will hint a few only, each of which will be perceived to be a source of innumerable others.

In the first place, it forfeits the respect and confidence of other nations, and all the advantages connected with national character. An individual who is observed to be inconstant to his plans, or perhaps to carry on his affairs without any plan at all, is marked at once by all prudent people as a speedy victim to his own unsteadiness and folly. His more friendly neighbors may pity him, but all will decline to connect their fortunes with his; and not a few will seize the opportunity of making their fortunes out of his. One nation is to another what one individual is to another; with this melancholy distinction, perhaps, that the former, with fewer of the benevolent emotions than the latter, are under fewer restraints also from taking undue advantage from the indiscretions of each other. Every nation, consequently, whose affairs betray a want of wisdom and stability, may calculate on every loss which can be sustained from the more systematic policy of its wiser neighbors. But the best instruction on this subject is unhappily conveyed to America by the example of her own situation. She finds that she is held in no respect by her friends; that she is the derision of her enemies; and that she is a prey to every nation which has an interest in speculating on her fluctuating councils and embarrassed affairs.

The internal effects of a mutable policy are still more calamitous. It poisons the blessings of liberty itself. It will be of little avail to the people that the laws are made by men of their own choice if the laws be so voluminous that they cannot be read, or so incoherent that they cannot be understood; if they be repealed or revised before they are promulgated, or undergo such incessant changes that no man, who knows what the law is today, can guess what it will be tomorrow. Law is defined to be a rule of action; but how can that be a rule, which is little known, and less fixed?

Another effect of public instability is the unreasonable advantage it gives to the sagacious, the enterprising, and the moneyed few over the industrious and uninformed mass of the people. Every new regulation concerning commerce or revenue, or in any manner affecting the value of the different species of property, presents a new harvest to those who watch the change, and can trace its consequences; a harvest, reared not by themselves, but by the toils and cares of the great body of their fellow-citizens. This is a state of things in which it may be said with some truth that laws are made for the *few*, not for the *many*.

In another point of view, great injury results from an unstable government. The want of confidence in the public councils damps every useful undertaking, the success and profit of which may depend on a continuance of existing arrangements. What prudent merchant will hazard his fortunes in any new branch of commerce when he knows not but that his plans may be rendered unlawful before they can be executed? What farmer or manufacturer will lay himself out for the encouragement given to any particular cultivation or establishment, when he can have no assurance that his preparatory labors and advances will not render him a victim to an inconstant government? In a word, no great improvement or laudable enterprise can go forward which requires the auspices of a steady system of national policy.

But the most deplorable effect of all is that diminution of attachment and reverence which steals into the hearts of the people towards a political system which betrays so many marks of infirmity, and disappoints so many of their flattering hopes. No government, any more than an individual, will long be respected without being truly respectable; nor be truly respectable without possessing a certain portion of order and stability.

Federalist 63
James Madison

To the Anti-Federalists, the Senate's six-year term and smaller number smacked of aristocracy. But to Publius, the selection of senators by state legislatures was a built-in protection for state interests. As a footnote to this argument, in making senatorial elections popular, the Seventeenth Amendent in 1913 changed not just the Senate, but the entire architecture of the Founders' Constitution.

MARCH 1, 1788

The Senate Continued

A *fifth* desideratum, illustrating the utility of a senate, is the want of a due sense of national character. Without a select and stable member of the government, the esteem of foreign powers will not only be forfeited by an unenlightened and variable policy, proceeding from the causes already mentioned, but the national councils will not possess that sensibility to the opinion of the world   5
which is perhaps not less necessary in order to merit than it is to obtain its respect and confidence.

An attention to the judgment of other nations is important to every government for two reasons: the one is that independently of the merits of any particular plan or measure, it is desirable, on various accounts, that it should   10
appear to other nations as the offspring of a wise and honorable policy; the second is that in doubtful cases, particularly where the national councils may be warped by some strong passion or momentary interest, the presumed or known opinion of the impartial world may be the best guide that can be followed. What has not America lost by her want of character with foreign   15
nations; and how many errors and follies would she not have avoided, if the justice and propriety of her measures had, in every instance, been previously tried by the light in which they would probably appear to the unbiased part of mankind?

James Madison, "No. 63: The Senate Continued," in Clinton Rossiter, ed., *The Federalist Papers* (New York: Mentor, 1999), 380–88.

Yet however requisite a sense of national character may be, it is evident that it can never be sufficiently possessed by a numerous and changeable body. It can only be found in a number so small that a sensible degree of the praise and blame of public measures may be the portion of each individual; or in an assembly
5   so durably invested with public trust that the pride and consequence of its members may be sensibly incorporated with the reputation and prosperity of the community. The half-yearly representatives of Rhode Island would probably have been little affected in their deliberations on the iniquitous measures of that State by arguments drawn from the light in which such measures would be
10 viewed by foreign nations, or even by the sister States; whilst it can scarcely be doubted that if the concurrence of a select and stable body had been necessary, a regard to national character alone would have prevented the calamities under which that misguided people is now laboring.

I add, as a *sixth* defect, the want, in some important cases, of a due responsibility
15 in the government to the people, arising from that frequency of elections which in other cases produces this responsibility. This remark will, perhaps, appear not only new, but paradoxical. It must nevertheless be acknowledged, when explained, to be as undeniable as it is important.

Responsibility, in order to be reasonable, must be limited to objects within
20 the power of the responsible party, and in order to be effectual, must relate to operations of that power, of which a ready and proper judgment can be formed by the constituents. The objects of government may be divided into two general classes: the one depending on measures which have singly an immediate and sensible operation; the other depending on a succession of
25 well-chosen and well-connected measures, which have a gradual and perhaps unobserved operation. The importance of the latter description to the collective and permanent welfare of every country needs no explanation. And yet it is evident that an assembly elected for so short a term as to be unable to provide more than one or two links in a chain of measures, on which the general
30 welfare may essentially depend, ought not to be answerable for the final result any more than a steward or tenant, engaged for one year, could be justly made to answer for places or improvements which could not be accomplished in less than half a dozen years. Nor is it possible for the people to estimate the *share* of influence which their annual assemblies may respectively have on events
35 resulting from the mixed transactions of several years. It is sufficiently difficult, at any rate, to preserve a personal responsibility in the members of a *numerous* body, for such acts of the body as have an immediate, detached, and palpable operation on its constituents.

The proper remedy for this defect must be an additional body in the legislative department, which, having sufficient permanency to provide for such objects as require a continued attention, and a train of measures, may be justly and effectually answerable for the attainment of those objects.

Thus far I have considered the circumstances which point out the necessity   5
of a well-constructed Senate only as they relate to the representatives of the people. To a people as little blinded by prejudice or corrupted by flattery as those whom I address, I shall not scruple to add that such an institution may be sometimes necessary as a defense to the people against their own temporary errors and delusions. As the cool and deliberate sense of the community   10
ought, in all governments, and actually will, in all free governments, ultimately prevail over the views of its rulers; so there are particular moments in public affairs when the people, stimulated by some irregular passion, or some illicit advantage, or misled by the artful misrepresentations of interested men, may call for measures which they themselves will afterwards be the most ready to   15
lament and condemn. In these critical moments, how salutary will be the interference of some temperate and respectable body of citizens, in order to check the misguided career and to suspend the blow meditated by the people against themselves, until reason, justice, and truth can regain their authority over the public mind? What bitter anguish would not the people of Athens   20
have often escaped if their government had contained so provident a safeguard against the tyranny of their own passions? Popular liberty might then have escaped the indelible reproach of decreeing to the same citizens the hemlock on one day and statues on the next.

It may be suggested that a people spread over an extensive region cannot,   25
like the crowded inhabitants of a small district, be subject to the infection of violent passions or to the danger of combining in pursuit of unjust measures. I am far from denying that this is a distinction of peculiar importance. I have, on the contrary, endeavored in a former paper to show that it is one of the principal recommendations of a confederated republic. At the same time,   30
this advantage ought not to be considered as superseding the use of auxiliary precautions. It may even be remarked that the same extended situation which will exempt the people of America from some of the dangers incident to lesser republics will expose them to the inconveniency of remaining for a longer time under the influence of those misrepresentations which the combined industry   35
of interested men may succeed in distributing among them.

It adds no small weight to all these considerations to recollect that history informs us of no long-lived republic which had not a senate. Sparta, Rome, and Carthage are, in fact, the only states to whom that character can be applied. In each of the two first there was a senate for life. The constitution of the senate in the last is less known. Circumstantial evidence makes it probable that it was not different in this particular from the two others.

5   It is at least certain that it had some quality or other which rendered it an anchor against popular fluctuations; and that a smaller council, drawn out of the senate, was appointed not only for life, but filled up vacancies itself. These examples, though as unfit for the imitation as they are repugnant to the genius of America, are, notwithstanding, when compared with the fugitive

10 and turbulent existence of other ancient republics, very instructive proofs of the necessity of some institution that will blend stability with liberty. I am not unaware of the circumstances which distinguish the American from other popular governments, as well ancient as modern; and which render extreme circumspection necessary, in reasoning from the one case to the other. But

15 after allowing due weight to this consideration it may still be maintained that there are many points of similitude which render these examples not unworthy of our attention. Many of the defects, as we have seen, which can only be supplied by a senatorial institution, are common to a numerous assembly frequently elected by the people, and to the people themselves. There are others

20 peculiar to the former which require the control of such an institution. The people can never wilfully betray their own interests; but they may possibly be betrayed by the representatives of the people; and the danger will be evidently greater where the whole legislative trust is lodged in the hands of one body of men than where the concurrence of separate and dissimilar bodies is required

25 in every public act.

The difference most relied on between the American and other republics consists in the principle of representation, which is the pivot on which the former move, and which is supposed to have been unknown to the latter, or at least to the ancient part of them. The use which has been made of this

30 difference, in reasonings contained in former papers, will have shown that I am disposed neither to deny its existence nor to undervalue its importance. I feel the less restraint, therefore, in observing that the position concerning the ignorance of the ancient governments on the subject of representation is by no means precisely true in the latitude commonly given to it. Without entering

35 into a disquisition which here would be misplaced, I will refer to a few known facts in support of what I advance.

In the most pure democracies of Greece, many of the executive functions were performed, not by the people themselves, but by officers elected by the people, and *representing* the people in their *executive* capacity.

Prior to the reform of Solon, Athens was governed by nine Archons, annually *elected by the people at large*. The degree of power delegated to them seems to be left in great obscurity. Subsequent to that period we find an assembly, first of four, and afterwards of six hundred members, annually *elected by the people*; and *partially* representing them in their *legislative* capacity, since they were not only associated with the people in the function of making laws, but had the exclusive right of originating legislative propositions to the people. The senate of Carthage, also, whatever might be its power or the duration of its appointment, appears to have been elective by the suffrages of the people. Similar instances might be traced in most, if not all, the popular governments of antiquity.

Lastly, in Sparta we meet with the Ephori, and in Rome with the Tribunes; two bodies, small indeed in number, but annually *elected by the whole body of the people*, and considered as the *representatives* of the people, almost in their *plenipotentiary* capacity. The Cosmi of Crete were also annually *elected by the people*, and have been considered by some authors as an institution analogous to those of Sparta and Rome, with this difference only, that in the election of that representative body the right of suffrage was communicated to a part only of the people.

From these facts, to which many others might be added, it is clear that the principle of representation was neither unknown to the ancients nor wholly overlooked in their political constitutions. The true distinction between these and the American governments lies *in the total exclusion of the people in their collective capacity*, from any share in the *latter*, and not in the *total exclusion of the representatives of the people* from the administration of the *former*. The distinction, however, thus qualified, must be admitted to leave a most advantageous superiority in favor of the United States. But to insure to this advantage its full effect, we must be careful not to separate it from the other advantage, of an extensive territory. For it cannot be believed that any form of representative government could have succeeded within the narrow limits occupied by the democracies of Greece.

In answer to all these arguments, suggested by reason, illustrated by examples, and enforced by our own experience, the jealous adversary of the Constitution will probably content himself with repeating that a senate appointed not immediately by the people, and for the term of six years, must gradually acquire a dangerous preeminence in the government and finally transform it into a tyrannical aristocracy.

To this general answer the general reply ought to be sufficient, that liberty may be endangered by the abuses of liberty as well as by the abuses of power; that there are numerous instances of the former as well as of the latter; and that the former, rather than the latter, is apparently most to be apprehended by the United States. But a more particular reply may be given.

Before such a revolution can be affected, the Senate, it is to be observed,
5   must in the first place corrupt itself; must next corrupt the State legislatures, must then corrupt the House of Representatives, and must finally corrupt the people at large. It is evident that the Senate must be first corrupted before it can attempt an establishment of tyranny. Without corrupting the State legislatures it cannot prosecute the attempt because the periodical change of
10 members would otherwise regenerate the whole body. Without exerting the means of corruption with equal success on the House of Representatives, the opposition of that co-equal branch of the government would inevitably defeat the attempt; and without corrupting the people themselves a succession of new representatives would speedily restore all things to their pristine order. Is
15 there any man who can seriously persuade himself that the proposed Senate can, by any possible means within the compass of human address, arrive at the object of a lawless ambition through all these obstructions?

If reason condemns the suspicion, the same sentence is pronounced by experience. The constitution of Maryland furnishes the most apposite example.
20 The Senate of that State is elected, as the federal Senate will be, indirectly by the people, and for a term less by one year only than the federal Senate. It is distinguished, also, by the remarkable prerogative of filling up its own vacancies within the term of its appointment, and at the same time is not under the control of any such rotation as is provided for the federal Senate. There are
25 some other lesser distinctions which would expose the former to colorable objections that do not lie against the latter. If the federal Senate, therefore, really contained the danger which has been so loudly proclaimed, some symptoms at least of a like danger ought by this time to have been betrayed by the Senate of Maryland, but no such symptoms have appeared. On the
30 contrary, the jealousies at first entertained by men of the same description with those who view with terror the correspondent part of the federal Constitution have been gradually extinguished by the progress of the experiment; and the Maryland constitution is daily deriving, from the salutary operation of this part of it, a reputation in which it will probably not be rivaled by that of any
35 State in the Union.

But if anything could silence the jealousies on this subject, it ought to be the British example. The Senate there, instead of being elected for a term of six years, and of being unconfined to particular families or fortunes, is an hereditary assembly of opulent nobles. The House of Representatives, instead of being elected for two years, and by the whole body of the people, is elected for seven years, and, in very great proportion, by a very small proportion of the people. Here, unquestionably, ought to be seen in full display the aristocratic usurpations and tyranny which are at some future period to be exemplified in the United States. Unfortunately, however, for the anti-federal argument, the British history informs us that this hereditary assembly has not been able to defend itself against the continual encroachments of the House of Representatives, and that it no sooner lost the support of the monarch than it was actually crushed by the weight of the popular branch.

As far as antiquity can instruct us on this subject, its examples support the reasoning which we have employed. In Sparta, the Ephori, the annual representatives of the people, were found an overmatch for the senate for life, continually gained on its authority and finally drew all power into their own hands. The Tribunes of Rome who were the representatives of the people prevailed, it is well known, in almost every contest with the senate for life, and in the end gained the most complete triumph over it. The fact is the more remarkable as unanimity was required in every act of the Tribunes, even after their number was augmented to ten. It proves the irresistible force possessed by that branch of a free government, which has the people on its side. To these examples might be added that of Carthage, whose senate, according to the testimony of Polybius, instead of drawing all power into its vortex had, at the commencement of the second Punic War, lost almost the whole of its original portion.

Besides the conclusive evidence resulting from this assemblage of facts that the federal Senate will never be able to transform itself, by gradual usurpations, into an independent and aristocratic body, we are warranted in believing that if such a revolution should ever happen from causes which the foresight of man cannot guard against, the House of Representatives, with the people on their side, will at all times be able to bring back the Constitution to its primitive form and principles. Against the force of the immediate representatives of the people nothing will be able to maintain even the constitutional authority of the Senate, but such a display of enlightened policy, and attachment to the public good, as will divide with that branch of the legislature the affections and support of the entire body of the people themselves.

FEDERALIST 70
ALEXANDER HAMILTON

To prevent the president from becoming monarchical, Anti-Federalists recommended a plural executive, shorter terms, and a one-term limit. Publius argues for the presidency as structured in the Constitution, and explains the necessity of an energetic executive.

MARCH 14, 1788

THE EXECUTIVE DEPARTMENT FURTHER CONSIDERED

There is an idea, which is not without its advocates, that a vigorous executive is inconsistent with the genius of republican government. The enlightened well-wishers to this species of government must at least hope that the supposition is destitute of foundation; since they can never admit its truth, without at the same time admitting the condemnation of their own principles. Energy 5
in the executive is a leading character in the definition of good government. It is essential to the protection of the community against foreign attacks; it is not less essential to the steady administration of the laws; to the protection of property against those irregular and high-handed combinations which sometimes interrupt the ordinary course of justice; to the security of liberty 10
against the enterprises and assaults of ambition, of faction, and of anarchy. Every man the least conversant in Roman history knows how often that republic was obliged to take refuge in the absolute power of a single man, under the formidable title of dictator, as well against the intrigues of ambitious individuals who aspired to the tyranny, and the seditions of whole classes of 15
the community whose conduct threatened the existence of all government, as against the invasions of external enemies who menaced the conquest and destruction of Rome.

There can be no need, however, to multiply arguments or examples on this head. A feeble executive implies a feeble execution of the government. A feeble execution 20

Alexander Hamilton, "No. 70: The Executive Department Further Considered," in Clinton Rossiter, ed., *The Federalist Papers* (New York: Mentor, 1999), 421–29.

is but another phrase for a bad execution; and a government ill executed, whatever it may be in theory, must be, in practice, a bad government.

Taking it for granted, therefore, that all men of sense will agree in the necessity of an energetic executive, it will only remain to inquire, what are the
5   ingredients which constitute this energy? How far can they be combined with those other ingredients which constitute safety in the republican sense? And how far does this combination characterize the plan which has been reported by the convention?

The ingredients which constitute energy in the executive are unity; duration;
10 an adequate provision for its support; and competent powers.

The ingredients which constitute safety in the republican sense are a due dependence on the people, and a due responsibility.

Those politicians and statesmen who have been the most celebrated for the soundness of their principles and for the justness of their views have declared
15 in favor of a single executive and a numerous legislature. They have, with great propriety, considered energy as the most necessary qualification of the former, and have regarded this as most applicable to power in a single hand; while they have, with equal propriety, considered the latter as best adapted to deliberation and wisdom, and best calculated to conciliate the confidence of the people and
20 to secure their privileges and interests.

That unity is conducive to energy will not be disputed. Decision, activity, secrecy, and dispatch will generally characterize the proceedings of one man in a much more eminent degree than the proceedings of any greater number; and in proportion as the number is increased, these qualities will be diminished.

25 This unity may be destroyed in two ways: either by vesting the power in two or more magistrates of equal dignity and authority, or by vesting it ostensibly in one man, subject in whole or in part to the control and cooperation of others, in the capacity of counselors to him. Of the first, the two consuls of Rome may serve as an example; of the last, we shall find examples in the constitutions
30 of several of the States. New York and New Jersey, if I recollect right, are the only States which have entrusted the executive authority wholly to single men. Both these methods of destroying the unity of the executive have their partisans; but the votaries of an executive council are the most numerous. They are both liable, if not to equal, to similar objections, and may in most
35 lights be examined in conjunction.

The experience of other nations will afford little instruction on this head. As far, however, as it teaches anything, it teaches us not to be enamored of plurality in the executive. We have seen that the Achaeans, on an experiment of two Praetors, were induced to abolish one. The Roman history records many instances of mischiefs to the republic from the dissensions between the consuls, and between the military tribunes, who were at times substituted for the consuls. But it gives us no specimens of any peculiar advantages derived to the state from the circumstance of the plurality of those magistrates. That the dissensions between them were not more frequent or more fatal is matter of astonishment, until we advert to the singular position in which the republic was almost continually placed, and to the prudent policy pointed out by the circumstances of the state, and pursued by the consuls, of making a division of the government between them. The patricians engaged in a perpetual struggle with the plebeians for the preservation of their ancient authorities and dignities; the consuls, who were generally chosen out of the former body, were commonly united by the personal interest they had in the defense of the privileges of their order. In addition to this motive of union, after the arms of the republic had considerably expanded the bounds of its empire, it became an established custom with the consuls to divide the administration between themselves by lot—one of them remaining at Rome to govern the city and its environs, the other taking command in the more distant provinces. This expedient must no doubt have had great influence in preventing those collisions and rivalships which might otherwise have embroiled the peace of the republic.

But quitting the dim light of historical research, attaching ourselves purely to the dictates of reason and good sense, we shall discover much greater cause to reject than to approve the idea of plurality in the executive, under any modification whatever.

Wherever two or more persons are engaged in any common enterprise or pursuit, there is always danger of difference of opinion. If it be a public trust or office in which they are clothed with equal dignity and authority, there is peculiar danger of personal emulation and even animosity. From either, and especially from all these causes, the most bitter dissensions are apt to spring. Whenever these happen, they lessen the respectability, weaken the authority, and distract the plans and operations of those whom they divide. If they should unfortunately assail the supreme executive magistracy of a country, consisting of a plurality of persons, they might impede or frustrate the most important measures of the government in the most critical emergencies of the state. And what is still worse, they might split the community into the most violent and irreconcilable factions, adhering differently to the different individuals who composed the magistracy.

Men often oppose a thing merely because they have had no agency in planning it, or because it may have been planned by those whom they dislike. But if they have been consulted, and have happened to disapprove, opposition then becomes, in their estimation, an indispensable duty of self-love. They seem to
5   think themselves bound in honor, and by all the motives of personal infallibility, to defeat the success of what has been resolved upon contrary to their sentiments. Men of upright, benevolent tempers have too many opportunities of remarking, with horror, to what desperate lengths this disposition is sometimes carried, and how often the great interests of society are sacrificed to the vanity, to the
10   conceit, and to the obstinacy of individuals, who have credit enough to make their passions and their caprices interesting to mankind. Perhaps the question now before the public may, in its consequences, afford melancholy proofs of the effects of this despicable frailty, or rather detestable vice, in the human character.

15   Upon the principles of a free government, inconveniences from the source just mentioned must necessarily be submitted to in the formation of the legislature; but it is unnecessary, and therefore unwise, to introduce them into the constitution of the executive. It is here too that they may be most pernicious. In the legislature, promptitude of decision is oftener an evil than a benefit.
20   The differences of opinion, and the jarrings of parties in that department of the government, though they may sometimes obstruct salutary plans, yet often promote deliberation and circumspection, and serve to check excesses in the majority. When a resolution too is once taken, the opposition must be at an end. That resolution is a law, and resistance to it punishable. But no
25   favorable circumstances palliate or atone for the disadvantages of dissension in the executive department. Here they are pure and unmixed. There is no point at which they cease to operate. They serve to embarrass and weaken the execution of the plan or measure to which they relate, from the first step to the final conclusion of it. They constantly counteract those qualities in the
30   executive which are the most necessary ingredients in its composition—vigor and expedition, and this without any counterbalancing good. In the conduct of war, in which the energy of the executive is the bulwark of the national security, everything would be to be apprehended from its plurality.

It must be confessed that these observations apply with principal weight to the
35   first case supposed—that is, to a plurality of magistrates of equal dignity and authority, a scheme, the advocates for which are not likely to form a numerous sect; but they apply, though not with equal yet with considerable weight to the project of a council, whose concurrence is made constitutionally necessary to the operations of the ostensible executive. An artful cabal in that council

would be able to distract and to enervate the whole system of administration. If no such cabal should exist, the mere diversity of views and opinions would alone be sufficient to tincture the exercise of the executive authority with a spirit of habitual feebleness and dilatoriness.

But one of the weightiest objections to a plurality in the executive, and which lies as much against the last as the first plan is that it tends to conceal faults and destroy responsibility. Responsibility is of two kinds—to censure and to punishment. The first is the more important of the two, especially in an elective office. Men in public trust will much oftener act in such a manner as to render them unworthy of being any longer trusted, than in such a manner as to make them obnoxious to legal punishment. But the multiplication of the executive adds to the difficulty of detection in either case. It often becomes impossible, amidst mutual accusations, to determine on whom the blame or the punishment of a pernicious measure, or series of pernicious measures, ought really to fall. It is shifted from one to another with so much dexterity, and under such plausible appearances, that the public opinion is left in suspense about the real author. The circumstances which may have led to any national miscarriage or misfortune are sometimes so complicated that where there are a number of actors who may have had different degrees and kinds of agency, though we may clearly see upon the whole that there has been mismanagement, yet it may be impracticable to pronounce to whose account the evil which may have been incurred is truly chargeable.

"I was overruled by my council. The council were so divided in their opinions that it was impossible to obtain any better resolution on the point." These and similar pretexts are constantly at hand, whether true or false. And who is there that will either take the trouble or incur the odium of a strict scrutiny into the secret springs of the transaction? Should there be found a citizen zealous enough to undertake the unpromising task, if there happened to be a collusion between the parties concerned, how easy it is to clothe the circumstances with so much ambiguity as to render it uncertain what was the precise conduct of any of those parties.

In the single instance in which the governor of this State is coupled with a council—that is, in the appointment to offices, we have seen the mischiefs of it in the view now under consideration. Scandalous appointments to important offices have been made. Some cases, indeed, have been so flagrant that ALL PARTIES have agreed in the impropriety of the thing. When inquiry has been made, the blame has been laid by the governor on the members of the council, who, on their part, have charged it upon his nomination; while the people remain altogether at a loss to determine by whose influence their interests have been committed to hands so unqualified and so manifestly improper. In tenderness to individuals, I forbear to descend to particulars.

It is evident from these considerations that the plurality of the executive tends
5 to deprive the people of the two greatest securities they can have for the faithful exercise of any delegated power, *first*, the restraints of public opinion, which lose their efficacy, as well on account of the division of the censure attendant on bad measures among a number as on account of the uncertainty on whom it ought to fall; and, *second*, the opportunity of discovering with facility and
10 clearness the misconduct of the persons they trust, in order either to their removal from office or to their actual punishment in cases which admit of it.

In England, the king is a perpetual magistrate; and it is a maxim which has obtained for the sake of the public peace that he is unaccountable for his administration, and his person sacred. Nothing, therefore, can be wiser in
15 that kingdom than to annex to the king a constitutional council, who may be responsible to the nation for the advice they give. Without this, there would be no responsibility whatever in the executive department—an idea inadmissible in a free government. But even there the king is not bound by the resolutions of his council, though they are answerable for the advice they give. He is
20 the absolute master of his own conduct in the exercise of his office and may observe or disregard the counsel given to him at his sole discretion.

But in a republic where every magistrate ought to be personally responsible for his behavior in office, the reason which in the British Constitution dictates the propriety of a council not only ceases to apply, but turns against the
25 institution. In the monarchy of Great Britain, it furnishes a substitute for the prohibited responsibility of the Chief Magistrate, which serves in some degree as a hostage to the national justice for his good behavior. In the American republic, it would serve to destroy, or would greatly diminish, the intended and necessary responsibility of the Chief Magistrate himself.

30 The idea of a council to the executive, which has so generally obtained in the State constitutions, has been derived from that maxim of republican jealousy which considers power as safer in the hands of a number of men than of a single man. If the maxim should be admitted to be applicable to the case, I should contend that the advantage on that side would not counterbalance
35 the numerous disadvantages on the opposite side. But I do not think the rule at all applicable to the executive power. I clearly concur in opinion, in this particular, with a writer whom the celebrated Junius pronounces to be "deep, solid, and ingenious," that "the executive power is more easily confined when

it is one;" that it is far more safe there should be a single object for the jealousy and watchfulness of the people; and, in a word, that all multiplication of the executive is rather dangerous than friendly to liberty.

A little consideration will satisfy us that the species of security sought for in the multiplication of the executive is unattainable. Numbers must be so great   5 as to render combination difficult, or they are rather a source of danger than of security. The united credit and influence of several individuals must be more formidable to liberty than the credit and influence of either of them separately. When power, therefore, is placed in the hands of so small a number of men as to admit of their interests and views being easily combined in a   10 common enterprise, by an artful leader, it becomes more liable to abuse, and more dangerous when abused, than if it be lodged in the hands of one man, who, from the very circumstance of his being alone, will be more narrowly watched and more readily suspected, and who cannot unite so great a mass of influence as when he is associated with others. The decemvirs of Rome, whose   15 name denotes their number, were more to be dreaded in their usurpation than any ONE of them would have been. No person would think of proposing an executive much more numerous than that body; from six to a dozen have been suggested for the number of the council. The extreme of these numbers is not too great for an easy combination; and from such a combination America would   20 have more to fear than from the ambition of any single individual. A council to a magistrate, who is himself responsible for what he does, are generally nothing better than a clog upon his good intentions, are often the instruments and accomplices of his bad, and are almost always a cloak to his faults.

I forbear to dwell upon the subject of expense; though it be evident that if the   25 council should be numerous enough to answer the principal end aimed at by the institution, the salaries of the members, who must be drawn from their homes to reside at the seat of government, would form an item in the catalog of public expenditures too serious to be incurred for an object of equivocal utility.   30

I will only add that, prior to the appearance of the Constitution, I rarely met with an intelligent man from any of the States who did not admit, as the result of experience, that the UNITY of the executive of this State was one of the best of the distinguishing features of our Constitution.

Federalist 71
Alexander Hamilton

Publius continues his defense of the presidency under the Constitution.

March 18, 1788

The Duration in Office of the Executive

Duration in office has been mentioned as the second requisite to the energy of the executive authority. This has relation to two objects: to the personal firmness of the executive magistrate in the employment of his constitutional powers, and to the stability of the system of administration which may have been adopted under his auspices. With regard to the first, it must be evident   5
that the longer the duration in office, the greater will be the probability of obtaining so important an advantage. It is a general principle of human nature that a man will be interested in whatever he possesses, in proportion to the firmness or precariousness of the tenure by which he holds it; will be less attached to what he holds by a momentary or uncertain title, than to   10
what he enjoys by a durable or certain title; and, of course, will be willing to risk more for the sake of the one than for the sake of the other. This remark is not less applicable to a political privilege, or honor, or trust, than to any article of ordinary property. The inference from it is that a man acting in the capacity of chief magistrate, under a consciousness that in a   15
very short time he *must* lay down his office, will be apt to feel himself too little interested in it to hazard any material censure or perplexity from the independent exertion of his powers, or from encountering the ill-humors, however transient, which may happen to prevail, either in a considerable part of the society itself, or even in a predominant faction in the legislative   20
body. If the case should only be that he *might* lay it down, unless continued by a new choice, and if he should be desirous of being continued, his wishes, conspiring with his fears, would tend still more powerfully to corrupt his

---

Alexander Hamilton, "No. 71: The Duration in Office of the Executive," in Clinton Rossiter, ed., *The Federalist Papers* (New York: Mentor, 1999), 429–34.

integrity, or debase his fortitude. In either case, feebleness and irresolution must be the characteristics of the station.

There are some who would be inclined to regard the servile pliancy of the executive to a prevailing current, either in the community or in the
5 legislature, as its best recommendation. But such men entertain very crude notions, as well of the purposes for which government was instituted, as of the true means by which the public happiness may be promoted. The republican principle demands that the deliberate sense of the community should govern the conduct of those to whom they entrust the management
10 of their affairs; but it does not require an unqualified complaisance to every sudden breeze of passion, or to every transient impulse which the people may receive from the arts of men, who flatter their prejudices to betray their interests. It is a just observation that the people commonly *intend* the PUBLIC GOOD. This often applies to their very errors. But their good sense
15 would despise the adulator who should pretend that they always *reason right* about the *means* of promoting it. They know from experience that they sometimes err; and the wonder is that they so seldom err as they do, beset as they continually are by the wiles of parasites and sycophants, by the snares of the ambitious, the avaricious, the desperate, by the artifices of men who
20 possess their confidence more than they deserve it, and of those who seek to possess rather than to deserve it. When occasions present themselves in which the interests of the people are at variance with their inclinations, it is the duty of the persons whom they have appointed to be the guardians of those interests to withstand the temporary delusion in order to give them
25 time and opportunity for more cool and sedate reflection. Instances might be cited in which a conduct of this kind has saved the people from very fatal consequences of their own mistakes, and has procured lasting monuments of their gratitude to the men who had courage and magnanimity enough to serve them at the peril of their displeasure.

30 But however inclined we might be to insist upon an unbounded complaisance in the executive to the inclinations of the people, we can with no propriety contend for a like complaisance to the humors of the legislature. The latter may sometimes stand in opposition to the former, and at other times the people may be entirely neutral. In either supposition, it is certainly desirable
35 that the executive should be in a situation to dare to act his own opinion with vigor and decision.

The same rule which teaches the propriety of a partition between the various branches of power teaches likewise that this partition ought to be so contrived as to render the one independent of the other. To what

purpose separate the executive or the judiciary from the legislative, if both
the executive and the judiciary are so constituted as to be at the absolute
devotion of the legislative? Such a separation must be merely nominal, and
incapable of producing the ends for which it was established. It is one thing
to be subordinate to the laws, and another to be dependent on the legislative   5
body. The first comports with, the last violates, the fundamental principles
of good government; and, whatever may be the forms of the Constitution,
unites all power in the same hands. The tendency of the legislative authority
to absorb every other has been fully displayed and illustrated by examples in
some preceding numbers. In governments purely republican, this tendency   10
is almost irresistible. The representatives of the people, in a popular assembly,
seem sometimes to fancy that they are the people themselves, and betray
strong symptoms of impatience and disgust at the least sign of opposition
from any other quarter; as if the exercise of its rights, by either the executive
or judiciary, were a breach of their privilege and an outrage to their dignity.   15
They often appear disposed to exert an imperious control over the other
departments; and as they commonly have the people on their side, they
always act with such momentum as to make it very difficult for the other
members of the government to maintain the balance of the Constitution.

It may perhaps be asked how the shortness of the duration in office can affect   20
the independence of the executive on the legislature, unless the one were
possessed of the power of appointing or displacing the other. One answer
to this inquiry may be drawn from the principle already remarked—that is,
from the slender interest a man is apt to take in a short-lived advantage, and
the little inducement it affords him to expose himself, on account of it, to   25
any considerable inconvenience or hazard. Another answer, perhaps more
obvious, though not more conclusive, will result from the consideration
of the influence of the legislative body over the people, which might be
employed to prevent the re-election of a man who, by an upright resistance
to any sinister project of that body, should have made himself obnoxious to   30
its resentment.

It may be asked also whether a duration of four years would answer the end
proposed; and if it would not, whether a less period, which would at least be
recommended by greater security against ambitious designs, would not, for
that reason, be preferable to a longer period which was, at the same time, too   35
short for the purpose of inspiring the desired firmness and independence of
the magistrate.

It cannot be affirmed that a duration of four years, or any other limited
duration, would completely answer the end proposed; but it would contribute

towards it in a degree which would have a material influence upon the spirit and character of the government. Between the commencement and termination of such a period there would always be a considerable interval in which the prospect of annihilation would be sufficiently remote not to
5 have an improper effect upon the conduct of a man endowed with a tolerable portion of fortitude; and in which he might reasonably promise himself that there would be time enough before it arrived to make the community sensible of the propriety of the measures he might incline to pursue. Though it be probable that, as he approached the moment when the public were, by
10 a new election, to signify their sense of his conduct, his confidence, and with it his firmness, would decline; yet both the one and the other would derive support from the opportunities which his previous continuance in the station had afforded him, of establishing himself in the esteem and goodwill of his constituents. He might, then, hazard with safety, in proportion to the proofs
15 he had given of his wisdom and integrity, and to the title he had acquired to the respect and attachment of his fellow-citizens. As on the one hand, a duration of four years will contribute to the firmness of the executive in a sufficient degree to render it a very valuable ingredient in the composition, so, on the other, it is not long enough to justify any alarm for the public
20 liberty. If a British House of Commons, from the most feeble beginnings, *from the mere power of assenting or disagreeing to the imposition of a new tax*, have, by rapid strides, reduced the prerogatives of the crown and the privileges of the nobility within the limits they conceived to be compatible with the principles of a free government, while they raised themselves to the
25 rank and consequence of a coequal branch of the legislature; if they have been able, in one instance, to abolish both the royalty and the aristocracy, and to overturn all the ancient establishments, as well in the Church as State; if they have been able, on a recent occasion, to make the monarch tremble at the prospect of an innovation attempted by them, what would
30 be to be feared from an elective magistrate of four years' duration with the confined authorities of a President of the United States? What, but that he might be unequal to the task which the Constitution assigns him? I shall only add that if his duration be such as to leave a doubt of his firmness, that doubt is inconsistent with a jealousy of his encroachments.

FEDERALIST 72
ALEXANDER HAMILTON

Anti-Federalists argued that an executive without term limits could, through demagoguery, keep office for as long as he could manipulate the public. Publius counters that re-eligibility will encourage good behavior. Subsequently, the Twenty-Second Amendment, enacted in 1951, limited the presidency to two terms.

MARCH 21, 1788

THE SAME SUBJECT CONTINUED, AND RE-ELIGIBILITY OF THE EXECUTIVE CONSIDERED

The administration of government, in its largest sense, comprehends all the operations of the body politic, whether legislative, executive, or judiciary; but in its most usual and perhaps its most precise signification, it is limited to executive details, and falls peculiarly within the province of the executive department. The actual conduct of foreign negotiations, the preparatory   5
plans of finance, the application and disbursement of the public monies in conformity to the general appropriations of the legislature, the arrangement of the army and navy, the directions of the operations of war—these, and other matters of a like nature, constitute what seems to be most properly understood by the administration of government. The persons, therefore, to   10
whose immediate management these different matters are committed ought to be considered as the assistants or deputies of the Chief Magistrate, and on this account they ought to derive their offices from his appointment, at least from his nomination, and ought to be subject to his superintendence. This view of the subject will at once suggest to us the intimate connection   15
between the duration of the executive magistrate in office and the stability of the system of administration. To reverse and undo what has been done by

---

Alexander Hamilton, "No. 72: The Same Subject Continued, and Re-eligibility of the Executive Considered," in Clinton Rossiter, ed., *The Federalist Papers* (New York: Mentor, 1999), 434–39.

a predecessor is very often considered by a successor as the best proof he can give of his own capacity and desert; and in addition to this propensity, where the alteration has been the result of public choice, the person substituted is warranted in supposing that the dismission of his predecessor has proceeded
5   from a dislike to his measures; and that the less he resembles him, the more he will recommend himself to the favor of his constituents. These considerations, and the influence of personal confidences and attachments, would be likely to induce every new President to promote a change of men to fill the subordinate stations; and these causes together could not fail to occasion a disgraceful and
10   ruinous mutability in the administration of the government.

With a positive duration of considerable extent, I connect the circumstances of re-eligibility. The first is necessary to give the officer himself the inclination and the resolution to act his part well, and to the community time and leisure to observe the tendency of his measures, and thence to form an experimental
15   estimate of their merits. The last is necessary to enable the people, when they see reason to approve of his conduct, to continue him in the station in order to prolong the utility of his talents and virtues, and to secure to the government the advantage of permanency in a wise system of administration.

Nothing appears more plausible at first sight, nor more ill-founded upon close
20   inspection, than a scheme which in relation to the present point has had some respectable advocates—I mean that of continuing the Chief Magistrate in office for a certain time, and then excluding him from it, either for a limited period or forever after. This exclusion, whether temporary or perpetual, would have nearly the same effects, and these effects would be for the most part rather
25   pernicious than salutary.

One ill effect of the exclusion would be a diminution of the inducements to good behavior. There are few men who would not feel much less zeal in the discharge of a duty when they were conscious that the advantage of the station with which it was connected must be relinquished at a determinate period,
30   than when they were permitted to entertain a hope of *obtaining*, by *meriting*, a continuance of them. This position will not be disputed so long as it is admitted that the desire of reward is one of the strongest incentives of human conduct; or that the best security for the fidelity of mankind is to make their interest coincide with their duty. Even the love of fame, the ruling passion of
35   the noblest minds, which would prompt a man to plan and undertake extensive and arduous enterprises for the public benefit, requiring considerable time to mature and perfect them, if he could flatter himself with the prospect of being allowed to finish what he had begun, would, on the contrary, deter him from the undertaking, when he foresaw that he must quit the scene before he could

accomplish the work, and must commit that, together with his own reputation, to hands which might be unequal or unfriendly to the task. The most to be expected from the generality of men, in such a situation, is the negative merit of not doing harm, instead of the positive merit of doing good.

Another ill effect of the exclusion would be the temptation to sordid views, to peculation, and, in some instances, to usurpation. An avaricious man who might happen to fill the office, looking forward to a time when he must at all events yield up the advantages he enjoyed, would feel a propensity not easy to be resisted by such a man to make the best use of his opportunities while they lasted, and might not scruple to have recourse to the most corrupt expedients to make the harvest as abundant as it was transitory; though the same man, probably, with a different prospect before him, might content himself with the regular perquisites of his situation, and might even be unwilling to risk the consequences of an abuse of his opportunities. His avarice might be a guard upon his avarice. Add to this that the same man might be vain or ambitious, as well as avaricious. And if he could expect to prolong his honors by his good conduct, he might hesitate to sacrifice his appetite for them to his appetite for gain. But with the prospect before him of approaching and inevitable annihilation, his avarice would be likely to get the victory over his caution, his vanity, or his ambition.

An ambitious man, too, finding himself seated on the summit of his country's honors, looking forward to the time at which he must descend from the exalted eminence forever, and reflecting that no exertion of merit on his part could save him from the unwelcome reverse, would be much more violently tempted to embrace a favorable conjuncture for attempting the prolongation of his power, at every personal hazard, than if he had the probability of answering the same end by doing his duty.

Would it promote the peace of the community, or the stability of the government, to have half a dozen men who had had credit enough to raise themselves to the seat of the supreme magistracy wandering among the people like discontented ghosts and sighing for a place which they were destined never more to possess?

A third ill effect of the exclusion would be the depriving the community of the advantage of the experience gained by the Chief Magistrate in the exercise of his office. That experience is the parent of wisdom is an adage the truth of which is recognized by the wisest as well as the simplest of mankind. What more desirable or more essential than this quality in the governors of nations? Where more desirable or more essential than in the first magistrate of a nation?

Can it be wise to put this desirable and essential quality under the ban of the Constitution, and to declare that the moment it is acquired, its possessor shall be compelled to abandon the station in which it was acquired and to which it is adapted? This, nevertheless, is the precise import of all those regulations
5   which exclude men from serving their country, by the choice of their fellow-citizens, after they have by a course of service fitted themselves for doing it with a greater degree of utility.

A fourth ill effect of the exclusion would be the banishing men from stations in which, in certain emergencies of the State, their presence might be of the
10 greatest moment to the public interest or safety. There is no nation which has not, at one period or another, experienced an absolute necessity of the services of particular men in particular situations, perhaps it would not be too strong to say, to the preservation of its political existence. How unwise, therefore, must be every such self-denying ordinance as serves to prohibit a nation from
15 making use of its own citizens in the manner best suited to its exigencies and circumstances! Without supposing the personal essentiality of the man, it is evident that a change of the Chief Magistrate, at the breaking out of a war, or at any similar crisis, for another, even of equal merit, would at all times be detrimental to the community, inasmuch as it would substitute inexperience
20 to experience, and would tend to unhinge and set afloat the already settled train of the administration.

A fifth ill effect of the exclusion would be that it would operate as a constitutional interdiction of stability in the administration. By *necessitating* a change of men, in the first office in the nation, it would necessitate a muta-
25 bility of measures. It is not generally to be expected that men will vary and measures remain uniform. The contrary is the usual course of things. And we need not be apprehensive that there will be too much stability, while there is even the option of changing; nor need we desire to prohibit the people from continuing their confidence where they think it may be safely placed, and
30 where, by constancy on their part, they may obviate the fatal inconveniences of fluctuating councils and a variable policy.

These are some of the disadvantages which would flow from the principle of exclusion. They apply most forcibly to the scheme of a perpetual exclusion; but when we consider that even a partial one would always render the readmission
35 of the person a remote and precarious object, the observations which have been made will apply nearly as fully to one case as to the other.

What are the advantages promised to counterbalance these disadvantages? They are represented to be: 1st, greater independence in the magistrate; 2nd, greater security to the people. Unless the exclusion be perpetual, there will be no pretense to infer the first advantage. But even in that case, may he have no object beyond his present station to which he may sacrifice his independence? May he have no connections, no friends, for whom he may sacrifice it? May he not be less willing, by a firm conduct, to make personal enemies, when he acts under the impression that a time is fast approaching, on the arrival of which he not only MAY, but MUST, be exposed to their resentments, upon an equal, perhaps upon an inferior, footing? It is not an easy point to determine whether his independence would be most promoted or impaired by such an arrangement.

As to the second supposed advantage, there is still greater reason to entertain doubts concerning it. If the exclusion were to be perpetual, a man of irregular ambition, of whom alone there could be reason in any case to entertain apprehension, would, with infinite reluctance, yield to the necessity of taking his leave forever of a post in which his passion for power and preeminence had acquired the force of habit. And if he had been fortunate or adroit enough to conciliate the goodwill of the people, he might induce them to consider as a very odious and unjustifiable restraint upon themselves a provision which was calculated to debar them of the right of giving a fresh proof of their attachment to a favorite. There may be conceived circumstances in which this disgust of the people, seconding the thwarted ambition of such a favorite, might occasion greater danger to liberty than could ever reasonably be dreaded from the possibility of a perpetuation in office by the voluntary suffrages of the community exercising a constitutional privilege.

There is an excess of refinement in the idea of disabling the people to continue in office men who had entitled themselves, in their opinion, to approbation and confidence; the advantages of which are at best speculative and equivocal, and are overbalanced by disadvantages far more certain and decisive.

Federalist 73
Alexander Hamilton

Although all legislation originates in Congress, the executive plays an integral role through the veto power.

March 21, 1788

The Provision for the Support of the Executive, and the Veto Power

The third ingredient towards constituting the vigor of the executive authority is an adequate provision for its support. It is evident that without proper attention to this article, the separation of the executive from the legislative department would be merely nominal and nugatory. The legislature, with a discretionary power over the salary and emoluments of the Chief Magistrate, 5
could render him as obsequious to their will as they might think proper to make him. They might, in most cases, either reduce him by famine, or tempt him by largesses, to surrender at discretion his judgment to their inclinations. These expressions, taken in all the latitude of the terms, would no doubt convey more than is intended. There are men who could neither be distressed nor won 10
into a sacrifice of their duty; but this stern virtue is the growth of few soils; and in the main it will be found that a power over a man's support is a power over his will. If it were necessary to confirm so plain a truth by facts, examples would not be wanting, even in this country, of the intimidation or seduction of the executive by the terrors or allurements of the pecuniary arrangements 15
of the legislative body.

It is not easy, therefore, to commend too highly the judicious attention which has been paid to this subject in the proposed Constitution. It is there provided that "The President of the United States shall, at stated times, receive for his services a compensation *which shall neither be increased nor diminished during* 20
the period for which he shall have been elected, and he *shall not receive within*

Alexander Hamilton, "No. 73: The Provision for the Support of the Executive, and the Veto Power," in Clinton Rossiter, ed., *The Federalist Papers* (New York: Mentor, 1999), 439–45.

that period any other emolument from the United States, or any of them." It is impossible to imagine any provision which would have been more eligible than this. The legislature, on the appointment of a President, is once for all to declare what shall be the compensation for his services during the time
5   for which he shall have been elected. This done, they will have no power to alter it, either by increase or diminution, till a new period of service by a new election commences. They can neither weaken his fortitude by operating on his necessities, nor corrupt his integrity by appealing to his avarice. Neither the Union, nor any of its members, will be at liberty to give, nor will he be at liberty
10 to receive, any other emolument than that which may have been determined by the first act. He can, of course, have no pecuniary inducement to renounce or desert the independence intended for him by the Constitution.

The last of the requisites to energy which have been enumerated are competent powers. Let us proceed to consider those which are proposed to be vested in
15 the President of the United States.

The first thing that offers itself to our observation is the qualified negative of the President upon the acts or resolutions of the two houses of the legislature; or, in other words, his power of returning all bills with objections to have the effect of preventing their becoming laws, unless they should afterwards be ratified by
20 two thirds of each of the component members of the legislative body.

The propensity of the legislative department to intrude upon the rights, and to absorb the powers, of the other departments has been already more than once suggested. The insufficiency of a mere parchment delineation of the boundaries of each has also been remarked upon; and the necessity of furnishing each with
25 constitutional arms for its own defense has been inferred and proved. From these clear and indubitable principles results the propriety of a negative, either absolute or qualified, in the executive upon the acts of the legislative branches. Without the one or the other, the former would be absolutely unable to defend himself against the depredations of the latter. He might gradually be stripped
30 of his authorities by successive resolutions or annihilated by a single vote. And in the one mode or the other, the legislative and executive powers might speedily come to be blended in the same hands. If even no propensity had ever discovered itself in the legislative body to invade the rights of the executive, the rules of just reasoning and theoretic propriety would of themselves teach us
35 that the one ought not to be left to the mercy of the other but ought to possess a constitutional and effectual power of self-defense.

But the power in question has a further use. It not only serves as a shield to the executive, but it furnishes an additional security against the enaction of improper laws. It establishes a salutary check upon the legislative body, calculated to guard the community against the effects of faction, precipitancy, or of any impulse unfriendly to the public good, which may happen to influence a majority of that body.

The propriety of a negative has, upon some occasions, been combated by an observation that it was not to be presumed a single man would possess more virtue and wisdom than a number of men; and that unless this presumption should be entertained, it would be improper to give the executive magistrate any species of control over the legislative body.

But this observation, when examined, will appear rather specious than solid. The propriety of the thing does not turn upon the supposition of superior wisdom or virtue in the executive, but upon the supposition that the legislature will not be infallible; that the love of power may sometimes betray it into a disposition to encroach upon the rights of other members of the government; that a spirit of faction may sometimes pervert its deliberations; that impressions of the moment may sometimes hurry it into measures which itself, on maturer reflection, would condemn. The primary inducement to conferring the power in question upon the executive is to enable him to defend himself; the secondary one is to increase the chances in favor of the community against the passing of bad laws, through haste, inadvertence, or design. The oftener the measure is brought under examination, the greater the diversity in the situations of those who are to examine it, the less must be the danger of those errors which flow from want of due deliberation, or of those missteps which proceed from the contagion of some common passion or interest. It is far less probable that culpable views of any kind should infect all the parts of the government at the same moment and in relation to the same object than that they should by turns govern and mislead every one of them.

It may perhaps be said that the power of preventing bad laws includes that of preventing good ones; and may be used to the one purpose as well as to the other. But this objection will have little weight with those who can properly estimate the mischiefs of that inconstancy and mutability in the laws, which form the greatest blemish in the character and genius of our governments. They will consider every institution calculated to restrain the excess of law-making, and to keep things in the same state in which they happen to be at any given period as much more likely to do good than harm; because it is favorable to greater stability in the system of legislation. The injury which may possibly be done by defeating a few good laws will be amply compensated by the advantage of preventing a number of bad ones.

Nor is this all. The superior weight and influence of the legislative body in a free government and the hazard to the executive in a trial of strength with that body afford a satisfactory security that the negative would generally be employed with great caution; and that there would oftener be room for a

5   charge of timidity than of rashness in the exercise of it. A king of Great Britain, with all his train of sovereign attributes, and with all the influence he draws from a thousand sources, would, at this day, hesitate to put a negative upon the joint resolutions of the two houses of Parliament. He would not fail to exert the utmost resources of that influence to strangle a measure disagreeable

10   to him, in its progress to the throne, to avoid being reduced to the dilemma of permitting it to take effect, or of risking the displeasure of the nation by an opposition to the sense of the legislative body. Nor is it probable that he would ultimately venture to exert his prerogative, but in a case of manifest propriety, or extreme necessity. All well-informed men in that kingdom will accede to

15   the justness of this remark. A very considerable period has elapsed since the negative of the crown has been exercised.

If a magistrate so powerful and so well fortified as a British monarch would have scruples about the exercise of the power under consideration, how much greater caution may be reasonably expected in a President of the United States,

20   clothed for the short period of four years with the executive authority of a government wholly and purely republican?

It is evident that there would be greater danger of his not using his power when necessary, than of his using it too often, or too much. An argument, indeed, against its expediency, has been drawn from this very source. It has

25   been represented, on this account, as a power odious in appearance, useless in practice. But it will not follow, that because it might be rarely exercised, it would never be exercised. In the case for which it is chiefly designed, that of an immediate attack upon the constitutional rights of the executive, or in a case in which the public good was evidently and palpably sacrificed, a man of

30   tolerable firmness would avail himself of his constitutional means of defense, and would listen to the admonitions of duty and responsibility. In the former supposition, his fortitude would be stimulated by his immediate interest in the power of his office; in the latter, by the probability of the sanction of his constituents who, though they would naturally incline to the legislative body

35   in a doubtful case, would hardly suffer their partiality to delude them in a very plain case. I speak now with an eye to a magistrate possessing only a common share of firmness. There are men who, under any circumstances, will have the courage to do their duty at every hazard.

But the convention have pursued a mean in this business, which will both facilitate the exercise of the power vested in this respect in the executive magistrate, and make its efficacy to depend on the sense of a considerable part of the legislative body. Instead of an absolute negative, it is proposed to give the executive the qualified negative already described. This is a power which would be much more readily exercised than the other. A man who might be afraid to defeat a law by his single VETO might not scruple to return it for reconsideration, subject to being finally rejected only in the event of more than one third of each house concurring in the sufficiency of his objections. He would be encouraged by the reflection that if his opposition should prevail, it would embark in it a very respectable proportion of the legislative body whose influence would be united with his in supporting the propriety of his conduct in the public opinion. A direct and categorical negative has something in the appearance of it more harsh, and more apt to irritate, than the mere suggestion of argumentative objections to be approved or disapproved by those to whom they are addressed. In proportion as it would be less apt to offend, it would be more apt to be exercised; and for this very reason it may in practice be found more effectual. It is to be hoped that it will not often happen that improper views will govern so large a proportion as two thirds of both branches of the legislature at the same time; and this, too, in defiance of the counterpoising weight of the executive. It is at any rate far less probable that this should be the case than that such views should taint the resolutions and conduct of a bare majority. A power of this nature in the executive will often have a silent and unperceived, though forcible, operation. When men, engaged in unjustifiable pursuits, are aware that obstructions may come from a quarter which they cannot control, they will often be restrained by the bare apprehension of opposition from doing what they would with eagerness rush into if no such external impediments were to be feared.

This qualified negative, as has been elsewhere remarked, is in this State vested in a council, consisting of the governor, with the chancellor and judges of the Supreme Court, or any two of them. It has been freely employed upon a variety of occasions, and frequently with success. And its utility has become so apparent, that persons who, in compiling the Constitution, were violent opposers of it, have from experience become its declared admirers.

I have in another place remarked that the convention, in the formation of this part of their plan, had departed from the model of the constitution of this State in favor of that of Massachusetts. Two strong reasons may be imagined for this preference. One is that the judges, who are to be the interpreters of the law, might receive an improper bias from having given a previous opinion in their revisionary capacities; the other is that by being often associated with the executive, they might be induced to embark too far in the political views of that magistrate, and thus a dangerous combination might by degrees be cemented

5 between the executive and judiciary departments. It is impossible to keep the judges too distinct from every other avocation than that of expounding the laws. It is peculiarly dangerous to place them in a situation to be either corrupted or influenced by the executive.

FEDERALIST 74
ALEXANDER HAMILTON

The president can act "with secrecy and dispatch," two qualities which the legislature and the judiciary will never possess.

MARCH 25, 1788

THE COMMAND OF THE MILITARY AND NAVAL FORCES, AND THE PARDONING POWER OF THE EXECUTIVE

The President of the United States is to be "commander-in-chief of the army and navy of the United States, and of the militia of the several States *when called into the actual service* of the United States." The propriety of this provision is so evident in itself and it is at the same time so consonant to the precedents of the State constitutions in general, that little need be said to explain or enforce it.　5 Even those of them which have in other respects coupled the Chief Magistrate with a council have for the most part concentrated the military authority in him alone. Of all the cares or concerns of government, the direction of war most peculiarly demands those qualities which distinguish the exercise of power by a single hand. The direction of war implies the direction of the common　10 strength; and the power of directing and employing the common strength forms a usual and essential part in the definition of the executive authority.

"The President may require the opinion, in writing, of the principal officer in each of the executive departments, upon any subject relating to the duties of their respective officers." This I consider as a mere redundancy in the plan, as　15 the right for which it provides would result of itself from the office.

He is also to be authorized "to grant reprieves and pardons for offenses against the United States, *except in cases of impeachment*." Humanity and good policy conspire to dictate that the benign prerogative of pardoning should be as little as possible fettered or embarrassed. The criminal code of every country partakes　20

Alexander Hamilton, "No. 74: The Command of the Military and Naval Forces, and the Pardoning Power of the Executive," in Clinton Rossiter, ed., *The Federalist Papers* (New York: Mentor, 1999), 445–48.

so much of necessary severity that without an easy access to exceptions in favor of unfortunate guilt, justice would wear a countenance too sanguinary and cruel. As the sense of responsibility is always strongest in proportion as it is undivided, it may be inferred that a single man would be most ready to
5   attend to the force of those motives which might plead for a mitigation of the rigor of the law, and least apt to yield to considerations which were calculated to shelter a fit object of its vengeance. The reflection that the fate of a fellow-creature depended on his *sole fiat* would naturally inspire scrupulousness and caution; the dread of being accused of weakness or connivance would
10   beget equal circumspection, though of a different kind. On the other hand, as men generally derive confidence from their numbers, they might often encourage each other in an act of obduracy, and might be less sensible to the apprehension of suspicion or censure for an injudicious or affected clemency. On these accounts, one man appears to be a more eligible dispenser of the
15   mercy of government than a body of men.

The expediency of vesting the power of pardoning in the President has, if I mistake not, been only contested in relation to the crime of treason. This, it has been urged, ought to have depended upon the assent of one, or both, of the branches of the legislative body. I shall not deny that there are strong
20   reasons to be assigned for requiring in this particular the concurrence of that body or of a part of it. As treason is a crime leveled at the immediate being of the society when the laws have once ascertained the guilt of the offender, there seems a fitness in referring the expediency of an act of mercy towards him to the judgment of the legislature. And this ought the rather to be the case, as
25   the supposition of the connivance of the Chief Magistrate ought not to be entirely excluded. But there are also strong objections to such a plan. It is not to be doubted that a single man of prudence and good sense is better fitted, in delicate conjunctures, to balance the motives which may plead for and against the remission of the punishment than any numerous body whatever. It
30   deserves particular attention that treason will often be connected with seditions which embrace a large proportion of the community, as lately happened in Massachusetts. In every such case we might expect to see the representation of the people tainted with the same spirit which had given birth to the offense. And when parties were pretty equally matched, the secret sympathy of the
35   friends and favorers of the condemned, availing itself of the good nature and weakness of others, might frequently bestow impunity where the terror of an example was necessary. On the other hand, when the sedition had proceeded from causes which had inflamed the resentments of the major party, they might often be found obstinate and inexorable, when policy demanded a

conduct of forbearance and clemency. But the principal argument for reposing the power of pardoning in this case in the Chief Magistrate is this: in seasons of insurrection or rebellion, there are often critical moments when a well-timed offer of pardon to the insurgents or rebels may restore the tranquility of the commonwealth; and which, if suffered to pass unimproved, it may never be   5 possible afterwards to recall. The dilatory process of convening the legislature, or one of its branches, for the purpose of obtaining its sanction to the measure, would frequently be the occasion of letting slip the golden opportunity. The loss of a week, a day, an hour, may sometimes be fatal. If it should be observed that a discretionary power with a view to such contingencies might   10 be occasionally conferred upon the President, it may be answered in the first place that it is questionable, whether, in a limited Constitution, that power could be delegated by law; and in the second place, that it would generally be impolitic beforehand to take any step which might hold out the prospect of impunity. A proceeding of this kind, out of the usual course, would be likely   15 to be construed into an argument of timidity or of weakness, and would have a tendency to embolden guilt.

Essay XI
Brutus

Here Brutus criticizes the power granted by the Constitution to an independent judiciary.

January 31, 1788

The nature and extent of the judicial power of the United States, proposed to be granted by this constitution, claims our particular attention.

Much has been said and written upon the subject of this new system on both sides, but I have not met with any writer, who has discussed the judicial powers with any degree of accuracy. And yet it is obvious, that we can form but very   5
imperfect ideas of the manner in which this government will work, or the effect it will have in changing the internal police and mode of distributing justice at present subsisting in the respective states, without a thorough investigation of the powers of the judiciary and of the manner in which they will operate. This government is a complete system, not only for making, but for executing laws.   10
And the courts of law, which will be constituted by it, are not only to decide upon the constitution and the laws made in pursuance of it, but by officers subordinate to them to execute all their decisions. The real effect of this system of government, will therefore be brought home to the feelings of the people, through the medium of the judicial power. It is, moreover, of great importance,   15
to examine with care the nature and extent of the judicial power, because those who are to be vested with it, are to be placed in a situation altogether unprecedented in a free country. They are to be rendered totally independent, both of the people and the legislature, both with respect to their offices and salaries. No errors they may commit can be corrected by any power above them, if any   20
such power there be, nor can they be removed from office for making ever so many erroneous adjudications.

Anonymous, "Essays, of Brutus, XI," January 31, 1788, in Herbert J. Storing, ed., *The Complete Anti-Federalist*, Vol. 2 (Chicago: University of Chicago Press, 1981), 417–22.

The only causes for which they can be displaced, is, conviction of treason, bribery, and high crimes and misdemeanors.

This part of the plan is so modeled, as to authorize the courts, not only to carry into execution the powers expressly given, but where these are wanting or
5 ambiguously expressed, to supply what is wanting by their own decisions.

That we may be enabled to form a just opinion on this subject, I shall, in considering it,

1st. Examine the nature and extent of the judicial powers—and

2d. Inquire, whether the courts who are to exercise them, are so constituted
10 as to afford reasonable ground of confidence, that they will exercise them for the general good....

In article 3d, section 2d, it is said, "The judicial power shall extend to all cases in law and equity arising under this constitution, the laws of the United States, and treaties made, or which shall be made, under their authority, etc."...

15 This article...vests the judicial with a power to resolve all questions that may arise on any case on the construction of the constitution, either in law or in equity.

1st. They are authorized to determine all questions that may arise upon the meaning of the constitution in law. This article vests the courts with authority
20 to give the constitution a legal construction, or to explain it according to the rules laid down for construing a law.—These rules give a certain degree of latitude of explanation. According to this mode of construction, the courts are to give such meaning to the constitution as comports best with the common, and generally received acceptation of the words in which it is expressed, regarding
25 their ordinary and popular use, rather than their grammatical propriety. Where words are dubious, they will be explained by the context....

2d. The judicial are not only to decide questions arising upon the meaning of the constitution in law, but also in equity.

By this they are empowered, to explain the constitution according to the reason-
30 ing spirit of it, without being confined to the words or letter....

From these remarks, the authority and business of the courts of law, under this clause, may be understood.

They will give the sense of every article of the constitution, that may from time to time come before them. And in their decisions they will not confine
35 themselves to any fixed or established rules, but will determine, according to

what appears to them, the reason and spirit of the constitution. The opinions of the supreme court, whatever they may be, will have the force of law; because there is no power provided in the constitution, that can correct their errors, or control their adjudications. From this court there is no appeal. And I conceive the legislature themselves, cannot set aside a judgment of this court, because they are authorized by the constitution to decide in the last resort. The legislature must be controlled by the constitution, and not the constitution by them. They have therefore no more right to set aside any judgment pronounced upon the construction of the constitution, than they have to take from the president, the chief command of the army and navy, and commit it to some other person. The reason is plain; the judicial and executive derive their authority from the same source, that the legislature do theirs; and therefore in all cases, where the constitution does not make the one responsible to, or controllable by the other, they are altogether independent of each other.

The judicial power will operate to affect, in the most certain, but yet silent and imperceptible manner, what is evidently the tendency of the constitution:—I mean, an entire subversion of the legislative, executive and judicial powers of the individual states. Every adjudication of the supreme court, on any question that may arise upon the nature and extent of the general government, will affect the limits of the state jurisdiction. In proportion as the former enlarge the exercise of their powers, will that of the latter be restricted.

That the judicial power of the United States, will lean strongly in favor of the general government, and will give such an explanation to the constitution, as will favor an extension of its jurisdiction, is very evident from a variety of considerations.

1st. The constitution itself strongly countenances such a mode of construction. Most of the articles in this system, which convey powers of any considerable importance, are conceived in general and indefinite terms, which are either equivocal, ambiguous, or which require long definitions to unfold the extent of their meaning. The two most important powers committed to any government, those of raising money, and of raising and keeping up troops, have already been considered, and shown to be unlimited by any thing but the discretion of the legislature. The clause which vests the power to pass all laws which are proper and necessary, to carry the powers given into execution, it has been shown, leaves the legislature at liberty, to do every thing, which in their judgment is best. It is said, I know, that this clause confers no power on the legislature, which they would not have had without it—though I believe this is not the fact, yet, admitting it to be, it implies that the constitution is not to receive an

explanation strictly, according to its letter; but more power is implied than is expressed. And this clause, if it is to be considered, as explanatory of the extent of the powers given, rather than giving a new power, is to be understood as declaring, that in construing any of the articles conveying power, the spirit,
5   intent and design of the clause, should be attended to, as well as the words in their common acceptation.

This constitution gives sufficient color for adopting an equitable construction, if we consider the great end and design it professedly has in view—these appear from its preamble to be, "to form a more perfect union, establish justice, ensure
10   domestic tranquility, provide for the common defense, promote the general welfare, and secure the blessings of liberty to ourselves and posterity." The design of this system is here expressed, and it is proper to give such a meaning to the various parts, as will best promote the accomplishment of the end; this idea suggests itself naturally upon reading the preamble, and will countenance the
15   court in giving the several articles such a sense, as will the most effectually promote the ends the constitution had in view—how this manner of explaining the constitution will operate in practice, shall be the subject of future inquiry.

2d. Not only will the constitution justify the courts in inclining to this mode of explaining it, but they will be interested in using this latitude of interpre-
20   tation. Every body of men invested with office are tenacious of power; they feel interested, and hence it has become a kind of maxim, to hand down their offices, with all its rights and privileges, unimpaired to their successors; the same principle will influence them to extend their power, and increase their rights; this of itself will operate strongly upon the courts to give such a meaning to the
25   constitution in all cases where it can possibly be done, as will enlarge the sphere of their own authority. Every extension of the power of the general legislature, as well as of the judicial powers, will increase the powers of the courts; and the dignity and importance of the judges, will be in proportion to the extent and magnitude of the powers they exercise. I add, it is highly probable the emolu-
30   ment of the judges will be increased, with the increase of the business they will have to transact and its importance. From these considerations the judges will be interested to extend the powers of the courts, and to construe the constitution as much as possible, in such a way as to favor it; and that they will do it, appears probable.

35   3d. Because they will have precedent to plead, to justify them in it. It is well known, that the courts in England, have by their own authority, extended their jurisdiction far beyond the limits set them in their original institution, and by the laws of the land....

When the courts will have a precedent before them of a court which extended its jurisdiction in opposition to an act of the legislature, is it not to be expected that they will extend theirs, especially when there is nothing in the constitution expressly against it? and they are authorized to construe its meaning, and are not under any control?   5

This power in the judicial, will enable them to mold the government, into almost any shape they please....

Federalist 78
Alexander Hamilton

Defending the idea of judicial review—the authority of the courts to declare a law unconstitutional—Publius denies that it leads to judicial supremacy. The courts must never substitute "will" for "judgment," as all branches of government answer to the Constitution.

June 14, 1788

The Judiciary Department

We proceed now to an examination of the judiciary department of the proposed government.

In unfolding the defects of the existing Confederation, the utility and necessity of a federal judicature have been clearly pointed out. It is the less necessary to recapitulate the considerations there urged as the propriety of the institution 5 in the abstract is not disputed; the only questions which have been raised being relative to the manner of constituting it, and to its extent. To these points, therefore, our observations shall be confined.

The manner of constituting it seems to embrace these several objects: 1st. The mode of appointing the judges. 2nd. The tenure by which they are to hold 10 their places. 3rd. The partition of the judiciary authority between different courts and their relations to each other.

First. As to the mode of appointing the judges: this is the same with that of appointing the officers of the Union in general and has been so fully discussed in the two last numbers that nothing can be said here which would not be 15 useless repetition.

Second. As to the tenure by which the judges are to hold their places: this chiefly concerns their duration in office, the provisions for their support, the precautions for their responsibility.

Alexander Hamilton, "No. 78: The Judiciary Department," in Clinton Rossiter, ed., *The Federalist Papers* (New York: Mentor, 1999), 463–71.

According to the plan of the convention, all judges who may be appointed by the United States are to hold their offices *during good behavior*, which is conformable to the most approved of the State constitutions, and among the rest, to that of this State. Its propriety having been drawn into question by the adversaries of that plan is no light symptom of the rage for objection which disorders their imaginations and judgments. The standard of good behavior for the continuance in office of the judicial magistracy is certainly one of the most valuable of the modern improvements in the practice of government. In a monarchy it is an excellent barrier to the despotism of the prince; in a republic it is a no less excellent barrier to the encroachments and oppressions of the representative body. And it is the best expedient which can be devised in any government to secure a steady, upright, and impartial administration of the laws.

Whoever attentively considers the different departments of power must perceive that, in a government in which they are separated from each other, the judiciary, from the nature of its functions, will always be the least dangerous to the political rights of the Constitution; because it will be least in a capacity to annoy or injure them. The executive not only dispenses the honors but holds the sword of the community. The legislature not only commands the purse but prescribes the rules by which the duties and rights of every citizen are to be regulated. The judiciary, on the contrary, has no influence over either the sword or the purse; no direction either of the strength or of the wealth of the society, and can take no active resolution whatever. It may truly be said to have neither FORCE nor WILL but merely judgment; and must ultimately depend upon the aid of the executive arm even for the efficacy of its judgments.

This simple view of the matter suggests several important consequences. It proves incontestably that the judiciary is beyond comparison the weakest of the three departments of power; that it can never attack with success either of the other two; and that all possible care is requisite to enable it to defend itself against their attacks. It equally proves that though individual oppression may now and then proceed from the courts of justice, the general liberty of the people can never be endangered from that quarter; I mean so long as the judiciary remains truly distinct from both the legislature and the executive. For I agree that "there is no liberty if the power of judging be not separated from the legislative and executive powers." And it proves, in the last place, that as liberty can have nothing to fear from the judiciary alone, but would have everything to fear from its union with either of the other departments; that as all the effects of such a union must ensue from a dependence of the former on the latter, notwithstanding a nominal and apparent separation;

that as, from the natural feebleness of the judiciary, it is in continual jeopardy of being overpowered, awed, or influenced by its coordinate branches; and that as nothing can contribute so much to its firmness and independence as permanency in office, this quality may therefore be justly regarded as an indispensable ingredient in its constitution, and, in a great measure, as the 5 citadel of the public justice and the public security.

The complete independence of the courts of justice is peculiarly essential in a limited Constitution. By a limited Constitution, I understand one which contains certain specified exceptions to the legislative authority; such, for instance, as that it shall pass no bills of attainder, no *ex post facto* laws, and the 10 like. Limitations of this kind can be preserved in practice no other way than through the medium of courts of justice, whose duty it must be to declare all acts contrary to the manifest tenor of the Constitution void. Without this, all the reservations of particular rights or privileges would amount to nothing.

Some perplexity respecting the rights of the courts to pronounce legislative acts 15 void, because contrary to the Constitution, has arisen from an imagination that the doctrine would imply a superiority of the judiciary to the legislative power. It is urged that the authority which can declare the acts of another void must necessarily be superior to the one whose acts may be declared void. As this doctrine is of great importance in all the American constitutions, a brief 20 discussion of the grounds on which it rests cannot be unacceptable.

There is no position which depends on clearer principles than that every act of a delegated authority, contrary to the tenor of the commission under which it is exercised, is void. No legislative act, therefore, contrary to the Constitution, can be valid. To deny this would be to affirm that the deputy is greater than his 25 principal; that the servant is above his master; that the representatives of the people are superior to the people themselves; that men acting by virtue of powers may do not only what their powers do not authorize, but what they forbid.

If it be said that the legislative body are themselves the constitutional judges of their own powers and that the construction they put upon them is conclusive 30 upon the other departments it may be answered that this cannot be the natural presumption where it is not to be collected from any particular provisions in the Constitution. It is not otherwise to be supposed that the Constitution could intend to enable the representatives of the people to substitute their *will* to that of their constituents. It is far more rational to suppose that the 35 courts were designed to be an intermediate body between the people and the legislature in order, among other things, to keep the latter within the limits assigned to their authority. The interpretation of the laws is the proper and

peculiar province of the courts. A constitution is, in fact, and must be regarded by the judges as, a fundamental law. It therefore belongs to them to ascertain its meaning as well as the meaning of any particular act proceeding from the legislative body. If there should happen to be an irreconcilable variance between
5   the two, that which has the superior obligation and validity ought, of course, to be preferred; or, in other words, the Constitution ought to be preferred to the statute, the intention of the people to the intention of their agents.

Nor does this conclusion by any means suppose a superiority of the judicial to the legislative power. It only supposes that the power of the people is superior
10   to both, and that where the will of the legislature, declared in its statutes, stands in opposition to that of the people, declared in the Constitution, the judges ought to be governed by the latter rather than the former. They ought to regulate their decisions by the fundamental laws rather than by those which are not fundamental.

15   This exercise of judicial discretion in determining between two contradictory laws is exemplified in a familiar instance. It not uncommonly happens that there are two statutes existing at one time, clashing in whole or in part with each other and neither of them containing any repealing clause or expression. In such a case, it is the province of the courts to liquidate and fix their meaning
20   and operation. So far as they can, by any fair construction, be reconciled to each other, reason and law conspire to dictate that this should be done; where this is impracticable, it becomes a matter of necessity to give effect to one in exclusion of the other. The rule which has obtained in the courts for determining their relative validity is that the last in order of time shall be
25   preferred to the first. But this is a mere rule of construction, not derived from any positive law but from the nature and reason of the thing. It is a rule not enjoined upon the courts by legislative provision but adopted by themselves, as consonant to truth and propriety, for the direction of their conduct as interpreters of the law. They thought it reasonable that between the interfering
30   acts of an *equal* authority that which was the last indication of its will should have the preference.

But in regard to the interfering acts of a superior and subordinate authority of an original and derivative power, the nature and reason of the thing indicate the converse of that rule as proper to be followed. They teach us that the prior
35   act of a superior ought to be preferred to the subsequent act of an inferior and subordinate authority; and that accordingly, whenever a particular statute contravenes the Constitution, it will be the duty of the judicial tribunals to adhere to the latter and disregard the former.

It can be of no weight to say that the courts, on the pretense of a repugnancy, may substitute their own pleasure to the constitutional intentions of the legislature. This might as well happen in the case of two contradictory statutes; or it might as well happen in every adjudication upon any single statute. The courts must declare the sense of the law; and if they should be disposed to   5
exercise WILL instead of JUDGMENT, the consequence would equally be the substitution of their pleasure to that of the legislative body. The observation, if it proved anything, would prove that there ought to be no judges distinct from that body.

If, then, the courts of justice are to be considered as the bulwarks of a limited   10
Constitution against legislative encroachments, this consideration will afford a strong argument for the permanent tenure of judicial offices, since nothing will contribute so much as this to that independent spirit in the judges which must be essential to the faithful performance of so arduous a duty.

This independence of the judges is equally requisite to guard the Constitution   15
and the rights of individuals from the effects of those ill humors which the arts of designing men, or the influence of particular conjunctures, sometimes disseminate among the people themselves, and which, though they speedily give place to better information, and more deliberate reflection, have a tendency, in the meantime, to occasion dangerous innovations in the government, and   20
serious oppressions of the minor party in the community. Though I trust the friends of the proposed Constitution will never concur with its enemies, in questioning that fundamental principle of republican government which admits the right of the people to alter or abolish the established Constitution whenever they find it inconsistent with their happiness; yet it is not to be   25
inferred from this principle that the representatives of the people, whenever a momentary inclination happens to lay hold of a majority of their constituents incompatible with the provisions in the existing Constitution would, on that account, be justifiable in a violation of those provisions; or that the courts would be under a greater obligation to connive at infractions in this shape   30
than when they had proceeded wholly from the cabals of the representative body. Until the people have, by some solemn and authoritative act, annulled or changed the established form, it is binding upon themselves collectively, as well as individually; and no presumption, or even knowledge of their sentiments, can warrant their representatives in a departure from it prior to   35
such an act. But it is easy to see that it would require an uncommon portion of fortitude in the judges to do their duty as faithful guardians of the Constitution, where legislative invasions of it had been instigated by the major voice of the community.

But it is not with a view to infractions of the Constitution only that the independence of the judges may be an essential safeguard against the effects of occasional ill humors in the society. These sometimes extend no farther than to the injury of the private rights of particular classes of citizens, by unjust
5   and partial laws. Here also the firmness of the judicial magistracy is of vast importance in mitigating the severity and confining the operation of such laws. It not only serves to moderate the immediate mischiefs of those which may have been passed but it operates as a check upon the legislative body in passing them; who, perceiving that obstacles to the success of iniquitous
10 intention are to be expected from the scruples of the courts, are in a manner compelled, by the very motives of the injustice they meditate, to qualify their attempts. This is a circumstance calculated to have more influence upon the character of our governments than but few may be aware of. The benefits of the integrity and moderation of the judiciary have already been felt in more
15 States than one; and though they may have displeased those whose sinister expectations they may have disappointed, they must have commanded the esteem and applause of all the virtuous and disinterested. Considerate men of every description ought to prize whatever will tend to beget or fortify that temper in the courts; as no man can be sure that he may not be tomorrow the
20 victim of a spirit of injustice, by which he may be a gainer today. And every man must now feel that the inevitable tendency of such a spirit is to sap the foundations of public and private confidence and to introduce in its stead universal distrust and distress.

That inflexible and uniform adherence to the rights of the Constitution, and of
25 individuals, which we perceive to be indispensable in the courts of justice, can certainly not be expected from judges who hold their offices by a temporary commission. Periodical appointments, however regulated, or by whomsoever made, would, in some way or other, be fatal to their necessary independence. If the power of making them was committed either to the executive or legislature
30 there would be danger of an improper complaisance to the branch which possessed it; if to both, there would be an unwillingness to hazard the displeasure of either; if to the people, or to persons chosen by them for the special purpose, there would be too great a disposition to consult popularity to justify a reliance that nothing would be consulted but the Constitution and the laws.

35 There is yet a further and a weighty reason for the permanency of the judicial offices which is deducible from the nature of the qualifications they require. It has been frequently remarked with great propriety that a voluminous code of laws is one of the inconveniences necessarily connected with the advantages of a free government. To avoid an arbitrary discretion in the courts, it is

indispensable that they should be bound down by strict rules and precedents which serve to define and point out their duty in every particular case that comes before them; and it will readily be conceived from the variety of controversies which grow out of the folly and wickedness of mankind that the records of those precedents must unavoidably swell to a very considerable bulk   5 and must demand long and laborious study to acquire a competent knowledge of them. Hence it is that there can be but few men in the society who will have sufficient skill in the laws to qualify them for the stations of judges. And making the proper deductions for the ordinary depravity of human nature, the number must be still smaller of those who unite the requisite integrity with   10 the requisite knowledge. These considerations apprise us that the government can have no great option between fit characters; and that a temporary duration in office which would naturally discourage such characters from quitting a lucrative line of practice to accept a seat on the bench would have a tendency to throw the administration of justice into hands less able and less well quali-   15 fied to conduct it with utility and dignity. In the present circumstances of this country and in those in which it is likely to be for a long time to come, the disadvantages on this score would be greater than they may at first sight appear; but it must be confessed that they are far inferior to those which present themselves under the other aspects of the subject.   20

Upon the whole, there can be no room to doubt that the convention acted wisely in copying from the models of those constitutions which have established *good behavior* as the tenure of their judicial offices, in point of duration; and that so far from being blamable on this account, their plan would have been inexcusably defective if it had wanted this important feature   25 of good government. The experience of Great Britain affords an illustrious comment on the excellence of the institution.

Marbury v. Madison
John Marshall (1755–1835)

Thomas Jefferson's election as president is often called the "Revolution of 1800," because it marked the first peaceful transfer of power from one political party to another. Despite its uniquely pacific character, the election's aftermath was marked by partisan rancor. The day before Jefferson took office, President John Adams commissioned fifty-eight Federalist judges. Upon assuming office Jefferson ordered his Secretary of State, James Madison, to withhold their commissions. One of them, William Marbury, brought a case that eventually reached the Supreme Court, where Chief Justice John Marshall wrote an opinion that established the power of judicial review.

1803

Mr. Chief Justice Marshall delivered the Opinion of the Court:

…1st. Has the applicant a right to the commission he demands?

2d. If he has a right, and that right has been violated, do the laws of his country afford him a remedy?

3d. If they do afford him a remedy, is it a mandamus issuing from this court?… 5

It is…the opinion of the Court,

1st. That by signing the commission of Mr. Marbury, the President of the United States appointed him a justice of peace for the county of Washington, in the District of Columbia; and that the seal of the United States, affixed thereto by the Secretary of State, is conclusive testimony of the verity of the signature, and 10 of the completion of the appointment; and that the appointment conferred on him a legal right to the office for the space of five years.

2d. That, having this legal title to the office, he has a consequent right to the commission; a refusal to deliver which is a plain violation of that right, for which the laws of his country afford him a remedy. 15

---

5 U.S. (1 Cranch) 137 (1803).

It remains to be inquired whether,

3d. He is entitled to the remedy for which he applies. This depends on,

1st. The nature of the writ applied for; and,

2d. The power of this court.

5   This, then, is a plain case for a mandamus, either to deliver the commission, or a copy of it from the record; and it only remains to be inquired,

Whether it can issue from this court....

The act to establish the judicial courts of the United States authorizes the Supreme Court "to issue writs of mandamus in cases warranted by the prin-
10   ciples and usages of law, to any courts appointed, or persons holding office, under the authority of the United States."

The Secretary of State, being a person holding an office under the authority of the United States, is precisely within the letter of the description, and if this court is not authorized to issue a writ of mandamus to such an officer, it must
15   be because the law is unconstitutional, and therefore absolutely incapable of conferring the authority, and assigning the duties which its words purport to confer and assign.

The constitution vests the whole judicial power of the United States in one Supreme Court, and such inferior courts as congress shall, from time to time,
20   ordain and establish. This power is expressly extended to all cases arising under the laws of the United States; and, consequently, in some form, may be exercised over the present case; because the right claimed is given by a law of the United States.

In the distribution of this power it is declared that "the Supreme Court shall have
25   original jurisdiction in all cases affecting ambassadors, other public ministers and consuls, and those in which a state shall be a party. In all other cases, the Supreme Court shall have appellate jurisdiction."

It has been insisted, at the bar, that as the original grant of jurisdiction, to the Supreme and inferior courts, is general, and the clause, assigning original
30   jurisdiction to the Supreme Court, contains no negative or restrictive words, the power remains to the legislature, to assign original jurisdiction to that court in other cases than those specified in the article which has been recited; provided those cases belong to the judicial power of the United States.

If it had been intended to leave it in the discretion of the legislature to apportion
35   the judicial power between the supreme and inferior courts according to the will of that body, it would certainly have been useless to have proceeded further

than to have defined the judicial power, and the tribunals in which it should be vested. The subsequent part of the section is mere surplusage, is entirely without meaning, if such is to be the construction. If congress remains at liberty to give this court appellate jurisdiction, where the constitution has declared their jurisdiction shall be original; and original jurisdiction where the constitution has declared it shall be appellate; the distribution of jurisdiction, made in the constitution, is form without substance....

It is the essential criterion of appellate jurisdiction, that it revises and corrects the proceedings in a cause already instituted, and does not create that cause. Although, therefore, a mandamus may be directed to courts, yet to issue such a writ to an officer for the delivery of a paper, is in effect the same as to sustain an original action for that paper, and, therefore, seems not to belong to appellate, but to original jurisdiction. Neither is it necessary in such a case as this, to enable the court to exercise its appellate jurisdiction.

The authority, therefore, given to the Supreme Court, by the act establishing the judicial courts of the United States, to issue writs of mandamus to public officers, appears not to be warranted by the constitution; and it becomes necessary to inquire whether a jurisdiction so conferred can be exercised.

The question, whether an act, repugnant to the constitution, can become the law of the land, is a question deeply interesting to the United States; but, happily, not of an intricacy proportioned to its interest. It seems only necessary to recognize certain principles, supposed to have been long and well established, to decide it.

That the people have an original right to establish, for their future government, such principles, as, in their opinion, shall most conduce to their own happiness is the basis on which the whole American fabric has been erected. The exercise of this original right is a very great exertion; nor can it, nor ought it, to be frequently repeated. The principles, therefore, so established, are deemed fundamental. And as the authority from which they proceed is supreme, and can seldom act, they are designed to be permanent.

This original and supreme will organizes the government, and assigns to different departments their respective powers. It may either stop here, or establish certain limits not to be transcended by those departments.

The government of the United States is of the latter description. The powers of the legislature are defined and limited; and that those limits may not be mistaken, or forgotten, the constitution is written. To what purpose are powers limited, and to what purpose is that limitation committed to writing, if these limits may, at any time, be passed by those intended to be restrained? The distinction between

a government with limited and unlimited powers is abolished, if those limits do not confine the persons on whom they are imposed, and if acts prohibited and acts allowed, are of equal obligation. It is a proposition too plain to be contested, that the constitution controls any legislative act repugnant to it; or,
5   that the legislature may alter the constitution by an ordinary act.

Between these alternatives there is no middle ground. The constitution is either a superior paramount law, unchangeable by ordinary means, or it is on a level with ordinary legislative acts, and, like other acts, is alterable when the legislature shall please to alter it.

10   If the former part of the alternative be true, then a legislative act contrary to the constitution is not law: if the latter part be true, then written constitutions are absurd attempts, on the part of the people, to limit a power in its own nature illimitable.

Certainly all those who have framed written constitutions contemplate them as forming the fundamental and paramount law of the nation, and, consequently,
15   the theory of every such government must be, that an act of the legislature, repugnant to the constitution, is void.

This theory is essentially attached to a written constitution, and, is consequently, to be considered, by this court, as one of the fundamental principles of our society. It is not therefore to be lost sight of in the further consideration of this subject.

20   If an act of the legislature, repugnant to the constitution, is void, does it, notwithstanding its invalidity, bind the courts, and oblige them to give it effect? Or, in other words, though it be not law, does it constitute a rule as operative as if it was a law? This would be to overthrow in fact what was established in theory; and would seem, at first view, an absurdity too gross to be insisted on.
25   It shall, however, receive a more attentive consideration.

It is emphatically the province and duty of the judicial department to say what the law is. Those who apply the rule to particular cases, must of necessity expound and interpret that rule. If two laws conflict with each other, the courts must decide on the operation of each.

30   So if a law be in opposition to the constitution; if both the law and the constitution apply to a particular case, so that the court must either decide that case conformably to the law, disregarding the constitution; or conformably to the constitution, disregarding the law; the court must determine which of these conflicting rules governs the case. This is of the very essence of judicial duty.

35   If, then, the courts are to regard the constitution, and the constitution is superior to any ordinary act of the legislature, the constitution, and not such ordinary act, must govern the case to which they both apply.

Those, then, who controvert the principle that the constitution is to be considered, in court, as a paramount law, are reduced to the necessity of maintaining that courts must close their eyes on the constitution, and see only the law.

This doctrine would subvert the very foundation of all written constitutions. 5
It would declare that an act which, according to the principles and theory of our government, is entirely void, is yet, in practice, completely obligatory. It would declare that if the legislature shall do what is expressly forbidden, such act, notwithstanding the express prohibition, is in reality effectual. It would be giving to the legislature a practical and real omnipotence, with the same breath 10
which professes to restrict their powers within narrow limits. It is prescribing limits, and declaring that those limits may be passed at pleasure.

That it thus reduces to nothing what we have deemed the greatest improvement on political institutions, a written constitution, would of itself be sufficient, in America, where written constitutions have been viewed with so much reverence, 15
for rejecting the construction. But the peculiar expressions of the constitution of the United States furnish additional arguments in favor of its rejection.

The judicial power of the United States is extended to all cases arising under the constitution.

Could it be the intention of those who gave this power, to say that in using it the 20
constitution should not be looked into? That a case arising under the constitution should be decided without examining the instrument under which it arises?

This is too extravagant to be maintained.

In some cases, then, the constitution must be looked into by the judges. And if they can open it at all, what part of it are they forbidden to read or to obey? 25

There are many other parts of the constitution which serve to illustrate this subject.

It is declared that "no tax or duty shall be laid on articles exported from any state." Suppose a duty on the export of cotton, of tobacco, or of flour; and a suit instituted to recover it. Ought judgment to be rendered in such a case? Ought 30
the judges to close their eyes on the constitution, and only see the law?

The constitution declares "that no bill of attainder or ex post facto law shall be passed."

If, however, such a bill should be passed, and a person should be prosecuted under it; must the court condemn to death those victims whom the constitution 35
endeavors to preserve?

"No person," says the constitution, "shall be convicted of treason unless on the testimony of two witnesses to the same overt act, or on confession in open court."

Here the language of the constitution is addressed especially to the courts. It prescribes, directly for them, a rule of evidence not to be departed from. If the legislature should change that rule, and declare one witness, or a confession out of court, sufficient for conviction, must the constitutional principle yield to the legislative act?

From these, and many other selections which might be made, it is apparent, that the framers of the constitution contemplated that instrument as a rule for the government of courts, as well as of the legislature.

Why otherwise does it direct the judges to take an oath to support it? This oath certainly applies in an especial manner, to their conduct in their official character. How immoral to impose it on them, if they were to be used as the instruments, and the knowing instruments, for violating what they swear to support!...

It is also not entirely unworthy of observation, that in declaring what shall be the supreme law of the land, the constitution itself is first mentioned; and not the laws of the United States generally, but those only which shall be made in pursuance of the constitution, have that rank.

Thus, the particular phraseology of the constitution of the United States confirms and strengthens the principle, supposed to be essential to all written constitutions, that a law repugnant to the constitution is void; and that courts, as well as other departments, are bound by that instrument.

VII

The Founders on Slavery, the Rise of the Positive Good School, and the Roots of the Secession Crisis

For the Founders, equality meant that every human being is born free from the arbitrary or non-consensual political rule of any other human being. All legitimate government is hence necessarily based on the consent of the governed. The continued existence of slavery, the most extreme form of denying consent, was thus the great original flaw in the American constitutional order. It is why Thomas Jefferson wrote, "I tremble for my country when I reflect that God is just." In a similar vein, Abraham Lincoln would later describe slavery as the "cancer" in the American body politic.

It is obvious from the official documents and private statements collected in this section that the Founders agreed that slavery was a moral evil because it violated the principle of equality. The overwhelming consensus of the Founders was that *all* human beings are created equal. Some Founders, like Jefferson, tentatively thought that there was a difference in abilities between blacks and whites. Others, such as Alexander Hamilton, thought there was no real difference in abilities between the two races. But all the Founders held that there was no difference in the equal natural rights of human beings, that the eradication of slavery would be a great good, and that slavery was corrupting to masters and slaves alike. There was no argument in the founding for the perpetuation of slavery as a good in itself.

The Founders believed that the anti-slavery measures undertaken in the Northwest Ordinance and the Constitution placed slavery, in Lincoln's words, "in the course of ultimate extinction." But why did they not simply eliminate slavery themselves?

The Founders faced a number of serious obstacles to emancipation. They recognized slavery as a great evil, but any measures they undertook to remove the evil must be consistent with the first purpose of government—the self-preservation of individuals and the political community. It was necessary to end slavery in a way that secured the rights of all. Some Founders, especially Jefferson, had a sort of optimistic Enlightenment faith in the progress of opinions that recognized the equal natural rights of all. But in the end, fears relating to self-preservation, the selfish human passions that incline us to exploit other human beings, and concerns over how to make good citizens of emancipated slaves proved more powerful than the growth of anti-slavery opinion.

The controversy over the admission of Missouri into the Union was, in Jefferson's words, "like a fire bell in the night." In one way the Missouri Compromise of 1820, which forbade the existence of slavery in the Louisiana Purchase except in Missouri itself, continued the restrictive policy regarding slavery put in place by the Founders. But it also signaled that public opinion was not becoming progressively anti-slavery.

The rise of the idea that slavery was a positive good in the 1830s indicated that those like Jefferson, who believed that popular opinion would naturally move in an anti-slavery direction, had been mistaken. The great theorist of the positive good argument was John C. Calhoun. He maintained that the Founders had indeed believed in the equality of all human beings and that they desired to eradicate slavery in America, but rejected their belief in equality as erroneous and pernicious. He proposed to remedy America's flawed founding with a new political science based on the purported truth that blacks are fundamentally unequal to whites and that slavery is positively beneficial for slaves and masters alike. In Calhoun's teaching, the "rights" of states—the Founders would not have spoken of states having rights—are sundered from the rights of individuals. Calhoun's ideas were to form the basis of the argument for secession.

The failure to pass the Wilmot Proviso banning slavery in the territories acquired in the war with Mexico, and the rapid deterioration of the Compromise of 1850, followed the growing acceptance of the positive good theory. The political battles over the Wilmot Proviso, and later the passage of the Kansas-Nebraska Act, led to the destruction of the Whig party and the birth of the Republican party. It was the work of Abraham Lincoln to ensure that the latter returned the nation to the doctrine of equality as understood by the Founders.

JOHN GRANT
Assistant Professor of Politics
Hillsdale College

Draft of the
Declaration of Independence
Thomas Jefferson

Thomas Jefferson's first draft of the Declaration of Independence contained a critique of King George III's involvement in the slave trade. Although not approved by the entire Second Continental Congress, it indicates that the leading Founders understood the slavery issue in moral terms.

1776

…He has waged cruel war against human nature itself, violating its most sacred rights of life and liberty in the persons of a distant people who never offended him, captivating and carrying them into slavery in another hemisphere, or to incur miserable death in their transportation thither. This piratical warfare, the opprobrium of *infidel* powers, is the warfare of the CHRISTIAN king of 5 Great Britain. Determined to keep open a market where MEN should be bought and sold, he has prostituted his negative for suppressing every legislative attempt to prohibit or to restrain this execrable commerce: and that this assemblage of horrors might want no fact of distinguished die, he is now exciting those very people to rise in arms among us, and to purchase that 10 liberty of which *he* has deprived them, by murdering the people upon whom *he* also obtruded them; thus paying off former crimes committed against the *liberties* of one people, with crimes which he urges them to commit against the *lives* of another.…

Thomas Jefferson, "Original Rough Draught," in Julian P. Boyd, ed., *The Papers of Thomas Jefferson*, Vol. 1 (Princeton, NJ: Princeton University Press, 1950–1992), 426.

THE NORTHWEST ORDINANCE
CONGRESS OF THE CONFEDERATION

Passed when only a single state outlawed slavery, the anti-slavery stance of the Northwest Ordinance—barring slavery in the territories, and thus in future states—gave weight to Abraham Lincoln's later argument that the Founders sought to place slavery "in the course of ultimate extinction."

JULY 13, 1787

ARTICLE VI

…There shall be neither slavery nor involuntary servitude in the said territory, otherwise than in the punishment of crimes, whereof the party shall have been duly convicted: *Provided always,* That any person escaping into the same, from whom labor or service is lawfully claimed in any one of the original States, such fugitive may be lawfully reclaimed, and conveyed to the person 5 claiming his or her labor or service as aforesaid.…

George Washington, John Adams, Benjamin Franklin, Alexander Hamilton, and James Madison on Slavery

None of the leading Founders ever declared slavery to be a just or beneficial institution. In fact, they hoped to see the slave trade eradicated, and eventually the entire institution of slavery made illegal.

George Washington
Letter to Robert Morris
APRIL 12, 1786

"…[T]here is not a man living who wishes more sincerely than I do, to see a plan adopted for the abolition of it.…"

John Adams
Letter to Robert J. Evans
JUNE 8, 1819

"…Every measure of prudence, therefore, ought to be assumed for the eventual total extirpation of slavery from the United States.… I have, through my whole life, held the practice of slavery in…abhorrence.…"

Benjamin Franklin
An Address to the Public from the Pennsylvania Society
NOVEMBER 9, 1789

"…Slavery is such an atrocious debasement of human nature, that its very extirpation, if not performed with solicitous care, may sometimes open a source of serious evils.…"

George Washington, "To Robert Morris," April 12, 1786, in W. W. Abbot et al., eds., *The Papers of George Washington, 1748–1799,* "Confederation Series," Vol. 4 (Charlottesville, VA: University of Virginia Press, 1976–present), 16.

John Adams, "To Robert J. Evans," June 8, 1819, in Adrienne Koch et al., eds., *Selected Writings of John and John Quincy Adams* (New York: Knopf, 1946), 209–10.

Benjamin Franklin, "An Address to the Public from the Pennsylvania Society for Promoting the Abolition of Slavery, and the Relief of Free Negroes Unlawfully Held in Bondage," November 9, 1789, in John Bigelow, ed., *The Works of Benjamin Franklin*, Vol. 12 (New York: G. P. Putnam's Sons, 1904), 157–58.

Alexander Hamilton
Philo Camillus no. 2

August 1795

"...The laws of certain states which give an ownership in the service of negroes as personal property, constitute a similitude between them and other articles of personal property, and thereby subject them to the right of capture by war. But being men, by the laws of God and nature, they were capable of acquiring

5   liberty—and when the captor in war, to whom by the capture the ownership was transferred, thought fit to give them liberty, the gift was not only valid, but irrevocable...."

James Madison
Speech at the Constitutional Convention

June 6, 1787

"...We have seen the mere distinction of color made in the most enlightened period of time, a ground of the most oppressive dominion ever exercised by

10   man over man...."

Alexander Hamilton, "Philo Camillus no. 2," August 1795, in Harold C. Syrett, ed., *The Papers of Alexander Hamilton*, Vol. 19 (New York: Columbia University Press, 1961–present), 101–2.

James Madison, "Speech at the Constitutional Convention," June 6, 1787, in Max Farrand, ed., *Records of the Federal Convention of 1787*, Vol. 1 (New Haven, CT: Yale University Press, 1937), 135.

Notes on the State of Virginia Query xviii: Manners
Thomas Jefferson

The primary author of the Declaration of Independence, Thomas Jefferson was well aware that his ownership of slaves violated the principles he espoused.

1784

The particular customs and manners that may happen to be received in that State?

It is difficult to determine on the standard by which the manners of a nation may be tried, whether *catholic* or *particular*. It is more difficult for a native to bring to that standard the manners of his own nation, familiarized to him by habit. There must doubtless be an unhappy influence on the manners of our people produced by the existence of slavery among us. The whole commerce 5
between master and slave is a perpetual exercise of the most boisterous passions, the most unremitting despotism on the one part, and degrading submissions on the other. Our children see this, and learn to imitate it; for man is an imitative animal. This quality is the germ of all education in him. From his cradle to his grave he is learning to do what he sees others do. If a parent could 10
find no motive either in his philanthropy or his self-love, for restraining the intemperance of passion towards his slave, it should always be a sufficient one that his child is present. But generally it is not sufficient. The parent storms, the child looks on, catches the lineaments of wrath, puts on the same airs in the circle of smaller slaves, gives a loose to the worst of passions, and thus nursed, 15
educated, and daily exercised in tyranny, cannot but be stamped by it with odious peculiarities. The man must be a prodigy who can retain his manners and morals undepraved by such circumstances. And with what execration should the statesman be loaded, who, permitting one half the citizens thus to trample on the rights of the other, transforms those into despots, and these 20

Thomas Jefferson, "Query XVIII: Manners," from *Notes on the State of Virginia,* in A.A. Lipscomb and A.E. Bergh, eds., *The Writings of Thomas Jefferson,* Vol. 2 (Washington, D.C.: Thomas Jefferson Memorial Association, 1907), 225–28.

into enemies, destroys the morals of the one part, and the *amor patriae* of the other. For if a slave can have a country in this world, it must be any other in preference to that in which he is born to live and labor for another; in which he must lock up the faculties of his nature, contribute as far as depends on

5   his individual endeavors to the evanishment of the human race, or entail his own miserable condition on the endless generations proceeding from him. With the morals of the people, their industry also is destroyed. For in a warm climate, no man will labor for himself who can make another labor for him. This is so true, that of the proprietors of slaves a very small proportion indeed

10   are ever seen to labor. And can the liberties of a nation be thought secure when we have removed their only firm basis, a conviction in the minds of the people that these liberties are of the gift of God? That they are not to be violated but with His wrath? Indeed I tremble for my country when I reflect that God is just; that his justice cannot sleep forever; that considering numbers, nature

15   and natural means only, a revolution of the wheel of fortune, an exchange of situation is among possible events; that it may become probable by supernatural interference! The Almighty has no attribute which can take side with us in such a contest. But it is impossible to be temperate and to pursue this subject through the various considerations of policy, of morals, of history

20   natural and civil. We must be contented to hope they will force their way into every one's mind. I think a change already perceptible, since the origin of the present revolution. The spirit of the master is abating, that of the slave rising from the dust, his condition mollifying, the way I hope preparing, under the auspices of heaven, for a total emancipation, and that this is disposed, in the

25   order of events, to be with the consent of the masters, rather than by their extirpation.

LETTER TO JOHN JAY
ALEXANDER HAMILTON

Alexander Hamilton, a founder of the New York Manumission Society, writes to John Jay, a co-founder of the Society and then-president of Congress, arguing that slaves should be allowed to fight for the American cause in the War for Independence, earning their "freedom with their muskets." Eventually, some 5,000 blacks served as soldiers in the war.

MARCH 14, 1779

DEAR SIR:

Colonel Laurens, who will have the honor of delivering you this letter, is on his way to South Carolina, on a project, which I think, in the present situation of affairs there, is a very good one and deserves every kind of support and encouragement. This is to raise two, three, or four battalions of 5 negroes; with the assistance of the government of that state, by contributions from the owners in proportion to the number they possess. If you should think proper to enter upon the subject with him, he will give you a detail of his plan. He wishes to have it recommended by Congress to the state; and, as an inducement, that they would engage to take those battalions into 10 Continental pay.

It appears to me, that an expedient of this kind, in the present state of Southern affairs, is the most rational, that can be adopted, and promises very important advantages. Indeed, I hardly see how a sufficient force can be collected in that quarter without it; and the enemy's operations there are 15 growing infinitely serious and formidable. I have not the least doubt, that the negroes will make very excellent soldiers, with proper management; and I will venture to pronounce, that they cannot be put in better hands than those of Mr. Laurens. He has all the zeal, intelligence, enterprise, and every other qualification requisite to succeed in such an undertaking. It is a 20

Alexander Hamilton, "To John Jay," March 14, 1779, in Harold C. Syrett, ed., *The Papers of Alexander Hamilton*, Vol. 2 (New York: Columbia University Press, 1961–present), 17–18.

maxim with some great military judges, that with sensible officers soldiers can hardly be too stupid; and on this principle it is thought that the Russians would make the best troops in the world, if they were under other officers than their own. The King of Prussia is among the number who maintain
5 this doctrine and has a very emphatical saying on the occasion, which I do not exactly recollect. I mention this, because I frequently hear it objected to the scheme of embodying negroes that they are too stupid to make soldiers. This is so far from appearing to me a valid objection that I think their want of cultivation (for their natural faculties are probably as good as ours) joined
10 to that habit of subordination which they acquire from a life of servitude, will make them sooner become soldiers than our White inhabitants. Let officers be men of sense and sentiment, and the nearer the soldiers approach to machines perhaps the better.

I foresee that this project will have to combat much opposition from prejudice
15 and self-interest. The contempt we have been taught to entertain for the blacks, makes us fancy many things that are founded neither in reason nor experience; and an unwillingness to part with property of so valuable a kind will furnish a thousand arguments to show the impracticability or pernicious tendency of a scheme which requires such a sacrifice. But it should be considered, that if
20 we do not make use of them in this way, the enemy probably will; and that the best way to counteract the temptations they will hold out will be to offer them ourselves. An essential part of the plan is to give them their freedom with their muskets. This will secure their fidelity, animate their courage, and I believe will have a good influence upon those who remain, by opening
25 a door to their emancipation. This circumstance, I confess, has no small weight in inducing me to wish the success of the project; for the dictates of humanity and true policy equally interest me in favor of this unfortunate class of men. . . .

FEDERALIST 54
JAMES MADISON

James Madison here gives voice to the understanding of the South regarding the three-fifths clause of the Constitution, which required that three-fifths of the slaves in each state be counted for purposes of representation. This clause had a strange history. Most Southerners argued that slaves should be counted as full persons for voting purposes, while Northerners opposed to slavery advocated that they not be counted at all. Here Madison's "Southerner" presents the compromise position with approval, but in the process admits much of its moral illogic.

FEBRUARY 12, 1788

THE APPORTIONMENT OF MEMBERS AMONG THE STATES

..."We subscribe to the doctrine," might one of our Southern brethren observe, "that representation relates more immediately to persons, and taxation more immediately to property, and we join in the application of this distinction to the case of our slaves. But we must deny the fact that slaves are considered merely as property, and in no respect whatever as persons. 5 The true state of the case is that they partake of both these qualities: being considered by our laws, in some respects, as persons, and in other respects as property. In being compelled to labor, not for himself, but for a master; in being vendible by one master to another master; and in being subject at all times to be restrained in his liberty and chastised in his body, by the capricious 10 will of another—the slave may appear to be degraded from the human rank, and classed with those irrational animals which fall under the legal denomination of property. In being protected, on the other hand, in his life and in his limbs, against the violence of all others, even the master of his labor and his liberty; and in being punishable himself for all violence committed against others—the 15

James Madison, "No. 54: The Apportionment of Members Among the States," in Clinton Rossiter, ed., *The Federalist Papers* (New York: Mentor, 1999), 334–35.

slave is no less evidently regarded by the law as a member of the society, not as a part of the irrational creation; as a moral person, not as a mere article of property. The federal Constitution, therefore, decides with great propriety on the case of our slaves, when it views them in the mixed character of persons and of property. This is in fact their true character. It is the character bestowed on them by the laws under which they live; and it will not be denied that these are the proper criterion; because it is only under the pretext that the laws have transformed the Negroes into subjects of property that a place is disputed them in the computation of numbers; and it is admitted that if the laws were to restore the rights which have been taken away, the Negroes could no longer be refused an equal share of representation with the other inhabitants....

LETTER TO THE ENGLISH ANTI-SLAVERY SOCIETY
JOHN JAY (1745–1829)

In 1777, John Jay's first attempt to abolish slavery in New York failed. In 1788, the state banned the importation of slaves. By 1799, the New York Manumission Society advocated for a bill, signed into law that year by then-Governor Jay, specifying that as of July 4, all children born to slave parents would be freed by a certain age. Less than a year after the Constitutional Convention, Jay addresses concerns from his British counterparts that anti-slavery progress in America is too slow.

JUNE 1788

GENTLEMEN:

Our society has been favored with your letter of the 1st of May last, and are happy that efforts so honorable to the nation are making in your country to promote the cause of justice and humanity relative to the Africans. That they who know the value of liberty, and are blessed with the enjoyment of it, ought not to subject others to slavery, is, like most other moral precepts, more generally 5 admitted in theory than observed in practice. This will continue to be too much the case while men are impelled to action by their passions rather than their reason, and while they are more solicitous to acquire wealth than to do as they would be done by. Hence it is that India and Africa experience unmerited oppression from nations which have been long distinguished by their attachment 10 to their civil and religious liberties, but who have expended not much less blood and treasure in violating the rights of others than in defending their own. The United States are far from being irreproachable in this respect. It undoubtedly is very inconsistent with their declarations on the subject of human rights to permit a single slave to be found within their jurisdiction, and we confess the 15 justice of your strictures on that head.

Permit us, however, to observe, that although consequences ought not to deter us from doing what is right, yet that it is not easy to persuade men in general

John Jay, "Jay to the English Anti-Slavery Society," June 21, 1788, in Henry Phelps Johnston, ed., *The Correspondence and Public Papers of John Jay*, Vol. 3 (New York: Da Capo Press, 1971), 340–44.

to act on that magnanimous and disinterested principle. It is well known that errors, either in opinion or practice, long entertained or indulged, are difficult to eradicate, and particularly so when they have become, as it were, incorporated in the civil institutions and domestic economy of a whole people.

5   Prior to the great revolution, the great majority or rather the great body of our people had been so long accustomed to the practice and convenience of having slaves, that very few among them even doubted the propriety and rectitude of it. Some liberal and conscientious men had, indeed, by their conduct and writings, drawn the lawfulness of slavery into question, and they made converts to that

10 opinion; but the number of those converts compared with the people at large was then very inconsiderable. Their doctrines prevailed by almost insensible degrees, and was like the little lump of leaven which was put into three measures of meal: even at this day, the whole mass is far from being leavened, though we have good reason to hope and to believe that if the natural operations of truth

15 are constantly watched and assisted, but not forced and precipitated, that end we all aim at will finally be attained in this country.

The Convention which formed and recommended the new Constitution had an arduous task to perform, especially as local interests, and in some measure local prejudices, were to be accommodated. Several of the States conceived

20 that restraints on slavery might be too rapid to consist with their particular circumstances; and the importance of union rendered it necessary that their wishes on that head should, in some degree, be gratified.

It gives us pleasure to inform you, that a disposition favorable to our views and wishes prevails more and more, and that it has already had an influence on our

25 laws. When it is considered how many of the legislators in the different States are proprietors of slaves, and what opinions and prejudices they have imbibed on the subject from their infancy, a sudden and total stop to this species of oppression is not to be expected.

We will cheerfully cooperate with you in endeavoring to procure advocates for

30 the same cause in other countries, and perfectly approve and commend your establishing a correspondence in France. It appears to have produced the desired effect; for Mons. De Varville, the secretary of a society for the like benevolent purpose at Paris, is now here, and comes instructed to establish a correspondence with us, and to collect such information as may promote our common views.

35 He delivered to our society an extract from the minutes of your proceedings, dated 8th of April last, recommending him to our attention, and upon that occasion they passed the resolutions of which the enclosed are copies.

We are much obliged by the pamphlets enclosed with your letter, and shall constantly make such communications to you as may appear to us interesting.

By a report of the committee for superintending the school we have established in this city for the education of negro children, we find that proper attention is paid to it, and that scholars are now taught in it. By the laws of this State, masters may now liberate healthy slaves of a proper age without giving security that they shall not become a parish charge; and the exportation as well as importation of them is prohibited. The State has also manumitted such as became its property by confiscation; and we have reason to expect that the maxim, that every man, of whatever color, is to be presumed to be free until the contrary be shown, will prevail in our courts of justice. Manumissions daily become more common among us; and the treatment which slaves in general meet with in this State is very little different from that of other servants....

LETTER TO HENRI GREGOIRE
THOMAS JEFFERSON

The Constitution specified that Congress could not prohibit the importation of slaves until 1808. President Jefferson signed the bill to bring about this prohibition in March 1807 and it went into effect on January 1, 1808. Writing here a year later, he maintains hopes for an end to slavery itself.

FEBRUARY 25, 1809

SIR:

I have received the favor of your letter of August 17th, and with it the volume you were so kind as to send me on the "Literature of Negroes." Be assured that no person living wishes more sincerely than I do, to see a complete refutation of the doubts I have myself entertained and expressed on the grade of understanding allotted to them by nature, and to find that in this respect they are on   5
a par with ourselves. My doubts were the result of personal observation on the limited sphere of my own State, where the opportunities for the development of their genius were not favorable, and those of exercising it still less so. I expressed them therefore with great hesitation; but whatever be their degree of talent it is no measure of their rights. Because Sir Isaac Newton was superior to others in   10
understanding, he was not therefore lord of the person or property of others. On this subject they are gaining daily in the opinions of nations, and hopeful advances are making towards their re-establishment on an equal footing with the other colors of the human family. I pray you therefore to accept my thanks for the many instances you have enabled me to observe of respectable intel-   15
ligence in that race of men, which cannot fail to have effect in hastening the day of their relief; and to be assured of the sentiments of high and just esteem and consideration which I tender to yourself with all sincerity.

Thomas Jefferson, "To Henri Gregoire," February 25, 1809, in Paul Leicester Ford, ed., *The Works of Thomas Jefferson*, Vol. 9 (New York: G. P. Putnam's Sons, 1904–5), 246–47.

Speech on Reception of Abolition Petitions
John C. Calhoun (1782–1850)

The number of slaves in America had grown from 700,000 in 1790 to over two million in 1830. Northern opposition to slavery was growing in the 1820s and 1830s, as it became clear that hopes for a withering away of slavery were unrealistic. This elicited a similarly strong response from slavery's foremost advocates. In 1836, the House of Representatives passed a "gag rule" that tabled abolition discussions. Here, Senator John C. Calhoun champions a similar resolution in the Senate. His argument became the linchpin of what came to be called the "positive good" school of thought regarding slavery, one all but absent from the debates of the two previous generations.

FEBRUARY 6, 1837

… I do not belong, said Mr. Calhoun, to the school which holds that aggression is to be met by concession. Mine is the opposite creed, which teaches that encroachments must be met at the beginning, and that those who act on the opposite principle are prepared to become slaves. In this case, in particular, I hold concession or compromise to be fatal. If we concede an inch, concession would follow concession—compromise would follow compromise, until our ranks would be so broken that effectual resistance would be impossible. We must meet the enemy on the frontier, with a fixed determination of maintaining our position at every hazard. Consent to receive these insulting petitions, and the next demand will be that they be referred to a committee in order that they may be deliberated and acted upon. At the last session we were modestly asked to receive them, simply to lay them on the table, without any view to ulterior action…. I then said, that the next step would be to refer the petition to a committee, and I already see indications that such is now the intention. If we yield, that will be followed by another, and we will thus proceed, step by step, to the final consummation of the object of these petitions. We are now told

John C. Calhoun, "Speech on the Reception of Abolition Petitions," February 6, 1837, in Richard Kenner Cralle, ed., *The Works of John C. Calhoun,* Vol. 2 (New York: D. Appleton & Co., 1888), 626–27, 628–33.

that the most effectual mode of arresting the progress of abolition is, to reason
it down; and with this view it is urged that the petitions ought to be referred to
a committee. That is the very ground which was taken at the last session in the
other House, but instead of arresting its progress it has since advanced more
5   rapidly than ever. The most unquestionable right may be rendered doubtful,
if once admitted to be a subject of controversy, and that would be the case in
the present instance. The subject is beyond the jurisdiction of Congress—they
have no right to touch it in any shape or form, or to make it the subject of
deliberation or discussion....

10   As widely as this incendiary spirit has spread, it has not yet infected this body,
or the great mass of the intelligent and business portion of the North; but
unless it be speedily stopped, it will spread and work upwards till it brings
the two great sections of the Union into deadly conflict. This is not a new
impression with me. Several years since, in a discussion with one of the Senators
15   from Massachusetts (Mr. Webster), before this fell spirit had showed itself, I
then predicted that the doctrine of the proclamation and the Force Bill,—that
this Government had a right, in the last resort, to determine the extent of its
own powers, and enforce its decision at the point of the bayonet, which was
so warmly maintained by that Senator, would at no distant day arouse the
20   dormant spirit of abolitionism. I told him that the doctrine was tantamount
to the assumption of unlimited power on the part of the Government, and
that such would be the impression on the public mind in a large portion of the
Union. The consequence would be inevitable. A large portion of the Northern
States believed slavery to be a sin, and would consider it as an obligation of
25   conscience to abolish it if they should feel themselves in any degree responsible
for its continuance,—and that this doctrine would necessarily lead to the belief
of such responsibility. I then predicted that it would commence as it has with
this fanatical portion of society, and that they would begin their operations
on the ignorant, the weak, the young, and the thoughtless,—and gradually
30   extend upwards till they would become strong enough to obtain political
control, when he and others holding the highest stations in society, would,
however reluctant, be compelled to yield to their doctrines, or be driven into
obscurity. But four years have since elapsed, and all this is already in a course
of regular fulfilment.

35   Standing at the point of time at which we have now arrived, it will not be more
difficult to trace the course of future events now than it was then. They who
imagine that the spirit now abroad in the North, will die away of itself without
a shock or convulsion, have formed a very inadequate conception of its real
character; it will continue to rise and spread, unless prompt and efficient

measures to stay its progress be adopted. Already it has taken possession of the pulpit, of the schools, and, to a considerable extent, of the press; those great instruments by which the mind of the rising generation will be formed.

However sound the great body of the non-slaveholding States are at present, in the course of a few years they will be succeeded by those who will have been   5 taught to hate the people and institutions of nearly one-half of this Union, with a hatred more deadly than one hostile nation ever entertained towards another. It is easy to see the end. By the necessary course of events, if left to themselves, we must become, finally, two people. It is impossible under the deadly hatred which must spring up between the two great sections, if the present causes   10 are permitted to operate unchecked, that we should continue under the same political system. The conflicting elements would burst the Union asunder, powerful as are the links which hold it together. Abolition and the Union cannot co-exist. As the friend of the Union I openly proclaim it,—and the sooner it is known the better. The former may now be controlled, but in a   15 short time it will be beyond the power of man to arrest the course of events. We of the South will not, cannot surrender our institutions. To maintain the existing relations between the two races, inhabiting that section of the Union, is indispensable to the peace and happiness of both. It cannot be subverted without drenching the country in blood, and extirpating one or the other of   20 the races.... But let me not be understood as admitting, even by implication, that the existing relations between the two races in the slaveholding States is an evil:—far otherwise; I hold it to be a good, as it has thus far proved itself to be to both, and will continue to prove so if not disturbed by the fell spirit of abolition. I appeal to facts. Never before has the black race of Central Africa,   25 from the dawn of history to the present day, attained a condition so civilized and so improved, not only physically, but morally and intellectually....

In the mean time, the white or European race has not degenerated. It has kept pace with its brethren in other sections of the Union where slavery does not exist. It is odious to make comparison; but I appeal to all sides whether the   30 South is not equal in virtue, intelligence, patriotism, courage, disinterestedness, and all the high qualities which adorn our nature....

But I take higher ground. I hold that in the present state of civilization, where two races of different origin, and distinguished by color, and other physical differences, as well as intellectual, are brought together, the relation now   35 existing in the slaveholding States between the two, is, instead of an evil, a good—a positive good. I feel myself called upon to speak freely upon the subject where the honor and interests of those I represent are involved. I hold then, that there never has yet existed a wealthy and civilized society in which

one portion of the community did not, in point of fact, live on the labor of
the other. Broad and general as is this assertion, it is fully borne out by history.
This is not the proper occasion, but if it were, it would not be difficult to trace
the various devices by which the wealth of all civilized communities has been
5   so unequally divided, and to show by what means so small a share has been
allotted to those by whose labor it was produced, and so large a share given
to the non-producing classes. The devices are almost innumerable, from the
brute force and gross superstition of ancient times, to the subtle and artful
fiscal contrivances of modern. I might well challenge a comparison between
10   them and the more direct, simple, and patriarchal mode by which the labor of
the African race is, among us, commanded by the European. I may say with
truth, that in few countries so much is left to the share of the laborer, and so
little exacted from him, or where there is more kind attention paid to him in
sickness or infirmities of age. Compare his condition with the tenants of the
15   poor houses in the more civilized portions of Europe—look at the sick, and
the old and infirm slave, on one hand, in the midst of his family and friends,
under the kind superintending care of his master and mistress, and compare it
with the forlorn and wretched condition of the pauper in the poor house. But
I will not dwell on this aspect of the question; I turn to the political; and here
20   I fearlessly assert that the existing relation between the two races in the South,
against which these blind fanatics are waging war, forms the most solid and
durable foundation on which to rear free and stable political institutions. It is
useless to disguise the fact. There is and always has been in an advanced stage
of wealth and civilization, a conflict between labor and capital. The condition
25   of society in the South exempts us from the disorders and dangers resulting
from this conflict; and which explains why it is that the political condition of
the slaveholding States has been so much more stable and quiet than that of
the North....

Surrounded as the slaveholding States are with such imminent perils, I rejoice
30   to think that our means of defense are ample, if we shall prove to have the
intelligence and spirit to see and apply them before it is too late. All we want
is concert, to lay aside all party differences, and unite with zeal and energy in
repelling approaching dangers. Let there be concert of action, and we shall
find ample means of security without resorting to secession or disunion. I
35   speak with full knowledge and a thorough examination of the subject, and for
one, see my way clearly.... I dare not hope that any thing I can say will arouse
the South to a due sense of danger; I fear it is beyond the power of mortal voice
to awaken it in time from the fatal security into which it has fallen.

Speech on the Oregon Bill
John C. Calhoun

Even worse than political errors such as the Northwest Ordinance, John C. Calhoun argues here, are theoretical errors, chief of which is the equality principle of the Declaration of Independence.

JUNE 27, 1848

... I turn now to my friends of the South, and ask: What are you prepared to do? If neither the barriers of the constitution nor the high sense of right and justice should prove sufficient to protect you, are you prepared to sink down into a state of acknowledged inferiority; to be stripped of your dignity of equals among equals, and be deprived of your equality of rights in this federal partnership of States? If so, you are woefully degenerated from your sires, and will well deserve to change condition with your slaves;—but if not, prepare to meet the issue. The time is at hand, if the question should not be speedily settled, when the South must rise up, and bravely defend herself, or sink down into base and acknowledged inferiority; and it is because I clearly perceive that this period is favorable for settling it, if it is ever to be settled, that I am in favor of pressing the question now to a decision—not because I have any desire whatever to embarrass either party in reference to the Presidential election. At no other period could the two great parties into which the country is divided be made to see and feel so clearly and intensely the embarrassment and danger caused by the question. Indeed, they must be blind not to perceive that there is a power in action that must burst asunder the ties that bind them together, strong as they are, unless it should be speedily settled. Now is the time, if ever. Cast your eyes to the North, and mark what is going on there; reflect on the tendency of events for the last three years in reference to this the most vital of all questions, and you must see that no time should be lost.

I am thus brought to the question, How can the question be settled? It can, in my opinion, be finally and permanently adjusted but one way,—and that

John C. Calhoun, "On the Oregon Bill," June 27, 1848, in Richard Kenner Cralle, ed., *The Works of John C. Calhoun,* Vol. 4 (New York: D. Appleton & Co., 1888), 503–12.

is on the high principles of justice and the constitution. Fear not to leave it to them. The less you do the better. If the North and South cannot stand together on their broad and solid foundation, there is none other on which they can. If the obligations of the constitution and justice be too feeble to
5   command the respect of the North, how can the South expect that she will regard the far more feeble obligations of an act of Congress? Nor should the North fear that, by leaving it where justice and the constitution leave it, she would be excluded from her full share of the territories. In my opinion, if it be left there, climate, soil, and other circumstances would fix the line between
10 the slaveholding and non-slaveholding States in about 36° 30'. It may zigzag a little, to accommodate itself to circumstances—sometimes passing to the north, and at others passing to the south of it; but that would matter little, and would be more satisfactory to all, and tend less to alienation between the two great sections, than a rigid, straight, artificial line, prescribed by an act of
15 Congress.

And here, let me say to Senators form the North;—you make a great mistake in supposing that the portion which might fall to the south of whatever line might be drawn, if left to soil, and climate, and circumstances to determine, would be closed to the white labor of the North, because it could not mingle
20 with slave labor without degradation. The fact is not so. There is no part of the world were agricultural, mechanical, and other descriptions of labor are more respected than in the South, with the exception of two descriptions of employment—that of menial and body servants. No Southern man—not the poorest or the lowest—will, under any circumstance, submit to perform either
25 of them. He has too much pride for that, and I rejoice that he has. They are unsuited to the spirit of a freeman. But the man who would spurn them feels not the least degradation to work in the same field with his slave; or to be employed to work with them in the same field or in any mechanical operation; and, when so employed, they claim the right,—and are admitted,
30 in the country portion of the South—of sitting at the table of their employers. Can as much, on the score of equality, be said of the North? With us the two great divisions of society are not the rich and poor, but white and black; and all the former, the poor as well as the rich, belong to the upper class, and are respected and treated as equals, if honest and industrious; and hence have a
35 position and pride of character of which neither poverty nor misfortune can deprive them.

But I go further, and hold that justice and the constitution are the easiest and safest guard on which the question can be settled, regarded in reference to party. It may be settled on that ground simply by non-action—by leaving the territories free and open to the emigration of all the world, so long as they continue so,—and when they become States, to adopt whatever constitution they please, with the single restriction, to be republican, in order to their admission into the Union. If a party cannot safely take this broad and solid position and successfully maintain it, what other can it take and maintain?   5 If it cannot maintain itself by an appeal to the great principles of justice, the constitution, and self-government, to what other, sufficiently strong to uphold them in public opinion, can they appeal? I greatly mistake the character of the people of this Union, if such an appeal would not prove successful, if either party should have the magnanimity to step forward, and boldly make it. It   10 would, in my opinion, be received with shouts of approbation by the patriotic and intelligent in every quarter. There is a deep feeling pervading the country that the Union and our political institutions are in danger, which such a course would dispel, and spread joy over the land.

Now is the time to take the step, and bring about a result so devoutly to be   15 wished. I have believed, from the beginning, that this was the only question sufficiently potent to dissolve the Union, and subvert our system of government; and that the sooner it was met and settled, the safer and better for all. I have never doubted but that, if permitted to progress beyond a certain point, its settlement would become impossible, and am under deep conviction that it   20 is now rapidly approaching it,—and that if it is ever to be averted, it must be done speedily. In uttering these opinions I look to the whole. If I speak earnestly, it is to save and protect all. As deep as is the stake of the South in the Union and our political institutions, it is not deeper than that of the North. We shall be as well prepared and as capable of meeting whatever may come,   25 as you.

Now, let me say, Senators, if our Union and system of government are doomed to perish, and we to share the fate of so many great people who have gone before us, the historian, who, in some future day, may record the events ending in so calamitous a result, will devote his first chapter to the ordinance of 1787,   30 lauded as it and its authors have been, as the first of that series which led to it. His next chapter will be devoted to the Missouri compromise, and the next to the present agitation. Whether there will be another beyond, I know not. It will depend on what we may do.

If he should possess a philosophical turn of mind, and be disposed to look   35 to more remote and recondite causes, he will trace it to a proposition which originated in a hypothetical truism, but which, as now expressed and now understood, is the most false and dangerous of all political errors. The proposition to which I allude, has become an axiom in the minds of a vast

many on both sides of the Atlantic, and is repeated daily from tongue to tongue, as an established and incontrovertible truth; it is,—that "all men are born free and equal." I am not afraid to attack error, however deeply it may be intrenched, or however widely extended, whenever it becomes my duty to do
5   so, as I believe it to be on this subject and occasion.

Taking the proposition literally (it is in that sense it is understood), there is not a word of truth in it. It begins with "all men are born," which is utterly untrue. Men are not born. Infants are born. They grow to be men. And concludes with asserting that they are born "free and equal," which is not less false.
10   They are not born free. While infants they are incapable of freedom, being destitute alike of the capacity of thinking and acting, without which there can be no freedom. Besides, they are necessarily born subject to their parents, and remain so among all people, savage and civilized, until the development of their intellect and physical capacity enables them to take care of themselves.
15   They grow to all the freedom of which the condition in which they were born permits, by growing to be men. Nor is it less false that they are born "equal." They are not so in any sense in which it can be regarded; and thus, as I have asserted, there is not a word of truth in the whole proposition, as expressed and generally understood.

20   If we trace it back, we shall find the proposition differently expressed in the Declaration of Independence. That asserts that "all men are created equal." The form of expression, though less dangerous, is not less erroneous. All men are not created. According to the Bible, only two—a man and a woman—ever were—and of these one was pronounced subordinate to the other. All others
25   have come into the world by being born, and in no sense, as I have shown, either free or equal. But this form of expression being less striking and popular, has given way to the present, and under the authority of a document put forth on so great an occasion, and leading to such important consequences, has spread far and wide, and fixed itself deeply in the public mind. It was
30   inserted in our Declaration of Independence without any necessity. It made no necessary part of our justification in separating from the parent country, and declaring ourselves independent. Breach of our chartered privileges, and lawless encroachment on our acknowledged and well-established rights by the parent country, were the real causes,—and of themselves sufficient, without resorting
35   to any other, to justify the step. Nor had it any weight in constructing the governments which were substituted in the place of the colonial. They were formed of the old materials and on practical and well-established principles, borrowed for the most part from our own experience and that of the country from which we sprang.

If the proposition be traced still further back, it will be found to have been adopted from certain writers in government who had attained much celebrity in the early settlement of these States, and with whose writings all the prominent actors in our revolution were familiar. Among these, Locke and Sydney were prominent. But they expressed it very differently. According to their expression, "all men in the state of nature were free and equal." From this the others were derived; and it was this to which I referred when I called it a hypothetical truism;—to understand why, will require some explanation.

Man, for the purpose of reasoning, may be regarded in three different states: in a state of individuality; that is, living by himself apart from the rest of his species. In the social; that is, living in society, associated with others of his species. And in the political; that is, living under government. We may reason as to what would be his rights and duties in either, without taking into consideration whether he could exist in it or not. It is certain, that in the first, the very supposition that he lived apart and separated from all others would make him free and equal. No one in such a state could have the right to command or control another. Every man would be his own master, and might do just as he pleased. But it is equally clear, that man cannot exist in such a state; that he is by nature social, and that society is necessary, not only to the proper development of all his faculties, moral and intellectual, but to the very existence of his race. Such being the case, the state is a purely hypothetical one; and when we say all men are free and equal in it, we announce a mere hypothetical truism; that is, a truism resting on a mere supposed stake that cannot exist, and of course one of little or no practical value.

But to call it a state of nature was a great misnomer, and has led to dangerous errors; for that cannot justly be called a state of nature which is so opposed to the constitution of man as to be inconsistent with the existence of his race and the development of the high faculties, mental and moral, with which he is endowed by his Creator.

Nor is the social state of itself his natural state; for society can no more exist without government, in one form or another, than man without society. It is the political, then, which includes the social, that is his natural state. It is the one for which his Creator formed him,—into which he is impelled irresistibly,—and in which only his race can exist and all its faculties be fully developed.

Such being the case, it follows that any, the worst form of government, is better than anarchy; and that individual liberty, or freedom, must be subordinate to whatever power may be necessary to protect society against anarchy within

or destruction from without; for the safety and well-being of society is as paramount to individual liberty, as the safety and well-being of the race is to that of individuals; and in the same proportion the power necessary for the safety of society is paramount to individual liberty. On the contrary, government has
5   no right to control individual liberty beyond what is necessary to the safety and well-being of society. Such is the boundary which separates the power of government and the liberty of the citizen or subject in the political state, which, as I have shown, is the natural state of man—the only one in which his race can exist, and the one in which he is born, lives, and dies.

10 It follows from this that all the quantum of power on the part of the government, and of liberty on that of individuals, instead of being equal in all cases, must necessarily be very unequal among different people, according to their different conditions. For just in proportion as a people are ignorant, stupid, debased, corrupt, exposed to violence within, and danger from without,
15 the power necessary for government to possess, in order to preserve society against anarchy and destruction, becomes greater and greater, and individual liberty less and less, until the lowest condition is reached,—when absolute and despotic power becomes necessary on the part of the government, and individual liberty extinct. So, on the contrary, just as a people rise in the scale
20 of intelligence, virtue, and patriotism, and the more perfectly they become acquainted with the nature of government, the ends for which it was ordered, and how it ought to be administered, and the less the tendency to violence and disorder within, and danger from abroad,—the power necessary for government becomes less and less, and individual liberty greater and greater.
25 Instead, then, of all men having the same right to liberty and equality, as is claimed by those who hold that they are all born free and equal, liberty is the noble and highest reward bestowed on mental and moral development, combined with favorable circumstances. Instead, then, of liberty and equality being born with men,—instead of all men and all classes and descriptions
30 being equally entitled to them, they are high prizes to be won, and are in their most perfect state, not only the highest reward that can be bestowed on our race, but the most difficult to be won,—and when won, the most difficult to be preserved.

They have been made vastly more so by the dangerous error I have attempted
35 to expose,—that all men are born free and equal,—as if those high qualities belonged to man without effort to acquire them, and to all equally alike, regardless of their intellectual and moral condition. The attempt to carry into practice this, the most dangerous of all political errors, and to bestow on all,— without regard to their fitness either to acquire or maintain liberty,—that

unbounded and individual liberty supposed to belong to man in the hypothetical and misnamed state of nature, has done more to retard the cause of liberty and civilization, and is doing more at present, than all other causes combined. While it is powerful to pull down governments, it is still more powerful to prevent their construction on proper principles. It is the leading cause among those which have placed Europe in its present anarchical condition, and which mainly stands in the way of reconstructing good governments in the place of those which have been overthrown,—threatening thereby the quarter of the globe most advanced in progress and civilization with hopeless anarchy,—to be followed by military despotism. Nor are we exempt from its disorganizing effects. We now begin to experience the danger of admitting so great an error to have a place in the declaration of our independence. For a long time it lay dormant; but in the process of time it began to germinate, and produce its poisonous fruits. It had strong hold on the mind of Mr. Jefferson, the author of that document, which caused him to take an utterly false view of the subordinate relation of the black to the white race in the South; and to hold, in consequence, that the latter, though utterly unqualified to possess liberty, were as fully entitled to both liberty and equality as the former; and that to deprive them of it was unjust and immoral. To this error, his proposition to exclude slavery from the territory northwest of the Ohio may be traced,—and to that of the ordinance of 1787,—and through it the deep and dangerous agitation which now threatens to engulf, and will certainly engulf, if not speedily settled, our political institutions, and involve the country in countless woes.

LETTER TO JOHN HOLMES
THOMAS JEFFERSON

*Awakened to the looming crisis over slavery by the Missouri Compromise,
Thomas Jefferson foresees in this letter that the Compromise was far from
the final word on the matter.*

APRIL 22, 1820

I thank you, dear Sir, for the copy you have been so kind as to send me of the
letter to your constituents on the Missouri question. It is a perfect justification
to them. I had for a long time ceased to read newspapers, or pay any attention to
public affairs, confident they were in good hands, and content to be a passenger
in our bark to the shore from which I am not distant. But this momentous   5
question, like a fire bell in the night, awakened and filled me with terror. I
considered it at once as the knell of the Union. It is hushed, indeed, for the
moment. But this is a reprieve only, not a final sentence. A geographical line,
coinciding with a marked principle, moral and political, once conceived and
held up to the angry passions of men, will never be obliterated; and every new   10
irritation will mark it deeper and deeper. I can say, with conscious truth, that
there is not a man on earth who would sacrifice more than I would to relieve
us from this heavy reproach, in any *practicable* way. The cession of that kind
of property, for so it is misnamed, is a bagatelle which would not cost me a
second thought, if, in that way, a general emancipation and *expatriation* could   15
be effected; and gradually, and with due sacrifices, I think it might be. But as
it is, we have the wolf by the ears, and we can neither hold him, nor safely let
him go. Justice is in one scale, and self-preservation in the other. Of one thing
I am certain, that as the passage of slaves from one State to another, would not
make a slave of a single human being who would not be so without it, so their   20
diffusion over a greater surface would make them individually happier, and
proportionally facilitate the accomplishment of their emancipation, by dividing
the burden on a greater number of coadjutors. An abstinence too, from this act

---

Thomas Jefferson, "To John Holmes," April 22, 1820, in Paul Leicester Ford, ed., *The Works of
Thomas Jefferson,* Vol. 10 (New York: G. P. Putnam's Sons, 1904–5), 157–58.

of power, would remove the jealousy excited by the undertaking of Congress to regulate the condition of the different descriptions of men composing a State. This certainly is the exclusive right of every State, which nothing in the constitution has taken from them and given to the General Government.
5   Could Congress, for example, say, that the non-freemen of Connecticut shall be freemen, or that they shall not emigrate into any other State?

I regret that I am now to die in the belief, that the useless sacrifice of themselves by the generation of 1776, to acquire self-government and happiness to their country, is to be thrown away by the unwise and unworthy passions of their
10   sons, and that my only consolation is to be, that I live not to weep over it. If they would but dispassionately weigh the blessings they will throw away, against an abstract principle more likely to be effected by union than by scission, they would pause before they would perpetrate this act of suicide on themselves, and of treason against the hopes of the world. To yourself, as the faithful advocate
15   of the Union, I tender the offering of my high esteem and respect.

LETTER TO EDWARD EVERETT
JAMES MADISON

In this 1830 response to Massachusetts statesman Edward Everett, James Madison maintains that a state does not possess the authority to strike down as unconstitutional an act of the federal government. The contrary doctrine, known as nullification, would take on later significance.

AUGUST 28, 1830

I have duly received your letter in which you refer to the "nullifying doctrine," advocated as a constitutional right by some of our distinguished fellow citizens; and to the proceedings of the Virginia Legislature in 98 and 99, as appealed to in behalf of that doctrine; and you express a wish for my ideas on those subjects.

I am aware of the delicacy of the task in some respects; and the difficulty in   5
every respect of doing full justice to it. But having in more than one instance complied with a like request from other friendly quarters, I do not decline a sketch of the views which I have been led to take of the doctrine in question, as well as some others connected with them; and of the grounds from which it appears that the proceedings of Virginia have been misconceived by those   10
who have appealed to them. In order to understand the true character of the Constitution of the United States the error, not uncommon, must be avoided of viewing it through the medium either of a consolidated Government or of a confederated Government whilst it is neither the one nor the other, but a mixture of both. And having in no model the similitudes and analogies applicable to   15
other systems of Government it must more than any other be its own interpreter, according to its text and *the facts of the case.*

From these it will be seen that the characteristic peculiarities of the Constitution are 1. The mode of its formation, 2. The division of the supreme powers of Government between the States in their united capacity and the States in their   20
individual capacities.

James Madison, "Letter to Edward Everett," August 28, 1830, in Ralph Ketcham, ed., *Selected Writings of James Madison* (Indianapolis, IN: Hackett, 2006), 340–48.

1. It was formed, not by the Governments of the component States, as the Federal Government for which it was substituted was formed; nor was it formed by a majority of the people of the United States as a single community in the manner of a consolidated Government.

5   It was formed by the States—that is by the people in each of the States, acting in their highest sovereign capacity; and formed, consequently by the same authority which formed the State Constitutions.

Being thus derived from the same source as the Constitutions of the States, it has within each State, the same authority as the Constitution of the State; and is as much a Constitution, in the strict sense of the term, within its prescribed sphere, as the Constitutions of the States are within their respective spheres; but with this obvious and essential difference, that being a compact among the States in their highest sovereign capacity, and constituting the people thereof one people for certain purposes, it cannot be altered or annulled at the will of the States individually, as the Constitution of a State may be at its individual will.

2. And that it divides the supreme powers of Government between the Government of the United States, and the Governments of the individual States, is stamped on the face of the instrument; the powers of war and of taxation, of commerce and of treaties, and other enumerated powers vested in the Government of the United States being of as high and sovereign a character as any of the powers reserved to the State Governments

Nor is the Government of the United States created by the Constitution, less a Government in the strict sense of the term, within the sphere of its powers, than the Governments created by the constitutions of the States are within their several spheres. It is like them organized into Legislative, Executive, and Judiciary Departments. It operates like them, directly on persons and things. And, like them, it has at command a physical force for executing the powers committed to it. The concurrent operation in certain cases is one of the features marking the peculiarity of the system.

Between these different constitutional Governments—the one operating in all the States, the others operating separately in each, with the aggregate powers of Government divided between them, it could not escape attention that controversies would arise concerning the boundaries of jurisdiction; and that some provision ought to be made for such occurrences. A political system that does not provide for a peaceable and authoritative termination of occurring controversies, would not be more than the shadow of a Government; the object and end of a real Government being the substitution of law and order for uncertainty confusion, and violence.

That to have left a final decision in such cases to each of the States, then thirteen and already twenty-four, could not fail to make the Constitution and laws of the United States different in different States was obvious; and not less obvious, that this diversity of independent decisions, must altogether distract the Government of the Union and speedily put an end to the Union itself. A uniform authority   5
of the laws, is in itself a vital principle. Some of the most important laws could not be partially executed. They must be executed in all the States or they could be duly executed in none. An impost or an excise, for example, if not in force in some States, would be defeated in others. It is well known that this was among the lessons of experience which had a primary influence in bringing about the   10
existing Constitution. A loss of its general authority would moreover revive the exasperating questions between the States holding ports for foreign commerce and the adjoining States without them, to which are now added all the inland States necessarily carrying on their foreign commerce through other States.

To have made the decisions under the authority of the individual States, co-   15
ordinate in all cases with decisions under the authority of the United States would unavoidably produce collisions incompatible with the peace of society, and with that regular and efficient administration which is the essence of free Governments. Scenes could not be avoided in which a ministerial officer of the United States and the correspondent officer of an individual State, would have   20
rencounters in executing conflicting decrees, the result of which would depend on the comparative force of the local posse attending them, and that a casualty depending on the political opinions and party feelings in different States.

To have referred every clashing decision under the two authorities for a final decision to the States as parties to the Constitution, would be attended with   25
delays, with inconveniences, and with expenses amounting to a prohibition of the expedient, not to mention its tendency to impair the salutary veneration for a system requiring such frequent interpositions, nor the delicate questions which might present themselves as to the form of stating the appeal, and as to the Quorum for deciding it.   30

To have trusted to negotiation, for adjusting disputes between the Government of the United States and the State Governments as between independent and separate sovereignties, would have lost sight altogether of a Constitution and Government for the Union; and opened a direct road from a failure of that resort, to the ultima ratio between nations wholly independent of and alien   35
to each other. If the idea had its origin in the process of adjustment between separate branches of the same Government the analogy entirely fails. In the case of disputes between independent parts of the same Government neither part being able to consummate its will, nor the Governor to proceed without a

concurrence of the parts, necessity brings about an accommodation. In disputes between a State Government and the Government of the United States the case is practically as well as theoretically different; each party possessing all the Departments of an organized Government, Legislative, Executive, and Judiciary;
5   and having each a physical force to support its pretensions. Although the issue of negotiation might sometimes avoid this extremity, how often would it happen among so many States, that an unaccommodating spirit in some would render that resource unavailing? A contrary supposition would not accord with a knowledge of human nature or the evidence of our own political history.

10   The Constitution, not relying on any of the preceding modifications for its safe and successful operation, has expressly declared on the one hand; 1. "That the Constitution, and the laws made in pursuance thereof, and all Treaties made under the authority of the United States shall be the supreme law of the land; 2. That the judges of every State shall be bound thereby, anything in the
15   Constitution or laws of any State to the contrary notwithstanding; 3. That the judicial power of the United States shall extend to all cases in law and equity arising under the Constitution, the laws of the United States and Treaties made under their authority etc."

On the other hand, as a security of the rights and powers of the States in their
20   individual capacities, against an undue preponderance of the powers granted to the Government over them in their united capacity, the Constitution has relied on, 1. The responsibility of the Senators and Representatives in the Legislature of the United States to the Legislatures and people of the States. 2. The responsibility of the President to the people of the United States; and 3. The liability of the
25   Executive and Judiciary functionaries of the United States to impeachment by the Representatives of the people of the States, in one branch of the Legislature of the United States and trial by the Representatives of the States, in the other branch; the State functionaries, Legislative, Executive, and Judiciary, being at the same time in their appointment and responsibility, altogether independent of the
30   agency or authority of the United States.

How far this structure of the Government of the United States be adequate and safe for its objects, time alone can absolutely determine. Experience seems to have shown that whatever may grow out of future stages of our national career, there is as yet a sufficient control in the popular will over the Executive and
35   Legislative Departments of the Government. When the Alien and Sedition laws were passed in contravention to the opinions and feelings of the community, the first elections that ensued put an end to them. And whatever may have been the character of other acts in the judgment of many of us, it is but true that they have generally accorded with the views of a majority of the States and of the people.

At the present day it seems well understood that the laws which have created most dissatisfaction have had a like sanction without doors; and that whether continued varied or repealed, a like proof will be given of the sympathy and responsibility of the Representative Body to the Constituent Body. Indeed, the great complaint now is, not against the want of this sympathy and responsibility, but against the results of them in the legislative policy of the nation.

With respect to the Judicial power of the United States and the authority of the Supreme Court in relation to the boundary of jurisdiction between the Federal and the State Governments. I may be permitted to refer to the number of the "Federalist" for the light in which the subject was regarded by its writer, at the period when the Constitution was depending; and it is believed that the same was the prevailing view then taken of it, that the same view has continued to prevail, and that it does so at this time notwithstanding the eminent exceptions to it.

But it is perfectly consistent with the concession of this power to the Supreme Court, in cases falling within the course of its functions, to maintain that the power has not always been rightly exercised. To say nothing of the period, happily a short one, when judges in their seats did not abstain from intemperate and party harangues, equally at variance with their duty and their dignity, there have been occasional decisions from the Bench which have incurred serious and extensive disapprobation. Still it would seem that, with but few exceptions, the course of the judiciary has been hitherto sustained by the predominant sense of the nation.

Those who have denied or doubted the supremacy of the judicial power of the United States and denounce at the same time nullifying power in a State, seem not to have sufficiently adverted to the utter inefficiency of a supremacy in a law of the land, without a supremacy in the exposition and execution of the law; nor to the destruction of all equipoise between the Federal Government and the State governments, if, whilst the functionaries of the Federal Government are directly or indirectly elected by and responsible to the States and the functionaries of the States are in their appointments and responsibility wholly independent of the United States no constitutional control of any sort belonged to the United States over the States. Under such an organization it is evident that it would be in the power of the States individually, to pass unauthorized laws, and to carry them into complete effect, anything in the Constitution and laws of the United States to the contrary notwithstanding. This would be a nullifying power in its plenary character; and whether it had its final effect, through the Legislative, Executive, or Judiciary organ of the State, would be equally fatal to the constitutional relation between the two Governments.

Should the provisions of the Constitution as here reviewed be found not to secure the Government and rights of the States against usurpations and abuses

on the part of the United States the final resort within the purview of the
Constitution lies in an amendment of the Constitution according to a process
applicable by the States.

And in the event of a failure of every constitutional resort, and an accumulation
5   of usurpations and abuses, rendering passive obedience and non-resistance a
greater evil, than resistance and revolution, there can remain but one resort,
the last of all, an appeal from the cancelled obligations of the constitutional
compact, to original rights and the law of self-preservation. This is the ultima
ratio under all Government whether consolidated, confederated, or a compound
10   of both; and it cannot be doubted that a single member of the Union, in the
extremity supposed, but in that only would have a right, as an extra and ultra
constitutional right, to make the appeal.

This brings us to the expedient lately advanced, which claims for a single
State a right to appeal against an exercise of power by the Government of the
15   United States decided by the State to be unconstitutional, to the parties of the
Constitution, compact; the decision of the State to have the effect of nullifying
the act of the Government of the United States unless the decision of the State
be reversed by three-fourths of the parties.

The distinguished names and high authorities which appear to have asserted
20   and given a practical scope to this doctrine, entitle it to a respect which it might
be difficult otherwise to feel for it.

If the doctrine were to be understood as requiring the three-fourths of the States
to sustain, instead of that proportion to reverse, the decision of the appealing
State, the decision to be without effect during the appeal, it would be sufficient
25   to remark, that this extra constitutional course might well give way to that
marked out by the Constitution which authorizes two-thirds of the States to
institute and three-fourths to effectuate, an amendment of the Constitution
establishing a permanent rule of the highest authority in place of an irregular
precedent of construction only.

30   But it is understood that the nullifying doctrine imports that the decision of
the State is to be presumed valid, and that it overrules the law of the United
States unless overruled by three-fourths of the States.

Can more be necessary to demonstrate the inadmissibility of such a doctrine
than that it puts it in the power of the smallest fraction over one-fourth of the
35   United States—that is, of seven States out of twenty-four—to give the law and
even the Constitution to seventeen States, each of the seventeen having as parties
to the Constitution an equal right with each of the seven to expound it and to

insist on the exposition. That the seven might, in particular instances be right and the seventeen wrong, is more than possible. But to establish a positive and permanent rule giving such a power to such a minority over such a majority, would overturn the first principle of free Government and in practice necessarily overturn the Government itself. 5

It is to be recollected that the Constitution was proposed to the people of the States as a *whole*, and unanimously adopted by the States as a *whole*, it being a part of the Constitution that not less than three-fourths of the States should be competent to make any alteration in what had been unanimously agreed to. So great is the caution on this point, that in two cases when peculiar interests 10 were at stake, a proportion even of three-fourths is distrusted, and unanimity required to make an alteration.

When the Constitution was adopted as a whole, it is certain that there were many parts which if separately proposed, would have been promptly rejected. It is far from impossible, that every part of the Constitution might be rejected 15 by a majority, and yet, taken together as a whole be unanimously accepted. Free constitutions will rarely if ever be formed without reciprocal concessions; without articles conditioned on and balancing each other. Is there a constitution of a single State out of the twenty-four that would bear the experiment of having its component parts submitted to the people and separately decided on? 20

What the fate of the Constitution of the United States would be if a small proportion of States could expunge parts of it particularly valued by a large majority, can have but one answer.

The difficulty is not removed by limiting the doctrine to cases of construction. How many cases of that sort, involving cardinal provisions of the Constitution, 25 have occurred? How many now exist? How many may hereafter spring up? How many might be ingeniously created, if entitled to the privilege of a decision in the mode proposed?

Is it certain that the principle of that mode would not reach farther than is contemplated. If a single State can of right require three-fourths of its co- 30 States to overrule its exposition of the Constitution, because that proportion is authorized to amend it, would the plea be less plausible that, as the Constitution was unanimously established, it ought to be unanimously expounded?

The reply to all such suggestions seems to be unavoidable and irresistible, that the Constitution is a compact; that its text is to be expounded according to the 35 provision for expounding it, making a part of the compact; and that none of the parties can rightfully renounce the expounding provision more than any other part. When such a right accrues, as it may accrue, it must grow out of abuses of the compact releasing the sufferers from their fealty to it.

In favor of the nullifying claim for the States individually, it appears, as you observe, that the proceedings of the Legislature of Virginia in 98 and 99 against
5   the Alien and Sedition Acts are much dwelt upon.

It may often happen, as experience proves, that erroneous constructions, not anticipated, may not be sufficiently guarded against in the language used; and it is due to the distinguished individuals who have misconceived the intention of those proceedings to suppose that the meaning of the Legislature, though
10   well comprehended at the time, may not now be obvious to those unacquainted with the contemporary indications and impressions.

But it is believed that by keeping in view the distinction between the Government of the States and the States in the sense in which they were parties to the Constitution; between the rights of the parties, in their concurrent and in their
15   individual capacities; between the several modes and objects of interposition against the abuses of power, and especially between interpositions within the purview of the Constitution and interpositions appealing from the Constitution to the rights of nature paramount to all Constitutions; with these distinctions kept in view, and an attention, always of explanatory use, to the views and
20   arguments which were combated, a confidence is felt, that the Resolutions of Virginia, as vindicated in the Report on them, will be found entitled to an exposition, showing a consistency in their parts and an inconsistency of the whole with the doctrine under consideration.

That the Legislature could not have intended to sanction such a doctrine is to
25   be inferred from the debates in the House of Delegates, and from the address of the two Houses to their constituents on the subject of the resolutions. The tenor of the debates which were ably conducted and are understood to have been revised for the press by most, if not all, of the speakers, discloses no reference whatever to a constitutional nght in an individual State to arrest
30   by force the operation of a law of the United States concert among the States for redress against the alien and sedition laws, as acts of usurped power, was a leading sentiment, and the attainment of a concert the immediate object of the course adopted by the Legislature, which was that of inviting the other States "to *concur* in declaring the acts to be unconstitutional, and to *cooperate* by the
35   necessary and proper measures in maintaining unimpaired the authorities rights and liberties reserved to the States respectively and to the people." That by the necessary and proper measures to be *concurrently* and cooperatively taken, were meant measures known to the Constitution, particularly the ordinary control

of the people and Legislatures of the States over the Government of the United States cannot be doubted; and the interposition of this control as the event showed was equal to the occasion.

It is worthy of remark, and explanatory of the intentions of the Legislature, that the words "not law, but utterly null, void, and of no force or effect," which had   5
followed, in one of the Resolutions, the word "unconstitutional," were struck out by common consent. Though the words were in fact but synonymous with "unconstitutional," yet to guard against a misunderstanding of this phrase as more than declaratory of opinion, the word unconstitutional alone was retained, as not liable to that danger.   10

The published address of the Legislature to the people their constituents affords another conclusive evidence of its views. The address warns them against the encroaching spirit of the General Government, argues the unconstitutionality of the alien and sedition acts, points to other instances in which the constitutional limits had been overleaped; dwells upon the dangerous mode of deriving   15
power by implications; and in general presses the necessity of watching over the consolidating tendency of the Federal policy. But nothing is said that can be understood to look to means of maintaining the rights of the States beyond the regular ones within the forms of the Constitution.

If any farther lights on the subject could be needed, a very strong one is   20
reflected in the answers to the Resolutions by the States which protested against them. The main objection to these, beyond a few general complaints against the inflammatory tendency of the resolutions was directed against the assumed authority of a State Legislature to declare a law of the United States unconstitutional, which they pronounced an unwarrantable interference   25
with the exclusive jurisdiction of the Supreme Court of the United States. Had the resolutions been regarded as avowing and maintaining a right in an individual State, to arrest by force the execution of a law of the United States it must be presumed that it would have been a conspicuous object of their denunciation.   30

The Missouri Compromise

The sectional struggle over slavery came to a head in 1820. With eleven free states and eleven slave states, if Missouri entered the Union as a slave state, the balance of power would shift toward the South. After several months of debate, a compromise emerged: Maine would enter the Union as a free state, Missouri as a slave state. Additionally, slavery was prohibited in the territory of the Louisiana Purchase north of Missouri's southern border.

March 6, 1820

An Act to authorize the people of the Missouri territory to form a constitution and state government, and for the admission of such state into the Union on an equal footing with the original states, and to prohibit slavery in certain territories.

Be it enacted by the Senate and House of Representatives of the United States of America, in Congress assembled, That the inhabitants of that portion of the Missouri Territory included within the boundaries hereinafter designated, be, and they are hereby, authorized to form for themselves a constitution and state government, and to assume such name as they shall deem proper; and the said state, when formed, shall be admitted into the Union, upon an equal footing with the original states, in all respects whatsoever. 5 … 10

Section 2. *And be it further enacted,* That the said state shall consist of all the territory included within the following boundaries, to wit: Beginning in the middle of the Mississippi river, on the parallel of thirty-six degrees of north latitude; thence west, along that parallel of latitude, to the St. Francois river; thence up, and following the course of that river, in the middle of the main channel thereof, to the parallel of latitude of thirty-six degrees and thirty minutes; thence west, along the same, to a point where the said parallel is intersected by a meridian line passing through the middle of the mouth of the Kansas river, where the same empties into the Missouri river, 15 … 20

Act of March 6, 1820, ch. 22, 22 *Stat.* 545–58.

thence, from the point aforesaid north, along the said meridian line, to the intersection of the parallel of latitude which passes through the rapids of the river Des Moines, making the said line to correspond with the Indian boundary line; thence east, from the point of intersection last aforesaid, along
5   the said parallel of latitude, to the middle of the channel of the main fork of the said river Des Moines; thence down and along the middle of the main channel of the said river Des Moines, to the mouth of the same, where it empties into the Mississippi river; thence, due east, to the middle of the main channel of the Mississippi river; thence down, and following the course of
10 the Mississippi river, in the middle of the main channel thereof, to the place of beginning: *Provided,* The said state shall ratify the boundaries aforesaid; *And provided also,* That the said state shall have concurrent jurisdiction on the river Mississippi, and every other river bordering on the said state, so far as the said rivers shall form a common boundary to the said state; and
15 any other state or states, now or hereafter to be formed and bounded by the same, such rivers to be common to both; and that the river Mississippi, and the navigable rivers and waters leading into the same, shall be common highways, and for ever free, as well to the inhabitants of the said state as to other citizens of the United States, without any tax, duty, impost, or toll,
20 therefor, imposed by the said state.

SECTION 3. *And be it further enacted,* That all free white male citizens of the United States, who shall have arrived at the age of twenty-one years, and have resided in said territory three months previous to the day of election, and all other persons qualified to vote for representatives to the general assembly of
25 the said territory, shall be qualified to be elected, and they are hereby qualified and authorized to vote, and choose representatives to form a convention, who shall be apportioned amongst the several counties as follows:

From the county of Howard, five representatives. From the county of Cooper, three representatives. From the county of Montgomery, two representatives.
30 From the county of Pike, one representative. From the county of Lincoln, one representative. From the county of St. Charles, three representatives. From the county of Franklin, one representative. From the county of St. Louis, eight representatives. From the county of Jefferson, one representative. From the county of Washington, three representatives. From the county of St. Genevieve,
35 four representatives. From the county of Madison, one representative. From the county of Cape Girardeau, five representatives. From the county of New Madrid, two representatives. From the county of Wayne, and that portion of the county of Lawrence which falls within the boundaries herein designated, one representative.

And the election for the representatives aforesaid shall be holden on the first Monday, and two succeeding days of May next, throughout the several counties aforesaid in the said territory, and shall be, in every respect, held and conducted in the same manner, and under the same regulations as is prescribed by the laws of the said territory regulating elections therein for members of the general   5
assembly, except that the returns of the election in that portion of Lawrence county included in the boundaries aforesaid, shall be made to the county of Wayne, as is provided in other cases under the laws of said territory.

SECTION 4. *And be it further enacted*, That the members of the convention thus duly elected, shall be, and they are hereby authorized to meet at the seat of   10
government of said territory on the second Monday of the month of June next; and the said convention, when so assembled, shall have power and authority to adjourn to any other place in the said territory, which to them shall seem best for the convenient transaction of their business; and which convention, when so met, shall first determine by a majority of the whole number elected, whether it   15
be, or be not, expedient at that time to form a constitution and state government for the people within the said territory, as included within the boundaries above designated; and if it be deemed expedient, the convention shall be, and hereby is, authorized to form a constitution and state government; or, if it be deemed more expedient, the said convention shall provide by ordinance for electing   20
representatives to form a constitution or frame of government; which said representatives shall be chosen in such manner, and in such proportion as they shall designate; and shall meet at such time and place as shall be prescribed by the said ordinance; and shall then form for the people of said territory, within the boundaries aforesaid, a constitution and state government: *Provided*,   25
That the same, whenever formed, shall be republican, and not repugnant to the constitution of the United States; and that the legislature of said state shall never interfere with the primary disposal of the soil by the United States, nor with any regulations Congress may find necessary for securing the title in such soil to the *bona fide* purchasers; and that no tax shall be imposed on lands the   30
property of the United States; and in no case shall non-resident proprietors be taxed higher than residents.

SECTION 5. *And be it further enacted*, That until the next general census shall be taken, the said state shall be entitled to one representative in the House of Representatives of the United States.   35

SECTION 6. *And be it further enacted*, That the following propositions be, and the same are hereby, offered to the convention of the said territory of Missouri, when formed, for their free acceptance or rejection, which, if accepted by the convention, shall be obligatory upon the United States:

First. That section numbered sixteen in every township, and when such section has been sold, or otherwise disposed of, other lands equivalent thereto, and as contiguous as may be, shall be granted to the state for the use of the inhabitants of such township, for the use of schools.

5   *Second.* That all salt springs, not exceeding twelve in number, with six sections of land adjoining to each, shall be granted to the said state for the use of said state, the same to be selected by the legislature of the said state, on or before the first day of January, in the year one thousand eight hundred and twenty-five; and the same, when so selected, to be used under such terms, conditions, and
10 regulations, as the legislature of said state shall direct: *Provided,* That no salt spring, the right whereof now is, or hereafter shall be, confirmed or adjudged to any individual or individuals, shall, by this section, be granted to the said state: *And provided also,* That the legislature shall never sell or lease the same, at any one time, for a longer period than ten years, without the consent of
15 Congress.

Third. That five per cent. of the net proceeds of the sale of lands lying within the said territory or state, and which shall be sold by Congress, from and after the first day of January next, after deducting all expenses incident to the same, shall be reserved for making public roads and canals, of which three fifths
20 shall be applied to those objects within the state, under the direction of the legislature thereof; and the other two fifths in defraying, under the direction of Congress, the expenses to be incurred in making of a road or roads, canal or canals, leading to the said state.

Fourth. That four entire sections of land be, and the same are hereby, granted
25 to the said state, for the purpose of fixing their seat of government thereon; which said sections shall, under the direction of the legislature of said state, be located, as near as may be, in one body, at any time, in such townships and ranges as the legislature aforesaid may select, on any of the public lands of the United States: *Provided,* That such locations shall be made prior to the public
30 sale of the lands of the United States surrounding such location.

Fifth. That thirty-six sections, or one entire township, which shall be designated by the President of the United States, together with the other lands heretofore reserved for that purpose, shall be reserved for the use of a seminary of learning, and vested in the legislature of said state, to be appropriated solely to the
35 use of such seminary by the said legislature: *Provided,* That the five foregoing propositions herein offered, are on the condition that the convention of the said state shall provide, by an ordinance, irrevocable without the consent of the United States, that every and each tract of land sold by the United States,

from and after the first day of January next, shall remain exempt from any tax laid by order or under the authority of the state, whether for state, county, or township, or any other purpose whatever, for the term of five years from and after the day of sale; *And further*, That the bounty lands granted, or hereafter to be granted, for military services during the late war, shall, while they continue   5
to be held by the patentees, or their heirs, remain exempt as aforesaid from taxation for the term of three years of from and after the date of the patents respectively.

SECTION 7. *And be it further enacted*, That in case a constitution and state government shall be formed for the people of the said territory of Missouri,   10
the said convention or representatives, as soon thereafter as may be, shall cause a true and attested copy of such constitution, or frame of state government, as shall be formed or provided, to be transmitted to Congress.

SECTION 8. *And be it further enacted*. That in all that territory ceded by France to the United States, under the name of Louisiana, which lies north of thirty-   15
six degrees and thirty minutes north latitude, not included within the limits of the state, contemplated by this act, slavery and involuntary servitude, otherwise than in the punishment of crimes, whereof the parties shall have been duly convicted, shall be, and is hereby, forever prohibited: *Provided always*, That any person escaping into the same, from whom laborr or service is lawfully   20
claimed, in any state or territory of the United States, such fugitive may be lawfully reclaimed and conveyed to the person claiming his or her labor or service as aforesaid.

THE WILMOT PROVISO

Early on in the Mexican-American War, America gained control over a vast swath of new territory extending from the Great Plains to the Pacific Ocean. In 1846, Congressman David Wilmot proposed a ban on slavery across the region, angering those who advocated on behalf of slavery's westward expansion.

AUGUST 8, 1846

Provided, That, as an express and fundamental condition to the acquisition of any territory from the Republic of Mexico by the United States, by virtue of any treaty which may be negotiated between them, and to the use by the Executive of the moneys herein appropriated, neither slavery nor involuntary servitude shall ever exist in any part of said territory, except for crime, whereof   5
the party shall first be duly convicted.

David Wilmot, "The Wilmot Proviso," August 8, 1846, in Thomas Hart Benton, ed., *Abridgment of the Debates of Congress, from 1789 to 1856*, Vol. 15 (New York: D. Appleton & Co., 1861), 646.

The Constitution and the Union
Daniel Webster (1782–1852)

Daniel Webster began representing Massachusetts in the U.S. Senate in 1813, and by the 1830s had attained a national reputation—in part as a result of his Senate debates with nullification proponent Senator Robert Hayne of South Carolina. Webster spent the final decade of his life attempting to avert the growing sectional divide, never wavering in his defense of Union. In this speech he restated his longstanding conviction that "Peaceable secession is an utter impossibility." He died two years later, in 1852, with the nation divided.

March 7, 1850

Mr. President:

I wish to speak today, not as a Massachusetts man, nor as a Northern man, but as an American, and a member of the Senate of the United States. It is fortunate that there is a Senate of the United States; a body not yet moved from its propriety, not lost to a just sense of its own dignity and its own high responsibilities, and a body to which the country looks, with confidence, for wise, moderate, patriotic, and healing counsels. It is not to be denied that we live in the midst of strong agitations, and are surrounded by very considerable dangers to our institutions and government. The imprisoned winds are let loose. The East, the North, and the stormy South combine to throw the whole sea into commotion, to toss its billows to the skies, and disclose its profoundest depths. I do not affect to regard myself, Mr. President, as holding, or as fit to hold, the helm in this combat with the political elements; but I have a duty to perform, and I mean to perform it with fidelity,—not without a sense of existing dangers, but not without hope. I have a part to act, not for my own security or safety, for I am looking out for no fragment upon which to float away from the wreck, if wreck there must be, but for the good of the whole, and the preservation of all; and there is that which will keep me to my duty during this struggle, whether

Daniel Webster, "The Constitution and the Union," March 7, 1850, in Charles M. Wiltse et al., eds., *The Papers of Daniel Webster*, Vol. 2 (Hanover, NH: Dartmouth College, 1975–1989), 515–16, 520–22, 540–41, 543–44, 546–48, 550–51.

the sun and the stars shall appear, or shall not appear for many days. I speak today for the preservation of the Union. "Hear me for my cause." I speak to-day, out of a solicitous and anxious heart, for the restoration to the country of that quiet and that harmony which make the blessings of this Union so rich,

5   and so dear to us all. These are the topics that I propose to myself to discuss; these are the motives, and the sole motives, that influence me in the wish to communicate my opinions to the Senate and the country; and if I can do any thing, however little, for the promotion of these ends, I shall have accomplished all that I expect....

10   Now, Sir, upon the general nature and influence of slavery there exists a wide difference of opinion between the northern portion of this country and the southern. It is said on the one side, that, although not the subject of any injunction or direct prohibition in the New Testament, slavery is a wrong; that it is founded merely in the right of the strongest; and that it is an oppression,

15   like unjust wars, like all those conflicts by which a powerful nation subjects a weaker to its will; and that, in its nature, whatever may be said of it in the modifications which have taken place, it is not according to the meek spirit of the Gospel. It is not "kindly affectioned"; it does not "seek another's, and not its own"; it does not "let the oppressed go free." These are sentiments that are

20   cherished, and of late with greatly augmented force, among the people of the Northern States. They have taken hold of the religious sentiment of that part of the country, as they have, more or less, taken hold of the religious feeling of a considerable portion of mankind. The South, upon the other side, having been accustomed to this relation between two races all their lives, from their

25   birth, having been taught, in general, to treat the subjects of this bondage with care and kindness, and I believe, in general, feeling great kindness for them, have not taken the view of the subject which I have mentioned. There are thousands of religious men, with consciences as tender as any of their brethren at the North, who do not see the unlawfulness of slavery; and there are more

30   thousands, perhaps, that, whatsoever they may think of it in its origin, and as a matter depending upon natural right, yet take things as they are, and, finding slavery to be an established relation of the society in which they live, can see no way in which, let their opinions on the abstract question be what they may, it is in the power of the present generation to relieve themselves from this relation.

35   And candor obliges me to say, that I believe they are just as conscientious, many of them, and the religious people, all of them, as they are at the North who hold different opinions.

The honorable Senator from South Carolina the other day alluded to the separation of that great religious community, the Methodist Episcopal

Church. That separation was brought about by differences of opinion upon this particular subject of slavery. I felt great concern, as that dispute went on, about the result. I was in hopes that the difference of opinion might be adjusted, because I looked upon that religious denomination as one of the great props of religion and morals throughout the whole country, from Maine to Georgia, 5 and westward to our utmost western boundary. The result was against my wishes and against my hopes. I have read all their proceedings and all their arguments; but I have never yet been able to come to the conclusion that there was any real ground for that separation; in other words, that any good could be produced by that separation. I must say I think there was some want of candor 10 or charity. Sir, when a question of this kind seizes on the religious sentiments of mankind, and comes to be discussed in religious assemblies of the clergy and laity, there is always to be expected, or always to be feared, a great degree of excitement. It is in the nature of man, manifested by his whole history, that religious disputes are apt to become warm in proportion to the strength of the 15 convictions which men entertain of the magnitude of the questions at issue. In all such disputes, there will sometimes be found men with whom everything is absolute; absolutely wrong, or absolutely right. They see the right clearly; they think others ought so to see it, and they are disposed to establish a broad line of distinction between what is right and what is wrong. They are not seldom 20 willing to establish that line upon their own convictions of truth and justice; and are ready to mark and guard it by placing along it a series of dogmas, as lines of boundary on the earth's surface are marked by posts and stones. There are men who, with clear perceptions, as they think, of their own duty, do not see how too eager a pursuit of one duty may involve them in the violation of 25 others, or how too warm an embracement of one truth may lead to a disregard of other truths equally important. As I heard it stated strongly, not many days ago, these persons are disposed to mount upon some particular duty, as upon a war-horse, and to drive furiously on and upon and over all other duties that may stand in the way. There are men who, in reference to disputes of that sort, 30 are of the opinion that human duties may be ascertained with the exactness of mathematics. They deal with morals as with mathematics; and they think what is right may be distinguished from what is wrong with the precision of an algebraic equation. They have, therefore, none too much charity towards others who differ from them. They are apt, too, to think that nothing is good 35 but what is perfect, and that there are no compromises or modifications to be made in consideration of difference of opinion or in deference to other men's judgment. If their perspicacious vision enables them to detect a spot on the face of the sun, they think that a good reason why the sun should be struck down from heaven. They prefer the chance of running into utter darkness to 40

living in heavenly light, if that heavenly light be not absolutely without any imperfection. There are impatient men; too impatient always to give heed to the admonition of St. Paul, that we are not to "do evil that good may come"; too impatient to wait for the slow progress of moral causes in the improvement
5   of mankind....

Mr. President, in the excited times in which we live, there is found to exist a state of crimination and recrimination between the North and South. There are lists of grievances produced by each; and those grievances, real or supposed, alienate the minds of one portion of the country from the other, exasperate the
10   feelings, and subdue the sense of fraternal affection, patriotic love, and mutual regard. I shall bestow a little attention, Sir, upon these various grievances existing on the one side and on the other. I begin with complaints of the South. I will not answer, further than I have, the general statements of the honorable Senator from South Carolina, that the North has prospered at the expense of
15   the South in consequence of the manner of administering this government, in the collecting of its revenues, and so forth. These are disputed topics, and I have no inclination to enter into them. But I will allude to the other complaints of the South, and especially to one which has in my opinion just foundation; and that is, that there has been found at the North, among individuals and
20   among legislators, a disinclination to perform fully their constitutional duties in regard to the return of persons bound to service who have escaped into the free States. In that respect, the South, in my judgment, is right, and the North is wrong. Every member of every Northern legislature is bound by oath, like every other officer in the country, to support the Constitution of the United
25   States; and the article of the Constitution which says to these States that they shall deliver up fugitives from service is as binding in honor and conscience as any other article. No man fulfils his duty in any legislature who sets himself to find excuses, evasions, escapes from this constitutional obligation. I have always thought that the Constitution addressed itself to the legislatures of the States or
30   to the States themselves. It says that those persons escaping to other States "shall be delivered up," and I confess I have always been of the opinion that it was an injunction upon the States themselves. When it is said that a person escaping into another State, and coming therefore within the jurisdiction of that State, shall be delivered up, it seems to me the import of the clause is, that the State
35   itself, in obedience to the Constitution, shall cause him to be delivered up. That is my judgment. I have always entertained that opinion, and I entertain it now. But when the subject, some years ago, was before the Supreme Court of the United States, the majority of the judges held that the power to cause fugitives from service to be delivered up was a power to be exercised under the authority

of this government. I do not know, on the whole, that it may not have been a fortunate decision. My habit is to respect the result of judicial deliberations and the solemnity of judicial decisions. As it now stands, the business of seeing that these fugitives are delivered up resides in the power of Congress and the national judicature, and my friend at the head of the Judiciary Committee has 5 a bill on the subject now before the Senate, which, with some amendments to it, I propose to support, with all its provisions, to the fullest extent. And I desire to call the attention of all sober-minded men at the North, of all conscientious men, of all men who are not carried away by some fanatical idea or some false impression, to their constitutional obligations. I put it to all the sober and sound 10 minds at the North as a question of morals and a question of conscience. What right have they, in their legislative capacity or any other capacity, to endeavor to get round this Constitution, to embarrass the free exercise of the rights secured by the Constitution; to the persons whose slaves escape from them? None at all; none at all. Neither in the forum of conscience, nor before the face of the 15 Constitution, are they, in my opinion justified in such an attempt. Of course it is a matter for their consideration. They probably, in the excitement of the times, have not stopped to consider of this. They have followed what seemed to be the current of thought and of motives, as the occasion arose, and they have neglected to investigate fully the real question, and to consider their 20 constitutional obligations; which, as I am sure, if they did consider, they would fulfil with alacrity. I repeat, therefore, Sir, that here is a well-founded ground of complaint against the North, which ought to be removed, which it is now in the power of the different departments of this government to remove; which calls for the enactment of proper laws authorizing the judicature of this government, 25 in the several States, to do all that is necessary for the recapture of fugitive slaves and for their restoration to those who claim them. Wherever I go, and whenever I speak on the subject, and when I speak here I desire to speak to the whole North, I say that the South has been injured in this respect, and has a right to complain; and the North has been too careless of what I think the Constitution 30 peremptorily and emphatically enjoins upon her as a duty....

Then, Sir, there are the Abolition societies, of which I am unwilling to speak, but in regard to which I have very clear notions and opinions. I do not think them useful. I think their operations for the last twenty years have produced nothing good or valuable. At the same time, I believe thousands of their members 35 to be honest and good men, perfectly well-meaning men. They have excited feelings; they think they must do something for the cause of liberty; and, in their sphere of action, they do not see what else they can do than to contribute to an Abolition press, or an Abolition society, or to pay an Abolition lecturer.

I do not mean to impute gross motives even to the leaders of these societies; but I am not blind to the consequences of their proceedings. I cannot but see what mischiefs their interference with the South has produced. And is it not plain to every man? Let any gentleman who entertains doubts on this point

5   recur to the debates in the Virginia House of Delegates in 1832, and he will see with what freedom a proposition made by Mr. Jefferson Randolph for the gradual abolition of slavery was discussed in that body. Every one spoke of slavery as he thought; very ignominious and disparaging names and epithets were applied to it. The debates in the House of Delegates on that occasion, I

10 believe, were all published. They were read by every colored man who could read; and to those who could not read, those debates were read by others. At that time Virginia was not unwilling or unafraid to discuss this question, and to let that part of her population know as much of the discussion as they could learn. That was in 1832. As has been said by the honorable member from

15 South Carolina, these Abolition societies commenced their course of action in 1835. It is said, I do not know how true it may be, that they sent incendiary publications into the slave States; at any rate, they attempted to arouse, and did arouse, a very strong feeling; in other words, they created great agitation in the North against Southern slavery. Well, what was the result? The bonds of

20 the slaves were bound more firmly than before, their rivets were more strongly fastened. Public opinion, which in Virginia had begun to be exhibited against slavery, and was opening out for the discussion of the question, drew back and shut itself up in its castle. I wish to know whether anybody in Virginia can now talk openly as Mr. Randolph, Governor McDowell, and others talked in 1832

25 and sent their remarks to the press? We all know the fact, and we all know the cause; and every thing that these agitating people have done has been, not to enlarge, but to restrain, not to set free, but to bind faster, the slave population of the South....

Mr. President, I should much prefer to have heard from every member on this
30 floor declarations of opinion that this Union could never be dissolved, than the declaration of opinion by anybody that, in any case, under the pressure of any circumstances, such a dissolution was possible. I hear with distress and anguish the word "secession," especially when it falls from the lips of those who are patriotic, and known to the country, and known all over the world, for

35 their political services. Secession! Peaceable secession! Sir, your eyes and mine are never destined to see that miracle. The dismemberment of this vast country without convulsion! The breaking up of the fountains of the great deep without ruffling the surface! Who is so foolish, I beg everybody's pardon, as to expect to see any such thing? Sir, he who sees these States, now revolving in harmony

around a common center, and expects to see them quit their places and fly off without convulsion, may look the next hour to see heavenly bodies rush from their spheres, and jostle against each other in the realms of space, without causing the wreck of the universe. There can be no such thing as peaceable secession. Peaceable secession is an utter impossibility. Is the great Constitution under which we live, covering this whole country, is it to be thawed and melted away by secession, as the snows on the mountain melt under the influence of a vernal sun, disappear almost unobserved, and run off? No, Sir! No, Sir! I will not state what might produce the disruption of the Union; but, Sir, I see as plainly as I see the sun in heaven what that disruption itself must produce; I see that it must produce war, and such a war as I will not describe, *in its twofold character.*

Peaceable secession! Peaceable secession! The concurrent agreement of all the members of this great republic to separate! A voluntary separation, with alimony on one side and on the other. Why, what would be the result? Where is the line to be drawn? What States are to secede? What is to remain American? What am I to be? An American no longer? Am I to become a sectional man, a local man, a separatist, with no country in common with the gentlemen who sit around me here, or who fill the other house of Congress? Heaven forbid! Where is the flag of the republic to remain? Where is the eagle still to tower? or is he to cower, and shrink, and fall to the ground? Why, Sir, our ancestors, our fathers and our grandfathers, those of them that are yet living amongst us with prolonged lives, would rebuke and reproach us; and our children and our grandchildren would cry out shame upon us, if we of this generation should dishonor these ensigns of the power of the government and the harmony of that Union which is every day felt among us with so much joy and gratitude. What is to become of the army? What is to become of the navy? What is to become of the public lands? How is each of the thirty States to defend itself? I know, although the idea has not been stated distinctly, there is to be, or it is supposed possible that there will be, a Southern Confederacy. I do not mean, when I allude to this statement, that any one seriously contemplates such a state of things. I do not mean to say that it is true, but I have heard it suggested elsewhere, that the idea has been entertained, that, after the dissolution of this Union, a Southern Confederacy might be formed. I am sorry, Sir, that it has ever been thought of, talked of, or dreamed of, in the wildest flights of human imagination. But the idea, so far as it exists, must be of a separation, assigning the slave States to one side and the free States to the other. Sir, I may express myself too strongly, perhaps, but there are impossibilities in the natural as well as in the physical world, and I hold the idea of a separation of these States, those that are free to form one government, and those that are slave-holding to form another, as such an impossibility. We

could not separate the States by any such line, if we were to draw it. We could not sit down here today and draw a line of separation that would satisfy any five men in the country. There are natural causes that would keep and tie us together, and there are social and domestic relations which we could not break
5 if we would, and which we should not if we could.

Sir, nobody can look over the face of this country at the present moment, nobody can see where its population is the most dense and growing, without being ready to admit, and compelled to admit, that ere long the strength of America will be in the Valley of the Mississippi. Well, now, Sir, I beg to inquire
10 what the wildest enthusiast has to say on the possibility of cutting that river in two, and leaving free States at its source and on its branches, and slave States down near its mouth, each forming a separate government? Pray, Sir, let me say to the people of this country, that these things are worthy of their pondering and of their consideration. Here, Sir, are five millions of freemen in the free
15 States north of the river of Ohio. Can any body suppose that this population can be severed, by a line that divides them from the territory of a foreign and an alien government, down somewhere, the Lord knows where, upon the lower banks of the Mississippi? What would become of Missouri? Will she join the *arrondissement* of the slave States? Shall the man from the Yellow Stone and
20 the Platte be conncected, in the new republic, with the man who lives on the southern extremity of the Cape of Florida? Sir, I am ashamed to pursue this line of remark. I dislike it, I have an utter disgust for it. I would rather hear of natural blasts and mildews, war, pestilence, and famine, than to hear gentlemen talk of secession. To break up this great government! to dismember this glorious
25 country! to astonish Europe with an act of folly such as Europe for two centuries has never beheld in any government or any people! No, Sir! no, Sir! There will be no secession! Gentlemen are not serious when they talk of secession....

And now, Mr. President, I draw these observations to a close. I have spoken freely, and I meant to do so. I have sought to make no display. I have sought
30 to enliven the occasion by no animated discussion, nor have I attempted any train of elaborate argument. I have wished only to speak my sentiments, fully and at length, being desirous, once and for all, to let the Senate know, and to let the country know, the opinions and sentiments which I entertain on all these subjects. These opinions are not likely to be suddenly changed. If there
35 be any future service that I can render to the country, consistently with these sentiments and opinions, I shall cheerfully render it. If there be not, I shall still be glad to have had an opportunity to disburden myself from the bottom of my heart, and to make known every political sentiment that therein exists.

And now, Mr. President, instead of speaking of the possibility or utility of secession, instead of dwelling in those caverns of darkness, instead of groping with those ideas so full of all that is horrid and horrible, let us come out into the light of day; let us enjoy the fresh air of Liberty and Union; let us cherish those hopes which belong to us; let us devote ourselves to those great objects 5 that are fit for our consideration and our action; let us raise our conceptions to the magnitude and the importance of the duties that devolve upon us; let our comprehension be as broad as the country for which we act, our aspirations as high as its certain destiny; let us not be pigmies in a case that calls for men. Never did there devolve on any generation of men higher trusts than now 10 devolve upon us, for the preservation of this Constitution and the harmony and peace of all who are destined to live under it. Let us make our generation one of the strongest and brightest links in that golden chain which is destined, I fondly believe, to grapple the people of all the States to this Constitution for ages to come. We have a great, popular constitutional government, guarded 15 by law and by judicature, and defended by the affections of the whole people. No monarchical throne presses these States together, no iron chain of military power encircles them; they live and stand under a government popular in its form, representative in its character, founded upon principles of equality, and so constructed, we hope, as to last for ever. In all its history it has been beneficent; 20 it has trodden down no man's liberty; it has crushed no State. Its daily respiration is liberty and patriotism; its yet youthful veins are full of enterprise, courage, and honorable love of glory and renown. Large before, the country has now, by recent events, become vastly larger. This republic now extends, with a vast breadth, across the whole continent. The two great seas of the world wash the 25 one and the other shore. We realize, on a mighty scale, the beautiful description of the ornamental border of the buckler of Achilles:—

> "Now, the broad shield complete, the artist crowned
> With his last hand, and poured the ocean round;
> In living silver seemed the waves to roll,   30
> And beat the buckler's verge, and bound the whole."

ALABAMA SLAVE CODE OF 1852

Growth in the slave population and threats from abolitionists led Southern states to adopt new slave codes in the mid-nineteenth century. Alabama's revised code, adopted in 1852 and in effect until the end of the Civil War, built on a previous code from 1833.

1852

CHAPTER III. PATROLS.

§983. All white male owners of slaves, below the age of sixty years, and all other free white persons, between the ages of eighteen and forty-five years, who are not disabled by sickness or bodily infirmity, except commissioned officers in the militia, and persons exempt by law from the performance of militia duty, are subject to perform patrol duty.... 5

§990. Each detachment must patrol such parts of the precinct as in their judgment is necessary, at least once a week at night, during their term of service, and oftener, when required so to do by a justice of the peace; or when informed, by a credible person, of evidences of insubordination, or threatened outbreak, or insurrection of the slaves; or of any contemplated unlawful assembly of slaves 10 or free negroes....

§992. The patrol has power to enter, in a peaceable manner, upon any plantation; to enter by force, if necessary, all negro cabins or quarters, kitchens and out houses, and to apprehend all slaves who may there by found, not belonging to the plantation or household, without a pass from their owner or overseer; or 15 strolling from place to place, without authority.

§993. The patrol has power to punish slaves found under the circumstances recited in the preceding section, by stripes, not exceeding thirty-nine.

"Title 13, Chapters 3, 4," in Arthur P. Bagby, et al., eds., *The Code of Alabama* (Montgomery, AL: Brittain and De Wold, 1852), 234–42.

§994. It is the duty of the patrol, on receiving information that any person is harboring a runaway slave, to make search for such slave, and if found, to apprehend and take him before a justice of the peace, who, if the owner is unknown, must commit him to jail.

5   §995. If the patrol find any slave from home without a pass, and under circumstances creating the belief that he is a runaway, they must detain him in custody, and give information thereof to the owner, if known; and if unknown, or without their precinct, deliver him up to a justice, who must commit him to jail for safe keeping....

10   §998. The leader of each patrol must, at the expiration of each term of service, make report in writing, and upon oath, to the justice, of the number of times his detachment has patrolled, and of the absence, without sufficient excuse, of any member of the detachment at the times designated for patrolling, and failure to perform patrol duty; and thereupon it is the duty of the justice to cite
15   such delinquents to appear at a time and place designated by him, and show cause why a fine should not be imposed against him; and upon their failure to appear, or to render a sufficient excuse, they must each be fined ten dollars for each omission, for which execution may issue....

§1004. The patrol, if sued for any act done in the performance of patrol duty,
20   may give this law in evidence under the general issue; but are liable in damages, to any person aggrieved, for any unnecessary violence committed under color of performing patrol duty, either by unnecessarily breaking or entering houses, or for any excessive punishment inflicted on any slave.

Chapter IV. Slaves and Free Negroes.

Article I. Slaves.

§1005. No master, overseer, or other person having the charge of a slave, must
25   permit such slave to hire himself to another person, or to hire his own time, or to go at large, unless in a corporate town, by consent of the authorities thereof, evidenced by an ordinance of the corporation; and every such offense is a misdemeanor, punishable by fine not less than twenty nor more than one hundred dollars.

30   §1006. No master, overseer, or head of a family must permit any slave to be or remain at his house, out house, or kitchen, without leave of the owner or overseer, above four hours at any one time; and for every such offense he forfeits ten dollars, to be recovered before any justice of the peace, by any person who may sue for the same.

§1007. Any owner or overseer of a plantation, or householder, who knowingly permits more than five negroes, other than his own, to be and remain at his house, plantation, or quarter, at any one time, forfeits ten dollars for each and every one over that number, to the use of any one who may sue for the same, before any justice of the peace; unless such assemblage is for the worship of   5 almighty God, or for burial service, and with the consent of the owner or overseer of such slaves.

§1008. No slave must go beyond the limits of the plantation on which he resides, without a pass, or some letter or token from his master or overseer, giving him authority to go and return from a certain place; and if found violating this   10 law, may be apprehended and punished, not exceeding twenty stripes, at the discretion of any justice before whom he may be taken.

§1009. If any slave go upon the plantation, or enter the house or out house of any person, without permission in writing from his master or overseer, or in the prosecution of his lawful business, the owner or overseer of such plantation or   15 householder may give, or order such slave to be given, ten lashes on his bare back.

§1010. Any railroad company in whose car or vehicle, and the master or owner of any steamboat, or vessel, in which a slave is transported or carried, without the written authority of the owner or person in charge of such slave, forfeits to the owner the sum of fifty dollars; and if such slave is lost, is liable for his value,   20 and all reasonable expenses attending the prosecution of the suit....

§1012. No slave can keep or carry a gun, powder, shot, club, or other weapon, except the tools given him to work with, unless ordered by his master or overseer to carry such weapon from one place to another. Any slave found offending against the provisions of this section, may be seized, with such weapon, by   25 any one, and carried before any justice, who, upon proof of the offense, must condemn the weapon to the use of such person, and direct that the slave receive thirty-nine lashes on his bare back.

§1013. Any justice of the peace may, within his own county, grant permission in writing to any slave, on the application of his master or overseer, to carry and   30 use a gun and ammunition within his master's plantation....

§1015. Riots, routs, unlawful assemblies, trespasses, and seditious speeches by a slave, are punished, by the direction of any justice before whom he may be carried, with stripes not exceeding one hundred.

§1016. Any person having knowledge of the commission of any offense by a   35 slave against the law, may apprehend him, and take him before a justice of the peace for trial....

§1018. No slave can own property, and any property purchased or held by a slave, not claimed by the master or owner, must be sold by order of any justice of the peace; one half the proceeds of the sale, after the payment of costs and necessary expenses, to be paid to the informer, and the residue to the county
5   treasury.

§1019. Any slave who writes for, or furnishes any other slave with any pass or free paper, on conviction before any justice of the peace, must receive one hundred lashes on his bare back.

§1020. Not more than five male slaves shall assemble together at any place off
10   the plantation, or place to which they belong, with or without passes or permits to be there, unless attended by the master or overseer of such slaves, or unless such slaves are attending the public worship of God, held by white persons.

§1021. It is the duty of all patrols, and all officers, civil and military, to disperse all such unlawful assemblies; and each of the slaves constituting such unlawful
15   assembly, must be punished by stripes, not exceeding ten; and for the second offense, may be punished with thirty-nine stripes, at the discretion of any justice of the peace before whom he may be brought.

§1022. Any slave who preaches, exhorts, or harangues any assembly of slaves, or of slaves and free persons of color, without a license to preach or exhort from
20   some religious society of the neighborhood, and in the presence of five slave-holders, must, for the first offense, be punished with thirty-nine lashes, and for the second, with fifty lashes; which punishment may be inflicted by any officer of a patrol company, or by the order of any justice of the peace.

§1023. Runaway slaves may be apprehended by any person, and carried before
25   any justice of the peace, who must either commit them to the county jail, or send them to the owner, if known; who must, for every slave so apprehended, pay the person apprehending him six dollars, and all reasonable charges.

§1024. Any justice of the peace receiving information that three or more runaway slaves are lurking and hid in swamps, or other obscure places, may, by
30   warrant, reciting the names of the slaves, and their owners, if known, direct a leader of the patrol of the district, and if there be none, then any other suitable person, to summon, and take with him such power as may be necessary to apprehend such runaway; and if taken, to deliver them to the owner or commit them to the jail of his proper county.

35   §1025. For such apprehension and delivery to the owner, or committal to jail, the parties so apprehending shall be entitled to twenty dollars for each slave, to be paid by the owner....

§1027. On the reception of a runaway slave, the sheriff must, without delay, cause advertisement to be made in a newspaper, published in the county, if there be one, if not, in the one published nearest to the court house of such county, giving an accurate description of the person of the slave, his supposed age, the information contained in the warrant in relation to the slave, and his owner, and such other facts important to the identification of the slave, as the sheriff may be able to obtain from the slave, or from any other source, which must be continued for six months, once a week, if the slave is not sooner reclaimed by the owner....

ARTICLE II. FREE NEGROES.

§1033. Every free colored person who has come to this state since the first day of February, one thousand eight hundred and thirty-two, and has been admonished by any sheriff, justice of the peace, or other judicial officer, that he cannot, by law, remain in this state; and does not, within thirty days, depart therefrom, must, on conviction, be punished by imprisonment in the penitentiary for two years; and shall have thirty days after his discharge from the penitentiary to leave the state; and on failing to do so, must be imprisoned in the penitentiary for five years....

§1035. If any free person of color is at any time found at an unlawful assembly of slaves, he forfeits twenty dollars, to any person who will sue for the same, before any justice of the peace; and for the second offense, must, in addition thereto, be punished with ten stripes. All justices of the peace, sheriffs, and constables, are charged with the execution of this law....

§1038. Any free person of color who writes for, or furnishes a slave with a pass, is guilty of a misdemeanor, and, on conviction, must be fined not less than fifty dollars, and be imprisoned not less than six months.

§1039. Any free person of color who writes for, or furnishes any slave a pass, with the intent to enable such slave to escape from his master, is guilty of a felony, and, on conviction, must be imprisoned in the penitentiary not less than three, nor more than seven years....

§1041. Any free person of color, who buys of, or sells to, any slave, any article, or commodity whatever, without a written permission from the master, or overseer of such slave, designating the article so to be bought, or sold, is guilty of a misdemeanor, and must, upon conviction, before any justice of the peace of the county where such offense is committed, be punished with thirty-nine stripes.

§1042. Any free person of color, found in company with any slave, in any kitchen, out house, or negro quarter, without a written permission from the owner, or overseer of such slave, must, for every such offense, receive fifteen lashes; and for every subsequent offense, thirty-nine lashes; which may be inflicted by the owner or overseer of the slave, or by any officer or member of any patrol company.

5   §1043. If any free person of color permits a slave to be, or remain in his house, or out house, or about his premises, without permission, in writing, from the owner, or overseer of the slave, he shall be punished as provided in the preceding section.

§1044. Any free person of color, who preaches, exhorts, or harangues any
10   assembly of slaves, or of slaves and free persons of color, unless in the presence of five slaveholders, and licensed to preach or exhort by some religious society of the neighborhood, must, for the first offense, receive thirty-nine lashes, and for the second offense, fifty lashes, by the order of any justice of the county, before whom the offender may be carried.

VIII
CRISIS OF
CONSTITUTIONAL GOVERNMENT

The political contest between Abraham Lincoln and Stephen Douglas encompassed far more than a seat in the United States Senate or even the presidency itself. At stake in the 1850s was the very character of American self-government.

In 1854, Congress enacted the Kansas-Nebraska Act, the brainchild of Douglas, then-chairman of the Senate's Committee on the Territories. The Act organized these vast territories, a necessary prelude to settlement (and railroad development, which was Douglas's original motivation), but did so in a way that placed the slavery issue in a state of permanent agitation that would persist until the Civil War. This land had been made forever free as part of the Missouri Compromise of 1820, but under Kansas-Nebraska the people of these territories would settle the slavery question for themselves.

Douglas championed this new doctrine of "popular sovereignty" as a way to put slavery to rest as a national issue. The principle of popular sovereignty is, in Douglas's words, that the people of any state or territory "should be left perfectly free to form and regulate their domestic institutions in their own way, and that no limitation should be placed upon that right in any form." It is the principle of absolute majority rule, even if the majority wants to reduce a minority to chattel slavery. The majority can do as it pleases, and the function of the government is only to secure that right and effectuate the will of the majority.

Lincoln, then a railroad attorney and a former one-term congressman, did not dispute the "sacred right of self-government," but he insisted that democratic politics must be tied to the moral purposes of the republic. To divorce democratic means from just ends is to "blow out the moral lights around us," he said in his first debate with Douglas. What Lincoln called "our ancient faith" is most perfectly expressed in the Declaration of Independence. Its central premise is the principle of natural equality, the belief that "no man is good enough to govern another man, without that other's consent." Self-government is only possible when it is grounded in this transcendent moral principle. Such a principle must be universal in its application; otherwise it is untenable. Genuine self-government and slavery can never coexist. As a violation of our ancient faith, slavery can only be considered a moral evil.

Lincoln saw in the Kansas-Nebraska Act an attempt to remove the idea of moral truth as the basis of American political life. It embodied the belief that slavery is simply an issue of local property regulation, rather than one of fundamental moral principle. Douglas himself asserted that "the great principle" of popular sovereignty "is the right of every community to judge and decide for itself, whether a thing is right or wrong." Right and wrong are detached from transcendent moral truth and are instead defined by the will of the strongest, here the majority. When the majority finds that enslaving the minority is in its interest, then slavery is a moral right. Freedom and slavery are, under popular sovereignty, moral equivalents.

Lincoln saw in popular sovereignty a greater threat to free self-government than all the histrionics of the most radical southern defenders of slavery. While the latter had few respectable adherents outside the South, Douglas's popular sovereignty was gaining adherents in the North, including some influential anti-slavery leaders. What made popular sovereignty so dangerous, Lincoln warned, was that it covered itself in "the sacred right of self-government," which every American cherishes, but then warped it by removing its moral foundation, so that self-government meant nothing more than the process of popular political decision-making. If public opinion came to accept Douglas's understanding of self-government, Lincoln believed, slavery would be nationalized. Southerners would continue to promote slavery, for it would be in their interest to do so, but Northerners, taught to "care not" by Douglas, would not risk peace, prosperity, and Union to resist slavery's expansion.

The moral foundations of free self-government were at the core of the political battle between Lincoln and Douglas. The readings in this section illustrate these conflicting views of free self-government, and serve as a reminder that this issue is a permanent feature of American political life, and perhaps the most fundamental.

KEVIN PORTTEUS
Assistant Professor of Politics
Hillsdale College

SPEECH ON THE
KANSAS-NEBRASKA ACT
ABRAHAM LINCOLN

Supporters of the Compromise of 1850 lauded it as a continuation of the Missouri Compromise, which had helped maintain peace for thirty years. But four years later, the Missouri Compromise was eviscerated by the Kansas-Nebraska Act. Authored by Democratic Senator Stephen Douglas, it was in fact two provisions, one providing for the territory of Nebraska and the other for the new territory of Kansas. Breaking with the Missouri Compromise's ban on slavery in this part of the country, it established the policy of "popular sovereignty": Slavery would be voted on by the citizens of each territory, and made legal or illegal according to the will of the majority. For Abraham Lincoln, this policy struck at the very heart of free government.

OCTOBER 16, 1854

... The repeal of the Missouri Compromise, and the propriety of its restoration, constitute the subject of what I am about to say....

I think, and shall try to show, that it is wrong; wrong in its direct effect, letting slavery into Kansas and Nebraska—and wrong in its prospective principle, allowing it to spread to every other part of the wide world, where men can be   5
found inclined to take it.

This *declared* indifference, but as I must think, covert *real* zeal for the spread of slavery, I can not but hate. I hate it because of the monstrous injustice of slavery itself. I hate it because it deprives our republican example of its just influence in the world—enables the enemies of free institutions, with plausibility, to taunt   10
us as hypocrites—causes the real friends of freedom to doubt our sincerity, and especially because it forces so many really good men amongst ourselves into an open war with the very fundamental principles of civil liberty—criticising the Declaration of Independence, and insisting that there is no right principle of action but *self-interest*.   15

Abraham Lincoln, "Speech at Peoria, Illinois," October 16, 1854, in Roy P. Basler, ed., *The Collected Works of Abraham Lincoln*, Vol. 2 (New Brunswick, NJ: Rutgers University Press, 1953), 248, 255–56, 265–76. Reprinted with the permission of the Abraham Lincoln Association, Springfield, IL.

Before proceeding, let me say I think I have no prejudice against the Southern people. They are just what we would be in their situation. If slavery did not now exist amongst them, they would not introduce it. If it did now exist amongst us, we should not instantly give it up. This I believe of the masses north and south.

5   Doubtless there are individuals, on both sides, who would not hold slaves under any circumstances; and others who would gladly introduce slavery anew, if it were out of existence. We know that some southern men do free their slaves, go north, and become tip-top abolitionists; while some northern ones go south, and become most cruel slave-masters.

10   When southern people tell us they are no more responsible for the origin of slavery, than we; I acknowledge the fact. When it is said that the institution exists; and that it is very difficult to get rid of it, in any satisfactory way, I can understand and appreciate the saying. I surely will not blame them for not doing what I should not know how to do myself. If all earthly power were given me, I should not know
15   what to do, as to the existing institution. My first impulse would be to free all the slaves, and send them to Liberia,—to their own native land. But a moment's reflection would convince me, that whatever of high hope, (as I think there is) there may be in this, in the long run, its sudden execution is impossible. If they were all landed there in a day, they would all perish in the next ten days; and there
20   are not surplus shipping and surplus money enough in the world to carry them there in many times ten days. What then? Free them all, and keep them among us as underlings? Is it quite certain that this betters their condition? I think I would not hold one in slavery, at any rate; yet the point is not clear enough for me to denounce people upon. What next? Free them, and make them politically and
25   socially, our equals? My own feelings will not admit of this; and if mine would, we well know that those of the great mass of white people will not. Whether this feeling accords with justice and sound judgment, is not the sole question, if indeed, it is any part of it. A universal feeling, whether well or ill-founded, can not be safely disregarded. We can not, then, make them equals. It does seem to
30   me that systems of gradual emancipation might be adopted; but for their tardiness in this, I will not undertake to judge our brethren of the south.

When they remind us of their constitutional rights, I acknowledge them, not grudgingly, but fully, and fairly; and I would give them any legislation for the reclaiming of their fugitives, which should not, in its stringency, be more likely
35   to carry a free man into slavery, than our ordinary criminal laws are to hang an innocent one.

But all this; to my judgment, furnishes no more excuse for permitting slavery to go into our own free territory, than it would for reviving the African slave trade by law. The law which forbids the bringing of slaves *from* Africa; and that which has so long forbid the taking them *to* Nebraska, can hardly be distinguished on any moral principle; and the repeal of the former could find quite as plausible excuses as that of the latter.

The arguments by which the repeal of the Missouri Compromise is sought to be justified, are these: 5

First, that the Nebraska country needed a territorial government.

Second, that in various ways, the public had repudiated it, and demanded the repeal; and therefore should not now complain of it.

And lastly, that the repeal establishes a principle, which is intrinsically right.

I will attempt an answer to each of them in its turn....   10

But one great argument in the support of the repeal of the Missouri Compromise, is still to come. That argument is "the sacred right of self-government." It seems our distinguished Senator has found great difficulty in getting his antagonists, even in the Senate to meet him fairly on this argument—some poet has said

"Fools rush in where angels fear to tread."   15

At the hazard of being thought one of the fools of this quotation, I meet that argument—I rush in, I take that bull by the horns.

I trust I understand, and truly estimate the right of self-government. My faith in the proposition that each man should do precisely as he pleases with all which is exclusively his own, lies at the foundation of the sense of justice there is in 20 me. I extend the principles to communities of men, as well as to individuals. I so extend it, because it is politically wise, as well as naturally just; politically wise, in saving us from broils about matters which do not concern us. Here, or at Washington, I would not trouble myself with the oyster laws of Virginia, or the cranberry laws of Indiana.   25

The doctrine of self-government is right—absolutely and eternally right—but it has no just application, as here attempted. Or perhaps I should rather say that whether it has such just application depends upon whether a negro is *not* or *is* a man. If he is *not* a man, why in that case, he who *is* a man may, as a matter of self-government, do just as he pleases with him. But if the negro *is* a man, 30 is it not to that extent, a total destruction of self-government, to say that he too shall not govern *himself*? When the white man governs himself that is self-government; but when he governs himself, and also governs *another* man, that is *more* than self-government—that is despotism. If the negro is a *man*, why then my ancient faith teaches me that "all men are created equal;" and that there can 35 be no moral right in connection with one man's making a slave of another.

Judge Douglas frequently, with bitter irony and sarcasm, paraphrases our argument by saying "The white people of Nebraska are good enough to govern themselves, *but they are not good enough to govern a few miserable negroes!!*"

Well I doubt not that the people of Nebraska are, and will continue to be as
5 good as the average of people elsewhere. I do not say the contrary. What I do say is, that no man is good enough to govern another man, *without that other's consent.* I say this is the leading principle—the sheet anchor of American republicanism. Our Declaration of Independence says:

"We hold these truths to be self evident: that all men are created equal; that
10 they are endowed by their Creator with certain inalienable rights; that among these are life, liberty and the pursuit of happiness. That to secure these rights, governments are instituted among men, DERIVING THEIR JUST POWERS FROM THE CONSENT OF THE GOVERNED."

I have quoted so much at this time merely to show that according to our
15 ancient faith, the just powers of governments are derived from the consent of the governed. Now the relation of masters and slaves is, PRO TANTO, a total violation of this principle. The master not only governs the slave without his consent; but he governs him by a set of rules altogether different from those which he prescribes for himself. Allow ALL the governed an equal voice in the
20 government, and that, and that only is self-government.

Let it not be said I am contending for the establishment of political and social equality between the whites and blacks. I have already said the contrary. I am not now combating the argument of NECESSITY, arising from the fact that the blacks are already amongst us; but I am combating what is set up as MORAL argu-
25 ment for allowing them to be taken where they have never yet been—arguing against the EXTENSION of a bad thing, which where it already exists, we must of necessity, manage as we best can.

In support of his application of the doctrine of self-government, Senator Douglas has sought to bring to his aid the opinions and examples of our revolutionary
30 fathers. I am glad he has done this. I love the sentiments of those old-time men; and shall be most happy to abide by their opinions. He shows us that when it was in contemplation for the colonies to break off from Great Britain, and set up a new government for themselves, several of the states instructed their delegates to go for the measure PROVIDED EACH STATE SHOULD BE ALLOWED TO
35 REGULATE ITS DOMESTIC CONCERNS IN ITS OWN WAY. I do not quote; but this in substance. This was right. I see nothing objectionable in it. I also think it probable that it had some reference to the existence of slavery amongst them. I will not deny that it had. But had it, in any reference to the carrying of

slavery into NEW COUNTRIES? That is the question; and we will let the fathers themselves answer it.

This same generation of men, and mostly the same individuals of the generation, who declared this principle—who declared independence—who fought the war of the revolution through—who afterwards made the constitution 5 under which we still live—these same men passed the ordinance of '87, declaring that slavery should never go to the north-west territory. I have no doubt Judge Douglas thinks they were very inconsistent in this. It is a question of discrimination between them and him. But there is not an inch of ground left for his claiming that their opinions—their example—their authority—are on 10 his side in this controversy.

Again, is not Nebraska, while a territory, a part of us? Do we not own the country? And if we surrender the control of it, do we not surrender the right of self-government? It is part of ourselves. If you say we shall not control it because it is ONLY part, the same is true of every other part; and when all the parts are 15 gone, what has become of the whole? What is then left of us? What use for the general government, when there is nothing left for it [to] govern?

But you say this question should be left to the people of Nebraska, because they are more particularly interested. If this be the rule, you must leave it to each individual to say for himself whether he will have slaves. What better moral 20 right have thirty-one citizens of Nebraska to say, that the thirty-second shall not hold slaves, than the people of the thirty-one States have to say that slavery shall not go into the thirty-second State at all?

But if it is a sacred right for the people of Nebraska to take and hold slaves there, it is equally their sacred right to buy them where they can buy them cheapest; 25 and that undoubtedly will be on the coast of Africa; provided you will consent to not hang them for going there to buy them. You must remove this restriction too, from the sacred right of self-government. I am aware you say that taking slaves from the States to Nebraska, does not make slaves of freemen; but the African slave-trader can say just as much. He does not catch free negroes and 30 bring them here. He finds them already slaves in the hands of their black captors, and he honestly buys them at the rate of about a red cotton handkerchief a head. This is very cheap, and it is a great abridgement of the sacred right of self-government to hang men for engaging in this profitable trade!

Another important objection to this application of the right of self-government, 35 is that it enables the first FEW, to deprive the succeeding MANY, of a free exercise of the right of self-government. The first few may get slavery IN, and the subsequent many cannot easily get it OUT. How common is the remark now in the slave States—"If we were only clear of our slaves, how much better it would be for us." They are actually deprived of the privilege of governing themselves as they would, by the action of a very few, in the beginning. The same thing was true of the whole nation at the time our constitution was formed.

5   Whether slavery shall go into Nebraska, or other new territories, is not a matter of exclusive concern to the people who may go there. The whole nation is interested that the best use shall be made of these territories. We want them for the homes of free white people. This they cannot be, to any considerable extent, if slavery shall be planted within them. Slave States are places for poor
10   white people to remove FROM; not to remove TO. New free States are the places for poor people to go to and better their condition. For this use, the nation needs these territories.

Still further; there are constitutional relations between the slave and free States, which are degrading to the latter. We are under legal obligations to catch and
15   return their runaway slaves to them—a sort of dirty, disagreeable job, which I believe, as a general rule the slave-holders will not perform for one another. Then again, in the control of the government—the management of the partnership affairs—they have greatly the advantage of us. By the constitution, each State has two Senators—each has a number of Representatives; in proportion
20   to the number of its people—and each has a number of presidential electors, equal to the whole number of its Senators and Representatives together. But in ascertaining the number of the people, for this purpose, five slaves are counted as being equal to three whites. The slaves do not vote; they are only counted and so used, as to swell the influence of the white people's votes. The
25   practical effect of this is more aptly shown by a comparison of the States of South Carolina and Maine. South Carolina has six representatives, and so has Maine; South Carolina has eight presidential electors, and so has Maine. This is precise equality so far; and, of course they are equal in Senators, each having two. Thus in the control of the government, the two States are equals
30   precisely. But how are they in the number of their white people? Maine has 581,813—while South Carolina has 274,567. Maine has twice as many as South Carolina, and 32,679 over. Thus each white man in South Carolina is more than the double of any man in Maine. This is all because South Carolina, besides her free people, has 384,984 slaves. The South Carolinian has precisely
35   the same advantage over the white man in every other free State, as well as in Maine. He is more than the double of any one of us in this crowd. The same advantage, but not to the same extent, is held by all the citizens of the slave States, over those of the free; and it is an absolute truth, without an exception, that there is no voter in any slave State, but who has more legal power

in the government, than any voter in any free State. There is no instance of exact equality; and the disadvantage is against us the whole chapter through. This principle, in the aggregate, gives the slave States, in the present Congress, twenty additional representatives—being seven more than the whole majority by which they passed the Nebraska bill.   5

Now all this is manifestly unfair; yet I do not mention it to complain of it, in so far as it is already settled. It is in the constitution; and I do not, for that cause, or any other cause, propose to destroy, or alter, or disregard the constitution. I stand to it, fairly, fully, and firmly.

But when I am told I must leave it altogether to OTHER PEOPLE to say whether   10 new partners are to be bred up and brought into the firm, on the same degrading terms against me, I respectfully demur. I insist, that whether I shall be a whole man, or only, the half of one, in comparison with others, is a question in which I am somewhat concerned; and one which no other man can have a sacred right of deciding for me. If I am wrong in this—if it really be a sacred   15 right of self-government, in the man who shall go to Nebraska, to decide whether he will be the EQUAL of me or the DOUBLE of me, then after he shall have exercised that right, and thereby shall have reduced me to a still smaller fraction of a man than I already am, I should like for some gentleman deeply skilled in the mysteries of sacred rights, to provide himself with a microscope,   20 and peep about, and find out, if he can, what has become of my sacred rights! They will surely be too small for detection with the naked eye.

Finally, I insist, that if there is ANY THING which it is the duty of the WHOLE PEOPLE to never entrust to any hands but their own, that thing is the preservation and perpetuity, of their own liberties, and institutions. And if they shall think,   25 as I do, that the extension of slavery endangers them, more than any, or all other causes, how recreant to themselves, if they submit the question, and with it, the fate of their country, to a mere hand-full of men, bent only on temporary self-interest. If this question of slavery extension were an insignificant one—one having no power to do harm—it might be shuffled aside in this way. But being,   30 as it is, the great Behemoth of danger, shall the strong gripe of the nation be loosened upon him, to entrust him to the hands of such feeble keepers?

I have done with this mighty argument, of self-government. Go, sacred thing! Go in peace.

But Nebraska is urged as a great Union-saving measure. Well I too, go for   35 saving the Union. Much as I hate slavery, I would consent to the extension of it rather than see the Union dissolved, just as I would consent to any GREAT evil, to avoid a GREATER one. But when I go to Union saving, I must believe, at least, that the means I employ has some adaptation to the end. To my mind, Nebraska has no such adaptation.

"It hath no relish of salvation in it."

5

It is an aggravation, rather, of the only one thing which ever endangers the Union. When it came upon us, all was peace and quiet. The nation was looking to the forming of new bonds of Union; and a long course of peace and prosperity seemed to lie before us. In the whole range of possibility, there scarcely appears to me to have been any thing, out of which the slavery agitation could have been revived, except the very project of repealing the Missouri

10

compromise. Every inch of territory we owned, already had a definite settlement of the slavery question, and by which, all parties were pledged to abide. Indeed, there was no uninhabited country on the continent, which we could acquire; if we except some extreme northern regions, which are wholly out of the question. In this state of case, the genius of Discord himself, could scarcely

15

have invented a way of again getting us by the ears, but by turning back and destroying the peace measures of the past. The councils of that genius seem to have prevailed, the Missouri compromise was repealed; and here we are, in the midst of a new slavery agitation, such, I think, as we have never seen before. Who is responsible for this? Is it those who resist the measure; or those who, cause-

20

lessly, brought it forward, and pressed it through, having reason to know, and, in fact, knowing it must and would be so resisted? It could not but be expected by its author, that it would be looked upon as a measure for the extension of slavery, aggravated by a gross breach of faith. Argue as you will, and long as you will, this is the naked FRONT and ASPECT, of the measure. And in this aspect, it

25

could not but produce agitation. Slavery is founded in the selfishness of man's nature—opposition to it, is his love of justice. These principles are an eternal antagonism; and when brought into collision so fiercely, as slavery extension brings them, shocks, and throes, and convulsions must ceaselessly follow. Repeal the Missouri compromise—repeal all compromises—repeal the declaration of

30

independence—repeal all past history, you still can not repeal human nature. It still will be the abundance of man's heart, that slavery extension is wrong; and out of the abundance of his heart, his mouth will continue to speak.

The structure, too, of the Nebraska bill is very peculiar. The people are to decide the question of slavery for themselves; but WHEN they are to decide; or HOW

35

they are to decide; or whether, when the question is once decided, it is to remain so, or is it to be subject to an indefinite succession of new trials, the law does not say, Is it to be decided by the first dozen settlers who arrive there? or is it to await the arrival of a hundred? Is it to be decided by a vote of the people? or a vote of the legislature? or, indeed by a vote of any sort? To these questions, the law gives no answer. There is a mystery about this; for when a member proposed to give the legislature express authority to exclude slavery, it was hooted down by the friends of the bill. This fact is worth remembering. Some yankees, in the east, are sending emigrants to Nebraska, to exclude slavery from it; and, so far as I can judge, they expect the question to be decided by voting, in some way or other. But the Missourians are awake too. They are within a stone's throw of the contested ground. They hold meetings, and pass resolutions, in which not the slightest allusion to voting is made. They resolve that slavery already exists in the territory; that more shall go there; that they, remaining in Missouri will protect it; and that abolitionists shall be hung, or driven away. Through all this, bowie-knives and six-shooters are seen plainly enough; but never a glimpse of the ballot-box. And, really, what is to be the result of this? Each party WITHIN, having numerous and determined backers WITHOUT, is it not probable that the contest will come to blows, and bloodshed? Could there be a more apt invention to bring about collision and violence, on the slavery question, than this Nebraska project is? I do not charge, or believe, that such was intended by Congress; but if they had literally formed a ring, and placed champions within it to fight out the controversy, the fight could be no more likely to come off, than it is. And if this fight should begin, is it likely to take a very peaceful, Union-saving turn? Will not the first drop of blood so shed, be the real knell of the Union?

The Missouri Compromise ought to be restored. For the sake of the Union, it ought to be restored. We ought to elect a House of Representatives which will vote its restoration. If by any means, we omit to do this, what follows? Slavery may or may not be established in Nebraska. But whether it be or not, we shall have repudiated—discarded from the councils of the Nation—the SPIRIT of COMPROMISE; for who after this will ever trust in a national compromise? The spirit of mutual concession—that spirit which first gave us the constitution, and which has thrice saved the Union—we shall have strangled and cast from us forever. And what shall we have in lieu of it? The South flushed with triumph and tempted to excesses; the North, betrayed, as they believe, brooding on wrong and burning for revenge. One side will provoke; the other resent. The one will taunt, the other defy; one agrees, the other retaliates. Already a few in the North, defy all constitutional restraints, resist the execution of the fugitive slave law, and even menace the institution of slavery in the States where it exists.

Already a few in the South, claim the constitutional right to take to and hold slaves in the free states—demand the revival of the slave trade; and demand a treaty with Great Britain by which fugitive slaves may be reclaimed from Canada. As yet they are but few on either side. It is a grave question for the lovers of the

Union, whether the final destruction of the Missouri Compromise, and with it the spirit of all compromise will or will not embolden and embitter each of these, and fatally increase the numbers of both.

But restore the compromise, and what then? We thereby restore the national
5   faith, the national confidence, the national feeling of brotherhood. We thereby reinstate the spirit of concession and compromise—that spirit which has never failed us in past perils, and which may be safely trusted for all the future. The south ought to join in doing this. The peace of the nation is as dear to them as to us. In memories of the past and hopes of the future, they share as largely
10   as we. It would be on their part, a great act—great in its spirit, and great in its effect. It would be worth to the nation a hundred years' purchase of peace and prosperity. And what of sacrifice would they make? They only surrender to us, what they gave us for a consideration long, long ago; what they have not now, asked for, struggled or cared for; what has been thrust upon them, not less to
15   their own astonishment than to ours.

But it is said we cannot restore it; that though we elect every member of the lower house, the Senate is still against us. It is quite true, that of the Senators who passed the Nebraska bill, a majority of the whole Senate will retain their seats in spite of the elections of this and the next year. But if at these elections,
20   their several constituencies shall clearly express their will against Nebraska, will these senators disregard their will? Will they neither obey, nor make room for those who will?

But even if we fail to technically restore the compromise, it is still a great point to carry a popular vote in favor of the restoration. The moral weight of such a vote
25   can not be estimated too highly. The authors of Nebraska are not at all satisfied with the destruction of the compromise—an endorsement of this PRINCIPLE, they proclaim to be the great object. With them, Nebraska alone is a small matter—to establish a principle, for FUTURE USE, is what they particularly desire.

That future use is to be the planting of slavery wherever in the wide world, local
30   and unorganized opposition can not prevent it. Now if you wish to give them this endorsement—if you wish to establish this principle—do so. I shall regret it; but it is your right. On the contrary if you are opposed to the principle— intend to give it no such endorsement—let no wheedling, no sophistry, divert you from throwing a direct vote against it.

35   Some men, mostly whigs, who condemn the repeal of the Missouri Com- promise, nevertheless hesitate to go for its restoration, lest they be thrown in company with the abolitionist. Will they allow me as an old whig to tell them good humoredly, that I think this is very silly? Stand with anybody that stands

RIGHT. Stand with him while he is right and PART with him when he goes wrong. Stand WITH the abolitionist in restoring the Missouri Compromise; and stand AGAINST him when he attempts to repeal the fugitive slave law. In the latter case you stand with the southern disunionist. What of that? you are still right. In both cases you are right. In both cases you oppose the dangerous extremes. In   5 both you stand on middle ground and hold the ship level and steady. In both you are national and nothing less than national. This is good old whig ground. To desert such ground, because of any company, is to be less than a whig—less than a man—less than an American.

I particularly object to the NEW position which the avowed principle of this   10 Nebraska law gives to slavery in the body politic. I object to it because it assumes that there CAN be MORAL RIGHT in the enslaving of one man by another. I object to it as a dangerous dalliance for a few people—a sad evidence that, feeling prosperity we forget right—that liberty, as a principle, we have ceased to revere. I object to it because the fathers of the republic eschewed, and rejected   15 it. The argument of "Necessity" was the only argument they ever admitted in favor of slavery; and so far, and so far only as it carried them, did they ever go. They found the institution existing among us, which they could not help; and they cast blame upon the British King for having permitted its introduction. BEFORE the constitution, they prohibited its introduction into the north-western   20 Territory—the only country we owned, then free from it. AT the framing and adoption of the constitution, they forbore to so much as mention the word "slave" or "slavery" in the whole instrument. In the provision for the recovery of fugitives, the slave is spoken of as a "PERSON HELD TO SERVICE OR LABOR." In that prohibiting the abolition of the African slave trade for twenty years, that   25 trade is spoken of as "The migration or importation of such persons as any of the States NOW EXISTING, shall think proper to admit," etc. These are the only provisions alluding to slavery. Thus, the thing is hid away, in the constitution, just as an afflicted man hides away a wen or a cancer, which he dares not cut out at once, lest he bleed to death; with the promise, nevertheless, that the cutting   30 may begin at the end of a given time. Less than this our fathers COULD not do; and NOW they WOULD not do. Necessity drove them so far, and farther, they would not go. But this is not all. The earliest Congress, under the constitution, took the same view of slavery. They hedged and hemmed it in to the narrowest limits of necessity.   35

In 1794, they prohibited an out-going slave-trade—that is, the taking of slaves FROM the United States to sell.

In 1798, they prohibited the bringing of slaves from Africa, INTO the Mississippi Territory—this territory then comprising what are now the States of Mississippi and Alabama. This was TEN YEARS before they had the authority to do the same thing as to the States existing at the adoption of the constitution.

In 1800 they prohibited AMERICAN CITIZENS from trading in slaves between foreign countries—as, for instance, from Africa to Brazil.

5   In 1803 they passed a law in aid of one or two State laws, in restraint of the internal slave trade.

In 1807, in apparent hot haste, they passed the law, nearly a year in advance, to take effect the first day of 1808—the very first day the constitution would permit—prohibiting the African slave trade by heavy pecuniary and corporal
10   penalties.

In 1820, finding these provisions ineffectual, they declared the trade piracy, and annexed to it, the extreme penalty of death. While all this was passing in the general government, five or six of the original slave States had adopted systems of gradual emancipation; and by which the institution was rapidly becoming
15   extinct within these limits.

Thus we see, the plain unmistakable spirit of that age, towards slavery, was hostility to the PRINCIPLE, and toleration, ONLY BY NECESSITY.

But NOW it is to be transformed into a "sacred right." Nebraska brings it forth, places it on the high road to extension and perpetuity; and, with a pat on its
20   back, says to it, "Go, and God speed you." Henceforth it is to be the chief jewel of the nation—the very figure-head of the ship of State. Little by little, but steadily as man's march to the grave, we have been giving up the OLD for the NEW faith. Near eighty years ago we began by declaring that all men are created equal; but now from that beginning we have run down to the other
25   declaration, that for SOME men to enslave OTHERS is a "sacred right of self-government." These principles can not stand together. They are as opposite as God and mammon; and whoever holds to the one, must despise the other. When Pettit, in connection with his support of the Nebraska bill, called the Declaration of Independence "a self-evident lie" he only did what consistency
30   and candor require all other Nebraska men to do. Of the forty odd Nebraska Senators who sat present and heard him, no one rebuked him. Nor am I apprised that any Nebraska newspaper, or any Nebraska orator, in the whole nation, has ever yet rebuked him. If this had been said among Marion's men, Southerners though they were, what would have become of the man who said
35   it? If this had been said to the men who captured André, the man who said it, would probably have been hung sooner than André was. If it had been said in old Independence Hall, seventy-eight years ago, the very door-keeper would have throttled the man, and thrust him into the street.

Let no one be deceived. The spirit of seventy-six and the spirit of Nebraska, are utter antagonisms; and the former is being rapidly displaced by the latter.

Fellow countrymen—Americans south, as well as north, shall we make no effort to arrest this? Already the liberal party throughout the world, express the apprehension "that the one retrograde institution in America, is undermining   5
the principles of progress, and fatally violating the noblest political system the world ever saw." This is not the taunt of enemies, but the warning of friends. Is it quite safe to disregard it—to despise it? Is there no danger to liberty itself, in discarding the earliest practice, and first precept of our ancient faith? In our greedy chase to make profit of the negro, let us beware, lest we "cancel and tear to pieces" even the white man's charter of freedom.   10

Our republican robe is soiled, and trailed in the dust. Let us repurify it. Let us turn and wash it white, in the spirit, if not the blood, of the Revolution. Let us turn slavery from its claims of "moral right," back upon its existing legal rights, and its arguments of "necessity." Let us return it to the position our fathers gave it; and there let it rest in peace. Let us re-adopt the Declaration of Independence,   15
and with it, the practices, and policy, which harmonize with it. Let north and south—let all Americans—let all lovers of liberty everywhere—join in the great and good work. If we do this, we shall not only have saved the Union; but we shall have so saved it, as to make, and to keep it, forever worthy of the saving. We shall have so saved it, that the succeeding millions of free happy people, the   20
world over, shall rise up, and call us blessed, to the latest generations....

REPUBLICAN PARTY PLATFORM
OF 1856

*Northern anger toward the Kansas-Nebraska Act reached its zenith in the
late spring of 1854, when various anti-slavery forces coalesced in Jackson,
Michigan. Organized around the principles of the Declaration of Independence, the Republican Party was born out of this meeting. It would adopt
a platform two years later that called for repeal of the Kansas-Nebraska
Act and restoration of the Missouri Compromise.*

JUNE 17, 1856

This convention of delegates, assembled in pursuance of a call addressed to
the people of the United States, without regard to past political differences
or divisions, who are opposed to the repeal of the Missouri Compromise, to
the policy of the present Administration, to the extension of slavery into free
territory; in favor of the admission of Kansas as a free state, of restoring the   5
action of the Federal government to the principles of Washington and Jefferson;
and who purpose to unite in presenting candidates for the offices of President
and Vice-President, do resolve as follows:

Resolved, That the maintenance of the principles promulgated in the Declaration
of Independence, and embodied in the federal constitution, is essential to the   10
preservation of our Republican institutions, and that the federal constitution,
the rights of the states, and the union of the states, shall be preserved.

Resolved, That with our republican fathers we hold it to be a self-evident
truth that all men are endowed with the inalienable right to life, liberty, and
the pursuit of happiness, and that the primary object and ulterior design of   15
our Federal government were, to secure these rights to all persons within its
exclusive jurisdiction; that as our republican fathers, when they had abolished
slavery in all our national territory, ordained that no person should be deprived

"1856.—Republican Platform," June 17, 1856, in Thomas Valentine Cooper and Hector Tyndale
Fenton, eds., *American Politics (Non-Partisan) from the Beginning to Date*, Vol. 2 (Philadelphia:
Fireside Publishing Company, 1892), 39–40.

of life, liberty, or property, without due process of law, it becomes our duty
to maintain this provision of the constitution against all attempts to violate
it for the purpose of establishing slavery in any territory of the United States,
by positive legislation, prohibiting its existence or extension therein. That we
5 deny the authority of Congress, of a territorial legislature, of any individual or
association of individuals, to give legal existence to slavery in any territory of
the United States, while the present constitution shall be maintained.

Resolved, That the constitution confers upon Congress sovereign power over the
territories of the United States for their government, and that in the exercise of
10 this power it is both the right and the imperative duty of Congress to prohibit
in the territories those twin relics of barbarism—polygamy and slavery.

Resolved, That while the constitution of the United States was ordained and
established, in order to form a more perfect union, establish justice, insure
domestic tranquility, provide for the common defense, promote the general
15 welfare, and secure the blessings of liberty, and contains ample provision for
the protection of the life, liberty, and property of every citizen, the dearest
constitutional rights of the people of Kansas have been fraudulently and violently
taken from them; their territory has been invaded by an armed force; spurious
and pretended legislative, judicial, and executive officers have been set over them,
20 by whose usurped authority, sustained by the military power of the government,
tyrannical and unconstitutional laws have been enacted and enforced; the
rights of the people to keep and bear arms have been infringed; test oaths of
an extraordinary and entangling nature have been imposed as a condition of
exercising the right of suffrage and holding office; the right of an accused person
25 to a speedy and public trial by an impartial jury has been denied; the right of
the people to be secure in their persons, houses, papers, and effects, against
unreasonable searches and seizures, has been violated; they have been deprived of
life, liberty, and property without due process of law; that the freedom of speech
and of the press has been abridged; the right to choose their representatives has
30 been made of no effect; murders, robberies, and arsons have been instigated
and encouraged, and the offenders have been allowed to go unpunished; that
all these things have been done with the knowledge, sanction, and procurement
of the present national administration; and that for this high crime against the
constitution, the Union, and humanity, we arraign that administration, the
35 President, his advisers, agents, supporters, apologists, and accessories, either
before or after the facts, before the country and before the world; and that it is
our fixed purpose to bring the actual perpetrators of these atrocious outrages,
and their accomplices, to a sure and condign punishment thereafter.

Resolved, That Kansas should be immediately admitted as a state of this Union, with her present free constitution, as at once the most effectual way of securing to her citizens the enjoyment of the rights and privileges to which they are entitled, and of ending the civil strife now raging in her territory.

Resolved, That the highwayman's plea, that "might makes right," embodied in   5
the Ostend circular, was in every respect unworthy of American diplomacy, and would bring shame and dishonor upon any government or people that gave it their sanction.

Resolved, That a railroad to the Pacific ocean, by the most central and practicable route, is imperatively demanded by the interests of the whole country, and   10
that the Federal government ought to render immediate and efficient aid in its construction, and, as an auxiliary thereto, to the immediate construction of an emigrant road on the line of the railroad.

Resolved, That appropriations of Congress for the improvement of rivers and harbors of a national character, required for the accommodation and security   15
of our existing commerce, are authorized by the constitution, and justified by the obligation of government to protect the lives and property of its citizens.

Resolved, That we invite the affiliation and cooperation of the men of all parties, however differing from us in other respects, in support of the principles herein declared; and believing that the spirit of our institutions, as well as the constitution   20
of our country, guarantees liberty of conscience and equality of rights among citizens, we oppose all proscriptive legislation affecting their security.

DRED SCOTT v. SANDFORD
ROGER TANEY (1777–1864)

*Like Stephen Douglas, Supreme Court Chief Justice Roger Taney believed
that his response to the slavery controversy would resolve the issue. His ruling
in* Dred Scott v. Sandford *had the opposite result, throwing the country
into even greater turmoil. The case was brought by a slave, Dred Scott, who
was taken by his master into territory in which slavery was illegal. Asked
to rule simply on whether Scott's residency in a free territory meant that he
should be granted freedom, the Court ruled that Congress had no power
to regulate slavery in the territories and that persons of African descent
could not be citizens, rendering both the Missouri Compromise and the
Compromise of 1850 unconstitutional.*

1857

MR. CHIEF JUSTICE TANEY DELIVERED THE OPINION OF THE COURT: . . .

. . . The question is simply this: can a negro, whose ancestors were imported into
this country and sold as slaves, become a member of the political community
formed and brought into existence by the Constitution of the United States,
and as such become entitled to all the rights, and privileges, and immunities,
guaranteed by that instrument to the citizen. One of these rights is the privilege of   5
suing in a court of the United States in the cases specified in the Constitution.

It will be observed, that the plea applies to that class of persons only whose
ancestors were negroes of the African race, and imported into this country, and
sold and held as slaves. The only matter in issue before the court, therefore, is,
whether the descendants of such slaves, when they shall be emancipated, or   10
who are born of parents who had become free before their birth, are citizens of
a state, in the sense in which the word "citizen" is used in the Constitution of
the United States. And this being the only matter in dispute on the pleadings,
the court must be understood as speaking in this opinion of that class only; that
is, of those persons who are the descendants of Africans who were imported   15
into this country and sold as slaves. . . .

---

60 U.S. (19 How.) 393 (1857).

We proceed to examine the case as presented by the pleadings.

The words "people of the United States" and "citizens" are synonymous terms, and mean the same thing. They both describe the political body who, according to our republican institutions, form the sovereignty, and who hold the power

5   and conduct the government through their representatives. They are what we familiarly call the "sovereign people," and every citizen is one of this people, and a constituent member of this sovereignty. The question before us is, whether the class of persons described in the plea in abatement compose a portion of this people, and are constituent members of this sovereignty. We think they

10   are not, and that they are not included, and were not intended to be included, under the word "citizens" in the Constitution, and can, therefore, claim none of the rights and privileges which that instrument provides for and secures to citizens of the United States. On the contrary, they were at that time considered as a subordinate and inferior class of beings, who had been subjugated by the

15   dominant race, and whether emancipated or not, yet remained subject to their authority, and had no rights or privileges but such as those who held the power and the government might choose to grant them.

It is not the province of the court to decide upon the justice or injustice, the policy or impolicy of these laws. The decision of that question belonged to the

20   political or law-making power; to those who formed the sovereignty and framed the Constitution. The duty of the court is to interpret the instrument they have framed, with the best lights we can obtain on the subject, and to administer it as we find it, according to its true intent and meaning when it was adopted.

In discussing this question, we must not confound the rights of citizenship

25   which a state may confer within its own limits, and the rights of citizenship as a member of the Union. It does not by any means follow, because he has all the rights and privileges of a citizen of a State, that he must be a citizen of the United States. He may have all of the rights and privileges of the citizen of a State, and yet not be entitled to the rights and privileges of a citizen in any other

30   State. For, previous to the adoption of the Constitution of the United States, every State had the undoubted right to confer on whomsoever it pleased the character of a citizen, and to endow him with all its rights. But this character, of course, was confined to the boundaries of the State, and gave him no rights or privileges in other States beyond those secured to him by the laws of nations

35   and the comity of States. Nor have the several States surrendered the power of conferring these rights and privileges by adopting the Constitution of the United States. Each State may still confer them upon an alien, or any one it thinks proper, or upon any class or description of persons; yet he would not be a citizen in the sense in which that word is used in the Constitution of the

United States, nor entitled to sue as such in one of its courts, nor to the privileges and immunities of a citizen in the other States. The rights which he would
acquire would be restricted to the State which gave them. The Constitution has
conferred on Congress the right to establish an uniform rule of naturalization,
and this right is evidently exclusive, and has always been held by this court to   5
be so. Consequently, no State, since the adoption of the Constitution, can, by
naturalizing an alien, invest him with the rights and privileges secured to a citizen
of a State under the federal government, although, so far as the State alone was
concerned, he would undoubtedly be entitled to the rights of a citizen, and
clothed with all the rights and immunities which the Constitution and laws of   10
the State attached to that character.

It is very clear, therefore, that no State can, by any Act or law of its own,
passed since the adoption of the Constitution, introduce a new member into
the political community created by the Constitution of the United States. It
cannot make him a member of this community by making him a member of   15
its own. And for the same reason it cannot introduce any person, or description of persons, who were not intended to be embraced in this new political
family, which the Constitution brought into existence, but were intended to
be excluded from it.

The question then arises, whether the provisions of the Constitution, in relation   20
to the personal rights and privileges to which the citizen of a state should be
entitled, embraced the negro African race, at that time in this country, or who
might afterwards be imported, who had then or should afterwards be made free
in any State; and to put it in the power of a single State to make him a citizen
of the United States, and endue him with the full rights of citizenship in every   25
other State without their consent. Does the Constitution of the United States
act upon him whenever he shall be made free under the laws of a State, and
raised there to the rank of a citizen, and immediately clothe him with all the
privileges of a citizen in every other State, and in its own courts?

The court think the affirmative of these propositions cannot be maintained.   30
And if it cannot, the plaintiff in error could not be a citizen of the State of
Missouri, within the meaning of the Constitution of the United States, and,
consequently, was not entitled to sue in its courts.

It is true, every person, and every class and description of persons, who were at
the time of the adoption of the Constitution recognized as citizens in the several   35
States, became also citizens of this new political body; but none other; it was
formed by them, and for them and their posterity, but for no one else. And the
personal rights and privileges guaranteed to citizens of this new sovereignty were

intended to embrace those only who were then members of the several state communities, or who should afterwards, by birthright or otherwise, become members, according to the provisions of the Constitution and the principles on which it was founded. It was the union of those who were at that time members of distinct and separate political communities into one political family, whose power, for certain specified purposes, was to extend over the whole territory of the United States. And it gave to each citizen rights and privileges outside of his State which he did not before possess, and placed him in every other State upon a perfect equality with its own citizens as to rights of person and rights of property; it made him a citizen of the United States.

It becomes necessary, therefore, to determine who were citizens of the several States when the Constitution was adopted. And in order to do this, we must recur to the governments and institutions of the thirteen Colonies, when they separated from Great Britain and formed new sovereignties, and took their places in the family of independent nations. We must inquire who, at that time, were recognized as the people or citizens of a State, whose rights and liberties had been outraged by the English Government; and who declared their independence, and assumed the powers of government to defend their rights by force of arms.

In the opinion of the court, the legislation and histories of the times, and the language used in the Declaration of Independence, show, that neither the class of persons who had been imported as slaves, nor their descendants, whether they had become free or not, were then acknowledged as a part of the people, nor intended to be included in the general words used in that memorable instrument.

It is difficult at this day to realize the state of public opinion in relation to that unfortunate race, which prevailed in the civilized and enlightened portions of the world at the time of the Declaration of Independence, and when the Constitution of the United States was framed and adopted. But the public history of every European nation displays it, in a manner too plain to be mistaken.

They had for more than a century before been regarded as beings of an inferior order; and altogether unfit to associate with the white race, either in social or political relations; and so far inferior, that they had no rights which the white man was bound to respect; and that the negro might justly and lawfully be reduced to slavery for his benefit. He was bought and sold, and treated as an ordinary article of merchandise and traffic, whenever a profit could be made by it. This opinion was at that time fixed and universal in the civilized portion of the white race. It was regarded as an axiom in morals as well as in politics, which no one thought of disputing, or supposed to be open to dispute; and men in every grade and position in society daily and habitually acted upon it in their private pursuits, as well as in matters of public concern, without doubting for a moment the correctness of this opinion.

And in no nation was this opinion more firmly fixed or more uniformly acted upon than by the English government and English people. They not only seized them on the coast of Africa, and sold them or held them in slavery for their own use; but they took them as ordinary articles of merchandise to every country where they could make a profit on them, and were far more extensively engaged in this commerce than any other nation in the world.

The opinion thus entertained and acted upon in England was naturally impressed upon the colonies they founded on this side of the Atlantic. And, accordingly, a negro of the African race was regarded by them as an article of property, and held, and bought and sold as such, in every one of the thirteen Colonies which united in the Declaration of Independence, and afterwards formed the Constitution of the United States. The slaves were more or less numerous in the different Colonies, as slave labor was found more or less profitable. But no one seems to have doubted the correctness of the prevailing opinion of the time.

The legislation of the different Colonies furnishes positive and indisputable proof of this fact....

The language of the Declaration of Independence is equally conclusive.

It begins by declaring that, "when in the course of human events it becomes necessary for one people to dissolve the political bands which have connected them with another, and to assume among the powers of the earth the separate and equal station to which the laws of nature and nature's God entitle them, a decent respect for the opinions of mankind requires that they should declare the causes which impel them to the separation."

It then proceeds to say: "We hold these truths to be self-evident: that all men are created equal; that they are endowed by their Creator with certain inalienable rights; that among them is life, liberty, and pursuit of happiness; that to secure these rights, governments are instituted, deriving their just powers from the consent of the governed."

The general words above quoted would seem to embrace the whole human family, and if they were used in a similar instrument at this day, would be so understood. But it is too clear for dispute, that the enslaved African race were not intended to be included, and formed no part of the people who framed and adopted this Declaration; for if the language, as understood in that day, would

embrace them, the conduct of the distinguished men who framed the Declaration of Independence would have been utterly and flagrantly inconsistent with the principles they asserted; and instead of the sympathy of mankind, to which they so confidently appealed, they would have deserved and received universal
5   rebuke and reprobation.

Yet the men who framed this Declaration were great men—high in literary acquirements—high in their sense of honor, and incapable of asserting principles inconsistent with those on which they were acting. They perfectly understood the meaning of the language they used, and how it would be understood by
10   others; and they knew that it would not, in any part of the civilized world, be supposed to embrace the negro race, which, by common consent, had been excluded from civilized governments and the family of nations, and doomed to slavery. They spoke and acted according to the then established doctrines and principles, and in the ordinary language of the day, and no one misunderstood
15   them. The unhappy black race were separated from the white by indelible marks, and laws long before established, and were never thought of or spoken of except as property, and when the claims of the owner or the profit of the trader were supposed to need protection.

This state of public opinion had undergone no change when the Constitution
20   was adopted, as is equally evident from its provisions and language.

The brief preamble sets forth by whom it was formed, for what purposes, and for whose benefit and protection. It declares that it is formed by the people of the United States; that is to say, by those who were members of the different political communities in the several States; and its great object is declared to
25   be to secure the blessings of liberty to themselves and their posterity. It speaks in general terms of the people of the United States, and of citizens of the several States, when it is providing for the exercise of the powers granted or the privileges secured to the citizen. It does not define what description of persons are intended to be included under these terms, or who shall be regarded as a
30   citizen and one of the people. It uses them as terms so well understood that no further description or definition was necessary.

But there are two clauses in the Constitution which point directly and specifically to the negro race as a separate class of persons, and show clearly that they were not regarded as a portion of the people or citizens of the government
35   then formed.

One of these clauses reserves to each of the thirteen States the right to import slaves until the year 1808, if it thinks proper. And the importation which it thus sanctions was unquestionably of persons of the race of which we are speaking, as the traffic in slaves in the United States had always been confined to them. And by the other provision the States pledge themselves to each other to maintain the right of property of the master, by delivering up to him any slave who may have escaped from his service, and be found within their respective territories. By the first above-mentioned clause, therefore, the right to purchase and hold   5 this property is directly sanctioned and authorized for twenty years by the people who framed the Constitution. And by the second, they pledge themselves to maintain and uphold the right of the master in the manner specified, as long as the government they then formed should endure. And these two provisions show, conclusively, that neither the description of persons therein referred to,   10 nor their descendants, were embraced in any of the other provisions of the Constitution; for certainly these two clauses were not intended to confer on them or their posterity the blessings of liberty, or any of the personal rights so carefully provided for the citizen....

We proceed, therefore, to inquire whether the facts relied on by the plaintiff   15 entitled him to his freedom.

The case, as he himself states it, on the record, brought here by his writ of error, is this:

The plaintiff was a negro slave, belonging to Dr. Emerson, who was a surgeon in the Army of the United States. In the year 1834, he took the plaintiff from   20 the State of Missouri to the military post at Rock Island, in the State of Illinois, and held him there as a slave until the month of April or May, 1836. At the time last mentioned, said Dr. Emerson removed the plaintiff from said military post at Rock Island to the military post at Fort Snelling, situated on the west bank of the Mississippi River, in the Territory known as Upper Louisiana,   25 acquired by the United States of France, and situated north of the latitude of thirty-six degrees thirty minutes north, and north of the State of Missouri. Said Dr. Emerson held the plaintiff in slavery at said Fort Snelling, from said last mentioned date until the year 1838.

In the year 1835, Harriet, who is named in the second count of the plaintiff's   30 declaration, was negro slave of Major Taliaferro, who belonged to the Army of the United States. In that year, 1835, said Major Taliaferro took said Harriet to said Fort Snelling, a military post, situated as hereinbefore stated, and kept her there as a slave until the year 1836, and then sold and delivered her as a slave, at said Fort Snelling, unto the said Dr. Emerson hereinbefore named. Said Dr.   35 Emerson held said Harriet in slavery at said Fort Snelling, until the year 1838.

In the year 1836, the plaintiff and Harriet intermarried, at Fort Snelling, with the consent of Dr. Emerson, who then claimed to be their master and owner.

Eliza and Lizzie, named in the third count of the plaintiff's declaration, are the fruit of that marriage. Eliza is about fourteen years old, and was born on board the steamboat Gipsey, north of the north line of the State of Missouri, and upon the River Mississippi. Lizzie is about seven years old, and was born in the State
5 of Missouri, at the military post called Jefferson Barracks.

In the year 1838, said Dr. Emerson removed the plaintiff and said Harriet, and their said daughter Eliza, from said Fort Snelling, to the State of Missouri, where they have ever since resided.

Before the commencement of this suit, said Dr. Emerson sold and conveyed
10 the plaintiff, and Harriet, Eliza, and Lizzie, to the defendant, as slaves, and the defendant has ever since claimed to hold them, and each of them, as slaves.

In considering this part of the controversy, two questions arise: 1st. Was he, together with his family, free in Missouri by reason of the stay in the territory of the United States hereinbefore mentioned? And 2d. If they were not, is Scott
15 himself free by reason of his removal to Rock Island, in the State of Illinois, as stated in the above admissions?

We proceed to examine the first question.

The Act of Congress, upon which the plaintiff relies, declares that slavery and involuntary servitude, except as a punishment for crime, shall be forever
20 prohibited in all that part of the territory ceded by France, under the name of Louisiana, which lies north of thirty-six degrees thirty minutes north latitude, and not included within the limits of Missouri. And the difficulty which meets us at the threshold of this part of the inquiry is, whether Congress was authorized to pass this law under any of the powers granted to it by the Constitution; for
25 if the authority is not given by that instrument, it is the duty of this court to declare it void and inoperative, and incapable of conferring freedom upon one who is held as a slave under the laws of any one of the States.

The counsel for the plaintiff has laid much stress upon that article in the Constitution which confers on Congress the power "to dispose of and make all needful
30 rules and regulations respecting the territory or other property belonging to the United States;" but, in the judgment of the court, that provision has no bearing on the present controversy, and the power there given, whatever it may be, is confined, and was intended to be confined, to the territory which at that time belonged to, or was claimed by, the United States, and was within their
35 boundaries as settled by the Treaty with Great Britain, and can have no influence upon a territory afterwards acquired from a foreign government. It was a special provision for a known and particular Territory, and to meet a present emergency, and nothing more.

A brief summary of the history of the times, as well as the careful and measured terms in which the article is framed, will show the correctness of this proposition….

This was the state of things when the Constitution of the United States was formed. The territory ceded by Virginia belonged to the several confederated States as common property, and they had united in establishing in it a system of government and jurisprudence, in order to prepare it for admission as States, according to the terms of the cession. They were about to dissolve this federative Union, and to surrender a portion of their independent sovereignty to a new government, which, for certain purposes, would make the people of the several States one people, and which was to be supreme and controlling within its sphere of action throughout the United States; but this government was to be carefully limited in its powers, and to exercise no authority beyond those expressly granted by the Constitution, or necessarily to be implied from the language of the instrument, and the objects it was intended to accomplish; and as this league of States would, upon the adoption of the new government, cease to have any power over the territory, and the Ordinance they had agreed upon be incapable of execution, and a mere nullity, it was obvious that some provision was necessary to give the new government sufficient power to enable it to carry into effect the objects for which it was ceded, and the compacts and agreements which the States had made each other in the exercise of their powers of sovereignty. It was necessary that the lands should be sold to pay the war debt; that a government and system of jurisprudence should be maintained in it, to protect the citizens of the United States, who should migrate to the Territory, in their rights of person and of property. It was also necessary that the new government, about to be adopted, should be authorized to maintain the claim of the United States to the unappropriated lands in North Carolina and Georgia, which had not then been ceded, but the cession of which was confidently anticipated upon some terms that would be arranged between the general government and these two States. And, moreover, there were many articles of value besides this property in land, such as arms, military stores, munitions, and ships of war, which were the common property of the States, when acting in their independent characters as confederates, which neither the new government nor any one else would have a right to take possession of, or control, without authority from them; and it was to place these things under the guardianship and protection of the new government, and to clothe it with the necessary powers, that the clause was inserted in the Constitution which give Congress the power "to dispose of and make all needful rules and regulations respecting the territory or other property belonging to the United States." It was intended for a specific purpose, to provide for the things we have mentioned. It was to transfer to the new government the property then held in common by

the States, and to give to that government power to apply it to the objects for which it had been destined by mutual agreement among the States before their league was dissolved. It applied only to the property which the States held in common at that time, and has no reference whatever to any territory or other
5   property which the new sovereignty might afterwards itself acquire....

The Constitution has always been remarkable for the felicity of its arrangement of different subjects, and the perspicuity and appropriateness of the language it uses. But if this clause is construed to extend to territory acquired by the present government from a foreign nation, outside of the limits of any charter
10   from the British Government to a Colony, it would be difficult to say, why it was deemed necessary to give the government the power to sell any vacant lands belonging to the sovereignty which might be found within it; and if this was necessary, why the grant of this power should precede the power to legislate over it and establish a government there; and still more difficult to say, why it
15   was deemed necessary so specially and particularly to grant the power to make needful rules and regulations in relation to any personal or movable property it might acquire there. For the words, "other property", necessarily, by every known rule of interpretation, must mean property of a different description from territory or land. And the difficulty would perhaps be insurmountable in
20   endeavoring to account for the last member of the sentence, which provides that "nothing in this Constitution shall be so construed as to prejudice any claims of the United States or any particular State," or to say how any particular State could have claims in or to a Territory ceded by a foreign government, or to account for associating this provision with the preceding provisions of the
25   clause, with which it would appear to have no connection....

Whether, therefore, we take the particular clause in question, by itself, or in connection with the other provisions of the Constitution, we think it clear, that it applies only to the particular territory of which we have spoken, and cannot, by any just rule of interpretation, be extended to a territory which the
30   new government might afterwards obtain from a foreign nation. Consequently, the power which Congress may have lawfully exercised in this territory, while it remained under a territorial government, and which may have been sanctioned by judicial decision, can furnish no justification and no argument to support a similar exercise of power over territory afterwards acquired by the Federal
35   Government. We put aside, therefore, any argument, drawn from precedents, showing the extent of the power which the general government exercised over slavery in this territory, as altogether inapplicable to the case before us....

No one, we presume, will question the correctness of that opinion; nor is there anything in conflict with it in the opinion now given. The point decided in the case cited has no relation to the question now before the court. That depended on the construction of the 3rd article of the Constitution, in relation to the judiciary of the United States, and the power which Congress might exercise in a territory in organizing the Judicial Department of the government. The case before us depends upon other and different provisions of the Constitution, altogether separate and   5 apart from the one above mentioned. The question as to what courts Congress may ordain or establish in a territory to administer laws which the Constitution authorizes it to pass, and what laws it is or is not authorized by the Constitution to pass, are widely different—are regulated by different and separate articles of the Constitution, and stand upon different principles. And we are satisfied that no   10 one who reads attentively the page in Peters' Reports to which we have referred, can suppose that the attention of the court was drawn for a moment to the question now before this court, or that it meant in that case to say that Congress had a right to prohibit a citizen of the United States from taking any property which he lawfully held, into a Territory of the United States.   15

This brings us to examine by what provision of the Constitution the present federal government under its delegated and restricted powers, is authorized to acquire territory outside of the original limits of the United States, and what powers it may exercise therein over the person or property of a citizen of the United States, while it remains a territory, and until it shall be admitted as one   20 of the States of the Union.

There is certainly no power given by the Constitution to the Federal Government to establish or maintain Colonies bordering on the United States or at a distance, to be ruled and governed at its own pleasure; nor to enlarge its territorial limits in any way, except by the admission of new States. That power is   25 plainly given; and if a new State is admitted it needs no further legislation by Congress, because the Constitution itself defines the relative rights and powers and duties of the State, and the citizens of the State, and the Federal Government. But no power is given to acquire a Territory to be held and governed permanently in that character.   30

And indeed the power exercised by Congress to acquire territory and establish a government there, according to its own unlimited discretion, was viewed with great jealousy by the leading statesmen of the day. And in the Federalist, No. 38, written by *Mr. Madison*, he speaks of the acquisition of the Northwestern Territory by the confederated States, by the cession from Virginia and the   35 establishment of a government there, as an exercise of power not warranted by the Articles of Confederation, and dangerous to the liberties of the people. And he urges the adoption of the Constitution as a security and safeguard against such an exercise of power.

We do not mean, however, to question the power of Congress in this respect. The power to expand the territory of the United States by the admission of new States is plainly given; and in the construction of this power by all the departments of the government, it has been held to authorize the acquisition

5   of territory, not fit for admission at the time, but to be admitted as soon as its population and situation would entitle it to admission. It is acquired to become a State, and not to be held as a colony and governed by Congress with absolute authority; and as the propriety of admitting a new State is committed to sound discretion of Congress, the power to acquire territory for that purpose, to be

10   held by the United States until it is in a suitable condition to become a state upon an equal footing with the other States, must rest upon the same discretion. It is a question for the Political Department of the government, and not the judicial; and whatever the Political Department of the government shall recognize as within the limits of the United States, the Judicial Department is

15   also bound to recognize, and to administer in it the laws of the United States, so far as they apply, and to maintain in the territory the authority and rights of the government, and also the personal rights and rights of property of individual citizens, as secured by the Constitution. All we mean to say on this point is, that, as there is no express regulation in the Constitution defining the power which

20   the general government may exercise over the person or property of a citizen in a territory thus acquired, the court must necessarily look to the provisions and principles of the Constitution, and its distribution of powers, for the rules and principles by which its decision must be governed.

Taking this rule to guide us, it may be safely assumed that citizens of the United

25   States who migrate to a territory belonging to the people of the United States, cannot be ruled as mere colonists, dependent upon the will of the general government, and to be governed by any laws it may think proper to impose. The principle upon which our governments rest, and upon which alone they continue to exist, is the union of States, sovereign and independent within

30   their own limits in their internal and domestic concerns, and bound together as one people by a general government, possessing certain enumerated and restricted powers, delegated to it by the people of the several States, and exercising supreme authority within the scope of the powers granted to it, throughout the dominion of the United States. A power, therefore, in the general government

35   to obtain and hold Colonies and dependent Territories, over which they might legislate without restriction, would be inconsistent with its own existence in its present form. Whatever it acquires, it acquires for the benefit of the people of the several States who created it. It is their trustee acting for them, and charged with the duty of promoting the interests of the whole people of the Union in

40   the exercise of the powers specifically granted.

At the time when the Territory in question was obtained by cession from France, it contained no population fit to be associated together and admitted as a State; and it therefore was absolutely necessary to hold possession of it as a Territory belonging to the United States until it was settled and inhabited by a civilized community capable of self-government, and in a condition to be admitted on equal   5 terms with the other States as a member of the Union. But, as we have before said, it was acquired by the general government as the representative and trustee of the people of the United States, and it must, therefore, be held in that character for their common and equal benefit; for it was the people of the several States, acting through the agent and representative, the Federal Government, who in fact acquired   10 the territory in question, and the government holds it for their common use until it shall be associated with the other States as a member of the Union.

But until that time arrives, it is undoubtedly necessary that some government should be established, in order to organize society, and to protect the inhabitants in their persons and property; and as the people of the United States could act in   15 this matter only through the government which represented them, and through which they spoke and acted when the territory was obtained, it was not only within the scope of its powers, but it was its duty to pass such laws and establish such a government as would enable those by whose authority they acted to reap the advantages anticipated from its acquisition, and to gather there a population   20 which would enable it to assume the position to which it was destined among the States of the Union. The power to acquire, necessarily carries with it the power to preserve and apply to the purposes for which it was acquired. The form of government to be established necessarily rested in the discretion of Congress. It was their duty to establish the one that would be best suited for the protec-   25 tion and security of the citizens of the United States and other inhabitants who might be authorized to take up their abode there, and that must always depend upon the existing condition of the Territory, as to the number and character of its inhabitants, and their situation in the Territory. In some cases a government, consisting of persons appointed by the Federal Government, would best subserve   30 the interests of the Territory, when the inhabitants were few and scattered, and new to one another. In other instances, it would be more advisable to commit the powers of self-government to the people who had settled in the territory, as being the most competent to determine what was best for their own interests. But some form of civil authority would be absolutely necessary to organize and   35 preserve civilized society, and prepare it to become a state; and what is the best form must always depend on the condition of the territory at the time, and the choice of the mode must depend upon the exercise of a discretionary power by Congress acting within the scope of its constitutional authority, and not infring- ing upon the rights of person or rights of property of the citizen who might go   40 there to reside or for any other lawful purpose. It was acquired by the exercise of this discretion and it must be held and governed in like manner, until it is fitted to be a state.

But the power of Congress over the person or property of a citizen can never be a
5   mere discretionary power under our Constitution and form of government. The powers of the government and the rights and privileges of the citizen are regulated and plainly defined by the Constitution itself. And when the territory becomes a part of the United States, the Federal Government enters into possession in the character impressed upon it by those who created it. It enters upon it with its
10   powers over the citizen strictly defined, and limited by the Constitution, from which it derives its own existence, and by virtue of which alone it continues to exist and act as a government and sovereignty. It has no power of any kind beyond it; and it cannot, when it enters a territory of the United States, put off its character, and assume discretionary or despotic powers which the Constitution
15   has denied to it. It cannot create for itself a new character separated from the citizens of the United States, and the duties it owes them under the provisions of the Constitution. The territory being a part of the United States, the government and the citizen both enter it under the authority of the Constitution, with their respective rights defined and marked out; and the Federal Government
20   can exercise no power over his person or property, beyond what that instrument confers, nor lawfully deny any right which it has reserved.

A reference to a few of the provisions of the Constitution will illustrate this proposition.

For example, no one, we presume, will contend that Congress can make any
25   law in a territory respecting the establishment of religion or the free exercise thereof, or abridging the freedom of speech or of the press, or the right of the people of the territory peaceably to assemble and to petition the government for the redress of grievances.

Nor can Congress deny to the people the right to keep and bear arms, nor the
30   right to trial by jury, nor compel anyone to be a witness against himself in a criminal proceeding.

These powers, and others in relation to rights of person, which it is not necessary here to enumerate, are, in express and positive terms, denied to the general government; and the rights of private property have been guarded with
35   equal care. Thus the rights of property are united with the rights of person, and placed on the same ground by the fifth amendment to the Constitution, which provides that no person shall be deprived of life, liberty and property, without due process of law. And an Act of Congress which deprives a citizen of

the United States of his liberty or property, merely because he came himself or brought his property into a particular Territory of the United States, and who had committed no offense against the laws, could hardly be dignified with the name of due process of law.

So, too, it will hardly be contended that Congress could by law quarter a soldier in a house in a territory without the consent of the owner, in time of peace; nor in time of war, but in a manner prescribed by law. Nor could they by law forfeit the property of a citizen in a territory who was convicted of treason, for a longer period than the life of the person convicted; nor take private property for public use without just compensation.

The powers over person and property of which we speak are not only not granted to Congress, but are in express terms denied, and they are forbidden to exercise them. And this prohibition is not confined to the States, but the words are general, and extend to the whole territory over which the Constitution gives it power to legislate, including those portions of it remaining under territorial government, as well as that covered by States. It is a total absence of power everywhere within the dominion of the United States, and places the citizens of a territory, so far as these rights are concerned, on the same footing with citizens of the States, and guards them as firmly and plainly against any inroads which the general government might attempt, under the plea of implied or incidental powers. And if Congress itself cannot do this—if it is beyond the powers conferred on the Federal Government—it will be admitted, we presume, that it could not authorize a territorial government to exercise them. It could confer no power on any local government, established by its authority, to violate the provisions of the Constitution.

It seems, however, to be supposed, that there is a difference between property in a slave and other property, and that different rules may be applied to it in expounding the Constitution of the United States. And the laws and usages of nations, and the writings of eminent jurists upon the relation of master and slave and their mutual rights and duties, and the powers which governments may exercise over it, have been dwelt upon in the argument.

But in considering the question before us, it must be borne in mind that there is no law of nations standing between the people of the United States and their government and interfering with their relation to each other. The powers of the government, and the rights of the citizen under it, are positive and practical regulations plainly written down. The people of the United States have delegated to it certain enumerated powers, and forbidden it to exercise others. It has no power over the person or property of a citizen but what the citizens

of the United States have granted. And no laws or usages of other nations, or reasoning of statesmen or jurists upon the relations of master and slave, can enlarge the powers of the government, or take from the citizens the rights they have reserved. And if the Constitution recognizes the right of property of the
5   master in a slave, and makes no distinction between that description of property and other property owned by a citizen, no tribunal, acting under the authority of the United States, whether it be legislative, executive, or judicial, has a right to draw such a distinction, or deny to it the benefit of the provisions and guarantees which have been provided for the protection of private property
10   against the encroachments of the government.

Now, as we have already said in an earlier part of this opinion, upon a different point, the right of property in a slave is distinctly and expressly affirmed in the Constitution. The right to traffic in it, like an ordinary article of merchandise and property, was guaranteed to the citizens of the United States, in every State
15   that might desire it, for twenty years. And the government in express terms is pledged to protect it in all future time, if the slave escapes from his owner. This is done in plain words—too plain to be misunderstood. And no word can be found in the Constitution which gives Congress a greater power over slave property, or which entitles property of that kind to less protection that property
20   of any other description. The only power conferred is the power coupled with the duty of guarding and protecting the owner in his rights.

Upon these considerations, it is the opinion of the court that the Act of Congress which prohibited a citizen from holding and owning property of this kind in the territory of the United States north of the line therein mentioned, is not
25   warranted by the Constitution, and is therefore void; and that neither Dred Scott himself, nor any of his family, were made free by being carried into this territory; even if they had been carried there by the owner, with the intention of becoming a permanent resident.

We have so far examined the case, as it stands under the Constitution of the
30   United States, and the powers thereby delegated to the Federal Government.

But there is another point in the case which depends on state power and state law. And it is contended, on the part of the plaintiff, that he is made free by being taken to Rock Island, in the State of Illinois, independently of his residence in the territory of the United States; and being so made free, he was not again
35   reduced to a state of slavery by being brought back to Missouri.

Our notice of this part of the case will be very brief; for the principle on which it depends was decided in this court, upon much consideration, in the case of *Strader et al. v. Graham*, reported in 10th Howard, 82. In that case, the slaves had been taken from Kentucky to Ohio, with the consent of the owner, and afterwards brought back to Kentucky. And this court held that their *status* or condition, as free or slave, depended upon the laws of Kentucky, when they were brought back into that State, and not of Ohio; and that this court had no jurisdiction to revise the judgment of a state court upon its own laws. This was the point directly before the court, and the decision that this court had not jurisdiction, turned upon it, as will be seen by the report of the case.

So in this case: as Scott was a slave when taken into the State of Illinois by his owner, and was there held as such, and brought back in that character, his *status*, as free or slave, depended on the laws of Missouri, and not of Illinois....

Upon the whole, therefore, it is the judgment of this court, that it appears by the record before us that the plaintiff in error is not a citizen of Missouri, in the sense in which that word is used in the Constitution; and that the Circuit Court of the United States, for that reason, had no jurisdiction in the case, and could give no judgment in it.

Its judgment for the defendant must, consequently, be reversed, and a mandate issued directing the suit to be dismissed for want of jurisdiction.

Speech on the
Dred Scott Decision
Abraham Lincoln

Abraham Lincoln argues that Chief Justice Taney's opinion in Dred Scott v.
Sandford *violated America's first principles and rewrote American history.*

June 26, 1857

...And now as to the Dred Scott decision. That decision declares two propositions—first, that a negro cannot sue in the U.S. Courts; and secondly, that
Congress cannot prohibit slavery in the Territories. It was made by a divided
court—dividing differently on the different points. Judge Douglas does not discuss
the merits of the decision; and, in that respect, I shall follow his example, believing   5
I could no more improve on McLean and Curtis, than he could on Taney.

He denounces all who question the correctness of that decision, as offering
violent resistance to it. But who resists it? Who has, in spite of the decision,
declared Dred Scott free, and resisted the authority of his master over him?

Judicial decisions have two uses—first, to absolutely determine the case   10
decided, and secondly, to indicate to the public how other similar cases will
be decided when they arise. For the latter use, they are called "precedents" and
"authorities."

We believe, as much as Judge Douglas, (perhaps more) in obedience to, and
respect for the judicial department of government. We think its decisions   15
on Constitutional questions, when fully settled, should control, not only
the particular cases decided, but the general policy of the country, subject
to be disturbed only by amendments of the Constitution as provided in that
instrument itself. More than this would be revolution. But we think the Dred
Scott decision is erroneous. We know the court that made it, has often over-   20
ruled its own decisions, and we shall do what we can to have it to over-rule
this. We offer no *resistance* to it.

Abraham Lincoln, "Speech at Springfield, Illinois," June 26, 1857, in Roy P. Basler, ed., *The Collected Works of Abraham Lincoln,* Vol. 2 (New Brunswick, NJ: Rutgers University Press, 1953), 400–407. Reprinted with the permission of the Abraham Lincoln Association, Springfield, IL.

Judicial decisions are of greater or less authority as precedents, according to circumstances. That this should be so, accords both with common sense, and the customary understanding of the legal profession.

If this important decision had been made by the unanimous concurrence of the
5 judges, and without any apparent partisan bias, and in accordance with legal public expectation, and with the steady practice of the departments throughout our history, and had been in no part, based on assumed historical facts which are not really true; or, if wanting in some of these, it had been before the court more than once, and had there been affirmed and re-affirmed through a course
10 of years, it then might be, perhaps would be, factious, nay, even revolutionary, to not acquiesce in it as a precedent.

But when, as it is true we find it wanting in all these claims to the public confidence, it is not resistance, it is not factious, it is not even disrespectful, to treat it as not having yet quite established a settled doctrine for the country—But
15 Judge Douglas considers this view awful. Hear him:

"The courts are the tribunals prescribed by the Constitution and created by the authority of the people to determine, expound and enforce the law. Hence, whoever resists the final decision of the highest judicial tribunal, aims a deadly blow to our whole Republican system of government—a blow, which
20 if successful would place all our rights and liberties at the mercy of passion, anarchy and violence. I repeat, therefore, that if resistance to the decisions of the Supreme Court of the United States, in a matter like the points decided in the Dred Scott case, clearly within their jurisdiction as defined by the Constitution, shall be forced upon the country as a political issue, it will become a distinct
25 and naked issue between the friends and the enemies of the Constitution—the friends and the enemies of the supremacy of the laws."

Why this same Supreme Court once decided a national bank to be constitutional; but General Jackson, as President of the United States, disregarded the decision, and vetoed a bill for a re-charter, partly on constitutional ground, declaring that
30 each public functionary must support the Constitution, "*as he understands it.*" But hear the General's own words. Here they are, taken from his veto message:

"It is maintained by the advocates of the bank, that its constitutionality, in all its features, ought to be considered as settled by precedent, and by the decision of the Supreme Court. To this conclusion I cannot assent. Mere precedent is a
35 dangerous source of authority, and should not be regarded as deciding questions of constitutional power, except where the acquiescence of the people and the States can be considered as well settled. So far from this being the case on this subject, an argument against the bank might be based on precedent. One

Congress in 1791, decided in favor of a bank; another in 1811, decided against it. One Congress in 1815 decided against a bank; another in 1816 decided in its favor. Prior to the present Congress, therefore the precedents drawn from that source were equal. If we resort to the States, the expressions of legislative, judicial and executive opinions against the bank have been probably to those 5 in its favor as four to one. There is nothing in precedent, therefore, which if its authority were admitted, ought to weigh in favor of the act before me."

I drop the quotations merely to remark that all there ever was, in the way of precedent up to the Dred Scott decision, on the points therein decided, had been against that decision. But hear General Jackson further— 10

"If the opinion of the Supreme court covered the whole ground of this act, it ought not to control the coordinate authorities of this Government. The Congress, the executive and the court, must each for itself be guided by its own opinion of the Constitution. Each public officer, who takes an oath to support the Constitution, swears that he will support it as he understands it, and not 15 as it is understood by others."

Again and again have I heard Judge Douglas denounce that bank decision, and applaud General Jackson for disregarding it. It would be interesting for him to look over his recent speech, and see how exactly his fierce philippics against us for resisting Supreme Court decisions, fall upon his own head. It will 20 call to his mind a long and fierce political war in this country, upon an issue which, in his own language, and, of course, in his own changeless estimation, was "a distinct and naked issue between the friends and the enemies of the Constitution," and in which war he fought in the ranks of the enemies of the Constitution. 25

I have said, in substance, that the Dred Scott decision was, in part; based on assumed historical facts which were not really true; and I ought not to leave the subject without giving some reasons for saying this; I therefore give an instance or two, which I think fully sustain me. Chief Justice Taney, in delivering the opinion of the majority of the Court, insists at great length that negroes were 30 no part of the people who made, or for whom was made, the Declaration of Independence, or the Constitution of the United States.

On the contrary, Judge Curtis, in his dissenting opinion, shows that in five of the then thirteen states, to wit, New Hampshire, Massachusetts, New York, New Jersey and North Carolina, free negroes were voters, and, in proportion to their 35 numbers, had the same part in making the Constitution that the white people had. He shows this with so much particularity as to leave no doubt of its truth; and, as a sort of conclusion on that point, holds the following language:

"The Constitution was ordained and established by the people of the United States, through the action, in each State, of those persons who were qualified by its laws to act thereon in behalf of themselves and all other citizens of the State. In some of the States, as we have seen, colored persons were among
5   those qualified by law to act on the subject. These colored persons were not only included in the body of 'the people of the United States,' by whom the Constitution was ordained and established; but in at least five of the States they had the power to act, and, doubtless, did act, by their suffrages, upon the question of its adoption."

10   Again, Chief Justice Taney says: "It is difficult, at this day to realize the state of public opinion in relation to that unfortunate race, which prevailed in the civilized and enlightened portions of the world at the time of the Declaration of Independence, and when the Constitution of the United States was framed and adopted." And again, after quoting from the Declaration, he says: "The general
15   words above quoted would seem to include the whole human family, and if they were used in a similar instrument at this day, would be so understood."

In these the Chief Justice does not directly assert, but plainly assumes, as a fact, that the public estimate of the black man is more favorable *now* than it was in the days of the Revolution. This assumption is a mistake. In some trifling
20   particulars, the condition of that race has been ameliorated; but, as a whole, in this country, the change between then and now is decidedly the other way; and their ultimate destiny has never appeared so hopeless as in the last three or four years. In two of the five States—New Jersey and North Carolina—that then gave the free negro the right of voting, the right has since been taken away; and in a
25   third—New York—it has been greatly abridged; while it has not been extended, so far as I know, to a single additional State, though the number of the States has more than doubled. In those days, as I understand, masters could, at their own pleasure, emancipate their slaves; but since then, such legal restraints have been made upon emancipation, as to amount almost to prohibition. In those days,
30   Legislatures held the unquestioned power to abolish slavery in their respective States; but now it is becoming quite fashionable for State Constitutions to withhold that power from the Legislatures. In those days, by common consent, the spread of the black man's bondage to new countries was prohibited; but now, Congress decides that it *will* not continue the prohibition, and the Supreme
35   Court decides that it *could* not if it would. In those days, our Declaration of Independence was held sacred by all, and thought to include all; but now, to aid in making the bondage of the negro universal and eternal, it is assailed, and sneered at, and construed, and hawked at, and torn, till, if its framers could rise from their graves, they could not at all recognize it. All the powers of earth seem

rapidly combining against him. Mammon is after him; ambition follows, and philosophy follows, and the Theology of the day is fast joining the cry. They have him in his prison house; they have searched his person, and left no prying instrument with him. One after another they have closed the heavy iron doors upon him, and now they have him, as it were, bolted in with a lock of a hundred keys, which can never be unlocked without the concurrence of every key; the keys in the hands of a hundred different men, and they scattered to a hundred different and distant places; and they stand musing as to what invention, in all the dominions of mind and matter, can be produced to make the impossibility of his escape more complete than it is.

It is grossly incorrect to say or assume, that the public estimate of the negro is more favorable now than it was at the origin of the government.

Three years and a half ago, Judge Douglas brought forward his famous Nebraska bill. The country was at once in a blaze. He scorned all opposition, and carried it through Congress. Since then he has seen himself superseded in a Presidential nomination, by one endorsing the general doctrine of his measure, but at the same time standing clear of the odium of its untimely agitation, and its gross breach of national faith; and he has seen that successful rival Constitutionally elected, not by the strength of friends, but by the division of adversaries, being in a popular minority of nearly four hundred thousand votes. He has seen his chief aids in his own State, Shields and Richardson, politically speaking, successively tried, convicted, and executed, for an offense not their own, but his. And now he sees his own case, standing next on the docket for trial.

There is a natural disgust in the minds of nearly all white people, to the idea of an indiscriminate amalgamation of the white and black races; and Judge Douglas evidently is basing his chief hope, upon the chances of being able to appropriate the benefit of this disgust to himself. If he can, by much drumming and repeating, fasten the odium of that idea upon his adversaries, he thinks he can struggle through the storm. He therefore clings to this hope, as a drowning man to the last plank. He makes an occasion for lugging it in from the opposition to the Dred Scott decision. He finds the Republicans insisting that the Declaration of Independence includes ALL men, black as well as white; and forthwith he boldly denies that it includes negroes at all, and proceeds to argue gravely that all who contend it does, do so only because they want to vote, and eat, and sleep, and marry with negroes! He will have it that they cannot be consistent else. Now I protest against that counterfeit logic which concludes that, because I do not want a black woman for a *slave* I must necessarily want her for a *wife*. I need not have her for either, I can just leave her alone. In some respects she certainly is not my equal; but in her natural right to eat the bread she earns with her own hands without asking leave of any one else, she is my equal, and the equal of all others.

Chief Justice Taney, in his opinion in the Dred Scott case, admits that the language of the Declaration is broad enough to include the whole human family,

5   but he and Judge Douglas argue that the authors of that instrument did not intend to include negroes, by the fact that they did not at once, actually place them on an equality with the whites. Now this grave argument comes to just nothing at all, by the other fact, that they did not at once, *or ever afterwards*, actually place all white people on an equality with one or another. And this is

10   the staple argument of both the Chief Justice and the Senator, for doing this obvious violence to the plain unmistakable language of the Declaration. I think the authors of that notable instrument intended to include *all* men, but they did not intend to declare all men equal *in all respects*. They did not mean to say all were equal in color, size, intellect, moral developments, or social capacity.

15   They defined with tolerable distinctness, in what respects they did consider all men created equal—equal in "certain inalienable rights, among which are life, liberty, and the pursuit of happiness." This they said, and this meant. They did not mean to assert the obvious untruth, that all were then actually enjoying that equality, nor yet, that they were about to confer it immediately upon them. In

20   fact they had no power to confer such a boon. They meant simply to declare the *right*, so that the *enforcement* of it might follow as fast as circumstances should permit. They meant to set up a standard maxim for free society, which should be familiar to all, and revered by all; constantly looked to, constantly labored for, and even though never perfectly attained, constantly approximated, and

25   thereby constantly spreading and deepening its influence, and augmenting the happiness and value of life to all people of all colors everywhere. The assertion that "all men are created equal" was of no practical use in effecting our separation from Great Britain; and it was placed in the Declaration, nor for that, but for future use. Its authors meant it to be, thank God, it is now proving itself, a

30   stumbling block to those who in after times might seek to turn a free people back into the hateful paths of despotism. They knew the proneness of prosperity to breed tyrants, and they meant when such should reappear in this fair land and commence their vocation they should find left for them at least one hard nut to crack.

35   I have now briefly expressed my view of the *meaning* and *objects* of that part of the Declaration of Independence which declares that "all men are created equal."

Now let us hear Judge Douglas' view of the same subject, as I find it in the printed report of his late speech. Here it is:

"No man can vindicate the character, motives and conduct of the signers of the Declaration of Independence, except upon the hypothesis that they referred to the white race alone, and not to the African, when they declared all men to have been created equal—that they were speaking of British subjects on this continent being equal to British subjects born and residing in Great   5
Britain—that they were entitled to the same inalienable rights, and among them were enumerated life, liberty and the pursuit of happiness. The Declaration was adopted for the purpose of justifying the colonists in the eyes of the civilized world in withdrawing their allegiance from the British crown, and dissolving their connection with the mother country."   10

My good friends, read that carefully over some leisure hour, and ponder well upon it—see what a mere wreck—mangled ruin—it makes of our once glorious Declaration.

"They were speaking of British subjects on this continent being equal to British subjects born and residing in Great Britain!" Why, according to this, not only   15
negroes but white people outside of Great Britain and America are not spoken of in that instrument. The English, Irish and Scotch, along with white Americans, were included to be sure, but the French, Germans and other white people of the world are all gone to pot along with the Judge's inferior races.

I had thought the Declaration promised something better than the condition of   20
British subjects; but no, it only meant that we should be *equal* to them in their own oppressed and *unequal* condition. According to that, it gave no promise that having kicked off the King and Lords of Great Britain, we should not at once be saddled with a King and Lords of our own.

I had thought the Declaration contemplated the progressive improvement in the   25
condition of all men everywhere; but no, it merely "was adopted for the purpose of justifying the colonists in the eyes of the civilized world in withdrawing their allegiance from the British crown, and dissolving their connection with the mother country." Why, that object having been effected some eighty years ago, the Declaration is of no practical use now—mere rubbish—old wadding left   30
to rot on the battle-field after the victory is won.

I understand you are preparing to celebrate the "Fourth," tomorrow week. What for? The doings of that day had no reference to the present; and quite half of you are not even descendants of those who were referred to at that day. But I suppose you will celebrate; and will even go so far as to read the Declaration.   35
Suppose after you read it once in the old fashioned way, you read it once more with Judge Douglas' version. It will then run thus: "We hold these truths to

be self-evident that all British subjects who were on this continent eighty-one years ago, were created equal to all British subjects born and *then* residing in Great Britain."

5   And now I appeal to all—to Democrats as well as others,—are you really willing that the Declaration shall be thus frittered away?—thus left no more, at most, than an interesting memorial of the dead past? thus shorn of its vitality, and practical value; and left without the *germ* or even the *suggestion* of the individual rights of man in it? . . .

A HOUSE DIVIDED
ABRAHAM LINCOLN

Abraham Lincoln delivered this speech upon his nomination as the Republican candidate for the U.S. Senate in Illinois, where he would square off against incumbent Senator Stephen Douglas. Drawing the leading metaphor from a passage in the Gospel of Matthew, Lincoln held that pro-slavery forces—Douglas, Franklin Pierce (president when the Kansas-Nebraska Act was adopted), Roger Taney, and James Buchanan (president when Dred Scott *was decided)—were working in concert to effect a national policy legalizing slavery in all states and territories. Papers throughout the North reprinted the text of the speech, propelling Lincoln to new prominence.*

JUNE 16, 1858

MR. PRESIDENT AND GENTLEMEN OF THE CONVENTION:

If we could first know *where* we are, and *whither* we are tending, we could then better judge *what* to do, and *how* to do it.

We are now far into the *fifth* year, since a policy was initiated, with the *avowed* object, and *confident* promise, of putting an end to slavery agitation.

Under the operation of that policy, that agitation has not only, *not ceased*, but   5
has *constantly augmented.*

In *my* opinion, it *will* not cease, until a *crisis* shall have been reached, and passed.

"A house divided against itself cannot stand."

I believe this government cannot endure, permanently half *slave* and half *free.*   10

I do not expect the Union to be *dissolved*—I do not expect the house to *fall*—but I *do* expect it will cease to be divided.

It will become *all* one thing, or *all* the other.

Abraham Lincoln, "'A House Divided': Speech at Springfield, Illinois," June 16, 1858, in Roy P. Basler, ed., *The Collected Works of Abraham Lincoln*, Vol. 2 (New Brunswick, NJ: Rutgers University Press, 1953), 461–66. Reprinted with the permission of the Abraham Lincoln Association, Springfield, IL.

Either the *opponents* of slavery, will arrest the further spread of it, and place it where the public mind shall rest in the belief that it is in the course of ultimate extinction; or its *advocates* will push it forward, till it shall become alike lawful in *all* the States, *old* as well as *new*—*North* as well as *South*.

5   Have we no *tendency* to the latter condition?

Let any one who doubts, carefully contemplate that now almost complete legal combination—piece of *machinery* so to speak—compounded of the Nebraska doctrine, and the Dred Scott decision. Let him consider not only *what work* the machinery is adapted to do, and *how well* adapted; but also, let him study
10   the *history* of its construction, and trace, if he can, or rather *fail*, if he can, to trace the evidences of design, and concert of action, among its chief bosses, from the beginning.

But, so far, *Congress* only, had acted; and an *endorsement* by the people, *real* or apparent, was indispensable, to *save* the point already gained, and give chance
15   for more.

The new year of 1854 found slavery excluded from more than half the States by State Constitutions, and from most of the national territory by Congressional prohibition.

Four days later, commenced the struggle, which ended in repealing that Con-
20   gressional prohibition.

This opened all the national territory to slavery; and was the first point gained.

This necessity had not been overlooked; but had been provided for, as well as might be, in the notable argument of "*squatter sovereignty*," otherwise called "*sacred right of self government*," which latter phrase, though expressive of the
25   only rightful basis of any government, was so perverted in this attempted use of it as to amount to just this: That if any *one* man, choose to enslave *another*, no *third* man shall be allowed to object.

That argument was incorporated into the Nebraska Bill itself, in the language which follows: "*It being the true intent and meaning of this act not to legislate*
30   *slavery into any Territory or state, not to exclude it therefrom; but to leave the people thereof perfectly free to form and regulate their domestic institutions in their own way, subject only to the Constitution of the United States.*"

Then opened the roar of loose declamation in favor of "Squatter Sovereignty" and "Sacred right of self government."

35   "But," said opposition members, "let us be more *specific*—let us *amend* the bill so as to expressly declare that the people of the territory *may* exclude

slavery." "Not we," said the friends of the measure; and down they voted the amendment.

While the Nebraska bill was passing through congress, a *law case*, involving the question of a negro's freedom, by reason of his owner having voluntarily taken him first into a free state and then a territory covered by the congressional pro- 5 hibition, and held him as a slave, for a long time in each, was passing through the U. S. Circuit Court for the District of Missouri; and both Nebraska bill and law suit were brought to a decision in the same month of May, 1854. The negro's name was "Dred Scott," which name now designates the decision finally made in the case.   10

Before the *then* next Presidential election, the law case came *to*, and was argued *in* the Supreme Court of the United States; but the *decision* of it was deferred until *after* the election. Still, *before* the election, Senator Trumbull, on the floor of the Senate, requests the leading advocate of the Nebraska Bill to state his *opinion* whether the people of a territory can constitutionally exclude slavery from their 15 limits; and the latter answers, "That is a question for the Supreme Court."

The election came. Mr. Buchanan was elected, and the *endorsement*, such as it was, secured. That was the *second* point gained. The endorsement, however, fell short of a clear popular majority by nearly four hundred thousand votes, and so, perhaps, was not overwhelmingly reliable and satisfactory.   20

The *outgoing* President, in his last annual message, as impressively as possible *echoed back* upon the people the *weight* and *authority* of the endorsement.

The Supreme Court met again; *did not* announce their decision, but ordered a re-argument.

The Presidential inauguration came, and still no decision of the court; but the 25 *incoming* President, in his inaugural address, fervently exhorted the people to abide by the forthcoming decision, *whatever it might be.*

Then, in a few days, came the decision.

The reputed author of the Nebraska bill finds an early occasion to make a speech at this capitol endorsing the Dred Scott Decision, and vehemently denouncing 30 all opposition to it.

The new President, too, seizes the early occasion of the Silliman letter to *endorse* and strongly *construe* that decision, and to express his *astonishment* that any different view had ever been entertained.

At length a squabble springs up between the President and the author of the 35 Nebraska bill, on the *mere* question of *fact*, whether the Lecompton constitu-

tion was or was not, in any just sense, made by the people of Kansas; and in
that squabble the latter declares that all he wants is a fair vote for the people,
and that he *cares* not whether slavery be voted *down* or voted *up*. I do not
understand his declaration that he cares not whether slavery be voted down or
5   voted up, to be intended by him other than as an *apt definition* of the *policy* he
would impress upon the public mind—the *principle* for which he declares he
has suffered much, and is ready to suffer to the end.

And well may he cling to that principle. If he has any parental feeling, well
may he cling to it. That principle, is the only *shred* left of his original Nebraska
10   doctrine. Under the Dred Scott decision, "squatter sovereignty" squatted out
of existence, tumbled down like temporary scaffolding—like the mold at the
foundry served through one blast and fell back into loose sand—helped to carry
an election, and then was kicked to the winds. His late *joint* struggle with the
Republicans, against the Lecompton Constitution, involves nothing of the
15   original Nebraska doctrine. That struggle was made on a point, the right of a
people to make their own constitution, upon which he and the Republicans
have never differed.

The several points of the Dred Scott decision, in connection with Senator
Douglas' "care not" policy, constitute the piece of machinery, in its *present* state
20   of advancement. This was the third point gained.

The *working* points of that machinery are:

First, that no negro slave, imported as such from Africa, and no descendant of
such slave can ever be a *citizen* of any State, in the sense of that term as used in
the Constitution of the United States.

25   This point is made in order to deprive the negro, in every possible event, of
the benefit of this provision of the United States Constitution, which declares
that—

"The citizens of each State shall be entitled to all privileges and immunities of
citizens in the several States."

30   Secondly, that "subject to the Constitution of the United States," neither *Congress*
nor a *Territorial Legislature* can exclude slavery from any United States territory.

This point is made in order that individual men may *fill up* the territories with
slaves, without danger of losing them as property, and thus to enhance the
chances of *permanency* to the institution through all the future.

35   Thirdly, that whether the holding a negro in actual slavery in a free State, makes
him free, as against the holder, the United States courts will not decide, but

will leave to be decided by the courts of any slave State the negro may be forced into by the master.

This point is made, not to be pressed *immediately*; but, if acquiesced in for a while, and apparently *endorsed* by the people at an election, *then* to sustain the logical conclusion that what Dred Scott's master might lawfully do with Dred Scott, in the free State of Illinois, every other master may lawfully do with any other *one*, or one *thousand* slaves, in Illinois, or in any other free State.

Auxiliary to all this, and working hand in hand with it, the Nebraska doctrine, or what is left of it, is to *educate* and *mold* public opinion, at least *Northern* public opinion, not to *care* whether slavery is voted *down* or voted *up*.

This shows exactly where we now *are*; and *partially* also, whither we are tending.

It will throw additional light on the latter, to go back, and run the mind over the string of historical facts already stated. Several things will *now* appear less *dark* and *mysterious* than they did *when* they were transpiring. The people were to be left "perfectly free" "subject only to the Constitution." What the *Constitution* had to do with it, outsiders could not *then* see. Plainly enough *now*, it was an exactly fitted *niche*, for the Dred Scott decision to afterwards come in, and declare the *perfect freedom* of the people, to be just no freedom at all.

Why was the amendment, expressly declaring the right of the people to exclude slavery, voted down? Plainly enough *now*, the adoption of it, would have spoiled the niche for the Dred Scott decision.

Why was the Court decision held up? Why, even a Senator's individual opinion withheld, till *after* the Presidential election? Plainly enough *now*, the speaking out *then* would have damaged the "*perfectly free*" argument upon which the election was to be carried.

Why the *outgoing* President's felicitation on the endorsement? Why the delay of a reargument? Why the incoming President's *advance* exhortation in favor of the decision?

These things *look* like the cautious *patting* and *petting* of a spirited horse, preparatory to mounting him, when it is dreaded that he may give the rider a fall.

And why the hasty after endorsements of the decision by the President and others?

We can not absolutely *know* that all these exact adaptations are the result of preconcert. But when we see a lot of framed timbers, different portions of which we know have been gotten out at different times and places and by different workmen—Stephen, Franklin, Roger and James, for instance—and when we see

these timbers joined together, and see they exactly make the frame of a house or a mill, all the tenons and mortices exactly fitting, and all the lengths and proportions of the different pieces exactly adapted to their respective places, and not a piece too many or too few—not omitting even scaffolding—or, if a
5   single piece be lacking, we see the place in the frame exactly fitted and prepared to yet bring such piece in—in *such* a case, we find it impossible to not *believe* that Stephen and Franklin and Roger and James all understood one another from the beginning, and all worked upon a common *plan* or *draft* drawn up before the first lick was struck....

Speech at Chicago
Stephen Douglas (1813–1861)

As the primary author of the Kansas-Nebraska Act and the most vocal defender of the Dred Scott *decision, Stephen Douglas traveled extensively promoting the concept of popular sovereignty, which he equated with republican self-government. The national reputation he garnered in the process would, he hoped, serve him well in a future presidential bid.*

July 9, 1858

…Fellow-citizens, while I devoted my best energies—all my energies, mental and physical—to the vindication of the great principle, and whilst the result has been such as will enable the people of Kansas to come into the Union with such a constitution as they desire, yet the credit of this great moral victory is to be divided among a large number of men of various and different political creeds.   5
I was rejoiced when I found in this great contest the Republican party coming up manfully and sustaining the principle that the people of each Territory, when coming into the Union, have the right to decide for themselves whether slavery shall or shall not exist within their limits. I have seen the time when that principle was controverted. I have seen the time when all parties did not recognize the   10
right of a people to have slavery or freedom, to tolerate or prohibit slavery as they deemed best, but claimed that power for the Congress of the United States, regardless of the wishes of the people to be affected by it; and when I found upon the Crittenden-Montgomery bill the Republicans and Americans of the North, and I may say, too, some glorious Americans and old-line Whigs from the   15
South, like Crittenden and his patriotic associates, joined with a portion of the Democracy to carry out and vindicate the right of the people to decide whether slavery should or should not exist within the limits of Kansas, I was rejoiced within my secret soul, for I saw an indication that the American people, when they came to understand the principle, would give it their cordial support….   20

Stephen Douglas, "Speech of Senator Douglas, On the Occasion of his Public Reception at Chicago," July 9, 1858, in Stephen Douglas, Abraham Lincoln, *Political Debates between Abraham Lincoln and Stephen A. Douglas* (New York: G. P. Putnam's Sons, 1912), 16–23, 30–35.

I regard the great principle of popular sovereignty as having been vindicated and made triumphant in this land as a permanent rule of public policy in the organization of Territories and the admission of new States. Illinois took her position upon this principle many years ago. You all recollect that in 1850,

5   after the passage of the Compromise measures of that year, when I returned to my home there was great dissatisfaction expressed at my course in supporting those measures. I appeared before the people of Chicago at a mass meeting, and vindicated each and every one of those measures; and by reference to my speech on that occasion, which was printed and circulated broadcast throughout the State

10   at the time, you will find that I then and there said that those measures were all founded upon the great principle that every people ought to possess the right to form and regulate their own domestic institutions in their own way, and that, that right being possessed by the people of the States, I saw no reason why the same principle should not be extended to all of the Territories of the United States.

15   A general election was held in this State a few months afterwards, for members of the Legislature, pending which all these questions were thoroughly canvassed and discussed, and the nominees of the different parties instructed in regard to the wishes of their constituents upon them. When that election was over, and the Legislature assembled, they proceeded to consider the merits of those Compromise

20   measures, and the principles upon which they were predicated. And what was the result of their action? They passed resolutions, first repealing the Wilmot Proviso instructions, and in lieu thereof adopted another resolution, in which they declared the great principle which asserts the right of the people to make their own form of government and establish their own institutions. That resolution is as follows:

25   *Resolved*, That our liberty and independence are based upon the right of the people to form for themselves such a government as they may choose; that this great principle, the birthright of freemen, the gift of Heaven, secured to us by the blood of our ancestors, ought to be secured to future generations, and no limitation ought to be applied to this power in the organization of any Territory

30   of the United States, of either Territorial Government or State Constitution, provided the Government so established shall be republican, and in conformity with the Constitution of the United States.

That resolution, declaring the great principle of self-government as applicable to the Territories and new States, passed the House of Representatives of this State by

35   a vote of sixty-one in the affirmative, to only four in the negative. Thus you find that an expression of public opinion—enlightened, educated, intelligent public opinion—on this question, by the representatives of Illinois in 1851, approaches nearer to unanimity than has ever been obtained on any controverted question. That resolution was entered on the journal of the Legislature of the State of

Illinois, and it has remained there from that day to this, a standing instruction to her Senators, and a request to her Representatives, in Congress to carry out that principle in all future cases. Illinois, therefore, stands pre-eminent as the State which stepped forward early and established a platform applicable to this slavery question, concurred in alike by Whigs and Democrats, in which it was declared to be the wish of our people that thereafter the people of the Territories should be left perfectly free to form and regulate their domestic institutions in their own way, and that no limitation should be placed upon that right in any form.

Hence what was my duty in 1854, when it became necessary to bring forward a bill for the organization of the Territories of Kansas and Nebraska? Was it not my duty, in obedience to the Illinois platform, to your standing instructions to your Senators, adopted with almost entire unanimity, to incorporate in that bill the great principle of self-government, declaring that it was "the true intent and meaning of the Act not to legislate slavery into any State or Territory, or to exclude it therefrom, but to leave the people thereof perfectly free to form and regulate their domestic institutions in their own way, subject only to the Constitution of the United States?" I did incorporate that principle in the Kansas-Nebraska Bill, and perhaps I did as much as any living man in the enactment of that bill, thus establishing the doctrine in the public policy of the country. I then defended that principle against assaults from one section of the Union. During this last winter it became my duty to vindicate it against assaults from the other section of the Union. I vindicated it boldly and fearlessly, as the people of Chicago can bear witness, when it was assailed by Free-soilers; and during this winter I vindicated and defended it as boldly and fearlessly when it was attempted to be violated by the almost united South. I pledged myself to you on every stump in Illinois in 1854, I pledged myself to the people of other States north and south, wherever I spoke; and in the United States Senate and elsewhere, in every form in which I could reach the public mind or the public ear, I gave the pledge that I, so far as the power should be in my hands, would vindicate the principle of the right of the people to form their own institutions, to establish free States or slave States as they chose, and that that principle should never be violated either by fraud, by violence, by circumvention, or by any other means, if it was in my power to prevent it. I now submit to you, my fellow-citizens, whether I have not redeemed that pledge in good faith. Yes, my friends, I have redeemed it in good faith; and it is a matter of heartfelt gratification to me to see these assembled thousands here tonight bearing their testimony to the fidelity with which I have advocated that principle, and redeemed my pledges in connection with it.

I will be entirely frank with you. My object was to secure the right of the people of each State and of each Territory, north or south, to decide the question for

themselves, to have slavery or not, just as they chose; and my opposition to the Lecompton Constitution was not predicated upon the ground that it was a pro-slavery constitution, nor would my action have been different had it been a Free-soil constitution. My speech against the Lecompton fraud was made on
5   the 9th of December, while the vote on the slavery clause in that constitution was not taken until the 21st of the same month, nearly two weeks after. I made my speech against the Lecompton monstrosity solely on the ground that it was a violation of the fundamental principles of free government; on the ground that it was not the act and deed of the people of Kansas; that it did not embody their
10   will; that they were averse to it; and hence I denied the right of Congress to force it upon them, either as a free State or a slave State. I deny the right of Congress to force a slaveholding State upon an unwilling people. I deny their right to force a free State upon an unwilling people. I deny their right to force a good thing upon a people who are unwilling to receive it. The great principle is the right of
15   every community to judge and decide for itself whether a thing is right or wrong, whether it would be good or evil for them to adopt it; and the right of free action, the right of free thought, the right of free judgment, upon the question is dearer to every true American than any other under a free government. My objection to the Lecompton contrivance was that it undertook to put a constitution on the
20   people of Kansas against their will, in opposition to their wishes, and thus violated the great principle upon which all our institutions rest. It is no answer to this argument to say that slavery is an evil, and hence should not be tolerated. You must allow the people to decide for themselves whether it is a good or an evil. You allow them to decide for themselves whether they desire a Maine liquor law or not;
25   you allow them to decide for themselves what kind of common schools they will have, what system of banking they will adopt, or whether they will adopt any at all; you allow them to decide for themselves the relations between husband and wife, parent and child, guardian and ward,—in fact, you allow them to decide for themselves all other questions: and why not upon this question? Whenever you
30   put a limitation upon the right of any people to decide what laws they want, you have destroyed the fundamental principle of self-government....

But I am equally free to say that the reason assigned by Mr. Lincoln for resisting the decision of the Supreme Court in the Dred Scott case does not in itself meet my approbation. He objects to it because that decision declared that a negro
35   descended from African parents, who were brought here and sold as slaves, is not and cannot be a citizen of the United States. He says it is wrong because it deprives the negro of the benefits of that clause of the Constitution which says that citizens of one State shall enjoy all the privileges and immunities of citizens of the several States; in other words, he thinks it wrong because it deprives the
40   negro of the privileges, immunities, and rights of citizenship, which pertain,

according to that decision, only to the white man. I am free to say to you that in my opinion this government of ours is founded on the white basis. It was made by the white man, for the benefit of the white man, to be administered by white men, in such manner as they should determine. It is also true that a negro, an Indian, or any other man of inferior race to a white man should be permitted 5 to enjoy, and humanity requires that he should have, all the rights, privileges, and immunities which he is capable of exercising consistent with the safety of society. I would give him every right and every privilege which his capacity would enable him to enjoy, consistent with the good of the society in which he lived. But you ask me, What are these rights and these privileges? My answer is, that 10 each State must decide for itself the nature and extent of these rights. Illinois has decided for herself. We have decided that the negro shall not be a slave, and we have at the same time decided that he shall not vote, or serve on juries, or enjoy political privileges. I am content with that system of policy which we have adopted for ourselves. I deny the right of any other State to complain of our 15 policy in that respect, or to interfere with it, or to attempt to change it. On the other hand, the State of Maine has decided that in that State a negro man may vote on an equality with the white man. The sovereign power of Maine had the right to prescribe that rule for herself. Illinois has no right to complain of Maine for conferring the right of negro suffrage, nor has Maine any right to interfere 20 with or complain of Illinois because she has denied negro suffrage.

The State of New York has decided by her constitution that a negro may vote, provided that he own $250 worth of property, but not otherwise. The rich negro can vote, but the poor one cannot. Although that distinction does not commend itself to my judgment, yet I assert that the sovereign power of New York had a 25 right to prescribe that form of the elective franchise. Kentucky, Virginia, and other States have provided that negroes, or a certain class of them in those States, shall be slaves, having neither civil nor political rights. Without endorsing the wisdom of that decision, I assert that Virginia has the same power, by virtue of her sovereignty, to protect slavery within her limits as Illinois has to banish it 30 forever from our own borders. I assert the right of each State to decide for itself on all these questions, and I do not subscribe to the doctrine of my friend Mr. Lincoln, that uniformity is either desirable or possible. I do not acknowledge that the States must all be free or must all be slave.

I do not acknowledge that the negro must have civil and political rights every- 35 where or nowhere. I do not acknowledge that the Chinese must have the same rights in California that we would confer upon him here. I do not acknowledge that the coolie imported into this country must necessarily be put upon an equality with the white race. I do not acknowledge any of these doctrines of uniformity in the local and domestic regulations in the different States. 40

Thus you see, my fellow-citizens, that the issues between Mr. Lincoln and myself, as respective candidates for the United States Senate, as made up, are direct, unequivocal, and irreconcilable. He goes for uniformity in our domestic institutions, for a war of sections, until one or the other shall be subdued. I go

5 for the great principle of the Kansas-Nebraska Bill,—the right of the people to decide for themselves.

On the other point, Mr. Lincoln goes for a warfare upon the Supreme Court of the United States because of their judicial decision in the Dred Scott case. I yield obedience to the decisions in that court,—to the final determination of

10 the highest judicial tribunal known to our Constitution. He objects to the Dred Scott decision because it does not put the negro in the possession of the rights of citizenship on an equality with the white man. I am opposed to negro equality. I repeat that this nation is a white people,—a people composed of European descendants, a people that have established this government for themselves and

15 their posterity,—and I am in favor of preserving, not only the purity of the blood, but the purity of the government from any mixture or amalgamation with inferior races. I have seen the effects of this mixture of superior and inferior races, this amalgamation of white men and Indians and negroes; we have seen it in Mexico, in Central America, in South America, and in all the Spanish-American States;

20 and its result has been degeneration, demoralization, and degradation below the capacity for self-government.

I am opposed to taking any step that recognizes the negro man or the Indian as the equal of the white man. I am opposed to giving him a voice in the administration of the government. I would extend to the negro and the Indian

25 and to all dependent races every right, every privilege, and every immunity consistent with the safety and welfare of the white races; but equality they never should have, either political or social, or in any other respect whatever.

My friends, you see that the issues are distinctly drawn. I stand by the same platform that I have so often proclaimed to you and to the people of Illinois

30 heretofore. I stand by the Democratic organization, yield obedience to its usages, and support its regular nominations. I endorse and approve the Cincinnati platform, and I adhere to and intend to carry out, as part of that platform, the great principle of self-government, which recognizes the right of the people in each State and Territory to decide for themselves their domestic institutions.

35 In other words, if the Lecompton issue shall arise again, you have only to turn back and see where you have found me during the last six months, and then rest assured that you will find me in the same position, battling for the same principle, and vindicating it from assault from whatever quarter it may come, so long as I have the power to do it....

Seventh Lincoln–Douglas Debate

Abraham Lincoln and Stephen Douglas agreed to debate in all nine of the state's congressional districts, with their recent speeches in Chicago and Springfield counting as the opening salvos. Seven debates ensued, each lasting three hours. This seventh and last debate, held in Alton, drew more than 5,000 spectators. Local and national papers—most in the service of one of the two main parties—reprinted each speech, leading to widespread circulation. After the debates concluded, Lincoln published an edited version. The book's popularity throughout the North paved the way for his eventual presidential campaign.

OCTOBER 15, 1858

SENATOR DOUGLAS'S SPEECH

...The issue thus being made up between Mr. Lincoln and myself on three points, we went before the people of the State. During the following seven weeks, between the Chicago speeches and our first meeting at Ottawa, he and I addressed large assemblages of the people in many of the central counties. In my speeches I confined myself closely to those three positions which he had 5 taken controverting his proposition that this Union could not exist as our fathers made it, divided into free and slave States, controverting his proposition of a crusade against the Supreme Court because of the Dred Scott decision, and controverting his proposition that the Declaration of Independence included and meant the negroes as well as the white men, when it declared all men to 10 be created equal. I supposed at that time that these propositions constituted a distinct issue between us, and that the opposite positions we had taken upon them we would be willing to be held to in every part of the State. I never intended to waver one hair's breadth from that issue either in the north or the

Abraham Lincoln and Stephen Douglas, "Seventh and Last Debate with Stephen A. Douglas at Alton, Illinois," October 15, 1858, in Roy P. Basler, ed., *The Collected Works of Abraham Lincoln,* Vol. 3 (New Brunswick, NJ: Rutgers University Press, 1953), 285–87, 296–97, 301–2, 304, 307–8, 312–16, 318–20, 322–23. Reprinted with the permission of the Abraham Lincoln Association, Springfield, IL.

south, or wherever I should address the people of Illinois. I hold that when the
time arrives that I cannot proclaim my political creed in the same terms not
only in the northern but the southern part of Illinois, not only in the northern
but the southern States, and wherever the American flag waves over American
5   soil, that then there must be something wrong in that creed. So long as we live
under a common constitution, so long as we live in a confederacy of sovereign
and equal States, joined together as one for certain purposes, that any political
creed is radically wrong which cannot be proclaimed in every State, and every
section of that Union alike. I took up Mr. Lincoln's three propositions in my
10   several speeches, analyzed them, and pointed out what I believed to be the radical
errors contained in them. First, in regard to his doctrine that this government
was in violation of the law of God which says, that a house divided against itself
cannot stand, I repudiated it as a slander upon the immortal framers of this
constitution. I then said, have often repeated, and now again assert, that in my
15   opinion our government can endure forever, divided into free and slave States as
our fathers made it,—each State having the right to prohibit, abolish or sustain
slavery just as it pleases. This government was made upon the great basis of the
sovereignty of the States, the right of each State to regulate its own domestic
institutions to suit itself, and that right was conferred with understanding and
20   expectation that inasmuch as each locality had separate interests, each locality
must have different and distinct local and domestic institutions, corresponding
to its wants and interests. Our fathers knew when they made the government,
that the laws and institutions which were well adapted to the green mountains
of Vermont, were unsuited to the rice plantations of South Carolina. They
25   knew then, as well as we know now, that the laws and institutions which would
be well adapted to the beautiful prairies of Illinois would not be suited to the
mining regions of California. They knew that in a Republic as broad as this,
having such a variety of soil, climate and interest, there must necessarily be a
corresponding variety of local laws—the policy and institutions of each State
30   adapted to its condition and wants. For this reason this Union was established
on the right of each State to do as it pleased on the question of slavery, and
every other question; and the various States were not allowed to complain of,
much less interfere, with the policy of their neighbors.

Suppose the doctrine advocated by Mr. Lincoln and the abolitionists of this
35   day had prevailed when the Constitution was made, what would have been
the result? Imagine for a moment that Mr. Lincoln had been a member of the
convention that framed the Constitution of the United States, and that when
its members were about to sign that wonderful document, he had arisen in
that convention as he did at Springfield this summer, and addressing himself

to the President, had said, "a house divided against itself cannot stand; this government divided into free and slave States cannot endure, they must all be free or all be slave, they must all be one thing or all the other, otherwise, it is a violation of the law of God, and cannot continue to exist;"—suppose Mr. Lincoln had convinced that body of sages, that that doctrine was sound, what would have been the result? Remember that the Union was then composed of thirteen States, twelve of which were slaveholding and one free. Do you think that the one free State would have outvoted the twelve slaveholding States, and thus have secured the abolition of slavery? On the other hand, would not the twelve slaveholding States have outvoted the one free State, and thus have fastened slavery, by a Constitutional provision, on every foot of the American Republic forever? You see that if this abolition doctrine of Mr. Lincoln had prevailed when the government was made, it would have established slavery as a permanent institution, in all the States whether they wanted it or not, and the question for us to determine in Illinois now as one of the free States is, whether or not we are willing, having become the majority section, to enforce a doctrine on the minority, which we would have resisted with our heart's blood had it been attempted on us when we were in a minority. How has the South lost her power as the majority section in this Union, and how have the free States gained it, except under the operation of that principle which declares the right of the people of each State and each territory to form and regulate their domestic institutions in their own way. It was under that principle that slavery was abolished in New Hampshire, Rhode Island, Connecticut, New York, New Jersey, and Pennsylvania; it was under that principle that one half of the slaveholding States became free; it was under that principle that the number of free States increased until from being one out of twelve States, we have grown to be the majority of States of the whole Union, with the power to control the House of Representatives and Senate, and the power, consequently, to elect a President by Northern votes without the aid of a Southern State. Having obtained this power under the operation of that great principle, are you now prepared to abandon the principle and declare that merely because we have the power you will wage a war against the Southern States and their institutions until you force them to abolish slavery everywhere....

But the Abolition party really think that under the Declaration of Independence the negro is equal to the white man, and that negro equality is an inalienable right conferred by the Almighty, and hence, that all human laws in violation of it are null and void. With such men it is no use for me to argue. I hold that the signers of the Declaration of Independence had no reference to negroes at all when they declared all men to be created equal. They did not mean negro, nor the savage Indians, nor the Fejee Islanders, nor any other barbarous race. They were speaking of white men. They alluded to men of European birth and European descent—to white men, and to none others, when they declared that doctrine. I hold that this Government was established on the white basis. It

5 was established by white men for the benefit of white men and their posterity forever, and should be administered by white men, and none others. But it does not follow, by any means, that merely because the negro is not a citizen, and merely because he is not our equal, that, therefore, he should be a slave. On the contrary, it does follow, that we ought to extend to the negro race, and to

10 all other dependent races all the rights, all the privileges, and all the immuni- ties which they can exercise consistently with the safety of society. Humanity requires that we should give them all these privileges; Christianity commands that we should extend those privileges to them. The question then arises what are those privileges, and what is the nature and extent of them. My answer is

15 that that is a question which each State must answer for itself. We in Illinois have decided it for ourselves. We tried slavery, kept it up for twelve years, and finding that it was not profitable we abolished it for that reason, and became a free State. We adopted in its stead the policy that a negro in this State shall not be a slave and shall not be a citizen. We have a right to adopt that policy.

20 For my part I think it is a wise and sound policy for us. You in Missouri must judge for yourselves whether it is a wise policy for you. If you choose to follow our example, very good; if you reject it, still well, it is your business, not ours. So with Kentucky. Let Kentucky adopt a policy to suit herself. If we do not like it we will keep away from it, and if she does not like ours let her stay at home,

25 mind her own business and let us alone. If the people of all the States will act on that great principle, and each State mind its own business, attend to its own affairs, take care of its own negroes and not meddle with its neighbors, then there will be peace between the North and the South, the East and the West, throughout the whole Union. Why can we not thus have peace? Why should

30 we thus allow a sectional party to agitate this country, to array the North against the South, and convert us into enemies instead of friends, merely that a few ambitious men may ride into power on a sectional hobby? How long is it since these ambitious Northern men wished for a sectional organization? Did any one of them dream of a sectional party as long as the North was the weaker section

35 and the South the stronger? Then all were opposed to sectional parties; but the moment the North obtained the majority in the House and Senate by the admission of California, and could elect a President without the aid of Southern votes, that moment ambitious Northern men formed a scheme to excite the North against the South, and make the people be governed in their votes by

40 geographical lines, thinking that the North, being the stronger section, would

outvote the South, and consequently they, the leaders, would ride into office on a sectional hobby. I am told that my hour is out. It was very short.

Mr. Lincoln's Reply

…At Galesburg the other day, I said in answer to Judge Douglas, that three years ago there never had been a man, so far as I knew or believed, in the whole world, who had said that the Declaration of Independence did not include negroes in the term "all men." I reassert it today. I assert that Judge Douglas and all his friends may search the whole records of the country, and it will be a matter of great astonishment to me if they shall be able to find that one human being three years ago had ever uttered the astounding sentiment that the term "all men" in the Declaration did not include the negro. Do not let me be misunderstood. I know that more than three years ago there were men who, finding this assertion constantly in the way of their schemes to bring about the ascendancy and perpetuation of slavery, *denied the truth of it.* I know that Mr. Calhoun and all the politicians of his school denied the truth of the Declaration. I know that it ran along in the mouths of some Southern men for a period of years, ending at last in that shameful though rather forcible declaration of Pettit of Indiana, upon the floor of the United States Senate, that the Declaration of Independence was in that respect "a self-evident lie," rather than a self-evident truth. But I say, with a perfect knowledge of all this hawking at the Declaration without directly attacking it, that three years ago there never had lived a man who had ventured to assail it in the sneaking way of pretending to believe it and then asserting it did not include the negro. I believe the first man who ever said it was Chief Justice Taney in the Dred Scott case, and the next to him was our friend Stephen A. Douglas. And now it has become the catch-word of the entire party. I would like to call upon his friends everywhere to consider how they have come in so short a time to view this matter in a way so entirely different from their former belief? to ask whether they are not being borne along by an irresistible current—whither, they know not?…

And when this new principle—this new proposition that no human being ever thought of three years ago,—is brought forward, *I combat it* as having an evil tendency, if not an evil design; I combat it as having a tendency to dehumanize the negro—to take away from him the right of ever striving to be a man. I combat it as being one of the thousand things constantly done in these days to prepare the public mind to make property, and nothing but property of the *negro in all the States of this Union.*…

Again; the institution of slavery is only mentioned in the Constitution of the United States two or three times, and in neither of these cases does the word

"slavery" or "negro race" occur; but covert language is used each time, and for a purpose full of significance. What is the language in regard to the prohibition of the African slave trade? It runs in about this way: "The migration or importation of such persons as any of the States now existing shall think proper to
5   admit, shall not be prohibited by the Congress prior to the year one thousand eight hundred and eight."

The next allusion in the Constitution to the question of slavery and the black race, is on the subject of the basis of representation, and there the language used is, "Representatives and direct taxes shall be apportioned among the several
10   States which may be included within this Union, according to their respective numbers, which shall be determined by adding to the whole number of free persons, including those bound to service for a term of years, and excluding Indians not taxed—three-fifths of all other persons."

It says "persons," not slaves, not negroes; but this "three-fifths" can be applied
15   to no other class among us than the negroes.

Lastly, in the provision for the reclamation of fugitive slaves it is said: "No person held to service or labor in one State under the laws thereof escaping into another, shall in consequence of any law or regulation therein, be discharged from such service or labor, but shall be delivered up, on claim of the party to
20   whom such service or labor may be due." There again there is no mention of the word "negro" or of slavery. In all three of these places, being the only allusions to slavery in the instrument, covert language is used. Language is used not suggesting that slavery existed or that the black race were among us. And I understand the contemporaneous history of those times to be that covert lan
25   guage was used with a purpose, and that purpose was that in our Constitution, which it was hoped and is still hoped will endure forever—when it should be read by intelligent and patriotic men, after the institution of slavery had passed from among us—there should be nothing on the face of the great charter of liberty suggesting that such a thing as negro slavery had ever existed among
30   us. This is part of the evidence that the fathers of the Government expected and intended the institution of slavery to come to an end. They expected and intended that it should be in the course of ultimate extinction. And when I say that I desire to see the further spread of it arrested I only say I desire to see that done which the fathers have first done. When I say I desire to see it placed
35   where the public mind will rest in the belief that it is in the course of ultimate extinction, I only say I desire to see it placed where they placed it. It is not true that our fathers, as Judge Douglas assumes, made this government part slave and part free. Understand the sense in which he puts it. He assumes that slavery is a rightful thing within itself,—was introduced by the framers of the

Constitution. The exact truth is, that they found the institution existing among us, and they left it as they found it. But in making the government they left this institution with many clear marks of disapprobation upon it. They found slavery among them and they left it among them because of the difficulty— the absolute impossibility of its immediate removal. And when Judge Douglas asks me why we cannot let it remain part slave and part free as the fathers of the government made, it he asks a question based upon an assumption which is itself a falsehood; and I turn upon him and ask him the question, when the policy that the fathers of the government had adopted in relation to this element among us was the best policy in the world—the only wise policy—the only policy that we can ever safely continue upon—that will ever give us peace unless this dangerous element masters us all and becomes a national institution—*I turn upon him and ask him why he could not let it alone?* I turn and ask him why he was driven to the necessity of introducing a *new policy* in regard to it? He has himself said he introduced a new policy. He said so in his speech on the 22d of March of the present year, 1858. I ask him why he could not let it remain where our fathers placed it? I ask too of Judge Douglas and his friends why we shall not again place this institution upon the basis on which the fathers left it? I ask you when he infers that I am in favor of setting the free and slave States at war, when the institution was placed in that attitude by those who made the constitution, *did they make any war?* If we had no war out of it when thus placed, wherein is the ground of belief that we shall have war out of it if we return to that policy? Have we had any peace upon this matter springing from any other basis? I maintain that we have not. I have proposed nothing more than a return to the policy of the fathers….

I have stated upon former occasions, and I may as well state again, what I understand to be the real issue in this controversy between Judge Douglas and myself. On the point of my wanting to make war between the free and the slave States, there has been no issue between us. So, too, when he assumes that I am in favor of introducing a perfect social and political equality between the white and black races. These are false issues, upon which Judge Douglas has tried to force the controversy. There is no foundation in truth for the charge that I maintain either of these propositions. The real issue in this controversy—the one pressing upon every mind—is the sentiment on the part of one class that looks upon the institution of slavery *as a wrong*, and of another class that *does not* look upon it as a wrong. The sentiment that contemplates the institution of slavery in this country as a wrong is the sentiment of the Republican party. It is the sentiment around which all their actions—all their arguments circle—from which all their propositions radiate. They look upon it as being a moral, social and political wrong; and while they contemplate it as such, they nevertheless

have due regard for its actual existence among us, and the difficulties of getting rid of it in any satisfactory way and to all the constitutional obligations
thrown about it. Yet having a due regard for these, they desire a policy in regard
to it that looks to its not creating any more danger. They insist that it should
5   as far as may be, *be treated* as a wrong, and one of the methods of treating it
as a wrong is to *make provision that it shall grow no larger.* They also desire a
policy that looks to a peaceful end of slavery at sometime, as being wrong.
These are the views they entertain in regard to it as I understand them; and all
their sentiments—all their arguments and propositions are brought within this
10   range. I have said and I repeat it here, that if there be a man amongst us who
does not think that the institution of slavery is wrong in any one of the aspects
of which I have spoken, he is misplaced and ought not to be with us. And if
there be a man amongst us who is so impatient of it as a wrong as to disregard
its actual presence among us and the difficulty of getting rid of it suddenly in a
15   satisfactory way, and to disregard the constitutional obligations thrown about
it, that man is misplaced if he is on our platform. We disclaim sympathy with
him in practical action. He is not placed properly with us.

On this subject of treating it as a wrong, and limiting its spread, let me say a
word. Has any thing ever threatened the existence of this Union save and except
20   this very institution of Slavery? What is it that we hold most dear amongst
us? Our own liberty and prosperity. What has ever threatened our liberty and
prosperity save and except this institution of Slavery? If this is true, how do you
propose to improve the condition of things by enlarging Slavery—by spreading
it out and making it bigger? You may have a wen or a cancer upon your person
25   and not be able to cut it out lest you bleed to death; but surely it is no way to
cure it, to engraft it and spread it over your whole body. That is no proper way
of treating what you regard a wrong. You see this peaceful way of dealing with
it as a wrong—restricting the spread of it, and not allowing it to go into new
countries where it has not already existed. That is the peaceful way, the old-
30   fashioned way, the way in which the fathers themselves set us the example.

On the other hand, I have said there is a sentiment which treats it as *not* being
wrong. That is the Democratic sentiment of this day. I do not mean to say that
every man who stands within that range positively asserts that it is right. That
class will include all who positively assert that it is right, and all who like Judge
35   Douglas treat it as indifferent and do not say it is either right or wrong. These
two classes of men fall within the general class of those who do not look upon
it as a wrong. And if there be among you anybody who supposes that he as a
Democrat, can consider himself "as much opposed to slavery as anybody," I
would like to reason with him. You never treat it as a wrong. What other thing

that you consider as a wrong, do you deal with as you deal with that? Perhaps you *say* it is wrong, *but your leader never does, and you quarrel with anybody who says it is wrong*. Although you pretend to say so yourself you can find no fit place to deal with it as a wrong. You must not say anything about it in the free States, *because it is not here*. You must not say anything about it in the slave States, *because it is there*. You must not say anything about it in the pulpit, because that is religion and has nothing to do with it. You must not say anything about it in politics, *because that will disturb the security of "my place."* There is no place to talk about it as being a wrong, although you say yourself it *is* a wrong. But finally you will screw yourself up to the belief that if the people of the slave States should adopt a system of gradual emancipation on the slavery question, you would be in favor of it. You would be in favor of it. You say that is getting it in the right place, and you would be glad to see it succeed. But you are deceiving yourself. You all know that Frank Blair and Gratz Brown, down there in St. Louis, undertook to introduce that system in Missouri. They fought as valiantly as they could for the system of gradual emancipation which you pretend you would be glad to see succeed. Now I will bring you to the test. After a hard fight they were beaten, and when the news came over here you threw up your hats and *hurrahed for Democracy*. More than that, take all the argument made in favor of the system you have proposed, and it carefully excludes the idea that there is anything wrong in the institution of slavery. The arguments to sustain that policy carefully excluded it. Even here today you heard Judge Douglas quarrel with me because I uttered a wish that it might sometime come to an end. Although Henry Clay could say he wished every slave in the United States was in the country of his ancestors, I am denounced by those pretending to respect Henry Clay for uttering a wish that it might sometime, in some peaceful way, come to an end. The Democratic policy in regard to that institution will not tolerate the merest breath, the slightest hint, of the least degree of wrong about it. Try it by some of Judge Douglas' arguments. He says he "don't care whether it is voted up or voted down" in the Territories. I do not care myself in dealing with that expression, whether it is intended to be expressive of his individual sentiments on the subject, or only of the national policy he desires to have established. It is alike valuable for my purpose. Any man can say that who does not see anything wrong in slavery, but no man can logically say it who does see a wrong in it; because no man can logically say he don't care whether a wrong is voted up or voted down. He may say he don't care whether an indifferent thing is voted up or down, but he must logically have a choice between a right thing and a wrong thing. He contends that whatever community wants slaves has a right to have them. So they have if it is not a wrong. But if it is a wrong, he cannot say people have a right to do wrong. He says that upon the

score of equality, slaves should be allowed to go in a new Territory, like other property. This is strictly logical if there is no difference between it and other property. If it and other property are equal, his argument is entirely logical. But if you insist that one is wrong and the other right, there is no use to institute
5   a comparison between right and wrong. You may turn over everything in the Democratic policy from beginning to end, whether in the shape it takes on the statute book, in the shape it takes in the Dred Scott decision, in the shape it takes in conversation or the shape it takes in short maxim-like arguments—it everywhere carefully excludes the idea that there is anything wrong in it.

10   That is the real issue. That is the issue that will continue in this country when these poor tongues of Judge Douglas and myself shall be silent. It is the eternal struggle between these two principles—right and wrong—throughout the world. They are the two principles that have stood face to face from the beginning of time; and will ever continue to struggle. The one is the common right
15   of humanity and the other the divine right of kings. It is the same principle in whatever shape it develops itself. It is the same spirit that says, "You work and toil and earn bread, and I'll eat it." No matter in what shape it comes, whether from the mouth of a king who seeks to bestride the people of his own nation and live by the fruit of their labor, or from one race of men as an apology for
20   enslaving another race, it is the same tyrannical principle. I was glad to express my gratitude at Quincy, and I re-express it here to Judge Douglas—*that he looks to no end of the institution of slavery.* That will help the people to see where the struggle really is. It will hereafter place with us all men who really do wish the wrong may have an end. And whenever we can get rid of the fog which obscures
25   the real question—when we can get Judge Douglas and his friends to avow a policy looking to its perpetuation—we can get out from among them that class of men and bring them to the side of those who treat it as a wrong. Then there will soon be an end of it, and that end will be its "ultimate extinction." Whenever the issue can be distinctly made, and all extraneous matter thrown out so
30   that men can fairly see the real difference between the parties, this controversy will soon be settled, and it will be done peaceably too. There will be no war, no violence. It will be placed again where the wisest and best men of the world, placed it. Brooks of South Carolina once declared that when this Constitution was framed, its framers did not look to the institution existing until this day.
35   When he said this, I think he stated a fact that is fully borne out by the history of the times. But he also said they were better and wiser men than the men of these days; yet the men of these days had experience which they had not, and by the invention of the cotton gin it became a necessity in this country that slavery should be perpetual. I now say that willingly or unwillingly, purposely

or without purpose, Judge Douglas has been the most prominent instrument in changing the position of the institution of slavery which the fathers of the government expected to come to an end ere this—*and putting it upon Brooks' cotton gin basis,*—placing it where he openly confesses he has no desire there shall ever be an end of it.... 5

Mr. Douglas's Reply

Mr. Lincoln has concluded his remarks by saying that there is not such an Abolitionist as I am in all America. If he could make the Abolitionists of Illinois believe that, he would not have much show for the Senate. Let him make the Abolitionists believe the truth of that statement and his political back is broken. 10

His first criticism upon me is the expression of his hope that the war of the administration will be prosecuted against me and the Democratic party of his State with vigor. He wants that war prosecuted with vigor; I have no doubt of it. His hopes of success, and the hopes of his party depend solely upon it. They have no chance of destroying the Democracy of this State except by the 15 aid of federal patronage. He has all the federal office-holders here as his allies, running separate tickets against the Democracy to divide the party although the leaders all intend to vote directly the Abolition ticket, and only leave the green-horns to vote this separate ticket who refuse to go into the Abolition camp. There is something really refreshing in the thought that Mr. Lincoln is 20 in favor of prosecuting one war vigorously. It is the first war I ever knew him to be in favor of prosecuting. It is the first war that I ever knew him to believe to be just or constitutional. When the Mexican war [was] being waged, and the American army was surrounded by the enemy in Mexico, he thought that war was unconstitutional, unnecessary and unjust. He thought it was not com- 25 menced on the right *spot*.

When I made an incidental allusion of that kind in the joint discussion over at Charleston some weeks ago, Lincoln, in replying, said that I, Douglas, had charged him with voting against supplies for the Mexican war, and then he reared up, full length, and swore that he never voted against the supplies—that 30 it was a slander—and caught hold of Ficklin, who sat on the stand, and said, "Here, Ficklin, tell the people that it is a lie." Well, Ficklin, who had served in Congress with him, stood up and told them all that he recollected about it. It was that when George Ashmun, of Massachusetts, brought forward a resolution declaring the war unconstitutional, unnecessary, and unjust, that Lincoln had 35 voted for it. "Yes," said Lincoln, "I did." Thus he confessed that he voted that the war was wrong, that our country was in the wrong, and consequently that

the Mexicans were in the right; but charged that I had slandered him by saying that he voted against the supplies. I never charged him with voting against
the supplies in my life, because I knew that he was not in Congress when they
were voted. The war was commenced on the 13th day of May, 1846, and on
5   that day we appropriated in Congress ten millions of dollars and fifty thousand
men to prosecute it. During the same session we voted more men and more
money, and at the next session we voted more men and more money, so that
by the time Mr. Lincoln entered Congress we had enough men and enough
money to carry on the war, and had no occasion to vote any more. When he
10   got into the House, being opposed to the war, and not being able to stop the
supplies, because they had all gone forward, all he could do was to follow the
lead of Corwin, and prove that the war was not begun on the right spot, and
that it was unconstitutional, unnecessary, and wrong. Remember, too, that
this he did after the war had been begun. It is one thing to be opposed to the
15   declaration of a war, another and very different thing to take sides with the
enemy against your own country after the war has been commenced. Our army
was in Mexico at the time, many battles had been fought; our citizens, who
were defending the honor of their country's flag, were surrounded by the dag-
gers, the guns and the poison of the enemy. Then it was that Corwin made his
20   speech in which he declared that the American soldiers ought to be welcomed
by the Mexicans with bloody hands and hospitable graves; then it was that
Ashmun and Lincoln voted in the House of Representatives that the war was
unconstitutional and unjust; and Ashmun's resolution, Corwin's speech, and
Lincoln's vote were sent to Mexico and read at the head of the Mexican army,
25   to prove to them that there was a Mexican party in the Congress of the United
States who were doing all in their power to aid them. That a man who takes
sides with the common enemy against his own country in time of war should
rejoice in a war being made on me now, is very natural. And in my opinion,
no other kind of a man would rejoice in it....

30   Mr. Lincoln tries to avoid the main issue by attacking the truth of my proposition, that our fathers made this government divided into free and slave States,
recognizing the right of each to decide all its local questions for itself. Did they
not thus make it? It is true that they did not establish slavery in any of the States,
or abolish it in any of them; but finding thirteen States twelve of which were
35   slave and one free, they agreed to form a government uniting them together, as
they stood divided into free and slave States, and to guarantee forever to each
State the right to do as it pleased on the slavery question. Having thus made
the government, and conferred this right upon each State forever, I assert that
this government can exist as they made it, divided into free and slave States, if

any one State chooses to retain slavery. He says that he looks forward to a time when slavery shall be abolished everywhere. I look forward to a time when each State shall be allowed to do as it pleases. If it chooses to keep slavery forever, it is not my business, but its own; if it chooses to abolish slavery, it is its own business—not mine. I care more for the great principle of self-government, 5 the right of the people to rule, than I do for all the negroes in Christendom. I would not endanger the perpetuity of this Union. I would not blot out the great inalienable rights of the white men for all the negroes that ever existed. Hence, I say, let us maintain this government on the principles that our fathers made it, recognizing the right of each State to keep slavery as long as its people 10 determine, or to abolish it when they please. But Mr. Lincoln says that when our fathers made this government they did not look forward to the state of things now existing; and therefore he thinks the doctrine was wrong; and he quotes Brooks, of South Carolina, to prove that our fathers then thought that probably slavery would be abolished, by each State acting for itself before this 15 time. Suppose they did; suppose they did not foresee what has occurred,—does that change the principles of our government? They did not probably foresee the telegraph that transmits intelligence by lightning, nor did they foresee the railroads that now form the bonds of union between the different States, or the thousand mechanical inventions that have elevated mankind. But do these 20 things change the principles of the government? Our fathers, I say, made this government on the principle of the right of each State to do as it pleases in its own domestic affairs, subject to the constitution, and allowed the people of each to apply to every new change of circumstances such remedy as they may see fit to improve their condition. This right they have for all time to come.... 25

The Dividing Line between Federal and Local Authority: Popular Sovereignty in the Territories
Stephen Douglas

In September 1857, pro-slavery forces in Kansas drafted the Lecompton Constitution. Their anti-slavery opponents declared the document invalid, as they had not participated in its creation. Adhering to the principle of popular sovereignty, Stephen Douglas rejected the Lecompton Constitution and called for Kansans to draft a new document. Northern Democrats, dismayed by the armed conflict in Kansas, supported his position; Southern Democrats looked on it as an act of betrayal. Douglas took every opportunity to explain his position in hopes of re-unifying his party. This speech was published in Harper's New Monthly Magazine.

SEPTEMBER 1859

Under our complex system of government it is the first duty of American states-men to mark distinctly the dividing line between Federal and Local Authority. To do this with accuracy involves an inquiry, not only into the powers and duties of the Federal Government under the Constitution, but also into the rights, privileges, and immunities of the people of the Territories, as well as of the States 5 composing the Union. The relative powers and functions of the Federal and State governments have become well understood and clearly defined by their practical operation and harmonious action for a long series of years; while the disputed question —involving the right of the people of the Territories to govern themselves in respect to their local affairs and internal polity—remains a fruitful 10 source of partisan strife and sectional controversy. The political organization which was formed in 1854, and has assumed the name of the Republican Party, is based on the theory that African slavery, as it exists in this country, is an evil of such magnitude—social, moral, and political—as to justify and require the exertion of the entire power and influence of the Federal Government to the 15 full extent that the Constitution, according to their interpretation, will permit for its ultimate extinction....

Stephen Douglas, "The Dividing Line between Federal and Local Authority: Popular Sovereignty in the Territories," *Harper's New Monthly Magazine* 19, no. 112 (September 1859): 519, 521–24, 527–29, 537.

This dividing line between Federal and Local authority was familiar to the framers of the Constitution. It is clearly defined and distinctly marked on every page of history which records the great events of that immortal struggle between the American Colonies and the British Government, which resulted
5 in the establishment of our national independence. In the beginning of that struggle the Colonies neither contemplated nor desired independence. In all their addresses to the Crown, and to the Parliament, and to the people of Great Britain, as well as to the people of America, they averred that as loyal British subjects they deplored the causes which impelled their separation from the par-
10 ent country. They were strongly and affectionately attached to the Constitution, civil and political institutions and jurisprudence of Great Britain, which they proudly claimed as the birth-right of all Englishmen, and desired to transmit them unimpaired as a precious legacy to their posterity. For a long series of years they remonstrated against the violation of their inalienable rights of self-
15 government under the British Constitution, and humbly petitioned for the redress of their grievances.

They acknowledged and affirmed their allegiance to the Crown, their affection for the people, and their devotion to the Constitution of Great Britain; and their only complaint was that they were not permitted to enjoy the rights and
20 privileges of self-government, in the management of their internal affairs and domestic concerns, in accordance with the guarantees of that Constitution and of the colonial charters granted by the Crown in pursuance of it. They conceded the right of the Imperial government to make all laws and perform all acts concerning the colonies, which were in their nature *Imperial* and not
25 *Colonial*—which affected the general welfare of the Empire, and did not in-terfere with the "internal polity" of the Colonies. They recognized the right of the Imperial government to declare war and make peace; to coin money and determine its value; to make treaties and conduct intercourse with foreign na-tions; to regulate commerce between the several colonies, and between each
30 colony and the parent country, and with foreign countries; and in general they recognized the right of the Imperial government of Great Britain to exercise all the powers and authority which, under our Federal Constitution, are delegated by the people of the several States to the Government of the United States.

Recognizing and conceding to the Imperial government all these powers—
35 *including the right to institute governments for the colonies*, by granting charters under which the inhabitants residing within the limits of any specified Territory might be organized into a political community, with a government consisting of its appropriate departments, executive, legislative, and judicial; conceding all these powers, the colonies emphatically denied that the Imperial government

had any rightful authority to impose taxes upon them without their consent, or to interfere with their internal polity; claiming that it was the birth-right of all Englishmen—inalienable when formed into a political community—to exercise and enjoy all the rights, privileges, and immunities of self-government in respect to all matters and things, which were Local and not General—Internal and not   5 External—Colonial and not Imperial—as fully as if they were inhabitants of England, with a fair representation in Parliament.

Thus it appears that our fathers of the Revolution were contending, not for Independence in the first instance, but for the inestimable right of Local Self-Government under the British Constitution; the right of every distinct   10 political community—dependent Colonies, Territories, and Provinces, as well as sovereign States—to make their own local laws, form their own domestic institutions, and manage their own internal affairs in their own way, subject only to the Constitution of Great Britain as the paramount law of the Empire.

The government of Great Britain had violated this inalienable right of local   15 self-government by a long series of acts on a great variety of subjects. The first serious point of controversy arose on the slavery question as early as 1699, which continued a fruitful source of irritation until the Revolution, and formed one of the causes for the separation of the colonies from the British Crown.

For more than forty years the Provincial Legislature of Virginia had passed   20 laws for the protection and encouragement of African slavery within her limits. This policy was steadily pursued until the white inhabitants of Virginia became alarmed for their own safety, in view of the numerous and formidable tribes of Indian savages which surrounded and threatened the feeble white settlements, while ship-loads of African savages were being daily landed in their midst. In   25 order to check and restrain a policy which seemed to threaten the very existence of the colony, the Provincial Legislature enacted a law imposing a tax upon every slave who should be brought into Virginia. The British merchants, who were engaged in the African slave-trade, regarding this legislation as injurious to their interests and in violation of their rights, petitioned the King of England   30 and his Majesty's ministers to annul the obnoxious law and protect them in their right to carry their slaves into Virginia and all other British colonies which were the common property of the Empire—acquired by the common blood and common treasure—and from which a few adventurers who had settled on the Imperial domain by his Majesty's sufferance, had no right to exclude them   35 or discriminate against their property by a mere Provincial enactment. Upon a full consideration of the subject the King graciously granted the prayer of the petitioners; and accordingly issued peremptory orders to the Royal Governor of Virginia, and to the Governors of all the other British colonies in America, forbidding them to sign or approve any Colonial or Provincial enactment injurious to the African Slave-Trade, unless such enactment should contain a clause suspending its operation until his Majesty's pleasure should be made known in the premises.

5   Judge Tucker, in his Appendix to Blackstone, refers to thirty-one acts of the Provincial Legislature of Virginia, passed at various periods from 1662 to 1772, upon the subject of African slavery, showing conclusively that Virginia always considered this as one of the questions affecting her "internal polity," over which she, in common with the other colonies, claimed "the right of exclusive
10 legislation in their Provincial Legislatures" within their respective limits. Some of these acts, particularly those which were enacted prior to the year 1699, were evidently intended to foster and encourage, as well as to regulate and control African slavery, as one of the domestic institutions of the colony. The act of 1699, and most of the enactments subsequent to that date, were as obviously
15 designed to restrain and check the growth of the institution with the view of confining it within the limit of the actual necessities of the community, or its ultimate extinction, as might be deemed most conducive to the public interests, by a system of unfriendly legislation, such as imposing a tax on all slaves introduced into the colony, which was increased and renewed from time to
20 time, as occasion required, until the period of the Revolution. Many of these acts never took effect, in consequence of the King withholding his assent, even after the Governor had approved the enactment, in cases where it contained a clause suspending its operation until his Majesty's pleasure should be made known in the premises.

25 In 1772 the Provincial Legislature of Virginia, after imposing another tax of five per cent, on all slaves imported into the colony, petitioned the King to remove all those restraints which inhibited his Majesty's Governors assenting to such laws as might check so very pernicious a commerce as slavery. Of this petition Judge Tucker says:

30 "The following extract from a petition to the Throne, presented from the House of Burgesses of Virginia, April 1st, 1772, will show the sense of the people of Virginia on the subject of slavery at that period:

"'The importation of slaves into the colony from the coast of Africa hath long been considered as a trade of great inhumanity; and under its present encour-
35 agement we have too much reason to fear will endanger the very existence of your Majesty's American dominions.'"

Mark the ominous words! Virginia tells the King of England in 1772, four years prior to the Declaration of Independence, that his Majesty's American dominions are in danger: Not because of the Stamp duties—not because of the tax on Tea—not because of his attempts to collect revenue in America! These have since been deemed sufficient to justify rebellion and revolution. But none of these are referred to by Virginia in her address to the Throne—there being another wrong which, in magnitude and enormity, so far exceeded these and all other causes of complaint that the very existence of his Majesty's American dominions depended upon it! That wrong consisted in forcing African slavery upon a dependent colony without her consent, and in opposition to the wishes of her own people!

The people of Virginia at that day did not appreciate the force of the argument used by the British merchants, who were engaged in the African slave-trade, and which was afterward endorsed, at least by implication, by the King and his Ministers; that the colonies were the common property of the Empire—acquired by the common blood and treasure—and therefore all British subjects had the right to carry their slaves into the colonies and hold them in defiance of the local law and in contempt of the wishes and safety of the colonies.

The people of Virginia not being convinced by this process of reasoning, still adhered to the doctrine which they held in common with their sister colonies, that it was the birth-right of all freemen—inalienable when formed into political communities—to exercise exclusive legislation in respect to all matters pertaining to their internal polity—slavery not excepted; and rather than surrender this great right they were prepared to withdraw their allegiance from the Crown.

Again referring to this petition to the King, the same learned Judge adds:

"This petition produced no effect, as appears from the first clause of our [Virginia] Constitution, where, among other acts of misrule, the inhuman use of the Royal negative in refusing us [the people of Virginia] permission to exclude slavery from us by law, is enumerated among the reasons for separating from Great Britain."

This clause in the Constitution of Virginia, referring to the inhuman use of the Royal negative, in refusing the Colony of Virginia permission to exclude slavery from her limits by law as one of the reasons for separating from Great Britain, was adopted on the 12th day of June, 1776, three weeks and one day previous to the Declaration of Independence by the Continental Congress; and after remaining in force as a part of the Constitution for a period of fifty-four years, was re-adopted, without alteration, by the Convention which framed the new Constitution in 1830, and then ratified by the people as a part of the new Constitution; and was again re-adopted by the Convention which amended the Constitution in 1850, and again ratified by the people as a part of the

amended Constitution, and at this day remains a portion of the fundamental law of Virginia—proclaiming to the world and to posterity that one of the reasons for separating from Great Britain was "the inhuman use of the Royal negative in refusing us [the Colony of Virginia] permission to exclude slavery
5   from us by law!"

The legislation of Virginia on this subject may be taken as a fair sample of the legislative enactments of each of the thirteen Colonies, showing conclusively that slavery was regarded by them all as a domestic question to be regarded and determined by each Colony to suit itself, without the intervention of the British
10   Parliament or "the inhuman use of the Royal negative." Each Colony passed a series of enactments, beginning at an early period of its history and running down to the commencement of the Revolution, either protecting, regulating, or restraining African Slavery within its respective limits and in accordance with their wishes and supposed interests. North and South Carolina, following the
15   example of Virginia, at first encouraged the introduction of slaves, until the number increased beyond their wants and necessities, when they attempted to check and restrain the further growth of the institution, by imposing a high rate of taxation upon all slaves which should be brought into those colonies; and finally, in 1764, South Carolina passed a law imposing a penalty of one
20   hundred pounds (or five hundred dollars) for every negro slave subsequently introduced into that Colony.

The Colony of Georgia was originally founded on strict anti-slavery principles, and rigidly maintained this policy for a series of years, until the inhabitants became convinced by experience, that, with their climate and productions, slave
25   labor, if not essential to their existence, would prove beneficial and useful to their material interests. Maryland and Delaware protected and regulated African Slavery as one of their domestic institutions. Pennsylvania, under the advice of William Penn, substituted fourteen years' service and perpetual adscript to the soil for hereditary slavery, and attempted to legislate, not for the total abolition
30   of slavery, but for the sanctity of marriage among slaves, and for their personal security. New Jersey, New York, and Connecticut, recognized African Slavery as a domestic institution lawfully existing within their respective limits, and passed the requisite laws for its control and regulation.

Rhode Island provided by law that no slave should serve more than ten years,
35   at the end of which time he was to be set free; and if the master should refuse to let him go free, or sold him elsewhere for a longer period of service, he was subject to a penalty of forty pounds, which was supposed at that period to be nearly double the value of the slave.

Massachusetts imposed heavy taxes upon all slaves brought into the Colony, and provided in some instances for sending the slaves back to their native land; and finally prohibited the introduction of any more slaves into the Colony under any circumstances.

When New Hampshire passed laws which were designed to prevent the introduction of any more slaves, the British Cabinet issued the following order to Governor Wentworth: "You are not to give your assent to, or pass any law imposing duties upon Negroes imported into New Hampshire."

While the legislation of the several Colonies exhibits dissimilarity of views, founded on a diversity of interests, on the merits and policy of slavery, it shows conclusively that they all regarded it as a domestic question affecting their internal polity in respect to which they were entitled to a full and exclusive power of legislation in the several provincial Legislatures. For a few years immediately preceding the American Revolution the African Slave-Trade was encouraged and stimulated by the British Government and carried on with more vigor by the English merchants than at any other period in the history of the Colonies; and this fact, taken in connection with the extraordinary claim asserted in the Memorable Preamble to the act repealing the Stamp duties, that "Parliament possessed the right to bind the Colonies in all cases whatsoever," not only in respect to all matters affecting the general welfare of the empire, but also in regard to the domestic relations and internal polity of the Colonies—produced a powerful impression upon the minds of the colonists, and imparted peculiar prominence to the principle involved in the controversy.

Hence the enactments by the several colonial Legislatures calculated and designed to restrain and prevent the increase of slaves; and, on the other hand, the orders issued by the Crown instructing the Colonial Governors not to sign or permit any legislative enactment prejudicial or injurious to the African Slave-Trade, unless such enactment should contain a clause suspending its operation until the royal pleasure should be made known in the premises; or, in other words, until the King should have an opportunity of annulling the acts of the colonial Legislatures by the "inhuman use of the Royal negative."

Thus the policy of the Colonies on the slavery question had assumed a direct antagonism to that of the British Government; and this antagonism not only added to the importance of the principle of local self-government in the Colonies, but produced a general concurrence of opinion and action in respect to the question of slavery in the proceedings of the Continental Congress, which assembled at Philadelphia for the first time on the 5th of September, 1774.

On the 14th of October the Congress adopted a Bill of Rights for the Colonies, in the form of a series of resolutions, in which, after conceding to the
British Government the power to regulate commerce and do such other things
as affected the general welfare of the empire without interfering with the
5   internal polity of the Colonies, they declared "That they are entitled to a free
and exclusive power in their several provincial Legislatures, where their right
of representation can alone be preserved, in all cases of taxation and internal
polity." Having thus defined the principle for which they were contending, the
Congress proceeded to adopt the following "Peaceful Measures," which they still
10   hoped would be sufficient to induce compliance with their just and reasonable
demands. These "Peaceful Measures" consisted of addresses to the King, to the
Parliament, and to the people of Great Britain, together with an Association
of Non-Intercourse to be observed and maintained so long as their grievances
should remain unredressed.

15   The second article of this Association, which was adopted without opposition
and signed by the Delegates from all the Colonies, was in these words:

"That we will neither import nor purchase any slave imported after the first day
of December next; after which time we will wholly discontinue the Slave-Trade,
and will neither be concerned in it ourselves, nor will we hire our vessels, nor
20   sell our commodities or manufactures to those who are engaged in it."

This Bill of Rights, together with these articles of association, were subsequently
submitted to and adopted by each of the thirteen Colonies in their respective
Provincial Legislatures.

Thus was distinctly formed between the Colonies and the parent country
25   that issue upon which the Declaration of Independence was founded and the
battles of the Revolution were fought. It involved the specific claim on the part
of the Colonies—denied by the King and Parliament—to the exclusive right
of legislation touching all local and internal concerns, *slavery included*. This
being the principle involved in the contest, a majority of the Colonies refused
30   to permit their Delegates to sign the Declaration of Independence except upon
the distinct condition and express reservation to each Colony of the exclusive
right to manage and control its local concerns and police regulations without
the intervention of any general Congress which might be established for the
United Colonies....

35   Let us pause at this point for a moment, and inquire whether it be just to those
illustrious patriots and sages who formed the Constitution of the United States,
to assume that they intended to confer upon Congress that unlimited and arbitrary power over the people of the American Territories, which they had resisted

with their blood when claimed by the British Parliament over British Colonies in America? Did they confer upon Congress the right to bind the people of the American Territories in all cases whatsoever, after having fought the battles of the Revolution against a "Preamble" declaring the right of Parliament "to bind the Colonies in all cases whatsoever?"   5

If, as they contended before the Revolution, it was the birth-right of all English-men, inalienable when formed into political communities, to exercise exclusive power of legislation in their local legislatures in respect to all things affecting their internal polity—slavery not excepted—did not the same right, after the Revolution, and by virtue of it, become the birth-right of all Americans, in like   10 manner inalienable when organized into political communities—no matter by what name, whether Colonies, Territories, Provinces, or new States?

Names often deceive persons in respect to the nature and substance of things. A signal instance of this kind is to be found in that clause of the Constitution which says: 15

"Congress shall have power to dispose of, and make all needful rules and regulations respecting the territory or other property belonging to the United States."

This being the only clause of the Constitution in which the word "territory" appears, that fact alone has doubtless led many persons to suppose that the   20 right of Congress to establish temporary governments for the Territories, in the sense in which the word is now used, must be derived from it, overlooking the important and controlling facts that at the time the Constitution was formed the word "territory" had never been used or understood to designate a political community or government of any kind in any law, compact, deed cession, or   25 public document; but had invariably been used either in its geographical sense to describe the superficial area of a State or district of country, as in the Virginia deed of cession of the "territory or *tract of country*" northwest of the River Ohio; or as meaning land in its character as property, in which latter sense it appears in the clause of the Constitution referred to, when providing for the disposition   30 of the "territory or other property belonging to the United States." These facts, taken in connection with the kindred one that during the whole period of the Confederation and the formation of the Constitution the temporary govern-ments which we now call "Territories," were invariably referred to in the deeds of cession, laws, compacts, plans of government, resolutions of congress, public   35 records, and authentic documents as "States," or "new States," conclusively show that the words "territory and other property" in the Constitution were used to designate the unappropriated lands and other property which the United

States owned, and not the people who might become residents on those lands, and be organized into political communities after the United States had parted with their title.

It is from this clause of the Constitution alone that Congress derives the power
5   to provide for the surveys and sale of the public lands and all other property belonging to the United States, not only in the Territories, but also in the several States of the Union. But for this provision Congress would have no power to authorize the sale of the public lands, military sites, old ships, cannon, muskets, or other property, real or personal, which belong to the United States and are
10   no longer needed for any public purpose. It refers exclusively to property in contradistinction to persons and communities. It confers the same power "to make all needful rules and regulations" in the States as in the Territories, and extends wherever there may be any land or other property belonging to the United States to be regulated or disposed of; but does not authorize Congress
15   to control or interfere with the domestic institutions and internal polity of the people (either in the States or the Territories) who may reside upon lands which the United States once owned. Such a power, had it been vested in Congress, would annihilate the sovereignty and freedom of the States as well as the great principle of self-government in the Territories, wherever the United States
20   happen to own a portion of the public lands within their respective limits, as, at present, in the States of Alabama, Florida, Mississippi, Louisiana, Arkansas, Missouri, Illinois, Indiana, Ohio, Michigan, Wisconsin, Iowa, Minnesota, California, and Oregon, and in the Territories of Washington, Nebraska, Kansas, Utah, and New Mexico. The idea is repugnant to the spirit and genius of our
25   complex system of government; because it effectually blots out the dividing line between Federal and Local authority which forms an essential barrier for the defense of the independence of the States and the liberties of the people against Federal invasion. With one anomalous exception, all the powers conferred on Congress are *Federal*, and not *Municipal*, in their character—affecting
30   the general welfare of the whole country without interfering with the internal polity of the people—and can be carried into effect by laws which apply alike to States and Territories. The exception, being in derogation of one of the fundamental principles of our political system (because it authorizes the Federal Government to control the municipal affairs and internal polity of the people
35   in certain specified, limited localities), was not left to vague inference or loose construction, nor expressed in dubious or equivocal language; but is found plainly written in that Section of the Constitution which says:

"Congress shall have power to exercise exclusive legislation in all cases whatsoever, over such district (not exceeding ten miles square) as may, by cession of particular States, and the acceptance of Congress, become the seat of the government of the United States, and to exercise like authority over all places purchased by the consent of the Legislature of the State in which the same shall be, for the erection of forts, magazines, arsenals, dock-yards, and other needful buildings." 5

No such power "to exercise exclusive legislation in all cases whatsoever," nor indeed any legislation in any case whatsoever, is conferred on Congress in respect to the municipal affairs and internal polity, either of the States or of the Territories. On the contrary, after the Constitution had been finally adopted, with its Federal powers delegated, enumerated, and defined, in order to guard in all future 10 time against any possible infringement of the reserved rights of the States, or of the people, an amendment was incorporated into the Constitution which marks the dividing line between Federal and Local authority so directly and indelibly that no lapse of time, no partisan prejudice, no sectional aggrandizement, no frenzied fanaticism can efface it. The amendment is in these words: 15

"The powers not delegated to the United States by the Constitution, nor prohibited by it to the States, are reserved to the States respectively, or to the people."

This view of the subject is confirmed, if indeed any corroborative evidence is required, by reference to the proceedings and debates of the Federal Conven- 20 tion, as reported by Mr. Madison. On the 18th of August, after a series of resolutions had been adopted as the basis of the proposed Constitution and referred to the Committee of Detail for the purpose of being put in proper form, the record says:

"Mr. Madison submitted, in order to be referred to the Committee of Detail, 25 the following powers, as proper to be added to those of the General Legislature (Congress):

"To dispose of the unappropriated lands of the United States.

"To institute temporary governments for the new States arising therein.

"To regulate affairs with the Indians, as well within as without the limits of the 30 United States.

"To exercise exclusively legislative authority at the seat of the general government, and over a district around the same not exceeding—square miles, the consent of the Legislature of the State or States comprising the same being first obtained."

Here we find the original and rough draft of these several powers as they now 35 exist, in their revised form, in the Constitution. The provision empowering

Congress "to dispose of the unappropriated lands of the United States" was modified and enlarged so as to include "other property belonging to the United States," and to authorize Congress to "make all needful rules and regulations" for the preservation, management, and sale of the same.

5 The provision empowering Congress "to institute temporary governments for the new States arising in the unappropriated lands of the United States," taken in connection with the one empowering Congress "to exercise exclusively Legislative authority at the seat of the general government, and over a district of country around the same," clearly shows the difference in the extent and nature
10 of the powers intended to be conferred to the new States or Territories on the one hand, and in the District of Columbia on the other. In the one case it was proposed to authorize Congress "to institute temporary governments for the new States," or Territories, as they are now called, just as our Revolutionary fathers recognized the right of the British crown to institute local governments
15 for the colonies, by issuing charters, under which the people of the colonies were "entitled (according to the Bill of Rights adopted by the Continental Congress) to a free and exclusive power of legislation, in their several Provincial Legislatures, where their right of representation can alone be preserved, in all cases of taxation and internal polity;" while, in the other case, it was proposed to authorize
20 Congress to exercise, exclusively, legislative authority over the municipal and internal polity of the people residing within the district which should be ceded for that purpose as the seat of the general government.

Each of these provisions was modified and perfected by the Committees of Detail and Revision, as will appear by comparing them with the corresponding
25 clauses as finally incorporated into the Constitution. The provision to authorize Congress to institute temporary governments for the new States or Territories, and to provide for their admission into the Union, appears in the Constitution in this form:

"New States may be admitted by the Congress into this Union."

30 The power to admit "*new States*" and "to make all laws which shall be necessary and proper" to that end, may fairly be construed to include the right to institute temporary governments for such new States or Territories, the same as Great Britain could rightfully institute similar governments for the colonies; but certainly not to authorize Congress to legislate in respect to their municipal
35 affairs and internal concerns, without violating that great fundamental principle in defense of which the battles of the Revolution were fought....

This exposition of the history of these measures shows conclusively that the authors of the Compromise Measures of 1850, and of the Kansas-Nebraska Act of 1854, as well as the members of the Continental Congress of 1774, and the founders of our system of government subsequent to the Revolution, regarded the people of the Territories and Colonies as political Communities which were entitled to a free and exclusive power of legislation in their Provincial legislatures, where their representation could alone be preserved, in all cases of taxation and internal polity. This right pertains to the people collectively as a law-abiding and peaceful community, and not to the isolated individuals who may wander upon the public domain in violation of law. It can only be exercised where there are inhabitants sufficient to constitute a government, and capable of performing its various functions and duties—a fact to be ascertained and determined by Congress. Whether the number shall be fixed at ten, fifteen, or twenty thousand inhabitants does not affect the principle.

The principle, under our political system, is *that every distinct political Community, loyal to the Constitution and the Union, is entitled to all the rights, privileges, and immunities of self-government in respect to their local concerns and internal polity, subject only to the Constitution of the United States.*

ADDRESS AT COOPER INSTITUTE
ABRAHAM LINCOLN

With an eye to the Republican presidential nomination of 1860, Abraham Lincoln campaigned vigorously across the North. Responding to Stephen Douglas's "Dividing Line" speech, he used this address to claim the mantle of America's Founders for the Republican Party. Employing original research on the anti-slavery views of "our fathers," Lincoln cast himself as a conservative. The speech caught the attention of the Eastern political establishment, while at the same time distinguishing him from the radical abolitionists.

FEBRUARY 27, 1860

...But enough! *Let all who believe that "our fathers, who framed the Government under which we live, understood this question just as well, and even better, than we do now," speak as they spoke, and act as they acted upon it. This is all Republicans ask—all Republicans desire—in relation to slavery. As those fathers marked it, so let it be again marked, as an evil not to be extended, but to be tolerated and protected* 5 *only because of and so far as its actual presence among us makes that toleration and protection a necessity. Let all the guarantees those fathers gave it, be, not grudgingly, but fully and fairly maintained.* For this Republicans contend, and with this, so far as I know or believe, they will be content.

And now, if they would listen—as I suppose they will not—I would address a 10 few words to the Southern people....

Your purpose, then, plainly stated, is, that you will destroy the Government, unless you be allowed to construe and enforce the Constitution as you please, on all points in dispute between you and us. You will rule or ruin in all events.

This, plainly stated, is your language. Perhaps you will say the Supreme Court 15 has decided the disputed Constitutional question in your favor. Not quite so.

Abraham Lincoln, "Address at Cooper Institute, New York City," February 27, 1860, in Roy P. Basler, ed., *The Collected Works of Abraham Lincoln,* Vol. 3 (New Brunswick, NJ: Rutgers University Press, 1953), 535, 543–50. Reprinted with the permission of the Abraham Lincoln Association, Springfield, IL.

But waiving the lawyer's distinction between dictum and decision, the Court have decided the question for you in a sort of way. The Court have substantially said, it is your Constitutional right to take slaves into the federal territories, and to hold them there as property. When I say the decision was made in a sort of
5   way, I mean it was made in a divided Court, by a bare majority of the Judges, and they not quite agreeing with one another in the reasons for making it; that it is so made as that its avowed supporters disagree with one another about its meaning, and that it was mainly based upon a mistaken statement of fact—the statement in the opinion that "the right of property in a slave is distinctly and
10   expressly affirmed in the Constitution."

An inspection of the Constitution will show that the right of property in a slave is not "*distinctly* and *expressly* affirmed" in it. Bear in mind, the Judges do not pledge their judicial opinion that such right is *impliedly* affirmed in the Constitution; but they pledge their veracity that it is "*distinctly* and *expressly*" affirmed
15   there—"distinctly," that is, not mingled with anything else—"expressly," that is, in words meaning just that, without the aid of any inference, and susceptible of no other meaning.

If they had only pledged their judicial opinion that such right is affirmed in the instrument by implication, it would be open to others to show that neither
20   the word "slave" nor "slavery" is to be found in the Constitution, nor the word "property" even, in any connection with language alluding to the things slave, or slavery, and that wherever in that instrument the slave is alluded to, he is called a "person;"—and wherever his master's legal right in relation to him is alluded to, it is spoken of as "service or labor which may be due,"—as a debt
25   payable in service or labor. Also, it would be open to show, by contemporaneous history, that this mode of alluding to slaves and slavery, instead of speaking of them, was employed on purpose to exclude from the Constitution the idea that there could be property in man.

To show all this, is easy and certain.

30   When this obvious mistake of the Judges shall be brought to their notice, is it not reasonable to expect that they will withdraw the mistaken statement, and reconsider the conclusion based upon it?

And then it is to be remembered that "our fathers, who framed the Government under which we live"—the men who made the Constitution—decided
35   this same Constitutional question in our favor, long ago—decided it without division among themselves, when making the decision; without division among themselves about the meaning of it after it was made, and, so far as any evidence is left, without basing it upon any mistaken statement of facts.

Under all these circumstances, do you really feel yourselves justified to break up this Government, unless such a court decision as yours is, shall be at once submitted to as a conclusive and final rule of political action? But you will not abide the election of a Republican President! In that supposed event, you say, you will destroy the Union; and then, you say, the great crime of having destroyed it will be upon us! That is cool. A highwayman holds a pistol to my ear, and mutters through his teeth, "Stand and deliver, or I shall kill you, and then you will be a murderer!"

To be sure, what the robber demanded of me—my money—was my own; and I had a clear right to keep it; but it was no more my own than my vote is my own; and the threat of death to me, to extort my money, and the threat of destruction to the Union, to extort my vote, can scarcely be distinguished in principle.

A few words now to Republicans. *It is exceedingly desirable that all parts of this great Confederacy shall be at peace, and in harmony, one with another. Let us Republicans do our part to have it so. Even though much provoked, let us do nothing through passion and ill temper. Even though the southern people will not so much as listen to us, let us calmly consider their demands, and yield to them if, in our deliberate view of our duty, we possibly can.* Judging by all they say and do, and by the subject and nature of their controversy with us, let us determine, if we can, what will satisfy them.

Will they be satisfied if the Territories be unconditionally surrendered to them? We know they will not. In all their present complaints against us, the Territories are scarcely mentioned. Invasions and insurrections are the rage now. Will it satisfy them, if, in the future, we have nothing to do with invasions and insurrections? We know it will not. We so know, because we know we never had anything to do with invasions and insurrections; and yet this total abstaining does not exempt us from the charge and the denunciation.

The question recurs, what will satisfy them? Simply this: We must not only let them alone, but we must, somehow, convince them that we do let them alone. This, we know by experience, is no easy task. We have been so trying to convince them from the very beginning of our organization, but with no success. In all our platforms and speeches we have constantly protested our purpose to let them alone; but this has had no tendency to convince them. Alike unavailing to convince them, is the fact that they have never detected a man of us in any attempt to disturb them.

These natural, and apparently adequate means all failing, what will convince them? This, and this only: cease to call slavery *wrong*, and join them in calling it *right*. And this must be done thoroughly—done in *acts* as well as in *words*.

Silence will not be tolerated—we must place ourselves avowedly with them. Senator Douglas's new sedition law must be enacted and enforced, suppressing all declarations that slavery is wrong, whether made in politics, in presses, in pulpits, or in private. We must arrest and return their fugitive slaves with
5   greedy pleasure. We must pull down our Free State constitutions. The whole atmosphere must be disinfected from all taint of opposition to slavery, before they will cease to believe that all their troubles proceed from us.

I am quite aware they do not state their case precisely in this way. Most of them would probably say to us, "Let us alone, *do* nothing to us, and say what you
10 please about slavery." But we do let them alone—have never disturbed them— so that, after all, it is what we say, which dissatisfies them. They will continue to accuse us of doing, until we cease saying.

I am also aware they have not, as yet, in terms, demanded the overthrow of our Free-State Constitutions. Yet those Constitutions declare the wrong of slavery,
15 with more solemn emphasis, than do all other sayings against it; and when all these other sayings shall have been silenced, the overthrow of these Constitutions will be demanded, and nothing be left to resist the demand. It is nothing to the contrary, that they do not demand the whole of this just now. Demanding what they do, and for the reason they do, they can voluntarily stop nowhere
20 short of this consummation. Holding, as they do, that slavery is morally right, and socially elevating, they cannot cease to demand a full national recognition of it, as a legal right, and a social blessing.

Nor can we justifiably withhold this, on any ground save our conviction that slavery is wrong. If slavery is right, all words, acts, laws, and constitutions against
25 it, are themselves wrong, and should be silenced, and swept away. If it is right, we cannot justly object to its nationality—its universality; if it is wrong, they cannot justly insist upon its extension—its enlargement. All they ask, we could readily grant, if we thought slavery right; all we ask, they could as readily grant, if they thought it wrong. Their thinking it right, and our thinking it wrong, is
30 the precise fact upon which depends the whole controversy. Thinking it right, as they do, they are not to blame for desiring its full recognition, as being right; but, thinking it wrong, as we do, can we yield to them? Can we cast our votes with their view, and against our own? In view of our moral, social, and political responsibilities, can we do this?

35 Wrong as we think slavery is, we can yet afford to let it alone where it is, because that much is due to the necessity arising from its actual presence in the nation; but can we, while our votes will prevent it, allow it to spread into the National Territories, and to overrun us here in these Free States? If our sense

of duty forbids this, then let us stand by our duty, fearlessly and effectively. Let us be diverted by none of those sophistical contrivances wherewith we are so industriously plied and belabored—contrivances such as groping for some middle ground between the right and the wrong, vain as the search for a man who should be neither a living man nor a dead man—such as a policy of "don't   5 care" on a question about which all true men do care—such as Union appeals beseeching true Union men to yield to Disunionists, reversing the divine rule, and calling, not the sinners, but the righteous to repentance—such as invocations to Washington, imploring men to unsay what Washington said, and undo what Washington did.   10

Neither let us be slandered from our duty by false accusations against us, nor frightened from it by menaces of destruction to the Government nor of dungeons to ourselves. LET US HAVE FAITH THAT RIGHT MAKES MIGHT, AND IN THAT FAITH, LET US, TO THE END, DARE TO DO OUR DUTY AS WE UNDERSTAND IT.

IX
SECESSION AND CIVIL WAR

To secure their Creator-endowed natural rights, Americans constituted a form of government that addressed two distinct but related sets of questions:

First, what regime will best secure those rights? That is: Who will rule in the United States? By what institutions will they rule? Finally, what way of life shall they pursue?

Second, what kind of polity will best secure those rights? That is: How centralized will this system of government be? How extensive is its territory? How large is its population?

The ancient Greek city-states had been centralized but small; the ancient empires and the feudal polities of Christian Europe had been large but decentralized. Modern states combined the size of some empires and many feudal realms with the centralization of the city state; built for war and wealth, they crushed the older kinds of polities in Europe. Americans solved the regime problem—the tyranny of king and of Parliament—with republicanism. The people would rule with national and state governing institutions based upon the principle of representation, enabling them to pursue happiness via religious, political, and economic liberty.

Americans solved the statism problem with federalism—what Publius called the "compound" republic. In this system, the national government would wield carefully enumerated powers—exerted on individuals within each state—but the state governments and the people would command the remainder of governing powers. A national Senate comprised of representatives selected by the state legislatures would guard the rights of the states in the nation's capital, linking the two levels of government together.

This solution marked centralization, but only a carefully measured centralization. The nation needed defense from the powerful statist empires of Europe; its federal government therefore also needed the revenues generated by a nationwide commercial market enforced by governments respecting property rights. Most political life existed for active citizens in their own towns, counties, and states.

The Constitution makes this polity republican through and through; not only the national but the state constitutions must adhere to the republican form of government and no other. This presented a problem. A few years after ratification, James Madison wrote: "In proportion as slavery prevails in a State, the Government, however democratic in name, must be aristocratic in fact. The power lies in a part instead of the whole; in the hands of property, not of numbers. All the ancient popular governments were, for this reason, aristocracies. The majority were slaves.... The Southern States of America are on the same principle aristocracies." Madison and the other Founders had hoped that slavery would disappear over time, removing this regime flaw, this self-contradiction in the American political architecture.

But Southern statesmen demurred, with increasing vehemence, in the decades subsequent to the founding. As the readings in this section reveal, the soon-to-be-president and vice-president of the Confederate States of America resoundingly affirmed slavery as the regime foundation of the new entity. All men are not created equal, they claimed; like convicts, lunatics, children, and apprentices, black slaves "by their nature are not fit to govern themselves," Senator Jefferson Davis stated. Moreover, the Southern statesmen defended their fundamentally aristocratic regime with a polity reminiscent of the Articles of Confederation. The pretense of "states' sovereignty" protected the regime of the slaveholders; at the same time, Davis argued, sovereignty should not prevail in the territories controlled by the American national government. There, the property rights of slave owners—exercised over the persons of their alleged racial inferiors—must trump the popular sovereignty propounded by Senator Stephen Douglas.

Against the regime of slave-holding aristocrats, Abraham Lincoln made his comprehensive rejoinder, recalling Americans to the moral foundation of the Founders—the principle of equal unalienable rights for all human beings—while also recalling them to the republican form of government and to the federal polity the Founders had designed for the protection of those rights.

To the Confederates' anti-republican regime challenge, Lincoln responded by proclaiming the slaves free only in those states that had rebelled, and did so as a strictly military measure. The formal abolition of slavery as a constitutionally protected feature of the regime had to await an amendment—not long in coming, after the Civil War.

Against the Confederates' challenge to the polity of federalism, Lincoln fought the war itself on the basis of preserving the Union. A disunited North America filled with medium-sized states with conflicting regimes might well have mimicked perennially war-torn Europe, as the Founders had feared. America bled for union—but perhaps, as Lincoln said, no more than black slaves had bled for their masters, and unquestionably much less, we might add, than Europeans would bleed in the next century.

WILL MORRISEY
Professor of Politics
William and Patricia LaMothe Professor
in the U.S. Constitution
Hillsdale College

REPLY IN THE SENATE TO WILLIAM SEWARD
JEFFERSON DAVIS (1808–1889)

The Senate of 1860 looked little like the Senate of 1790, its proceedings having degenerated into unbridled partisanship. Several years before this debate, South Carolina Congressman Preston Brooks savagely beat Massachusetts Senator Charles Sumner following anti-slavery remarks on the Senate floor. The South had few defenders more tenacious than Mississippi's Senator Jefferson Davis. He had opposed the Compromise of 1850 and hoped for the annexation of much of northern Mexico, which he believed a natural place to expand Southern interests. Here, in response to New York Senator William Seward, Davis makes clear that, like John C. Calhoun, he rejects the equality principle of the Declaration.

FEBRUARY 29, 1860

...When the Senator from New York closed the studied and elaborate address which he delivered today, I rose for the purpose, not of replying to all the points which he had made, wherein I found rather those generalities not sufficiently glittering to delude, but only for the purpose of noticing some of the salient positions which he assumed, and to one of which the Senator from Illinois has 5 very happily responded—that wherein he charged the Democratic party with having violated its faith which was pledged in 1850. The Senator from Illinois performed his duty on two occasions: first, his duty to the whole country, when he moved an amendment which he believed would bring to it peace and a permanent settlement of a grave question; next, he performed the duty 10 which he owed to himself; for when the Congress enacted measures against the voice of certain southern Senators and members, and pledged themselves to the policy of non-intervention with slavery in the Territories, he, being a party to that transaction, owed it to himself, and discharged a duty which it imposed upon his honor, when he moved to repeal the restriction in palpable violation 15

Jefferson Davis, "Reply to William H. Seward," February 29, 1860, in Lynda L. Crist et al., eds., *The Papers of Jefferson Davis*, Vol. 6 (Baton Rouge: Louisiana State University Press, 1971–present), 278–84.

of the agreement which was then made. He has answered well as to that point, and I have nothing to add.

But the Senator from New York invokes us by his love for the Union, and in the spirit of fraternity. I have nothing to object to the tone in which he has 5 addressed us, but I wish we could have acts instead of words. Faith might follow something more significant than high-sounding professions of attachment to the Union, and fraternity to its various members. If the Senator would show to us, by his adherence to the Constitution, and his faithful maintenance of the oath he has taken to support it, that we may rely on the pledge which he gives 10 us that the Republican party, bound by its oath, cannot trespass on the rights of any section, our faith might follow, however far behind, such manifestations upon his own part of the good faith which he proclaims to be within the breast of his political party.

But are we to believe these mere professions of the lips whilst he proclaims 15 opposition to one of the most marked features of the Constitution? whilst he and those with whom he is associated, not only here, but at home, are endeavoring to trample under foot the laws of the United States enacted in conformity with the Constitution, and to secure one of its provisions—a provision so significant that it has been remarked, and is a part of history, that the Union could not have 20 been formed if it had not been incorporated in the Constitution? The oaths of such men become cheap as custom-house oaths, and we are asked to stake our future security on the mere guarantee which such an oath gives!

But the Senator from New York arraigns those who speak in a certain contingency of providing for their own safety out of the Union, as being in opposition 25 to his love for the Union; and he manifests his incapacity to understand our doctrine of State rights by the very simile which he employs when he speaks of our fathers building a temple wherein they had a collision of opinion as to whether the marble should be white or whether it should be manifold in its color, and at last agreed together—forgetful that our fathers were occupied in 30 providing a common agent for the States, not building up a central government to look over them. The States remained each its own temple. They made an agent. Their controversy was as to the functions and powers of that agent—not as to the nature of the temple in which they should preserved their liberties. That temple is the State governments. Beneath that we sit down as under our 35 own vine and fig tree, secure in our power to maintain our rights.

But the Senator asks, how is it that, whilst we are professing this general fraternity and adherence to the Union, we still assert that if one of his party is elected President, we are ready to dissolve the Union? I do not know who has made that assertion, if it has been made. However, the language employed may have imperfectly conveyed the idea that the position was assumed as the Senator fairly presented it, under the conviction that they spoke of those who sought the Government to use it for their destruction. That was the provocation, that was the contingency, however it may have been expressed, that was the idea   5 I have seen embodied in every resolution of that kind wherever it has been passed. To ask us that we shall sit still, under such a Government, is as though we were to be asked to sit in this Senate Chamber, whilst we knew that some one was destroying the foundation on which it rested; to ask us to rely upon the durability which that foundation had when the building was constructed;   10 to rely confidently on the strength we knew it once to possess, even when we had been advertised that that foundation was being destroyed. Are we not advertised that the Senator and those with whom he cooperates are assailing our constitutional rights? How, then, can we sit quietly? If, instead of sitting here to admire the panel and the pilaster and the typical decorations of the ceiling,   15 one, aware that the foundation was being undermined, should walk out of the Chamber, would you arraign him for endeavoring to destroy the building, or would you level your charges against the sapper and miner who was at work on its foundation? That is the proposition.

Who has been more industrious, patient, and skillful, as a sapper and miner   20 against the foundations of the Constitution, than the Senator himself? Who has been in advance of him in the fiery charge on the rights of the States, and in assuming to the Federal Government the power to crush and to coerce them? Even today he has repeated his doctrines. He tells us this is a Government which we will learn is not merely a Government of the States, but a Government of each   25 individual of the people of the United States; and he refers to that doctrine of coercion which the great mind of Hamilton (the mighty intellect of New York, which, in his day, like a lens, gathered in all which could illuminate the subject upon which his mind was concentrated) said was a proposition not to provide for a union of the States, but for their destruction. Such was the view which he   30 who led the forces of the strong Government party took of this idea of enabling the Federal Government to coerce a State. Here the Senator, in advance of that, still mistaking the fundamental principles on which our Government rests, talks about the individual masses coercing the sovereign States of this Union. Sir, when it comes to that, there will be an "irrepressible conflict" indeed; and   35 I have now the faith I have before announced, that, when it comes to that, he will find men loyal to the Government and true to its institutions, residing around his own home, who will arrest his footsteps, and hold him prisoner in the name of liberty and the Constitution.

There is nothing, Mr. President, which has led men to greater confusion of ideas than this term of "free States" and "slave States;" and I trusted that the Senator, with his discriminating and logical mind, was going to give us something tangible, instead of dealing in a phrase never applicable. He applied another; but
5   what was his phrase? "Capital States" and "labor States." And where is the State in which nobody labors? The fallacy upon which the Senator hung adjective after adjective was, that all the labor of the southern States was performed by negroes. Did he not know that the negroes formed but a small part of the people of the southern States? Did he suppose nobody labored but a negro, there? If so, he
10 was less informed than I had previously believed him to be. Negro slavery exists in the South, and by the existence of negro slavery, the white man is raised to the dignity of a freeman and an equal. Nowhere else will you find every white man superior to menial service. Nowhere else will you find every white man recognized so far as an equal as never to be excluded from any man's house or any
15 man's table. Your own menial who blacks your boots, drives your carriage, who wears your livery, and is your own in every sense of the word, is not your equal; and such is society wherever negro slavery is not the substratum on which the white race is elevated to its true dignity. We, however, have no theory to press upon you; we leave you to such institutions as you may prefer; but when you
20 assail ours, we come to the vindication of our institutions by showing you that all your phrases are false; that we are the freemen. With us, and with us alone, as I believe, the white man attains to his true dignity in the Government. So much for the great fallacy on which the Senator's argument hangs, that the labor of the South is all negro labor, and that the white man must there be degraded
25 if he labors; or that we have no laboring white men. I do not know which is his opinion; one of the two. The Senator has himself resided in a southern State, and therefore I say I believed him to be better informed before he spoke. I must suppose him to be as ignorant as his speech would indicate. No man, however, who has seen any portion of southern society, can entertain any such
30 opinion as that which he presents; and it is in order that the statement he has made may not go out to deceive those less informed than himself, that I offer at this time the correction.

The Senator makes a rather hackneyed argument, that, in asserting our right to go into the Territory and enjoy it, we are seeking to take exclusive possession
35 of it. I shall not dwell on that point further than to say that we have sought to exclude nobody. We have sought not to usurp the Territory to our exclusive possession; we have sought that government should be instituted in order that every person and property might be protected that went into it—the white man coming from the North, and the white man coming from the South, both

meeting on an equality in the Territory, and each with whatever property he may hold under the laws of his State and the Constitution of the United States. Such is our position. It is to array a prejudice, which does not justly attach to us, to assume that we have ever sought to exclude any citizen from any State or Territory from going into any Territory and there possessing all the rights which we claim to ourselves.

We have heard time and again this session the same point made against the Democratic party, that they were hedging themselves behind the decision of the Supreme Court. If this had been presented in the beginning, it might have had some fairness; but, after years of conflict, and after we had found it utterly impossible ever to reach a conclusion satisfactory to both sides—in other words, to enact a law which would answer the purpose—we then agreed to postpone a question judicial in its character, and thus agreed to be bound, legislatively and politically, by the decision which that judicial question should receive. Now, the Senator pleads to the jurisdiction, as though we had ever asserted that the Supreme Court could decide a political question; but he was bound in honor, and so were all who acted with him, to abide by the decision of an umpire to which they had themselves referred the case. We are willing to abide by it. We but claim from them that to which we pledged ourselves, and that to which they were mutually pledged when this position was taken by the two Houses of Congress.

But the Senator in his zeal depicts the negro slave of the South as a human being reduced to the condition of a mere chattel. Is it possible that the Senator did not know that the negro slave in every southern State was still a person, protected by all the laws which punish crime in other persons? Could the Senator have failed to know that no master could take the life of or maim his slave without being held responsible under the criminal laws of any southern State, and held to a responsibility as rigid as though that negro had been a white man? How, then, is it asserted that these are not persons in the eye of the law, not protected by the law as persons. The venerable Senator from Kentucky knows very well that this is not law in any State of the Union where slaves are held, but that everywhere they are protected; that the criminal law covers them as perfectly as it covers the white man....

... Several southern Senators around have spoken to me to the effect that in each of their States the protection is secured, and a suit may be instituted at common law for assault and battery, to protect a negro as well as a white man. The condition of slavery with us is, in a word, Mr. President, nothing but the form of civil government instituted for a class of people not fit to govern themselves. It is exactly what in every State exists in some form or other. It is just that kind of control which is extended in every northern State over its convicts, its lunatics, its minors, its apprentices. It is but a form of civil government for those who by their nature are not fit to govern themselves. We recognize the fact of the inferiority stamped upon that race of men by the Creator, and from the cradle to the grave, our Government, as a civil institution, marks that inferiority. In their subject and dependent state, they are not the objects of cruelty as they would be if left to the commission of crime, for which they should be incarcerated in penitentiaries and work-houses, and put under hired overseers, having no interest in them and no relation to them, no affiliation, growing out of the associations of childhood and the tender care of age. Is there nothing of the balm needed in the Senator's own State, that he must needs go abroad to seek objects for his charity and philanthropy? What will he say of those masses in New York now memorializing for something very like an agrarian law? What will he say to the throngs of beggars who crowd the streets of his great commercial emporium? What will he say to the multitudes collected in the penitentiaries and prisons of his own State? I seek not, sir, to inquire into the policy and propriety of the institutions of other States; I assume not to judge of their fitness; it belongs to the community to judge, and I know not under what difficulties they may have been driven to what I cannot approve; but never, sir, in all my life, have I seen anything that so appealed to every feeling of humanity and manliness, as the suffering of the poor children imprisoned in your juvenile penitentiaries—imprisoned before they were old enough to know the nature of crime—there held to such punishment as we never inflict save upon those of mature years. I arraign you not for this: I know not what your crowded population and increasing wants may demand; I know not how far it may be the necessary result of crime which follows in the footsteps of misery; I know not how far the parents have become degraded, and how far the children have become outcast, and how far it may have devolved on the State to take charge of them; but, I thank my God, that in the state of society where I reside, we have no scenes so revolting as these.

Why then not address yourselves to the evils which you have at home? Why not confine your inquiries to the remedial measures which will relieve the suffering of and stop the progress of crime among your own people? Very intent in looking into the distance for the mote in your brother's eye, is it to be wondered that we turn back and point to the beam in your own?

REPLY IN THE SENATE TO STEPHEN DOUGLAS
JEFFERSON DAVIS

A month before this speech, the Democratic National Convention had convened in Charleston, South Carolina. When the delegates failed to adopt an explicitly pro-slavery platform, the Convention dissolved. Rival Southern and Northern Conventions reconvened in June 1860, each nominating their own presidential candidate: Stephen Douglas for the North and John Breckinridge for the South. With the Democratic vote thus divided, the Republican candidate was widely expected to win the 1860 election. Here Davis laments the Kansas-Nebraska solution, explaining how Douglas, once a Southern hero, had become a villain.

MAY 17, 1860

...It is this confusion of ideas, it is this confounding of terms, this changing of language, this applying of special meanings to words, out of which, I think, a large portion of the dispute arises. For instance, it is claimed that President Pierce, in using the phrase "existing and incipient States," meant to include all Territories, and thus that he had bound me to a doctrine which precluded my strictures on what I termed squatter sovereignty. This all arises from the misuse of language. An incipient State, according to my idea, is the territorial condition at the moment it changes into that of a State. It is when the people assemble in convention to form a constitution as a State, that they are in the condition of an incipient State. Various names were applied to the Territories at an earlier period. Sometimes they were called "new States," because they were expected to be States; sometimes they were called "States in embryo," and it requires a determination of the language that is employed before it is possible to arrive at any conclusion as to the differences of understanding between gentlemen. Therefore it was, and, I think, very properly, (but not, as the Senator supposes, that I wanted to catechize him,) that I asked him what he meant by non-intervention, before I commenced these remarks.

Jefferson Davis, "Reply to Stephen A. Douglas," May 17, 1860, in Lynda L. Crist et al., eds., *The Papers of Jefferson Davis*, Vol. 6 (Baton Rouge: Louisiana State University Press, 1971–present), 322.

In the same line of errors was the confusion which resulted in his assuming that the evils I described as growing out of his doctrine on the plains of Kansas, were a denunciation, on my part, of the bill called the Kansas-Nebraska bill. At the time that bill passed, I did not foresee all the evils which have resulted from the
5 doctrine based upon it, but which I do not think it contains. I am not willing now to turn on those who were in a position which compelled them to act and made them responsible, and to divest myself of any responsibility which belongs to any opinion I entertained. I will not seek to judge after the fact and hold the measure up against those who had to judge before me. Therefore I will frankly
10 avow that I should have sustained that bill if I had been in the Senate; but I did not foresee or apprehend such evils as immediately grew up on the plains of Kansas. I looked then, as our fathers had looked before, to the settlement of the question of what institutions should exist there, as one to be determined by soil and climate, and by the pleasure of those who should voluntarily go into
15 the country. Such, however, was not the case. The form of the Kansas-Nebraska bill invited to a controversy—not foreseen.

SOUTH CAROLINA
SECESSION DECLARATION

In December 1860, South Carolina announced its departure from the United States of America, citing Abraham Lincoln's election as a primary cause. Six states quickly followed South Carolina's lead, and on February 4, 1861, they banded together to form the Confederate States of America.

DECEMBER 24, 1860

DECLARATION OF THE IMMEDIATE CAUSES WHICH INDUCE AND JUSTIFY THE SECESSION OF SOUTH CAROLINA FROM THE FEDERAL UNION

The People of the State of South Carolina, in Convention assembled, on the 26th day of April, A.D., 1852, declared that the frequent violations of the Constitution of the United States, by the Federal Government, and its encroachments upon the reserved rights of the States, fully justified this State in then withdrawing from the Federal Union; but in deference to the opinions   5
and wishes of the other slaveholding States, she forbore at that time to exercise this right. Since that time, these encroachments have continued to increase, and further forbearance ceases to be a virtue.

And now the State of South Carolina having resumed her separate and equal place among nations, deems it due to herself, to the remaining United States of   10
America, and to the nations of the world, that she should declare the immediate causes which have led to this act.

In the year 1765, that portion of the British Empire embracing Great Britain, undertook to make laws for the government of that portion composed of the thirteen American Colonies. A struggle for the right of self-government ensued,   15
which resulted, on the 4th July, 1776, in a Declaration, by the Colonies, "that they are, and of right ought to be, FREE AND INDEPENDENT; and that, as free and independent States, they have full power to levy war, conclude peace,

South Carolina Convention, *Declaration of the Immediate Causes which Induce and Justify the Secession of South Carolina from the Federal Union* (Charleston, SC: Evans and Cogswell, 1860), 3–11.

contract alliances, establish commerce, and to do all other acts and things which independent States may of right do."

They further solemnly declared that whenever any "form of government becomes destructive of the ends for which it was established, it is the right of
5 the people to alter or abolish it, and to institute a new government." Deeming the Government of Great Britain to have become destructive of these ends, they declared that the Colonies "are absolved from all allegiace to the British Crown, and that all political connection between them and the State of Great Britain is, and ought to be, totally dissolved."

10 In pursuance of this Declaration of Independence, each of the thirteen States proceeded to exercise its separate sovereignty; adopted for itself a Constitution, and appointed officers for the administration of government in all its depart-ments—Legislative, Executive and Judicial. For purposes of defense, they united their arms and their counsels; and, in 1778, they entered into a League known
15 as the Articles of Confederation, whereby they agreed to entrust the adminis-tration of their external relations to a common agent, known as the Congress of the United States, expressly declaring, in the first article, "that each State retains its sovereignty, freedom and independence, and every power, jurisdiction and right which is not, by this Confederation, expressly delegated to the United
20 States in Congress assembled."

Under this Confederation the War of the Revolution was carried on, and on the 3d September, 1783, the contest ended, and a definitive Treaty was signed by Great Britain, in which she acknowledged the Independence of the Colonies in the following terms:

25 "*Article* 1.—His Britannic Majesty acknowledges the said United States, viz: New Hampshire, Massachusetts Bay, Rhode Island and Providence Plantations, Connecticut, New York, New Jersey, Pennsylvania, Delaware, Maryland, Virginia, North Carolina, South Carolina and Georgia, to be FREE, SOVEREIGN AND INDEPENDENT STATES; that he treats them as such; and for himself, his
30 heirs and successors, relinquishes all claims to the government, propriety and territorial rights of the same and every part thereof."

Thus were established the two great principles asserted by the Colonies, name-ly: the right of a State to govern itself; and the right of a people to abolish a Government when it becomes destructive of the ends for which it was
35 instituted. And concurrent with the establishment of these principles, was the fact, that each Colony became and was recognized by the mother Country as a FREE, SOVEREIGN AND INDEPENDENT STATE.

In 1787, Deputies were appointed by the States to revise the Articles of Confederation, and on 17th September, 1787, these Deputies recommended, for the adoption of the States, the Articles of Union, known as the Constitution of the United States.

The parties to whom this Constitution was submitted, were the several sovereign States; they were to agree or disagree, and when nine of them agreed, the compact was to take effect among those concurring; and the General Government, as the common agent, was then invested with their authority.

If only nine of the thirteen States had concurred, the other four would have remained as they then were—separate, sovereign States, independent of any of the provisions of the Constitution. In fact, two of the States did not accede to the Constitution until long after it had gone into operation among the other eleven; and during that interval, they each exercised the functions of an independent nation.

By this Constitution, certain duties were imposed upon the several States, and the exercise of certain of their powers were restrained, which necessarily implied their continued existence as sovereign States. But, to remove all doubt, an amendment was added, which declared that the powers not delegated to the United States by the Constitution, nor prohibited by it to the States, are reserved to the States, respectively, or to the people. On 23d May, 1788, South Carolina, by a Convention of her people, passed an Ordinance assenting to this Constitution, and afterwards altered her own Constitution, to conform herself to the obligations she had undertaken.

Thus was established, by compact between the States, a Government, with definite objects and powers, limited to the express words of the grant. This limitation left the whole remaining mass of power subject to the clause reserving it to the States or to the people, and rendered unnecessary any specification of reserved rights.

We hold that the Government thus established is subject to the two great principles asserted in the Declaration of Independence; and we hold further, that the mode of its formation subjects it to a third fundamental principle, namely: the law of compact. We maintain that in every compact between two or more parties, the obligation is mutual; that the failure of one of the contracting parties to perform a material part of the agreement, entirely releases the obligation of the other; and that where no arbiter is provided, each party is remitted to his own judgment to determine the fact of failure, with all its consequences.

In the present case, that fact is established with certainty. We assert, that fourteen of the States have deliberately refused for years past to fulfil their constitutional obligations, and we refer to their own Statutes for the proof.

The Constitution of the United States, in its 4th Article, provides as follows:

"No person held to service or labor in one State, under the laws thereof, escaping into another, shall, in consequence of any law or regulation therein, be discharged from such service or labor, but shall be delivered up, on claim of the
5   party to whom such service or labor may be due."

This stipulation was so material to the compact, that without it that compact would not have been made. The greater number of the contracting parties held slaves, and they had previously evinced their estimate of the value of such a stipulation by making it a condition in the Ordinance for the government of
10   the territory ceded by Virginia, which now composes the States north of the Ohio river.

The same article of the Constitution stipulates also for rendition by the several States of fugitives from justice from the other States.

The General Government, as the common agent, passed laws to carry into
15   effect these stipulations of the States. For many years these laws were executed. But an increasing hostility on the part of the non-slaveholding States to the Institution of Slavery has led to a disregard of their obligations, and the laws of the General Government have ceased to effect the objects of the Constitution. The States of Maine, New Hampshire, Vermont, Massachusetts, Connecticut,
20   Rhode Island, New York, Pennsylvania, Illinois, Indiana, Michigan, Wisconsin and Iowa, have enacted laws which either nullify the Acts of Congress or render useless any attempt to execute them. In many of these States the fugitive is discharged from the service or labor claimed, and in none of them has the State Government complied with the stipulation made in the Constitution.
25   The State of New Jersey, at an early day, passed a law in conformity with her constitutional obligation; but the current of anti-slavery feeling has led her more recently to enact laws which render inoperative the remedies provided by her own law and by the laws of Congress. In the State of New York even the right of transit for a slave has been denied by her tribunals; and the States
30   of Ohio and Iowa have refused to surrender to justice fugitives charged with murder, and with inciting servile insurrection in the State of Virginia. Thus the constitutional compact has been deliberately broken and disregarded by the non-slaveholding States, and the consequence follows that South Carolina is released from her obligation.

35   The ends for which this Constitution was framed are declared by itself to be "to form a more perfect union, establish justice, insure domestic tranquility, provide for the common defense, promote the general welfare, and secure the blessings of liberty to ourselves and our posterity."

These ends it endeavored to accomplish by a Federal Government, in which each State was recognized as an equal, and had separate control over its own institutions. The right of property in slaves was recognized by giving to free persons distinct political rights, by giving them the right to represent, and burthening them with direct taxes for three-fifths of their slaves; by authorizing 5 the importation of slaves for twenty years; and by stipulating for the rendition of fugitives from labor.

We affirm that these ends for which this Government was instituted have been defeated, and the Government itself has been made destructive of them by the action of the non-slaveholding States. Those States have assumed the right 10 of deciding upon the propriety of our domestic institutions; and have denied the rights of property established in fifteen of the States and recognized by the Constitution; they have denounced as sinful the institution of Slavery; they have permitted the open establishment among them of societies, whose avowed object is to disturb the peace and to eloign the property of the citizens of other 15 States. They have encouraged and assisted thousands of our slaves to leave their homes; and those who remain, have been incited by emissaries, books and pictures to servile insurrection.

For twenty-five years this agitation has been steadily increasing, until it has now secured to its aid the power of the Common Government. Observing the *forms* 20 of the Constitution, a sectional party has found within that article establishing the Executive Department, the means of subverting the Constitution itself. A geographical line has been drawn across the Union, and all the States north of that line have united in the election of a man to the high office of President of the United States whose opinions and purposes are hostile to slavery. He is to 25 be entrusted with the administration of the Common Government, because he has declared that that "Government cannot endure permanently half slave, half free," and that the public mind must rest in the belief that Slavery is in the course of ultimate extinction.

This sectional combination for the subversion of the Constitution, has been 30 aided in some of the States by elevating to citizenship, persons, who, by the Supreme Law of the land, are incapable of becoming citizens; and their votes have been used to inaugurate a new policy, hostile to the South, and destructive of its peace and safety.

On the 4th March next, this party will take possession of the Government. It 35 has announced, that the South shall be excluded from the common Territory; that the Judicial Tribunals shall be made sectional, and that a war must be waged against slavery until it shall cease throughout the United States.

The Guarantees of the Constitution will then no longer exist; the equal rights of the States will be lost. The slaveholding States will no longer have the power of self-government, or self-protection, and the Federal Government will have become their enemy.

5   Sectional interest and animosity will deepen the irritation, and all hope of remedy is rendered vain, by the fact that public opinion at the North has invested a great political error with the sanctions of a more erroneous religious belief.

We, therefore, the people of South Carolina, by our delegates, in Convention
10   assembled, appealing to the Supreme Judge of the world for the rectitude of our intentions, have solemnly declared that the Union heretofore existing between this State and the other States of North America, is dissolved, and that the State of South Carolina has resumed her position among the nations of the world, as a separate and independent State; with full power to levy war, conclude peace,
15   contract alliances, establish commerce, and to do all other acts and things which independent States may of right do.

To Dissolve the Union between the State of South Carolina and other States united with her under the compact entitled "The Constitution of the United States of America."

20   *We, the People of the State of South Carolina, in Convention assembled, do declare and ordain, and it is hereby declared and ordained,*

That the Ordinance adopted by us in Convention, on the twenty-third day of May, in the year of our Lord one thousand seven hundred and eighty-eight, whereby the Constitution of the United States of America was ratified, and
25   also, all Acts and parts of Acts of the General Assembly of this State, ratifying amendments of the said Constitution, are hereby repealed; and that the union now subsisting between South Carolina and other States, under the name of "The United States of America," is hereby dissolved.

CORNERSTONE SPEECH
ALEXANDER STEPHENS (1812–1883)

*Former Senator Jefferson Davis became president of the Confederate govern-
ment, while former Georgia Congressman Alexander Stephens became vice
president. Three weeks after Abraham Lincoln's inauguration, Stephens delivered this speech in Savannah, identifying the cornerstone of the Confederacy
as an idea opposite to the equality principle of the American founding.*

MARCH 21, 1861

At half past seven o'clock on Thursday evening, the largest audience ever
assembled at the Athenaeum was in the house, waiting most impatiently for
the appearance of the orator of the evening, Honorable A. H. Stephens, Vice-
President of the Confederate States of America. The committee, with invited
guests, were seated on the stage, when, at the appointed hour, the Honorable   5
C. C. Jones, Mayor, and the speaker, entered, and were greeted by the immense
assemblage with deafening rounds of applause.

The Mayor then, in a few pertinent remarks, introduced Mr. Stephens, stating
that at the request of a number of the members of the convention, and citizens
of Savannah and the State, now here, he had consented to address them upon   10
the present state of public affairs....

Mr. STEPHENS rose and said:

...[W]e are passing through one of the greatest revolutions in the annals of
the world. Seven States have within the last three months thrown off an old
government and formed a new. This revolution has been signally marked, up   15
to this time, by the fact of its having been accomplished without the loss of a
single drop of blood.

Alexander Stephens, "Sketch of the Corner-Stone Speech," March 21, 1861, in Henry Cleveland,
ed., *Alexander H. Stephens, in Public and Private: With Letters and Speeches, Before, During, and Since
the War* (Philadelphia: National Publishing Co., 1866), 717–23, 726, 728–29.

This new constitution, or form of government, constitutes the subject to which your attention will be partly invited. In reference to it, I make this first general remark. It amply secures all our ancient rights, franchises, and liberties. All the great principles of Magna Charta are retained in it. No citizen is deprived of life, liberty, or property, but by the judgment of his peers under the laws of the land. The great principle of religious liberty, which was the honor and pride of the old constitution, is still maintained and secured. All the essentials of the old constitution, which have endeared it to the hearts of the American people, have been preserved and perpetuated. Some changes have been made.... Some of these I should have preferred not to have seen made; but these, perhaps, meet the cordial approbation of a majority of this audience, if not an overwhelming majority of the people of the Confederacy. Of them, therefore, I will not speak. But other important changes do meet my cordial approbation. They form great improvements upon the old constitution. So, taking the whole new constitution, I have no hesitancy in giving it as my judgment that it is decidedly better than the old.

Allow me briefly to allude to some of these improvements. The question of building up class interests, or fostering one branch of industry to the prejudice of another under the exercise of the revenue power, which gave us so much trouble under the old constitution, is put at rest forever under the new. We allow the imposition of no duty with a view of giving advantage to one class of persons, in any trade or business, over those of another. All, under our system, stand upon the same broad principles of perfect equality. Honest labor and enterprise are left free and unrestricted in whatever pursuit they may be engaged.... This old thorn of the tariff, which was the cause of so much irritation in the old body politic, is removed forever from the new.

Again, the subject of internal improvements, under the power of Congress to regulate commerce, is put at rest under our system. The power claimed by construction under the old constitution, was at least a doubtful one— it rested solely upon construction. We of the South, generally apart from considerations of constitutional principles, opposed its exercise upon grounds of its inexpediency and injustice. Notwithstanding this opposition, millions of money, from the common treasury had been drawn for such purposes. Our opposition sprang from no hostility to commerce, or all necessary aids for facilitating it. With us it was simply a question, upon *whom* the burden should fall. In Georgia, for instance, we have done as much for the cause of internal improvements as any other portion of the country according to population and means.... All this was done to open an outlet for our products of the interior, and those to the west of us, to reach the marts of the world. No State was in greater need of such facilities than Georgia, but we did not ask that these works should be made by appropriations out of the common treasury. The cost of the grading, the superstructure, and equipments of our roads, was borne by those who entered on the enterprise.... What justice was there in taking this money, which our people paid into the common treasury on the importation of our iron, and applying it to the improvement of rivers and harbors elsewhere?

The true principle is to subject the commerce of every locality, to whatever burdens may be necessary to facilitate it. If Charleston harbor needs improvement, let the commerce of Charleston bear the burden. If the mouth of the Savannah river has to be cleared out, let the seagoing navigation which is benefitted by it, bear the burden. So with the mouths of the Alabama and Mississippi river. Just as the products of the interior, our cotton, wheat, corn, and other articles, have to bear the necessary rates of freight over our railroads to reach the seas. This is again the broad principle of perfect equality and justice. And it is especially set forth and established in our new constitution....

But not to be tedious in enumerating the numerous changes for the better, allow me to allude to one other—though last, not least. The new constitution has put at rest, *forever*, all the agitating questions relating to our peculiar institution—African slavery as it exists amongst us—the proper *status* of the negro in our form of civilization. This was the immediate cause of the late rupture and present revolution. Jefferson in his forecast, had anticipated this, as the "rock upon which the old Union would split." He was right. What was conjecture with him, is now a realized fact. But whether he fully comprehended the great truth upon which that rock *stood* and *stands*, may be doubted. The prevailing ideas entertained by him and most of the leading statesmen at the time of the formation of the old constitution, were that the enslavement of the African was in violation of the laws of nature; that it was wrong in *principle*, socially, morally, and politically. It was an evil they knew not well how to deal with, but the general opinion of the men of that day was that, somehow or other in the order of Providence, the institution would be evanescent and pass away. This idea, though not incorporated in the constitution, was the prevailing idea at that time. The constitution, it is true, secured every essential guarantee to the institution while it should last, and hence no argument can be justly urged against the constitutional guarantees thus secured, because of the common sentiment of the day. Those ideas, however, were fundamentally wrong. They rested upon the assumption of the equality of races. This was an error. It was a sandy foundation, and the government built upon it fell when the "storm came and the wind blew."

Our new government is founded upon exactly the opposite idea; its foundations are laid, its corner-stone rests upon the great truth, that the negro is not equal to the white man; that slavery—subordination to the superior race—is his natural and normal condition.

5   This, our new government, is the first, in the history of the world, based upon this great physical, philosophical, and moral truth. This truth has been slow in the process of its development, like all other truths in the various departments of science. It has been so even amongst us. Many who hear me, perhaps, can recollect well, that this truth was not generally admitted, even within their

10   day. The errors of the past generation still clung to many as late as twenty years ago. Those at the North, who still cling to these errors, with a zeal above knowledge, we justly denominate fanatics. All fanaticism springs from an aberration of the mind—from a defect in reasoning. It is a species of insanity. One of the most striking characteristics of insanity, in many instances, is

15   forming correct conclusions from fancied or erroneous premises; so with the anti-slavery fanatics; their conclusions are right if their premises were. They assume that the negro is equal, and hence conclude that he is entitled to equal privileges and rights with the white man. If their premises were correct, their conclusions would be logical and just—but their premise being wrong, their

20   whole argument fails. I recollect once of having heard a gentleman from one of the northern States, of great power and ability, announce in the House of Representatives, with imposing effect, that we of the South would be compelled, ultimately, to yield upon this subject of slavery, that it was as impossible to war successfully against a principle in politics, as it was in physics or mechanics.

25   That the principle would ultimately prevail. That we, in maintaining slavery as it exists with us, were warring against a principle, a principle founded in nature, the principle of the equality of men. The reply I made to him was, that upon his own grounds, we should, ultimately, succeed, and that he and his associates, in this crusade against our institutions, would ultimately fail.

30   The truth announced, that it was as impossible to war successfully against a principle in politics as it was in physics and mechanics, I admitted; but told him that it was he, and those acting with him, who were warring against a principle. They were attempting to make things equal which the Creator had made unequal.

35   In the conflict thus far, success has been on our side, complete throughout the length and breadth of the Confederate States. It is upon this, as I have stated, our social fabric is firmly planted; and I cannot permit myself to doubt the ultimate success of a full recognition of this principle throughout the civilized and enlightened world.

As I have stated, the truth of this principle may be slow in development, as all truths are and ever have been, in the various branches of science. It was so with the principles announced by Galileo—it was so with Adam Smith and his principles of political economy. It was so with Harvey, and his theory of the circulation of the blood. It is stated that not a single one of the medical 5 profession, living at the time of the announcement of the truths made by him, admitted them. Now, they are universally acknowledged. May we not, therefore, look with confidence to the ultimate universal acknowledgment of the truths upon which our system rests? It is the first government ever instituted upon the principles in strict conformity to nature, and the ordination of Providence, 10 in furnishing the materials of human society. Many governments have been founded upon the principle of the subordination and serfdom of certain classes of the same race; such were and are in violation of the laws of nature. Our system commits no such violation of nature's laws. With us, all of the white race, however high or low, rich or poor, are equal in the eye of the law. Not 15 so with the negro. Subordination is his place. He, by nature, or by the curse against Canaan, is fitted for that condition which he occupies in our system. The architect in the construction of buildings, lays the foundation with the proper material—the granite; then comes the brick or the marble. The substratum of our society is made of the material fitted by nature for it, and by experience we 20 know, that it is best, not only for the superior, but for the inferior race, that it should be so. It is, indeed, in conformity with the ordinance of the Creator. It is not for us to inquire into the wisdom of his ordinances, or to question them. For his own purposes, he has made one race to differ from another, as he has made "one star to differ from another star in glory." 25

The great objects of humanity are best attained when there is conformity to his laws and decrees, in the formation of governments as well as in all things else. Our confederacy is founded upon principles in strict conformity with these laws. This stone which was rejected by the first builders "is become the chief of the corner"—the real "corner-stone"—in our new edifice. 30

I have been asked, what of the future? It has been apprehended by some that we would have arrayed against us the civilized world. I care not who or how many they may be against us, when we stand upon the eternal principles of truth, *if we are true to ourselves and the principles for which we contend*, we are obliged to, and must triumph. 35

Thousands of people who begin to understand these truths are not yet completely out of the shell; they do not see them in their length and breadth. We hear much of the civilization and christianization of the barbarous tribes of Africa. In my judgment, those ends will never be attained, but by first teaching them the lesson taught to Adam, that "in the sweat of his brow he should eat his bread," and teaching them to work, and feed, and clothe themselves....

...Looking to the distant future, and, perhaps, not very far distant either, it is not beyond the range of possibility, and even probability, that all the great
5 States of the north-west will gravitate this way, as well as Tennessee, Kentucky, Missouri, Arkansas, etc. Should they do so, our doors are wide enough to receive them, but not until they are ready to assimilate with us in principle.

The process of disintegration in the old Union may be expected to go on with almost absolute certainty if we pursue the right course. We are now the
10 nucleus of a growing power which, if we are true to ourselves, our destiny, and high mission, will become the controlling power on this continent. To what extent accessions will go on in the process of time, or where it will end, the future will determine.... Such are some of the glimpses of the future as I catch them....

15 In olden times the olive branch was considered the emblem of peace; we will send to the nations of the earth another and far more potential emblem of the same, the cotton plant. The present duties were levied with a view of meeting the present necessities and exigencies, in preparation for war, if need be; but if we have peace, and he hoped we might, and trade should resume its proper
20 course, a duty of ten per cent. upon foreign importations it was thought might be sufficient to meet the expenditures of the government. If some articles should be left on the free list, as they now are, such as breadstuffs, etc., then, of course, duties upon others would have to be higher—but in no event to an extent to embarrass trade and commerce. He concluded in an earnest appeal
25 for union and harmony, on part of all the people in support of the common cause, in which we were all enlisted, and upon the issues of which such great consequences depend.

If, said he, we are true to ourselves, true to our cause, true to our destiny, true to our high mission, in presenting to the world the highest type of civilization ever
30 exhibited by man—there will be found in our lexicon no such word as fail.

Mr. Stephens took his seat, amid a burst of enthusiasm and applause, such as the Athenaeum has never had displayed within its walls, within "the recollection of the oldest inhabitant."

FAREWELL ADDRESS TO THE SENATE
JEFFERSON DAVIS

Most Southern members of Congress followed their states into secession. In this farewell speech, Senator Jefferson Davis expresses admiration for the late Senator John C. Calhoun, author of the nullification doctrine, and suprisingly invokes the Declaration of Independence in his cause.

JANUARY 21, 1861

I rise, Mr. President, for the purpose of announcing to the Senate that I have satisfactory evidence that the State of Mississippi, by a solemn ordinance of her people in convention assembled, has declared her separation from the United States. Under these circumstances, of course my functions are terminated here. It has seemed to me proper, however, that I should appear in the Senate to announce   5
that fact to my associates, and I will say but very little more. The occasion does not invite me to go into argument; and my physical condition would not permit me to do so if it were otherwise; and yet it seems to become me to say something on the part of the State I here represent, on an occasion so solemn as this.

It is known to Senators who have served with me here, that I have for many years   10
advocated, as an essential attribute of State sovereignty, the right of a State to secede from the Union. Therefore, if I had not believed there was justifiable cause; if I had thought that Mississippi was acting without sufficient provocation, or without an existing necessity, I should still, under my theory of the Government, because of my allegiance to the State of which I am a citizen, have been bound by   15
her action. I, however, may be permitted to say that I do think she has justifiable cause, and I approve of her act. I conferred with her people before that act was taken, counseled them then that if the state of things which they apprehended should exist when the convention met, they should take the action which they have now adopted.   20

I hope none who hear me will confound this expression of mine with the advocacy of the right of a State to remain in the Union, and to disregard its constitutional

Jefferson Davis, "Farewell Address," January 21, 1861, in Lynda L. Crist et al., eds., *The Papers of Jefferson Davis*, Vol. 7 (Baton Rouge: Louisiana State University Press, 1971–present), 18–22.

obligations by the nullification of the law. Such is not my theory. Nullification and secession, so often confounded, are indeed antagonistic principles. Nullification is a remedy which it is sought to apply within the Union, and against the agent of the States. It is only to be justified when the agent has violated his constitutional
5   obligation, and a State, assuming to judge for itself, denies the right of the agent thus to act, and appeals to the other States of the Union for a decision; but when the States themselves, and when the people of the States, have so acted as to convince us that they will not regard our constitutional rights, then, and then for the first time, arises the doctrine of secession in its practical application.

10 A great man who now reposes with his fathers, and who has been often arraigned for a want of fealty to the Union, advocated the doctrine of nullification, because it preserved the Union. It was because of his deep-seated attachment to the Union, his determination to find some remedy for existing ills short of a severance of the ties which bound South Carolina to the other States, that Mr. Calhoun advocated
15 the doctrine of nullification, which he proclaimed to be peaceful, to be within the limits of State power, not to disturb the Union, but only to be a means of bringing the agent before the tribunal of the States for their judgment.

Secession belongs to a different class of remedies. It is to be justified upon the basis that the States are sovereign. There was a time when none denied it. I hope
20 the time may come again, when a better comprehension of the theory of our Government, and the inalienable rights of the people of the States, will prevent any one from denying that each State is a sovereign, and thus may reclaim the grants which it has made to any agent whomsoever.

I therefore say I concur in the action of the people of Mississippi, believing it to be
25 necessary and proper, and should have been bound by their action if my belief had been otherwise; and this brings me to the important point which I wish on this last occasion to present to the Senate. It is by this confounding of nullification and secession that the name of a great man, whose ashes now mingle with his mother earth, has been invoked to justify coercion against a seceded State. The phrase "to
30 execute the laws," was an expression which General Jackson applied to the case of a State refusing to obey the laws while yet a member of the Union. That is not the case which is now presented. The laws are to be executed over the United States, and upon the people of the United States. They have no relation to any foreign country. It is a perversion of terms, at least it is a great misapprehension of the
35 case, which cites that expression for application to a State which has withdrawn from the Union. You may make war on a foreign State. If it be the purpose of gentlemen, they may make war against a State which has withdrawn from the Union; but there are no laws of the United States to be executed within the limits of a seceded State. A State finding herself in the condition in which Mississippi
40 has judged she is, in which her safety requires that she should provide for the

maintenance of her rights out of the Union, surrenders all the benefits, (and they are known to be many,) deprives herself of the advantages, (they are known to be great,) severs all the ties of affection, (and they are close and enduring,) which have bound her to the Union; and thus divesting herself of every benefit, taking upon herself every burden, she claims to be exempt from any power to execute the laws of the United States within her limits.

I well remember an occasion when Massachusetts was arraigned before the bar of the Senate, and when then the doctrine of coercion was rife and to be applied against her because of the rescue of a fugitive slave in Boston. My opinion then was the same that it is now. Not in a spirit of egotism, but to show that I am not influenced in my opinion because the case is my own, I refer to that time and that occasion as containing the opinion which I then entertained, and on which my present conduct is based. I then said, if Massachusetts, following her through a stated line of conduct, chooses to take the last step which separates her from the Union, it is her right to go, and I will neither vote one dollar nor one man to coerce her back; but will say to her, God speed, in memory of the kind associations which once existed between her and the other States.

It has been a conviction of pressing necessity, it has been a belief that we are to be deprived in the Union of the rights which our fathers bequeathed to us, which has brought Mississippi into her present decision. She has heard proclaimed the theory that all men are created free and equal, and this made the basis of an attack upon her social institutions; and the sacred Declaration of Independence has been invoked to maintain the position of the equality of the races. That Declaration of Independence is to be construed by the circumstances and purposes for which it was made. The communities were declaring their independence; the people of those communities were asserting that no man was born—to use the language of Mr. Jefferson—booted and spurred to ride over the rest of mankind; that men were created equal—meaning the men of the political community; that there was no divine right to rule; that no man inherited the right to govern; that there were no classes by which power and place descended to families, but that all stations were equally within the grasp of each member of the body-politic. These were the great principles they announced; these were the purposes for which they made their declaration; these were the ends to which their enunciation was directed. They have no reference to the slave; else, how happened it that among the items of arraignment made against George III was that he endeavored to do just what the North has been endeavoring of late to do—to stir up insurrection among our slaves? Had the Declaration announced that the negroes were free and equal, how was the Prince to be arraigned for stirring up insurrection among them? And how was this to be enumerated among the high crimes which caused the colonies to sever their connection with the mother country? When our Constitution was formed, the same idea was rendered more palpable, for there we find provision made for that very class of persons as property; they were not put upon the footing of equality with white men—not even upon that of paupers and convicts; but, so far as representation was concerned, were discriminated against as a lower caste,

5   only to be represented in the numerical proportion of three fifths.

Then, Senators, we recur to the compact which binds us together; we recur to the principles upon which our Government was founded; and when you deny them, and when you deny to us the right to withdraw from a Government which thus perverted threatens to be destructive of our rights, we but tread in the path

10 of our fathers when we proclaim our independence, and take the hazard. This is done not in hostility to others, not to injure any section of the country, not even for our own pecuniary benefit; but from the high and solemn motive of defending and protecting the rights we inherited, and which it is our sacred duty to transmit unshorn to our children.

15 I find in myself, perhaps, a type of the general feeling of my constituents towards yours. I am sure I feel no hostility to you, Senators from the North. I am sure there is not one of you, whatever sharp discussion there may have been between us, to whom I cannot now say, in the presence of my God, I wish you well; and such, I am sure, is the feeling of the people whom I represent towards those

20 whom you represent. I therefore feel that I but express their desire when I say I hope, and they hope, for peaceful relations with you, though we must part. They may be mutually beneficial to us in the future, as they have been in the past, if you so will it. The reverse may bring disaster on every portion of the country; and if you will have it thus, we will invoke the God of our fathers, who delivered

25 them from the power of the lion, to protect us from the ravages of the bear; and thus, putting our trust in God and in our own firm hearts and strong arms, we will vindicate the right as best we may.

In the course of my service here, associated at different times with a great variety of Senators, I see now around me some with whom I have served long; there have

30 been points of collision; but whatever of offense there has been to me, I leave here; I carry with me no hostile remembrance. Whatever offense I have given which has not been redressed, or for which satisfaction has not been demanded, I have, Senators, in this hour of our parting, to offer you my apology for any pain which, in heat of discussion, I have inflicted. I go hence unencumbered

35 of the remembrance of any injury received, and having discharged the duty of making the only reparation in my power for any injury offered.

Mr. President, and Senators, having made the announcement which the occasion seemed to me to require, it only remains to me to bid you a final adieu.

FIRST INAUGURAL ADDRESS
ABRAHAM LINCOLN

Abraham Lincoln's First Inaugural Address, delivered a month after the formation of the Confederacy, served as a final plea for Americans to reunite. Lincoln makes clear that he has no intention to change the status of slavery in the states where it exists, having no constitutional authority to do so. He makes equally clear that secession is not a constitutional option.

MARCH 4, 1861

FELLOW CITIZENS OF THE UNITED STATES:

In compliance with a custom as old as the government itself, I appear before you to address you briefly, and to take, in your presence, the oath prescribed by the Constitution of the United States, to be taken by the President "before he enters on the execution of this office."

I do not consider it necessary, at present for me to discuss those matters of administration about which there is no special anxiety, or excitement. 5

Apprehension seems to exist among the people of the Southern States, that by the accession of a Republican Administration, their property, and their peace, and personal security, are to be endangered. There has never been any reasonable cause for such apprehension. Indeed, the most ample evidence to the contrary 10 has all the while existed, and been open to their inspection. It is found in nearly all the published speeches of him who now addresses you. I do but quote from one of those speeches when I declare that "I have no purpose, directly or indirectly, to interfere with the institution of slavery in the States where it exists. I believe I have no lawful right to do so, and I have no inclination to do 15 so." Those who nominated and elected me did so with full knowledge that I had made this, and many similar declarations, and had never recanted them. And more than this, they placed in the platform, for my acceptance, and as a law to themselves, and to me, the clear and emphatic resolution which I now read:

Abraham Lincoln, "First Inaugural Address—Final Text," March 4, 1861, in Roy P. Basler, ed., *The Collected Works of Abraham Lincoln*, Vol. 4 (New Brunswick, NJ: Rutgers University Press, 1953), 262–71. Reprinted with the permission of the Abraham Lincoln Association, Springfield, IL.

"*Resolved*, That the maintenance inviolate of the rights of the States, and especially the right of each State to order and control its own domestic institutions
according to its own judgment exclusively, is essential to that balance of power
on which the perfection and endurance of our political fabric depend; and
5   we denounce the lawless invasion by armed force of the soil of any State or
Territory, no matter under what pretext, as among the gravest of crimes."

I now reiterate these sentiments: and in doing so, I only press upon the public
attention the most conclusive evidence of which the case is susceptible, that
the property, peace and security of no section are to be in anywise endan-
10   gered by the now incoming Administration. I add too, that all the protection
which, consistently with the Constitution and the laws, can be given, will
be cheerfully given to all the States when lawfully demanded, for whatever
cause—as cheerfully to one section, as to another.

There is much controversy about the delivering up of fugitives from service or
15   labor. The clause I now read is as plainly written in the Constitution as any
other of its provisions:

"No person held to service or labor in one State, under the laws thereof,
escaping into another, shall, in consequence of any law or regulation therein,
be discharged from such service or labor, but shall be delivered up on claim of
20   the party to whom such service or labor may be due."

It is scarcely questioned that this provision was intended by those who made
it, for the reclaiming of what we call fugitive slaves; and the intention of the
law-giver is the law. All members of Congress swear their support to the whole
Constitution—to this provision as much as to any other. To the proposition,
25   then, that slaves whose cases come within the terms of this clause, "shall be
delivered up," their oaths are unanimous. Now, if they would make the effort
in good temper, could they not, with nearly equal unanimity, frame and pass
a law, by means of which to keep good that unanimous oath?

There is some difference of opinion whether this clause should be enforced by
30   national or by state authority; but surely that difference is not a very material
one. If the slave is to be surrendered, it can be of but little consequence to him,
or to others, by which authority it is done. And should any one, in any case, be
content that his oath shall go unkept, on a merely unsubstantial controversy
as to *how* it shall be kept?

35   Again, in any law upon this subject, ought not all the safeguards of liberty
known in civilized and humane jurisprudence to be introduced, so that a free
man be not, in any case, surrendered as a slave? And might it not be well, at

the same time, to provide by law for the enforcement of that clause in the Constitution which guarantees that "The citizens of each State shall be entitled to all previleges and immunities of citizens in the several States?"

I take the official oath today, with no mental reservations, and with no purpose to construe the Constitution or laws, by any hypercritical rules. And while I do not choose now to specify particular acts of Congress as proper to be enforced, I do suggest, that it will be much safer for all, both in official and private stations, to conform to, and abide by, all those acts which stand unrepealed, than to violate any of them, trusting to find impunity in having them held to be unconstitutional.

It is seventy-two years since the first inauguration of a President under our national Constitution. During that period fifteen different and greatly distinguished citizens, have, in succession, administered the executive branch of the government. They have conducted it through many perils; and, generally, with great success. Yet, with all this scope for precedent, I now enter upon the same task for the brief constitutional term of four years, under great and peculiar difficulty. A disruption of the Federal Union heretofore only menaced, is now formidably attempted.

I hold, that in contemplation of universal law, and of the Constitution, the Union of these States is perpetual. Perpetuity is implied, if not expressed, in the fundamental law of all national governments. It is safe to assert that no government proper, ever had a provision in its organic law for its own termination. Continue to execute all the express provisions of our national Constitution, and the Union will endure forever—it being impossible to destroy it, except by some action not provided for in the instrument itself.

Again, if the United States be not a government proper, but an association of States in the nature of contract merely, can it, as a contract, be peaceably unmade, by less than all the parties who made it? One party to a contract may violate it—break it, so to speak; but does it not require all to lawfully rescind it?

Descending from these general principles, we find the proposition that, in legal contemplation, the Union is perpetual, confirmed by the history of the Union itself. The Union is much older than the Constitution. It was formed in fact, by the Articles of Association in 1774. It was matured and continued by the Declaration of Independence in 1776. It was further matured and the faith of all the then thirteen States expressly plighted and engaged that it should be perpetual, by the Articles of Confederation in 1778. And finally, in 1787, one of the declared objects for ordaining and establishing the Constitution, was "*to form a more perfect union.*"

But if destruction of the Union, by one, or by a part only, of the States, be lawfully possible, the Union is less perfect than before the Constitution, having lost the vital element of perpetuity.

It follows from these views that no State, upon its own mere motion, can
5 lawfully get out of the Union,—that *resolves* and *ordinances* to that effect are legally void; and that acts of violence, within any State or States, against the authority of the United States, are insurrectionary or revolutionary, according to circumstances.

I therefore consider that, in view of the Constitution and the laws, the Union is
10 unbroken; and, to the extent of my ability, I shall take care, as the Constitution itself expressly enjoins upon me, that the laws of the Union be faithfully executed in all the States. Doing this I deem to be only a simple duty on my part; and I shall perform it, so far as practicable, unless my rightful masters, the American people, shall withhold the requisite means, or, in some authoritative
15 manner, direct the contrary. I trust this will not be regarded as a menace, but only as the declared purpose of the Union that it *will* constitutionally defend, and maintain itself.

In doing this there needs to be no bloodshed or violence; and there shall be none, unless it be forced upon the national authority. The power confided
20 to me, will be used to hold, occupy, and possess the property, and places belonging to the government, and to collect the duties and imposts; but beyond what may be necessary for these objects, there will be no invasion— no using of force against, or among the people anywhere. Where hostility to the United States, in any interior locality, shall be so great and so universal, as
25 to prevent competent resident citizens from holding the Federal offices, there will be no attempt to force obnoxious strangers among the people for that object. While the strict legal right may exist in the government to enforce the exercise of these offices, the attempt to do so would be so irritating, and so nearly impracticable with all, that I deem it better to forego, for the time, the
30 uses of such offices.

The mails, unless repelled, will continue to be furnished in all parts of the Union. So far as possible, the people everywhere shall have that sense of perfect security which is most favorable to calm thought and reflection. The course here indicated will be followed, unless current events, and experience, shall show a
35 modification, or change, to be proper; and in every case and exigency, my best discretion will be exercised, according to circumstances actually existing, and with a view and a hope of a peaceful solution of the national troubles, and the restoration of fraternal sympathies and affections.

That there are persons in one section, or another who seek to destroy the Union at all events, and are glad of any pretext to do it, I will neither affirm or deny; but if there be such, I need address no word to them. To those, however, who really love the Union, may I not speak?

Before entering upon so grave a matter as the destruction of our national fabric, with all its benefits, its memories, and its hopes, would it not be wise to ascertain precisely why we do it? Will you hazard so desperate a step, while there is any possibility that any portion of the ills you fly from, have no real existence? Will you, while the certain ills you fly to, are greater than all the real ones you fly from? Will you risk the commission of so fearful a mistake?

All profess to be content in the Union, if all constitutional rights can be maintained. Is it true, then, that any right, plainly written in the Constitution, has been denied? I think not. Happily the human mind is so constituted, that no party can reach to the audacity of doing this. Think, if you can, of a single instance in which a plainly written provision of the Constitution has ever been denied. If, by the mere force of numbers, a majority should deprive a minority of any clearly written constitutional right, it might, in a moral point of view, justify revolution—certainly would, if such right were a vital one. But such is not our case. All the vital rights of minorities, and of individuals, are so plainly assured to them, by affirmations and negations, guarranties and prohibitions, in the Constitution, that controversies never arise concerning them. But no organic law can ever be framed with a provision specifically applicable to every question which may occur in practical administration. No foresight can anticipate, nor any document of reasonable length contain express provisions for all possible questions. Shall fugitives from labor be surrendered by national or by State authority? The Constitution does not expressly say. *May* Congress prohibit slavery in the territories? The Constitution does not expressly say. *Must* Congress protect slavery in the territories? The Constitution does not expressly say.

From questions of this class spring all our constitutional controversies, and we divide upon them into majorities and minorities. If the minority will not acquiesce, the majority must, or the government must cease. There is no other alternative; for continuing the government, is acquiescence on one side or the other. If a minority, in such case, will secede rather than acquiesce, they make a precedent which, in turn, will divide and ruin them; for a minority of their own will secede from them, whenever a majority refuses to be controlled by such minority. For instance, why may not any portion of a new confederacy, a year or two hence, arbitrarily secede again, precisely as portions of the present Union now claim to secede from it. All who cherish disunion sentiments, are now being educated to the exact temper of doing this. Is there such perfect identity of interests among the States to compose a new Union, as to produce harmony only, and prevent renewed secession?

Plainly, the central idea of secession, is the essence of anarchy. A majority, held in restraint by constitutional checks, and limitations, and always changing
5   easily, with deliberate changes of popular opinions and sentiments, is the only true sovereign of a free people. Whoever rejects it, does, of necessity, fly to anarchy or to despotism. Unanimity is impossible; the rule of a minority, as a permanent arrangement, is wholly inadmissible; so that, rejecting the majority principle, anarchy, or despotism in some form, is all that is left.

10   I do not forget the position assumed by some, that constitutional questions are to be decided by the Supreme Court; nor do I deny that such decisions must be binding in any case, upon the parties to a suit, as to the object of that suit, while they are also entitled to very high respect and consideration, in all parallel cases, by all other departments of the government. And while it is
15   obviously possible that such decision may be erroneous in any given case, still the evil effect following it, being limited to that particular case, with the chance that it may be over-ruled, and never become a precedent for other cases, can better be borne than could the evils of a different practice. At the same time the candid citizen must confess that if the policy of the government, upon vital
20   questions, affecting the whole people, is to be irrevocably fixed by decisions of the Supreme Court, the instant they are made, in ordinary litigation between parties, in personal actions, the people will have ceased, to be their own rulers, having, to that extent, practically resigned their government, into the hands of that eminent tribunal. Nor is there, in this view, any assault upon the court,
25   or the judges. It is a duty, from which they may not shrink, to decide cases properly brought before them; and it is no fault of theirs, if others seek to turn their decisions to political purposes.

One section of our country believes slavery is *right*, and ought to be extended, while the other believes it is *wrong*, and ought not to be extended. This is the
30   only substantial dispute. The fugitive slave clause of the Constitution, and the law for the suppression of the foreign slave trade, are each as well enforced, perhaps, as any law can ever be in a community where the moral sense of the people imperfectly supports the law itself. The great body of the people abide by the dry legal obligation in both cases, and a few break over in each.
35   This, I think, cannot be perfectly cured; and it would be worse in both cases *after* the separation of the sections, than before. The foreign slave trade, now imperfectly suppressed, would be ultimately revived without restriction, in one section; while fugitive slaves, now only partially surrendered, would not be surrendered at all, by the other.

Physically speaking, we cannot separate. We cannot remove our respective sections from each other, nor build an impassable wall between them. A husband and wife may be divorced, and go out of the presence, and beyond the reach of each other; but the different parts of our country cannot do this. They cannot but remain face to face; and intercourse, either amicable or hostile, must continue between them. Is it possible then to make that intercourse more advantageous, or more satisfactory, *after* separation than *before*? Can aliens make treaties easier than friends can make laws? Can treaties be more faithfully enforced between aliens, than laws can among friends? Suppose you go to war, you cannot fight always; and when, after much loss on both sides, and no gain on either, you cease fighting, the identical old questions, as to terms of intercourse, are again upon you.

This country, with its institutions, belongs to the people who inhabit it. Whenever they shall grow weary of the existing government, they can exercise their *constitutional* right of amending it, or their *revolutionary* right to dismember, or overthrow it. I can not be ignorant of the fact that many worthy, and patriotic citizens are desirous of having the national constitution amended. While I make no recommendation of amendments, I fully recognize the rightful authority of the people over the whole subject, to be exercised in either of the modes prescribed in the instrument itself; and I should, under existing circumstances, favor, rather than oppose, a fair opportunity being afforded the people to act upon it.

I will venture to add that, to me, the convention mode seems preferable, in that it allows amendments to originate with the people themselves, instead of only permitting them to take, or reject, propositions, originated by others, not especially chosen for the purpose, and which might not be precisely such, as they would wish to either accept or refuse. I understand a proposed amendment to the Constitution—which amendment, however, I have not seen, has passed Congress, to the effect that the federal government, shall never interfere with the domestic institutions of the States, including that of persons held to service. To avoid misconstruction of what I have said, I depart from my purpose not to speak of particular amendments, so far as to say that, holding such a provision to now be implied constitutional law, I have no objection to its being made express, and irrevocable.

The Chief Magistrate derives all his authority from the people, and they have referred none upon him to fix terms for the separation of the States. The people themselves can do this also if they choose; but the executive, as such, has nothing to do with it. His duty is to administer the present government, as it came to his hands, and to transmit it, unimpaired by him, to his successor.

Why should there not be a patient confidence in the ultimate justice of the people? Is there any better, or equal hope, in the world? In our present differences, is either party without faith of being in the right? If the Almighty Ruler of nations, with his eternal truth and justice, be on your side of the
5 North, or on yours of the South, that truth, and that justice, will surely prevail, by the judgment of this great tribunal, the American people.

By the frame of the government under which we live, this same people have wisely given their public servants but little power for mischief; and have, with equal wisdom, provided for the return of that little to their own hands at very
10 short intervals.

While the people retain their virtue, and vigilance, no administration, by any extreme of wickedness or folly, can very seriously injure the government, in the short space of four years.

My countrymen, one and all, think calmly and *well*, upon this whole subject.
15 Nothing valuable can be lost by taking time. If there be an object to *hurry* any of you, in hot haste, to a step which you would never take *deliberately*, that object will be frustrated by taking time; but no good object can be frustrated by it. Such of you as are now dissatisfied, still have the old Constitution unimpaired, and, on the sensitive point, the laws of your own framing under
20 it; while the new administration will have no immediate power, if it would, to change either. If it were admitted that you who are dissatisfied, hold the right side in the dispute, there still is no single good reason for precipitate action. Intelligence, patriotism, Christianity, and a firm reliance on Him, who has never yet forsaken this favored land, are still competent to adjust, in the best
25 way, all our present difficulty.

In *your* hands, my dissatisfied fellow countrymen, and not in *mine*, is the momentous issue of civil war. The government will not assail *you*. You can have no conflict, without being yourselves the aggressors. *You* have no oath registered in Heaven to destroy the government, while *I* shall have the most solemn one
30 to "preserve, protect and defend it."

I am loath to close. We are not enemies, but friends. We must not be enemies. Though passion may have strained, it must not break our bonds of affection. The mystic chords of memory, stretching from every battle-field, and patriot grave, to every living heart and hearthstone, all over this broad land, will yet
35 swell the chorus of the Union, when again touched, as surely they will be, by the better angels of our nature.

Message to Congress in Special Session
Abraham Lincoln

On April 12, 1861, a Confederate commander informed the Union forces stationed at Fort Sumter, in the Charleston harbor, of his plans to attack. The Civil War began an hour later. President Abraham Lincoln immediately called for 75,000 volunteers. Four states from the upper South seceded over the following month. With Congress out of session, Lincoln led the military effort without congressional approval for nearly three months. In this speech to Congress, which convened on Independence Day, he depicts the Confederacy as a section of the Union in insurrection rather than a foreign nation requiring a declaration of war.

JULY 4, 1861

FELLOW-CITIZENS OF THE SENATE AND HOUSE OF REPRESENTATIVES:

Having been convened on an extraordinary occasion, as authorized by the Constitution, your attention is not called to any ordinary subject of legislation.

At the beginning of the present Presidential term, four months ago, the functions of the Federal Government were found to be generally suspended within the several States of South Carolina, Georgia, Alabama, Mississippi, Louisiana, and Florida, excepting only those of the Post Office Department.   5

Within these States, all the Forts, Arsenals, Dock-yards, Custom-houses, and the like, including the movable and stationary property in, and about them, had been seized, and were held in open hostility to this Government, excepting only Forts Pickens, Taylor, and Jefferson, on, and near the Florida coast, and   10
Fort Sumter, in Charleston harbor, South Carolina. The Forts thus seized had been put in improved condition; new ones had been built; and armed forces had been organized, and were organizing, all avowedly with the same hostile purpose.

Abraham Lincoln, "Message to Congress in Special Session," July 4, 1861, in Roy P. Basler, ed., *The Collected Works of Abraham Lincoln*, Vol. 4 (New Brunswick, NJ: Rutgers University Press, 1953), 421–41. Reprinted with the permission of the Abraham Lincoln Association, Springfield, IL.

The Forts remaining in the possession of the Federal government, in, and near, these States, were either besieged or menaced by warlike preparations; and especially Fort Sumter was nearly surrounded by well-protected hostile batteries, with guns equal in quality to the best of its own, and outnumbering the
5 latter as perhaps ten to one. A disproportionate share, of the Federal muskets and rifles, had somehow found their way into these States, and had been seized, to be used against the government. Accumulations of the public revenue, lying within them, had been seized for the same object. The Navy was scattered in distant seas; leaving but a very small part of it within the immediate reach
10 of the government. Officers of the Federal Army and Navy, had resigned in great numbers; and, of those resigning, a large proportion had taken up arms against the government. Simultaneously, and in connection, with all this, the purpose to sever the Federal Union, was openly avowed. In accordance with this purpose, an ordinance had been adopted in each of these States, declaring
15 the States, respectively, to be separated from the National Union. A formula for instituting a combined government of these states had been promulgated; and this illegal organization, in the character of confederate States was already invoking recognition, aid, and intervention, from Foreign Powers.

Finding this condition of things, and believing it to be an imperative duty upon
20 the incoming Executive, to prevent, if possible, the consummation of such attempt to destroy the Federal Union, a choice of means to that end became indispensable. This choice was made; and was declared in the Inaugural address. The policy chosen looked to the exhaustion of all peaceful measures, before a resort to any stronger ones. It sought only to hold the public places and property,
25 not already wrested from the Government, and to collect the revenue; relying for the rest, on time, discussion, and the ballot-box. It promised a continuance of the mails, at government expense, to the very people who were resisting the government; and it gave repeated pledges against any disturbance to any of the people, or any of their rights. Of all that which a president might constitution-
30 ally, and justifiably, do in such a case, everything was foreborne, without which, it was believed possible to keep the government on foot.

On the 5th of March, (the present incumbent's first full day in office) a letter of Major Anderson, commanding at Fort Sumter, written on the 28th of February, and received at the War Department on the 4th of March, was, by that
35 Department, placed in his hands. This letter expressed the professional opinion of the writer, that re-inforcements could not be thrown into that Fort within the time for his relief, rendered necessary by the limited supply of provisions, and with a view of holding possession of the same, with a force of less than twenty thousand good, and well-disciplined men. This opinion was concurred

in by all the officers of his command; and their *memoranda* on the subject, were made enclosures of Major Anderson's letter. The whole was immediately laid before Lieutenant General Scott, who at once concurred with Major Anderson in opinion. On reflection, however, he took full time, consulting with other officers, both of the Army and the Navy; and, at the end of four days, came reluctantly, but decidedly, to the same conclusion as before. He also stated at the same time that no such sufficient force was then at the control of the Government, or could be raised, and brought to the ground, within the time when the provisions in the Fort would be exhausted. In a purely military point of view, this reduced the duty of the administration, in the case, to the mere matter of getting the garrison safely out of the Fort.

It was believed, however, that to so abandon that position, under the circumstances, would be utterly ruinous; that the *necessity* under which it was to be done, would not be fully understood—that, by many, it would be construed as a part of a *voluntary* policy—that, at home, it would discourage the friends of the Union, embolden its adversaries, and go far to insure to the latter, a recognition abroad—that, in fact, it would be our national destruction consummated. This could not be allowed. Starvation was not yet upon the garrison; and ere it would be reached, *Fort Pickens* might be reinforced. This last, would be a clear indication of *policy*, and would better enable the country to accept the evacuation of Fort Sumter, as a military *necessity*. An order was at once directed to be sent for the landing of the troops from the Steamship Brooklyn, into Fort Pickens. This order could not go by land, but must take the longer, and slower route by sea. The first return news from the order was received just one week before the fall of Fort Sumter. The news itself was, that the officer commanding the Sabine, to which vessel the troops had been transferred from the Brooklyn, acting upon some *quasi* armistice of the late administration, (and of the existence of which, the present administration, up to the time the order was despatched, had only too vague and uncertain rumors, to fix attention) had refused to land the troops. To now re-inforce Fort Pickens, before a crisis would be reached at Fort Sumter was impossible—rendered so by the near exhaustion of provisions in the latter-named Fort. In precaution against such a conjuncture, the government had, a few days before, commenced preparing an expedition, as well adapted as might be, to relieve Fort Sumter, which expedition was intended to be ultimately used, or not, according to circumstances. The strongest anticipated case, for using it, was now presented; and it was resolved to send it forward. As had been intended, in this contingency, it was also resolved to notify the Governor of South Carolina, that he might expect an attempt would be made to provision the Fort; and that, if the attempt should not be resisted, there would be no effort to throw in men, arms, or ammunition, without further notice, or in case of an attack upon the Fort. This notice was accordingly given; whereupon the Fort was attacked, and bombarded to its fall, without even awaiting the arrival of the provisioning expedition.

5   It is thus seen that the assault upon, and reduction of, Fort Sumter, was, in no sense, a matter of self-defensce on the part of the assailants. They well knew that the garrison in the Fort could, by no possibility, commit aggression upon them. They knew—they were expressly notified—that the giving of bread to the few brave and hungry men of the garrison, was all which would on that occasion be
10   attempted, unless themselves, by resisting so much, should provoke more. They knew that this Government desired to keep the garrison in the Fort, not to assail them, but merely to maintain visible possession, and thus to preserve the Union from actual, and immediate dissolution—trusting, as herein-before stated, to time, discussion, and the ballot-box, for final adjustment; and they assailed,
15   and reduced the Fort, for precisely the reverse object—to drive out the visible authority of the Federal Union, and thus force it to immediate dissolution.

That this was their object, the Executive well understood; and having said to them in the inaugural address, "You can have no conflict without being yourselves the aggressors," he took pains, not only to keep this declaration
20   good, but also to keep the case so free from the power of ingenious sophistry, as that the world should not be able to misunderstand it. By the affair at Fort Sumter, with its surrounding circumstances, that point was reached. Then, and thereby, the assailants of the Government, began the conflict of arms, without a gun in sight, or in expectancy, to return their fire, save only the few in the
25   Fort, sent to that harbor, years before, for their own protection, and still ready to give that protection, in whatever was lawful. In this act, discarding all else, they have forced upon the country, the distinct issue: "Immediate dissolution, or blood."

And this issue embraces more than the fate of these United States. It presents
30   to the whole family of man, the question, whether a constitutional republic, or a democracy—a government of the people, by the same people—can, or cannot, maintain its territorial integrity, against its own domestic foes. It presents the question, whether discontented individuals, too few in numbers to control administration, according to organic law, in any case, can always, upon the
35   pretences made in this case, or on any other pretences, or arbitrarily, without any pretence, break up their Government, and thus practically put an end to free government upon the earth. It forces us to ask: "Is there, in all republics, this inherent, and fatal weakness?" "Must a government, of necessity, be too *strong* for the liberties of its own people, or too *weak* to maintain its own existence?"

So viewing the issue, no choice was left but to call out the war power of the Government; and so to resist force, employed for its destruction, by force, for its preservation.

The call was made; and the response of the country was most gratifying; surpassing, in unanimity and spirit, the most sanguine expectation. Yet none of the States commonly called Slave-states, except Delaware, gave a Regiment through regular State organization. A few regiments have been organized within some others of those states, by individual enterprise, and received into the government service. Of course the seceded States, so called, (and to which Texas had been joined about the time of the inauguration), gave no troops to the cause of the Union. The border States, so called, were not uniform in their actions; some of them being almost *for* the Union, while in others—as Virginia, North Carolina, Tennessee, and Arkansas—the Union sentiment was nearly repressed, and silenced. The course taken in Virginia was the most remarkable—perhaps the most important. A convention, elected by the people of that State, to consider this very question of disrupting the Federal Union, was in session at the capital of Virginia when Fort Sumter fell. To this body the people had chosen a large majority of *professed* Union men. Almost immediately after the fall of Sumter, many members of that majority went over to the original disunion minority, and, with them, adopted an ordinance for withdrawing the State from the Union. Whether this change was wrought by their great approval of the assault upon Sumter, or their great resentment at the government's resistance to that assault, is not definitely known. Although they submitted the ordinance, for ratification, to a vote of the people, to be taken on a day then somewhat more than a month distant, the convention, and the Legislature, (which was also in session at the same time and place) with leading men of the State, not members of either, immediately commenced acting, as if the State were already out of the Union. They pushed military preparations vigorously forward all over the state. They seized the United States Armory at Harper's Ferry, and the Navy-yard at Gosport, near Norfolk. They received—perhaps invited— into their state, large bodies of troops, with their warlike appointments, from the so-called seceded States. They formally entered into a treaty of temporary alliance, and co-operation with the so-called "Confederate States," and sent members to their Congress at Montgomery. And, finally, they permitted the insurrectionary government to be transferred to their capital at Richmond.

The people of Virginia have thus allowed this giant insurrection to make its nest within her borders; and this government has no choice left but to deal with it, *where* it finds it. And it has the less regret, as the loyal citizens have, in due form, claimed its protection. Those loyal citizens, this government is bound to recognize, and protect, as being Virginia.

In the border States, so called—in fact, the middle states—there are those who favor a policy which they call "armed neutrality"—that is, an arming of those states to prevent the Union forces passing one way, or the disunion, the other, over their soil. This would be disunion completed. Figuratively speaking, it would be the building of an impassable wall along the line of separation. And yet, not quite an impassable one; for, under the guise of neutrality, it would tie the hands of the Union men, and freely pass supplies from among them, to the insurrectionists, which it could not do as an open enemy. At a stroke, it would take all the trouble off the hands of secession, except only what proceeds from the external blockade. It would do for the disunionists that which, of all things, they most desire—feed them well, and give them disunion without a struggle of their own. It recognizes no fidelity to the Constitution, no obligation to maintain the Union; and while very many who have favored it are, doubtless, loyal citizens, it is, nevertheless, treason in effect.

Recurring to the action of the government, it may be stated that, at first, a call was made for seventy-five thousand militia; and rapidly following this, a proclamation was issued for closing the ports of the insurrectionary districts by proceedings in the nature of Blockade. So far all was believed to be strictly legal. At this point the insurrectionists announced their purpose to enter upon the practice of privateering.

Other calls were made for volunteers, to serve three years, unless sooner discharged; and also for large additions to the regular Army and Navy. These measures, whether strictly legal or not, were ventured upon, under what appeared to be a popular demand, and a public necessity; trusting, then as now, that Congress would readily ratify them. It is believed that nothing has been done beyond the constitutional competency of Congress.

Soon after the first call for militia, it was considered a duty to authorize the Commanding General, in proper cases, according to his discretion, to suspend the privilege of the writ of habeas corpus; or, in other words, to arrest, and detain, without resort to the ordinary processes and forms of law, such individuals as he might deem dangerous to the public safety. This authority has purposely been exercised but very sparingly. Nevertheless, the legality and propriety of what has been done under it, are questioned; and the attention of the country has been called to the proposition that one who is sworn to "take care that the laws be faithfully executed," should not himself violate them. Of course some consideration was given to the questions of power, and propriety, before this matter was acted upon. The whole of the laws which were required to be faithfully executed, were being resisted, and failing of execution, in nearly one-third of the States. Must they be allowed to finally fail of execution, even had it been perfectly clear, that by the use of the means necessary to their execution, some single law, made in such extreme tenderness of the citizen's liberty, that practically, it relieves more of the guilty, than of the innocent, should, to a very limited extent, be violated? To state the question more directly, are all the laws, *but one*, to go unexecuted, and the government itself go to pieces, lest that one be violated? Even in such a case, would not the official oath be broken, if the government should be overthrown, when it was believed that disregarding the single law, would tend to preserve it? But it was not believed that this question was presented. It was not believed that any law was violated. The provision of the Constitution that "The privilege of the writ of habeas corpus, shall not be suspended unless when, in cases of rebellion or invasion, the public safety may require it," is equivalent to a provision—is a provision—that such privilege may be suspended when, in cases of rebellion, or invasion, the public safety *does* require it. It was decided that we have a case of rebellion, and that the public safety does require the qualified suspension of the privilege of the writ which was authorized to be made. Now it is insisted that Congress, and not the Executive, is vested with this power. But the Constitution itself, is silent as to which, or who, is to exercise the power; and as the provision was plainly made for a dangerous emergency, it cannot be believed the framers of the instrument intended, that in every case, the danger should run its course, until Congress could be called together; the very assembling of which might be prevented, as was intended in this case, by the rebellion.

No more extended argument is now offered; as an opinion, at some length, will probably be presented by the Attorney General. Whether there shall be any legislation upon the subject, and if any, what, is submitted entirely to the better judgment of Congress.

The forbearance of this government had been so extraordinary, and so long continued, as to lead some foreign nations to shape their action as if they supposed the early destruction of our national Union was probable. While this, on discovery, gave the Executive some concern, he is now happy to say that the sovereignty, and rights of the United States, are now everywhere practically respected by foreign powers; and a general sympathy with the country is manifested throughout the world.

The reports of the Secretaries of the Treasury, War, and the Navy, will give the information in detail deemed necessary, and convenient for your deliberation, and action; while the Executive, and all the Departments, will stand ready to supply omissions, or to communicate new facts, considered important for you to know.

It is now recommended that you give the legal means for making this contest a short, and a decisive one; that you place at the control of the government, for the work, at least four hundred thousand men, and four hundred millions of dollars. That number of men is about one tenth of those of proper ages within

5   the regions where, apparently, *all* are willing to engage; and the sum is less than a twentythird part of the money value owned by the men who seem ready to devote the whole. A debt of six hundred millions of dollars *now*, is a less sum per head, than was the debt of our revolution, when we came out of that struggle; and the money value in the country, now bears even a greater proportion to

10 what it was *then*, than does the population. Surely each man has as strong a motive *now*, to *preserve* our liberties, as each had *then*, to *establish* them.

A right result, at this time, will be worth more to the world, than ten times the men, and ten times the money. The evidence reaching us from the country, leaves no doubt, that the material for the work is abundant; and that it needs only

15 the hand of legislation to give it legal sanction, and the hand of the Executive to give it practical shape and efficiency. One of the greatest perplexities of the government, is to avoid receiving troops faster than it can provide for them. In a word, the people will save their government, if the government itself, will do its part, only indifferently well.

20 It might seem, at first thought, to be of little difference whether the present movement at the South be called "secession" or "rebellion." The movers, however, well understand the difference. At the beginning, they knew they could never raise their treason to any respectable magnitude, by any name which implies *violation* of law. They knew their people possessed as much of moral sense, as

25 much of devotion to law and order, and as much pride in, and reverence for, the history, and government, of their common country, as any other civilized, and patriotic people. They knew they could make no advancement directly in the teeth of these strong and noble sentiments. Accordingly they commenced by an insidious debauching of the public mind. They invented an ingenious

30 sophism, which, if conceded, was followed by perfectly logical steps, through all the incidents, to the complete destruction of the Union. The sophism itself is, that any state of the Union may, *consistently* with the national Constitution, and therefore *lawfully*, and *peacefully*, withdraw from the Union, without the consent of the Union, or of any other state. The little disguise that the supposed

35 right is to be exercised only for just cause, themselves to be the sole judge of its justice, is too thin to merit any notice.

With rebellion thus sugar-coated, they have been drugging the public mind of their section for more than thirty years; and, until at length, they have brought many good men to a willingness to take up arms against the government the day *after* some assemblage of men have enacted the farcical pretence of taking their State out of the Union, who could have been brought to no such thing the day *before*.

This sophism derives much—perhaps the whole—of its currency, from the assumption, that there is some omnipotent, and sacred supremacy, pertaining to a *State*—to each State of our Federal Union. Our States have neither more, nor less power, than that reserved to them, in the Union, by the Constitution—no one of them ever having been a State *out* of the Union. The original ones passed into the Union even *before* they cast off their British colonial dependence; and the new ones each came into the Union directly from a condition of dependence, excepting Texas. And even Texas, in its temporary independence, was never designated a State. The new ones only took the designation of States, on coming into the Union, while that name was first adopted for the old ones, in, and by, the Declaration of Independence. Therein the "United Colonies" were declared to be "Free and Independent States"; but, even then, the object plainly was not to declare their independence of *one another*, or of the *Union*; but directly the contrary, as their mutual pledge, and their mutual action, before, at the time, and afterwards, abundantly show. The express plighting of faith, by each and all of the original thirteen, in the Articles of Confederation, two years later, that the Union shall be perpetual, is most conclusive. Having never been States, either in substance, or in name, *outside* of the Union, whence this magical omnipotence of "State rights," asserting a claim of power to lawfully destroy the Union itself? Much is said about the "sovereignty" of the States; but the word, even, is not in the national Constitution; nor, as is believed, in any of the State constitutions. What is a "sovereignty," in the political sense of the term? Would it be far wrong to define it "A political community, without a political superior"? Tested by this, no one of our States, except Texas, ever was a sovereignty. And even Texas gave up the character on coming into the Union; by which act, she acknowledged the Constitution of the United States, and the laws and treaties of the United States made in pursuance of the Constitution, to be, for her, the supreme law of the land. The States have their *status* IN the Union, and they have no other *legal status*. If they break from this, they can only do so against law, and by revolution. The Union, and not themselves separately, procured their independence, and their liberty. By conquest, or purchase, the Union gave each of them, whatever of independence, and liberty, it has. The Union is older than any of the States; and, in fact, it created them as States. Originally, some dependent colonies made the Union; and, in turn, the Union threw off their old dependence, for them, and made them States, such as they are. Not one of them ever had a State constitution, independent of the Union.

Of course, it is not forgotten that all the new States framed their constitutions, before they entered the Union; nevertheless, dependent upon, and preparatory to, coming into the Union.

Unquestionably the States have the powers, and rights, reserved to them in,
5 and by the National Constitution; but among these, surely, are not included all conceivable powers, however mischievous, or destructive; but, at most, such only, as were known in the world, at the time, as governmental powers; and certainly, a power to destroy the government itself, had never been known as a governmental—as a merely administrative power. This relative matter of
10 National power, and State rights, as a principle, is no other than the principle of *generality*, and *locality*. Whatever concerns the whole, should be confided to the whole—to the general government; while, whatever concerns *only* the State, should be left exclusively, to the State. This is all there is of original principle about it. Whether the National Constitution, in defining boundaries between
15 the two, has applied the principle with exact accuracy, is not to be questioned. We are all bound by that defining, without question.

What is now combatted, is the position that secession is *consistent* with the Constitution—is *lawful*, and *peaceful*. It is not contended that there is any express law for it; and nothing should ever be implied as law, which leads to
20 unjust, or absurd consequences. The nation purchased, with money, the countries out of which several of these States were formed. Is it just that they shall go off without leave, and without refunding? The nation paid very large sums, (in the aggregate, I believe, nearly a hundred millions) to relieve Florida of the aboriginal tribes. Is it just that she shall now be off without consent, or without
25 making any return? The nation is now in debt for money applied to the benefit of these so-called seceding States, in common with the rest. Is it just, either that creditors shall go unpaid, or the remaining States pay the whole? A part of the present national debt was contracted to pay the old debts of Texas. Is it just that she shall leave, and pay no part of this herself?

30 Again, if one State may secede, so may another; and when all shall have seceded, none is left to pay the debts. Is this quite just to creditors? Did we notify them of this sage view of ours, when we borrowed their money? If we now recognize this doctrine, by allowing the seceders to go in peace, it is difficult to see what we can do, if others choose to go, or to extort terms upon which they will
35 promise to remain.

The seceders insist that our Constitution admits of secession. They have assumed to make a National Constitution of their own, in which, of necessity, they have either *discarded*, or *retained*, the right of secession, as they insist, it exists in ours.

If they have discarded it, they thereby admit that, on principle, it ought not to be in ours. If they have retained, it by their own construction of ours they show that to be consistent they must secede from one another, whenever they shall find it the easiest way of settling their debts, or effecting any other selfish, or unjust object. The principle itself is one of disintegration, and upon which no government can possibly endure.

If all the States, save one, should assert the power to *drive* that one out of the Union, it is presumed the whole class of seceder politicians would at once deny the power, and denounce the act as the greatest outrage upon State rights. But suppose that precisely the same act, instead of being called "driving the one out," should be called "the seceding of the others from that one," it would be exactly what the seceders claim to do; unless, indeed, they make the point, that the one, because it is a minority, may rightfully do, what the others, because they are a majority, may not rightfully do. These politicians are subtle, and profound, on the rights of minorities. They are not partial to that power which made the Constitution, and speaks from the preamble, calling itself "We, the People."

It may well be questioned whether there is, today, a majority of the legally qualified voters of any State, except perhaps South Carolina, in favor of disunion. There is much reason to believe that the Union men are the majority in many, if not in every other one, of the so-called seceded States. The contrary has not been demonstrated in any one of them. It is ventured to affirm this, even of Virginia and Tennessee; for the result of an election, held in military camps, where the bayonets are all on one side of the question voted upon, can scarcely be considered as demonstrating popular sentiment. At such an election, all that large class who are, at once, *for* the Union, and *against* coercion, would be coerced to vote against the Union.

It may be affirmed, without extravagance, that the free institutions we enjoy, have developed the powers, and improved the condition, of our whole people, beyond any example in the world. Of this we now have a striking, and an impressive illustration. So large an army as the government has now on foot, was never before known, without a soldier in it, but who had taken his place there, of his own free choice. But more than this: there are many single Regiments whose members, one and another, possess full practical knowledge of all the arts, sciences, professions, and whatever else, whether useful or elegant, is known in the world; and there is scarcely one, from which there could not be selected, a President, a Cabinet, a Congress, and perhaps a Court, abundantly competent to administer the government itself. Nor do I say this is not true, also, in the army of our late friends, now adversaries, in this contest; but if it is, so much better the reason why the government, which has conferred such

benefits on both them and us, should not be broken up. Whoever, in any section, proposes to abandon such a government, would do well to consider, in
deference to what principle it is, that he does it—what better he is likely to
get in its stead—whether the substitute will give, or be intended to give, so
5   much of good to the people. There are some foreshadowings on this subject.
Our adversaries have adopted some Declarations of Independence, in which,
unlike the good old one, penned by Jefferson, they omit the words "all men are
created equal." Why? They have adopted a temporary national constitution, in
the preamble of which, unlike our good old one, signed by Washington, they
10   omit "We, the People," and substitute "We, the deputies of the sovereign and
independent States." Why? Why this deliberate pressing out of view, the rights
of men, and the authority of the people?

This is essentially a People's contest. On the side of the Union, it is a struggle
for maintaining in the world, that form, and substance of government, whose
15   leading object is, to elevate the condition of men—to lift artificial weights from
all shoulders—to clear the paths of laudable pursuit for all—to afford all, an
unfettered start, and a fair chance, in the race of life. Yielding to partial, and
temporary departures, from necessity, this is the leading object of the government for whose existence we contend.

20   I am most happy to believe that the plain people understand, and appreciate
this. It is worthy of note, that while in this, the government's hour of trial, large
numbers of those in the Army and Navy, who have been favored with the offices,
have resigned, and proved false to the hand which had pampered them, not one
common soldier, or common sailor is is known to have deserted his flag.

25   Great honor is due to those officers who remain true, despite the example of
their treacherous associates; but the greatest honor, and most important fact of
all, is the unanimous firmness of the common soldiers, and common sailors.
To the last man, so far as known, they have successfully resisted the traitorous
efforts of those, whose commands, but an hour before, they obeyed as absolute
30   law. This is the patriotic instinct of the plain people. They understand, without
an argument, that destroying the government, which was made by Washington,
means no good to them.

Our popular government has often been called an experiment. Two points in
it, our people have already settled—the successful *establishing*, and the success-
35   ful *administering* of it. One still remains—its successful *maintenance* against a
formidable internal attempt to overthrow it. It is now for them to demonstrate
to the world, that those who can fairly carry an election, can also suppress a
rebellion—that ballots are the rightful, and peaceful, successors of bullets; and

that when ballots have fairly, and constitutionally, decided, there can be no successful appeal, back to bullets; that there can be no successful appeal, except to
ballots themselves, at succeeding elections. Such will be a great lesson of peace;
teaching men that what they cannot take by an election, neither can they take
it by a war—teaching all, the folly of being the beginners of a war.   5

Lest there be some uneasiness in the minds of candid men, as to what is to be
the course of the government, towards the Southern States, *after* the rebellion
shall have been suppressed, the Executive deems it proper to say, it will be his
purpose then, as ever, to be guided by the Constitution, and the laws; and that
he probably will have no different understanding of the powers, and duties of   10
the Federal government, relatively to the rights of the States, and the people,
under the Constitution, than that expressed in the inaugural address.

He desires to preserve the government, that it may be administered for all, as
it was administered by the men who made it. Loyal citizens everywhere, have
the right to claim this of their government; and the government has no right to   15
withhold, or neglect it. It is not perceived that, in giving it, there is any coercion,
any conquest, or any subjugation, in any just sense of those terms.

The Constitution provides, and all the States have accepted the provision, that
"The United States shall guarantee to every State in this Union a republican form
of government." But, if a State may lawfully go out of the Union, having done   20
so, it may also discard the republican form of government; so that to prevent
its going out, is an indispensable *means*, to the *end*, of maintaining the guaranty
mentioned; and when an end is lawful and obligatory, the indispensable means
to it, are also lawful, and obligatory.

It was with the deepest regret that the Executive found the duty of employing   25
the war-power, in defense of the government, forced upon him. He could but
perform this duty, or surrender the existence of the government. No compromise, by public servants, could, in this case, be a cure; not that compromises are
not often proper, but that no popular government can long survive a marked
precedent, that those who carry an election, can only save the government from   30
immediate destruction, by giving up the main point, upon which the people
gave the election. The people themselves, and not their servants, can safely
reverse their own deliberate decisions. As a private citizen, the Executive could
not have consented that these institutions shall perish; much less could he, in
betrayal of so vast, and so sacred a trust, as these free people had confided to   35
him. He felt that he had no moral right to shrink; nor even to count the chances
of his own life, in what might follow. In full view of his great responsibility, he
has, so far, done what he has deemed his duty. You will now, according to your

own judgment, perform yours. He sincerely hopes that your views, and your action, may so accord with his, as to assure all faithful citizens, who have been disturbed in their rights, of a certain, and speedy restoration to them, under the Constitution, and the laws.

5   And having thus chosen our course, without guile, and with pure purpose, let us renew our trust in God, and go forward without fear, and with manly hearts.

THE EMANCIPATION PROCLAMATION
ABRAHAM LINCOLN

The Emancipation Proclamation, issued on September 22, 1862, promised emancipation for slaves residing in the Confederacy, unless the rebellious states returned to the Union by January 1 of the following year. The three-month deadline came and went, and slavery ceased to have legal sanction in much of the South. Although complete emancipation did not occur until the passage of the Thirteenth Amendment in 1865, Abraham Lincoln's actions earned him the nickname "The Great Emancipator."

JANUARY 1, 1863

BY THE PRESIDENT OF THE UNITED STATES OF AMERICA:

A PROCLAMATION.

Whereas, on the twenty-second day of September, in the year of our Lord one thousand eight hundred and sixty-two, a proclamation was issued by the President of the United States, containing, among other things, the following, to wit:

"That on the first day of January, in the year of our Lord one thousand eight hundred and sixty-three, all persons held as slaves within any State or desig- 5 nated part of a State, the people whereof shall then be in rebellion against the United States, shall be then, thenceforward, and forever free; and the Executive Government of the United States, including the military and naval authority thereof, will recognize and maintain the freedom of such persons, and will do no act or acts to repress such persons, or any of them, in any efforts they may 10 make for their actual freedom.

"That the Executive will, on the first day of January aforesaid, by proclamation, designate the States and parts of States, if any, in which the people thereof, respectively, shall then be in rebellion against the United States; and the fact that

Abraham Lincoln, "Emancipation Proclamation," January 1, 1863, in Roy P. Basler, ed., *The Collected Works of Abraham Lincoln*, Vol. 6 (New Brunswick, NJ: Rutgers University Press, 1953), 28–30. Reprinted with the permission of the Abraham Lincoln Association, Springfield, IL.

any State, or the people thereof, shall on that day be, in good faith, represented in the Congress of the United States by members chosen thereto at elections wherein a majority of the qualified voters of such State shall have participated, shall, in the absence of strong countervailing testimony, be deemed conclusive

5   evidence that such State, and the people thereof, are not then in rebellion against the United States."

Now, therefore I, Abraham Lincoln, President of the United States, by virtue of the power in me vested as Commander-in-Chief, of the Army and Navy of the United States in time of actual armed rebellion against authority and

10   government of the United States, and as a fit and necessary war measure for suppressing said rebellion, do, on this first day of January, in the year of our Lord one thousand eight hundred and sixty-three, and in accordance with my purpose so to do publicly proclaimed for the full period of one hundred days, from the day first above mentioned, order and designate as the States and

15   parts of States wherein the people thereof respectively, are this day in rebellion against the United States, the following, to wit:

Arkansas, Texas, Louisiana, (except the Parishes of St. Bernard, Plaquemines, Jefferson, St. John, St. Charles, St. James, Ascension, Assumption, Terrebonne, Lafourche, St. Mary, St. Martin, and Orleans, including the City of New

20   Orleans) Mississippi, Alabama, Florida, Georgia, South-Carolina, North-Carolina, and Virginia, (except the forty-eight counties designated as West Virginia, and also the counties of Berkley, Accomac, Northampton, Elizabeth-City, York, Princess Ann, and Norfolk, including the cities of Norfolk and Portsmouth); and which excepted parts are, for the present, left precisely as if

25   this proclamation were not issued.

And by virtue of the power, and for the purpose aforesaid, I do order and declare that all persons held as slaves within said designated States, and parts of States, are, and henceforward shall be free; and that the Executive government of the United States, including the military and naval authorities thereof, will

30   recognize and maintain the freedom of said persons.

And I hereby enjoin upon the people so declared to be free to abstain from all violence, unless in necessary self-defense; and I recommend to them that, in all cases when allowed, they labor faithfully for reasonable wages.

And I further declare and make known, that such persons of suitable condition,

35   will be received into the armed service of the United States to garrison forts, positions, stations, and other places, and to man vessels of all sorts in said service.

And upon this act, sincerely believed to be an act of justice, warranted by the Constitution, upon military necessity, I invoke the considerate judgment of mankind, and the gracious favor of Almighty God.

In witness whereof, I have hereunto set my hand and caused the seal of the United States to be affixed. 5

Done at the City of Washington, this first day of January, in the year of our Lord one thousand eight hundred and sixty-three, and of the Independence of the United States of America the eighty-seventh.

By the President:

ABRAHAM LINCOLN

WILLIAM H. SEWARD, *Secretary of State.*

GETTYSBURG ADDRESS
ABRAHAM LINCOLN

From July 1 to 3, 1863, 160,000 men from the Union and Confederate armies met at Gettysburg in southern Pennsylvania. It would prove to be the turning point of the war, but with more than 50,000 casualties from both sides it was among the most costly of battles. President Abraham Lincoln's speech, delivered four months later, lasted only two minutes. But it said as much or more about the Civil War than any book written since.

NOVEMBER 19, 1863

Four score and seven years ago our fathers brought forth, on this continent, a new nation, conceived in Liberty, and dedicated to the proposition that all men are created equal.

Now we are engaged in a great civil war, testing whether that nation, or any nation so conceived, and so dedicated, can long endure. We are met on a great   5
battle-field of that war. We have come to dedicate a portion of that field, as a final resting-place for those who here gave their lives, that that nation might live. It is altogether fitting and proper that we should do this.

But, in a larger sense, we can not dedicate—we can not consecrate—we can not hallow—this ground. The brave men, living and dead, who struggled here,   10
have consecrated it far above our poor power to add or detract. The world will little note, nor long remember what we say here, but it can never forget what they did here. It is for us the living, rather, to be dedicated here to the unfinished work which they who fought here have thus far so nobly advanced. It is rather for us to be here dedicated to the great task remaining before us—   15
that from these honored dead we take increased devotion to that cause for which they here gave the last full measure of devotion—that we here highly

Abraham Lincoln, "Gettysburg Address," November 19, 1863, in Roy P. Basler, ed., *The Collected Works of Abraham Lincoln*, Vol. 7 (New Brunswick, NJ: Rutgers University Press, 1953), 23. Reprinted with the permission of the Abraham Lincoln Association, Springfield, IL.

resolve that these dead shall not have died in vain—that this nation, under God, shall have a new birth of freedom—and that government of the people, by the people, for the people, shall not perish from the earth.

Second Inaugural Address
Abraham Lincoln

The South's surrender was a month away when Abraham Lincoln delivered his second inaugural. Lincoln looks back on the war and ahead to the task of rebuilding the nation. A little over a month later, he was assassinated.

March 4, 1865

Fellow Countrymen:

At this second appearing to take the oath of the presidential office, there is less occasion for an extended address than there was at the first. Then a statement, somewhat in detail, of a course to be pursued, seemed fitting and proper. Now, at the expiration of four years, during which public declarations have been constantly called forth on every point and phase of the great contest 5 which still absorbs the attention, and engrosses the energies of the nation, little that is new could be presented. The progress of our arms, upon which all else chiefly depends, is as well known to the public as to myself; and it is, I trust, reasonably satisfactory and encouraging to all. With high hope for the future, no prediction in regard to it is ventured. 10

On the occasion corresponding to this four years ago, all thoughts were anxiously directed to an impending civil-war. All dreaded it—all sought to avert it. While the inaugural address was being delivered from this place, devoted altogether to *saving* the Union without war, insurgent agents were in the city seeking to *destroy* it without war—seeking to dissolve the Union, and divide 15 effects, by negotiation. Both parties deprecated war; but one of them would *make* war rather than let the nation survive; and the other would *accept* war rather than let it perish. And the war came.

One eighth of the whole population were colored slaves, not distributed generally over the Union, but localized in the Southern part of it. These slaves 20

Abraham Lincoln, "Second Inaugural Address," March 4, 1865, in Roy P. Basler, ed., *The Collected Works of Abraham Lincoln*, Vol. 8 (New Brunswick, NJ: Rutgers University Press, 1953), 332–33. Reprinted with the permission of the Abraham Lincoln Association, Springfield, IL.

constituted a peculiar and powerful interest. All knew that this interest was, somehow, the cause of the war. To strengthen, perpetuate, and extend this interest was the object for which the insurgents would rend the Union, even by war; while the government claimed no right to do more than to restrict
5 the territorial enlargement of it. Neither party expected for the war, the magnitude, or the duration, which it has already attained. Neither anticipated that the *cause* of the conflict might cease with, or even before, the conflict itself should cease. Each looked for an easier triumph, and a result less fundamental and astounding. Both read the same Bible, and pray to the same God; and
10 each invokes His aid against the other. It may seem strange that any men should dare to ask a just God's assistance in wringing their bread from the sweat of other men's faces; but let us judge not that we be not judged. The prayers of both could not be answered; that of neither has been answered fully. The Almighty has His own purposes. "Woe unto the world because of
15 offenses! for it must needs be that offenses come; but woe to that man by whom the offense cometh!" If we shall suppose that American Slavery is one of those offenses which, in the providence of God, must needs come, but which, having continued through His appointed time, He now wills to remove, and that He gives to both North and South, this terrible war, as the woe due to
20 those by whom the offense came, shall we discern therein any departure from those divine attributes which the believers in a Living God always ascribe to Him? Fondly do we hope—fervently do we pray—that this mighty scourge of war may speedily pass away. Yet, if God wills that it continue, until all the wealth piled by the bond-man's two hundred and fifty years of unrequited
25 toil shall be sunk, and until every drop of blood drawn with the lash, shall be paid by another drawn with the sword, as was said three thousand years ago, so still it must be said "the judgments of the Lord, are true and righteous altogether."

With malice toward none; with charity for all; with firmness in the right, as
30 God gives us to see the right, let us strive on to finish the work we are in; to bind up the nation's wounds; to care for him who shall have borne the battle, and for his widow, and his orphan—to do all which may achieve and cherish a just, and a lasting peace, among ourselves, and with all nations.

X
THE PROGRESSIVE REJECTION
OF THE FOUNDING

It is impossible to understand the fate of the Founders' principles in American politics without perceiving how those principles have been replaced by those that animate today's administrative state. The administrative state in America emerged out of the dominant political ideas of the Progressive Era. As a practical matter, much of the infrastructure of today's system of property redistribution and centralized regulation was built during President Franklin D. Roosevelt's New Deal. But the intellectual foundation for the New Deal came a generation earlier, in the Progressive Era—a fact acknowledged by no less an authority than Franklin Roosevelt himself, who in his 1932 Commonwealth Club Address credited the ideas of Theodore Roosevelt and especially Woodrow Wilson as the source of his own plan for transforming American government.

While Progressivism was complex in the details espoused by a wide range of important figures in American history, in its essence it amounts to an argument in favor of progressing, or moving beyond, the political principles of the American founding. Progressives sought to enlarge vastly the scope of the national government for the purpose of responding to a set of economic and social conditions that, it was contended, could not have been envisioned during the founding era, and for which the Founders' limited, constitutional government was inadequate. While the Founders had posited what they held to be a permanent understanding of just government, based upon a fixed account of human nature, the Progressives countered that the ends and scope of government were to be defined anew in each historical epoch. They coupled this perspective of historical contingency with a deep faith in historical progress; they believed that government was becoming less of a danger to the governed due to historical evolution, and was also becoming more capable of solving the great array of problems besetting the human race.

This basic Progressive premise manifested itself in the thinking of the most influential Americans from the 1880s into the 1920s and beyond, and formed a common thread in the writings and speeches of well-known figures like Theodore Roosevelt, Woodrow Wilson, Robert La Follette, and John Dewey, as well as figures less well-known to contemporary students such as Herbert Croly and Frank Goodnow. These Progressives and their contemporaries took aim both at the Constitution, where the separation of powers inhibited the kind of activist central government that would be essential to implementing the Progressive policy agenda, and at the Declaration of Independence, which the Progressives rightly understood as setting the purpose for the Constitution itself. In its embrace of individual natural rights as the only legitimate purpose of government, the Declaration, Progressives knew, served as a formidable obstacle to their regulatory and redistributive policy aims. This explains why most of the theoretical works authored by Progressives begin with a critique of natural rights principles, and it makes understandable Wilson's admonition—in an address ostensibly honoring Thomas Jefferson—that "if you want to understand the real Declaration of Independence, do not repeat the preface." In other words, do not repeat that part of the Declaration that enshrines natural rights as the focal point of just government not only for the founding era, but for all time.

The Progressives' coupling of historical contingency with the doctrine of progress reveals how their movement was the means by which nineteenth-century German historicism was imported into the American political tradition. Among other things, American Progressives took from the Germans—and especially from the philosopher G. W. F. Hegel—their critique of natural rights and their organic or "living" notion of the national state. It was thus through the Progressives that the concept of a "living Constitution" entered the American lexicon.

In order to bring about the "living" conception of the Constitution, Progressives endorsed new ways of understanding America's traditional political institutions and advocated a variety of reforms. Both the proposed Progressive reforms and the broad principles that gave rise to them are evident in the selections included in this section. The principled critique of natural rights and the embrace of evolutionary constitutionalism are manifest in Dewey's *Liberalism and Social Action*, in Goodnow's *The American Conception of Liberty*, in Wilson's "Socialism and Democracy," and in Wilson's "What is Progress?" The argument for transforming American political institutions takes several forms: The presidency is discussed in Theodore Roosevelt's *Autobiography* and in the third chapter of Wilson's *Constitutional Government of the United States*, the judiciary in Theodore Roosevelt's "The Right of the People to Rule," the federal bureaucracy in Wilson's "The Study of Administration," and the party and electoral system in Croly's *Progressive Democracy*. This section also offers an important critique of Progressivism in President Calvin Coolidge's speech, "The Inspiration of the Declaration," delivered on the 150th anniversary of the Declaration of Independence.

RONALD J. PESTRITTO
Associate Professor of Politics
Charles and Lucia Shipley Professor
in the American Constitution
Hillsdale College

LIBERALISM AND SOCIAL ACTION
JOHN DEWEY (1859–1952)

As a leading Progressive scholar from the 1880s onward, John Dewey, who taught mainly at Columbia University, devoted much of his life to redefining the idea of education. His thought was influenced by German philosopher G. W. F. Hegel, and central to it was a denial of objective truth and an embrace of historicism and moral relativism. As such he was critical of the American founding.

1935

1. THE HISTORY OF LIBERALISM

… The natural beginning of the inquiry in which we are engaged is consideration of the origin and past development of liberalism. It is to this topic that the present chapter is devoted. The conclusion reached from a brief survey of history, namely, that liberalism has had a checkered career, and that it has meant in practice things so different as to be opposed to one another, might perhaps have been anticipated without prolonged examination of its past. But location and description of the ambiguities that cling to the career of liberalism will be of assistance in the attempt to determine its significance for today and tomorrow. 5

The use of the words liberal and liberalism to denote a particular social philosophy does not appear to occur earlier than the first decade of the nineteenth century. But the thing to which the words are applied is older. It might be traced back to Greek thought; some of its ideas, especially as to the importance of the free play of intelligence, may be found notably expressed in the funeral oration attributed to Pericles. But for the present purpose it is not necessary to go back of John Locke, the philosopher of the "glorious revolution" of 1688. The outstanding points of Locke's version of liberalism are that governments 10

15

John Dewey, "Liberalism and Social Action," in Jo Ann Boydston, ed., *The Papers of John Dewey: The Later Works, 1925–1953*, Vol. 11 (Carbondale, IL: Southern Illinois University, 1987), 6–16, 21–23, 25–27, 39–40. Reproduced with permission of Southern Illinois University Press in the format Textbook via Copyright Clearance Center.

are instituted to protect the rights that belong to individuals prior to political organization of social relations. These rights are those summed up a century later in the American Declaration of Independence: the rights of life, liberty and the pursuit of happiness. Among the "natural" rights especially emphasized
5   by Locke is that of property, originating, according to him, in the fact that an individual has "mixed" himself, through his labor, with some natural hitherto unappropriated object. This view was directed against levies on property made by rulers without authorization from the representatives of the people. The theory culminated in justifying the right of revolution. Since governments
10   are instituted to protect the natural rights of individuals, they lose claim to obedience when they invade and destroy these rights instead of safeguarding them: a doctrine that well served the aims of our forefathers in their revolt against British rule, and that also found an extended application in the French Revolution of 1789.

15   The impact of this earlier liberalism is evidently political. Yet one of Locke's greatest interests was to uphold toleration in an age when intolerance was rife, persecution of dissenters in faith almost the rule, and when wars, civil and between nations, had a religious color. In serving the immediate needs of England—and then those of other countries in which it was desired to substitute
20   representative for arbitrary government—it bequeathed to later social thought a rigid doctrine of natural rights inherent in individuals independent of social organization. It gave a directly practical import to the older semi-theological and semi-metaphysical conception of natural law as supreme over positive law and gave a new version of the old idea that natural law is the counterpart of
25   reason, being disclosed by the natural light with which man is endowed.

The whole temper of this philosophy is individualistic in the sense in which individualism is opposed to organized social action. It held to the primacy of the individual over the state not only in time but in moral authority. It defined the individual in terms of liberties of thought and action already possessed by
30   him in some mysterious ready-made fashion, and which it was the sole business of the state to safeguard. Reason was also made an inherent endowment of the individual, expressed in men's moral relations to one another, but not sustained and developed because of these relations. It followed that the great enemy of individual liberty was thought to be government because of its tendency to
35   encroach upon the innate liberties of individuals. Later liberalism inherited this conception of a natural antagonism between ruler and ruled, interpreted as a natural opposition between the individual and organized society. There still lingers in the minds of some the notion that there are two different "spheres" of action and of rightful claims; that of political society and that of the individual,

and that in the interest of the latter the former must be as contracted as possible. Not till the second half of the nineteenth century did the idea arise that government might and should be an instrument for securing and extending the liberties of individuals. This later aspect of liberalism is perhaps foreshadowed in the clauses of our Constitution that confer upon Congress power to provide   5
for "public welfare" as well as for public safety.

What has already been said indicates that with Locke the inclusion of the economic factor, property, among natural rights had a political animus. However, Locke at times goes so far as to designate as property everything that is included in "life, liberties and estates"; the individual has property in himself and in his   10
life and activities; property in this broad sense is that which political society should protect. The importance attached to the right of property within the political area was without doubt an influence in the later definitely economic formulation of liberalism. But Locke was interested in property already possessed. A century later industry and commerce were sufficiently advanced in   15
Great Britain so that interest centered in *production* of wealth, rather than in its possession. The conception of labor as the source of right in property was employed not so much to protect property from confiscation by the ruler (that right was practically secure in England) as to urge and justify freedom in the use and investment of capital and the right of laborers to move about and seek   20
new modes of employment—claims denied by the common law that came down from semi-feudal conditions. The earlier economic conception may fairly be called static; it was concerned with possessions and estates. The newer economic conception was dynamic. It was concerned with release of productivity and exchange from a cumbrous complex of restrictions that had the force of   25
law. The enemy was no longer the arbitrary special action of rulers. It was the whole system of common law and judicial practice in its adverse bearing upon freedom of labor, investment and exchange.

The transformation of earlier liberalism that took place because of this new interest is so tremendous that its story must be told in some detail. The concern   30
for liberty and for the individual, which was the basis of Lockeian liberalism, persisted; otherwise the newer theory would not have been liberalism. But liberty was given a very different practical meaning. In the end, the effect was to subordinate political to economic activity; to connect natural laws with the laws of production and exchange, and to give a radically new significance   35
to the earlier conception of reason. The name of Adam Smith is indissolubly connected with initiation of this transformation. Although he was far from being an unqualified adherent of the idea of *laissez faire*, he held that the activity of individuals, freed as far as possible from political restriction, is the

chief source of social welfare and the ultimate spring of social progress. He held that there is a "natural" or native tendency in every individual to better each his own estate through putting forth effort (labor) to satisfy his natural wants. Social welfare is promoted because the cumulative, but undesigned and 5   unplanned, effect of the convergence of a multitude of individual efforts is to increase the commodities and services put at the disposal of men collectively, of society. This increase of goods and services creates new wants and leads to putting forth new modes of productive energy. There is not only a native impulse to exchange, to "truck," but individuals are released by the processes of 10 exchange from the necessity for labor in order to satisfy all of the individual's own wants; through division of labor, productivity is enormously increased. Free economic processes thus bring about an endless spiral of ever increasing change, and through the guidance of an "invisible hand" (the equivalent of the doctrine of preestablished harmony so dear to the eighteenth century) the 15 efforts of individuals for personal advancement and personal gain accrue to the benefit of society, and create a continuously closer knit interdependence of interests.

The ideas and ideals of the new political economy were congruous with the increase of industrial activity that was marked in England even before the in- 20 vention of the steam engine. They spread rapidly. Their power was furthered when the great industrial and commercial expansion of England ensued in the wake of the substitution of mechanical for human energy, first in textiles and then in other occupations. Under the influence of the industrial revolution the old argument against political action as a social agency assumed a new form. 25 Such action was not only an invasion of individual liberty but it was in effect a conspiracy against the causes that bring about social progress. The Lockeian idea of natural laws took on a much more concrete, a more directly practical, meaning. Natural law was still regarded as something more fundamental than man-made law, which by comparison is artificial. But natural laws lost their 30 remote moral meaning. They were identified with the laws of free industrial production and free commercial exchange....

Economists developed the principle of the free economic activity of individuals; since this freedom was identified with absence of governmental action, conceived as an interference with natural liberty, the result was the formulation of *laissez* 35 *faire* liberalism. Bentham carried the same conception, though from a differ- ent point of view, into a vigorous movement for reform of the common law and judicial procedure by means of legislative action. The Mills developed the psychological and logical foundation implicit in the theories of the economists and of Bentham....

According to Bentham, the criterion of all law and of every administrative effort is its effect upon the sum of happiness enjoyed by the greatest possible number. In calculating this sum, every individual is to count as one and only as one. The mere formulation of the doctrine was an attack upon every inequality of status that had the sanction of law. In effect, it made the well-being of the individual the norm of political action in every area in which it operates. In effect, though not wholly in Bentham's express apprehension, it transferred attention from the well-being already possessed by individuals to one they might attain if there were a radical change in social institutions. For existing institutions enabled a small number of individuals to enjoy their pleasures at the cost of the misery of a much greater number. While Bentham himself conceived that the changes to be made in legal and political institutions were mainly negative, such as abolition of abuses, corruptions and inequalities, nevertheless (as we shall see later) there was nothing in his fundamental doctrine that stood in the way of using the power of government to create, constructively and positively, new institutions if and when it should appear that the latter would contribute more effectively to the well-being of individuals....

Bentham's theory led him to the view that all organized action is to be judged by its consequences, consequences that take effect in the lives of individuals. His psychology was rather rudimentary. It made him conceive of consequences as being atomic units of pleasures and pains that can be algebraically summed up. It is to this aspect of his doctrines that later writers, especially moralists, have chiefly devoted their critical attention. But this particular aspect of his theory, if we view it in the perspective of history, is an adventitious accretion. His enduring idea is that customs, institutions, law, social arrangements are to be judged on the basis of their consequences as these come home to the individuals that compose society. Because of his emphasis upon consequences, he made short work of the tenets of both of the two schools that had dominated, before his day, English political thought. He brushed aside, almost contemptuously, the conservative school that found the source of social wisdom in the customs and precedents of the past. This school has its counterpart in those empiricists of the present day who attack every measure and policy that is new and innovating on the ground that it does not have the sanction of experience, when what they really mean by "experience" is patterns of mind that were formed in a past that no longer exists.

But Bentham was equally aggressive in assault upon that aspect of earlier liberalism which was based upon the conception of inherent natural rights—following in this respect a clue given by David Hume. Natural rights and natural liberties exist only in the kingdom of mythological social zoology. Men do not obey laws

because they think these laws are in accord with a scheme of natural rights. They obey because they believe, rightly or wrongly, that the consequences of obeying are upon the whole better than the consequences of disobeying. If the consequences of existing rule become too intolerable, they revolt. An enlightened
5   self-interest will induce a ruler not to push too far the patience of subjects. The enlightened self-interest of citizens will lead them to obtain by peaceful means, as far as possible, the changes that will effect a distribution of political power and the publicity that will lead political authorities to work for rather than against the interests of the people—a situation which Bentham thought was realized
10 by government that is representative and based upon popular suffrage. But in any case, not natural rights but consequences in the lives of individuals are the criterion and measure of policy and judgment.

Because the liberalism of the economists and the Benthamites was adapted to contemporary conditions in Great Britain, the influence of the liberalism of the
15 school of Locke waned. By 1820 it was practically extinct. Its influence lasted much longer in the United States. We had no Bentham and it is doubtful whether he would have had much influence if he had appeared. Except for movements in codification of law, it is hard to find traces of the influence of Bentham in this country. As was intimated earlier, the philosophy of Locke bore much the
20 same relation to the American revolt of the colonies that it had to the British revolution of almost a century earlier. Up to, say, the time of the Civil War, the United States were predominantly agrarian. As they became industrialized, the philosophy of liberty of individuals, expressed especially in freedom of contract, provided the doctrine needed by those who controlled the economic system.
25 It was freely employed by the courts in declaring unconstitutional legislation that limited this freedom. The ideas of Locke embodied in the Declaration of Independence were congenial to our pioneer conditions that gave individuals the opportunity to carve their own careers. Political action was lightly thought of by those who lived in frontier conditions. A political career was very largely
30 annexed as an adjunct to the action of individuals in carving their own careers. The gospel of self-help and private initiative was practiced so spontaneously that it needed no special intellectual support....

Thus from various sources and under various influences there developed an inner split in liberalism. This cleft is one cause of the ambiguity from which
35 liberalism still suffers and which explains a growing impotency. These are still those who call themselves liberals who define liberalism in terms of the old opposition between the province of organized social action and the province of purely individual initiative and effort. In the name of liberalism they are jealous of every extension of governmental activity. They may grudgingly concede

the need of special measures of protection and alleviation undertaken by the state at times of great social stress, but they are the confirmed enemies of social legislation (even prohibition of child labor), as standing measures of political policy. Wittingly or unwittingly, they still provide the intellectual system of apologetics for the existing economic régime, which they strangely, it would seem ironically, uphold as a régime of individual liberty for all.

But the majority who call themselves liberals today are committed to the principle that organized society must use its powers to establish the conditions under which the mass of individuals can possess actual as distinct from merely legal liberty. They define their liberalism in the concrete in terms of a program of measures moving toward this end. They believe that the conception of the state which limits the activities of the latter to keeping order as between individuals and to securing redress for one person when another person infringes the liberty existing law has given him, is in effect simply a justification of the brutalities and inequities of the existing order. Because of this internal division within liberalism its later history is wavering and confused. The inheritance of the past still causes many liberals, who believe in a generous use of the powers of organized society to change the terms on which human beings associate together, to stop short with merely protective and alleviatory measures—a fact that partly explains why another school always refers to "reform" with scorn. It will be the object of the next chapter to portray the crisis in liberalism, the *impasse* in which it now almost finds itself, and through criticism of the deficiencies of earlier liberalism to suggest the way in which liberalism may resolve the crisis, and emerge as a compact, aggressive force.

2. The Crisis in Liberalism

The net effect of the struggle of early liberals to emancipate individuals from restriction imposed upon them by the inherited type of social organization was to pose a problem, that of a new social organization. The ideas of liberals set forth in the first third of the nineteenth century were potent in criticism and in analysis. They released forces that had been held in check. But analysis is not construction, and release of force does not of itself give direction to the force that is set free. Victorian optimism concealed for a time the crisis at which liberalism had arrived. But when that optimism vanished amid the conflict of nations, classes and races characteristic of the latter part of the nineteenth century—a conflict that has grown more intense with the passing years—the crisis could no longer be covered up. The beliefs and methods of earlier liberalism were ineffective when faced with the problems of social organization and integration. Their inadequacy is a large part of belief now so current that all liberalism is an outmoded doctrine. At the same time, insecurity and uncertainty in belief and purpose are powerful factors in generating dogmatic faiths that are profoundly hostile to everything to which liberalism in any possible formulation is devoted….

The earlier liberals lacked historic sense and interest. For a while this lack had an
5   immediate pragmatic value. It gave liberals a powerful weapon in their fight with reactionaries. For it enabled them to undercut the appeal to origin, precedent and past history by which the opponents of social change gave sacrosanct quality to existing inequities and abuses. But disregard of history took its revenge. It blinded the eyes of liberals to the fact that their own special interpretations
10   of liberty, individuality and intelligence were themselves historically conditioned, and were relevant only to their own time. They put forward their ideas as immutable truths good at all times and places; they had no idea of historic relativity, either in general or in its application to themselves.

When their ideas and plans were projected they were an attack upon the interests
15   that were vested in established institutions and that had the sanction of custom. The new forces for which liberals sought an entrance were incipient; the *status quo* was arrayed against their release. By the middle of the nineteenth century the contemporary scene had radically altered. The economic and political changes for which they strove were so largely accomplished that they had become in
20   turn the vested interest, and their doctrines, especially in the form of *laissez faire* liberalism, now provided the intellectual justification of the *status quo*. This creed is still powerful in this country. The earlier doctrine of "natural rights," superior to legislative action, has been given a definitely economic meaning by the courts, and used by judges to destroy social legislation passed in the inter-
25   est of a real, instead of purely formal, liberty of contract. Under the caption of "rugged individualism" it inveighs against all new social policies. Beneficiaries of the established economic régime band themselves together in what they call Liberty Leagues to perpetuate the harsh regimentation of millions of their fellows. I do not imply that resistance to change would not have appeared if
30   it had not been for the doctrines of earlier liberals. But had the early liberals appreciated the historic relativity of their own interpretation of the meaning of liberty, the later resistance would certainly have been deprived of its chief intellectual and moral support. The tragedy is that although these liberals were the sworn foes of political absolutism, they were themselves absolutists in the
35   social creed they formulated.

This statement does not mean, of course, that they were opposed to social change; the opposite is evidently the case. But it does mean they held that beneficial social change can come about in but one way, the way of private economic enterprise, socially undirected, based upon and resulting in the sanctity of private property—that is to say, freedom from social control. So today those who profess the earlier type of liberalism ascribe to this one factor all social betterment that has occurred; such as the increase in productivity and improved standards of living. The liberals did not try to prevent change, but they did try to limit its course to a single channel and to immobilize the channel.

If the early liberals had put forth their special interpretation of liberty as something subject to historic relativity they would not have frozen it into a doctrine to be applied at all times under all social circumstances. Specifically, they would have recognized that effective liberty is a function of the social conditions existing at any time. If they had done this, they would have known that as economic relations became dominantly controlling forces in setting the pattern of human relations, the necessity of liberty for individuals which they proclaimed will require social control of economic forces in the interest of the great mass of individuals. Because the liberals failed to make a distinction between purely formal or legal liberty and effective liberty of thought and action, the history of the last one hundred years is the history of non-fulfillment of their predictions….

The crisis in liberalism, as I said at the outset, proceeds from the fact that after early liberalism had done its work, society faced a new problem, that of social organization. Its work was to liberate a group of individuals, representing the new science and the new forces of productivity, from customs, ways of thinking, institutions, that were oppressive of the new modes of social action, however useful they may have been in their day. The instruments of analysis, of criticism, of dissolution, that were employed were effective for the work of release. But when it came to the problem of organizing the new forces and the individuals whose modes of life they radically altered into a coherent social organization, possessed of intellectual and moral directive power, liberalism was well-nigh impotent. The rise of national polities that pretend to represent the order, discipline and spiritual authority that will counteract social disintegration is a tragic comment upon the unpreparedness of older liberalism to deal with the new problem which its very success precipitated.

But the values of freed intelligence, of liberty, of opportunity for every individual to realize the potentialities of which he is possessed, are too precious to be sacrificed to a régime of despotism, especially when the régime is in such large measure merely the agent of a dominant economic class in its struggle to keep and extend the gains it has amassed at the expense of genuine social order, unity, and development. Liberalism has to gather itself together to formulate the ends to which it is devoted in terms of means that are relevant to the contemporary situation. The only form of enduring social organization that is now possible is

one in which the new forces of productivity are cooperatively controlled and used in the interest of the effective liberty and the cultural development of the individuals that constitute society. Such a social order cannot be established by an unplanned and external convergence of the actions of separate individuals,
5   each of whom is bent on personal private advantage. This idea is the Achilles heel of early liberalism. The idea that liberalism cannot maintain its ends and at the same time reverse its conception of the means by which they are to be attained is folly. The ends can now be achieved *only* by reversal of the means to which early liberalism was committed. Organized social planning, put into
10   effect for the creation of an order in which industry and finance are socially directed in behalf of institutions that provide the material basis for the cultural liberation and growth of individuals, is now the sole method of social action by which liberalism can realize its professed aims. Such planning demands in turn a new conception and logic of freed intelligence as a social force....

The American Conception of Liberty
Frank Goodnow (1859–1939)

Progressive political science was based on the assumption that society could be organized in such a way that social ills would disappear. Frank Goodnow, president of Johns Hopkins University and the first president of the American Political Science Association, helped pioneer the idea that separating politics from administration was the key to progress. In this speech, given at Brown University, he addresses the need to move beyond the ideas of the Founders.

1916

The end of the eighteenth century was marked by the formulation and general acceptance by thinking men in Europe of a political philosophy which laid great emphasis on individual private rights. Man was by this philosophy conceived of as endowed at the time of his birth with certain inalienable rights. Thus, Rousseau in his "Social Contract" treated man as primarily an individual and only   5
secondarily as a member of human society. Society itself was regarded as based upon a contract made between the individuals by whose union it was formed. At the time of making this contract these individuals were deemed to have reserved certain rights spoken of as "natural" rights. These rights could neither be taken away nor be limited without the consent of the individual affected.   10

Such a theory, of course, had no historical justification. There was no record of the making of any such contract as was postulated. It was impossible to assert, as a matter of fact even, that man existed first as an individual and that later he became, as the result of any act of volition on his part, a member of human society. But at a time when truth was sought usually through speculation   15
rather than observation, the absence of proof of the facts which lay at the basis of the theory did not seriously trouble those by whom it was formulated or accepted.

Frank Goodnow, *The American Conception of Liberty* (Providence, RI: Standard Printing Company, 1916), 9–13, 19–21, 29–31.

While there was no justification in fact for this social contract theory and this doctrine of natural rights, their acceptance by thinking men did nevertheless have an important influence upon the development of thought and in that way upon the actual conditions of human life. For these theories were not

5   only a philosophical explanation of the organization of society; they were at the same time the result of the then existing social conditions, and like most such theories were also an attempt to justify a course of conduct which was believed to be expedient.

At the end of the eighteenth century a great change was beginning in West-

10   ern Europe. The enlargement of the field of commercial transactions, due to the discovery and colonization of America and to the contact of Europe with Asia, particularly with India, had opened new spheres of activity to those minded for adventure. The invention of the steam engine and its application to manufacturing were rapidly changing industrial conditions. The fac-

15   tory system was in process of establishment and had already begun to displace domestic industry.

The new possibilities of reward for individual endeavor made men impatient of the restrictions on private initiative incident to an industrial and commercial system which was fast passing away. They therefore welcomed with eagerness

20   a political philosophy which, owing to the emphasis it placed upon private rights, would if acted upon have the effect of freeing them from what they regarded as hampering limitations on individual initiative.

This political philosophy was incorporated into the celebrated Declaration of the Rights of Man and of the Citizen promulgated in France on the eve of the

25   Revolution. A perusal of this remarkable document reveals the fact, however, that the reformers of France had not altogether emancipated themselves from the influences of their historical development. For almost every clause of the Declaration refers to rights under the law rather than to rights which were natural to and inherent in man.

30   The subsequent development in Europe of this private rights philosophy is along the lines thus marked out by the Declaration. The rights which men have been recognized as possessing have not been considered to be inherent rights, attaching to man at the time of his birth, so much as rights which find their origin in the law as adopted by that organ of government regarded as

35   representative of the society of which the individual man is a member.

In a word, man is regarded now throughout Europe, contrary to the view expressed by Rousseau, as primarily a member of society and secondarily as an individual. The rights which he possesses are, it is believed, conferred upon him, not by his Creator, but rather by the society to which he belongs. What they are is to be determined by the legislative authority in view of the needs of that society. Social expediency, rather than natural right, is thus to determine the sphere of individual freedom of action.

The development of this private rights philosophy has been, however, somewhat different in the United States. The philosophy of Rousseau was accepted in this country probably with even greater enthusiasm than was the case in Europe. The social and economic conditions of the Western World were, in the first place, more favorable than in Europe for its acceptance. There was at the time no well-developed social organization in this country. America was the land of the pioneer, who had to rely for most of his success upon his strong right arm. Such communities as did exist were loosely organized and separated one from another. Roads worthy of the name hardly existed and communication was possible only by rivers which were imperfectly navigable or over a sea which, when account is taken of the vessels then in use, was tempestuous in character.

Furthermore, the religious and moral influences in this country, which owed much to the Protestant Reformation, all favored the development of an extreme individualism. They emphasized personal responsibility and the salvation of the individual soul. It was the fate of the individual rather than that of the social group which appealed to the preacher or aroused the anxiety of the theologian. It was individual rather than social morality which was emphasized by the ethical teacher and received attention in moral codes. Everything, in a word, favored the acceptance of the theory of individual natural rights.

The result was the adoption in this country of a doctrine of unadulterated individualism. Every one had rights. Social duties were hardly recognized, or if recognized little emphasis was laid upon them. It was apparently thought that every one was able and willing to protect his rights, and that as a result of the struggle between men for their rights and of the compromise of what appeared to be conflicting rights would arise an effective social organization.

The rights with which it was believed that man was endowed by his Creator were, as was the case in France, set forth in bills of rights which formed an important part of American constitutions. The form in which they were stated in American bills of rights was subject to fewer qualifications than was the case in France. Their origin was found in nature rather than in the law. The development of these rights, further, has been quite different from the European development which has been noted. American courts, early in the history of the country, claimed and secured the general recognition of a power to declare unconstitutional and therefore void acts of legislation which, in their opinion, were not in conformity with these bills of rights. In their determination of these questions, American courts appear to have been largely influenced by the private rights conception of the prevalent political philosophy. The result has been that the private individual rights of American citizens have come to be formulated and defined, not by representative legislative bodies, as is now the rule in Europe, but by courts which have in the past been much under the influence of the political philosophy of the eighteenth century....

This general attitude towards private rights is, it seems to me, at the present time in process of modification. Whatever may have been formerly the advantages attaching to a private rights political philosophy—and that they were many I should be the last person to deny—this question of private rights has been reexamined with the idea of ascertaining whether, under the conditions of modern life, our traditional political philosophy should be retained.

The political philosophy of the eighteenth century was formulated before the announcement and acceptance of the theory of evolutionary development. The natural rights doctrine presupposed almost that society was static or stationary rather than dynamic or progressive in character. It was generally believed at the end of the eighteenth century that there was a social state which under all conditions and at all times would be absolutely ideal. The rights which man had were believed to come from his Creator. These rights consequently were the same then as they once had been and would always remain the same. Natural rights were in theory thus permanent and immutable. Natural rights being conceived of as eternal and immutable, the theory of natural rights did not permit of their amendment in view of a change in conditions.

The actual rights which at the close of the eighteenth century were recognized were, however, as a matter of fact influenced in large measure by the social and economic conditions of the time when the recognition was made. Those conditions have certainly been subjected to great modifications. The pioneer can no longer rely upon himself alone. Indeed with the increase of population and the conquest of the wilderness the pioneer has almost disappeared. The improvement in the means of communication, which has been one of the most marked changes that have occurred, has placed in close contact and relationship once separated and unrelated communities. The canal and the railway, the steamship and the locomotive, the telegraph and the telephone, we might add the motor car and the aeroplane, have all contributed to the formation of a social organization such as our forefathers never saw in their wildest dreams. The accumulation of capital, the concentration of industry with the accompanying increase in the size of the industrial unit and the loss of personal relations between employer and employed, have all brought about a constitution of society very different from that which was to be found a century and a quarter ago. Changed conditions, it has been thought, must bring in their train different conceptions of private rights if society is to be advantageously carried on. In other words, while insistence on individual rights may have been of great advantage at a time when the social organization was not highly developed, it may become a menace when social rather than individual efficiency is the necessary prerequisite of progress. For social efficiency probably owes more to the common realization of social duties than to the general insistence on privileges based on individual private rights. As our conditions have changed, as the importance of the social group has been realized, as it has been perceived that social efficiency must be secured if we are to attain and retain our place in the field of national competition which is practically coterminous with the world, the attitude of our courts on the one hand towards private rights and on the other hand towards social duties has gradually been changing. The general theory remains the same. Man is still said to be possessed of inherent natural rights of which he may not be deprived without his consent. The courts still now and then hold unconstitutional acts of legislature which appear to encroach upon those rights. At the same time the sphere of governmental action is continually widening and the actual content of individual private rights is being increasingly narrowed....

We no longer believe as we once believed that a good social organization can be secured merely through stressing our rights. The emphasis is being laid more and more on social duties. The efficiency of the social group is taking on in our eyes a greater importance that it once had. We are not, it is true, taking the view that the individual man lives for the state of which he is a member and that state efficiency is in some mysterious way an admirable end in and of itself.

But we have come to the conclusion that man under modern conditions is primarily a member of society and that only as he recognizes his duties as a member of society can he secure the greatest opportunities as an individual. While we do not regard society as an end in itself we do consider it as one of the most important means through which man may come into his own.

You are probably asking yourselves: What is the purpose of saying these things in this place? What connection have they with a great educational institution? My answer to these questions is this. Those who are in charge of such an institution are under a very solemn obligation. They are in some measure at any rate responsible for the beliefs of the coming generation of thinkers and of molders of public opinion. We teachers perhaps take ourselves too seriously at times. That I am willing to admit. We may not have nearly the influence which we think we have. Changes in economic conditions for which we are in no way responsible bring in their train regardless of what we teach changes in beliefs and opinions. But if we are unable to exercise great influence in the institution of positive changes, we can by acquainting ourselves with the changes in conditions and by endeavoring to accommodate our teaching to those changes, certainly refrain from impeding progress. This may be an over-modest estimate of the function of a teacher. At the same time it is an ideal the realization of which is not to be despised. For many universities have in the past been the homes of conservatism. New ideas have often knocked for a long time on the gates of learning before they have been permitted to enter. Even after they have passed the portal they are sometimes the object of a suspicion which it has taken years to allay.

So I repeat we teachers are in a measure responsible for the thoughts of the coming generation. This being the case, if under the conditions of modern life it is the social group rather than the individual which is increasing in importance, if it is true that greater emphasis should be laid on social duties and less on individual rights, it is the duty of the University to call the attention of the student to this fact and it is the duty of the student when he goes out into the world to do what in him lies to bring this truth home to his fellows.

WHAT IS PROGRESS?
WOODROW WILSON (1856–1924)

After earning a Ph.D. in both history and political science at Johns Hopkins University, Woodrow Wilson held various academic positions, culminating in the presidency of Princeton University. Throughout this period, he came to see the Constitution as a cumbersome instrument unfit for the government of a large and vibrant nation. This speech, delivered during his successful campaign for president in 1912 and included in a collection of speeches called The New Freedom, *puts forward the idea of an evolving or "living" constitution.*

1913

In that sage and veracious chronicle, "Alice Through the Looking-Glass," it is recounted how, on a noteworthy occasion, the little heroine is seized by the Red Chess Queen, who races her off at a terrific pace. They run until both of them are out of breath; then they stop, and Alice looks around her and says, "Why, we are just where we were when we started!" "Oh, yes," says the Red Queen; 5 "you have to run twice as fast as that to get anywhere else."

That is a parable of progress. The laws of this country have not kept up with the change of economic circumstances in this country; they have not kept up with the change of political circumstances; and therefore we are not even where we were when we started. We shall have to run, not until we are out of breath, but 10 until we have caught up with our own conditions, before we shall be where we were when we started; when we started this great experiment which has been the hope and the beacon of the world. And we should have to run twice as fast as any rational program I have seen in order to get anywhere else.

I am, therefore, forced to be a progressive, if for no other reason, because we 15 have not kept up with our changes of conditions, either in the economic field or in the political field. We have not kept up as well as other nations have. We

Woodrow Wilson, "What is Progress?" in *The New Freedom* (New York: Doubleday, Page, and Company, 1913), 33–54.

635

have not kept our practices adjusted to the facts of the case, and until we do, and unless we do, the facts of the case will always have the better of the argument; because if you do not adjust your laws to the facts, so much the worse for the laws, not for the facts, because law trails along after the facts. Only that law is

5 unsafe which runs ahead of the facts and beckons to it and makes it follow the will-o'-the-wisps of imaginative projects.

Business is in a situation in America which it was never in before; it is in a situation to which we have not adjusted our laws. Our laws are still meant for business done by individuals; they have not been satisfactorily adjusted to busi-

10 ness done by great combinations, and we have got to adjust them. I do not say we may or may not; I say we must; there is no choice. If your laws do not fit your facts, the facts are not injured, the law is damaged; because the law, unless I have studied it amiss, is the expression of the facts in legal relationships. Laws have never altered the facts; laws have always necessarily expressed the facts;

15 adjusted interests as they have arisen and have changed toward one another.

Politics in America is in a case which sadly requires attention. The system set up by our law and our usage doesn't work,—or at least it can't be depended on; it is made to work only by a most unreasonable expenditure of labor and pains. The government, which was designed for the people, has got into the hands of

20 bosses and their employers, the special interests. An invisible empire has been set up above the forms of democracy.

There are serious things to do. Does any man doubt the great discontent in this country? Does any man doubt that there are grounds and justifications for discontent? Do we dare stand still? Within the past few months we have

25 witnessed (along with other strange political phenomena, eloquently signifi-cant of popular uneasiness) on one side a doubling of the Socialist vote and on the other the posting on dead walls and hoardings all over the country of certain very attractive and diverting bills warning citizens that it was "better to be safe than sorry" and advising them to "let well enough alone." Apparently

30 a good many citizens doubted whether the situation they were advised to let alone was really well enough, and concluded that they would take a chance of being sorry. To me, these counsels of do-nothingism, these counsels of sitting still for fear something would happen, these counsels addressed to the hope-ful, energetic people of the United States, telling them that they are not wise

35 enough to touch their own affairs without marring them, constitute the most extraordinary argument of fatuous ignorance I ever heard. Americans are not yet cowards. True, their self-reliance has been sapped by years of submission to the doctrine that prosperity is something that benevolent magnates provide for them with the aid of the government; their self-reliance has been weakened,

but not so utterly destroyed that you can twit them about it. The American people are not naturally stand-patters. Progress is the word that charms their ears and stirs their hearts.

There are, of course, Americans who have not yet heard that anything is going on. The circus might come to town, have the big parade and go, without their catching a sight of the camels or a note of the calliope. There are people, even Americans, who never move themselves or know that anything else is moving.

A friend of mine who had heard of the Florida "cracker," as they call a certain ne'er-do-well portion of the population down there, when passing through the State in a train, asked some one to point out a "cracker" to him. The man asked replied, "Well, if you see something off in the woods that looks brown, like a stump, you will know it is either a stump or a cracker; if it moves, it is a stump."

Now, movement has no virtue in itself. Change is not worth while for its own sake. I am not one of those who love variety for its own sake. If a thing is good today, I should like to have it stay that way tomorrow. Most of our calculations in life are dependent upon things staying the way they are. For example, if, when you got up this morning, you had forgotten how to dress, if you had forgotten all about those ordinary things which you do almost automatically, which you can almost do half awake, you would have to find out what you did yesterday. I am told by the psychologists that if I did not remember who I was yesterday, I should not know who I am today, and that, therefore, my very identity depends upon my being able to tally today with yesterday. If they do not tally, then I am confused; I do not know who I am, and I have to go around and ask somebody to tell me my name and where I came from.

I am not one of those who wish to break connection with the past; I am not one of those who wish to change for the mere sake of variety. The only men who do that are the men who want to forget something, the men who filled yesterday with something they would rather not recollect today, and so go about seeking diversion, seeking abstraction in something that will blot out recollection, or seeking to put something into them which will blot out all recollection. Change is not worth while unless it is improvement. If I move out of my present house because I do not like it, then I have got to choose a better house, or build a better house, to justify the change.

It would seem a waste of time to point out that ancient distinction,—between mere change and improvement. Yet there is a class of mind that is prone to confuse them. We have had political leaders whose conception of greatness was

to be forever frantically doing something,—it mattered little what; restless, vociferous men, without sense of the energy of concentration, knowing only the energy of succession. Now, life does not consist of eternally running to a fire. There is no virtue in going anywhere unless you will gain something by being
5 there. The direction is just as important as the impetus of motion.

All progress depends on how fast you are going, and where you are going, and I fear there has been too much of this thing of knowing neither how fast we were going or where we were going. I have my private belief that we have been doing most of our progressiveness after the fashion of those things that in my
10 boyhood days we called "treadmills,"—a treadmill being a moving platform, with cleats on it, on which some poor devil of a mule was forced to walk forever without getting anywhere. Elephants and even other animals have been known to turn treadmills, making a good deal of noise, and causing certain wheels to go round, and I daresay grinding out some sort of product for somebody, but
15 without achieving much progress. Lately, in an effort to persuade the elephant to move, really, his friends tried dynamite. It moved,—in separate and scattered parts, but it moved.

A cynical but witty Englishman said, in a book, not long ago, that it was a mistake to say of a conspicuously successful man, eminent in his line of business,
20 that you could not bribe a man like that, because, he said, the point about such men is that they have been bribed—not in the ordinary meaning of that word, not in any gross, corrupt sense, but they have achieved their great success by means of the existing order of things and therefore they have been put under bonds to see that that existing order of things is not changed; they are bribed
25 to maintain the *status quo*.

It was for that reason that I used to say, when I had to do with the administration of an educational institution, that I should like to make the young gentlemen of the rising generation as unlike their fathers as possible. Not because their fathers lacked character or intelligence or knowledge or patriotism, but because
30 their fathers, by reason of their advancing years and their established position in society, had lost touch with the processes of life; they had forgotten what it was to begin; they had forgotten what it was to rise; they had forgotten what it was to be dominated by the circumstances of their life on their way up from the bottom to the top, and, therefore, they were out of sympathy with the creative,
35 formative and progressive forces of society.

Progress! Did you ever reflect that that word is almost a new one? No word comes more often or more naturally to the lips of modern man, as if the thing it stands for were almost synonymous with life itself, and yet men through many thousand years never talked or thought of progress. They thought in the other direction. Their stories of heroisms and glory were tales of the past. The ancestor wore the heavier armor and carried the larger spear. "There were giants in those days." Now all that has altered. We think of the future, not the past, as the more glorious time in comparison with which the present is nothing. Progress, development,—those are modern words. The modern idea is to leave the past and press onward to something new.

But what is progress going to do with the past, and with the present? How is it going to treat them? With ignominy, or respect? Should it break with them altogether, or rise out of them, with its roots still deep in the older time? What attitude shall progressives take toward the existing order, toward those institutions of conservatism, the Constitution, the laws, and the courts?

Are those thoughtful men who fear that we are now about to disturb the ancient foundations of our institutions justified in their fear? If they are, we ought to go very slowly about the processes of change. If it is indeed true that we have grown tired of the institutions which we have so carefully and sedulously built up, then we ought to go very slowly and very carefully about the very dangerous task of altering them. We ought, therefore, to ask ourselves, first of all, whether thought in this country is tending to do anything by which we shall retrace our steps, or by which we shall change the whole direction of our development?

I believe, for one, that you cannot tear up ancient rootages and safely plant the tree of liberty in soil which is not native to it. I believe that the ancient traditions of a people are its ballast; you cannot make a *tabula rasa* upon which to write a political program. You cannot take a new sheet of paper and determine what your life shall be tomorrow. You must knit the new into the old. You cannot put a new patch on an old garment without ruining it; it must be not a patch, but something woven into the old fabric, of practically the same pattern, of the same texture and intention. If I did not believe that to be progressive was to preserve the essentials of our institutions, I for one could not be a progressive.

One of the chief benefits I used to derive from being president of a university was that I had the pleasure of entertaining thoughtful men from all over the world. I cannot tell you how much has dropped into my granary by their presence. I had been casting around in my mind for something by which to draw several parts of my political thought together when it was my good fortune to entertain a very interesting Scotsman who had been devoting himself to the philosophical thought of the seventeenth century. His talk was so engaging that it was delightful to hear him speak of anything, and presently there came out of the unexpected region of his thought the thing I had been waiting for. He

called my attention to the fact that in every generation all sorts of speculation and thinking tend to fall under the formula of the dominant thought of the age. For example, after the Newtonian Theory of the universe had been developed, almost all thinking tended to express itself in the analogies of the Newtonian
5 Theory, and since the Darwinian Theory has reigned amongst us, everybody is likely to express whatever he wishes to expound in terms of development and accommodation to environment.

Now, it came to me, as this interesting man talked, that the Constitution of the United States had been made under the dominion of the Newtonian Theory. You
10 have only to read the papers of *The Federalist* to see that fact written on every page. They speak of the "checks and balances" of the Constitution, and use to express their idea the simile of the organization of the universe, and particularly of the solar system,—how by the attraction of gravitation the various parts are held in their orbits; and then they proceed to represent Congress, the Judiciary,
15 and the President as a sort of imitation of the solar system.

They were only following the English Whigs, who gave Great Britain its modern constitution. Not that those Englishmen analyzed the matter, or had any theory about it; Englishmen care little for theories. It was a Frenchman, Montesquieu, who pointed out to them how faithfully they had copied Newton's description
20 of the mechanism of the heavens.

The makers of our Federal Constitution read Montesquieu with true scientific enthusiasm. They were scientists in their way,—the best way of their age,—those fathers of the nation. Jefferson wrote of "the laws of Nature,"—and then by way of afterthought,—"and of Nature's God." And they constructed a government as
25 they would have constructed an orrery,—to display the laws of nature. Politics in their thought was a variety of mechanics. The Constitution was founded on the law of gravitation. The government was to exist and move by virtue of the efficacy of "checks and balances."

The trouble with the theory is that government is not a machine, but a living
30 thing. It falls, not under the theory of the universe, but under the theory of organic life. It is accountable to Darwin, not to Newton. It is modified by its environment, necessitated by its tasks, shaped to its functions by the sheer pressure of life. No living thing can have its organs offset against each other, as checks, and live. On the contrary, its life is dependent upon their quick co-
35 operation, their ready response to the commands of instinct or intelligence, their amicable community of purpose. Government is not a body of blind forces; it is a body of men, with highly differentiated functions, no doubt, in our modern day, of specialization, with a common task and purpose. Their cooperation

is indispensable, their warfare fatal. There can be no successful government without the intimate, instinctive coordination of the organs of life and action. This is not theory, but fact, and displays its force as fact, whatever theories may be thrown across its track. Living political constitutions must be Darwinian in structure and in practice. Society is a living organism and must obey the laws of life, not of mechanics; it must develop.

All that progressives ask or desire is permission—in an era when "development," "evolution," is the scientific word—to interpret the Constitution according to the Darwinian principle; all they ask is recognition of the fact that a nation is a living thing and not a machine.

Some citizens of this country have never got beyond the Declaration of Independence, signed in Philadelphia, July 4th, 1776. Their bosoms swell against George III, but they have no consciousness of the war for freedom that is going on today.

The Declaration of Independence did not mention the questions of our day. It is of no consequence to us unless we can translate its general terms into examples of the present day and substitute them in some vital way for the examples it itself gives, so concrete, so intimately involved in the circumstances of the day in which it was conceived and written. It is an eminently practical document, meant for the use of practical men; not a thesis for philosophers, but a whip for tyrants; not a theory of government, but a program of action. Unless we can translate it into the questions of our own day, we are not worthy of it, we are not the sons of the sires who acted in response to its challenge.

What form does the contest between tyranny and freedom take today? What is the special form of tyranny we now fight? How does it endanger the rights of the people, and what do we mean to do in order to make our contest against it effectual? What are to be the items of our new declaration of independence?

By tyranny, as we now fight it, we mean control of the law, of legislation and adjudication, by organizations which do not represent the people, by means which are private and selfish. We mean, specifically, the conduct of our affairs and the shaping of our legislation in the interest of special bodies of capital and those who organize their use. We mean the alliance, for this purpose, of political machines with selfish business. We mean the exploitation of the people by legal and political means. We have seen many of our governments under these influences cease to be representative governments, cease to be governments representative of the people, and become governments representative of special interests, controlled by machines, which in their turn are not controlled by the people.

Sometimes, when I think of the growth of our economic system, it seems to me as if, leaving our law just about where it was before any of the modern inventions or developments took place, we had simply at haphazard extended the family residence, added an office here and a workroom there, and a new set of sleeping rooms there, built up higher on our foundations, and put out little lean-tos on the side, until we have a structure that has no character whatever. Now, the problem is to continue to live in the house and yet change it.

Well, we are architects in our time, and our architects are also engineers. We don't have to stop using a railroad terminal because a new station is being built. We don't have to stop any of the processes of our lives because we are rearranging the structures in which we conduct those processes. What we have to undertake is to systematize the foundations of the house, then to thread all the old parts of the structure with the steel which will be laced together in modern fashion, accommodated to all the modern knowledge of structural strength and elasticity, and then slowly change the partitions, relay the walls, let in the light through new apertures, improve the ventilation; until finally, a generation or two from now, the scaffolding will be taken away, and there will be the family in a great building whose noble architecture will at last be disclosed, where men can live as a single community, cooperative as in a perfected, coordinated beehive, not afraid of any storm of nature, not afraid of any artificial storm, any imitation of thunder and lightning, knowing that the foundations go down to the bedrock of principle, and knowing that whenever they please they can change that plan again and accommodate it as they please to the altering necessities of their lives.

But there are a great many men who don't like the idea. Some wit recently said, in view of the fact that most of our American architects are trained in a certain *École* in Paris, that all American architecture in recent years was either bizarre or "Beaux Arts." I think that our economic architecture is decidedly bizarre; and I am afraid that there is a good deal to learn about matters other than architecture from the same source from which our architects have learned a great many things. I don't mean the School of Fine Arts at Paris, but the experience of France; for from the other side of the water men can now hold up against us the reproach that we have not adjusted our lives to modern conditions to the same extent that they have adjusted theirs. I was very much interested in some of the reasons given by our friends across the Canadian border for being very shy about the reciprocity arrangements. They said: "We are not sure whither these arrangements will lead, and we don't care to associate too closely with the economic conditions of the United States until those conditions are as modern as ours." And when I resented it, and asked for particulars, I had, in regard to many matters, to retire from the debate. Because I found that they had adjusted their regulations of economic development to conditions we had not yet found a way to meet in the United States.

Well, we have started now at all events. The procession is under way. The stand-patter doesn't know there is a procession. He is asleep in the back part of his house. He doesn't know that the road is resounding with the tramp of men going to the front. And when he wakes up, the country will be empty. He will be deserted, and he will wonder what has happened. Nothing has happened. The world has been going on. The world has a habit of going on. The world has a habit of leaving those behind who won't go with it. The world has always neglected stand-patters. And, therefore, the stand-patter does not excite my indignation; he excites my sympathy. He is going to be so lonely before it is all over. And we are good fellows, we are good company; why doesn't he come along? We are not going to do him any harm. We are going to show him a good time. We are going to climb the slow road until it reaches some upland where the air is fresher, where the whole talk of mere politicians is stilled, where men can look in each other's faces and see that there is nothing to conceal, that all they have to talk about they are willing to talk about in the open and talk about with each other; and whence, looking back over the road, we shall see at last that we have fulfilled our promise to mankind. We had said to all the world, "America was created to break every kind of monopoly, and to set men free, upon a footing of equality, upon a footing of opportunity, to match their brains and their energies." and now we have proved that we meant it.

Socialism and Democracy
Woodrow Wilson

Woodrow Wilson makes clear in this article the consequences of rejecting the idea of inherent natural rights for the idea that rights are a positive grant from government.

AUGUST 22, 1887

Is it possible that in practical America we are becoming sentimentalists? To judge by much of our periodical literature, one would think so. All resolution about great affairs seems now "sicklied o'er with a pale cast of thought." Our magazine writers smile sadly at the old-time optimism of their country; are themselves full of forebodings; expend much force and enthusiasm and strong 5 (as well as weak) English style in disclosing social evils and economics bugbears; are moved by a fine sympathy for the unfortunate and a fine anger against those who bring wrong upon their fellows: but where amidst all these themes for the conscience is there a theme for the courage of the reader? Where are the brave plans of reform which should follow such prologues? 10

No man with a heart can withhold sympathy from the laborer whose strength is wasted and whose hope is thwarted in the service of the heartless and close-fisted; but, then, no man with a head ought to speak that sympathy in the public prints unless he have some manly, thought-out ways of betterment to propose. One wearies easily, it must be confessed, of woeful-warnings; one 15 sighs often for a little tonic of actual thinking grounded in sane, clear-sighted perception of what is possible to be done. Sentiment is not despicable—it may be elevating and noble, it may be inspiring, and in some mental fields it is self-sufficing—but when uttered concerning great social and political questions it needs the addition of practical, initiative sense to keep it sweet and to prevent 20 its becoming insipid.

Woodrow Wilson, "Socialism and Democracy," August 22, 1887, in Arthur S. Link, ed., *The Papers of Woodrow Wilson*, Vol. 5 (Princeton, NJ: Princeton University Press, 1966–1993), 559–62.

I point these remarks particularly at current discussions of socialism, and principally of 'state socialism,' which is almost the only form of socialism seriously discussed among us, outside the Anti-Poverty Society. Is there not a plentiful lack of nerve and purpose in what we read and hear nowadays on this momen-
5   tous topic. One might be excused for taking and keeping the impression that there can be no great need for haste in the settlement of the questions mooted in connection with it, inasmuch as the debating of them has not yet passed beyond its rhetorical and pulpit stage. It is easy to make socialism, as theoretically developed by the greater and saner socialistic writers, intelligible not only,
10 but even attractive, as a conception; it is easy also to render it a thing of fear to timorous minds, and to make many signs of the times bear menace of it; the only hard task is to give it validity and strength as a program in practical politics. Yet the whole interest of socialism for those whose thinking extends beyond the covers of books and the paragraphs of periodicals lies in what it will
15 mean in practice. It is a question of practical politics, or else it is only a thesis for engaging discourse.

Even mere discoursers, one would think, would be attracted to treat of the practical means of realizing for society the principles of socialism, for much the most interesting and striking features of it emerge only when its actual
20 applications to concrete affairs are examined. These actual applications of it are the part of it which is much the most worth talking about,—even for those whose only object is to talk effectively.

Roundly described, socialism is a proposition that every community, by means of whatever forms of organization may be most effective for the purpose, see
25 to it for itself that each one of its members finds the employment for which he is best suited and is rewarded according to his diligence and merit, all proper surroundings of moral influence being secured to him by the public authority. 'State socialism' is willing to act through state authority as it is at present organized. It proposes that all idea of a limitation of public authority by individual
30 rights be put out of view, and that the State consider itself bound to stop only at what is unwise or futile in its universal superintendence alike of individual and of public interests. The thesis of the state socialist is, that no line can be drawn between private and public affairs which the State may not cross at will; that omnipotence of legislation is the first postulate of all just political theory.

35 Applied in a democratic state, such doctrine sounds radical, but not revolutionary. It is only a acceptance of the extremest logical conclusions deducible from democratic principles long ago received as respectable. For it is very clear that in fundamental theory socialism and democracy are almost if not quite one and the same. They both rest at bottom upon the absolute right of the community

to determine its own destiny and that of its members. Men as communities are supreme over men as individuals. Limits of wisdom and convenience to the public control there may be: limits of principle there are, upon strict analysis, none.

It is of capital importance to note this substantial correspondence of fundamental conception as between socialism and democracy: a whole system of practical politics may be erected upon it without further foundation. The germinal conceptions of democracy are as free from all thought of a limitation of the public authority as are the corresponding conceptions of socialism; the individual rights which the democracy of our own century has actually observed, were suggested to it by a political philosophy radically individualistic, but not necessarily democratic. Democracy is bound by no principle of its own nature to say itself nay as to the exercise of any power. Here, then, lies the point. The difference between democracy and socialism is not an essential difference, but only a practical difference—is a difference of *organization* and *policy*, not a difference of primary motive. Democracy has not undertaken the tasks which socialists clamor to have undertaken; but it refrains from them, not for lack of adequate principles or suitable motives, but for lack of adequate organization and suitable hardihood: because it cannot see its way clear to accomplishing them with credit. Moreover it may be said that democrats of today hold off from such undertakings because they are of today, and not of the days, which history very well remembers, when government had the temerity to try everything. The best thought of modern time having recognized a difference between social and political questions, democratic government, like all other governments, seeks to confine itself to those political concerns which have, in the eyes of the judicious, approved themselves appropriate to the sphere and capacity of public authority.

The socialist does not disregard the obvious lessons of history concerning overwrought government: at least he thinks he does not. He denies that he is urging the resumption of tasks which have been repeatedly shown to be impossible. He points to the incontrovertible fact that the economic and social conditions of life in our century are not only superficially but radically different from those of any other time whatever. Many affairs of life which were once easily to be handled by individuals have now become so entangled amongst the complexities of international trade relations, so confused by the multiplicity of news-voices, or so hoisted into the winds of speculation that only powerful combinations of wealth and influence can compass them. Corporations grow on every hand, and on every hand not only swallow and overawe individuals but also compete with governments. The contest is no longer between government and individuals;

it is now between government and dangerous combinations and individuals. Here is a monstrously changed aspect of the social world. In face of such circumstances, must not government lay aside all timid scruple and boldly make itself an agency for social reform as well as for political control?

5   'Yes,' says the democrat, 'perhaps it must. You know it is my principle, no less than yours, that every man shall have an equal chance with every other man: if I saw my way to it as a practical politician, I should be willing to go farther and superintend every man's use of his chance. But the means? The question with me is not whether the community has power to act as it may please in these
10   matters, but how it can act with practical advantage—a question of *policy*.'

A question of policy primarily, but also a question of organization, that is to say of *administration*.

The President of
the United States
Woodrow Wilson

*For Woodrow Wilson, constitutional checks and balances and the separation
of powers are indicative of the flawed thinking of America's Founders. They
are means of limiting government, when the fact is that government alone
can provide the peoples' needs. Wilson looks to the presidency—the singular
voice of the people—as the best hope for overcoming the old order.*

1908

It is difficult to describe any single part of a great governmental system without
describing the whole of it. Governments are living things and operate as organic
wholes. Moreover, governments have their natural evolution and are one thing
in one age, another in another. The makers of the Constitution constructed
the federal government upon a theory of checks and balances which was meant   5
to limit the operation of each part and allow to no single part or organ of it a
dominating force; but no government can be successfully conducted upon so
mechanical a theory. Leadership and control must be lodged somewhere; the
whole art of statesmanship is the art of bringing the several parts of government into effective cooperation for the accomplishment of particular common   10
objects,—and party objects at that. Our study of each part of our federal system,
if we are to discover our real government as it lives, must be made to disclose to
us its operative coordination as a whole: its places of leadership, its method of
action, how it operates, what checks it, what gives it energy and effect. Governments are what politicians make them, and it is easier to write of the President   15
than of the presidency....

Fortunately, the definitions and prescriptions of our constitutional law, though
conceived in the Newtonian spirit and upon the Newtonian principle, are sufficiently broad and elastic to allow for the play of life and circumstance. Though
they were Whig theorists, the men who framed the federal Constitution were   20
also practical statesmen with an experienced eye for affairs and a quick practical

Woodrow Wilson, "The President of the United States," in *Constitutional Government of the United
States* (New York: Columbia University Press, 1908), 54, 57, 59–60, 66–81.

sagacity in respect of the actual structure of government, and they have given us a thoroughly workable model. If it had in fact been a machine governed by mechanically automatic balances, it would have had no history; but it was not, and its history has been rich with the influences and personalities of the
5   men who have conducted it and made it a living reality. The government of the United States has had a vital and normal organic growth and has proved itself eminently adapted to express the changing temper and purposes of the American people from age to age.

That is the reason why it is easier to write of the President than of the presi-
10   dency. The presidency has been one thing at one time, another at another, varying with the man who occupied the office and with the circumstances that surrounded him....

Both men and circumstances have created these contrasts in the administration and influence of the office of President. We have all been disciples of Montes-
15   quieu, but we have also been practical politicians. Mr. Bagehot once remarked that it was no proof of the excellence of the Constitution of the United States that the Americans had operated it with conspicuous success because the Americans could run any constitution successfully; and, while the compliment is altogether acceptable, it is certainly true that our practical sense is more
20   noticeable than our theoretical consistency, and that, while we were once all constitutional lawyers, we are in these latter days apt to be very impatient of literal and dogmatic interpretations of constitutional principle.

The makers of the Constitution seem to have thought of the President as what the stricter Whig theorists wished the king to be: only the legal executive, the
25   presiding and guiding authority in the application of law and the execution of policy. His veto upon legislation was only his 'check' on Congress,—was a power of restraint, not of guidance. He was empowered to prevent bad laws, but he was not to be given an opportunity to make good ones. As a matter of fact he has become very much more. He has become the leader of his party
30   and the guide of the nation in political purpose, and therefore in legal action. The constitutional structure of the government has hampered and limited his action in these significant roles, but it has not prevented it. The influence of the President has varied with the men who have been Presidents and with the circumstances of their times, but the tendency has been unmistakably disclosed,
35   and springs out of the very nature of government itself. It is merely the proof that our government is a living, organic thing, and must, like every other gov- ernment, work out the close synthesis of active parts which can exist only when leadership is lodged in some one man or group of men. You cannot compound a successful government out of antagonisms. Greatly as the practice and influ-

ence of Presidents has varied, there can be no mistaking the fact that we have grown more and more inclined from generation to generation to look to the President as the unifying force in our complex system, the leader both of his party and of the nation. To do so is not inconsistent with the actual provisions of the Constitution; it is only inconsistent with a very mechanical theory of its meaning and intention. The Constitution contains no theories. It is as practical a document as Magna Carta....

As legal executive, his constitutional aspect, the President cannot be thought of alone. He cannot execute laws. Their actual daily execution must be taken care of by the several executive departments and by the now innumerable body of federal officials throughout the country. In respect of the strictly executive duties of his office the President may be said to administer the presidency in conjunction with the members of his cabinet, like the chairman of a commission. He is even of necessity much less active in the actual carrying out of the law than are his colleagues and advisers. It is therefore becoming more and more true, as the business of the government becomes more and more complex and extended, that the President is becoming more and more a political and less and less an executive officer. His executive powers are in commission, while his political powers more and more center and accumulate upon him and are in their very nature personal and inalienable.

Only the larger sort of executive questions are brought to him. Departments which run with easy routine and whose transactions bring few questions of general policy to the surface may proceed with their business for months and even years together without demanding his attention; and no department is in any sense under his direct charge. Cabinet meetings do not discuss detail: they are concerned only with the larger matters of policy or expediency which important business is constantly disclosing. There are no more hours in the President's day than in another man's. If he is indeed the executive, he must act almost entirely by delegation, and is in the hands of his colleagues. He is likely to be praised if things go well, and blamed if they go wrong; but his only real control is of the persons to whom he deputes the performance of executive duties. It is through no fault or neglect of his that the duties apparently assigned to him by the Constitution have come to be his less conspicuous, less important duties, and that duties apparently not assigned to him at all chiefly occupy his time and energy. The one set of duties it has proved practically impossible for him to perform; the other it has proved impossible for him to escape.

He cannot escape being the leader of his party except by incapacity and lack of personal force, because he is at once the choice of the party and of the nation. He is the party nominee, and the only party nominee for whom the whole

nation votes. Members of the House and Senate are representatives of localities, are voted for only by sections of voters, or by local bodies of electors like the members of the state legislatures. There is no national party choice except that of President. No one else represents the people as a whole, exercising a national
5   choice; and inasmuch as his strictly executive duties are in fact subordinated, so far at any rate as all detail is concerned, the President represents not so much the party's governing efficiency as its controlling ideals and principles. He is not so much part of its organization as its vital link of connection with the thinking nation. He can dominate his party by being spokesman for the real
10 sentiment and purpose of the country, by giving direction to opinion, by giving the country at once the information and the statements of policy which will enable it to form its judgments alike of parties and of men.

For he is also the political leader of the nation, or has it in his choice to be. The nation as a whole has chosen him, and is conscious that it has no other
15 political spokesman. His is the only national voice in affairs. Let him once win the admiration and confidence of the country, and no other single force can withstand him, no combination of forces will easily overpower him. His position takes the imagination of the country. He is the representative of no constituency, but of the whole people. When he speaks in his true character, he
20 speaks for no special interest. If he rightly interpret the national thought and boldly insist upon it, he is irresistible; and the country never feels the zest of action so much as when its President is of such insight and calibre. Its instinct is for unified action, and it craves a single leader. It is for this reason that it will often prefer to choose a man rather than a party. A President whom it trusts
25 can not only lead it, but form it to his own views.

It is the extraordinary isolation imposed upon the President by our system that makes the character and opportunity of his office so extraordinary. In him are centered both opinion and party. He may stand, if he will, a little outside party and insist as if it were upon the general opinion. It is with the instinctive feeling
30 that it is upon occasion such a man that the country wants that nominating conventions will often nominate men who are not their acknowledged leaders, but only such men as the country would like to see lead both its parties. The President may also, if he will, stand within the party counsels and use the advantage of his power and personal force to control its actual programs. He
35 may be both the leader of his party and the leader of the nation, or he may be one or the other. If he lead the nation, his party can hardly resist him. His office is anything he has the sagacity and force to make it.

That is the reason why it has been one thing at one time, another at another. The Presidents who have not made themselves leaders have lived no more truly on that account in the spirit of the Constitution than those whose force has told in the determination of law and policy. No doubt Andrew Jackson overstepped the bounds meant to be set to the authority of his office. It was certainly in direct contravention of the spirit of the Constitution that he should have refused to respect and execute decisions of the Supreme Court of the United States, and 5 no serious student of our history can righteously condone what he did in such matters on the ground that his intentions were upright and his principles pure. But the Constitution of the United States is not a mere lawyers' document: it is a vehicle of life, and its spirit is always the spirit of the age. Its prescriptions are clear and we know what they are; a written document makes lawyers of us 10 all, and our duty as citizens should make us conscientious lawyers, reading the text of the Constitution without subtlety or sophistication; but life is always your last and most authoritative critic.

Some of our Presidents have deliberately held themselves off from using the full power they might legitimately have used, because of conscientious scruples, 15 because they were more theorists than statesmen. They have held the strict literary theory of the Constitution, the Whig theory, the Newtonian theory, and have acted as if they thought that Pennsylvania Avenue should have been even longer than it is; that there should be no intimate communication of any kind between the Capitol and the White House; that the President as a man 20 was no more at liberty to lead the houses of Congress by persuasion than he was at liberty as President to dominate them by authority,—supposing that he had, what he has not, authority enough to dominate them. But the makers of the Constitution were not enacting Whig theory, they were not making laws with the expectation that, not the laws themselves, but their opinions, known 25 by future historians to lie back of them, should govern the constitutional action of the country. They were statesmen, not pedants, and their laws are sufficient to keep us to the paths they set us upon. The President is at liberty, both in law and conscience, to be as big a man as he can. His capacity will set the limit; and if Congress be overborne by him, it will be no fault of the makers of the 30 Constitution,—it will be from no lack of constitutional powers on its part, but only because the President has the nation behind him, and Congress has not. He has no means of compelling Congress except through public opinion.

That I say he has no means of compelling Congress will show what I mean, and that my meaning has no touch of radicalism or iconoclasm in it. There are 35 illegitimate means by which the President may influence the action of Congress. He may bargain with members, not only with regard to appointments, but also with regard to legislative measures. He may use his local patronage to assist members to get or retain their seats. He may interpose his powerful influence, in one covert way or another, in contests for places in the Senate. He may also overbear Congress by arbitrary acts which ignore the laws or virtually override them. He may even substitute his own orders for acts of Congress which he wants but cannot get. Such things are not only deeply immoral, they are destructive of the fundamental understandings of constitutional government and, therefore, of constitutional government itself. They are sure, moreover, in a country of free public opinion, to bring their own punishment, to destroy both the fame and the power of the man who dares to practise them. No honorable man includes such agencies in a sober exposition of the Constitution or allows himself to think of them when he speaks of the influences of "life" which govern each generation's use and interpretation of that great instrument, our sovereign guide and the object of our deepest reverence. Nothing in a system like ours can be constitutional which is immoral or which touches the good faith of those who have sworn to obey the fundamental law. The reprobation of all good men will always overwhelm such influences with shame and failure. But the personal force of the President is perfectly constitutional to any extent to which he chooses to exercise it, and it is by the clear logic of our constitutional practice that he has become alike the leader of his party and the leader of the nation.

The political powers of the President are not quite so obvious in their scope and character when we consider his relations with Congress as when we consider his relations to his party and to the nation. They need, therefore, a somewhat more critical examination. Leadership in government naturally belongs to its executive officers, who are daily in contact with practical conditions and exigencies and whose reputations alike for good judgment and for fidelity are at stake much more than are those of the members of the legislative body at every turn of the law's application. The law-making part of the government ought certainly to be very hospitable to the suggestions of the planning and acting part of it. Those Presidents who have felt themselves bound to adhere to the strict literary theory of the Constitution have scrupulously refrained from attempting to determine either the subjects or the character of legislation, except so far as they were obliged to decide for themselves, after Congress had acted, whether they should acquiesce in it or not. And yet the Constitution explicitly authorizes the President to recommend to Congress "such measures as he shall deem necessary and expedient," and it is not necessary to the integrity of even the literary theory of the Constitution to insist that such recommendations should be merely perfunctory. Certainly General Washington did not so regard them, and he stood much nearer the Whig theory than we do. A President's messages to Congress have no more weight or authority than their intrinsic reasonableness and importance give them: but that is their only constitutional limitation. The

Constitution certainly does not forbid the President to back them up, as General Washington did, with such personal force and influence as he may possess. Some of our Presidents have felt the need, which unquestionably exists in our system, for some spokesman of the nation as a whole, in matters of legislation no less than in other matters, and have tried to supply Congress with the leadership of suggestion, backed by argument and by iteration and by every legitimate appeal to public opinion. Cabinet officers are shut out from Congress; the President himself has, by custom, no access to its floor; many long-established barriers of precedent, though not of law, hinder him from exercising any direct influence upon its deliberations; and yet he is undoubtedly the only spokesman of the whole people. They have again and again, as often as they were afforded the opportunity, manifested their satisfaction when he has boldly accepted the role of leader, to which the peculiar origin and character of his authority entitle him. The Constitution bids him speak, and times of stress and change must more and more thrust upon him the attitude of originator of policies.

His is the vital place of action in the system, whether he accept it as such or not, and the office is the measure of the man,—of his wisdom as well as of his force. His veto abundantly equips him to stay the hand of Congress when he will. It is seldom possible to pass a measure over his veto, and no President has hesitated to use the veto when his own judgment of the public good was seriously at issue with that of the houses. The veto has never been suffered to fall into even temporary disuse with us. In England it has ceased to exist, with the change in the character of the executive. There has been no veto since Anne's day, because ever since the reign of Anne the laws of England have been originated either by ministers who spoke the king's own will or by ministers whom the king did not dare gainsay; and in our own time the ministers who formulate the laws are themselves the executive of the nation; a veto would be a negative upon their own power. If bills pass of which they disapprove, they resign and give place to the leaders of those who approve them. The framers of the Constitution made in our President a more powerful, because a more isolated, king than the one they were imitating; and because the Constitution gave them their veto in such explicit terms, our Presidents have not hesitated to use it, even when it put their mere individual judgment against that of large majorities in both houses of Congress. And yet in the exercise of the power to suggest legislation, quite as explicitly conferred upon them by the Constitution, some of our Presidents have seemed to have a timid fear that they might offend some law of taste which had become a constitutional principle.

In one sense their messages to Congress have no more authority than the letters of any other citizen would have. Congress can heed or ignore them as it pleases;

and there have been periods of our history when presidential messages were utterly without practical significance, perfunctory documents which few persons except the editors of newspapers took the trouble to read. But if the President has personal force and cares to exercise it, there is this tremendous difference
5   between his messages and the views of any other citizen, either outside Congress or in it: that the whole country reads them and feels that the writer speaks with an authority and a responsibility which the people themselves have given him.

The history of our cabinets affords a striking illustration of the progress of the idea that the President is not merely the legal head but also the political leader
10   of the nation. In the earlier days of the government it was customary for the President to fill his cabinet with the recognized leaders of his party. General Washington even tried the experiment which William of Orange tried at the very beginning of the era of cabinet government. He called to his aid the leaders of both political parties, associating Mr. Hamilton with Mr. Jefferson,
15   on the theory that all views must be heard and considered in the conduct of the government. That was the day in which English precedent prevailed, and English cabinets were made up of the chief political characters of the day. But later years have witnessed a marked change in our practice, in this as in many other things. The old tradition was indeed slow in dying out. It persisted with
20   considerable vitality at least until General Garfield's day, and may yet from time to time revive, for many functions of our cabinets justify it and make it desirable. But our later Presidents have apparently ceased to regard the cabinet as a council of party leaders such as the party they represent would have chosen. They look upon it rather as a body of personal advisers whom the President
25   chooses from the ranks of those whom he personally trusts and prefers to look to for advice. Our recent Presidents have not sought their associates among those whom the fortunes of party contest have brought into prominence and influence, but have called their personal friends and business colleagues to cabinet positions, and men who have given proof of their efficiency in private, not in
30   public, life,—bankers who had never had any place in the formal counsels of the party, eminent lawyers who had held aloof from politics, private secretaries who had shown an unusual sagacity and proficiency in handling public business; as if the President were himself alone the leader of his party, the members of his cabinet only his private advisers, at any rate advisers of his private choice. Mr.
35   Cleveland may be said to have been the first President to make this conception of the cabinet prominent in his choices, and he did not do so until his second administration. Mr. Roosevelt has emphasized the idea.

Upon analysis it seems to mean this: the cabinet is an executive, not a political body. The President cannot himself be the actual executive; he must therefore find, to act in his stead, men of the best legal and business gifts, and depend upon them for the actual administration of the government in all its daily activities. If he seeks political advice of his executive colleagues, he seeks it because he relies upon their natural good sense and experienced judgment, upon their knowledge of the country and its business and social conditions, upon their   5 sagacity as representative citizens of more than usual observation and discretion; not because they are supposed to have had any very intimate contact with politics or to have made a profession of public affairs. He has chosen, not representative politicians, but eminent representative citizens, selecting them rather for their special fitness for the great business posts to which he has assigned them   10 than for their political experience, and looking to them for advice in the actual conduct of the government rather than in the shaping of political policy. They are, in his view, not necessarily political officers at all.

It may with a great deal of plausibility be argued that the Constitution looks upon the President himself in the same way. It does not seem to make him   15 a prime minister or the leader of the nation's counsels. Some Presidents are, therefore, and some are not. It depends upon the man and his gifts. He may be like his cabinet, or he may be more than his cabinet. His office is a mere vantage ground from which he may be sure that effective words of advice and timely efforts at reform will gain telling momentum. He has the ear of the nation as   20 of course, and a great person may use such an advantage greatly. If he use the opportunity, he may take his cabinet into partnership or not, as he pleases; and so its character may vary with his. Self-reliant men will regard their cabinets as executive councils; men less self-reliant or more prudent will regard them as also political councils, and will wish to call into them men who have earned   25 the confidence of their party. The character of the cabinet may be made a nice index of the theory of the presidential office, as well as of the President's theory of party government; but the one view is, so far as I can see, as constitutional as the other.

One of the greatest of the President's powers I have not yet spoken of at all: 30 his control, which is very absolute, of the foreign relations of the nation. The initiative in foreign affairs, which the President possesses without any restriction whatever, is virtually the power to control them absolutely. The President cannot conclude a treaty with a foreign power without the consent of the Senate, but he may guide every step of diplomacy, and to guide diplomacy is to determine   35 what treaties must be made, if the faith and prestige of the government are to be maintained. He need disclose no step of negotiation until it is complete, and when in any critical matter it is completed the government is virtually committed. Whatever its disinclination, the Senate may feel itself committed also.

I have not dwelt upon this power of the President, because it has been decisively influential in determining the character and influence of the office at only two periods in our history; at the very first, when the government was young and had so to use its incipient force as to win the respect of the nations into whose
5   family it had thrust itself, and in our own day when the results of the Spanish War, the ownership of distant possessions, and many sharp struggles for foreign trade make it necessary that we should turn our best talents to the task of dealing firmly, wisely, and justly with political and commercial rivals. The President can never again be the mere domestic figure he has been throughout
10 so large a part of our history. The nation has risen to the first rank in power and resources. The other nations of the world look askance upon her, half in envy, half in fear, and wonder with a deep anxiety what she will do with her vast strength. They receive the frank professions of men like Mr. John Hay, whom we wholly trusted, with a grain of salt, and doubt what we were sure of, their
15 truthfulness and sincerity, suspecting a hidden design under every utterance he makes. Our President must always, henceforth, be one of the great powers of the world, whether he act greatly and wisely or not, and the best statesmen we can produce will be needed to fill the office of Secretary of State. We have but begun to see the presidential office in this light; but it is the light which will
20 more and more beat upon it, and more and more determine its character and its effect upon the politics of the nation. We can never hide our President again as a mere domestic officer. We can never again see him the mere executive he was in the thirties and forties. He must stand always at the front of our affairs, and the office will be as big and as influential as the man who occupies it.

25 How is it possible to sum up the duties and influence of such an office in such a system in comprehensive terms which will cover all its changeful aspects? In the view of the makers of the Constitution the President was to be legal executive; perhaps the leader of the nation; certainly not the leader of the party, at any rate while in office. But by the operation of forces inherent in the very
30 nature of government he has become all three, and by inevitable consequence the most heavily burdened officer in the world. No other man's day is so full as his, so full of the responsibilities which tax mind and conscience alike and demand an inexhaustible vitality. The mere task of making appointments to office, which the Constitution imposes upon the President, has come near to
35 breaking some of our Presidents down, because it is a never-ending task in a civil service not yet put upon a professional footing, confused with short terms of office, always forming and dissolving. And in proportion as the President ventures to use his opportunity to lead opinion and act as spokesman of the people in affairs the people stand ready to overwhelm him by running to him

with every question, great and small. They are as eager to have him settle a literary question as a political; hear him as acquiescently with regard to matters of
special expert knowledge as with regard to public affairs, and call upon him to
quiet all troubles by his personal intervention. Men of ordinary physique and
discretion cannot be Presidents and live, if the strain be not somehow relieved.   5
We shall be obliged always to be picking our chief magistrates from among wise
and prudent athletes,—a small class.

The future development of the presidency, therefore, must certainly, one would
confidently predict, run along such lines as the President's later relations with
his cabinet suggest. General Washington, partly out of unaffected modesty, no   10
doubt, but also out of the sure practical instinct which he possessed in so unusual
a degree, set an example which few of his successors seem to have followed in
any systematic manner. He made constant and intimate use of his colleagues in
every matter that he handled, seeking their assistance and advice by letter when
they were at a distance and he could not obtain it in person. It is well known to   15
all close students of our history that his greater state papers, even those which
seem in some peculiar and intimate sense his personal utterances, are full of
the ideas and the very phrases of the men about him whom he most trusted.
His rough drafts came back to him from Mr. Hamilton and Mr. Madison in
great part rephrased and rewritten, in many passages reconceived and given a   20
new color. He thought and acted always by the light of counsel, with a will
and definite choice of his own, but through the instrumentality of other minds
as well as his own. The duties and responsibilities laid upon the President by
the Constitution can be changed only by constitutional amendment,—a thing
too difficult to attempt except upon some greater necessity than the relief of an   25
overburdened office, even though that office be the greatest in the land; and it is
to be doubted whether the deliberate opinion of the country would consent to
make of the President a less powerful officer than he is. He can secure his own
relief without shirking any real responsibility. Appointments, for example, he
can, if he will, make more and more upon the advice and choice of his executive   30
colleagues; every matter of detail not only, but also every minor matter of counsel
or of general policy, he can more and more depend upon his chosen advisers to
determine; he need reserve for himself only the larger matters of counsel and
that general oversight of the business of the government and of the persons who
conduct it which is not possible without intimate daily consultations, indeed,   35
but which is possible without attempting the intolerable burden of direct control. This is, no doubt, the idea of their functions which most Presidents have
entertained and which most Presidents suppose themselves to have acted on;
but we have reason to believe that most of our Presidents have taken their duties

too literally and have attempted the impossible. But we can safely predict that as the multitude of the President's duties increases, as it must with the growth and widening activities of the nation itself, the incumbents of the great office will more and more come to feel that they are administering it in its truest pur-
5   pose and with greatest effect by regarding themselves as less and less executive officers and more and more directors of affairs and leaders of the nation,—men of counsel and of the sort of action that makes for enlightenment.

The Presidency: Making An Old Party Progressive
Theodore Roosevelt (1858–1919)

Theodore Roosevelt's ascension to the presidency in 1901, upon the assassination of William McKinley, marked the emergence of Progressivism on the national scene. From trust busting to railroad regulation, Roosevelt sought to expand federal power over a large swath of the American economy. In this excerpt from his autobiography, he offers a view of the Constitution that is compatible with his Progressive politics.

1913

… The most important factor in getting the right spirit in my Administration, next to the insistence upon courage, honesty, and a genuine democracy of desire to serve the plain people, was my insistence upon the theory that the executive power was limited only by specific restrictions and prohibitions appearing in the Constitution or imposed by the Congress under its Constitutional powers. 5 My view was that every executive officer, and above all every executive officer in high position, was a steward of the people bound actively and affirmatively to do all he could for the people, and not to content himself with the negative merit of keeping his talents undamaged in a napkin. I declined to adopt the view that what was imperatively necessary for the Nation could not be done by 10 the President unless he could find some specific authorization to do it. My belief was that it was not only his right but his duty to do anything that the needs of the Nation demanded unless such action was forbidden by the Constitution or by the laws. Under this interpretation of executive power I did and caused to be done many things not previously done by the President and the heads of 15 the departments. I did not usurp power, but I did greatly broaden the use of executive power. In other words, I acted for the public welfare, I acted for the common well-being of all our people, whenever and in whatever manner was necessary, unless prevented by direct constitutional or legislative prohibition.

Theodore Roosevelt, "The Presidency: Making an Old Party Progressive," in *The Rough Riders, An Autobiography* (New York: The Macmillan Company, 1913), 614–15, 643.

I did not care a rap for the mere form and show of power; I cared immensely for the use that could be made of the substance....

In internal affairs I cannot say that I entered the Presidency with any deliberately planned and far-reaching scheme of social betterment. I had, however,
5   certain strong convictions; and I was on the lookout for every opportunity of realizing those convictions. I was bent upon making the Government the most efficient possible instrument in helping the people of the United States to better themselves in every way, politically, socially, and industrially. I believed with all my heart in real and thoroughgoing democracy, and I wished to make this
10   democracy industrial as well as political, although I had only partially formulated the methods I believed we should follow. I believed in the people's rights, and therefore in National rights and States' rights just exactly to the degree in which they severally secured popular rights. I believed in invoking the National power with absolute freedom for every National need; and I believed that the
15   Constitution should be treated as the greatest document ever devised by the wit of man to aid a people in exercising every power necessary for its own betterment, and not as a straitjacket cunningly fashioned to strangle growth. As for the particular methods of realizing these various beliefs, I was content to wait and see what method might be necessary in each given case as it arose; and I
20   was certain that the cases would arise fast enough....

THE STUDY OF ADMINISTRATION
WOODROW WILSON

Writing a year before Congress created the Interstate Commerce Commission, the first independent regulatory agency, Woodrow Wilson argues in this article that it is only through such agencies—separate from the political process and independent of the electorate—that government can pursue its necessary ends.

NOVEMBER 2, 1886

I suppose that no practical science is ever studied where there is no need to know it. The very fact, therefore, that the eminently practical science of administration is finding its way into college courses in this country would prove that this country needs to know more about administration, were such proof of the fact required to make out a case. It need not be said, however, that we do not look into college programs for proof of this fact. It is a thing almost taken for granted among us, that the present movement called civil service reform must, after the accomplishment of its first purpose, expand into efforts to improve, not the *personnel* only, but also the organization and methods of our government offices: because it is plain that their organization and methods need improvement only less than their *personnel*. It is the object of administrative study to discover, first, what government can properly and successfully do, and, secondly, how it can do these proper things with the utmost possible efficiency and at the least possible cost either of money or of energy. On both these points there is obviously much need of light among us; and only careful study can supply that light.

Before entering on that study, however, it is needful:

I.   To take some account of what others have done in the same line; that is to say, of the history of the study.

II. To ascertain just what is its subject-matter.

III. To determine just what are the best methods by which to develop it, and the most clarifying political conceptions to carry with us into it.

Woodrow Wilson, "The Study of Administration," *Political Science Quarterly* 2 (July 1887): 197–222.

Unless we know and settle these things, we shall set out without chart or compass.

I.

The science of administration is the latest fruit of that study of the science of politics which was begun some twenty-two hundred years ago. It is a birth of
5　our own century, almost of our own generation.

Why was it so late in coming? Why did it wait till this too busy century of ours to demand attention for itself? Administration is the most obvious part of government; it is government in action; it is the executive, the operative, the most visible side of government, and is of course as old as government itself.
10　It is government in action, and one might very naturally expect to find that government in action had arrested the attention and provoked the scrutiny of writers of politics very early in the history of systematic thought.

But such was not the case. No one wrote systematically of administration as a branch of the science of government until the present century had passed its
15　first youth and had begun to put forth its characteristic flower of the systematic knowledge. Up to our own day all the political writers whom we now read had thought, argued, and dogmatized only about the *constitution* of government; about the nature of the state, the essence and seat of sovereignty, popular power and kingly prerogative; about the greatest meanings lying at the heart of govern-
20　ment, and the high ends set before the purpose of government by man's nature and man's aims. The central field of controversy was that great field of theory in which monarchy rode tilt against democracy, in which oligarchy would have built for itself strongholds of privilege, and in which tyranny sought opportunity to make good its claim to receive submission from all competitors. Amidst this
25　high warfare of principles, administration could command no pause for its own consideration. The question was always: Who shall make law, and what shall that law be? The other question, how law should be administered with enlightenment, with equity, with speed, and without friction, was put aside as "practical detail" which clerks could arrange after doctors had agreed upon principles.

30　That political philosophy took this direction was of course no accident, no chance preference or perverse whim of political philosophers. The philosophy of any time is, as Hegel says, "nothing but the spirit of that time expressed in abstract thought"; and political philosophy, like philosophy of every other kind, has only held up the mirror to contemporary affairs. The trouble in early times
35　was almost altogether about the constitution of government; and consequently that was what engrossed men's thoughts. There was little or no trouble about administration,—at least little that was heeded by administrators. The func-

tions of government were simple, because life itself was simple. Government went about imperatively and compelled men, without thought of consulting their wishes. There was no complex system of public revenues and public debts to puzzle financiers; there were, consequently, no financiers to be puzzled. No one who possessed power was long at a loss how to use it. The great and only question was: Who shall possess it? Populations were of manageable numbers; property was of simple sorts. There were plenty of farms, but no stocks and bonds: more cattle than vested interests.

I have said that all this was true of "early times"; but it was substantially true also of comparatively late times. One does not have to look back of the last century for the beginnings of the present complexities of trade and perplexities of commercial speculation, nor for the portentous birth of national debts. Good Queen Bess, doubtless, thought that the monopolies of the sixteenth century were hard enough to handle without burning her hands; but they are not remembered in the presence of the giant monopolies of the nineteenth century. When Blackstone lamented that corporations had no bodies to be kicked and no souls to be damned, he was anticipating the proper time for such regrets by a full century. The perennial discords between master and workmen which now so often disturb industrial society began before the Black Death and the Statute of Laborers; but never before our own day did they assume such ominous proportions as they wear now. In brief, if difficulties of governmental action are to be seen gathering in other centuries, they are to be seen culminating in our own.

This is the reason why administrative tasks have nowadays to be so studiously and systematically adjusted to carefully tested standards of policy, the reason why we are having now what we never had before, a science of administration. The weightier debates of constitutional principle are even yet by no means concluded; but they are no longer of more immediate practical moment than questions of administration. It is getting to be harder to *run* a constitution than to frame one.

Here is Mr. Bagehot's graphic, whimsical way of depicting the difference between the old and the new in administration:

"In early times, when a despot wishes to govern a distant province, he sends down a satrap on a grand horse, and other people on little horses; and very little is heard of the satrap again unless he send back some of the little people to tell what he has been doing. No great labor of superintendence is possible. Common rumor and casual report are the sources of intelligence. If it seems certain that the province is in a bad state, satrap No. 1 is recalled, and satrap

No. 2 sent out in his stead. In civilized countries the process is different. You erect a bureau in the province you want to govern; you make it write letters and copy letters; it sends home eight reports *per diem* to the head bureau in St. Petersburg. Nobody does a sum in the province without some one doing
5   the same sum in the capital, to "check" him, and see that he does it correctly. The consequence of this is, to throw on the heads of departments an amount of reading and labor which can only be accomplished by the greatest natural aptitude, the most efficient training, the most firm and regular industry."

There is scarcely a single duty of government which was once simple which is
10   not now complex; government once had but a few masters; it now has scores of masters. Majorities formerly only underwent government; they now conduct government. Where government once might follow the whims of a court, it must now follow the views of a nation.

And those views are steadily widening to new conceptions of state duty; so that,
15   at the same time that the functions of government are every day becoming more complex and difficult, they are also vastly multiplying in number. Administration is everywhere putting its hands to new undertakings. The utility, cheapness, and success of the government's postal service, for instance, point towards the early establishment of governmental control of the telegraph system. Or, even
20   if our government is not to follow the lead of the governments of Europe in buying or building both telegraph and railroad lines, no one can doubt that in some way it must make itself master of masterful corporations. The creation of national commissioners of railroads, in addition to the older state commissions, involves a very important and delicate extension of administrative functions.
25   Whatever hold of authority state or federal governments are to take upon corporations, there must follow cares and responsibilities which will require not a little wisdom, knowledge, and experience. Such things must be studied in order to be well done. And these, as I have said, are only a few of the doors which are being opened to offices of government. The idea of the state and the consequent
30   ideal of its duty are undergoing noteworthy change; and "the idea of the state is the conscience of administration." Seeing every day new things which the state ought to do, the next thing is to see clearly how it ought to do them.

This is why there should be a science of administration which shall seek to straighten the paths of government, to make its business less unbusinesslike, to
35   strengthen and purify its organization, and to crown its duties with dutifulness. This is one reason why there is such a science.

But where has this science grown up? Surely not on this side the sea. Not much impartial scientific method is to be discerned in our administrative practices. The

poisonous atmosphere of city government, the crooked secrets of state administration, the confusion, sinecurism, and corruption ever and again discovered
in the bureaux at Washington forbid us to believe that any clear conceptions of
what constitutes good administration are as yet very widely current in the United
States. No; American writers have hitherto taken no very important part in the   5
advancement of this science. It has found its doctors in Europe. It is not of our
making; it is a foreign science, speaking very little of the language of English or
American principle. It employs only foreign tongues; it utters none but what
are to our minds alien ideas. Its aims, its examples, its conditions, are almost
exclusively grounded in the histories of foreign races, in the precedents of foreign   10
systems, in the lessons of foreign revolutions. It has been developed by French
and German professors, and is consequently in all parts adapted to the needs of a
compact state, and made to fit highly centralized forms of government; whereas,
to answer our purposes, it must be adapted, not to a simple and compact, but
to a complex and multiform state, and made to fit highly decentralized forms   15
of government. If we would employ it, we must Americanize it, and that not
formally, in language merely, but radically, in thought, principle, and aim as
well. It must learn our constitutions by heart; must get the bureaucratic fever
out of its veins; must inhale much free American air.

If an explanation be sought why a science manifestly so susceptible of being   20
made useful to all governments alike should have received attention first in
Europe, where government has long been a monopoly, rather than in England
or the United States, where government has long been a common franchise, the
reason will doubtless be found to be twofold: first, that in Europe, just because
government was independent of popular assent, there was more governing to   25
be done; and, second, that the desire to keep government a monopoly made the
monopolists interested in discovering the least irritating means of governing.
They were, besides, few enough to adopt means promptly.

It will be instructive to look into this matter a little more closely. In speaking
of European governments I do not, of course, include England. She has not   30
refused to change with the times. She has simply tempered the severity of the
transition from a polity of aristocratic privilege to a system of democratic power
by slow measures of constitutional reform which, without preventing revolution, has confined it to paths of peace. But the countries of the continent for
a long time desperately struggled against all change, and would have diverted   35
revolution by softening the asperities of absolute government. They sought so
to perfect their machinery as to destroy all wearing friction, so to sweeten their
methods with consideration for the interests of the governed as to placate all
hindering hatred, and so assiduously and opportunely to offer their aid to all

classes of undertakings as to render themselves indispensable to the industrious. They did at last give the people constitutions and the franchise; but even after that they obtained leave to continue despotic by becoming paternal. They made themselves too efficient to be dispensed with, too smoothly operative to
5   be noticed, too enlightened to be inconsiderately questioned, too benevolent to be suspected, too powerful to be coped with. All this has required study; and they have closely studied it.

On this side the sea, we, the while, had known no great difficulties of government. With a new country, in which there was room and remunerative employ-
10 ment for everybody, with liberal principles of government and unlimited skill in practical politics, we were long exempted from the need of being anxiously careful about plans and methods of administration. We have naturally been slow to see the use or significance of those many volumes of learned research and painstaking examination into the ways and means of conducting govern-
15 ment which the presses of Europe have been sending to our libraries. Like a lusty child, government with us has expanded in nature and grown great in stature, but has also become awkward in movement. The vigor and increase of its life has been altogether out of proportion to its skill in living. It has gained strength, but it has not acquired deportment. Great, therefore, as has been our
20 advantage over the countries of Europe in point of ease and health of constitutional development, now that the time for more careful administrative adjustments and larger administrative knowledge has come to us, we are at a signal disadvantage as compared with the transatlantic nations; and this for reasons which I shall try to make clear.

25 Judging by the constitutional histories of the chief nations of the modern world, there may be said to be three periods of growth through which government has passed in all the most highly developed of existing systems, and through which it promises to pass in all the rest. The first of these periods is that of absolute rulers, and of an administrative system adapted to absolute rule; the second is that in which
30 constitutions are framed to do away with absolute rulers and substitute popular control, and in which administration is neglected for these higher concerns; and the third is that in which the sovereign people undertake to develop administration under this new constitution which has brought them into power.

Those governments are now in the lead in administrative practice which had
35 rulers still absolute but also enlightened when those modern days of political illumination came in which it was made evident to all but the blind that governors are properly only the servants of the governed. In such governments administration has been organized to subserve the general weal with the simplicity and effectiveness vouchsafed only to the undertakings of a single will.

Such was the case in Prussia, for instance, where administration has been most studied and most nearly perfected. Frederic the Great, stern and masterful as was his rule, still sincerely professed to regard himself as only the chief servant of the state, to consider his great office a public trust; and it was he who, building upon the foundations laid by his father, began to organize the public service of Prussia as in very earnest a service of the public. His no less absolute successor, Frederic William III, under the inspiration of Stein, again, in his turn, advanced the work still further, planning many of the broader structural features which give firmness and form to Prussian administration today. Almost the whole of the admirable system has been developed by kingly initiative.

Of similar origin was the practice, if not the plan, of modern French administration, with its symmetrical divisions of territory and its orderly gradations of office. The days of the Revolution—of the Constituent Assembly—were days of constitution-*writing*, but they can hardly be called days of constitution-*making*. The Revolution heralded a period of constitutional development,—the entrance of France upon the second of those periods which I have enumerated,—but it did not itself inaugurate such a period. It interrupted and unsettled absolutism, but did not destroy it. Napoleon succeeded the monarchs of France, to exercise a power as unrestricted as they had ever possessed.

The recasting of French administration by Napoleon is, therefore, my second example of the perfecting of civil machinery by the single will of an absolute ruler before the dawn of a constitutional era. No corporate, popular will could ever have effected arrangements such as those which Napoleon commanded. Arrangements so simple at the expense of local prejudice, so logical in their indifference to popular choice, might be decreed by a Constituent Assembly, but could be established only by the unlimited authority of a despot. The system of the year VIII was ruthlessly thorough and heartlessly perfect. It was, besides, in large part, a return to the despotism that had been overthrown.

Among those nations, on the other hand, which entered upon a season of constitution-making and popular reform before administration had received the impress of liberal principle, administrative improvement has been tardy and half-done. Once a nation has embarked in the business of manufacturing constitutions, it finds it exceedingly difficult to close out that business and open for the public a bureau of skilled, economical administration. There seems to be no end to the tinkering of constitutions. Your ordinary constitution will last you hardly ten years without repairs or additions; and the time for administrative detail comes late.

Here, of course, our examples are England and our own country. In the days of the Angevin kings, before constitutional life had taken root in the Great

Charter, legal and administrative reforms began to proceed with sense and vigor under the impulse of Henry II's shrewd, busy, pushing, indomitable spirit and purpose; and kingly initiative seemed destined in England, as elsewhere, to shape governmental growth at its will. But impulsive, errant Richard and

5 weak, despicable John were not the men to carry out such schemes as their father's. Administrative development gave place in their reigns to constitutional struggles; and Parliament became king before any English monarch had had the practical genius or the enlightened conscience to devise just and lasting forms for the civil service of the state.

10 The English race, consequently, has long and successfully studied the art of curbing executive power to the constant neglect of the art of perfecting executive methods. It has exercised itself much more in controlling than in energizing government. It has been more concerned to render government just and moderate than to make it facile, well-ordered, and effective. English and American

15 political history has been a history, not of administrative development, but of legislative oversight,—not of progress in governmental organization, but of advance in law-making and political criticism. Consequently, we have reached a time when administrative study and creation are imperatively necessary to the well-being of our governments saddled with the habits of a long period of

20 constitution-making. That period has practically closed, so far as the establishment of essential principles is concerned, but we cannot shake off its atmosphere. We go on criticizing when we ought to be creating. We have reached the third of the periods I have mentioned,—the period, namely, when the people have to develop administration in accordance with the constitutions they won for

25 themselves in a previous period of struggle with absolute power; but we are not prepared for the tasks of the new period.

Such an explanation seems to afford the only escape from blank astonishment at the fact that, in spite of our vast advantages in point of political liberty, and above all in point of practical political skill and sagacity, so many nations are

30 ahead of us in administrative organization and administrative skill. Why, for instance, have we but just begun purifying a civil service which was rotten full fifty years ago? To say that slavery diverted us is but to repeat what I have said—that flaws in our constitution delayed us.

Of course all reasonable preference would declare for this English and American

35 course of politics rather than for that of any European country. We should not like to have had Prussia's history for the sake of having Prussia's administrative skill; and Prussia's particular system of administration would quite suffocate us. It is better to be untrained and free than to be servile and systematic. Still there is no denying that it would be better yet to be both free in spirit and proficient

in practice. It is this even more reasonable preference which impels us to discover what there may be to hinder or delay us in naturalizing this much-to-be-desired science of administration.

What, then, is there to prevent?

Well, principally, popular sovereignty. It is harder for democracy to organize   5
administration than for monarchy. The very completeness of our most cherished political successes in the past embarrasses us. We have enthroned public opinion; and it is forbidden us to hope during its reign for any quick schooling of the sovereign in executive expertness or in the conditions of perfect functional balance in government. The very fact that we have realized popular   10
rule in its fulness has made the task of *organizing* that rule just so much the more difficult. In order to make any advance at all we must instruct and persuade a multitudinous monarch called public opinion,—a much less feasible undertaking than to influence a single monarch called a king. An individual sovereign will adopt a simple plan and carry it out directly: he will have but   15
one opinion, and he will embody that one opinion in one command. But this other sovereign, the people, will have a score of differing opinions. They can agree upon nothing simple: advance must be made through compromise, by a compounding of differences, by a trimming of plans and a suppression of too straightforward principles. There will be a succession of resolves running   20
through a course of years, a dropping fire of commands running through a whole gamut of modifications.

In government, as in virtue, the hardest of hard things is to make progress. Formerly the reason for this was that the single person who was sovereign was generally either selfish, ignorant, timid, or a fool,—albeit there was now and   25
again one who was wise. Nowadays the reason is that the many, the people, who are sovereign have no single ear which one can approach, and are selfish, ignorant, timid, stubborn, or foolish with the selfishness, the ignorances, the stubbornnesses, the timidities, or the follies of several thousand persons,— albeit there are hundreds who are wise. Once the advantage of the reformer   30
was that the sovereign's mind had a definite locality, that it was contained in one man's head, and that consequently it could be gotten at; though it was his disadvantage that the mind learned only reluctantly or only in small quantities, or was under the influence of some one who let it learn only the wrong things. Now, on the contrary, the reformer is bewildered by the fact that the sovereign's   35
mind has no definite locality, but is contained in a voting majority of several million heads; and embarrassed by the fact that the mind of this sovereign also is under the influence of favorites, who are none the less favorites in a good old-fashioned sense of the word because they are not persons by preconceived

opinions; *i.e.*, prejudices which are not to be reasoned with because they are not the children of reason.

Wherever regard for public opinion is a first principle of government, practical reform must be slow and all reform must be full of compromises. For wherever
5 public opinion exists it must rule. This is now an axiom half the world over, and will presently come to be believed even in Russia. Whoever would effect a change in a modern constitutional government must first educate his fellow-citizens to want *some* change. That done, he must persuade them to want the particular change he wants. He must first make public opinion willing to listen
10 and then see to it that it listen to the right things. He must stir it up to search for an opinion, and then manage to put the right opinion in its way.

The first step is not less difficult than the second. With opinions, possession is more than nine points of the law. It is next to impossible to dislodge them. Institutions which one generation regards as only a makeshift approximation to the realization
15 of a principle, the next generation honors as the nearest possible approximation to that principle, and the next worships the principle itself. It takes scarcely three generations for the apotheosis. The grandson accepts his grandfather's hesitating experiment as an integral part of the fixed constitution of nature.

Even if we had clear insight into all the political past, and could form out
20 of perfectly instructed heads a few steady, infallible, placidly wise maxims of government into which all sound political doctrine would be ultimately resolvable, *would the country act on them*? That is the question. The bulk of mankind is rigidly unphilosophical, and nowadays the bulk of mankind votes. A truth must become not only plain but also commonplace before it will be seen by the
25 people who go to their work very early in the morning; and not to act upon it must involve great and pinching inconveniences before these same people will make up their minds to act upon it.

And where is this unphilosophical bulk of mankind more multifarious in its composition than in the United States? To know the public mind of this country,
30 one must know the mind, not of Americans of the older stocks only, but also of Irishmen, of Germans, of negroes. In order to get a footing for new doctrine, one must influence minds cast in every mold of race, minds inheriting every bias of environment, warped by the histories of a score of different nations, warmed or chilled, closed or expanded by almost every climate of the globe.

35 So much, then, for the history of the study of administration, and the peculiarly difficult conditions under which, entering upon it when we do, we must undertake it. What, now, is the subject-matter of this study, and what are its characteristic objects?

II.

The field of administration is a field of business. It is removed from the hurry and strife of politics; it at most points stands apart even from the debatable ground of constitutional study. It is a part of political life only as the methods of the counting-house are a part of the life of society; only as machinery is part of the manufactured product. But it is, at the same time, raised very far 5 above the dull level of mere technical detail by the fact that through its greater principles it is directly connected with the lasting maxims of political wisdom, the permanent truths of political progress.

The object of administrative study is to rescue executive methods from the confusion and costliness of empirical experiment and set them upon foundations 10 laid deep in stable principle.

It is for this reason that we must regard civil-service reform in its present stages as but a prelude to a fuller administrative reform. We are now rectifying methods of appointment; we must go on to adjust executive functions more fitly and to prescribe better methods of executive organization and action. Civil-service 15 reform is thus but a moral preparation for what is to follow. It is clearing the moral atmosphere of official life by establishing the sanctity of public office as a public trust, and, by making service unpartisan, it is opening the way for making it businesslike. By sweetening its motives it is rendering it capable of improving its methods of work. 20

Let me expand a little what I have said of the province of administration. Most important to be observed is the truth already so much and so fortunately insisted upon by our civil-service reformers; namely, that administration lies outside the proper sphere of *politics*. Administrative questions are not political questions. Although politics sets the tasks for administration, it should not be suffered to 25 manipulate its offices.

This is distinction of high authority; eminent German writers insist upon it as of course. Bluntschli, for instance, bids us separate administration alike from politics and from law. Politics, he says, is state activity "in things great and universal," while "administration, on the other hand," is "the activity of the state in 30 individual and small things. Politics is thus the special province of the statesman, administration of the technical official." "Policy does nothing without the aid of administration"; but administration is not therefore politics. But we do not require German authority for this position; this discrimination between administration and politics is now, happily, too obvious to need further discussion. 35

There is another distinction which must be worked into all our conclusions, which, though but another side of that between administration and politics, is not quite so easy to keep sight of: I mean the distinction between *constitutional* and administrative questions, between those governmental adjustments which are essential to constitutional principle and those which are merely instrumental to the possibly changing purposes of a wisely adapting convenience.

5   One cannot easily make clear to every one just where administration resides in the various departments of any practicable government without entering upon particulars so numerous as to confuse and distinctions so minute as to distract. No lines of demarcation, setting apart administrative from non-administrative functions, can be run between this and that department of government without

10   being run up hill and down dale, over dizzy heights of distinction and through dense jungles of statutory enactment, hither and thither around "ifs" and "buts," "whens" and "howevers," until they become altogether lost to the common eye not accustomed to this sort of surveying, and consequently not acquainted with the use of the theodolite of logical discernment. A great deal of administration

15   goes about *incognito* to most of the world, being confounded now with political "management," and again with constitutional principle.

Perhaps this ease of confusion may explain such utterances as that of Niebuhr's: "Liberty," he says, "depends incomparably more upon administration than upon constitution." At first sight this appears to be largely true. Apparently facility in

20   the actual exercise of liberty does depend more upon administrative arrangements than upon constitutional guarantees; although constitutional guarantees alone secure the existence of liberty. But—upon second thought—is even so much as this true? Liberty no more consists in easy functional movement than intelligence consists in the ease and vigor with which the limbs of a strong man

25   move. The principles that rule within the man, or the constitution, are the vital springs of liberty or servitude. Because dependence and subjection are without chains, are lightened by every easy-working device of considerate, paternal government, they are not thereby transformed into liberty. Liberty cannot live apart from constitutional principle; and no administration, however perfect

30   and liberal its methods, can give men more than a poor counterfeit of liberty if it rest upon illiberal principles of government.

A clear view of the difference between the province of constitutional law and the province of administrative function ought to leave no room for misconception; and it is possible to name some roughly definite criteria upon which such a

35   view can be built. Public administration is detailed and systematic execution of public law. Every particular application of general law is an act of administration. The assessment and raising of taxes, for instance, the hanging of a criminal, the transportation and delivery of the mails, the equipment and recruiting of the army and navy, *etc.*, are all obviously acts of administration; but the general

laws which direct these things to be done are as obviously outside of and above administration. The broad plans of governmental action are not administrative; the detailed execution of such plans is administrative. Constitutions, therefore, properly concern themselves only with those instrumentalities of government which are to control general law. Our federal constitution observes this principle in saying nothing of even the greatest of the purely executive offices, and speaking only of that President of the Union who was to share the legislative and policy-making functions of government, only of those judges of highest jurisdiction who were to interpret and guard its principles, and not of those who were merely to give utterance to them.

This is not quite the distinction between Will and answering Deed, because the administrator should have and does have a will of his own in the choice of means for accomplishing his work. He is not and ought not to be a mere passive instrument. The distinction is between general plans and special means.

There is, indeed, one point at which administrative studies trench on constitutional ground—or at least upon what seems constitutional ground. The study of administration, philosophically viewed, is closely connected with the study of the proper distribution of constitutional authority. To be efficient it must discover the simplest arrangements by which responsibility can be unmistakably fixed upon officials; the best way of dividing authority without hampering it, and responsibility without obscuring it. And this question of the distribution of authority, when taken into the sphere of the higher, the originating functions of government, is obviously a central constitutional question. If administrative study can discover the best principles upon which to base such distribution, it will have done constitutional study an invaluable service. Montesquieu did not, I am convinced, say the last word on this head.

To discover the best principle for the distribution of authority is of greater importance, possibly, under a democratic system, where officials serve many masters, than under others where they serve but a few. All sovereigns are suspicious of their servants, and the sovereign people is no exception to the rule; but how is its suspicion to be allayed by *knowledge*? If that suspicion could but be clarified into wise vigilance, it would be altogether salutary; if that vigilance could be aided by the unmistakable placing of responsibility, it would be altogether beneficent. Suspicion in itself is never healthful either in the private or in the public mind. *Trust is strength* in all relations of life; and, as it is the office of the constitutional reformer to create conditions of trustfulness, so it is the office of the administrative organizer to fit administration with conditions of clear-cut responsibility which shall insure trustworthiness.

And let me say that large powers and unhampered discretion seem to me the indispensable conditions of responsibility. Public attention must be easily directed, in each case of good or bad administration, to just the man deserving of praise or blame. There is no danger in power, if only it be not irresponsible.

5   If it be divided, dealt out in shares to many, it is obscured; and if it be obscured, it is made irresponsible. But if it be centered in heads of the service and in heads of branches of the service, it is easily watched and brought to book. If to keep his office a man must achieve open and honest success, and if at the same time he feels himself intrusted with large freedom of discretion, the greater his power

10   the less likely is he to abuse it, the more is he nerved and sobered and elevated by it. The less his power, the more safely obscure and unnoticed does he feel his position to be, and the more readily does he relapse into remissness.

Just here we manifestly emerge upon the field of that still larger question,—the proper relations between public opinion and administration.

15   To whom is official trustworthiness to be disclosed, and by whom is it to be rewarded? Is the official to look to the public for his meed of praise and his push of promotion, or only to his superior in office? Are the people to be called in to settle administrative discipline as they are called in to settle constitutional principles? These questions evidently find their root in what is undoubtedly

20   the fundamental problem of this whole study. That problem is: What part shall public opinion take in the conduct of administration?

The right answer seems to be, that public opinion shall play the part of authoritative critic.

But the *method* by which its authority shall be made to tell? Our peculiar

25   American difficulty in organizing administration is not the danger of losing liberty, but the danger of not being able or willing to separate its essentials from its accidents. Our success is made doubtful by that besetting error of ours, the error of trying to do too much by vote. Self-government does not consist in having a hand in everything, any more than housekeeping consists necessarily

30   in cooking dinner with one's own hands. The cook must be trusted with a large discretion as to the management of the fires and the ovens.

In those countries in which public opinion has yet to be instructed in its privileges, yet to be accustomed to having its own way, this question as to the province of public opinion is much more readily soluble than in this country,

35   where public opinion is wide awake and quite intent upon having its own way anyhow. It is pathetic to see a whole book written by a German professor of political science for the purpose of saying to his countrymen, "Please try to have an opinion about national affairs"; but a public which is so modest may

at least be expected to be very docile and acquiescent in learning what things it has *not* a right to think and speak about imperatively. It may be sluggish, but it will not be meddlesome. It will submit to be instructed before it tries to instruct. Its political education will come before its political activity. In trying to instruct our own public opinion, we are dealing with a pupil apt to think itself quite sufficiently instructed beforehand.

The problem is to make public opinion efficient without suffering it to be meddlesome. Directly exercised, in the oversight of the daily details and in the choice of the daily means of government, public criticism is of course a clumsy nuisance, a rustic handling delicate machinery. But as superintending the greater forces of formative policy alike in politics and administration, public criticism is altogether safe and beneficent, altogether indispensable. Let administrative study find the best means for giving public criticism this control and for shutting it out from all other interference.

But is the whole duty of administrative study done when it has taught the people what sort of administration to desire and demand, and how to get what they demand? Ought it not to go on to drill candidates for the public service?

There is an admirable movement towards universal political education now afoot in this country. The time will soon come when no college of respectability can afford to do without a well-filled chair of political science. But the education thus imparted will go but a certain length. It will multiply the number of intelligent critics of government, but it will create no component body of administrators. It will prepare the way for the development of a sure-footed understanding of the general principles of government, but it will not necessarily foster skill in conducting government. It is an education which will equip legislators, perhaps, but not executive officials. If we are to improve public opinion, which is the motive power of government, we must prepare better officials as the *apparatus* of government. If we are to put in new boilers and to mend the fires which drive our governmental machinery, we must not leave the old wheels and joints and valves and bands to creak and buzz and clatter on as best they may at bidding of the new force. We must put in new running parts wherever there is the least lack of strength or adjustment. It will be necessary to organize democracy by sending up to the competitive examinations for the civil service men definitely prepared for standing liberal tests as to technical knowledge. A technically schooled civil service will presently have become indispensable.

I know that a corps of civil servants prepared by a special schooling and drilled, after appointment, into a perfected organization, with appropriate hierarchy and characteristic discipline, seems to a great many very thoughtful persons to

contain elements which might combine to make an offensive official class,—a distinct, semi-corporate body with sympathies divorced from those of a progressive, free-spirited people, and with hearts narrowed to the meanness of a bigoted officialism. Certainly such a class would be altogether hateful and
5   harmful in the United States. Any measure calculated to produce it would for us be measures of reaction and of folly.

But to fear the creation of a domineering, illiberal officialism as a result of the studies I am here proposing is to miss altogether the principle upon which I wish most to insist. That principle is, that administration in the United States
10   must be at all points sensitive to public opinion. A body of thoroughly trained officials serving during good behavior we must have in any case: that is a plain business necessity. But the apprehension that such a body will be anything un-American clears away the moment it is asked. What is to constitute good behavior? For that question obviously carries its own answer on its face. Steady,
15   hearty allegiance to the policy of the government they serve will constitute good behavior. That *policy* will have no taint of officialism about it. It will not be the creation of permanent officials, but of statesmen whose responsibility to public opinion will be direct and inevitable. Bureaucracy can exist only where the whole service of the state is removed from the common political life of the
20   people, its chiefs as well as its rank and file. Its motives, its objects, its policy, its standards, must be bureaucratic. It would be difficult to point out any examples of impudent exclusiveness and arbitrariness on the part of officials doing service under a chief of department who really served the people, as all our chiefs of departments must be made to do. It would be easy, on the other hand, to adduce
25   other instances like that of the influence of Stein in Prussia, where the leadership of one statesman imbued with true public spirit transformed arrogant and perfunctory bureaux into public-spirited instruments of just government.

The ideal for us is a civil service cultured and self-sufficient enough to act with sense and vigor, and yet so intimately connected with the popular thought, by
30   means of elections and constant public counsel, as to find arbitrariness of class spirit quite out of the question.

III.

Having thus viewed in some sort the subject-matter and the objects of this study of administration, what are we to conclude as to the methods best suited to it—the points of view most advantageous for it?

35   Government is so near us, so much a thing of our daily familiar handling, that we can with difficulty see the need of any philosophical study of it, or the exact points of such study, should it be undertaken. We have been on our feet too

long to study now the art of walking. We are a practical people, made so apt, so adept in self-government by centuries of experimental drill, that we are scarcely any longer capable of perceiving the awkwardness of the particular system we may be using, just because it is so easy for us to use any system. We do not study the art of governing: we govern. But mere unschooled genius for affairs will not save us from sad blunders in administration. Though democrats by long inheritance and repeated choice, we are still rather crude democrats. Old as democracy is, its organization on a basis of modern ideas and conditions is still an unaccomplished work. The democratic state has yet to be equipped for carrying those enormous burdens of administration which the needs of this industrial and trading age are so fast accumulating. Without comparative studies in government we cannot rid ourselves of the misconception that administration stands upon an essentially different basis in a democratic state from that on which it stands in a non-democratic state.

After such study we could grant democracy the sufficient honor of ultimately determining by debate all essential questions affecting the public weal, of basing all structures of policy upon the major will; but we would have found but one rule of good administration for all governments alike. So far as administrative functions are concerned, all governments have a strong structural likeness; more than that, if they are to be uniformly useful and efficient, they *must* have a strong structural likeness. A free man has the same bodily organs, the same executive parts, as the slave, however different may be his motives, his services, his energies. Monarchies and democracies, radically different as they are in other respects, have in reality much the same business to look to.

It is abundantly safe nowadays to insist upon this actual likeness of all governments, because these are days when abuses of power are easily exposed and arrested, in countries like our own, by a bold, alert, inquisitive, detective public thought and a sturdy popular self-dependence such as never existed before. We are slow to appreciate this; but it is easy to appreciate it. Try to imagine personal government in the United States. It is like trying to imagine a national worship of Zeus. Our imaginations are too modern for the feat.

But, besides being safe, it is necessary to see that for all governments alike the legitimate ends of administration are the same, in order not to be frightened at the idea of looking into foreign systems of administration for instruction and suggestion; in order to get rid of the apprehension that we might perchance blindly borrow something incompatible with our principles. That man is blindly astray who denounces attempts to transplant foreign systems into this country. It is impossible: they simply would not grow here. But why should we not use such parts of foreign contrivances as we want, if they be in any way serviceable?

We are in no danger of using them in a foreign way. We borrowed rice, but we do not eat it with chopsticks. We borrowed our whole political language from England, but we leave the words "king" and "lords" out of it. What did we ever originate, except the action of the federal government upon individuals and
5 some of the functions of the federal supreme court?

We can borrow the science of administration with safety and profit if only we read all fundamental differences of condition into its essential tenets. We have only to filter it through our constitutions, only to put it over a slow fire of criticism and distil away its foreign gases.

10 I know that there is a sneaking fear in some conscientiously patriotic minds that studies of European systems might signalize some foreign methods as better than some American methods; and the fear is easily to be understood. But it would scarcely be avowed in any just company.

It is the more necessary to insist upon thus putting away all prejudices against
15 looking anywhere in the world but at home for suggestions in this study, because nowhere else in the whole field of politics, it would seem, can we make use of the historical, comparative method more safely than in this province of administration. Perhaps the more novel the forms we study the better. We shall the sooner learn the peculiarities of our own methods. We can never learn either
20 our own weaknesses or our own virtues by comparing ourselves with ourselves. We are too used to the appearance and procedure of our own system to see its true significance. Perhaps even the English system is too much like our own to be used to the most profit in illustration. It is best on the whole to get entirely away from our own atmosphere and to be most careful in examining such
25 systems as those of France and Germany. Seeing our own institutions through such *media*, we see ourselves as foreigners might see us were they to look at us without preconceptions. Of ourselves, so long as we know only ourselves, we know nothing.

Let it be noted that it is the distinction, already drawn, between administra-
30 tion and politics which makes the comparative method so safe in the field of administration. When we study the administrative systems of France and Germany, knowing that we are not in search of *political* principles, we need not care a peppercorn for the constitutional or political reasons which Frenchmen or Germans give for their practices when explaining them to us. If I see a mur-
35 derous fellow sharpening a knife cleverly, I can borrow his way of sharpening the knife without borrowing his probable intention to commit murder with it; and so, if I see a monarchist dyed in the wool managing a public bureau well, I can learn his business methods without changing one of my republican

spots. He may serve his king; I will continue to serve the people; but I should like to serve my sovereign as well as he serves his. By keeping this distinction in view,—that is, by studying administration as a means of putting our own politics into convenient practice, as a means of making what is democratically politic towards all administratively possible towards each,—we are on perfectly safe ground, and can learn without error what foreign systems have to teach us. We thus devise an adjusting weight for our comparative method of study. We can thus scrutinize the anatomy of foreign governments without fear of getting any of their diseases into our veins; dissect alien systems without apprehension of blood-poisoning.

Our own politics must be the touchstone for all theories. The principles on which to base a science of administration for America must be principles which have democratic policy very much at heart. And, to suit American habit, all general theories must, as theories, keep modestly in the background, not in open argument only, but even in our own minds,—lest opinions satisfactory only to the standards of the library should be dogmatically used, as if they must be quite as satisfactory to the standards of practical politics as well. Doctrinaire devices must be postponed to tested practices. Arrangements not only sanctioned by conclusive experience elsewhere but also congenial to American habit must be preferred without hesitation to theoretical perfection. In a word, steady, practical statesmanship must come first, closet doctrine second. The cosmopolitan what-to-do must always be commanded by the American how-to-do-it.

Our duty is, to supply the best possible life to a *federal* organization, to systems within systems; to make town, city, county, state, and federal governments live with a like strength and an equally assured healthfulness, keeping each unquetionably its own master and yet making all interdependent and cooperative, combining independence with mutual helpfulness. The task is great and important enough to attract the best minds.

This interlacing of local self-government with federal self-government is quite a modern conception. It is not like the arrangements of imperial federation in Germany. There local government is not yet, fully, local *self*-government. The bureaucrat is everywhere busy. His efficiency springs out of *esprit de corps*, out of care to make ingratiating obeisance to the authority of a superior, or at best, out of the soil of a sensitive conscience. He serves, not the public, but an irresponsible minister. The question for us is, how shall our series of governments within governments be so administered that it shall always be to the interest of the public officer to serve, not his superior alone but the community also, with the best efforts of his talents and the soberest service of his conscience? How shall such service be made to his commonest interest by contributing abundantly to his sustenance, to his dearest interest by furthering his ambition, and to his highest interest by advancing his honor and establishing his character? And how shall this be done alike for the local part and for the national whole?

5   If we solve this problem we shall again pilot the world. There is a tendency—is there not?—a tendency as yet dim, but already steadily impulsive and clearly destined to prevail, towards, first the confederation of parts of empires like the British, and finally of great states themselves. Instead of centralization of power, there is to be wide union with tolerated divisions of prerogative. This is
10   a tendency towards the American type—of governments joined with governments for the pursuit of common purposes, in honorary equality and honorable subordination. Like principles of civil liberty are everywhere fostering like methods of government; and if comparative studies of the ways and means of government should enable us to offer suggestions which will practically com-
15   bine openness and vigor in the administration of such governments with ready docility to all serious, well-sustained public criticism, they will have approved themselves worthy to be ranked among the highest and most fruitful of the great departments of political study. That they will issue in such suggestions I confidently hope.

The Right of the People to Rule

Theodore Roosevelt

Theodore Roosevelt relinquished the presidency in 1908, believing that his Progressive legacy lay safely in the hands of his handpicked successor, William Howard Taft. Although Taft expanded many of Roosevelt's policies and succeeded in passing through Congress the Sixteenth Amendment, permitting a national income tax, Roosevelt challenged Taft in the 1912 Republican primary. Losing the nomination, he announced an independent candidacy under the banner of the Progressive or "Bull Moose" Party. In this campaign speech, he urges more direct power to the people through recall elections, referenda and initiatives, and direct primaries.

MARCH 20, 1912

The great fundamental issue now before the Republican party and before our people can be stated briefly. It is, Are the American people fit to govern themselves, to rule themselves, to control themselves? I believe they are. My opponents do not. I believe in the right of the people to rule. I believe the majority of the plain people of the United States will, day in and day out, make 5 fewer mistakes in governing themselves than any smaller class or body of men, no matter what their training, will make in trying to govern them. I believe, again, that the American people are, as a whole, capable of self-control and of learning by their mistakes. Our opponents pay lip-loyalty to this doctrine; but they show their real beliefs by the way in which they champion every device to 10 make the nominal rule of the people a sham.

I have scant patience with this talk of the tyranny of the majority. Whenever there is tyranny of the majority, I shall protest against it with all my heart and soul. But we are today suffering from the tyranny of minorities. It is a small minority that is grabbing our coal deposits, our water powers, and our harbor 15 fronts. A small minority is battening on the sale of adulterated foods and drugs. It is a small minority that lies behind monopolies and trusts. It is a small minor-

---

Theodore Roosevelt, "The Right of the People to Rule," *The Outlook* 100 (March 1912): 618–23.

ity that stands behind the present law of master and servant, the sweat-shops, and the whole calendar of social and industrial injustice. It is a small minority that is today using our convention system to defeat the will of a majority of the people in the choice of delegates to the Chicago Convention. The only
5   tyrannies from which men, women, and children are suffering in real life are the tyrannies of minorities.

If the majority of the American people were in fact tyrannous over the minority, if democracy had no greater self-control than empire, then indeed no written words which our forefathers put into the Constitution could stay that tyranny.

10 No sane man who has been familiar with the government of this country for the last twenty years will complain that we have had too much of the rule of the majority. The trouble has been a far different one—that, at many times and in many localities, there have held public office in the States and in the Nation men who have, in fact, served not the whole people, but some special
15 class or special interest. I am not thinking only of those special interests which by grosser methods, by bribery and crime, have stolen from the people. I am thinking as much of their respectable allies and figureheads, who have ruled and legislated and decided as if in some way the vested rights of privilege had a first mortgage on the whole United States, while the rights of all the people
20 were merely an unsecured debt. Am I overstating the case? Have our political leaders always, or generally, recognized their duty to the people as anything more than a duty to disperse the mob, see that the ashes are taken away, and distribute patronage? Have our leaders always, or generally, worked for the benefit of human beings, to increase the prosperity of all the people, to give to
25 each some opportunity of living decently and bringing up his children well? The questions need no answer.

Now there has sprung up a feeling deep in the hearts of the people—not of the bosses and professional politicians, not of the beneficiaries of special privilege—a pervading belief of thinking men that when the majority of the people do in fact,
30 as well as theory, rule, then the servants of the people will come more quickly to answer and obey, not the commands of the special interests, but those of the whole people. To reach toward that end the Progressives of the Republican party in certain States have formulated certain proposals for change in the form of the State government—certain new "checks and balances" which may check
35 and balance the special interests and their allies. That is their purpose. Now turn for a moment to their proposed methods.

First, there are the "initiative and referendum," which are so framed that if the Legislatures obey the command of some special interest, and obstinately refuse the will of the majority, the majority may step in and legislate directly. No

man would say that it was best to conduct all legislation by direct vote of the people—it would mean the loss of deliberation, of patient consideration—but, on the other hand, no one whose mental arteries have not long since hardened can doubt that the proposed changes are needed when the Legislatures refuse to carry out the will of the people. The proposal is a method to reach an un-   5
deniable evil. Then there is the recall of public officers—the principle that an officer chosen by the people who is unfaithful may be recalled by vote of the majority before he finishes his term. I will speak of the recall of judges in a moment—leave that aside—but as to the other officers, I have heard no argument advanced against the proposition, save that it will make the public officer   10
timid and always currying favor with the mob. That argument means that you can fool all the people all the time, and is an avowal of disbelief in democracy. If it be true—and I believe it is not—it is less important than to stop those public officers from currying favor with the interests. Certain States may need the recall, others may not; where the term of elective office is short it may be   15
quite needless; but there are occasions when it meets a real evil, and provides a needed check and balance against the special interests.

Then there is the direct primary—the real one, not the New York one—and that, too, the Progressives offer as a check on the special interests. Most clearly of all does it seem to me that this change is wholly good—for every State. The   20
system of party government is not written in our Constitutions, but it is none the less a vital and essential part of our form of government. In that system the party leaders should serve and carry out the will of their own party. There is no need to show how far that theory is from the facts, or to rehearse the vulgar thieving partnerships of the corporations and the bosses, or to show   25
how many times the real government lies in the hands of the boss, protected from the commands and the revenge of the voters by his puppets in office and the power of patronage. We need not be told how he is thus entrenched nor how hard he is to overthrow. The facts stand out in the history of nearly every State in the Union. They are blots on our political system. The direct primary   30
will give the voters a method ever ready to use, by which the party leader shall be made to obey their command. The direct primary, if accompanied by a stringent corrupt-practices act, will help break up the corrupt partnership of corporations and politicians.

My opponents charge that two things in my program are wrong because they   35
intrude into the sanctuary of the judiciary. The first is the recall of judges; and the second, the review by the people of judicial decisions on certain constitu-
tional questions. I have said again and again that I do not advocate the recall of judges in all States and in all communities. In my own State I do not advocate it or believe it to be needed, for in this State our trouble lies not with corrup-   40

tion on the bench, but with the effort by the honest but wrong headed judges to thwart the people in their struggle for social justice and fair-dealing. The integrity of our judges from Marshall to White and Holmes—and to Cullen and many others in our own State—is a fine page of American history. But—I
5 say it soberly—democracy has a right to approach the sanctuary of the courts when a special interest has corruptly found sanctuary there; and this is exactly what has happened in some of the States where the recall of the judges is a living issue. I would far more willingly trust the whole people to judge such a case than some special tribunal—perhaps appointed by the same power that chose
10 the judge—if that tribunal is not itself really responsible to the people and is hampered and clogged by the technicalities of impeachment proceedings.

I have stated that the courts of the several States—not always but often—have construed the "due process" clause of the State Constitutions as if it prohibited the whole people of the State from adopting methods of regulating the use of
15 property so that human life, particularly the lives of the working men, shall be safer, freer, and happier. No one can successfully impeach this statement. I have insisted that the true construction of "due process" is that pronounced by Justice Holmes in delivering the unanimous opinion of the Supreme Court of the United States, when he said:

20 "The police power extends to all the great public needs. It may be put forth in aid of what is sanctioned by usage, or held by the prevailing morality or strong and preponderant opinion to be greatly and immediately necessary to the public welfare."

I insist that the decision of the New York Court of Appeals in the Ives case,
25 which set aside the will of the majority of the people as to the compensation of injured workmen in dangerous trades, was intolerable and based on a wrong political philosophy. I urge that in such cases where the courts construe the due process clause as if property rights, to the exclusion of human rights, had a first mortgage on the Constitution, the people may, after sober deliberation, vote,
30 and finally determine whether the law which the court set aside shall be valid or not. By this method can be clearly and finally ascertained the preponderant opinion of the people which Justice Holmes makes the test of due process in the case of laws enacted in the exercise of the police power. The ordinary methods now in vogue of amending the Constitution have in actual practice proved
35 wholly inadequate to secure justice in such cases with reasonable speed, and cause intolerable delay and injustice, and those who stand against the changes I propose are champions of wrong and injustice, and of tyranny by the wealthy and the strong over the weak and the helpless.

So that no man may misunderstand me, let me recapitulate:

(1) I am not proposing anything in connection with the Supreme Court of the United States, or with the Federal Constitution.

(2) I am not proposing anything having any connection with ordinary suits, civil or criminal, as between individuals.

(3) I am not speaking of the recall of judges.

(4) I am proposing merely that in a certain class of cases involving the police power, when a State court has set aside as unconstitutional a law passed by the Legislature for the general welfare, the question of the validity of the law—which should depend, as Justice Holmes so well phrases it, upon the prevailing morality or preponderant opinion—be submitted for final determination to a vote of the people, taken after due time for consideration. And I contend that the people, in the nature of things, must be better judges of what is the preponderant opinion than the courts, and that the courts should not be allowed to reverse the political philosophy of the people. My point is well illustrated by a recent decision of the Supreme Court, holding that the Court would not take jurisdiction of a case involving the constitutionality of the initiative and referendum laws of Oregon. The ground of the decision was that such a question was not judicial in its nature, but should be left for determination to the other coordinate departments of the Government. Is it not equally plain that the question whether a given social policy is for the public good is not of a judicial nature, but should be settled by the Legislature, or in the final instance by the people themselves?

The President of the United States, Mr. Taft, devoted most of a recent speech to criticism of this proposition. He says that it "is utterly without merit or utility, and, instead of being…in the interest of all the people, and of the stability of popular government, is sowing the seeds of confusion and tyranny." (By this he of course means the tyranny of the majority, that is, the tyranny of the American people as a whole.) He also says that my proposal (which, as he rightly sees, is merely a proposal to give the people a real, instead of only a nominal, chance to construe and amend a State Constitution with reasonable rapidity) would make such amendment and interpretation "depend on the feverish, uncertain, and unstable determination of successive votes on different laws by temporary and changing majorities;" and that "it lays the axe at the foot of the tree of well-ordered freedom, and subjects the guarantees of life, liberty, and property without remedy to the fitful impulse of a temporary majority of an electorate."

This criticism is really less a criticism of my proposal than a criticism of all popular government. It is wholly unfounded, unless it is founded on the belief that the people are fundamentally untrustworthy. If the Supreme Court's definition of due process in relation to the police power is sound, then an act of

5 the Legislature to promote the collective interests of the community must be valid, if it embodies a policy held by the prevailing morality or a preponderant opinion to be necessary to the public welfare. This is the question that I propose to submit to the people. How can the prevailing morality or a preponderant opinion be better and more exactly ascertained than by a vote of the people?

10 The people must know better than the court what their own morality and their own opinion is. I ask that you, here, you and the others like you, you the people, be given the chance to state your own views of justice and public morality, and not sit meekly by and have your views announced for you by well-meaning adherents of outworn philosophies, who exalt the pedantry of formulas above

15 the vital needs of human life.

The object I have in view could probably be accomplished by an amendment of the State Constitutions taking away from the courts the power to review the Legislature's determination of a policy of social justice, by defining due process of law in accordance with the views expressed by Justice Holmes of the Supreme

20 Court. But my proposal seems to me more democratic and, I may add, less radical. For under the method I suggest the people may sustain the court as against the Legislature, whereas, if due process were defined in the Constitution, the decision of the Legislature would be final.

Mr. Taft's position is the position that has been held from the beginning of our

25 Government, although not always so openly held, by a large number of reputable and honorable men who, down at bottom, distrust popular government, and, when they must accept it, accept it with reluctance, and hedge it around with every species of restriction and check and balance, so as to make the power of the people as limited and as ineffective as possible. Mr. Taft fairly defines the

30 issue when he says that our Government is and should be a government of all the people by a representative part of the people. This is an excellent and moderate description of all oligarchy. It defines our Government as a government of all the people by a few of the people.

Mr. Taft, in his able speech, has made what is probably the best possible pre-

35 sentation of the case for those who feel in this manner. Essentially this view differs only in its expression from the view nakedly set forth by one of his supporters, Congressman Campbell. Congressman Campbell, in a public speech in New Hampshire, in opposing the proposition to give the people real and effective control over all their servants, including the judges, stated that this

was equivalent to allowing an appeal from the umpire to the bleachers. Doubt-less Congressman Campbell was not himself aware of the cynical truthfulness with which he was putting the real attitude of those for whom he spoke. But it unquestionably is their real attitude. Mr. Campbell's conception of the part the American people should play in self-government is that they should sit on the bleachers and pay the price of admission, but should have nothing to say as to the contest which is waged in the arena by the professional politicians. Apparently Mr. Campbell ignores the fact that the American people are not mere onlookers at a game, that they have a vital stake in the contest, and that democracy means nothing unless they are able and willing to show that they are their own masters.

I am not speaking jokingly, nor do I mean to be unkind; for I repeat that many honorable and well-meaning men of high character take this view, and have taken it from the time of the formation of the Nation. Essentially this view is that the Constitution is a straight-jacket to be used for the control of an unruly patient—the people. Now I hold that this view is not only false but mischievous, that our Constitutions are instruments designed to secure justice by securing the deliberate but effective expression of the popular will, that the checks and balances are valuable as far, and only so far, as they accomplish that deliberation, and that it is a warped and unworthy and improper construction of our form of government to see in it only a means of thwarting the popular will and of preventing justice. Mr. Taft says that "every class" should have a "voice" in the government. That seems to me a very serious misconception of the American political situation. The real trouble with us is that some classes have had too much voice. One of the most important of all the lessons to be taught and to be learned is that a man should vote, not as a representative of a class, but merely as a good citizen, whose prime interests are the same as those of all other good citizens. The belief in different classes, each having a voice in the Government, has given rise to much of our present difficulty; for whosoever believes in these separate classes, each with a voice, inevitably, even although unconsciously, tends to work, not for the good of the whole people, but for the protection of some special class—usually that to which he himself belongs.

The same principle applies when Mr. Taft says that the judiciary ought not to be "representative" of the people in the sense that the Legislature and the Executive are. This is perfectly true of the judge when he is performing merely the ordinary functions of a judge in suits between man and man. It is not true of the judge engaged in interpreting, for instance, the due process clause—where the judge is ascertaining the preponderant opinion of the people (as Judge Holmes states it). When he exercises that function he has no right to let his political philosophy reverse and thwart the will of the majority. In that function the judge must represent the people or he fails in the test the Supreme Court has laid down. Take the Workmen's Compensation Act here in New York. The legislators gave us a law in the interest of humanity and decency and fair dealing. In so doing they represented the people, and represented them well. Several judges declared that law Constitutional in our State, and several courts in other States declared similar laws Constitutional, and the Supreme Court of the Nation declared a similar law affecting men in inter-State business constitutional; but the highest court in the State of New York, the Court of Appeals, declared that we, the people of New York, could not have such a law. I hold that in this case the legislators and the judges alike occupied representative positions; the difference was merely that the former represented us well and the latter represented us ill. Remember that the legislators promised that law, and were returned by the people partly in consequence of such promise. That judgment of the people should not have been set aside unless it were irrational. Yet in the Ives case the New York Court of Appeals praised the policy of the law and the end it sought to obtain; and then declared that the people lacked power to do justice!

Mr. Taft again and again, in quotations I have given and elsewhere through his speech, expresses his disbelief in the people when they vote at the polls. In one sentence he says that the proposition gives "powerful effect to the momentary impulse of a majority of an electorate and prepares the way for the possible exercise of the grossest tyranny." Elsewhere he speaks of the "feverish uncertainty" and "unstable determination" of laws by "temporary and changing majorities;" and again he says that the system I propose "would result in suspension or application of Constitutional guarantees according to popular whim," which would destroy "all possible consistency" in Constitutional interpretation. I should much like to know the exact distinction that is to be made between what Mr. Taft calls "the fitful impulse of a temporary majority" when applied to a question such as that I raise and any other question. Remember that under my proposal to review a rule of decision by popular vote, amending or construing, to that extent, the Constitution, would certainly take at least two years from the time of the election of the Legislature which passed the act. Now, only four months elapse between the nomination and the election of a man as President, to fill for four years the most important office in the land. In one of Mr. Taft's speeches he speaks of "the voice of the people as coming next to the voice of God." Apparently, then, the decision of the people about the Presidency, after four months' deliberation, is to be treated as "next to the voice of God;" but if, after two years of sober thought, they decide that women and children shall be protected in industry, or men protected from excessive hours of labor under unhygienic conditions, or wage-workers compensated when they lose life or limb in the service of others, then their decision forthwith becomes a "whim" and "feverish" and "unstable" and an exercise of "the grossest tyranny" and the "laying of the axe to the foot of the tree of freedom." It seems absurd to speak of a conclusion reached by the people after two years' deliberation, after threshing the matter out before the Legislature, after threshing it out before the Governor, after threshing it out before the court and by the court, and then after full debate for four or six months, as "the fitful impulse of a temporary majority." If Mr. Taft's language correctly describes such action by the people, then he himself and all other Presidents have been elected by "the fitful impulse of a temporary majority;" then the Constitution of each State, and the Constitution of the Nation, have been adopted, and all amendments thereto have been adopted, by "the fitful impulse of a temporary majority." If he is right, it was "the fitful impulse of a temporary majority" which founded, and another fitful impulse which perpetuated, this Nation. Mr. Taft's position is perfectly clear. It is that we have in this country a special class of persons wiser than the people, who are above the people, who cannot be reached by the people, but who govern them and ought to govern them; and who protect various classes of the people from the whole people. That is the old, old doctrine which has been acted upon for thousands of years abroad; and which here in America has been acted upon sometimes openly, sometimes secretly, for forty years by many men in public and in private life, and I am sorry to say by many judges; a doctrine which has in fact tended to create a bulwark for privilege, a bulwark unjustly protecting special interests against the rights of the people as a whole. This doctrine is to me a dreadful doctrine; for its effect is, and can only be, to make the courts the shield of privilege against popular rights. Naturally, every upholder and beneficiary of crooked privilege loudly applauds the doctrine. It is behind the shield of that doctrine that crooked clauses creep into laws, that men of wealth and power control legislation. The men of wealth who praise this doctrine, this theory, would do well to remember that to its adoption by the courts is due the distrust so many of our wage-workers now feel for the courts. I deny that that theory has worked so well that we should continue it. I most earnestly urge that the evils and abuses it has produced cry aloud for remedy; and the only remedy is in fact to restore the power to govern directly to the people, and to make the public servant directly responsible to the whole people—and to no part of them, to no "class" of them.

Mr. Taft is very much afraid of the tyranny of majorities. For twenty-five years here in New York State, in our efforts to get social and industrial justice, we have suffered from the tyranny of a small minority. We have been denied, now

by one court, now by another, as in the Bakeshop Case, where the courts set aside the law limiting the hours of labor in bakeries—the "due process" clause again—as in the workmen's compensation act, as in the tenement-house cigar factory case—in all these and many other cases we have been denied by small
5   minorities, by a few worthy men of wrong political philosophy on the bench, the right to protect our people in their lives, their liberty, and their pursuit of happiness. As for "consistency"—why, the record of the courts, in such a case as the income tax for instance, is so full of inconsistencies as to make the fear expressed of "inconsistency" on the part of the people seem childish....

Progressive Democracy
Herbert Croly (1869–1930)

In this book, Herbert Croly, a leading Progressive theorist and founder of
The New Republic magazine, criticizes the Founders' fear of tyranny of the
majority and rejects their idea that government exists to protect individual
rights.

1915

Chapter XII: The Advent of Direct Government

...If economic, social, political and technical conditions had remained very
much as they were at the end of the eighteenth century, the purely democratic
political aspirations might never have obtained the chance of expression. Some
form of essentially representative government was at that time apparently the only
dependable kind of liberal political organization. It was imposed by the physical   5
and technical conditions under which government had to be conducted. Direct
government did not seem to be possible outside of city or tribal states, whose
population and area was sufficiently small to permit the actual assemblage of
the body politic at some particular place, either at regular intervals or in case
of an emergency. But in the case of states chiefly devoted to agriculture, whose   10
free citizens were distributed over a wide area, and were, in any event, too
numerous for actual assemblage in any one spot, it seemed necessary for the
people to delegate to a body of representatives the power required not merely
for public administration, but for the discussion of public questions, the adoption of public policies and the supervising of the administration itself. Some   15
form of a responsible representative government, that is, was prescribed by
fundamental economic and social conditions. The function was performed in
the several states according to the method best adapted to local traditions and
by the class which had proved itself capable of leadership.

In the twentieth century, however, these practical conditions of political associ-   20
ation have again changed, and have changed in a manner which enables

---

Herbert Croly, *Progressive Democracy* (New York: The Macmillan Company, 1914), 262–83.

the mass of the people to assume some immediate control of their political destinies. While it is more impossible than ever for the citizens of a modern industrial and agricultural state actually to assemble after the manner of a New England town-meeting, it is no longer necessary for them so to assemble. They
5   have abundant opportunities of communication and consultation without any actual meeting at one time and place. They are kept in constant touch with one another by means of the complicated agencies of publicity and intercourse which are afforded by the magazines, the press and the like. The active citizenship of the country meets every morning and evening and discusses the affairs
10 of the nation with the newspaper as an impersonal interlocutor. Public opinion has a thousand methods of seeking information and obtaining definite and effective expression which it did not have four generations ago. The community is broken up into innumerable smaller communities, each of which is united by common interests and ideas and each of which is seeking to bring a larger
15 number of people under the influence of its interests and ideas. Under such conditions the discussions which take place in a Congress or a Parliament no longer possess their former function. They no longer create and guide what public opinion there is. Their purpose rather is to provide a mirror for public opinion, to advertise and illuminate its constituent ideas and purposes, and to
20 confront the advocates of those ideas with the discipline of effective resistance and, perhaps, with the responsibilities of power. Phases of public opinion form, develop, gather to a head, assert their power and find their place chiefly by the activity of other more popular unofficial agencies. Thus the democracy has at its disposal a mechanism of developing and exchanging opinions, and
25 of reaching decisions, which is independent of representative assemblies, and which is, or may become, superior to that which it formerly obtained by virtue of occasional popular assemblages.

The adoption of the machinery of direct government is a legitimate expression of this change. After centuries of political development, in which
30 certain forms of representation were imposed upon progressive nations by conditions of practical efficiency, and in which these representative forms grew continually in variety and complexity, underlying conditions have again shifted. Pure democracy has again become not merely possible, but natural and appropriate. The attempt to return to it is no more retrogressive
35 than was the attempt to recover classic humanism after its eclipse during the Middle Ages. Society has been passing through a period of prodigious fertility, during which new social aspirations, purposes, instruments and activities have multiplied with unprecedented rapidity. If these new interests and activities are to be assimilated, they must be recognized and incorporated into the system

of government. As a consequence of the attempt to incorporate them into the system of government, society may seem to be yielding to the power of disintegrating economic and social forces. This appears to be the beginning of a reverse process of denationalization which will be equivalent to dissolution. Those who place any such interpretation upon the facts of modern social development and the corresponding political changes fail to understand their meaning. Increasingly direct popular political action is coming to have a function in the political organization of a modern society, because only in this way can the nation again become a master in its own house. Its very fecundity, and the enormous power which many of its offspring obtain, have compelled a democratic nation to adopt a more thoroughgoing method of promoting its integrity. As yet it is not making very much headway. It is distracted and disconcerted by its own fertility. It is terrified in particular by the capitalist and labor organizations to which it has given birth. But it will not continue to be disconcerted and terrified. It is adopting the very political instruments which are necessary for the purpose of keeping control of the increasingly numerous and increasingly powerful agencies of its own life. The attempt, far from being a reactionary reversion to an earlier political and social type, prepares the way, it may be hoped, for an advance towards a better and deeper social and political union, associated with direct popular political action and responsibility.

CHAPTER XIII: DIRECT *VERSUS* REPRESENTATIVE GOVERNMENT

In the preceding chapter I have submitted some reasons for believing that direct government is not retrogressive merely because its methods exhibit certain analogies to those used in city and tribal states. Neither does the fact that the electorate in a directly governed state has certain positive functions to perform in relation to legislation place upon such a state the stigma of reaction. Direct government cannot be fairly condemned as reactionary unless the exercise of the broad general responsibilities which it imposes upon the electorate proves inimical to the delegation of sufficient and specific additional responsibilities to other departments of the government. This second aspect of the matter still remains to be discussed. Will the advent of direct democracy result in any increase of the confusion and disorganization which prevails in the mechanism of American state representation? Or will the draught of self-confidence, which our local democracies are by way of swallowing, be communicated to the behavior of the rest of the political mechanism and invigorate the whole system? Will direct popular government commit the same fatal mistake which, to a greater or smaller extent, has already been committed by the national monarchies, by parliamentary government and by democratic legalism? Will it seek to appropriate or emasculate legislative or administrative functions which need to be delegated to other human agencies?

The critics of direct democracy can hardly be blamed for considering doubtful the answers to the foregoing questions. The American experiment in direct
5   democracy is still in its early youth. Its meaning and its tendencies cannot be demonstrated from experience. If the active political responsibilities which it grants to the electorate are redeemed in the negative and suspicious spirit which characterized the attitude of the American democracy towards its official organization during its long and barren alliance with legalism,
10 direct democracy will merely become a source of additional confusion and disorganization. On the other hand, if, as a consequence of its rupture with legalism, the American democracy undergoes a change of spirit, if the attempt to discharge new and responsible activities in connection with its own government brings with it a positive inspiration and genuine social energy,
15 the result may be to renovate American representative institutions and afford novel and desirable opportunities for effective political leadership. I prefer the second of these alternatives, but the preference can hardly be justified by a consideration of the results which have already been achieved in the directly governed states. It is born of an examination of the history, the needs and the
20 ideals of the American local democracies.

The more dogmatic partisans of direct government do not help us very much in making a decision between the foregoing alternatives. In fact, they seem not to understand that any such alternatives exist. They usually attach much the same automatic efficacy to the system of direct government that the Fathers
25 attached to constitutionalism and checks and balances. They have not, indeed, any declared intention of substituting direct for representative government. They admit verbally the necessity in a pure democracy of some effective delegation of specific governmental functions. But as a rule they devote very little attention and thought to the problem of a more powerful and efficient
30 mechanism of legislation and administration. They are preoccupied by the flagrant betrayal of the popular interest which took place under the traditional system, and they seem to think that the adoption of the initiative, referendum and the recall will not merely protect the popular interest, but liberate the popular will—even though the popular will lacks, as much as it has lacked in
35 the past, the impulse of positive social purposes.

Such an attitude toward the instruments of direct government is merely an-other expression of the old superstitious belief in political mechanics against which progressive democracy is bound to protest. If the people in the directly governed states consider the new instruments of democracy as fundamentally a safeguard against abuse and oppression, they may succeed in abolishing one kind of abuse and oppression, but only at the price of its being succeeded by other kinds. If they do not impose limits on their use of the instruments of direct government, based upon the conditions of their profitable service, it will prove to be a barren and mischievous addition to the stock of democratic political   5 institutions. The success of the new instruments as negative safeguards will be commensurate with their success as agencies for the realization of positive popular political purposes. Their serviceability as agencies for the realization of popular political purposes will depend upon the ability of democratic law-givers to associate with them an efficient method of delegating popular political   10 authority. Direct democracy, that is, has little meaning except in a community which is resolutely pursuing a vigorous social program. It must become one of a group of political institutions, whose object is fundamentally to invigorate and socialize the action of American public opinion.

The salient reasons which make it necessary to associate the advent of direct   15 democracy with the attempt to realize a positive social program have already been indicated. They are derived from the profound alterations in the balance of a political organization which is substituting a positive for a negative social policy. The abstract legalistic individualism of the Jeffersonian democracy had in theory no need of any machinery of direct popular control. The activity of   20 government was restricted, and its organs were emasculated, in the interest of a specific formulation of individual rights. Government was considered to be merely a form of temporary police supervision. Such a political system was placed in irons by the Law and lacked the power to do any harm. It really needed to operate somewhat independently of public opinion. Fermentation   25 of public opinion and active political and social experimentation could not accomplish anything of real social value. The essential popular needs were already safeguarded in the Law, which deserved vigilant protection and unquestioning obedience on the part of all good citizens. Effective popular control of such a government was unnecessary. Government was not intended   30 to be the instrument of important popular social purposes.

In its actual historical development the government soon became the instru-ment of important popular social purposes, and it was obliged to develop a corresponding method of popular control. But the popular social purposes which the State and Federal governments formerly attempted to realize   35 were derived from the old individualistic social economy, and the control supposed to be exercised by the partisan organizations was ineffective. A wholly new situation was created when the local democracies came to need and possess a genuinely social policy, which threw increased burdens upon the government, and commensurately increased its power. Under such conditions direct popular control over the mechanism of government became of essential importance. A negative individualistic social policy implies a weak and irresponsible government. A positive comprehensive social policy implies

5 a strong, efficient and responsible government. But a strong and efficient government, which exercises a large part of the authority of the state and which is not bound by the substantive provisions of the fundamental Law, might well be dangerous not only to individual civil rights, but to popular political rights. Every precaution should be adopted to keep it in sensitive

10 touch with public opinion. A lack of responsiveness to public opinion would tempt it to become domineering and oppressive, and would in the long run make its own work abortive as well as dangerous. A social policy is concerned in the most intimate and comprehensive way with the lives of the people. In order to be successful, it must rest on the basis of abundant and cordial

15 popular support.

The mechanism of direct government has, consequently, an essential function to perform in the organization of a social democracy. The realization of a genuine social policy necessitates the aggrandizement of the administrative and legislative branches of the government. Progressive democracy recognizes

20 the need of these instruments, but it recognizes the need of keeping control of them. A strong government with an affirmative policy and effective popular control are supplementary rather than hostile one to another. The realization of such a policy will in the long run demand both an efficient system of representation and an efficient method of direct popular supervision.

25 The friends of direct government do not usually advocate it, for the reasons indicated in the preceding paragraph. An exclusively representative government is to many of them a perfectly satisfactory form of democratic political organization. It is objectionable only because it has failed to be really representative. A recent convert to pure democracy, President Woodrow Wilson,

30 has expressed in the following words the reasons for his conversion: "If we felt we had genuine representative government in our state legislatures, no one would propose the initiative and the referendum in the United States. Our most ardent and successful advocates regard them as a sobering means of obtaining genuine representative action on the part of legislative bodies. They

35 do not mean to set anything aside. They mean to restore and to reinvigorate rather." And a much more radical critic of our traditional system, Professor J. Allen Smith, who also favors direct popular political action, asserts that "a government of the representative type, if responsive to public sentiment, would answer all the requirements of a democratic state."

The adoption of direct government may, it is true, end by reinvigorating representative government; but if so, the result will not be accomplished by refusing "to set anything aside." The first thing which must be set aside is the method of representation which has passed in this country under the name of representative government. Direct government will never reinvigorate our   5 existing state of political institutions. What it may accomplish is to supply energy to a new and better method of delegating popular political authority.

A statesman whose dominant object was the reorganization of existing state representative government would be foolish to depend upon the initiative and the referendum for the accomplishment of his purpose. There are a score of   10 ways in which American state government could be made more representative without any invocation of the instrument of direct government. The first condition of effective representation is the bestowal upon the representative body of some effective power and responsibility, which, as all admit, is precisely the condition which has been largely and increasingly absent from our so-called   15 representative institutions. Direct government does not automatically satisfy this need. On the contrary, as the experience of the state of Oregon sufficiently proves, its merely external addition to the existing machinery of representation tends, if anything, to attenuate still further the meagre responsibilities officially conferred on our state representative agencies.   20

So far as these state representative agencies are concerned, a representative value cannot be restored to them, because they were never intended to be and never have been representative in any self-respecting meaning of the word. A thoroughly representative government is essentially government by men rather than by Law. The active exercise of effective political responsibility is confided   25 to a body of the elect. They assume the same responsibility for the ultimate welfare of the state that the American system delegates to the Law and its official expounders. True, the legislative body may govern, just as the Law was permitted to govern, by virtue of an explicit or implied popular consent, but in a representative system popular power is exercised only to be delegated. For the   30 time being, complete legal responsibility for the public weal is conferred upon the legislature. Quite obviously no such responsibility has been conferred by the American system either upon the legislature or upon the legislature and executive together; and, to my mind, it cannot be expected that any exclusively representative system will be even fairly successful on any other terms.   35

The Progressive Republicans, who are advocating an increase of executive power and a closer cooperation between the executive and the legislature as the most effective means of reinvigorating the representative system, can make a very strong argument in its favor. They can make a stronger argument than

can those advocates of "pure" democracy who expect to develop a genuinely representative government by grafting the instruments of direct government on an essentially and fatally unrepresentative system. But they cannot make a strong enough argument. The cooperation between an executive and a
5   legislature, each of which derives its authority directly from the people, cannot be made properly operative except by some method of referring disputes to the common master—which means a considerable measure of direct government. Moreover, an American electorate would not submit for long to the increased power of the organs of government which would result from their cooperative
10 action, without the creation of some means of effective popular control. But even if these difficulties could be overcome, it is doubtful how far any system can be considered really representative which does not bestow complete responsibility for the public welfare upon the government. The government must have the power to determine the Law instead of being circumscribed by
15 the Law. Just in so far as its authority was curtailed, its sense of responsibility would be relaxed and its integrity would be undermined.

A purely representative system, such as that of the United Kingdom, seeks to accomplish the fundamental objects of government by a method opposed to that of the traditional American system. The former bestows complete legal
20 responsibility for the welfare of the state and the course of its development upon the elect in the expectation that thereby society will obtain the boon of rational guidance. "Representation is not," says Guizot, who was one of its most ardent advocates, "an arithmetical means employed to count individual wills, but a natural process, whereby public reason, which alone has the right
25 to govern modern society, may be extracted from the bosom of society itself." This account of the ultimate meaning of a purely representative system was accepted substantially by John Stuart Mill, although with certain significant modifications; and it manifestly constitutes the only justification for the enormous power and responsibility bestowed upon the legislative body. As
30 the result of their deliberations the action of the representatives must embody a program based upon the enduring and the binding interests of the nation.

The American constitutional system did not need to create a powerful organ of government whose wise leadership would help to extract reason from the bosom of society. That desirable result had already been accomplished. Reason
35 had been printed on the bosom of society in indelible ink by virtue of the embodiment in the Constitution of the great principles of legal morals. Its human purveyors were rather the judges than the legislature; and the business of the courts was not merely to declare the Word, but to keep the fire of political reason glowing in the political hearth. Under such a system executives

and legislatures were not supposed, and did not need, to be particularly reasonable—which is certainly a proof of the wisdom of the Fathers of the Republic. They needed most of all to be obedient and self-restrained. For if any effective method exists of extracting reason from the bosom of society, the human purveyors of this rational extract certainly require some oracular   5 writing for their guidance; and the more authoritative this oracle can be made, the better. So far as the object of political organization is to bring to the surface an already existing fund of reason, the method adopted by the founders of the American constitutional system may be preferred to the method characteristic of a purely representative system. The latter leaves the secretion   10 and extraction of reason much more to the operation of a clumsy mechanism. As an edifice of political rationalism, the record of the discussion and action of the British Parliament during the past century cannot be compared to the constitutional decisions of the Supreme Court of the United States; and this is true notwithstanding the fact that even in the latter some traces may be   15 occasionally discovered of the fallibility of that sovereign faculty.

Thus the difficulty with a purely representative government is similar to the difficulty which is involved in government by Law. The assumption made by the advocates of both of these systems is that society possesses at any one time a fund of social reason which, by virtue of its superiority to interested,   20 inexperienced and perverse counsel, is entitled to determine social action. The state should be organized chiefly for the purpose of giving control to this fund of social reason. The means whereby this control is exercised differs radically in the two systems; but we need not bother about their respective advantages or disadvantages. Neither of them meets the needs of a progressive democratic   25 society, because in a society of this kind no such fund of really authoritative social reason can be held to exist. There is a fund of social reason which should possess some authority; but it is so small compared to social aspirations and needs that a democratic society must be organized less to obey than to increase it. The work of extracting the stores of reason from the bosom of society must   30 be subordinated to the more fundamental object of augmenting the supply of social reason and improving its distribution. Legalism and purely representative government are unsuited to the needs of a thoroughgoing democracy, because their method of organization depends on popular obedience rather than popular education. The promotion and the diffusion of social reason cannot   35 be brought about without a reverence for orderly procedure and without the leadership of the elect; but the erection of legalism alone or of representation alone into a system is not sufficient to secure this most important of all political objects. The best chance of securing it opens up as a result a more thoroughly popular organization of the state. The electorate must be required as the result of its own actual experience and unavoidable responsibilities to develop those very qualities of intelligence, character, faith and sympathy which are necessary for the success of the democratic experiment.

5   Thus neither representative government nor government by law nor any combination between the two is competent to meet all the requirements of a democratic polity. A clear-sighted, self-confident and loyal democracy will keep in its own hands the active control of all the agents and instruments of its own fulfilment. The instinctive repugnance which the American
10 democracy has always exhibited to the delegation of too much power to any one of the separate departments of government is explicable and justifiable. No plebiscite can bestow authenticity upon an ostensibly democratic political system which approximates in practice to the exercise of executive omnipotence. No intermittent appeals to the people for their approbation can
15 wholly democratize a system which approximates in practice to the exercise of legislative omnipotence. No reverence for the law can guarantee political and social liberty to a body of democrats who confide their collective destiny to written formulas as expounded by a ruling body of lawyers. In practice each of these systems develops into a method of class government. The men to whom
20 the enormous power is delegated will use it, in part at least, to perpetuate the system which is so beneficial to themselves. But even if they were as wise as Solomon and as gallant and disinterested as Sir Galahad, the systems for which they spoke and acted would still be evading rather than meeting the democratic problem. None of these systems make the people actively responsible for their
25 own reasonableness and welfare. The people do not reap the advantages to which they are entitled, but if they did receive every possible advantage, they would not be earning it and could not keep what they received.

In all three of the principal departments of government, there are essential functions to be performed which must be delegated by a democracy to selected
30 men under conditions which make for technical efficiency and individual independence and self-respect. The Fathers of the Republic were fully justified both in keeping the powers distinguished, and in seeking to balance one against the other. Their mistake consisted in the methods adopted for preserving or readjusting the balance. The preservation of a balance depends upon the
35 harmonious development of several elements which enter into it; and as in the course of nature harmonious development is rare, the preservation of any such balance must usually be contrived by human insistence and intelligence. Only one part of a democratic system is entitled to exercise any such function—the electorate itself. The whole of a democratic political system is divided into

three parts, not merely or primarily as a protection to individual and popular liberties, but rather to provide an essential positive function for the people to perform—the function of recreating the unity which is necessarily compromised by the no less necessary specialization of governmental function. Such is the part which the people, or the closest possible approximation to the people, have to play in the process of their own nationalization or socialization. They must divide in order to act, to think, to rule, to move on and to aspire; but they must not impose upon any one of the resulting classifications or subdivisions the responsibility of ultimate social cohesion. That responsibility rests with the whole people, and its fulfilment depends upon popular intelligence, sympathy and faith.

Many sincere social democrats in this country, as well as in England or France, regard any such dependence upon direct government with the utmost repugnance. The industrial and social program of a democracy can, in their opinion, be accomplished with less friction and delay through the agency of an authoritative representative body. They are probably right in expecting that in the near future direct popular government will increase the difficulty of securing the adoption of many items in a desirable social program. But reformers of this class, like the conservatives, attach too much importance to the accomplishment and maintenance of specific results, and too little to the permanent moral welfare of the democracy. They are willing to have the people imposed upon in the interest of what is or is intended to be the popular benefit. An authoritative representative government, particularly one which is associated with inherited leadership and a strong party system, carries with it an enormous prestige. It is frequently in a position either to ignore, to circumvent or to wear down popular opposition. But a social program purchased at such a price is not worth what it costs. It makes no difference how benevolent the intention of the government may be or how wise its legislation. The program which is carried out by such means will do nothing to make the people worthy of their advantages. The result will either be popular servility or organized popular resistance or both. The country in which a benevolent government has succeeded in carrying out the most comprehensive social policy of modern times is the country in which a social democratic party, organized to overthrow the government, has succeeded in obtaining the support of a third of the electorate.

Social reformers must, consequently, be patient as well as eager and tenacious. A moderate program which is well understood and cordially supported by public opinion, and upon which the electorate has been in some measure specifically consulted, will be much more beneficial than a more extensive

program which is not so well understood, and which does not represent a genuine popular affirmation. From the beginning of civilization the people have been constantly imposed upon by moral or social or physical force in the real or supposed interest of their own welfare. The process will doubtless
5   have to continue in some measure; but if democracy means anything, it means popular liberation in precisely this respect. It means that social reformers must present their arguments primarily to the electorate, and welcome every good opportunity of allowing the electorate to pass judgment upon their proposals.

10 Our conclusion, then, is double-faced. Democracy implies and needs some method of representation which will be efficient and responsible enough to carry out a social policy, but which does not imply the delegation of its own ultimate discretionary power to any body of men or body of law. No such representative system can be found in the provisions of existing state
15 constitutions. An organization of the executive and legislative powers, which will give increased energy to both of them and which is adjusted to their cooperation both one with another and with a sufficient measure of direct government, is what is needed and must be contrived. The new organization will be intended first, last and always to promote political education. It must be
20 adapted to action, but the action must merely be the decisive temporary result of widespread popular fermentation. It must have the chance to be efficient, but only for the purpose of being educational. It must be able to educate, but primarily by the road of efficient action. The new system can accomplish nothing without human energy, intelligence, sacrifice and faith, but if those
25 qualities are present, it will make the best use of them.

The Inspiration of
the Declaration
Calvin Coolidge (1872–1933)

President Coolidge delivered this speech on the 150th anniversary of the Declaration of Independence. Rejecting Progressivism root and branch, he defends America's founding principles.

July 5, 1926

We meet to celebrate the birthday of America. The coming of a new life always excites our interest. Although we know in the case of the individual that it has been an infinite repetition reaching back beyond our vision, that only makes it the more wonderful. But how our interest and wonder increase when we behold the miracle of the birth of a new nation. It is to pay our tribute of reverence 5
and respect to those who participated in such a mighty event that we annually observe the fourth day of July. Whatever may have been the impression created by the news which went out from this city on that summer day in 1776, there can be no doubt as to the estimate which is now placed upon it. At the end of 150 years the four corners of the earth unite in coming to Philadelphia as to 10
a holy shrine in grateful acknowledgement of a service so great, which a few inspired men here rendered to humanity, that it is still the preeminent support of free government throughout the world.

Although a century and a half measured in comparison with the length of human experience is but a short time, yet measured in the life of governments and 15
nations it ranks as a very respectable period. Certainly enough time has elapsed to demonstrate with a great deal of thoroughness the value of our institutions and their dependability as rules for the regulation of human conduct and the advancement of civilization. They have been in existence long enough to become very well seasoned. They have met, and met successfully, the test of experience. 20

It is not so much then for the purpose of undertaking to proclaim new theories and principles that this annual celebration is maintained, but rather to reaffirm

---

Calvin Coolidge, "The Inspiration of the Declaration," in *Foundations of the Republic: Speeches and Addresses* (New York: Scribner's Sons, 1926), 441–54.

and reestablish those old theories and principles which time and the unerring logic of events have demonstrated to be sound. Amid all the clash of conflicting interests, amid all the welter of partisan politics, every American can turn for solace and consolation to the Declaration of Independence and the Constitution

5 of the United States with the assurance and confidence that those two great charters of freedom and justice remain firm and unshaken. Whatever perils appear, whatever dangers threaten, the Nation remains secure in the knowledge that the ultimate application of the law of the land will provide an adequate defense and protection.

10 It is little wonder that people at home and abroad consider Independence Hall as hallowed ground and revere the Liberty Bell as a sacred relic. That pile of bricks and mortar, that mass of metal, might appear to the uninstructed as only the outgrown meeting place and the shattered bell of a former time, useless now because of more modern conveniences, but to those who know they have become consecrated by

15 the use which men have made of them. They have long been identified with a great cause. They are the framework of a spiritual event. The world looks upon them, because of their associations of one hundred and fifty years ago, as it looks upon the Holy Land because of what took place there nineteen hundred years ago. Through use for a righteous purpose they have become sanctified.

20 It is not here necessary to examine in detail the causes which led to the American Revolution. In their immediate occasion they were largely economic. The colonists objected to the navigation laws which interfered with their trade, they denied the power of Parliament to impose taxes which they were obliged to pay, and they therefore resisted the royal governors and the royal forces which were

25 sent to secure obedience to these laws. But the conviction is inescapable that a new civilization had come, a new spirit had arisen on this side of the Atlantic more advanced and more developed in its regard for the rights of the individual than that which characterized the Old World. Life in a new and open country had aspirations which could not be realized in any subordinate position. A

30 separate establishment was ultimately inevitable. It had been decreed by the very laws of human nature. Man everywhere has an unconquerable desire to be the master of his own destiny.

We are obliged to conclude that the Declaration of Independence represented the movement of a people. It was not, of course, a movement from the top.

35 Revolutions do not come from that direction. It was not without the support of many of the most respectable people in the Colonies, who were entitled to all the consideration that is given to breeding, education, and possessions. It had the support of another element of great significance and importance to which I shall later refer. But the preponderance of all those who occupied a position

which took on the aspect of aristocracy did not approve of the Revolution and held toward it an attitude either of neutrality or open hostility. It was in no sense a rising of the oppressed and downtrodden. It brought no scum to the surface, for the reason that colonial society had developed no scum. The great body of the people were accustomed to privations, but they were free from depravity. If they had poverty, it was not of the hopeless kind that afflicts great cities, but the inspiring kind that marks the spirit of the pioneer. The American Revolution represented the informed and mature convictions of a great mass of independent, liberty-loving, God-fearing people who knew their rights, and possessed the courage to dare to maintain them.

The Continental Congress was not only composed of great men, but it represented a great people. While its members did not fail to exercise a remarkable leadership, they were equally observant of their representative capacity. They were industrious in encouraging their constituents to instruct them to support independence. But until such instructions were given they were inclined to withhold action.

While North Carolina has the honor of first authorizing its delegates to concur with other Colonies in declaring independence, it was quickly followed by South Carolina and Georgia, which also gave general instructions broad enough to include such action. But the first instructions which unconditionally directed its delegates to declare for independence came from the great Commonwealth of Virginia. These were immediately followed by Rhode Island and Massachusetts, while the other Colonies, with the exception of New York, soon adopted a like course.

This obedience of the delegates to the wishes of their constituents, which in some cases caused them to modify their previous positions, is a matter of great significance. It reveals an orderly process of government in the first place; but more than that, it demonstrates that the Declaration of Independence was the result of the seasoned and deliberate thought of the dominant portion of the people of the Colonies. Adopted after long discussion and as the result of the duly authorized expression of the preponderance of public opinion, it did not partake of dark intrigue or hidden conspiracy. It was well advised. It had about it nothing of the lawless and disordered nature of a riotous insurrection. It was maintained on a plane which rises above the ordinary conception of rebellion. It was in no sense a radical movement but took on the dignity of a resistance to illegal usurpations. It was conservative and represented the action of the colonists to maintain their constitutional rights which from time immemorial had been guaranteed to them under the law of the land.

When we come to examine the action of the Continental Congress in adopting the Declaration of Independence in the light of what was set out in that great

document and in the light of succeeding events, we can not escape the conclusion that it had a much broader and deeper significance than a mere secession of territory and the establishment of a new nation. Events of that nature have been taking place since the dawn of history. One empire after another has arisen,
5   only to crumble away as its constituent parts separated from each other and set up independent governments of their own. Such actions long ago became commonplace. They have occurred too often to hold the attention of the world and command the admiration and reverence of humanity. There is something beyond the establishment of a new nation, great as that event would be, in the
10 Declaration of Independence which has ever since caused it to be regarded as one of the great charters that not only was to liberate America but was everywhere to ennoble humanity.

It was not because it was proposed to establish a new nation, but because it was proposed to establish a nation on new principles, that July 4, 1776, has come
15 to be regarded as one of the greatest days in history. Great ideas do not burst upon the world unannounced. They are reached by a gradual development over a length of time usually proportionate to their importance. This is especially true of the principles laid down in the Declaration of Independence. Three very definite propositions were set out in its preamble regarding the nature of
20 mankind and therefore of government. These were the doctrine that all men are created equal, that they are endowed with certain inalienable rights, and that therefore the source of the just powers of government must be derived from the consent of the governed.

If no one is to be accounted as born into a superior station, if there is to be no
25 ruling class, and if all possess rights which can neither be bartered away nor taken from them by any earthly power, it follows as a matter of course that the practical authority of the Government has to rest on the consent of the governed. While these principles were not altogether new in political action, and were very far from new in political speculation, they had never been assembled before
30 and declared in such a combination. But remarkable as this may be, it is not the chief distinction of the Declaration of Independence. The importance of political speculation is not to be underestimated, as I shall presently disclose. Until the idea is developed and the plan made there can be no action.

It was the fact that our Declaration of Independence containing these immortal
35 truths was the political action of a duly authorized and constituted representative public body in its sovereign capacity, supported by the force of general opinion and by the armies of Washington already in the field, which makes it the most important civil document in the world. It was not only the principles declared, but the fact that therewith a new nation was born which was to be founded upon

those principles and which from that time forth in its development has actually maintained those principles, that makes this pronouncement an incomparable event in the history of government. It was an assertion that a people had arisen determined to make every necessary sacrifice for the support of these truths and by their practical application bring the War of Independence to a successful   5 conclusion and adopt the Constitution of the United States with all that it has meant to civilization.

The idea that the people have a right to choose their own rulers was not new in political history. It was the foundation of every popular attempt to depose an undesirable king. This right was set out with a good deal of detail by the Dutch   10 when as early as July 26, 1581, they declared their independence of Philip of Spain. In their long struggle with the Stuarts the British people asserted the same principles, which finally culminated in the Bill of Rights deposing the last of that house and placing William and Mary on the throne. In each of these cases sovereignty through divine right was displaced by sovereignty through   15 the consent of the people. Running through the same documents, though expressed in different terms, is the clear inference of inalienable rights. But we should search these charters in vain for an assertion of the doctrine of equality. This principle had not before appeared as an official political declaration of any nation. It was profoundly revolutionary. It is one of the corner stones of   20 American institutions.

But if these truths to which the declaration refers have not before been adopted in their combined entirety by national authority, it is a fact that they had been long pondered and often expressed in political speculation. It is generally assumed that French thought had some effect upon our public mind during Revolutionary   25 days. This may have been true. But the principles of our declaration had been under discussion in the Colonies for nearly two generations before the advent of the French political philosophy that characterized the middle of the eighteenth century. In fact, they come from an earlier date. A very positive echo of what the Dutch had done in 1581, and what the English were preparing to do, appears in   30 the assertion of the Reverend Thomas Hooker of Connecticut as early as 1638, when he said in a sermon before the General Court that—

"The foundation of authority is laid in the free consent of the people.

"The choice of public magistrates belongs unto the people by God's own allowance."   35

This doctrine found wide acceptance among the nonconformist clergy who later made up the Congregational Church. The great apostle of this movement was the Reverend John Wise, of Massachusetts. He was one of the leaders of the revolt against the royal governor Andros in 1687, for which he suffered imprisonment. He was a liberal in ecclesiastical controversies. He appears to have been familiar with the writings of the political scientist, Samuel Pufendorf, who was born in Saxony in 1632. Wise published a treatise, entitled "The Church's Quarrel Espoused," in 1710, which was amplified in another publication in 1717. In it he dealt with the principles of civil government. His works were reprinted in 1772 and have been declared to have been nothing less than a textbook of liberty for our Revolutionary fathers.

While the written word was the foundation, it is apparent that the spoken word was the vehicle for convincing the people. This came with great force and wide range from the successors of Hooker and Wise. It was carried on with a missionary spirit which did not fail to reach the Scotch-Irish of North Carolina, showing its influence by significantly making that Colony the first to give instructions to its delegates looking to independence. This preaching reached the neighborhood of Thomas Jefferson, who acknowledged that his "best ideas of democracy" had been secured at church meetings.

That these ideas were prevalent in Virginia is further revealed by the Declaration of Rights, which was prepared by George Mason and presented to the general assembly on May 27, 1776. This document asserted popular sovereignty and inherent natural rights, but confined the doctrine of equality to the assertion that "All men are created equally free and independent." It can scarcely be imagined that Jefferson was unacquainted with what had been done in his own Commonwealth of Virginia when he took up the task of drafting the Declaration of Independence. But these thoughts can very largely be traced back to what John Wise was writing in 1710. He said, "Every man must be acknowledged equal to every man." Again, "The end of all good government is to cultivate humanity and promote the happiness of all and the good of every man in all his rights, his life, liberty, estate, honor, and so forth...."

And again, "For as they have a power every man in his natural state, so upon combination they can and do bequeath this power to others and settle it according as their united discretion shall determine." And still again, "Democracy is Christ's government in church and state." Here was the doctrine of equality, popular sovereignty, and the substance of the theory of inalienable rights clearly asserted by Wise at the opening of the eighteenth century, just as we have the principle of the consent of the governed stated by Hooker as early as 1638.

When we take all these circumstances into consideration, it is but natural that the first paragraph of the Declaration of Independence should open with a

reference to Nature's God and should close in the final paragraphs with an appeal
to the Supreme Judge of the world and an assertion of a firm reliance on Divine
Providence. Coming from these sources, having as it did this background, it is
no wonder that Samuel Adams could say "The people seem to recognize this
resolution as though it were a decree promulgated from heaven."   5

No one can examine this record and escape the conclusion that in the great
outline of its principles the Declaration was the result of the religious teachings
of the preceding period. The profound philosophy which Jonathan Edwards
applied to theology, the popular preaching of George Whitefield, had aroused
the thought and stirred the people of the Colonies in preparation for this   10
great event. No doubt the speculations which had been going on in England,
and especially on the Continent, lent their influence to the general sentiment
of the times. Of course, the world is always influenced by all the experience
and all the thought of the past. But when we come to a contemplation of the
immediate conception of the principles of human relationship which went   15
into the Declaration of Independence we are not required to extend our search
beyond our own shores. They are found in the texts, the sermons, and the
writings of the early colonial clergy who were earnestly undertaking to instruct
their congregations in the great mystery of how to live. They preached equality
because they believed in the fatherhood of God and the brotherhood of man.   20
They justified freedom by the text that we are all created in the divine image,
all partakers of the divine spirit.

Placing every man on a plane where he acknowledged no superiors, where no
one possessed any right to rule over him, he must inevitably choose his own
rulers through a system of self-government. This was their theory of democracy.   25
In those days such doctrines would scarcely have been permitted to flourish
and spread in any other country. This was the purpose which the fathers
cherished. In order that they might have freedom to express these thoughts and
opportunity to put them into action, whole congregations with their pastors
had migrated to the colonies. These great truths were in the air that our people   30
breathed. Whatever else we may say of it, the Declaration of Independence was
profoundly American.

If this apprehension of the facts be correct, and the documentary evidence would
appear to verify it, then certain conclusions are bound to follow. A spring will
cease to flow if its source be dried up; a tree will wither if its roots be destroyed. In 35
its main features the Declaration of Independence is a great spiritual document.
It is a declaration not of material but of spiritual conceptions. Equality, liberty,
popular sovereignty, the rights of man—these are not elements which we can

see and touch. They are ideals. They have their source and their roots in the religious convictions. They belong to the unseen world. Unless the faith of the American people in these religious convictions is to endure, the principles of our Declaration will perish. We can not continue to enjoy the result if we
5   neglect and abandon the cause.

We are too prone to overlook another conclusion. Governments do not make ideals, but ideals make governments. This is both historically and logically true. Of course the government can help to sustain ideals and can create institutions through which they can be the better observed, but their source by their very
10   nature is in the people. The people have to bear their own responsibilities. There is no method by which that burden can be shifted to the government. It is not the enactment, but the observance of laws, that creates the character of a nation.

About the Declaration there is a finality that is exceedingly restful. It is often
15   asserted that the world has made a great deal of progress since 1776, that we have had new thoughts and new experiences which have given us a great advance over the people of that day, and that we may therefore very well discard their conclusions for something more modern. But that reasoning can not be applied to this great charter. If all men are created equal, that is final. If they are
20   endowed with inalienable rights, that is final. If governments derive their just powers from the consent of the governed, that is final. No advance, no progress can be made beyond these propositions. If anyone wishes to deny their truth or their soundness, the only direction in which he can proceed historically is not forward, but backward toward the time when there was no equality, no rights
25   of the individual, no rule of the people. Those who wish to proceed in that direction can not lay claim to progress. They are reactionary. Their ideas are not more modern, but more ancient, than those of the Revolutionary fathers.

In the development of its institutions America can fairly claim that it has remained true to the principles which were declared 150 years ago. In all the
30   essentials we have achieved an equality which was never possessed by any other people. Even in the less important matter of material possessions we have secured a wider and wider distribution of wealth. The rights of the individual are held sacred and protected by constitutional guarantees, which even the Government itself is bound not to violate. If there is any one thing among
35   us that is established beyond question, it is self-government—the right of the people to rule. If there is any failure in respect to any of these principles, it is because there is a failure on the part of individuals to observe them. We hold that the duly authorized expression of the will of the people has a divine sanction. But even in that we come back to the theory of John Wise that "Democracy

is Christ's government...." The ultimate sanction of law rests on the righteous authority of the Almighty.

On an occasion like this a great temptation exists to present evidence of the practical success of our form of democratic republic at home and the ever-broadening acceptance it is securing abroad. Although these things are well known, their frequent consideration is an encouragement and an inspiration. But it is not results and effects so much as sources and causes that I believe it is even more necessary constantly to contemplate. Ours is a government of the people. It represents their will. Its officers may sometimes go astray, but that is not a reason for criticizing the principles of our institutions. The real heart of the American Government depends upon the heart of the people. It is from that source that we must look for all genuine reform. It is to that cause that we must ascribe all our results.

It was in the contemplation of these truths that the fathers made their declaration and adopted their Constitution. It was to establish a free government, which must not be permitted to degenerate into the unrestrained authority of a mere majority or the unbridled weight of a mere influential few. They undertook the balance these interests against each other and provide the three separate independent branches, the executive, the legislative, and the judicial departments of the Government, with checks against each other in order that neither one might encroach upon the other. These are our guarantees of liberty. As a result of these methods enterprise has been duly protected from confiscation, the people have been free from oppression, and there has been an ever-broadening and deepening of the humanities of life.

Under a system of popular government there will always be those who will seek for political preferment by clamoring for reform. While there is very little of this which is not sincere, there is a large portion that is not well informed. In my opinion very little of just criticism can attach to the theories and principles of our institutions. There is far more danger of harm than there is hope of good in any radical changes. We do need a better understanding and comprehension of them and a better knowledge of the foundations of government in general. Our forefathers came to certain conclusions and decided upon certain courses of action which have been a great blessing to the world. Before we can understand their conclusions we must go back and review the course which they followed. We must think the thoughts which they thought. Their intellectual life centered around the meeting-house. They were intent upon religious worship. While there were always among them men of deep learning, and later those who had comparatively large possessions, the mind of the people was not so much engrossed in how much they knew, or how much they had, as in how they were going to live. While scantily provided with other literature, there was a wide acquaintance with the Scriptures. Over a period as great as that which measures the existence of our independence they were subject to this discipline not only in their religious life and educational training, but also in their political

5   thought. They were a people who came under the influence of a great spiritual development and acquired a great moral power.

No other theory is adequate to explain or comprehend the Declaration of Independence. It is the product of the spiritual insight of the people. We live in an age of science and of abounding accumulation of material things. These

10   did not create our Declaration. Our Declaration created them. The things of the spirit come first. Unless we cling to that, all our material prosperity, overwhelming though it may appear, will turn to a barren scepter in our grasp. If we are to maintain the great heritage which has been bequeathed to us, we must be like-minded as the fathers who created it. We must not sink into a pagan

15   materialism. We must cultivate the reverence which they had for the things that are holy. We must follow the spiritual and moral leadership which they showed. We must keep replenished, that they may glow with a more compelling flame, the altar fires before which they worshipped.

XI

INSTITUTIONALIZING
PROGRESSIVISM:
THE NEW DEAL AND
THE GREAT SOCIETY

Pick any three letters of the alphabet, economist Milton Friedman said, put them in any order, and in the acronym you will discover an unnecessary federal agency. The alphabet soup of federal regulatory and administrative agencies grew into what it is today largely during the administrations of Franklin D. Roosevelt and Lyndon B. Johnson, two presidents whose names are well-known by their initials. Ronald Reagan, who majored in economics in college during the Great Depression, came much later to see LBJ's Great Society, especially, as inimical to freedom. It was his cause as president, Reagan wrote, to undo the damage it had inflicted upon the country, and to reduce government to a size more in keeping with the principles of the American founding.

Franklin Roosevelt, influenced profoundly if indirectly by the previous generation of Progressive intellectuals, captured in a pragmatic tone the Progressive emphasis on necessitous change. His Commonwealth Club Address, one of the most influential of the twentieth century, is presented in his *Public Papers* with a heading indicative of his prevailing philosophy: "New Conditions Impose New Requirements Upon Government and Those Who Conduct Government." Economic depression and the collapse of the American financial sector required a "re-appraisal of values," Roosevelt said in this speech.

Even as he adduced a plan for action, Roosevelt outlined a larger project in the speech. Liberalism need not be fixated forever on just one threat. Rather, it must maintain dexterity of mission, such that whenever change happens, as inevitably it will, political actors can accommodate the changes and adjust to new necessities. History with a capital "H," the historicism dwelt upon in academic essays by Woodrow Wilson and others a generation before, takes on real meaning in this formulation, for Roosevelt gives politicians—himself to start with—a practical role, along with all others who will launch programs, projects, even domestic wars, against whatever would inhibit progress.

Twelve years after the Commonwealth Club Address, Roosevelt delivered his 1944 State of the Union Address. In it he said that the old rights of the original Bill of Rights had adequately protected the American people; however, with new threats, new solutions were needed. Of these old rights he said, "They were our rights to life and liberty." In response to new dangers, we must add the guarantee of "security." That will come, Roosevelt pledged, only with an extension of entitlement that entails the right to a job, a home, health care, and education. *The Wall Street Journal* offered its opinion of Roosevelt's curious use of the past tense in reference to the old rights: "Are, not were, Mr. President."

President John F. Kennedy's New Frontier and President Johnson's Great Society shared with the New Deal the underlying idea that the old individualistic understanding of rights was passé, and the new era necessitated a collective approach. Even more, for Johnson, it offered the opportunity in which, as he said in 1964 at the University of Michigan, Americans "can help build a society where the demands of morality, and the needs of the spirit, can be realized in the life of the Nation." America is rich and powerful, but it must become great through a process of societal and political evolution. Politics must be an agent for change, Johnson said; it must alleviate poverty, build community, and guarantee not just the opportunity for equality, but the "result." Declaring a "War on Poverty," Johnson built an arsenal of federal agencies. Costing five trillion dollars, with no alleviation of poverty to show for all that expense, that war's ramparts still remain. Medicaid, Medicare, food stamps, and Head Start, among many other federal agencies, were started by Johnson, and were then given even more money and sway by his successors, until 1980, when President Reagan insisted that the growth of government had to stop.

A direct response to Progressivism's underlying ideology, Reagan's First Inaugural Address in 1980 echoed his 1964 speech, "A Time for Choosing." In both, Reagan sees America's choice as between an ideology of government growth, rule by experts, and rampant redistributionism, on the one hand, and a belief in the power of the individual, rule by the people, and a return to limited government, on the other. We should not see a fat man standing beside a thin one, Reagan said in 1964, and conclude that the fat one got that way by taking advantage of the other. Progressivism encourages that outlook, and must be counteracted and overcome.

Just as Winston Churchill had stood athwart the ideologies of his day, so Ronald Reagan did in his. In many ways, the ideologies they fought were similar. A common characteristic of their foes was a Progressivism that would place power beyond control of the people. For the British statesman as well as the American, the U.S. Constitution was a citadel of strength upon which liberty-loving peoples everywhere could rely.

DAVID J. BOBB
Lecturer in Politics
Director, Allan P. Kirby, Jr. Center for
Constitutional Studies and Citizenship
Hillsdale College

COMMONWEALTH CLUB ADDRESS
FRANKLIN D. ROOSEVELT (1882–1945)

Delivered by Franklin Roosevelt to California's Commonwealth Club dur-
ing his first run for the White House, this speech was penned by Adolf Berle,
a noted scholar and a member of Roosevelt's "Brain Trust" who drew deeply
upon earlier Progressive thought, especially that of John Dewey.

SEPTEMBER 23, 1932

…I want to speak not of politics but of Government. I want to speak not of
parties, but of universal principles. They are not political, except in that larger
sense in which a great American once expressed a definition of politics, that
nothing in all of human life is foreign to the science of politics.

I do want to give you, however, a recollection of a long life spent for a large part   5
in public office. Some of my conclusions and observations have been deeply
accentuated in these past few weeks. I have traveled far—from Albany to the
Golden Gate. I have seen many people, and heard many things, and today,
when in a sense my journey has reached the half-way mark, I am glad of the
opportunity to discuss with you what it all means to me.   10

Sometimes, my friends, particularly in years such as these, the hand of discouragement falls upon us. It seems that things are in a rut, fixed, settled, that the
world has grown old and tired and very much out of joint. This is the mood of
depression, of dire and weary depression.

But then we look around us in America, and everything tells us that we are   15
wrong. America is new. It is in the process of change and development. It has
the great potentialities of youth, and particularly is this true of the great West,
and of this coast, and of California.

Franklin D. Roosevelt, "Campaign Address on Progressive Government at the Commonwealth
Club," September 23, 1932, in Samuel Irving Rosenman, ed., *The Public Papers and Addresses of*
Franklin D. Roosevelt, Vol. 1 (New York: Russell & Russell, 1938), 742–56.

I would not have you feel that I regard this as in any sense a new community. I have traveled in many parts of the world, but never have I felt the arresting thought of the change and development more than here, where the old, mystic East would seem to be near to us, where the currents of life and thought and commerce of
5   the whole world meet us. This factor alone is sufficient to cause man to stop and think of the deeper meaning of things, when he stands in this community.

But more than that, I appreciate that the membership of this club consists of men who are thinking in terms beyond the immediate present, beyond their own immediate tasks, beyond their own individual interest. I want to invite
10 you, therefore, to consider with me in the large, some of the relationships of Government and economic life that go deeply into our daily lives, our happiness, our future and our security.

The issue of Government has always been whether individual men and women will have to serve some system of Government or economics, or whether a system
15 of Government and economics exists to serve individual men and women. This question has persistently dominated the discussions of Government for many generations. On questions relating to these things men have differed, and for time immemorial it is probable that honest men will continue to differ.

The final word belongs to no man; yet we can still believe in change and in
20 progress. Democracy, as a dear old friend of mine in Indiana, Meredith Nicholson, has called it, is a quest, a never-ending seeking for better things, and in the seeking for these things and the striving for them, there are many roads to follow. But, if we map the course of these roads, we find that there are only two general directions.

25 When we look about us, we are likely to forget how hard people have worked to win the privilege of Government. The growth of the national Governments of Europe was a struggle for the development of a centralized force in the Nation, strong enough to impose peace upon ruling barons. In many instances the victory of the central Government, the creation of a strong central Government, was a
30 haven of refuge to the individual. The people preferred the master far away to the exploitation and cruelty of the smaller master near at hand.

But the creators of national Government were perforce ruthless men. They were often cruel in their methods, but they did strive steadily toward something that society needed and very much wanted, a strong central State able to keep the
35 peace, to stamp out civil war, to put the unruly nobleman in his place, and to permit the bulk of individuals to live safely. The man of ruthless force had his place in developing a pioneer country, just as he did in fixing the power of the central Government in the development of Nations. Society paid him well for

his services and its development. When the development among the Nations of Europe, however, had been completed, ambition and ruthlessness, having served their term, tended to overstep their mark.

There came a growing feeling that Government was conducted for the benefit of a few who thrived unduly at the expense of all. The people sought a balancing—   5 a limiting force. There came gradually, through town councils, trade guilds, national parliaments, by constitution and by popular participation and control, limitations on arbitrary power.

Another factor that tended to limit the power of those who ruled, was the rise of the ethical conception that a ruler bore a responsibility for the welfare of   10 his subjects.

The American colonies were born in this struggle. The American Revolution was a turning point in it. After the Revolution the struggle continued and shaped itself in the public life of the country. There were those who because they had seen the confusion which attended the years of war for American independence   15 surrendered to the belief that popular Government was essentially dangerous and essentially unworkable. They were honest people, my friends, and we can- not deny that their experience had warranted some measure of fear. The most brilliant, honest and able exponent of this point of view was Hamilton. He was too impatient of slow-moving methods. Fundamentally he believed that the   20 safety of the republic lay in the autocratic strength of its Government, that the destiny of individuals was to serve that Government, and that fundamentally a great and strong group of central institutions, guided by a small group of able and public spirited citizens, could best direct all Government.

But Mr. Jefferson, in the summer of 1776, after drafting the Declaration of   25 Independence turned his mind to the same problem and took a different view. He did not deceive himself with outward forms. Government to him was a means to an end, not an end in itself; it might be either a refuge and a help or a threat and a danger, depending on the circumstances. We find him carefully analyzing the society for which he was to organize a Government. "We have no   30 paupers. The great mass of our population is of laborers, our rich who cannot live without labor, either manual or professional, being few and of moderate wealth. Most of the laboring class possess property, cultivate their own lands, have families and from the demand for their labor, are enabled to exact from the rich and the competent such prices as enable them to feed abundantly, clothe   35 above mere decency, to labor moderately and raise their families."

These people, he considered, had two sets of rights, those of "personal compe- tency" and those involved in acquiring and possessing property. By "personal

competency" he meant the right of free thinking, freedom of forming and expressing opinions, and freedom of personal living, each man according to his own lights. To insure the first set of rights, a Government must so order its functions as not to interfere with the individual. But even Jefferson realized that the
5 exercise of the property rights might so interfere with the rights of the individual that the Government, without whose assistance the property rights could not exist, must intervene, not to destroy individualism, but to protect it.

You are familiar with the great political duel which followed; and how Hamilton, and his friends, building toward a dominant centralized power were at length
10 defeated in the great election of 1800, by Mr. Jefferson's party. Out of that duel came the two parties, Republican and Democratic, as we know them today.

So began, in American political life, the new day, the day of the individual against the system, the day in which individualism was made the great watchword of American life. The happiest of economic conditions made that day long and
15 splendid. On the Western frontier, land was substantially free. No one, who did not shirk the task of earning a living, was entirely without opportunity to do so. Depressions could, and did, come and go; but they could not alter the fundamental fact that most of the people lived partly by selling their labor and partly by extracting their livelihood from the soil, so that starvation and
20 dislocation were practically impossible. At the very worst there was always the possibility of climbing into a covered wagon and moving west where the untilled prairies afforded a haven for men to whom the East did not provide a place. So great were our natural resources that we could offer this relief not only to our own people, but to the distressed of all the world; we could invite immigration
25 from Europe, and welcome it with open arms. Traditionally, when a depression came a new section of land was opened in the West; and even our temporary misfortune served our manifest destiny.

It was in the middle of the nineteenth century that a new force was released and a new dream created. The force was what is called the industrial revolution, the
30 advance of steam and machinery and the rise of the forerunners of the modern industrial plant. The dream was the dream of an economic machine, able to raise the standard of living for everyone; to bring luxury within the reach of the humblest; to annihilate distance by steam power and later by electricity, and to release everyone from the drudgery of the heaviest manual toil. It was
35 to be expected that this would necessarily affect Government. Heretofore, Government had merely been called upon to produce conditions within which people could live happily, labor peacefully, and rest secure. Now it was called upon to aid in the consummation of this new dream. There was, however, a shadow over the dream. To be made real, it required use of the talents of men

of tremendous will and tremendous ambition, since by no other force could
the problems of financing and engineering and new developments be brought
to a consummation.

So manifest were the advantages of the machine age, however, that the United
States fearlessly, cheerfully, and, I think, rightly, accepted the bitter with the   5
sweet. It was thought that no price was too high to pay for the advantages
which we could draw from a finished industrial system. The history of the last
half century is accordingly in large measure a history of a group of financial
Titans, whose methods were not scrutinized with too much care, and who were
honored in proportion as they produced the results, irrespective of the means   10
they used. The financiers who pushed the railroads to the Pacific were always
ruthless, often wasteful, and frequently corrupt; but they did build railroads,
and we have them today. It has been estimated that the American investor paid
for the American railway system more than three times over in the process; but
despite this fact the net advantage was to the United States. As long as we had   15
free land; as long as population was growing by leaps and bounds; as long as
our industrial plants were insufficient to supply our own needs, society chose
to give the ambitious man free play and unlimited reward provided only that
he produced the economic plant so much desired.

During this period of expansion, there was equal opportunity for all and the   20
business of Government was not to interfere but to assist in the development of
industry. This was done at the request of business men themselves. The tariff was
originally imposed for the purpose of "fostering our infant industry," a phrase
I think the older among you will remember as a political issue not so long ago.
The railroads were subsidized, sometimes by grants of money, oftener by grants   25
of land; some of the most valuable oil lands in the United States were granted
to assist the financing of the railroad which pushed through the Southwest. A
nascent merchant marine was assisted by grants of money, or by mail subsidies,
so that our steam shipping might ply the seven seas. Some of my friends tell
me that they do not want the Government in business. With this I agree; but   30
I wonder whether they realize the implications of the past. For while it has
been American doctrine that the Government must not go into business in
competition with private enterprises, still it has been traditional, particularly
in Republican administrations, for business urgently to ask the Government to
put at private disposal all kinds of Government assistance. The same man who   35
tells you that he does not want to see the Government interfere in business—
and he means it, and has plenty of good reasons for saying so—is the first
to go to Washington and ask the Government for a prohibitory tariff on his
product. When things get just bad enough, as they did two years ago, he will

go with equal speed to the United States Government and ask for a loan; and the Reconstruction Finance Corporation is the outcome of it. Each group has sought protection from the Government for its own special interests, without realizing that the function of Government must be to favor no small group at
5   the expense of its duty to protect the rights of personal freedom and of private property of all its citizens.

In retrospect we can now see that the turn of the tide came with the turn of the century. We were reaching our last frontier; there was no more free land and our industrial combinations had become great uncontrolled and irresponsible
10   units of power within the State. Clear-sighted men saw with fear the danger that opportunity would no longer be equal; that the growing corporation, like the feudal baron of old, might threaten the economic freedom of individuals to earn a living. In that hour, our antitrust laws were born. The cry was raised against the great corporations. Theodore Roosevelt, the first great Republican
15   Progressive, fought a Presidential campaign on the issue of "trust busting" and talked freely about malefactors of great wealth. If the Government had a policy it was rather to turn the clock back, to destroy the large combinations and to return to the time when every man owned his individual small business.

This was impossible; Theodore Roosevelt, abandoning the idea of "trust busting,"
20   was forced to work out a difference between "good" trusts and "bad' trusts. The Supreme Court set forth the famous "rule of reason" by which it seems to have meant that a concentration of industrial power was permissible if the method by which it got its power, and the use it made of that power, were reasonable.

Woodrow Wilson, elected in 1912, saw the situation more clearly. Where
25   Jefferson had feared the encroachment of political power on the lives of individuals, Wilson knew that the new power was financial. He saw, in the highly centralized economic system, the despot of the twentieth century, on whom great masses of individuals relied for their safety and their livelihood, and whose irresponsibility and greed (if they were not controlled) would reduce them to
30   starvation and penury. The concentration of financial power had not proceeded so far in 1912 as it has today; but it had grown far enough for Mr. Wilson to realize fully its implications. It is interesting, now, to read his speeches. What is called "radical" today (and I have reason to know whereof I speak) is mild compared to the campaign of Mr. Wilson. "No man can deny," he said, "that
35   the lines of endeavor have more and more narrowed and stiffened; no man who knows anything about the development of industry in this country can have failed to observe that the larger kinds of credit are more and more difficult to obtain unless you obtain them upon terms of uniting your efforts with those who already control the industry of the country, and nobody can fail to observe

that every man who tries to set himself up in competition with any process of manufacture which has taken place under the control of large combinations of capital will presently find himself either squeezed out or obliged to sell and allow himself to be absorbed." Had there been no World War—had Mr. Wilson been able to devote eight years to domestic instead of to international affairs—   5 we might have had a wholly different situation at the present time. However, the then distant roar of European cannon, growing ever louder, forced him to abandon the study of this issue. The problem he saw so clearly is left with us as a legacy; and no one of us on either side of the political controversy can deny that it is a matter of grave concern to the Government.   10

A glance at the situation today only too clearly indicates that equality of opportunity as we have known it no longer exists. Our industrial plant is built; the problem just now is whether under existing conditions it is not overbuilt. Our last frontier has long since been reached, and there is practically no more free land. More than half of our people do not live on the farms or on lands   15 and cannot derive a living by cultivating their own property. There is no safety valve in the form of a Western prairie to which those thrown out of work by the Eastern economic machines can go for a new start. We are not able to invite the immigration from Europe to share our endless plenty. We are now providing a drab living for our own people.   20

Our system of constantly rising tariffs has at last reacted against us to the point of closing our Canadian frontier on the north, our European markets on the east, many of our Latin-American markets to the south, and a goodly propor-tion of our Pacific markets on the west, through the retaliatory tariffs of those countries. It has forced many of our great industrial institutions which exported   25 their surplus production to such countries, to establish plants in such countries, within the tariff walls. This has resulted in the reduction of the operation of their American plants, and opportunity for employment.

Just as freedom to farm has ceased, so also the opportunity in business has narrowed. It still is true that men can start small enterprises, trusting to native   30 shrewdness and ability to keep abreast of competitors; but area after area has been preempted altogether by the great corporations, and even in the fields which still have no great concerns, the small man starts under a handicap. The unfeeling statistics of the past three decades show that the independent busi-ness man is running a losing race. Perhaps he is forced to the wall; perhaps he   35 cannot command credit; perhaps he is "squeezed out," in Mr. Wilson's words, by highly organized corporate competitors, as your corner grocery man can tell you. Recently a careful study was made of the concentration of business in the United States. It showed that our economic life was dominated by some six

hundred odd corporations who controlled two-thirds of American industry. Ten million small business men divided the other third. More striking still, it appeared that if the process of concentration goes on at the same rate, at the end of another century we shall have all American industry controlled by a dozen
5   corporations, and run by perhaps a hundred men. Put plainly, we are steering a steady course toward economic oligarchy, if we are not there already.

Clearly, all this calls for a reappraisal of values. A mere builder of more industrial plants, a creator of more railroad systems, an organizer of more corporations, is as likely to be a danger as a help. The day of the great promoter or the financial
10 Titan, to whom we granted anything if only he would build, or develop, is over. Our task now is not discovery or exploitation of natural resources, or necessarily producing more goods. It is the soberer, less dramatic business of administering resources and plants already in hand, of seeking to reestablish foreign markets for our surplus production, of meeting the problem of underconsumption,
15 of adjusting production to consumption, of distributing wealth and products more equitably, of adapting existing economic organizations to the service of the people. The day of enlightened administration has come.

Just as in older times the central Government was first a haven of refuge, and then a threat, so now in a closer economic system the central and ambitious
20 financial unit is no longer a servant of national desire, but a danger. I would draw the parallel one step farther. We did not think because national Government had become a threat in the 18th century that therefore we should abandon the principle of national Government. Nor today should we abandon the principle of strong economic units called corporations, merely because their
25 power is susceptible of easy abuse. In other times we dealt with the problem of an unduly ambitious central Government by modifying it gradually into a constitutional democratic Government. So today we are modifying and controlling our economic units.

As I see it, the task of Government in its relation to business is to assist the
30 development of an economic declaration of rights, an economic constitutional order. This is the common task of statesman and business man. It is the minimum requirement of a more permanently safe order of things.

Happily, the times indicate that to create such an order not only is the proper policy of Government, but it is the only line of safety for our economic structures
35 as well. We know, now, that these economic units cannot exist unless prosperity is uniform, that is, unless purchasing power is well distributed throughout every group in the Nation. That is why even the most selfish of corporations for its own interest would be glad to see wages restored and unemployment ended

and to bring the Western farmer back to his accustomed level of prosperity and to assure a permanent safety to both groups. That is why some enlightened industries themselves endeavor to limit the freedom of action of each man and business group within the industry in the common interest of all; why business men everywhere are asking a form of organization which will bring the scheme 5 of things into balance, even though it may in some measure qualify the freedom of action of individual units within the business.

The exposition need not further be elaborated. It is brief and incomplete, but you will be able to expand it in terms of your own business or occupation without difficulty. I think everyone who has actually entered the economic struggle— 10 which means everyone who was not born to safe wealth—knows in his own experience and his own life that we have now to apply the earlier concepts of American Government to the conditions of today.

The Declaration of Independence discusses the problem of Government in terms of a contract. Government is a relation of give and take, a contract, perforce, if 15 we would follow the thinking out of which it grew. Under such a contract rulers were accorded power, and the people consented to that power on consideration that they be accorded certain rights. The task of statesmanship has always been the redefinition of these rights in terms of a changing and growing social order. New conditions impose new requirements upon Government and those who 20 conduct government.

I held, for example, in proceedings before me as Governor, the purpose of which was the removal of the Sheriff of New York, that under modern conditions it was not enough for a public official merely to evade the legal terms of official wrongdoing. He owed a positive duty as well. I said in substance that if he had 25 acquired large sums of money, he was when accused required to explain the sources of such wealth. To that extent this wealth was colored with a public interest. I said that in financial matters public servants should, even beyond private citizens, be held to a stern and uncompromising rectitude.

I feel that we are coming to a view through the drift of our legislation and our 30 public thinking in the past quarter century that private economic power is, to enlarge an old phrase, a public trust as well. I hold that continued enjoyment of that power by any individual or group must depend upon the fulfillment of that trust. The men who have reached the summit of American business life know this best; happily, many of these urge the binding quality of this greater 35 social contract.

The terms of that contract are as old as the Republic, and as new as the new economic order.

Every man has a right to life; and this means that he has also a right to make a comfortable living. He may by sloth or crime decline to exercise that right; but it may not be denied him. We have no actual famine or dearth; our industrial and agricultural mechanism can produce enough and to spare. Our Govern-
5   ment formal and informal, political and economic, owes to everyone an avenue to possess himself of a portion of that plenty sufficient for his needs, through his own work.

Every man has a right to his own property; which means a right to be assured, to the fullest extent attainable, in the safety of his savings. By no other means
10   can men carry the burdens of those parts of life which, in the nature of things, afford no chance of labor: childhood, sickness, old age. In all thought of property, this right is paramount; all other property rights must yield to it. If, in accord with this principle, we must restrict the operations of the speculator, the manipulator, even the financier, I believe we must accept the restriction as
15   needful, not to hamper individualism but to protect it.

These two requirements must be satisfied, in the main, by the individuals who claim and hold control of the great industrial and financial combinations which dominate so large a part of our industrial life. They have undertaken to be, not business men, but princes of property. I am not prepared to say that the system
20   which produces them is wrong. I am very clear that they must fearlessly and competently assume the responsibility which goes with the power. So many enlightened business men know this that the statement would be little more than a platitude, were it not for an added implication.

This implication is, briefly, that the responsible heads of finance and industry
25   instead of acting each for himself, must work together to achieve the common end. They must, where necessary, sacrifice this or that private advantage; and in reciprocal self-denial must seek a general advantage. It is here that formal Government—political Government, if you chose—comes in. Whenever in the pursuit of this objective the lone wolf, the unethical competitor, the reckless
30   promoter, the Ishmael or Insull whose hand is against every man's, declines to join in achieving an end recognized as being for the public welfare, and threatens to drag the industry back to a state of anarchy, the Government may properly be asked to apply restraint. Likewise, should the group ever use its collective power contrary to the public welfare, the Government must be swift to enter
35   and protect the public interest.

The Government should assume the function of economic regulation only as a last resort, to be tried only when private initiative, inspired by high responsibility, with such assistance and balance as Government can give, has finally failed.

As yet there has been no final failure, because there has been no attempt; and I decline to assume that this Nation is unable to meet the situation.

The final term of the high contract was for liberty and the pursuit of happiness. We have learned a great deal of both in the past century. We know that individual liberty and individual happiness mean nothing unless both are ordered in the sense that one man's meat is not another man's poison. We know that the old "rights of personal competency," the right to read, to think, to speak, to choose and live a mode of life, must be respected at all hazards. We know that liberty to do anything which deprives others of those elemental rights is outside the protection of any compact; and that Government in this regard is the maintenance of a balance, within which every individual may have a place if he will take it; in which every individual may find safety if he wishes it; in which every individual may attain such power as his ability permits, consistent with his assuming the accompanying responsibility.

All this is a long, slow task. Nothing is more striking than the simple innocence of the men who insist, whenever an objective is present, on the prompt production of a patent scheme guaranteed to produce a result. Human endeavor is not so simple as that. Government includes the art of formulating a policy, and using the political technique to attain so much of that policy as will receive general support; persuading, leading, sacrificing, teaching always, because the greatest duty of a statesman is to educate. But in the matters of which I have spoken, we are learning rapidly, in a severe school. The lessons so learned must not be forgotten, even in the mental lethargy of a speculative upturn. We must build toward the time when a major depression cannot occur again; and if this means sacrificing the easy profits of inflationist booms, then let them go; and good riddance.

Faith in America, faith in our tradition of personal responsibility, faith in our institutions, faith in ourselves demand that we recognize the new terms of the old social contract. We shall fulfill them, as we fulfilled the obligation of the apparent Utopia which Jefferson imagined for us in 1776, and which Jefferson, Roosevelt and Wilson sought to bring to realizations. We must do so, lest a rising tide of misery, engendered by our common failure, engulf us all. But failure is not an American habit; and in the strength of great hope we must all shoulder our common load.

DEMOCRATIC CONVENTION ADDRESS
FRANKLIN D. ROOSEVELT

Having launched the New Deal, an ambitious program of political and economic re-engineering aimed at ending the Great Depression, President Franklin D. Roosevelt accepted his party's nomination to run for a second term. In this speech at the 1936 Democratic Convention, he defends his programs—some of which had been struck down as unconstitutional by the Supreme Court—and tags opponents as "economic royalists."

JUNE 27, 1936

SENATOR ROBINSON, MEMBERS OF THE DEMOCRATIC CONVENTION, MY FRIENDS:

Here, and in every community throughout the land, we are met at a time of great moment to the future of the Nation. It is an occasion to be dedicated to the simple and sincere expression of an attitude toward problems, the determination of which will profoundly affect America.

I come not only as a leader of a party, not only as a candidate for high office, but as one upon whom many critical hours have imposed and still impose a grave responsibility. 5

For the sympathy, help and confidence with which Americans have sustained me in my task I am grateful. For their loyalty I salute the members of our great party, in and out of political life in every part of the Union. I salute those of other parties, especially those in the Congress of the United States who on so many occasions have put partisanship aside. I thank the Governors of the several States, their Legislatures, their State and local officials who participated unselfishly and regardless of party in our efforts to achieve recovery and destroy abuses. Above all I thank the millions of Americans who have borne disaster bravely and have dared to smile through the storm. 10 15

Franklin D. Roosevelt, "Acceptance of the Renomination for the Presidency," June 27, 1936, in in Samuel Irving Rosenman, ed., *The Public Papers and Addresses of Franklin D. Roosevelt*, Vol. 5 (New York: Russell & Russell, 1969), 230–36.

America will not forget these recent years, will not forget that the rescue was not a mere party task. It was the concern of all of us. In our strength we rose together, rallied our energies together, applied the old rules of common sense, and together survived.

5   In those days we feared fear. That was why we fought fear. And today, my friends, we have won against the most dangerous of our foes. We have conquered fear.

But I cannot, with candor, tell you that all is well with the world. Clouds of suspicion, tides of ill-will and intolerance gather darkly in many places. In our own land we enjoy indeed a fullness of life greater than that of most Nations.
10 But the rush of modern civilization itself has raised for us new difficulties, new problems which must be solved if we are to preserve to the United States the political and economic freedom for which Washington and Jefferson planned and fought.

Philadelphia is a good city in which to write American history. This is fitting
15 ground on which to reaffirm the faith of our fathers; to pledge ourselves to restore to the people a wider freedom; to give to 1936 as the founders gave to 1776—an American way of life.

That very word freedom, in itself and of necessity, suggests freedom from some restraining power. In 1776 we sought freedom from the tyranny of a political
20 autocracy—from the eighteenth century royalists who held special privileges from the crown. It was to perpetuate their privilege that they governed without the consent of the governed; that they denied the right of free assembly and free speech; that they restricted the worship of God; that they put the average man's property and the average man's life in pawn to the mercenaries of dynastic
25 power; that they regimented the people.

And so it was to win freedom from the tyranny of political autocracy that the American Revolution was fought. That victory gave the business of governing into the hands of the average man, who won the right with his neighbors to make and order his own destiny through his own Government. Political tyranny
30 was wiped out at Philadelphia on July 4, 1776.

Since that struggle, however, man's inventive genius released new forces in our land which reordered the lives of our people. The age of machinery, of railroads; of steam and electricity; the telegraph and the radio; mass production, mass distribution—all of these combined to bring forward a new civilization and
35 with it a new problem for those who sought to remain free.

For out of this modern civilization economic royalists carved new dynasties. New kingdoms were built upon concentration of control over material things.

Through new uses of corporations, banks and securities, new machinery of industry and agriculture, of labor and capital—all undreamed of by the fathers— the whole structure of modern life was impressed into this royal service.

There was no place among this royalty for our many thousands of small business men and merchants who sought to make a worthy use of the American system   5 of initiative and profit. They were no more free than the worker or the farmer. Even honest and progressive-minded men of wealth, aware of their obligation to their generation, could never know just where they fitted into this dynastic scheme of things.

It was natural and perhaps human that the privileged princes of these   10 new economic dynasties, thirsting for power, reached out for control over Government itself. They created a new despotism and wrapped it in the robes of legal sanction. In its service new mercenaries sought to regiment the people, their labor, and their property. And as a result the average man once more confronts the problem that faced the Minute Man.   15

The hours men and women worked, the wages they received, the conditions of their labor—these had passed beyond the control of the people, and were imposed by this new industrial dictatorship. The savings of the average family, the capital of the small business man, the investments set aside for old age—other people's money—these were tools which the new economic royalty used to dig   20 itself in.

Those who tilled the soil no longer reaped the rewards which were their right. The small measure of their gains was decreed by men in distant cities.

Throughout the Nation, opportunity was limited by monopoly. Individual initiative was crushed in the cogs of a great machine. The field open for free   25 business was more and more restricted. Private enterprise, indeed, became too private. It became privileged enterprise, not free enterprise.

An old English judge once said: "Necessitous men are not free men." Liberty requires opportunity to make a living—a living decent according to the standard of the time, a living which gives man not only enough to live by, but something   30 to live for.

For too many of us the political equality we once had won was meaningless in the face of economic inequality. A small group had concentrated into their own hands an almost complete control over other people's property, other people's money, other people's labor—other people's lives. For too many of us life was   35 no longer free; liberty no longer real; men could no longer follow the pursuit of happiness.

Against economic tyranny such as this, the American citizen could appeal only to the organized power of Government. The collapse of 1929 showed up the despotism for what it was. The election of 1932 was the people's mandate to end it. Under that mandate it is being ended.

5   The royalists of the economic order have conceded that political freedom was the business of the Government, but they have maintained that economic slavery was nobody's business. They granted that the Government could protect the citizen in his right to vote, but they denied that the Government could do anything to protect the citizen in his right to work and his right to live.

10 Today we stand committed to the proposition that freedom is no half-and-half affair. If the average citizen is guaranteed equal opportunity in the polling place, he must have equal opportunity in the market place.

These economic royalists complain that we seek to overthrow the institutions of America. What they really complain of is that we seek to take away their power.

15 Our allegiance to American institutions requires the overthrow of this kind of power. In vain they seek to hide behind the Flag and the Constitution. In their blindness they forget what the Flag and the Constitution stand for. Now, as always, they stand for democracy, not tyranny; for freedom, not subjection; and against a dictatorship by mob rule and the overprivileged alike.

20 The brave and clear platform adopted by this Convention, to which I heartily subscribe, sets forth that Government in a modern civilization has certain inescapable obligations to its citizens, among which are protection of the family and the home, the establishment of a democracy of opportunity, and aid to those overtaken by disaster.

25 But the resolute enemy within our gates is ever ready to beat down our words unless in greater courage we will fight for them.

For more than three years we have fought for them. This Convention, in every word and deed, has pledged that that fight will go on.

The defeats and victories of these years have given to us as a people a new
30 understanding of our Government and of ourselves. Never since the early days of the New England town meeting have the affairs of Government been so widely discussed and so clearly appreciated. It has been brought home to us that the only effective guide for the safety of this most worldly of worlds, the greatest guide of all, is moral principle.

35 We do not see faith, hope and charity as unattainable ideals, but we use them as stout supports of a Nation fighting the fight for freedom in a modern civilization.

Faith—in the soundness of democracy in the midst of dictatorships.

Hope—renewed because we know so well the progress we have made.

Charity—in the true spirit of that grand old word. For charity literally translated from the original means love, the love that understands, that does not merely share the wealth of the giver, but in true sympathy and 5 wisdom helps men to help themselves.

We seek not merely to make Government a mechanical implement, but to give it the vibrant personal character that is the very embodiment of human charity.

We are poor indeed if this Nation cannot afford to lift from every recess of American life the dread fear of the unemployed that they are not needed in 10 the world. We cannot afford to accumulate a deficit in the books of human fortitude.

In the place of the palace of privilege we seek to build a temple out of faith and hope and charity.

It is a sobering thing, my friends, to be a servant of this great cause. We try in our 15 daily work to remember that the cause belongs not to us, but to the people. The standard is not in the hands of you and me alone. It is carried by America. We seek daily to profit from experience, to learn to do better as our task proceeds.

Governments can err, Presidents do make mistakes, but the immortal Dante tells us that divine justice weighs the sins of the cold-blooded and the sins of 20 the warm-hearted in different scales.

Better the occasional faults of a Government that lives in a spirit of charity than the consistent omissions of a Government frozen in the ice of its own indifference.

There is a mysterious cycle in human events. To some generations much is 25 given. Of other generations much is expected. This generation of Americans has a rendezvous with destiny.

In this world of ours in other lands, there are some people, who, in times past, have lived and fought for freedom, and seem to have grown too weary to carry on the fight. They have sold their heritage of freedom for the illusion of a living. 30 They have yielded their democracy.

I believe in my heart that only our success can stir their ancient hope. They begin to know that here in America we are waging a great and successful war. It is not alone a war against want and destitution and economic demoralization. It is more than that; it is a war for the survival of democracy. We are fighting to 35 save a great and precious form of government for ourselves and for the world.

I accept the commission you have tendered me. I join with you. I am enlisted for the duration of the war.

What Good's a Constitution?
Winston Churchill (1874–1965)

Written soon after Franklin Roosevelt's Democratic Convention Address of 1936, this article by British statesman Winston Churchill points to the wide gulf between Churchill's and Roosevelt's economic views, even if five years later they would forge a close wartime alliance. Beyond their differences on economics, Churchill sees the American Constitution as an enduring source of strength for the American republic, not an obstacle to be overcome.

August 22, 1936

No one can think clearly or sensibly about this vast and burning topic without in the first instance making up his mind upon the fundamental issue. Does he value the State above the citizen, or the citizen above the State? Does a government exist for the individual, or do individuals exist for the government? One must recognize that the world today is deeply divided upon this. Some of the most powerful   5
nations and races have definitely chosen to subordinate the citizen or subject to the life of the State. In Russia, Germany and Italy we have this sombre, tremendous decision, expressed in varying forms. All nations agree that in time of war, where the life and independence of the country are at stake, every man and woman must be ready to work and, if need be, die in defense of these supreme objects; and that   10
the government must be empowered to call upon them to any extent.

But what we are now considering is the existence of this principle in times of peace and its erection into a permanent system to which the life of great communities must be made to conform. The argument is used that economic crises are only another form of war, and as they are always with us, or can always be   15
alleged to be with us, it is claimed that we must live our lives in a perpetual state of war, only without actual shooting, bayoneting or cannonading.

This is, of course, the Socialist view. As long as Socialists present themselves in an international guise as creators of a new world order, like the beehive or the

---

ant heap, with a new human heart to fit these novel conceptions, they could easily be beaten, and have been very effectively beaten both by argument and by nature. But when new forms of socialism arose which were grafted not upon world ideals but upon the strongest forms of nationalism, their success
5   was remarkable.

In Germany, for instance, the alliance between national patriotism, tradition and pride on the one hand, and discontent about the inequalities of wealth on the other, made the Weimar Constitution 'a scrap of paper'. Either of these two fierce, turbulent torrents separately might have been kept within bounds.
10 Joined together in a fierce confluence, they proved irresistible.

Once the rulers of a country can create a war atmosphere in time of peace, can allege that the State is in danger and appeal to all the noblest national instincts, as well as all the basest, it is only in very solidly established countries that the rights of the citizens can be preserved. In Germany these rights vanished almost
15 overnight. Today no one may criticize the dictatorship, either in speech or writing. Voters still go to the polls—in fact, are herded to the polls like sheep—but the method of election has become a fantastic travesty of popular government. A German can vote for the régime, but not against it. If he attempts to indicate disapproval, his ballot paper is reckoned as 'spoiled'.

20 The tyranny of the ruling junta extends into every department of life. Friends may not greet each other without invoking the name of Hitler. At least on certain days, the very meals that a family eats in the privacy of its home are regulated by decree. The shadow of an all-powerful State falls between parent and child, husband and wife. Love itself is fettered and confined. No marriage, no love
25 relation of any kind is permitted which offends against a narrow and arbitrary code based upon virulent race prejudice.

Nor is this all. Even in the sphere of religion the State must intervene. It comes between the priest and his penitent, between the worshipper and the God to whom he prays. And this last, by one of the curious ironies of history, in the
30 land of Luther.

To rivet this intolerable yoke upon the necks of the German people all the resources of propaganda have been utilized to magnify the sense of crisis and to exhibit sometimes France, sometimes Poland, sometimes Lithuania, always the Soviets and the Jews, as antagonists at whom the patriotic Teuton must
35 grind his teeth.

Much the same thing has happened in Russia. The powerful aid of national sentiment and imperialist aspirations has been invoked to buttress a decaying Communism.

In the United States, also, economic crisis has led to an extension of the activities of the Executive and to the pillorying, by irresponsible agitators, of certain groups and sections of the population as enemies of the rest. There have been efforts to exalt the power of the central government and to limit the rights of individuals. It has been sought to mobilize behind this reversal of the American   5
tradition, at once the selfishness of the pensioners, or would-be pensioners, of Washington, and the patriotism of all who wish to see their country prosperous once more.

It is when passions and cupidities are thus unleashed and, at the same time, the sense of public duty rides high in the hearts of all men and women of good will   10
that the handcuffs can be slipped upon the citizens and they can be brought into entire subjugation to the executive government. Then they are led to believe that, if they will only yield themselves, body, mind and soul, to the State, and obey unquestioningly its injunctions, some dazzling future of riches and power will open to them, either—as in Italy—by the conquest of the territories   15
of others, or—as in America—by a further liberation and exploitation of the national resources.

I take the opposite view. I hold that governments are meant to be, and must remain, the servants of the citizens; that states and federations only come into existence and can only by justified by preserving the 'life, liberty and the pursuit   20
of happiness' in the homes and families of individuals. The true right and power rest in the individual. He gives of his right and power to the State, expecting and requiring thereby in return to receive certain advantages and guarantees. I do not admit that an economic crisis can ever truly be compared with the kind of struggle for existence by races constantly under primordial conditions. I do   25
not think that modern nations in time of peace ought to regard themselves as if they were the inhabitants of besieged cities, liable to be put to the sword or led into slavery if they cannot make good their defense.

One of the greatest reasons for avoiding war is that it is destructive to liberty. But we must not be led into adopting for ourselves the evils of war in time of   30
peace upon any pretext whatever. The word 'civilization' means not only peace by the non-regimentation of the people such as is required in war. Civilization means that officials and authorities, whether uniformed or not, whether armed or not, are made to realize that they are servants and not masters.

Socialism or overweening State life, whether in peace or war, is only sharing   35
miseries and not blessings. Every self-respecting citizen in every country must be on his guard lest the rulers demand of him in time of peace sacrifices only tolerable in a period of war for national self-preservation.

I judge the civilization of any community by simple tests. What is the degree of freedom possessed by the citizen or subject? Can he think, speak and act freely under well-established, well-known laws? Can he criticize the executive government? Can he sue the State if it has infringed his rights? Are there also

5   great processes for changing the law to meet new conditions?

Judging by these standards, Great Britain and the United States can claim to be in the forefront of civilized communities. But we owe this only in part to the good sense and watchfulness of our citizens. In both our countries the character of the judiciary is a vital factor in the maintenance of the rights and liberties

10 of the individual citizen.

Our judges extend impartially to all men protection, not only against wrongs committed by private persons, but also against the arbitrary acts of public authority. The independence of the courts is, to all of us, the guarantee of freedom and the equal rule of law.

15 It must, therefore, be the first concern of the citizens of a free country to preserve and maintain the independence of the courts of justice, however inconvenient that independence may be, on occasion, to the government of the day.

But all this implies peace conditions, an atmosphere of civilization rather than militarization or officialization. It implies a balance and equipoise of society

20 which can be altered only gradually. It is so hard to build the structure of a vast economic community, and so easy to upset it and throw it into confusion. The onus must lie always upon those who propose a change, and the process of change is hardly ever beneficial unless it considers what is due to the past as well as what is claimed for the future.

25 It is for these reasons among many others that the founders of the American Republic in their Declaration of Independence inculcate as a duty binding upon all worthy sons of America 'a frequent recurrence to first principles'. Do not let us too readily brush aside the grand, simple affirmations of the past. All wisdom is not new wisdom. Let us never forget that the glory of the nineteenth

30 century was founded upon what seemed to be the successful putting down of those twin curses, anarchy and tyranny.

The question we are discussing is whether a fixed constitution is a bulwark or a fetter. From what I have written it is plain that I incline to the side of those who would regard it as a bulwark, and that I rank the citizen higher than the

35 State, and regard the State as useful only in so far as it preserves his inherent rights. All forms of tyranny are odious. It makes very little difference to the citizen, father of a family, head of a household, whether tyranny comes from a

royal or imperial despot, or from a Pope or Inquisitor, or from a military caste, or from an aristocratic or plutocratic oligarchy, or from a ring of employers, or a trade union, or a party caucus—or worst of all, from a terrified and infuriated mob. 'A man's a man for a' that.' The whole point is, whether he can make head against oppression in any of its Protean shapes, and defend the island of his home, his life and soul. And here is the point at which we may consider and contrast the constitutions of our respective countries.

It is very difficult for us in England to realize the kind of deadlock which has been reached in the United States. Imagine, for instance, the gigantic India Bill, passed through Parliament and for two or three years in active operation throughout the whole of India, suddenly being declared illegal by the law lords sitting as a tribunal. Imagine—to take an instance nearer home—some gigantic measure of insurance as big as our widows' pensions, health and employment insurance rolled together, which had deeply interwoven itself in the whole life of the people, upon which every kind of contract and business arrangement had been based, being declared to have no validity by a court of law. We simply cannot conceive it. Yet something very like that has occurred on your side of the Atlantic.

In our country an act of Parliament which, upon the advice of the ministers responsible for it, has received the royal assent is the law of the land. Its authority cannot be questioned by any court. There is no limit to the powers of Crown and Parliament. Even the gravest changes in our Constitution can in theory be carried out by simple majority votes in both Houses and the consequential assent of the Crown.

But we now watch the workings of a written Constitution enforced by a Supreme Court according to the letter of the law, under which anyone may bring a test case challenging not merely the interpretation of a law, but the law itself, and if the Court decides for the appellant, be he only an owner of a few chickens, the whole action of the Legislature and the Executive becomes to that extent null and void. We know that to modify the Constitution even in the smallest particular requires a two-thirds majority of the sovereign states forming the American Union. And this has been achieved, after prodigious struggles, on only a score of occasions during the whole history of the United States.

American citizens or jurists in their turn, gaze with wonder at our great British democracy expressing itself with plenary powers through a Government and Parliament controlled only by the fluctuating currents of public opinion. British Governments live from day to day only upon the approval of the House of Commons. There is no divorce between the Executive and the Legislature. The ministers, new or old, must be chosen from men and parties which in the aggregate will command a majority in the House of Commons. Parliament can, if it chooses, even prolong its own life beyond the statutory limit. Ministers may at any time advise the King to a sudden dissolution. Yet all classes and all parties have a deep, underlying conviction that these vast, flexible powers will not be abused, that the spirit of our unwritten Constitution will be respected at every stage.

To understand how this faith is justified, how the British people are able to enjoy a real stability of government without a written Constitution, it is necessary to consider the beginning of party politics in Britain. Whigs and Tories were almost equally concerned to assert the authority of Parliament as a check upon the Executive. With the Whigs this was a matter of fundamental principle; with the Tories it was a question of expediency, James II was a Catholic and his efforts to further the cause of his co-religionists alienated the great bulk of the Tory party, who were loyal to the Church of England. Then from the advent of William of Orange to the accession of George III, with a brief interval in the reign of Queen Anne, the Crown could do nothing without the Whigs and the government of the country was predominantly or exclusively in the hands of that party.

The Tories were thus vitally interested in preserving and extending the rights of the parliamentary opposition. In this way a jealous care for constitutional rights came to mark both the great parties of the State. And as to all men the Constitution represented security and freedom, none would consent willingly to any breach of it, even to gain a temporary advantage.

Modern times offer respect for law and constitutional usage. Nothing contributed so much to the collapse of the general strike ten years ago as the declaration by great lawyers that it was illegal. And the right of freedom of speech and publication is extended, under the Constitution, to those who in theory seek to overthrow established institutions by force of arms so long as they do not commit any illegal act.

Another factor making for stability is our permanent civil service. Governments come and go; parliamentary majorities fluctuate; but the civil servants remain. To new and inexperienced ministers they are 'guides, philosophers and friends'. Themselves untouched by the vicissitudes of party fortunes, they impart to the business of administration a real continuity.

On the whole, too, popular opinion acts as a guardian of the unwritten Constitution. Public chastisement would speedily overtake any minister, however powerful, who fell below the accepted standards of fair play or who descended to trickwork or dodgery.

When one considers the immense size of the United States and the extraordinary contrasts of climate and character which differentiate the forty-eight sovereign states of the American Union, as well as the inevitable conflict of interests between North and South and between East and West, it would seem that the participants of so vast a federation have the right to effectual guarantees upon the fundamental laws, and that these should not be easily changed to suit a particular emergency or fraction of the country. 5

The founders of the Union, although its corpus was then so much smaller, realized this with profound conviction. They did not think it possible to entrust legislation for so diverse a community and enormous an area to a simple majority. They were as well acquainted with the follies and intolerance of parliaments as with the oppression of princes. 'To control the powers and conduct of the legislature,' said a leading member of the Convention of 1787, 'by an overruling constitution was an improvement in the science and practice of government reserved to the American States.' 10 15

All the great names of American history can be invoked behind this principle. Why should it be considered obsolete? If today we are framing that constitution for a 'United States of Europe' for which so many thinkers on this side of the ocean aspire, fixed and almost unalterable guarantees would be required by the acceding nations. 20

It may well be that this very quality of rigidity, which is today thought to be so galling, has been a prime factor in founding the greatness of the United States. In the shelter of the Constitution nature has been conquered, a mighty continent has been brought under the sway of man, and an economic entity established, unrivalled in the whole history of the globe. 25

In this small island of Britain we make laws for ourselves. But if we had again attempted to apply this flexibility and freedom to the British Empire, and to frame an Imperial Constitution to make laws for the whole body, it would have been broken to pieces. Although we have a free, flexible Constitution at the centre and for the centre of the Empire, nothing is more rigid than the established practice—namely, that we claim no powers to interfere with the affairs of its self-governing component parts. No supreme court is needed to enforce this rule. We have learned the lessons of the past too well. 30

And here we must note a dangerous misuse of terminology. 'Taking the rigidity out of the American Constitution' means, and is intended to mean, new gigantic accessions of power to the dominating centre of government and giving it the means to make new fundamental laws enforceable upon all American citizens. 35

Such a departure in the British Empire by a chance parliamentary majority or even by aggregate Dominion parliamentary majorities, would shatter it to bits. The so-called 'rigidity' of the American Constitution is in fact the guarantee of freedom to its widespread component parts. That a set of persons, however eminent, carried into office upon some populist heave should have the power to make the will of a bare majority effective over the whole of the United States might cause disasters upon the greatest scale from which recovery would not be swift or easy.

I was reading the other day a recent American novel by Sinclair Lewis—*It Can't Happen Here*. Such books render a public service to the English-speaking world. When we see what has happened in Germany, Italy and Russia we cannot neglect their warning. This is an age in which the citizen requires more, and not less, legal protection in the exercise of his rights and' liberties.

That is doubtless why, after all the complaints against the rigidity of the United States Constitution and the threats of a presidential election on this issue, none of the suggested constitutional amendments has so far been adopted by the Administration. This may explain why the 'Nine Old Men' of the Supreme Court have not been more seriously challenged. But the challenge may come at a later date, though it would perhaps be wiser to dissociate it from any question of the age of the judges, lest it be the liberal element in the court which is weakened.

Now, at the end of these reflections, I must strike a minor and different note. The rigidity of the Constitution of the United States is the shield of the common man. But that rigidity ought not to be interpreted by pedants. In England we continually give new interpretation to the archaic language of our fundamental institutions, and this is no new thing in the United States. The judiciary have obligations which go beyond expounding the mere letter of the law. The Constitution must be made to work.

A true interpretation, however, of the British or the American Constitution is certainly not a chop-logic or pedantic interpretation. So august a body as the Supreme Court in dealing with law must also deal with the life of the United States, and words, however solemn, are only true when they preserve their vital relationship to facts. It would certainly be a great disaster, not only to the American Republic but to the whole world, if a violent collision should take place between the large majority of the American people and the great instrument of government which has so long presided over their expanding fortunes.

Annual Message
to Congress
Franklin D. Roosevelt

As victory in the Second World War looked more and more likely, President Franklin D. Roosevelt turned his attention to postwar America. In this speech he proposes a "second Bill of Rights."

January 11, 1944

... It is our duty now to begin to lay the plans and determine the strategy for the winning of a lasting peace and the establishment of an American standard of living higher than ever before known. We cannot be content, no matter how high that general standard of living may be, if some fraction of our people—whether it be one-third or one-fifth or one-tenth—is ill-fed, ill-clothed, ill-housed, and   5
insecure.

This Republic had its beginning, and grew to its present strength, under the protection of certain inalienable political rights—among them the right of free speech, free press, free worship, trial by jury, freedom from unreasonable searches and seizures. They were our rights to life and liberty.   10

As our Nation has grown in size and stature, however—as our industrial economy expanded—these political rights proved inadequate to assure us equality in the pursuit of happiness.

We have come to a clear realization of the fact that true individual freedom cannot exist without economic security and independence. "Necessitous men   15
are not free men." People who are hungry and out of a job are the stuff of which dictatorships are made.

In our day these economic truths have become accepted as self-evident. We have accepted, so to speak, a second Bill of Rights under which a new basis of security and prosperity can be established for all—regardless of station, race,   20
or creed.

Franklin D. Roosevelt, "Message on the State of the Union," 1944, in Samuel Irving Rosenman, ed., *The Public Papers and Addresses of Franklin D. Roosevelt*, Vol. 13 (New York: Harper, 1950), 40–42.

Among these are:

The right to a useful and remunerative job in the industries or shops or farms or mines of the Nation;

The right to earn enough to provide adequate food and clothing and
5   recreation;

The right of every farmer to raise and sell his products at a return which will give him and his family a decent living;

The right of every businessman, large and small, to trade in an atmosphere of freedom from unfair competition and domination by monopolies at home or
10   abroad;

The right of every family to a decent home;

The right to adequate medical care and the opportunity to achieve and enjoy good health;

The right to adequate protection from the economic fears of old age, sickness,
15   accident, and unemployment;

The right to a good education.

All of these rights spell security. And after this war is won we must be prepared to move forward, in the implementation of these rights, to new goals of human happiness and well-being.

20   America's own rightful place in the world depends in large part upon how fully these and similar rights have been carried into practice for our citizens. For unless there is security here at home there cannot be lasting peace in the world.

One of the great American industrialists of our day—a man who has rendered yeoman service to his country in this crisis—recently emphasized the grave
25   dangers of "rightist reaction" in this Nation. All clear-thinking businessmen share his concern. Indeed, if such reaction should develop—if history were to repeat itself and we were to return to the so-called "normalcy" of the 1920's—then it is certain that even though we shall have conquered our enemies on the battlefields abroad, we shall have yielded to the spirit of Fascism here at home.

30   I ask the Congress to explore the means for implementing this economic bill of rights—for it is definitely the responsibility of the Congress so to do. Many of these problems are already before committees of the Congress in the form of proposed legislation. I shall from time to time communicate with the Congress with respect to these and further proposals. In the event that no adequate program of progress
35   is evolved, I am certain that the Nation will be conscious of the fact.

Our fighting men abroad—and their families at home—expect such a program and have the right to insist upon it. It is to their demands that this Government should pay heed rather than to the whining demands of selfish pressure groups who seek to feather their nests while young Americans are dying.

The foreign policy that we have been following—the policy that guided us at   5
Moscow, Cairo, and Teheran—is based on the common sense principle which was best expressed by Benjamin Franklin on July 4, 1776: "We must all hang together, or assuredly we shall all hang separately."

I have often said that there are no two fronts for America in this war. There is only one front. There is one line of unity which extends from the hearts of   10
the people at home to the men of our attacking forces in our farthest outposts. When we speak of our total effort, we speak of the factory and the field, and the mine as well as of the battleground—we speak of the soldier and the civilian, the citizen and his Government.

Each and every one of us has a solemn obligation under God to serve this   15
Nation in its most critical hour—to keep this Nation great—to make this Nation greater in a better world.

COMMENCEMENT ADDRESS AT YALE UNIVERSITY
JOHN F. KENNEDY (1917–1963)

President John F. Kennedy's New Frontier policies were consistent with the policies of his Progressive predecessors. Current problems, he suggests in this speech, call for technical expertise rather than old ideas.

JUNE 11,1962

PRESIDENT GRISWOLD, MEMBERS OF THE FACULTY, GRADUATES AND THEIR FAMILIES, LADIES AND GENTLEMEN:

Let me begin by expressing my appreciation for the very deep honor which you have conferred upon me. As General de Gaulle occasionally acknowledges America to be the daughter of Europe, so I am pleased to come to Yale, the daughter of Harvard. It might be said now that I have the best of both worlds, a Harvard education and a Yale degree.   5

I am particularly glad to become a Yale man because as I think about my troubles, I find that a lot of them have come from other Yale men. Among businessmen, I have had a minor disagreement with Roger Blough, of the law school class of 1931, and I have had some complaints, too, from my friend Henry Ford, of the class of 1940. In journalism I seem to have a difference with John Hay   10
Whitney, of the class of 1926—and sometimes I also displease Henry Luce of the class of 1920, not to mention also William F. Buckley, Jr., of the class of 1950. I even have some trouble with my Yale advisers. I get along with them, but I am not always sure how they get along with each other.

I have the warmest feelings for Chester Bowles of the class of 1924, and for Dean   15
Acheson of the class of 1915, and my assistant, McGeorge Bundy, of the class of 1940. But I am not 100 percent sure that these three wise and experienced Yale men wholly agree with each other on every issue.

John F. Kennedy, "Commencement Address at Yale University," June 11, 1962, in *Public Papers of the Presidents of the United States: John F. Kennedy* (Washington, D.C.: Government Printing Office, 1962–64), 470–75.

So this administration which aims at peaceful cooperation among all Americans has been the victim of a certain natural pugnacity developed in this city among Yale men. Now that I, too, am a Yale man, it is time for peace. Last week at West Point, in the historic tradition of that Academy, I availed myself of the
5   powers of Commander in Chief to remit all sentences of offending cadets. In that same spirit, and in the historic tradition of Yale, let me now offer to smoke the clay pipe of friendship with all of my brother Elis, and I hope that they may be friends not only with me but even with each other.

In any event, I am very glad to be here and as a new member of the club, I
10 have been checking to see what earlier links existed between the institution of the Presidency and Yale. I found that a member of the class of 1878, William Howard Taft, served one term in the White House as preparation for becoming a member of this faculty. And a graduate of 1804, John C. Calhoun, regarded the Vice Presidency, quite naturally, as too lowly a status for a Yale alumnus—and
15 became the only man in history to ever resign that office.

Calhoun in 1804 and Taft in 1878 graduated into a world very different from ours today. They and their contemporaries spent entire careers stretching over 40 years in grappling with a few dramatic issues on which the Nation was sharply and emotionally divided, issues that occupied the attention of a generation
20 at a time: the national bank, the disposal of the public lands, nullification or union, freedom or slavery, gold or silver. Today these old sweeping issues very largely have disappeared. The central domestic issues of our time are more subtle and less simple. They relate not to basic clashes of philosophy or ideology but to ways and means of reaching common goals—to research for sophisticated
25 solutions to complex and obstinate issues. The world of Calhoun, the world of Taft had its own hard problems and notable challenges. But its problems are not our problems. Their age is not our age. As every past generation has had to disenthrall itself from an inheritance of truisms and stereotypes, so in our own time we must move on from the reassuring repetition of stale phrases to a new,
30 difficult, but essential confrontation with reality.

For the great enemy of the truth is very often not the lie—deliberate, contrived, and dishonest—but the myth—persistent, persuasive, and unrealistic. Too often we hold fast to the cliches of our forebears. We subject all facts to a prefabricated set of interpretations. We enjoy the comfort of opinion without
35 the discomfort of thought.

Mythology distracts us everywhere—in government as in business, in politics as in economics, in foreign affairs as in domestic affairs. But today I want to particularly consider the myth and reality in our national economy. In recent months many have come to feel, as I do, that the dialogue between the parties—between business and government, between the government and the public—is clogged by illusion and platitude and fails to reflect the true realities of contemporary American society.

I speak of these matters here at Yale because of the self-evident truth that a great   5
university is always enlisted against the spread of illusion and on the side of reality. No one has said it more clearly than your President Griswold: "Liberal learning is both a safeguard against false ideas of freedom and a source of true ones." Your role as university men, whatever your calling, will be to increase each new generation's grasp of its duties.   10

There are three great areas of our domestic affairs in which, today, there is a danger that illusion may prevent effective action. They are, first, the question of the size and the shape of the government's responsibilities; second, the question of public fiscal policy; and third, the matter of confidence, business confidence or public confidence, or simply confidence in America. I want to talk about   15
all three, and I want to talk about them carefully and dispassionately—and I emphasize that I am concerned here not with political debate but with finding ways to separate false problems from real ones.

If a contest in angry argument were forced upon it, no administration could shrink from response, and history does not suggest that American Presidents   20
are totally without resources in an engagement forced upon them because of hostility in one sector of society. But in the wider national interest, we need not partisan wrangling but common concentration on common problems. I come here to this distinguished university to ask you to join in this great task.

Let us take first the question of the size and shape of government. The myth   25
here is that government is big, and bad—and steadily getting bigger and worse. Obviously this myth has some excuse for existence. It is true that in recent history each new administration has spent much more money than its predecessor. Thus President Roosevelt outspent President Hoover, and with allowances for the special case of the Second World War, President Truman outspent President   30
Roosevelt. Just to prove that this was not a partisan matter, President Eisenhower then outspent President Truman by the handsome figure of $182 billion. It is even possible, some think, that this trend may continue.

But does it follow from this that big government is growing relatively bigger? It does not—for the fact is for the last fifteen years, the Federal Government—and   35
also the Federal debt—and also the Federal bureaucracy—have grown less rapidly than the economy as a whole. If we leave defense and space expenditures aside, the Federal Government since the Second World War has expanded less

than any other major sector of our national life—less than industry, less than commerce, less than agriculture, less than higher education, and very much less than the noise about big government.

The truth about big government is the truth about any other great activity—it is
5 complex. Certainly it is true that size brings dangers—but it is also true that size can bring benefits. Here at Yale which has contributed so much to our national progress in science and medicine, it may be proper for me to mention one great and little noticed expansion of government which has brought strength to our whole society—the new role of our Federal Government as the major patron of
10 research in science and in medicine. Few people realize that in 1961, in support of all university research in science and medicine, three dollars out of every four came from the Federal Government. I need hardly point out that this has taken place without undue enlargement of Government control—that American scientists remain second to none in their independence and in their individualism.

15 I am not suggesting that Federal expenditures cannot bring some measure of control. The whole thrust of Federal expenditures in agriculture have been related by purpose and design to control, as a means of dealing with the problems created by our farmers and our growing productivity. Each sector, my point is, of activity must be approached on its own merits and in terms of specific
20 national needs. Generalities in regard to Federal expenditures, therefore, can be misleading—each case, science, urban renewal, education, agriculture, natural resources, each case must be determined on its merits if we are to profit from our unrivaled ability to combine the strength of public and private purpose.

Next, let us turn to the problem of our fiscal policy. Here the myths are legion
25 and the truth hard to find. But let me take as a prime example the problem of the Federal budget. We persist in measuring our Federal fiscal integrity today by the conventional or administrative budget—with results which would be regarded as absurd in any business firm—in any country of Europe—or in any careful assessment of the reality of our national finances. The administrative
30 budget has sound administrative uses. But for wider purposes it is less helpful. It omits our special trust funds and the effect that they have on our economy; it neglects changes in assets and inventories. It cannot tell a loan from a straight expenditure—and worst of all it cannot distinguish between operating expenditures and long term investments.

35 This budget, in relation to the great problems of Federal fiscal policy which are basic to our economy in 1962, is not simply irrelevant; it can be actively misleading. And yet there is a mythology that measures all of our national soundness or unsoundness on the single simple basis of this same annual

administrative budget. If our Federal budget is to serve not the debate but the country, we must and will find ways of clarifying this area of discourse.

Still in the area of fiscal policy, let me say a word about deficits. The myth persists that Federal deficits create inflation and budget surpluses prevent it. Yet sizeable budget surpluses after the war did not prevent inflation, and persistent deficits   5 for the last several years have not upset our basic price stability. Obviously deficits are sometimes dangerous—and so are surpluses. But honest assessment plainly requires a more sophisticated view than the old and automatic cliche that deficits automatically bring inflation.

There are myths also about our public debt. It is widely supposed that this debt   10 is growing at a dangerously rapid rate. In fact, both the debt per person and the debt as a proportion of our gross national product have declined sharply since the Second World War. In absolute terms the national debt since the end of World War II has increased only eight percent, while private debt was increasing 305 percent, and the debts of State and local governments—on whom people   15 frequently suggest we should place additional burdens—the debts of State and local governments have increased 378 percent. Moreover, debts, public and private, are neither good nor bad, in and of themselves. Borrowing can lead to over-extension and collapse—but it can also lead to expansion and strength. There is no single, simple slogan in this field that we can trust.   20

Finally, I come to the matter of confidence. Confidence is a problem of myth and also a matter of truth—and this time let me take the truth of the matter first.

It is true—and of high importance—that the prosperity of this country depends on the assurance that all major elements within it will live up to their responsibilities. If business were to neglect its obligations to the public, if labor   25 were blind to all public responsibility, above all, if government were to abandon its obvious—and statutory—duty of watchful concern for our economic health—if any of these things should happen, then confidence might well be weakened and the danger of stagnation would increase. This is the true issue of confidence.   30

But there is also the false issue—and its simplest form is the assertion that any and all of the unfavorable turns of the speculative wheel—however temporary and however plainly speculative in character—are the result of, and I quote, "a lack of confidence in the national administration." This I must tell you, while comforting, is not wholly true. Worse, it obscures the reality—which is also   35 simple. The solid ground of mutual confidence is the necessary partnership of government with all of the sectors of our society in the steady quest for economic progress.

Corporate plans are not based on a political confidence in party leaders but on an economic confidence in the Nation's ability to invest and produce and consume. Business had full confidence in the administrations in power in 1929, 1954, 1958, and 1960—but this was not enough to prevent recession when business
5   lacked full confidence in the economy. What matters is the capacity of the Nation as a whole to deal with its economic problems and its opportunities.

The stereotypes I have been discussing distract our attention and divide our effort. These stereotypes do our Nation a disservice, not just because they are exhausted and irrelevant, but above all because they are misleading—because
10 they stand in the way of the solution of hard and complicated facts. It is not new that past debates should obscure present realities. But the damage of such a false dialogue is greater today than ever before simply because today the safety of all the world—the very future of freedom—depends as never before upon the sensible and clearheaded management of the domestic affairs of the
15 United States.

The real issues of our time are rarely as dramatic as the issues of Calhoun. The differences today are usually matters of degree. And we cannot understand and attack our contemporary problems in 1962 if we are bound by traditional labels and wornout slogans of an earlier era. But the unfortunate fact of the matter
20 is that our rhetoric has not kept pace with the speed of social and economic change. Our political debates, our public discourse—on current domestic and economic issues—too often bear little or no relation to the actual problems the United States faces.

What is at stake in our economic decisions today is not some grand warfare
25 of rival ideologies which will sweep the country with passion but the practical management of a modern economy. What we need is not labels and cliches but more basic discussion of the sophisticated and technical questions involved in keeping a great economic machinery moving ahead.

The national interest lies in high employment and steady expansion of output,
30 in stable prices, and a strong dollar. The declaration of such an objective is easy; their attainment in an intricate and interdependent economy and world is a little more difficult. To attain them, we require not some automatic response but hard thought. Let me end by suggesting a few of the real questions on our national agenda.

35 First, how can our budget and tax policies supply adequate revenues and preserve our balance of payments position without slowing up our economic growth?

Two, how are we to set our interest rates and regulate the flow of money in ways which will stimulate the economy at home, without weakening the dollar abroad? Given the spectrum of our domestic and international responsibilities, what should be the mix between fiscal and monetary policy?

Let me give several examples from my experience of the complexity of these matters and how political labels and ideological approaches are irrelevant to the solution.   5

Last week, a distinguished graduate of this school, Senator Proxmire, of the class of 1938, who is ordinarily regarded as a liberal Democrat, suggested that we should follow in meeting our economic problems a stiff fiscal policy, with emphasis on budget balance and an easy monetary policy with low interest rates in order to keep our economy going. In the same week, the Bank for   10 International Settlement in Basel, Switzerland, a conservative organization representing the central bankers of Europe suggested that the appropriate economic policy in the United States should be the very opposite; that we should follow a flexible budget policy, as in Europe, with deficits when the economy is down and a high monetary policy on interest rates, as in Europe, in order to 15 control inflation and protect goals. Both may be right or wrong. It will depend on many different factors.

The point is that this is basically an administrative or executive problem in which political labels or cliches do not give us a solution.

A well-known business journal this morning, as I journeyed to New Haven,   20 raised the prospects that a further budget deficit would bring inflation and encourage the flow of gold. We have had several budget deficits beginning with a twelve and a half billion dollars deficit in 1958, and it is true that in the fall of 1960 we had a gold dollar loss running at five billion dollars annually. This would seem to prove the case that a deficit produces inflation and that we lose   25 gold, yet there was no inflation following the deficit of 1958 nor has there been inflation since then.

Our wholesale price index since 1958 has remained completely level in spite of several deficits, because the loss of gold has been due to other reasons: price instability, relative interest rates, relative export-import balances, national   30 security expenditures—all the rest.

Let me give you a third and final example. At the World Bank meeting in September, a number of American bankers attending predicted to their European colleagues that because of the fiscal 1962 budget deficit, there would be a strong inflationary pressure on the dollar and a loss of gold. Their predictions on inflation 35 were shared by many in business and helped push the market up. The recent reality of noninflation helped bring it down. We have had no inflation because we have had other factors in our economy that have contributed to price stability.

I do not suggest that the Government is right and they are wrong. The fact of the matter is in the Federal Reserve Board and in the administration this fall, a similar view was held by many well-informed and disinterested men that inflation was the major problem that we would face in the winter of 1962. But
5   it was not. What I do suggest is that these problems are endlessly complicated and yet they go to the future of this country and its ability to prove to the world what we believe it must prove.

I am suggesting that the problems of fiscal and monetary policies in the sixties as opposed to the kinds of problems we faced in the thirties demand subtle
10 challenges for which technical answers, not political answers, must be provided. These are matters upon which government and business may and in many cases will disagree. They are certainly matters that government and business should be discussing in the most sober, dispassionate, and careful way if we are to maintain the kind of vigorous economy upon which our country depends.

15 How can we develop and sustain strong and stable world markets for basic commodities without unfairness to the consumer and without undue stimulus to the producer? How can we generate the buying power which can consume what we produce on our farms and in our factories? How can we take advantage of the miracles of automation with the great demand that it will put upon
20 highly skilled labor and yet offer employment to the half million of unskilled school dropouts each year who enter the labor market, eight million of them in the 1960's?

How do we eradicate the barriers which separate substantial minorities of our citizens from access to education and employment on equal terms with the rest?

25 How, in sum, can we make our free economy work at full capacity—that is, provide adequate profits for enterprise, adequate wages for labor, adequate utilization of plant, and opportunity for all?

These are the problems that we should be talking about—that the political parties and the various groups in our country should be discussing. They cannot
30 be solved by incantations from the forgotten past. But the example of Western Europe shows that they are capable of solution—that governments, and many of them are conservative governments, prepared to face technical problems without ideological preconceptions, can coordinate the elements of a national economy and bring about growth and prosperity—a decade of it.

35 Some conversations I have heard in our own country sound like old records, long-playing, left over from the middle thirties. The debate of the thirties had its great significance and produced great results, but it took place in a different

world with different needs and different tasks. It is our responsibility today to
live in our own world, and to identify the needs and discharge the tasks of the
1960's.

If there is any current trend toward meeting present problems with old
cliches, this is the moment to stop it—before it lands us all in a bog of sterile   5
acrimony.

Discussion is essential; and I am hopeful that the debate of recent weeks, though
up to now somewhat barren, may represent the start of a serious dialogue of
the kind which has led in Europe to such fruitful collaboration among all the
elements of economic society and to a decade of unrivaled economic progress.   10
But let us not engage in the wrong argument at the wrong time between the
wrong people in the wrong country—while the real problems of our own time
grow and multiply, fertilized by our neglect.

Nearly 150 years ago Thomas Jefferson wrote, "The new circumstances under
which we are placed call for new words, new phrases, and for the transfer of   15
old words to new objects." New words, new phrases, the transfer of old words
to new objects—that is truer today than it was in the time of Jefferson, because
the role of this country is so vastly more significant. There is a show in England
called "Stop the World, I Want to Get Off." You have not chosen to exercise
that option. You are part of the world and you must participate in these days   20
of our years in the solution of the problems that pour upon us, requiring the
most sophisticated and technical judgment; and as we work in consonance to
meet the authentic problems of our times, we will generate a vision and an
energy which will demonstrate anew to the world the superior vitality and the
strength of the free society.   25

Remarks at the University of Michigan
Lyndon B. Johnson (1908–1973)

In this commencement address, President Lyndon B. Johnson introduces his Progressive idea of a "Great Society."

May 22, 1964

President Hatcher, Governor Romney, Senators McNamara and Hart, Congressmen Meader and Staebler, and other members of the fine Michigan delegation, members of the graduating class, my fellow Americans:

It is a great pleasure to be here today. This university has been coeducational since 1870, but I do not believe it was on the basis of your accomplishments that a Detroit high school girl said, "In choosing a college, you first have to decide whether you want a coeducational school or an educational school."

Well, we can find both here at Michigan, although perhaps at different hours.   5

I came out here today very anxious to meet the Michigan student whose father told a friend of mine that his son's education had been a real value. It stopped his mother from bragging about him.

I have come today from the turmoil of your Capital to the tranquility of your campus to speak about the future of your country.   10

The purpose of protecting the life of our Nation and preserving the liberty of our citizens is to pursue the happiness of our people. Our success in that pursuit is the test of our success as a Nation.

For a century we labored to settle and to subdue a continent. For half a century we called upon unbounded invention and untiring industry to create an order   15
of plenty for all of our people.

The challenge of the next half century is whether we have the wisdom to use that wealth to enrich and elevate our national life, and to advance the quality of our American civilization.

Lyndon B. Johnson, "Remarks at the University of Michigan," May 22, 1964, in *Public Papers of the Presidents of the United States: Lyndon B. Johnson, 1963–64*, Vol. 1 (Washington, D.C.: Government Printing Office, 1965), 704–7.

Your imagination, your initiative, and your indignation will determine whether we build a society where progress is the servant of our needs, or a society where old values and new visions are buried under unbridled growth. For in your time we have the opportunity to move not only toward the rich society and 5   the powerful society, but upward to the Great Society.

The Great Society rests on abundance and liberty for all. It demands an end to poverty and racial injustice, to which we are totally committed in our time. But that is just the beginning.

The Great Society is a place where every child can find knowledge to enrich his 10   mind and to enlarge his talents. It is a place where leisure is a welcome chance to build and reflect, not a feared cause of boredom and restlessness. It is a place where the city of man serves not only the needs of the body and the demands of commerce but the desire for beauty and the hunger for community.

It is a place where man can renew contact with nature. It is a place which honors 15   creation for its own sake and for what it adds to the understanding of the race. It is a place where men are more concerned with the quality of their goals than the quantity of their goods.

But most of all, the Great Society is not a safe harbor, a resting place, a final objective, a finished work. It is a challenge constantly renewed, beckoning 20   us toward a destiny where the meaning of our lives matches the marvelous products of our labor.

So I want to talk to you today about three places where we begin to build the Great Society—in our cities, in our countryside, and in our classrooms.

Many of you will live to see the day, perhaps fifty years from now, when there 25   will be 400 million Americans—four-fifths of them in urban areas. In the remainder of this century urban population will double, city land will double, and we will have to build homes, highways, and facilities equal to all those built since this country was first settled. So in the next forty years we must rebuild the entire urban United States.

30   Aristotle said: "Men come together in cities in order to live, but they remain together in order to live the good life." It is harder and harder to live the good life in American cities today.

The catalog of ills is long: there is the decay of the centers and the despoiling of the suburbs. There is not enough housing for our people or transportation for 35   our traffic. Open land is vanishing and old landmarks are violated.

Worst of all expansion is eroding the precious and time honored values of community with neighbors and communion with nature. The loss of these values breeds loneliness and boredom and indifference.

Our society will never be great until our cities are great. Today the frontier of imagination and innovation is inside those cities and not beyond their borders.

New experiments are already going on. It will be the task of your generation to make the American city a place where future generations will come, not only to live but to live the good life.

I understand that if I stayed here tonight I would see that Michigan students are really doing their best to live the good life.

This is the place where the Peace Corps was started. It is inspiring to see how all of you, while you are in this country, are trying so hard to live at the level of the people.

A second place where we begin to build the Great Society is in our countryside. We have always prided ourselves on being not only America the strong and America the free, but America the beautiful. Today that beauty is in danger. The water we drink, the food we eat, the very air that we breathe, are threatened with pollution. Our parks are overcrowded, our seashores overburdened. Green fields and dense forests are disappearing.

A few years ago we were greatly concerned about the "Ugly American." Today we must act to prevent an ugly America.

For once the battle is lost, once our natural splendor is destroyed, it can never be recaptured. And once man can no longer walk with beauty or wonder at nature his spirit will wither and his sustenance be wasted.

A third place to build the Great Society is in the classrooms of America. There your children's lives will be shaped. Our society will not be great until every young mind is set free to scan the farthest reaches of thought and imagination. We are still far from that goal.

Today, eight million adult Americans, more than the entire population of Michigan, have not finished five years of school. Nearly twenty million have not finished eight years of school. Nearly fifty-four million—more than one-quarter of all America—have not even finished high school.

Each year more than 100,000 high school graduates, with proved ability, do not enter college because they cannot afford it. And if we cannot educate today's youth, what will we do in 1970 when elementary school enrollment will be five million greater than 1960? And high school enrollment will rise by five million. College enrollment will increase by more than three million.

In many places, classrooms are overcrowded and curricula are outdated. Most of our qualified teachers are underpaid, and many of our paid teachers are unqualified. So we must give every child a place to sit and a teacher to learn from. Poverty must not be a bar to learning, and learning must offer an escape from poverty.

But more classrooms and more teachers are not enough. We must seek an educational system which grows in excellence as it grows in size. This means better training for our teachers. It means preparing youth to enjoy their hours of leisure as well as their hours of labor. It means exploring new techniques of teaching, to find new ways to stimulate the love of learning and the capacity for creation.

These are three of the central issues of the Great Society. While our Government has many programs directed at those issues, I do not pretend that we have the full answer to those problems.

But I do promise this: We are going to assemble the best thought and the broadest knowledge from all over the world to find those answers for America. I intend to establish working groups to prepare a series of White House conferences and meetings—on the cities, on natural beauty, on the quality of education, and on other emerging challenges. And from these meetings and from this inspiration and from these studies we will begin to set our course toward the Great Society.

The solution to these problems does not rest on a massive program in Washington, nor can it rely solely on the strained resources of local authority. They require us to create new concepts of cooperation, a creative federalism, between the National Capital and the leaders of local communities.

Woodrow Wilson once wrote: "Every man sent out from his university should be a man of his Nation as well as a man of his time."

Within your lifetime powerful forces, already loosed, will take us toward a way of life beyond the realm of our experience, almost beyond the bounds of our imagination.

For better or for worse, your generation has been appointed by history to deal with those problems and to lead America toward a new age. You have the chance never before afforded to any people in any age. You can help build a society where the demands of morality, and the needs of the spirit, can be realized in the life of the Nation.

So, will you join in the battle to give every citizen the full equality which God enjoins and the law requires, whatever his belief, or race, or the color of his skin?

Will you join in the battle to give every citizen an escape from the crushing weight of poverty?

Will you join in the battle to make it possible for all nations to live in enduring peace—as neighbors and not as mortal enemies ?

Will you join in the battle to build the Great Society, to prove that our material progress is only the foundation on which we will build a richer life of mind and spirit?

There are those timid souls who say this battle cannot be won; that we are condemned to a soulless wealth. I do not agree. We have the power to shape the civilization that we want. But we need your will, your labor, your hearts, if we are to build that kind of society.

Those who came to this land sought to build more than just a new country. They sought a new world. So I have come here today to your campus to say that you can make their vision our reality. So let us from this moment begin our work so that in the future men will look back and say: It was then, after a long and weary way, that man turned the exploits of his genius to the full enrichment of his life.

Thank you. Goodbye.

Commencement Address at Howard University
Lyndon B. Johnson

In this commencement address, President Lyndon B. Johnson calls for a
redefinition of equality.

June 4, 1965

Dr. Nabrit, my fellow Americans:

I am delighted at the chance to speak at this important and this historic institution. Howard has long been an outstanding center for the education of Negro Americans. Its students are of every race and color and they come from many countries of the world. It is truly a working example of democratic excellence.   5

Our earth is the home of revolution. In every corner of every continent men charged with hope contend with ancient ways in the pursuit of justice. They reach for the newest of weapons to realize the oldest of dreams, that each may walk in freedom and pride, stretching his talents, enjoying the fruits of the earth.

Our enemies may occasionally seize the day of change, but it is the banner of   10
our revolution they take. And our own future is linked to this process of swift and turbulent change in many lands in the world. But nothing in any country touches us more profoundly, and nothing is more freighted with meaning for our own destiny than the revolution of the Negro American.

In far too many ways American Negroes have been another nation: deprived of   15
freedom, crippled by hatred, the doors of opportunity closed to hope.

In our time change has come to this Nation, too. The American Negro, acting with impressive restraint, has peacefully protested and marched, entered the courtrooms and the seats of government, demanding a justice that has long been denied. The voice of the Negro was the call to action. But it is a tribute   20

Lyndon B. Johnson, "Commencement Address at Howard University: 'To Fulfill These Rights,'" June 4, 1965, in *Public Papers of the Presidents of the United States: Lyndon B. Johnson, 1965*, Vol. 2 (Washington, D.C.: Government Printing Office, 1966), 635–40.

to America that, once aroused, the courts and the Congress, the President and most of the people, have been the allies of progress.

LEGAL PROTECTION FOR HUMAN RIGHTS

Thus we have seen the high court of the country declare that discrimination
5   based on race was repugnant to the Constitution, and therefore void. We have seen in 1957, and 1960, and again in 1964, the first civil rights legislation in this Nation in almost an entire century.

As majority leader of the United States Senate, I helped to guide two of these bills through the Senate. And, as your President, I was proud to sign the third.
10   And now very soon we will have the fourth—a new law guaranteeing every American the right to vote.

No act of my entire administration will give me greater satisfaction than the day when my signature makes this bill, too, the law of this land.

The voting rights bill will be the latest, and among the most important, in a
15   long series of victories. But this victory—as Winston Churchill said of another triumph for freedom—"is not the end. It is not even the beginning of the end. But it is, perhaps, the end of the beginning."

That beginning is freedom; and the barriers to that freedom are tumbling down. Freedom is the right to share, share fully and equally, in American society—to
20   vote, to hold a job, to enter a public place, to go to school. It is the right to be treated in every part of our national life as a person equal in dignity and promise to all others.

FREEDOM IS NOT ENOUGH

But freedom is not enough. You do not wipe away the scars of centuries by say-ing: Now you are free to go where you want, and do as you desire, and choose
25   the leaders you please.

You do not take a person who, for years, has been hobbled by chains and liberate him, bring him up to the starting line of a race and then say, "you are free to compete with all the others," and still justly believe that you have been completely fair.

Thus it is not enough just to open the gates of opportunity. All our citizens
30   must have the ability to walk through those gates.

This is the next and the more profound stage of the battle for civil rights. We seek not just freedom but opportunity. We seek not just legal equity but human ability, not just equality as a right and a theory but equality as a fact and equality as a result.

For the task is to give twenty million Negroes the same chance as every other American to learn and grow, to work and share in society, to develop their abilities—physical, mental and spiritual, and to pursue their individual happiness.

To this end equal opportunity is essential, but not enough, not enough. Men and women of all races are born with the same range of abilities. But ability is   5 not just the product of birth. Ability is stretched or stunted by the family that you live with, and the neighborhood you live in—by the school you go to and the poverty or the richness of your surroundings. It is the product of a hundred unseen forces playing upon the little infant, the child, and finally the man.

Progress for Some

This graduating class at Howard University is witness to the indomitable deter-   10 mination of the Negro American to win his way in American life.

The number of Negroes in schools of higher learning has almost doubled in fifteen years. The number of non-white professional workers has more than doubled in ten years. The median income of Negro college women tonight exceeds that of white college women. And there are also the enormous accomplishments of   15 distinguished individual Negroes—many of them graduates of this institution, and one of them the first lady ambassador in the history of the United States.

These are proud and impressive achievements. But they tell only the story of a growing middle class minority, steadily narrowing the gap between them and their white counterparts.   20

A Widening Gulf

But for the great majority of Negro Americans—the poor, the unemployed, the uprooted, and the dispossessed—there is a much grimmer story. They still, as we meet here tonight, are another nation. Despite the court orders and the laws, despite the legislative victories and the speeches, for them the walls are rising and the gulf is widening.   25

Here are some of the facts of this American failure.

Thirty-five years ago the rate of unemployment for Negroes and whites was about the same. Tonight the Negro rate is twice as high.

In 1948 the eight percent unemployment rate for Negro teenage boys was actually less than that of whites. By last year that rate had grown to twenty-three   30 percent, as against thirteen percent for whites unemployed.

Between 1949 and 1959, the income of Negro men relative to white men declined in every section of this country. From 1952 to 1963 the median income of Negro families compared to white actually dropped from fifty-seven percent to fifty-three percent.

In the years 1955 through 1957, twenty-two percent of experienced Negro workers were out of work at some time during the year. In 1961 through 1963
5 that proportion had soared to twenty-nine percent.

Since 1947 the number of white families living in poverty has decreased twenty-seven percent while the number of poorer nonwhite families decreased only three percent.

The infant mortality of nonwhites in 1940 was seventy percent greater than
10 whites. Twenty-two years later it was ninety percent greater.

Moreover, the isolation of Negro from white communities is increasing, rather than decreasing as Negroes crowd into the central cities and become a city within a city.

Of course Negro Americans as well as white Americans have shared in our rising
15 national abundance. But the harsh fact of the matter is that in the battle for true equality too many—far too many—are losing ground every day.

The Causes of Inequality

We are not completely sure why this is. We know the causes are complex and subtle. But we do know the two broad basic reasons. And we do know that we have to act.

20 First, Negroes are trapped—as many whites are trapped—in inherited, gateless poverty. They lack training and skills. They are shut in, in slums, without decent medical care. Private and public poverty combine to cripple their capacities.

We are trying to attack these evils through our poverty program, through our education program, through our medical care and our other health programs,
25 and a dozen more of the Great Society programs that are aimed at the root causes of this poverty.

We will increase, and we will accelerate, and we will broaden this attack in years to come until this most enduring of foes finally yields to our unyielding will.

But there is a second cause—much more difficult to explain, more deeply
30 grounded, more desperate in its force. It is the devastating heritage of long years of slavery; and a century of oppression, hatred, and injustice.

Special Nature of Negro Poverty

For Negro poverty is not white poverty. Many of its causes and many of its cures are the same. But there are differences—deep, corrosive, obstinate differences—

radiating painful roots into the community, and into the family, and the nature of the individual.

These differences are not racial differences. They are solely and simply the consequence of ancient brutality, past injustice, and present prejudice. They are anguishing to observe. For the Negro they are a constant reminder of oppression. For the white they are a constant reminder of guilt. But they must be faced and they must be dealt with and they must be overcome, if we are ever to reach the time when the only difference between Negroes and whites is the color of their skin.

Nor can we find a complete answer in the experience of other American minorities. They made a valiant and a largely successful effort to emerge from poverty and prejudice.

The Negro, like these others, will have to rely mostly upon his own efforts. But he just can not do it alone. For they did not have the heritage of centuries to overcome, and they did not have a cultural tradition which had been twisted and battered by endless years of hatred and hopelessness, nor were they excluded— these others—because of race or color—a feeling whose dark intensity is matched by no other prejudice in our society.

Nor can these differences be understood as isolated infirmities. They are a seamless web. They cause each other. They result from each other. They reinforce each other.

Much of the Negro community is buried under a blanket of history and circumstance. It is not a lasting solution to lift just one corner of that blanket. We must stand on all sides and we must raise the entire cover if we are to liberate our fellow citizens.

THE ROOTS OF INJUSTICE

One of the differences is the increased concentration of Negroes in our cities. More than seventy-three percent of all Negroes live in urban areas compared with less than seventy percent of the whites. Most of these Negroes live in slums. Most of these Negroes live together—a separated people.

Men are shaped by their world. When it is a world of decay, ringed by an invisible wall, when escape is arduous and uncertain, and the saving pressures of a more hopeful society are unknown, it can cripple the youth and it can desolate the men.

There is also the burden that a dark skin can add to the search for a productive place in our society. Unemployment strikes most swiftly and broadly at the Negro, and this burden erodes hope. Blighted hope breeds despair. Despair brings indifferences to the learning which offers a way out. And despair, coupled with indifferences, is often the source of destructive rebellion against the fabric of society.

There is also the lacerating hurt of early collision with white hatred or prejudice, distaste or condescension. Other groups have felt similar intolerance. But
5   success and achievement could wipe it away. They do not change the color of a man's skin. I have seen this uncomprehending pain in the eyes of the little, young Mexican-American schoolchildren that I taught many years ago. But it can be overcome. But, for many, the wounds are always open.

Family Breakdown

Perhaps most important—its influence radiating to every part of life—is the
10 breakdown of the Negro family structure. For this, most of all, white America must accept responsibility. It flows from centuries of oppression and persecution of the Negro man. It flows from the long years of degradation and discrimination, which have attacked his dignity and assaulted his ability to produce for his family.

This, too, is not pleasant to look upon. But it must be faced by those whose
15 serious intent is to improve the life of all Americans.

Only a minority—less than half—of all Negro children reach the age of eighteen having lived all their lives with both of their parents. At this moment, tonight, little less than two-thirds are at home with both of their parents. Probably a majority of all Negro children receive federally-aided public assistance sometime
20 during their childhood.

The family is the cornerstone of our society. More than any other force it shapes the attitude, the hopes, the ambitions, and the values of the child. And when the family collapses it is the children that are usually damaged. When it happens on a massive scale the community itself is crippled.

25 So, unless we work to strengthen the family, to create conditions under which most parents will stay together—all the rest: schools, and playgrounds, and public assistance, and private concern, will never be enough to cut completely the circle of despair and deprivation.

To Fulfill these Rights

There is no single easy answer to all of these problems.

30 Jobs are part of the answer. They bring the income which permits a man to provide for his family.

Decent homes in decent surroundings and a chance to learn—an equal chance to learn—are part of the answer.

Welfare and social programs better designed to hold families together are part of the answer.

Care for the sick is part of the answer.

An understanding heart by all Americans is another big part of the answer.

And to all of these fronts—and a dozen more—I will dedicate the expanding   5
efforts of the Johnson administration.

But there are other answers that are still to be found. Nor do we fully understand even all of the problems. Therefore, I want to announce tonight that this fall I intend to call a White House conference of scholars, and experts, and outstanding Negro leaders—men of both races—and officials of Government at every level.   10

This White House conference's theme and title will be "To Fulfill These Rights."

Its object will be to help the American Negro fulfill the rights which, after the long time of injustice, he is finally about to secure.

To move beyond opportunity to achievement.   15

To shatter forever not only the barriers of law and public practice, but the walls which bound the condition of many by the color of his skin.

To dissolve, as best we can, the antique enmities of the heart which diminish the holder, divide the great democracy, and do wrong—great wrong—to the children of God.   20

And I pledge you tonight that this will be a chief goal of my administration, and of my program next year, and in the years to come. And I hope, and I pray, and I believe, it will be a part of the program of all America.

What is Justice

For what is justice?

It is to fulfill the fair expectations of man.   25

Thus, American justice is a very special thing. For, from the first, this has been a land of towering expectations. It was to be a nation where each man could be ruled by the common consent of all—enshrined in law, given life by institutions, guided by men themselves subject to its rule. And all—all of every station and origin—would be touched equally in obligation and in liberty.   30

Beyond the law lay the land. It was a rich land, glowing with more abundant promise than man had ever seen. Here, unlike any place yet known, all were to share the harvest.

And beyond this was the dignity of man. Each could become whatever his qualities of mind and spirit would permit—to strive, to seek, and, if he could, to find his happiness.

This is American justice. We have pursued it faithfully to the edge of our
5   imperfections, and we have failed to find it for the American Negro.

So, it is the glorious opportunity of this generation to end the one huge wrong of the American Nation and, in so doing, to find America for ourselves, with the same immense thrill of discovery which gripped those who first began to realize that here, at last, was a home for freedom.

10 All it will take is for all of us to understand what this country is and what this country must become.

The Scripture promises: "I shall light a candle of understanding in thine heart, which shall not be put out."

Together, and with millions more, we can light that candle of understanding
15 in the heart of all America.

And, once lit, it will never again go out.

A Time for Choosing
Ronald Reagan (1911–2004)

In this nationally televised speech in support of Barry Goldwater, the 1964 Republican Party presidential candidate, Ronald Reagan challenges the Progressive principles behind President Lyndon B. Johnson's Great Society. The speech propelled Reagan to national prominence.

October 27, 1964

I am going to talk of controversial things. I make no apology for this. I have been talking on this subject for ten years, obviously under the administration of both parties. I mention this only because it seems impossible to legitimately debate the issues of the day without being subjected to name-calling and the application of labels. Those who deplore use of the terms "pink" and "leftist"   5
are themselves guilty of branding all who oppose their liberalism as right wing extremists. How long can we afford the luxury of this family fight when we are at war with the most dangerous enemy ever known to man?

If we lose that war, and in so doing lose our freedom, it has been said history will record with the greatest astonishment that those who had the most to lose did   10
the least to prevent its happening. The guns are silent in this war but frontiers fall while those who should be warriors prefer neutrality. Not too long ago two friends of mine were talking to a Cuban refugee. He was a businessman who had escaped from Castro. In the midst of his tale of horrible experiences, one of my friends turned to the other and said, "We don't know how lucky we are."   15
The Cuban stopped and said, "How lucky you are? I had some place to escape to." And in that sentence he told the entire story. If freedom is lost here there is no place to escape to.

It's time we asked ourselves if we still know the freedoms intended for us by the Founding Fathers. James Madison said, "We base all our experiments on   20
the capacity of mankind for self-government." This idea that government

Ronald Reagan, "A Time for Choosing," 1964, in Alfred A. Bolitzer et al., eds., *A Time for Choosing: The Speeches of Ronald Reagan, 1961–1982* (Chicago: Regnery, 1983), 41–57.

was beholden to the people, that it had no other source of power except the sovereign people, is still the newest, most unique idea in all the long history of man's relation to man. For almost two centuries we have proved man's capacity for self-government, but today we are told we must choose between a left and
5   a right or, as others suggest, a third alternative, a kind of safe middle ground. I suggest to you there is no left or right, only an up or down. Up to the maximum of individual freedom consistent with law and order, or down to the ant heap of totalitarianism; and regardless of their humanitarian purpose those who would sacrifice freedom for security have, whether they know it or not, chosen this
10 downward path. Plutarch warned, "The real destroyer of the liberties of the people is he who spreads among them bounties, donations, and benefits."

Today there is an increasing number who can't see a fat man standing beside a thin one without automatically coming to the conclusion the fat man got that way by taking advantage of the thin one. So they would seek the answer to all
15 the problems of human need through government. Howard K. Smith of television fame has written, "The profit motive is outmoded. It must be replaced by the incentives of the welfare state." He says, "The distribution of goods must be effected by a planned economy."

Another articulate spokesman for the welfare state defines liberalism as meeting
20 the material needs of the masses through the full power of centralized government. I for one find it disturbing when a representative refers to the free men and women of this country as the masses, but beyond this the full power of centralized government was the very thing the Founding Fathers sought to minimize. They knew you don't control things; you can't control the economy
25 without controlling *people*. So we have come to a time for choosing. Either we accept the responsibility for our own destiny, or we abandon the American Revolution and confess that an intellectual belief in a far-distant capitol can plan our lives for us better than we can plan them ourselves.

Already the hour is late. Government has laid its hand on health, housing, farming,
30 industry, commerce, education, and, to an ever-increasing degree, interferes with the people's right to know. Government tends to grow; government programs take on weight and momentum, as public servants say, always with the best of intentions, "What greater service we could render if only we had a little more money and a little more power." But the truth is that outside of its legitimate function,
35 government does nothing as well or as economically as the private sector of the economy. What better example do we have of this than government's involvement in the farm economy over the last thirty years. One-fourth of farming has seen a steady decline in the per capita consumption of everything it produces. That one-fourth is regulated and subsidized by government.

In contrast, the three-fourths of farming unregulated and unsubsidized has seen a twenty-one percent increase in the per capita consumption of all its produce. Since 1955 the cost of the farm program has nearly doubled. Direct payment to farmers is eight times as great as it was nine years ago, but farm income remains unchanged while farm surplus is bigger. In that same period we have seen a   5 decline of five million in the farm population, but an increase in the number of Department of Agriculture employees.

There is now one such employee for every thirty farms in the United States, and still they can't figure how sixty-six shiploads of grain headed for Austria could disappear without a trace, and Billy Sol Estes never left shore. Three years ago   10 the government put into effect a program to curb the over-production of feed grain. Now, two and a half billion dollars later, the corn crop is one hundred million bushels bigger than before the program started. And the cost of the program prorates out to forty-three dollars for every dollar bushel of corn we don't grow. Nor is this the only example of the price we pay for government   15 meddling. Some government programs with the passage of time take on a sacrosanct quality.

One such considered above criticism, sacred as motherhood, is TVA. This program started as a flood control project; the Tennessee Valley was periodically ravaged by destructive floods. The Army Engineers set out to solve this problem.   20 They said that it was possible that once in 500 years there could be a total capacity flood that would inundate some six hundred thousand acres. Well, the engineers fixed that. They made a permanent lake which inundated a million acres. This solved the problem of floods, but the annual interest on the TVA debt is five times as great as the annual flood damage they sought to correct.   25

Of course, you will point out that TVA gets electric power from the impounded waters, and this is true, but today eighty-five percent of TVA's electricity is generated in coal-burning steam plants. Now perhaps you'll charge that I'm overlooking the navigable waterway that was created, providing cheap barge traffic, but the bulk of the freight barged on that waterway is coal being shipped to the TVA   30 steam plants, and the cost of maintaining that channel each year would pay for shipping all of the coal by rail, and there would be money left over.

One last argument remains: the prosperity produced by such large programs of government spending. Certainly there are few areas where more spending has taken place. The Labor Department lists fifty percent of the 169 counties in the   35 Tennessee Valley as permanent areas of poverty, distress, and unemployment.

Meanwhile, back in the city, under Urban Renewal, the assault on freedom carries on. Private property rights have become so diluted that public interest is anything a few planners decide it should be. In Cleveland, Ohio, to get a project under way, city officials reclassified eighty-four buildings as substandard in spite of the fact their own inspectors had previously pronounced these buildings sound. The owners stood by and watched twenty-six million dollars

5   worth of property as it was destroyed by the headache ball. Senate Bill 628 says: "Any property, be it home or commercial structure, can be declared slum or blighted and the owner has no recourse at law. The Law Division of the Library of Congress and the General Accounting Office have said that the Courts will have to rule against the owner."

10   HOUSING. In one key Eastern city a man owning a blighted area sold his property to Urban Renewal for several million dollars. At the same time, he submitted his own plan for the rebuilding of this area and the government sold him back his own property for twenty-two percent of what they paid. Now the government announces, "We are going to build subsidized housing in the

15   thousands where we have been building in the hundreds." At the same time FHA and the Veterans Administration reveal they are holding 120 thousand housing units reclaimed from mortgage foreclosure, mostly because the low down payment and the easy terms brought the owners to a point where they realized the unpaid balance on the homes amounted to a sum greater than the

20   homes were worth, so they just walked out the front door, possibly to take up residence in newer subsidized housing, again with little or no down payment and easy terms.

Some of the foreclosed homes have already been bulldozed into the earth, others, it has been announced, will be refurbished and put on sale for down

25   payments as low as $100 and thirty-five years to pay. This will give the bulldozers a second crack. It is in the area of social welfare that government has found its most fertile growing bed. So many of us accept our responsibility for those less fortunate. We are susceptible to humanitarian appeals.

Federal welfare spending is today ten times greater than it was in the dark depths

30   of the Depression. Federal, state, and local welfare combined spend forty-five billion dollars a year. Now the government has announced that twenty percent, some 9.3 million families, are poverty-stricken on the basis that they have less than a $3,000 a year income.

If this present welfare spending was prorated equally among these poverty-

35   stricken families, we could give each family more than $4,500 a year. Actually, direct aid to the poor averages less than $600 per family. There must be some administrative overhead somewhere. Now, are we to believe that another billion dollar program added to the half a hundred programs and the forty-five billion

dollars, will, through some magic, end poverty? For three decades we have tried to solve unemployment by government planning, without success. The more the plans fail, the more the planners plan.

The latest is the Area Redevelopment Agency, and in two years less than one-half of one percent of the unemployed could attribute new jobs to this agency, and the cost to the taxpayer for each job found was $5,000. But beyond the great bureaucratic waste, what are we doing to the people we seek to help?

Recently a judge told me of an incident in his court. A fairly young woman with six children, pregnant with her seventh, came to him for a divorce. Under his questioning it became apparent her husband did not share this desire. Then the whole story came out. Her husband was a laborer earning $250 a month. By divorcing him she could get an eighty dollars raise. She was eligible for $350 a month from the Aid to Dependent Children Program. She had been talked into the divorce by two friends who had already done this very thing. But any time we question the schemes of the do-gooders, we are denounced as being opposed to their humanitarian goal. It seems impossible to legitimately debate their solutions with the assumption that all of us share the desire to help those less fortunate. They tell us we are always against, never for anything. Well, it isn't so much that liberals are ignorant. It's just that they know so much that isn't so.

We are for a provision that destitution should not follow unemployment by reason of old age. For that reason we have accepted Social Security as a step toward meeting that problem. However, we are against the irresponsibility of those who charge that any criticism or suggested improvement of the program means we want to end payment to those who depend on Social Security for a livelihood.

Fiscal Irresponsibility. We have been told in millions of pieces of literature and press releases that Social Security is an insurance program, but the executives of Social Security appeared before the Supreme Court in the case of *Nestor* v. *Fleming* and proved to the Court's satisfaction that it is not insurance but is a welfare program, and Social Security dues are a tax for the general use of the government. Well it can't be both: insurance and welfare. Later, appearing before a Congressional Committee, they admitted that Social Security is today 298 billion dollars in the red. This fiscal irresponsibility has already caught up with us.

Faced with a bankruptcy, we find that today a young man in his early twenties, going to work at less than an average salary, will, with his employer, pay into Social Security an amount which could provide the young man with a retirement insurance policy guaranteeing $220 a month at age sixty-five, and the government promises him $127.

Now, are we so lacking in business sense that we cannot put this program on a sound actuarial basis, so that those who do depend on it won't come to the
5 cupboard and find it bare, and at the same time can't we introduce voluntary features so that those who can make better provision for themselves are allowed to do so? Incidentally, we might also allow participants in Social Security to name their own beneficiaries, which they cannot do in the present program. These are not insurmountable problems.

10 Youth Aid Plans. We have today thirty million workers protected by industrial and union pension funds that are soundly financed by some seventy billion dollars invested in corporate securities and income earning real estate. I think we are for telling our senior citizens that no one in this country should be denied medical care for lack of funds, but we are against forcing all citizens into
15 a compulsory government program regardless of need. Now the government has turned its attention to our young people, and suggests that it can solve the problem of school dropouts and juvenile delinquency through some kind of revival of the old C.C.C. camps. The suggested plan prorates out to a cost of $4,700 a year for each young person we want to help. We can send them to
20 Harvard for $2,700 a year. Of course, don't get me wrong—I'm not suggesting Harvard as the answer to juvenile delinquency.

We are for an international organization where the nations of the world can legitimately seek peace. We are against subordinating American interests to an organization so structurally unsound that a two-thirds majority can be mustered
25 in the U.N. General Assembly among nations representing less than ten percent of the world population.

Is there not something of hypocrisy in assailing our allies for so-called vestiges of colonialism while we engage in a conspiracy of silence about the peoples enslaved by the Soviet in the satellite nations? We are for aiding our allies by
30 sharing our material blessings with those nations which share our fundamental beliefs. We are against doling out money, government to government, which ends up financing socialism all over the world.

We set out to help nineteen war-ravaged countries at the end of World War II. We are now helping 107. We have spent 146 billion dollars. Some of that
35 money bought a two million dollar yacht for Haile Selassie. We bought dress suits for Greek undertakers. We bought one thousand TV sets with twenty-three-inch screens for a country where there is no electricity, and some of our foreign aid funds provided extra wives for Kenya government officials. When

Congress moved to cut foreign aid they were told that if they cut it one dollar they endangered national security, and then Senator Harry Byrd revealed that since its inception foreign aid has rarely spent its allotted budget. It has today $21 billion in unexpended funds.

Some time ago Dr. Howard Kershner was speaking to the Prime Minister of Lebanon. The Prime Minister told him proudly that his little country balanced its budget each year. It had no public debt, no inflation, a modest tax rate, and had increased its gold holdings from seventy to 120 million dollars. When he finished, Dr. Kershner said, "Mr. Prime Minister, my country hasn't balanced its budget twenty-eight out of the last forty years. My country's debt is greater than the combined debt of all the nations of the world. We have inflation, we have a tax rate that takes from the private sector a percentage of income greater than any civilized nation has ever taken and survived. We have lost gold at such a rate that the solvency of our currency is in danger. Do you think that my country should continue to give your country millions of dollars each year?" The Prime Minister smiled and said, "No, but if you are foolish enough to do it, we are going to keep on taking the money."

NINE STALLS FOR ONE BULL. And so we built a model stock farm in Lebanon, and we built nine stalls for each bull. I find something peculiarly appropriate in that. We have in our vaults $15 billion in gold. We don't own an ounce. Foreign dollar claims against that gold total $27 billion. In the last six years, fifty-two nations have bought $7 billion worth of our gold and all fifty-two are receiving foreign aid.

Because no government ever voluntarily reduces itself in size, government programs once launched never go out of existence. A government agency is the nearest thing to eternal life we'll ever see on this earth. The United States Manual takes twenty-five pages to list by name every Congressman and Senator, and all the agencies controlled by Congress. It then lists the agencies coming under the Executive Branch, and this requires 520 pages.

Since the beginning of the century our gross national product has increased by thirty-three times. In the same period the cost of federal government has increased 234 times, and while the work force is only one and one-half times greater, federal employees number nine times as many. There are now two and one-half million federal employees. No one knows what they all do. One Congressman found out what one of them does. This man sits at a desk in Washington. Documents come to him each morning. He reads them, initials them, and passes them on to the proper agency. One day a document arrived he wasn't supposed to read, but he read it, initialled it and passed it on. Twenty-four hours later it arrived back at his desk with a memo attached that said, "You weren't supposed to read this. Erase your initials, and initial the erasure."

While the federal government is the great offender, the idea filters down. During a period in California when our population has increased ninety percent, the cost of state government has gone up 862 percent and the number of employees 500 percent. Governments, state and local, now employ one out of six of the nation's work force. If the rate of increase of the last three years continues, by 1970 one-fourth of the total work force will be employed by government. Already we have a permanent structure so big and complex it is virtually beyond the control of Congress and the comprehension of the people, and tyranny inevitable follows when this permanent structure usurps the policy-making function that belongs to elected officials.

One example of this occurred when Congress was debating whether to lend the United Nations $100 million. While they debated, the State Department gave the United Nations $217 million and the United Nations used part of that money to pay the delinquent dues of Castro's Cuba.

Under bureaucratic regulations adopted with no regard to the wish of the people, we have lost much of our Constitutional freedom. For example, federal agents can invade a man's property without a warrant, can impose a fine without a formal hearing, let alone a trial by jury, and can seize and sell his property at auction to enforce payment of that fine.

RIGHTS BY DISPENSATION. An Ohio deputy fire marshal sentenced a man to prison after a secret proceeding in which the accused was not allowed to have a lawyer present. The Supreme Court upheld that sentence, ruling that it was an administrative investigation of incidents damaging to the economy. Someplace a perversion has taken place. Our natural unalienable rights are now presumed to be a dispensation of government, divisible by a vote of the majority. The greatest good for the greatest number is a high-sounding phrase but contrary to the very basis of our nation, unless it is accompanied by recognition that we have certain rights which cannot be infringed upon, even if the individual stands outvoted by all of his fellow citizens. Without this recognition, majority rule is nothing more than mob rule.

It is time we realized that socialism can come without overt seizure of property or nationalization of private business. It matters little that you hold the title to your property or business if government can dictate policy and procedure and holds life and death power over your business. The machinery of this power already exists. Lowell Mason, former anti-trust law enforcer for the Federal Trade Commission, has written "American business is being harassed, bled and even blackjacked under a preposterous crazy quilt system of laws." There are so many that the government literally can find some charge to bring against any concern it chooses to prosecute. Are we safe in our books and records?

The natural gas producers have just been handed a 428-page questionnaire by the Federal Power Commission. It weights ten pounds. One firm has estimated it will take 70,000 accountant man-hours to fill out this questionnaire, and it must be done in quadruplicate. The Power Commission says it must have it to determine whether a proper price is being charged for gas. The National Labor Relations Board ruled that a business firm could not discontinue its shipping department even though it was more efficient and economical to subcontract this work out.

The Supreme Court has ruled the government has the right to tell a citizen what he can grow on his own land for his own use. The Secretary of Agriculture has asked for the right to imprison farmers who violate their planting quotas. One business firm has been informed by the Internal Revenue Service that it cannot take a tax deduction for its institutional advertising because this advertising espoused views not in the public interest.

A child's prayer in a school cafeteria endangers religious freedom, but the people of the Amish religion in the State of Ohio, who cannot participate in Social Security because of their religious beliefs, have had their livestock seized and sold at auction to enforce payment of Social Security dues.

We approach a point of no return when government becomes so huge and entrenched that we fear the consequences of upheaval and just go along with it. The federal government accounts for one-fifth of the industrial capacity of the nation, one-fourth of all construction, holds or guarantees one-third of all mortgages, owns one-third of the land, and engages in some nineteen thousand businesses covering half a hundred different lines. The Defense Department runs 269 supermarkets. They do a gross business of $730 million a year, and lose $150 million. The government spends $11 million an hour every hour of the twenty-four and pretends we had a tax cut while it pursues a policy of planned inflation that will more than wipe out any benefit with depreciation of our purchasing power.

We need true tax reform that will at least make a start toward restoring for our children the American dream that wealth is denied to no one, that each individual has the right to fly as high as his strength and ability will take him. The economist Sumner Schlicter has said, "If a visitor from Mars looked at our tax policy, he would conclude it had been designed by a Communist spy to make free enterprise unworkable." But we cannot have such reform while our tax policy is engineered by people who view the tax as a means of achieving changes in our social structure. Senator [Joseph S.] Clark (D.-Pa.) says the tax issue is a class issue, and the government must use the tax to redistribute the wealth and earnings downward.

5   KARL MARX. On January 15th in the White House, the President [Lyndon Johnson] told a group of citizens they were going to take all the money they thought was being unnecessarily spent, "take it from the haves and give it to the have-nots who need it so much." When Karl Marx said this he put it:... "from each according to his ability, to each according to his need."

10   Have we the courage and the will to face up to the immorality and discrimination of the progressive surtax, and demand a return to traditional proportionate taxation? Many decades ago the Scottish economist, John Ramsey McCulloch, said, "The moment you abandon the cardinal principle of exacting from all individuals the same proportion of their income or their property, you are at

15 sea without a rudder or compass and there is no amount of injustice or folly you may not commit."

No nation has survived the tax burden that reached one-third of its national income. Today in our country the tax collector's share is thirty-seven cents of every dollar earned. Freedom has never been so fragile, so close to slipping from our

20 grasp. I wish I could give you some magic formula, but each of us must find his own role. One man in Virginia found what he could do, and dozens of business firms have followed his lead. Concerned because his two hundred employees seemed unworried about government extravagance he conceived the idea of taking all of their withholding out of only the fourth paycheck each month. For

25 three paydays his employees received their full salary. On the fourth payday all withholding was taken. He has one employee who owes him $4.70 each fourth payday. It only took one month to produce two hundred conservatives.

Are you willing to spend time studying the issues, making yourself aware, and then conveying that information to family and friends? Will you resist the

30 temptation to get a government handout for your community? Realize that the doctor's fight against socialized medicine is your fight. We can't socialize the doctors without socializing the patients. Recognize that government invasion of public power is eventually an assault upon your own business. If some among you fear taking a stand because you are afraid of reprisals from customers,

35 clients, or even government, recognize that you are just feeding the crocodile hoping he'll eat you last.

If all of this seems like a great deal of trouble, think what's at stake. We are faced with the most evil enemy mankind has known in his long climb from the swamp to the stars. There can be no security anywhere in the free world if there is not fiscal and economic stability within the United States. Those who ask us to trade our freedom for the soup kitchen of the welfare state are architects of a policy of accommodation. They tell us that by avoiding a direct confrontation with the enemy he will learn to love us and give up his evil ways. 5 All who oppose this idea are blanket indicted as war-mongers. Well, let us set one thing straight, there is no argument with regard to peace and war. It is cheap demagoguery to suggest that anyone would want to send other people's sons to war. The only argument is with regard to the best way to avoid war. There is only one sure way—surrender. 10

APPEASEMENT OR COURAGE? The spectre our well-meaning liberal friends refuse to face is that their policy of accommodation is appeasement, and appeasement does not give you a choice between peace and war, only between fight and surrender. We are told that the problem is too complex for a simple answer. They are wrong. There is no easy answer, but there is a simple answer. We 15 must have the courage to do what we know is morally right, and this policy of accommodation asks us to accept the greatest possible immorality. We are being asked to buy our safety from the threat of "the bomb" by selling into permanent slavery our fellow human beings enslaved behind the Iron Curtain, to tell them to give up their hope of freedom because we are ready to make a 20 deal with their slave masters.

Alexander Hamilton warned us that a nation which can prefer disgrace to danger is prepared for a master and deserves one. Admittedly there is a risk in any course we follow. Choosing the high road cannot eliminate that risk. Already some of the architects of accommodation have hinted what their decision will be if their 25 plan fails and we are faced with the final ultimatum. The English commentator [Kenneth] Tynan has put it this way: he would rather live on his knees than die on his feet. Some of our own have said "Better Red than dead." If we are to believe that nothing is worth the dying, when did this begin? Should Moses have told the children of Israel to live in slavery rather than dare the wilderness? 30 Should Christ have refused the Cross? Should the patriots at Concord Bridge have refused to fire the shot heard 'round the world? Are we to believe that all the martyrs of history died in vain?

You and I have a rendezvous with destiny. We can preserve for our children this, the last best hope of man on earth, or we can sentence them to take the 35 first step into a thousand years of darkness. If we fail, at least let our children and our children's children say of us we justified our brief moment here. We did all that could be done.

FIRST INAUGURAL ADDRESS
RONALD REAGAN

Breaking with historical precedent, Ronald Reagan's first inauguration was held on the Capitol's West Front, allowing him to refer in his speech to the presidential memorials and to Arlington National Cemetery in the distance. The first post-New Deal president to challenge the principles of the New Deal, Reagan presents his opposition in terms of reviving the idea of consent of the governed.

JANUARY 20, 1981

SENATOR HATFIELD, MR. CHIEF JUSTICE, MR. PRESIDENT, VICE PRESIDENT BUSH, VICE PRESIDENT MONDALE, SENATOR BAKER, SPEAKER O'NEILL, REVEREND MOOMAW, AND MY FELLOW CITIZENS:

To a few of us here today, this is a solemn and most momentous occasion; and yet, in the history of our nation, it is a commonplace occurrence. The orderly transfer of authority as called for in the Constitution routinely takes place as it has for almost two centuries and few of us stop to think how unique we really are. In the eyes of many in the world, this every-four-year ceremony we accept   5
as normal is nothing less than a miracle.

Mr. President, I want our fellow citizens to know how much you did to carry on this tradition. By your gracious cooperation in the transition process, you have shown a watching world that we are a united people pledged to maintaining a political system which guarantees individual liberty to a greater degree than   10
any other, and I thank you and your people for all your help in maintaining the continuity which is the bulwark of our Republic.

The business of our nation goes forward. These United States are confronted with an economic affliction of great proportions. We suffer from the longest and one of the worst sustained inflations in our national history. It distorts our   15

Ronald Reagan, "First Inaugural Address," January 20, 1981, in John Gabriel Hunt, ed., *The Inaugural Addresses of the Presidents* (New York: Gramercy, 1995), 471–78.

economic decisions, penalizes thrift, and crushes the struggling young and the fixed-income elderly alike. It threatens to shatter the lives of millions of our people.

5   Idle industries have cast workers into unemployment, causing human misery and personal indignity. Those who do work are denied a fair return for their labor by a tax system which penalizes successful achievement and keeps us from maintaining full productivity.

But great as our tax burden is, it has not kept pace with public spending. For decades, we have piled deficit upon deficit, mortgaging our future and our
10 children's future for the temporary convenience of the present. To continue this long trend is to guarantee tremendous social, cultural, political, and economic upheavals.

You and I, as individuals, can, by borrowing, live beyond our means, but for only a limited period of time. Why, then, should we think that collectively, as
15 a nation, we are not bound by that same limitation?

We must act today in order to preserve tomorrow. And let there be no misunderstanding—we are going to begin to act, beginning today.

The economic ills we suffer have come upon us over several decades. They will not go away in days, weeks, or months, but they will go away. They will go away
20 because we, as Americans, have the capacity now, as we have had in the past, to do whatever needs to be done to preserve this last and greatest bastion of freedom.

In this present crisis, government is not the solution to our problem.

From time to time, we have been tempted to believe that society has become too complex to be managed by self-rule, that government by an elite group is
25 superior to government for, by, and of the people. But if no one among us is capable of governing himself, then who among us has the capacity to govern someone else? All of us together, in and out of government, must bear the burden. The solutions we seek must be equitable, with no one group singled out to pay a higher price.

30 We hear much of special interest groups. Our concern must be for a special interest group that has been too long neglected. It knows no sectional boundaries or ethnic and racial divisions, and it crosses political party lines. It is made up of men and women who raise our food, patrol our streets, man our mines and factories, teach our children, keep our homes, and heal us when we're
35 sick—professionals, industrialists, shopkeepers, clerks, cabbies, and truckdrivers. They are, in short, "We the people," this breed called Americans.

Well, this administration's objective will be a healthy, vigorous, growing economy that provides equal opportunity for all Americans, with no barriers born of bigotry or discrimination. Putting America back to work means putting all Americans back to work. Ending inflation means freeing all Americans from the terror of runaway living costs. All must share in the productive 5 work of this "new beginning" and all must share in the bounty of a revived economy. With the idealism and fair play which are the core of our system and our strength, we can have a strong and prosperous America at peace with itself and the world.

So, as we begin, let us take inventory. We are a nation that has a government— 10 not the other way around. And this makes us special among the nations of the earth. Our government has no power except that granted it by the people. It is time to check and reverse the growth of government which shows signs of having grown beyond the consent of the governed.

It is my intention to curb the size and influence of the federal establishment 15 and to demand recognition of the distinction between the powers granted to the federal government and those reserved to the states or to the people. All of us need to be reminded that the federal government did not create the states; the states created the federal government.

Now, so there will be no misunderstanding, it is not my intention to do away 20 with government. It is, rather, to make it work—work with us, not over us; to stand by our side, not ride on our back. Government can and must provide opportunity, not smother it; foster productivity, not stifle it.

If we look to the answer as to why, for so many years, we achieved so much, prospered as no other people on earth, it was because here, in this land, we 25 unleashed the energy and individual genius of man to a greater extent than has ever been done before. Freedom and the dignity of the individual have been more available and assured here than in any other place on earth. The price for this freedom at times has been high, but we have never been unwilling to pay that price. 30

It is no coincidence that our present troubles parallel and are proportionate to the intervention and intrusion in our lives that result from unnecessary and excessive growth of government. It is time for us to realize that we are too great a nation to limit ourselves to small dreams. We are not, as some would have us believe, doomed to an inevitable decline. I do not believe in a fate that will 35 fall on us no matter what we do. I do believe in a fate that will fall on us if we do nothing. So, with all the creative energy at our command, let us begin an era of national renewal. Let us renew our determination, our courage, and our strength. And let us renew our faith and our hope.

We have every right to dream heroic dreams. Those who say that we are in a time when there are no heroes just don't know where to look. You can see
5 heroes every day going in and out of factory gates. Others, a handful in number, produce enough food to feed all of us and then the world beyond. You meet heroes across a counter—and they are on both sides of that counter. There are entrepreneurs with faith in themselves and faith in an idea who create new jobs, new wealth and opportunity. They are individuals and families whose taxes
10 support the government and whose voluntary gifts support church, charity, culture, art, and education. Their patriotism is quiet but deep. Their values sustain our national life.

I have used the words "they" and "their" in speaking of these heroes. I could say "you" and "your" because I am addressing the heroes of whom I speak—you,
15 the citizens of this blessed land. Your dreams, your hopes, your goals are going to be the dreams, the hopes, and the goals of this administration, so help me God.

We shall reflect the compassion that is so much a part of your makeup. How can we love our country and not love our countrymen, and loving them,
20 reach out a hand when they fall, heal them when they are sick, and provide opportunities to make them self-sufficient so they will be equal in fact and not just in theory?

Can we solve the problems confronting us? Well, the answer is an unequivocal and emphatic "yes." To paraphrase Winston Churchill, I did not take the oath
25 I have just taken with the intention of presiding over the dissolution of the world's strongest economy.

In the days ahead I will propose removing the roadblocks that have slowed our economy and reduced productivity. Steps will be taken aimed at restoring the balance between the various levels of government. Progress may be slow—
30 measured in inches and feet, not miles—but we will progress. It is time to reawaken this industrial giant, to get government back within its means, and to lighten our punitive tax burden. And these will be our first priorities, and on these principles, there will be no compromise.

On the eve of our struggle for independence a man who might have been one
35 of the greatest among the Founding Fathers, Dr. Joseph Warren, president of the Massachusetts Congress, said to his fellow Americans, "Our country is in danger, but not to be despaired of.... On you depend the fortunes of America.

You are to decide the important questions upon which rests the happiness and the liberty of millions yet unborn. Act worthy of yourselves."

Well, I believe we, the Americans of today, are ready to act worthy of ourselves, ready to do what must be done to ensure happiness and liberty for ourselves, our children and our children's children.   5

And as we renew ourselves here in our own land, we will be seen as having greater strength throughout the world. We will again be the exemplar of freedom and a beacon of hope for those who do not now have freedom.

To those neighbors and allies who share our freedom, we will strengthen our historic ties and assure them of our support and firm commitment. We will   10
match loyalty with loyalty. We will strive for mutually beneficial relations. We will not use our friendship to impose on their sovereignty, for our own sovereignty is not for sale.

As for the enemies of freedom, those who are potential adversaries, they will be reminded that peace is the highest aspiration of the American people. We will   15
negotiate for it, sacrifice for it; we will not surrender for it—now or ever.

Our forbearance should never be misunderstood. Our reluctance for conflict should not be misjudged as a failure of will. When action is required to preserve our national security, we will act. We will maintain sufficient strength to prevail if need be, knowing that if we do so we have the best chance of never having   20
to use that strength.

Above all, we must realize that no arsenal, or no weapon in the arsenals of the world, is so formidable as the will and moral courage of free men and women. It is a weapon our adversaries in today's world do not have. It is a weapon that we as Americans do have. Let that be understood by those who practice terrorism   25
and prey upon their neighbors.

I am told that tens of thousands of prayer meetings are being held on this day, and for that I am deeply grateful. We are a nation under God, and I believe God intended for us to be free. It would be fitting and good, I think, if on each inauguration day in future years it should be declared a day of prayer.   30

This is the first time in history that this ceremony has been held, as you have been told, on the west front of the Capitol. Standing here, one faces a magnificent vista, opening up on this city's special beauty and history. At the end of this open mall are those shrines to the giants on whose shoulders we stand.

Directly in front of me, the monument to a monumental man: George   35
Washington, Father of Our Country. A man of humility who came to

greatness reluctantly. He led Americans out of revolutionary victory into infant nationhood. Off to one side, the stately memorial to Thomas Jefferson. The Declaration of Independence flames with his eloquence.

And then beyond the Reflecting Pool the dignified columns of the Lincoln
5   Memorial. Whoever would understand in his heart the meaning of America will find it in the life of Abraham Lincoln.

Beyond those monuments to heroism is the Potomac River, and on the far shore the sloping hills of Arlington National Cemetery with its row on row of simple white markers bearing crosses or stars of David. They add up to only a
10   tiny fraction of the price that has been paid for our freedom.

Each one of those markers is a monument to the kind of hero I spoke of earlier. Their lives ended in places called Belleau Wood, the Argonne, Omaha Beach, Salerno and halfway around the world on Guadalcanal, Tarawa, Pork Chop Hill, the Chosin Reservoir, and in a hundred rice paddies and jungles of a
15   place called Vietnam.

Under one such marker lies a young man—Martin Treptow—who left his job in a small town barber shop in 1917 to go to France with the famed Rainbow Division. There, on the western front, he was killed trying to carry a message between battalions under heavy artillery fire.

20   We are told that on his body was found a diary. On the flyleaf under the heading, "My Pledge," he had written these words: "America must win this war. Therefore, I will work, I will save, I will sacrifice, I will endure, I will fight cheerfully and do my utmost, as if the issue of the whole struggle depended on me alone."

The crisis we are facing today does not require of us the kind of sacrifice that
25   Martin Treptow and so many thousands of others were called upon to make. It does require, however, our best effort, and our willingness to believe in ourselves and to believe in our capacity to perform great deeds; to believe that together, with God's help, we can and will resolve the problems which now confront us.

30   And, after all, why shouldn't we believe that? We are Americans. God bless you, and thank you.